READINGS IN
CANADIAN
HISTORY

PRE-CONFEDERATION

READINGS IN
CANADIAN
HISTORY

FOURTH EDITION

R. Douglas Francis
Donald B. Smith
UNIVERSITY OF CALGARY

HARCOURT
BRACE
CANADA

Harcourt Brace & Company, Canada
Toronto Montreal Orlando Fort Worth San Diego
Philadelphia London Sydney Tokyo

Canadian Cataloguing in Publication Data

Main entry under title:

Readings in Canadian history

4th ed.
Contents: V. 1. Pre-Confederation — v. 2. Post-Confederation.
ISBN 0-7747-3245-8 (v. 1)
ISBN 0-7747-3246-6 (v. 2)

1. Canada - History. I. Francis, R. D. (R. Douglas),
1944- . II. Smith, Donald B., 1946- .

FC164.R43 1993   971   C93-093904-2

Publisher: Heather McWhinney
Editor and Marketing Manager: Daniel Brooks/Christopher Carson
Developmental Editor: Michael Bolton
Editorial Assistant: Susan Fisher
Director of Publishing Services: Jean Davies
Editorial Manager: Marcel Chiera
Supervising Editor: Semareh Al-Hillal
Production Manager: Sue-Ann Becker
Manufacturing Co-ordinator: Denise Wake
Copy Editor: Darlene Zeleney
Cover Design: Brett Miller
Interior Design: John Zehethofer
Typesetting and Assembly: True to Type Inc.
Printing and Binding: Best Gagné Book Manufacturers

Cover Art: *The Guide's Home, Algonquin Park*, 1914, by Arthur Lismer (1885–1969). Oil on canvas, 102.6 x 114.4 cm. Reproduced with the permission of the National Gallery of Canada, Ottawa.

♾ This book was printed in Canada on acid-free paper.

1 2 3 4 5   98 97 96 95 94

Preface

In this fourth edition of our two-volume *Readings in Canadian History*, as in the previous three editions, our concern has been to provide a collection of articles suitable for introductory Canadian history tutorials. This has meant selecting topics related to the major issues that are explored in such history courses, and providing useful readings of a general nature. We have once again included material that deals with the various regions of the country and, whenever possible, reflects new research interests among Canadian historians. Consequently, we have changed some of the topics and replaced many of the readings. Unfortunately, because of space limitations, the addition of new articles has forced us to drop several worthwhile readings that appeared in the third edition. Still, we trust that this edition will continue to meet the needs of introductory students in Canadian history.

This volume includes two or three selections on each of fifteen topics, thereby affording instructors flexibility in choosing readings. Short introductions to each topic set the readings in a historical context and offer suggestions for further reading. It is our hope that this reader will contribute to increased discussion in tutorials, as well as complement course lectures and, where applicable, textbooks. In particular, *Readings in Canadian History* can be used effectively in conjunction with the textbooks *Origins: Canadian History to Confederation*, 2nd ed. (Toronto: Holt, Rinehart and Winston, 1992) and *Destinies: Canadian History since Confederation*, 2nd ed. (Toronto: Holt, Rinehart and Winston, 1992), both by R. Douglas Francis, Richard Jones, and Donald B. Smith.

In preparing past editions of the readers, we and the publisher sought advice from a number of Canadian historians. Their comments were generously given and greatly improved the original outlines of the collections. We would like to thank, in particular, Douglas Baldwin, of Acadia University; Olive Dickason, of the University of Alberta; Carol Wilton-Siegel, of York University; John Eagle, of the University of Alberta; and Hugh Johnston, of Simon Fraser University. Many other individuals made valuable suggestions; we are indebted to John Belshaw, of Cariboo College; Margaret Conrad, of Acadia University; Beatrice Craig, of the University of Ottawa; Chad Gaffield, of the University of Ottawa; Marcel Martel, of Glendon College, York University; Thomas Socknat, of the University of Toronto; Robert Sweeny, of Memorial University; Duncan McDowell, of Carleton University; and Peter Ward, of the University of British Columbia. For the fourth edition, valuable reviews were provided by Wendy Wallace and Paul Whyte, of North Island College, and by Roger Hall, of the University of Western Ontario.

Heartfelt thanks also go to Dave Dimmell, Chris Carson, Dan Brooks, Michael Bolton, and Semareh Al-Hillal, of Harcourt Brace & Company, Canada, for their help and constant encouragement toward the completion of this fourth edition, and to Darlene Zeleney, who edited the book. Finally, we wish to thank those Canadian historians who consented to let their writings be included in this reader. Their ideas and viewpoints will greatly enrich the study and appreciation of Canadian history among first- and second-year university students.

Douglas Francis
Donald Smith
Department of History
University of Calgary

A Note from the Publisher

Thank you for selecting *Readings in Canadian History: Pre-Confederation*, Fourth Edition, by R. Douglas Francis and Donald B. Smith. The authors and the publisher have devoted considerable time to the careful development of this book. We appreciate your recognition of this effort and accomplishment.

We want to hear what you think about this edition of *Readings in Canadian History: Pre-Confederation*. Please take a few minutes to complete the stamped reply card at the back of the book. Your comments and suggestions will be valuable to us in the preparation of new editions.

Contents

List of Maps

Edward S. Curtis/Glenbow Archives, Calgary/NA-1700-139.

Depictions of Indians as savages wandering in the wilderness or as innocent children living gratefully off nature's bounty are cultural artifacts of Europe; they have little to do with the actual lives of Native Americans.

Richard White and William Cronon, "Ecological Change and Indian–White Relations"

The Native Peoples and Early European Contact

The Europeans who came to North America looked upon it as an empty continent, open for settlement. In reality, Amerindians claimed and inhabited almost every part of the "New World," from the Gulf of Mexico to the Arctic coast, from the Atlantic to the Pacific. There were more than fifty Amerindian groups in Canada alone.

In the pre-European period, there was neither a common designation for the country nor a common name for the native inhabitants. The "Indians" of Canada owed their allegiance to their family, their band, their village, their tribe, and — in the case of several tribes — their confederacy. But they had no concept of a pan-Indian identity. Each tribe spoke its own language and regarded its own members as "the people." This lack of a perceived common identity contributed to the Amerindians' failure to resist the Europeans. But other factors contributed as well; among them were the reliance of some Native groups on European manufactured trade goods; the fur-trade rivalries; the colonial wars; and the catastrophic drop in population that resulted from exposure to European diseases.

In their article "Ecological Change and Indian–White Relations," historians Richard White and William Cronon review the environmental implications of the relationship between Amerindians and Europeans in North America. In "The French Presence in Huronia: The Structure of Franco-Huron Relations in the First Half of the Seventeenth Century," anthropologist Bruce Trigger traces the fortunes of the Hurons, one of the Native groups that came into the closest contact with French fur traders in the seventeenth century.

Diamond Jenness's dated *Indians of Canada* (Ottawa: King's Printer, 1932; numerous editions since) must be supplemented by Olive Patricia Dickason's *Canada's First Nations: A History of Founding Peoples from Earliest Times* (Toronto: McClelland and Stewart, 1992). Alan D. McMillan has written a useful survey, *Native Peoples and Cultures of Canada: An Anthropological Overview* (Vancouver: Douglas and McIntyre, 1988). A good collection of articles on Canada's Native peoples, edited by R. Bruce Morrison and C. Roderick Wilson, is *Native Peoples: The Canadian Experience* (Toronto: McClelland and Stewart, 1986). Anthropologist

Alice B. Kehoe provides an overview in her *North American Indians: A Comprehensive Account*, 2nd ed. (Englewood Cliffs, N.J.: Prentice-Hall, 1992). Thomas Y. Canby's "The Search for the First Americans," *National Geographic* 156, 3 (September 1979): 330-63, is an interesting account of recent archaeological work in the Americas. Robert McGhee's *Ancient Canada* (Ottawa: Canadian Museum of Civilization, 1989) reviews what is currently known of Canada's First Nations and Inuit before the arrival of the Europeans.

A very good introduction to the subject of early French–Indian relations in the Americas is Olive Patricia Dickason's *The Myth of the Savage and the Beginnings of French Colonialism in the Americas* (Edmonton: University of Alberta Press, 1984). Other useful introductions are Alfred G. Bailey's *The Conflict of European and Eastern Algonkian Cultures, 1504-1700* (1937; second edition published by the University of Toronto Press, 1969); the short booklet by Bruce Trigger entitled *The Indians and the Heroic Age of New France*, Canadian Historical Association, Historical Booklet no. 30, rev. ed. (Ottawa: CHA, 1989) and his *Natives and Newcomers: Canada's 'Heroic Age' Reconsidered* (Kingston and Montreal: McGill-Queen's University Press, 1985); and the first chapter, entitled "Native Peoples and the Beginnings of New France to 1650," in John A. Dickinson and Brian Young, *A Short History of Quebec*, 2nd ed. (Toronto: Copp Clark Pitman, 1993), 2-26. An interesting popular account of early Amerindian–European contact is Robert McGhee's *Canada Rediscovered* (Ottawa: Canadian Museum of Civilization, 1991). Useful maps appear in R. Cole Harris, ed., *Historical Atlas of Canada*, vol. 1, *From the Beginning to 1800* (Toronto: University of Toronto Press, 1987).

Students interested in pursuing the subject further should consult James Axtell, ed., *The Indian Peoples of Eastern America: A Documentary History of the Sexes* (New York: Oxford, 1981) and his *The Invasion Within: The Contest of Cultures in Colonial North America* (New York: Oxford University Press, 1985); Cornelius Jaenen, *Friend and Foe: Aspects of French–Amerindian Cultural Contact in the Sixteenth and Seventeenth Centuries* (Toronto: McClelland and Stewart, 1976); Bruce Trigger, *Natives and Newcomers: Canada's "Heroic Age" Reconsidered* (Kingston and Montreal: McGill-Queen's University Press, 1985); and Denys Delâge, *Bitter Feast: Amerindians and Europeans in the American Northeast, 1600-64*, translated from the French by Jane Brierley (Vancouver: University of British Columbia Press, 1993).

Two interesting books on the early fur trade are Calvin Martin's *Keepers of the Game: Indian–Animal Relationships and the Fur Trade* (Berkeley, California: University of California Press, 1978) and Shepard Krech's edited work, *Indians, Animals and the Fur Trade: A Critique of Keepers of the Game* (Athens, Georgia: University of Georgia Press, 1981). Ramsay Cook reviews environmental questions in his "Cabbages Not Kings: Towards an Ecological Interpretation of Early Canadian History,"

Journal of Canadian Studies 25, 4 (Winter 1990/91): 5–16. For Cook's comments on the environment in Chief Donnacona's day (the mid-1530s), see "Donnacona Discovers Europe: Rereading Jacques Cartier's *Voyages*," in his *Voyages of Jacques Cartier* (Toronto: University of Toronto Press, 1993), ix–xli. Ecological issues in Native American history are examined in Christopher Vecsey and Robert W. Venables, eds., *American Indian Environments* (Syracuse, N.Y.: Syracuse University Press, 1980). A model study of ecological history in the early European contact period is William Cronon's *Changes in the Land: Indians, Colonists, and the Ecology of New England* (New York: Hill and Wong, 1983).

The Europeans' early attitudes to the question of Indian sovereignty are reviewed in Brian Slattery's "French Claims in North America, 1500–59," *Canadian Historical Review* 59 (1978): 139–69, and W.J. Eccles's "Sovereignty-Association, 1500–1783," *Canadian Historical Review* 65 (1984): 475–510. Leslie C. Green and Olive Dickason review the ideology of the European occupation of the Americas in *The Law of Nations and the New World* (Edmonton: University of Alberta Press, 1989).

How did the Europeans' view of land and nature differ from that of the First Nations? In what ways would their attitudes lead to misunderstandings with the Indians? The questions of Amerindian sovereignty and the right to self-determination are important issues today.

3

Ecological Change and Indian–White Relations

RICHARD WHITE and WILLIAM CRONON

Several themes should be kept in mind when surveying the environmental history of Indian–White relations in North America. The first is that a great many myths obscure the understanding of this subject. There has long been a tendency in the United States, encouraged by the environmental movement of the 1960s and 1970s, to view Indians as "original conservationists," people so intimately bound to the land that they have left no mark upon it (MacLeod 1936; Speck 1938; Deloria 1970:181–97; Jacobs 1972:19–30). Depictions of Indians as savages wandering in the wilderness or as innocent children living gratefully off nature's bounty are cultural artifacts of Europe; they have little to do with the actual lives of Native Americans (H.N. Smith 1950; Pearce 1953; Sheehan 1973; Slotkin 1973). Indeed, the very word *wilderness*, in the sense of a natural landscape unaffected by human use, has little meaning

From *Handbook of North American Indians*, vol. 4, *History of Indian-White Relations*, ed. Wilcomb E. Washburn; series ed. William Sturtevant (Washington: Smithsonian Institution Press, 1989), 417–27.

for most of aboriginal North America. To assert that Indians lived on pristine "virgin land" not only ignores the human influences that had long reshaped pre-Columbian North America but also "naturalizes" Indians in a way that denies both their histories and their cultures. Just as important, to portray Indians as "conservationists" or "ecologists" is fundamentally anachronistic (Martin 1978:157–88).

A second theme of Indian environmental history has to do with broad similarities in Indians' actual uses of the natural world. Given their diversity, it is dangerous to generalize about Indian land-use practices; nonetheless, certain common features emerge when they are contrasted with those of Europeans. Agriculture on the two continents differed dramatically. In Indian North America, in places where crops were raised, they were almost always integrated into hunting, fishing, and gathering economies that required more physical mobility than was typical of European communities. However intimate the relation of certain Plains peoples to the bison herds, no North American ungulate species had been fully domesticated, so that dairy products, woven textiles, and animal power sources were generally lacking. In many parts of the continent — the Arctic, Subarctic, much of the Great Basin, and the Northwest Coast — agriculture was not practiced at all, though nonagricultural subsistence practices differed radically in different regional environments. Throughout the continent, seasonal cycles, ecologically and culturally defined, governed the physical movement of Indian communities among different environmental sources of subsistence. Indian economies typically protected themselves from environmental fluctuations by incorporating a wide variety of different resources into these seasonal cycles. When one such resource failed to appear during a given season of the year, others were almost always available to support a community. These in turn were usually articulated in terms of a clear sexual division of labor in which (to overgeneralize) men concentrated on hunting and fishing, and women on horticulture and gathering (H. Driver 1969; Jorgensen 1980).

The ways Indians used the environment profoundly influenced the historical landscapes of North America. Indian activities brought changes to the continent's forests, grasslands, and deserts, whether by modifying vegetational assemblages, by encouraging or discouraging the spread of animal populations, or by creating habitats best suited to human settlements. The tools and methods Indian peoples used to gain food, shelter, and clothing before White contact varied widely. Some techniques, such as irrigation, were localized; other techniques, such as burning, were in use across the continent.

The notion that Indians passively "adapted" to their regional environments must be avoided. Natural systems clearly limited human uses of land, and in the trivial sense that Indians did not do the impossible, they adapted. But if regional environments were diverse, Indian uses of them were even more diverse. Nature offered not one, but many ways for human beings to live in a given region. More important, it gave no clues as to what might be an "optimum" way to live, for only culture could provide the values that defined what an optimum use of land might be. Indians were no more passive or "adaptive" in choosing such environmental values than Europeans were, and out of their choices and spiritual beliefs flowed the material changes they imposed upon the landscapes of North America.

The third theme of Indian environmental history is simply that anthropogenic change of North American landscapes accelerated with the arrival of the Europeans. The story of Indian–White relations cannot be framed solely in political or diplomatic or even cultural terms, for the very ground over which Indians and Euro-Americans were struggling shifted as they did so. Part of the process of environmental change involved incompatible uses of different habitats, as when Europeans imposed fences or fixed property boundaries on landscapes that had lacked them. Part of it derived from the reduction or elimination of indigenous species — species that had been fundamental to earlier Indian economies — as they experienced new and heavier human use; at the same time, the introduction of alien species shifted ecosystems and economies alike. And part of the process involved fundamental differences in Indian and European conceptions of spiritual nature.

Indian Conceptions of Nature

North American Indian conceptions of nature and culture generally intersect in two ways. On the one hand, human beings are part of nature by virtue of being biological beings living within a material world. On the other, natural beings such as plants and animals are also part of a human cultural world. Perhaps the clearest example of this can be found among the Algonquian peoples of the northern United States and Canada. Among both the Ojibwa and the East Cree, for instance, natural and cultural worlds overlap. In the Cree world game animals exist as persons who "participate simultaneously in two levels of reality, one 'natural' and one 'cultural'" (A. Tanner 1979:137). The interaction of hunters and game animals becomes a social relationship, often expressed in terms of friendship or love. In a properly conducted hunt the animals offer themselves voluntarily to be killed (A. Tanner 1979:138, 146, 148).

In consequence, the boundaries between human and nonhuman communities become difficult to define. Just as nature and culture shade into one another, so do natural and supernatural phenomena. One class of spirits exists as personified natural forces, while another class of spirits "own" or are "masters" of particular animal species (A. Tanner 1979:114–16, 139). Human beings thus act properly and successfully in nature not merely through practical environmental knowledge but also through spiritual relations with the masters of the game and with the animals themselves (A. Tanner 1979:122; Hallowell 1976:357–86; Black 1977, 1977a; Charlevoix 1744, 2:144; JR 50:289).

For Indian communities that view the world through these lenses, few distinctions are made between what outsiders might regard as common-sense environmental knowledge and those magical activities that induce an animal to surrender to a hunter. A hunting technique of the Winnebago, for example, involved shooting an arrow down the trail of the quarry deer the day before an actual hunt. The hunter did not regard the arrow falling on the trail as a preliminary to the hunt or as a substitute for hunting skills; the arrow and the subsequent hunt were an "indissoluble whole" and were employed only under well-defined conditions (Radin 1924:15–16). Similar ceremonies were used by the Navajo to request hunting success both from the Talking Gods who controlled game animals and from the animals themselves (W.W. Hill 1938:98). Among the Winnebago, the Navajo, and the Cree, then, the "practical" and the "spiritual" paralleled each other (A. Tanner 1979:134). Neither alone could make the hunt successful.

In the Southeast, this conception of the complex community relationships among animals, plants, and human beings became even more elaborate when applied to disease. Like many Indians, the Cherokee constructed their medical theories on the premise that animals caused illnesses as a way of retaliating against hunters whose activities were wanton, careless, or disrespectful of animal remains. Despite this dangerous power that animals could wield, human beings were not entirely defenseless against it, for a number of plant allies had agreed to furnish them with specific remedies against animal-induced disease. Much of Cherokee medicine involved selecting plants appropriate to the animal causing a particular illness. To treat sickness being sent by deer, for instance, doctors made a compound of four plants known in Cherokee as "Deer Ear," "Deer Shin," "Deer Eye," and "Deer Tongue" (Mooney 1890:47). The Cherokee thus established cultural congruences among the plants they saw as connected to certain animals and then used those plants to treat the diseases they thought those animals caused.

By using these techniques Native American groups sought to manipulate nature to serve their own purposes. This was particularly true among horticultural peoples, who established intricate symbolic schemes representing natural systems and their seasonal cycles that could be ritually manipulated. Such cultural systems differed (and continue to differ) profoundly in detail, but they were often based on perceived natural oppositions between earth and sky, winter and summer, male and female; these in turn were elaborated into cultural categories that could be applied to the entire natural world. The Creek, Cherokee, and other Southeast Indians, for example, conceived of the world in terms of an opposition between "upper" and "lower" worlds, with "this world" suspended between. It was the duty of Indian peoples to maintain the balance between the upper and lower worlds, by keeping separate those things that belonged to each. This task gave them what has been called an "almost obsessive concern with purity and pollution" (Hudson 1976:121) in their efforts to prevent the mixing of things from opposing categories.

As another example of such horticultural belief systems, the people of the Tewa Pueblos developed a quite different set of cultural classifications, but these too were inspired by natural oppositions. The Tewas elaborated their social organization and ritual cycle from natural dualities marked by the solar equinoxes and by the opposition between hot and cold temperatures. From those two sets of poles, ritual divisions could be applied to phenomena ranging from disease, to plants and animals, to society itself. The Tewa system of summer and winter chiefs reflects this duality (Oritz 1969:118–19).

Whether Indians understood their place in the natural environment   7
in terms of a series of social relationships among spirits, human beings, and nonhuman organisms, or in terms of ritual classificatory systems, they showed little reluctance about trying to control that environment. For the East Cree, "much of the religious thought of the hunters is concerned with the state of the natural environment, with how the environment may be controlled, and with the reason for failure when hunters are unable to exercise that control" (A. Tanner 1979:211). The same is even more true of agricultural peoples. The ritual cycle of the Tewas is designed to "harmonize man's relations with the spirits, and to ensure that the desired cyclical changes will continue to come about in nature" (Oritz 1969:98). Above all, their agricultural rituals are designed to procure rain (Oritz 1969:106). Similarly, the Pawnee quite literally believed that their ceremonial cycle perennially ensured that corn would grow and buffalo would prosper (Weltfish 1965). In all these ways, Indian religions and ritual practices confirmed the crucial role human beings played in facilitating the movement of natural cycles.

Indian Transformations of Landscape

One key determinant of Indian environmental influence was simple population density. In the Arctic and Subarctic, environmental conditions and social organization both contributed to the lowest population densities in North America, on the order of 1.7 persons per 100 square kilometers; this was lower than was typical of more temperate regions (*Handbook of North American Indians* [hereafter *HNAI*], vol. 6:141, 173, 275, 372, 534; *HNAI*, vol. 5:164, 206, 479–80, 486; Hallowell 1949; Krech 1978; Dobyns 1983:34–45). Because northern biological cycles moved between dramatic annual extremes in the relative abundance of subsistence resources, human numbers and impacts there remained small relative to places elsewhere on the continent. No agriculture was possible, so localized shifts in game animal populations probably remained the most significant human effects on natural landscapes. Anthropogenic forest fires may occasionally have affected wide areas of the Subarctic land-scape, but there is little evidence that the use of fire for hunting was widespread in the region (Flannery 1939:14, 167; Day 1953:338–39; *HNAI*, vol. 6:86).

South of the Subarctic, population densities were generally higher, ranging from perhaps a little over one person per 100 square kilometers in the deserts of Nevada to over 300 persons per 100 square kilometers in the more fertile areas of the East (Dobyns 1983:34–45). In the de-ciduous woodlands of the Northeast, Algonquian and Iroquoian peoples living in more temperate climates attained higher population densities in part by combining annual cycles of hunting and gathering with a horticultural cycle derived from the Meso-American corn-squash-bean cultigen complex. Crops were planted chiefly by Indian women during April and May, and a mixture of gathering, fishing, and small-game hunting sustained communities until the fall harvest. Villages would then break into smaller bands to participate in the fall and winter deer hunts, living off harvested corn when meat supplies fell short (Wallace 1970:49–75; Salisbury 1982:30–39; Cronon 1983:34–53).

Agricultural fields in the vicinity of permanent villages could become quite extensive, and these, combined with the effects of gathering wood for fuel, resulted in localized deforestation. After the soil fertility of such fields had begun to decline, they were abandoned and new lands cleared to replace them. The result was to maintain early successional stages in the vicinity of Indian villages, creating a patchy landscape of grass-lands, shrublands, and young woods. In addition, many communities followed the practice of setting fire to portions of the forest around them, opening up the landscape still further. The promotion of mixed grass-lands and young woods simultaneously provided forage for animals such as deer, hare, beaver, turkey, grouse, and quail. Although these species were not "domesticated" in any conventional sense of the word, Indians played a significant role in managing their numbers and use.

In the Southeast, similar alterations of the landscape reflected the agricultural and hunting demands of Indian peoples. The prehistoric peoples had concentrated their settlements and cleared fields along the terrace lands bordering major rivers; moving out from those bases, they hunted the surrounding forest and prairie lands. After epidemics had largely depopulated prehistoric centers, the nations who inhabited the region following European contact tended to live along smaller streams. There they still farmed terrace lands, but the old fields of the prehistoric people became prime hunting grounds. In the region as a whole, the distribution of fields and villages changed over time, but the overall pat-

8

tern remained the same: ribbons of fields ran along the terraces and were surrounded by hunting areas of forest, prairie, and abandoned fields.

Within this landscape, Southeast Indians acted to increase the abundance of those plants and animals they needed for food and clothing. To produce the corn, beans, and squash that formed the staples of their diets, they practiced swidden agriculture, cutting and burning existing vegetation to establish their fields. Within fields that contained beans as well as corn, nitrogen-fixing bacteria on the roots of the legumes replaced some of the nitrogen that corn extracted from the soil, but the beans never put back all that the corn took out. As fields declined in fertility, Indians abandoned them and cleared new ones. They were selective in their clearing, paying attention to soil quality and also, in some areas, sparing wild fruit and nut trees (Sauer 1971:181, 282–84). Under ideal conditions, this agriculture was remarkably productive and, when supplemented by hunting, fishing, and gathering, it provided the tribes of the Southeast with a secure subsistence.

The game that hunters took in upland forests and prairies had fewer direct connections than crops did with human alterations of the environment, but it too was influenced by the ways people modified habitats. Indians burned both to clear lands and to hunt game, but the influence of anthropogenic fire in creating deer habitats varied from region to region within the Southeast. In the upland pine-hardwood forests, burning appears to have encouraged herbaceous growth, particularly of those plants most palatable to deer (R. White 1938:10–11). On the prairies, old fields, and openings, the fires retarded normal successional patterns and maintained the edge habitats in which deer thrive. However, along the Gulf Plain, fire degraded rather than improved deer habitat. In this region, longleaf pine, a fire-resistant species, dominated a region that otherwise would have been oak-hickory forests with a higher average carrying capacity for deer. The combination of poor agricultural soils and scarce game made this perhaps the least inhabited section of the region (Chapman 1932; R. White 1983:11, Pyne 1982:112).

The Plains provide one of the most intriguing examples of Indian uses of the environment. This is a land of abundant grass and often catastrophic drought. Before the horse, the southern and central Plains were inhabited by Caddoan peoples who farmed the river valleys along its margins and who seasonally ventured out onto the plains to hunt buffalo. Permanent residents of the plains were confined to small groups of nomadic peoples, and even they apparently engaged in a more limited horticulture. The women — the horticulturalists of the tribes of the Plains margin — had by the late nineteenth century evolved a series of crop varieties that had been adjusted to local conditions over long periods of time (Will and Hyde 1964). These villagers too exerted pressure on the environment. Their activities gradually exhausted local timber supplies and diminished the fertility of cornfields, so they were forced to

9

move their settlements. Later, their widespread burning of the grasslands, together with the fires set by surrounding nomads, reduced the quantity of timber along stream and river margins where it would otherwise have existed. Because such environmental changes gradually undermined the subsistence base of the community itself, the life of such a village, barring attack from the outside, would appear to have been about 30 years (Wells 1970; R. White 1983:183–85).

In the Southwest and Great Basin, aridity set limits on human land use, but there too the environment hardly dictated a specific or optimal use. The Hopi, Apache, and Southern Paiute, for example, all shared desert environments, but their systems of land use differed significantly. Each modified the land to suit their needs. For instance, the desert around Black Mesa, where the Hopis built their villages, is hardly ideal for agriculture. The lands are high and dry, with the critical rainfall of July and August usually amounting to only three or four inches; that the Hopis even attempted agriculture under such conditions is remarkable. Once they did so, climate and the scarcity of water severely restricted when and where they could plant (Bradfield 1971:2).

Despite such conditions, environment by no means determined the cultural accommodations the Hopis made in responding to them. To compensate for aridity, the Hopis planted special varieties of corn with a greatly elongated mesocotyl and a single deeply thrusting radicle instead of seminal roots. The unusual mesocotyl and radicle allowed corn to germinate even when planted as much as 10 inches deep and to make maximum use of moisture preserved deep beneath the ground's sandy surface (Bradfield 1971:5–6). But such corn could not be planted everywhere. The Hopis had to select fields that successfully preserved the moisture from melting winter snows and also captured runoff from rain and snow elsewhere on the mesa. These fields were located on clay soils overlain by sand, and they dotted the valleys that were carved into the mesa's sides. The Hopis located their fields in these valleys by noting the size of key indicator plants, particularly the rabbit brush and its associated species. Such fields, barring catastrophic arroyo cutting, were the sites of an agriculture that was permanent rather than shifting, since floodwaters and the silt they carried fertilized as well as watered the fields. In the desert the Hopis constructed an agricultural economy that included not only corn, beans, and squash, but also cotton and, after contact with the Spanish, orchards (Bradfield 1971:12–19).

Farming clearly involves modifying the landscape, but Indians shaped the Southwest much more widely, if less dramatically, with fire. Fire drives by Apaches and Papagos of the Gila River system in the Sonoran Desert were apparently important in keeping grasslands from becoming chaparral. Apaches set fires as a hunting technique, and these fires in turn encouraged plant successions that helped increase game populations (Dobyns 1981:34–43). In the Great Basin, Indians also set fires to encourage the germination of wild plant seeds and the growth of wild tobacco (Steward 1933:281). Fires set by hunters in the Plateau culture area were major ecological factors in shaping foothill grasslands and mountain woodlands (Gruell 1985; Flores 1983:329; Arno 1985:82).

The barren high desert environment of the Great Basin demanded much of the people who lived there, and they of necessity forged a sub-sistence system that was at once alert to all possible food sources and flexible enough never entirely to depend on one or two. The Northern and Southern Paiute and Western Shoshone depended on mobility and flexibility to survive. They used a variety of fish, plants, and animals that were abundant and easily harvested only for brief periods. The Southern Paiute and Western Shoshone used their intricate knowledge of desert environments to gather what they could, storing one food when-ever possible to guard against the failure of another element in their elaborate seasonal cycle. No family or band could depend entirely on their own resources; boundaries were flexible and the population read-justed itself to seasonal scarcity or abundance. A poor yield of ricegrass in the territory of one Northern Paiute band, for example, required that band to move into the territory of another where food was more abundant. Such shifts were only temporary, since a poor yield of ricegrass rarely meant that other seasonal plant foods — say, the piñon crop in the fall — would fail to be plentiful in the migrant band's own territory. Although the various Paiute groups might seem to have been the people most forced to take the land as found, a closer look shows environmental manipulation even here. Many Northern Paiute groups burned vegetation to encourage wild plants, with some sowing seeds after the fires (Steward 1941:281; Downs 1966). The Owens Valley Paiutes burned to encourage the growth of certain desirable plants, and they increased the yield of several plants by practicing limited irrigation (Steward 1933, 1930:150).

In California, many of the techniques found among the Great Basin peoples occurred again. The Diegueño and Luiseño irrigated and cul-tivated wild plants (Bean and Lawton 1973:xv, xxvii). Far more than in the Great Basin, California Indians used fire to shape the environment. Indian fires in the Sacramento Valley and neighboring foothills reduced "brush cover to favor a parkland of grasses, trees, and intermittent stands of brush" (Lewis 1973:17). By maintaining early successional stages, In-dians provided a favorable environment for deer. Burning the chaparral was particularly important. After the fire had reduced woody species, a variety of grasses, forbs, and sprouts on regenerating chaparral provided an abundance of game food. In higher mountain regions, frequent ground fires set by Indians left the larger trees undamaged, destroyed needles and debris, encouraged shrubs and herbaceous plants, and maintained the forest as a parkland with open spaces between the trees. Such a forest provided more abundant animals and easier hunting. Regular burn-ing, by eliminating debris, reduced the likelihood that catastrophic crown

11

fires, which were capable of entirely destroying the forest, would occur (Lewis 1973:25–35, 1985).

In the coastal regions of the Pacific Northwest and along the major rivers that reached into the interior, the seasonal cycles of Indian peoples clearly centered on the annual spawning runs of salmon and steelhead, but subsistence extended beyond fishing. Around the fishing runs, many coastal peoples created an elaborate cycle of gathering and hunting. This cycle meant much more than simple variety in their diet; it was a hedge against those years in which salmon runs failed. This was true not only of the Coast Salish but also of the Kwakiutl, Haida, and other tribes farther north (Drucker and Heizer 1967). To increase the yields of this hunting and gathering system, Southern Coast Salish groups such as the Skagit, Snohomish, and Kikiallus significantly modified local environments. They burned the scattered prairies to increase yields of bracken (whose roots were ground to flour) and camas (whose bulbs were dried and stored). There is a little evidence that the Salish regularly burned forests, but prairie fires did occasionally spread into surrounding woods and could, under proper conditions, cause immense conflagrations. Burned-over sections of forest were common at White settlement. These fires helped to maintain the dominance of Douglas fir, the seedlings of which, unlike those of hemlock and cedar, could not grow unless the mature trees of the overstory were eliminated (R. White 1980).

If, then, one were to summarize the ways in which Indians modified North American landscapes prior to the start of European settlement, several subsistence practices would clearly be counted among the most important and widespread. Hunting and, where available, fishing were significant sources of food and clothing virtually everywhere on the continent, but their effects on local animal populations were determined by human population densities, the abundance of game species apart from Indian influence, and the extent to which hunter-gatherer economies were supplemented by horticulture. The agricultural activities of North, Southeast, and Southwest Indians yielded substantial landscape change not only on croplands themselves but also on old fields where different successional stages coexisted in a complex system of altered habitats. Everywhere on the continent, burning wood to cook food and warm lodges produced local deforestation. Much more dramatic was the use of fire to burn wild grasslands and forests. No single Indian practice contributed to more dramatic changes in North American environments.

Postcontact Environmental Change

DISEASE

The most immediate environmental change in Indian lives brought by European landings on American shores was also the most invisible and insidious: the introduction of pathogenic microorganisms against which Indians had virtually no immunity. Indian susceptibility to diseases like smallpox, chicken pox, measles, influenza, and malaria was a function of several phenomena. Most immediately, it was caused by their failure to maintain the historical transmission of antibodies from mother to child that is one of the species' most effective biological defenses against disease. That in turn resulted from their ancestors' passage through arctic environments where low winter temperatures and low population densities made it impossible for pathogens to survive, and from their lack of the domesticated animals with which Old World populations share several key disease organisms (Crosby 1972, 1976; McNeill 1976).

Wherever Indians encountered Europeans for any extended period of time, disease and depopulation were the eventual results. In the four decades following Columbus's arrival, massive epidemics killed millions of Indians in the Caribbean basin and in Central and South America. Although early epidemics are very poorly documented in North America, they were probably already beginning to occur to a limited degree in coastal areas during the sixteenth century and had brought significant depopulation by the early seventeenth century (Dobyns 1983). They recurred well into the nineteenth century among peoples with no previous experience of a particular disease. Mortality rates varied with the specific disease organism, population density, the season of the year, a community's historical immunity, and so on, but at their worst they could range as high as 80 or 90 percent. Some communities appear to have survived their encounters with disease more easily than others, and that tendency increased as historical exposure, mergers with other groups, and biological immunity rose. Nonetheless, as late as 1837, the Mandan of the Missouri River were virtually wiped out by smallpox (Crosby 1976:299).

The indirect effects of disease may have been at least as important as direct ones in bringing environmental change to North American habitats. The strain placed on economic subsistence practices, hierarchies of political power, and ritual belief systems in societies drastically reduced must have been quite extraordinary. Areas that had supported large populations, such as the major terraces of Southeastern rivers, or the coastal bays and salt marshes of the Northeast, suddenly became depopulated. Villages were forced to move into new alliances with each other, shuffling the decks of kin networks and political alliances to accommodate their altered circumstances. These changes, like depopulation itself, were bound to have significant effects on the ways Indians used the plants and animals around them.

THE FUR TRADE AND RESOURCE EXHAUSTION

The epidemics occurred at precisely the same time that Indian economies were being drawn into new trading relations with European merchants. Indian reasons for participating in the fur trade were diverse and numerous. They included the symbolic and ritual power attributed to certain European goods and the simple material attractions of European trade goods, whether those had to do with the sharpness of metal tools, the warmth and colorfulness of woolen fabrics, or the effectiveness of firearms in certain types of hunting and warfare. Alcohol rapidly came to have an extraordinary and destructive attraction to Indians, the reasons for which are not entirely clear (Vachon 1960; Stanley 1953; Miller and Hamell 1986). Precontact trading networks facilitated the movement of furs and European goods along known transport corridors; these in a sense simply expanded their repertoire to include new bundles of goods. Disruption of status systems in the wake of epidemic depopulation may well have contributed to the willingness of Indians to participate in the trade (Cronon 1983; Ceci 1977; Salisbury 1982).

14

Whatever the reasons, the net effect of the fur trade was to begin a process whereby the animals of the hunt gradually became trading commodities, although the older spiritual relations of the traditional hunt could persist long after animal furs had begun to be sold in European markets (A. Tanner 1979). The fur trade entailed the integration of European goods and traders into Indian gift relations and kin networks as much as it did the linkage of Indian economies to merchant capitalism and the North Atlantic economy ("The Hudson's Bay Company and Native People," *HNAI*, vol. 4). Complex hybrid economies and cultural exchanges resulted, and all had environmental consequences.

In association with European contact, but often far ahead of actual European settlement, major changes occurred in the distribution of North American fauna. Native species dwindled or disappeared and exotic species appeared in sizable numbers. Alterations in flora were even more far-reaching, but these changes tended to come after actual Euro-American settlement. The destruction of big game species did not begin immediately; there is evidence that some of these species were actually increasing in number and range during the period following contact. Bison appear to have been expanding east of the Mississippi, and white-tailed deer, taking advantage of the new habitats opened after riverine lands had been abandoned by peoples following epidemics, may also have increased their populations in the Southeast (Rostlund 1960; R. White 1983:10–11).

Although there is little doubt that local overhunting did occur in aboriginal North America, such overhunting never seriously threatened regional populations of game animals before the advent of the fur trade. The population of those animals whose pelts provided the basis for various fur trades — beaver all over the continent, white-tailed deer in the Southeast, buffalo on the Plains, and sea otter in the Northwest Coast and California — plummeted toward regional or total extinction (Matthiessen 1959). Not all this destruction was the work of Indian hunters, but they played a critical role.

Despite suggestions that Northern Algonquians engaged in a war of revenge against the beaver because they believed that the animal had wantonly caused epidemics, the bulk of available evidence suggests that Indians overhunted game animals in order to obtain the goods offered by Europeans (Martin 1978; Krech 1981). Indian demand for European goods, while quite real, was not automatically large enough to threaten game populations. Nor were native cultural and political barriers against overhunting rapidly and easily overcome. The stimulation of demand and the breakdown of safeguards against overhunting were the result not only of the fur trade but also of social and political developments that were altering the native landscapes of North America. Generalizations upon the environmental consequences of the trade are thus hazardous. Not only did the animals that traders sought differ from place to place and period to period, but the trade itself ranged from a relatively straightforward economic exchange in some areas to a single element in much larger political relationships elsewhere. Moreover, the trade itself cannot be taken in isolation; it was but a component of a larger Indian subsistence economy and had to exist in balance with it.

15

Overhunting as a response to the fur trade did not occur everywhere. Certain tribes — the Pawnees and Crows being perhaps the most notable — managed to control alcohol consumption and frustrated traders by keeping their trade within well-defined limits (Wishart 1979:6). Groups that were central to the imperial balance of power in North America, such as the Iroquois, received needed goods as gifts and thus were less dependent on the hunt.

For overhunting to occur, several conditions had to be met. Indians needed the technological capability to take game in numbers sufficient to threaten the survival of a species. They had to desire or require European goods in sufficient quantities to invest the labor necessary to hunt out game animals. During the hunt, they had to have access to the resources necessary to maintain hunters and their families if the fur-bearing animals themselves did not yield enough meat and garments for subsistence. They had to be able to hunt in a region without threat of disruptive attacks by other peoples. Finally, they had to be able to justify, within their own system of values, the elimination of entire species.

The first factor, technology, seems to be the least important. Northern Indians possessed a native technology and hunting techniques perfectly capable of eliminating the beaver before Whites came. Among buffalo hunters, the bow and arrow remained the preferred weapon even after the introduction of the gun. The horse more than the gun increased the efficiency of the hunt, but mounted hunters harvested the herds for years without seriously depleting them. Firearms did make overhunting of white-tailed deer easier, but hardly ensured their destruction (Martin 1978).

The second factor, demand for trade goods, could lead to depletion even when limited if exchange rates were high and furbearers few. Classic cases include the destruction of beaver in many tribal territories in the Northeast and the elimination of sea otters on the Northwest Coast. When Indian demand was inelastically low, as it often was, and game was abundant, trade might persist for years with only gradual or limited depletion. In the Great Lakes, where beaver and other game animals were abundant over much of the area, depletion of furbearers occurred gradually (Alcoze 1981; Kay 1977:158; Beauharnois and Hocquart 1737). Hunters quickly eliminated beaver and large game in the lands around the overcrowded refugee centers of people who had fled the Iroquois attacks, but game remained abundant elsewhere, both because Indian demand remained limited and because part of that demand could be met by gifts from rival European empires. Even after overhunting of the beaver had clearly occurred, Indians around Green Bay still quit hunting as soon as they had obtained their basic necessities, and if the requisite European goods were available from other sources, they often refused to hunt for furs at all (Kay 1979:402–403; Ray 1980).

When Indian demand for trade goods, for whatever reason, led to overhunting, Indian hunters had several alternatives. If depletion affected only some fur-bearing species, native hunters could simply turn their attention to other animals. With the decline of beaver, for example, first the Menominee and Winnebago and later the Sioux began hunting less valuable species, such as the muskrat, that remained abundant (Kay 1979:413; Anderson 1984:109). If alternative species were not able to support the trade, a group might take measures, either on their own or at the instigation of traders, to conserve or replace depleted species. Another response to the depletion of species was the organization of hunting territories of the Algonquian peoples of eastern Canada. The specific arrangements varied, and the details have been a matter of controversy (*HNAI*, vol. 6:25–26).

The third factor, access to resources, is evinced in the tendency of Indian hunters operating in depleted environments to become dependent on traders for food. Where animals such as the white-tailed deer or the buffalo were a source of both food and skins, overhunting eliminated a community's principal source of food supplies and clothing. Beyond this, traders often bought or harvested Indian foodstuffs themselves in order to pay advances to Indians short of supplies during the winter or spring. After gift exchanges gave way to credit transactions, Indians in debt could be induced to hunt more intensively. On the other hand, without food, Indians would be diverted from fur hunting to subsistence hunting or fishing (Bishop 1974:24, 183–86). Such dependence, of course, only increased as traders encouraged tribes such as the Ojibwa to move into regions of the Canadian Shield that, despite their respectable yield of furs, offered few of the other resources on which Ojibwa life depended.

Hunters in this situation quickly came to depend on traders not just for access to European goods but also for food and clothing (Ray 1974:147, 225; Bishop 1974:196).

The fourth factor, freedom from warfare, is important because moving onto new hunting grounds often meant infringing on lands already hunted by others. If the hunters already in possession of hunting lands resisted the incursions of new hunters, game depletion might be halted simply because borderland rivalry rendered the region too dangerous for fur hunting and thus protected animal populations. In such disputed zones, game populations could recover. This phenomenon appears to have taken place in the borderlands between the Sioux and Chippewa in the eighteenth and nineteenth centuries; in the southern borderlands of the Choctaw, Creek, and Chickasaw in the seventeenth and eighteenth centuries; and in portions of the Great Lakes region that were initially emptied of their inhabitants during the Iroquois wars of the seventeenth century (Hickerson 1965; R. White 1983).

17

These political constraints on overhunting vanished when Europeans moved in to establish peace. When the French secured an uneasy peace in Ontario and southern Michigan among the Ottawa, Mississauga (Ojibwa), Huron-Petun, and the Iroquois, for example, the result was overhunting. French traders complained that for the first time Indians were slaughtering all beavers in the area regardless of age. There was little sense in conserving shared lands or game if rivals would reap the benefits of so doing. Similarly, the Iroquois had complained during an earlier peace that Illinois hunters, contrary to accepted custom, were killing all beavers and sparing no breeding stock (Bacqueville de la Potherie 1722, 3:176–77; NYCD 9:162–63; Lahontan 1905, 1:82). Peace in the Southeast brought similar results among the Choctaw and Chickasaw in the eighteenth and early nineteenth centuries, where the victims were white-tailed deer (R. White 1983; Hatley 1977).

Once begun, the search for fresh hunting lands could instigate a cycle of overhunting, expansion, conflict, and eventually renewed overhunting, but none of these was inevitable. In emerging onto the Plains, groups such as the Teton Sioux, the Assiniboin, and Plains Cree in effect broke this cycle as they transformed their own economies and used the buffalo to become less dependent on European goods. Their connection to the fur trade before the last brief period of the robe trade was as provisioners of the northern fur trapping brigades, producing pemmican for their consumption. These tribes and others contributed to the demise of the buffalo, but their role was relatively minor. White Americans, more than Indians, were principally responsible for the destruction of the bison herds (Ray 1974:131–33, 147).

But the question still remains: even if the job of persuading Indians to overhunt was a long and complicated one, why didn't Indians do more to conserve the depleted animal species upon which their well-being increasingly depended? How did they justify the slaughter of entire species of animals? This is again a question that can only be answered for particular groups involved in particular aspects of the fur trade, but a look at the logic of two groups — Northern Algonquians in the beaver trade and Sioux in the buffalo trade — can perhaps clarify the general patterns.

For Northern Algonquians, beavers, like other animals, were under the control of masters of the game. Their abundance depended on human relations with these masters of the game and on the respect accorded individual animals. The decline of a species meant either that Indians had not observed proper ritual forms or that relations with the game master for that species had deteriorated. Two solutions suggested themselves. Conservation, one such response, appears to have been adopted among contemporary East Crees. Among the Crees, native beliefs about depletion have led to a hunting system that ensures the maintenance of desired species. Respect for the animals involves killing only those that are needed. Although a given territory may be hunted out almost completely, it is then allowed to go unhunted until game animals are once more abundant.

But there is no necessary correlation between such beliefs and modern conservation. Great Lakes Algonquians, for example, could just as consistently consider their increased hunting to be right and "necessary," since they still treated animal remains with respect and still killed only the number of animals needed to acquire goods that were "necessary" (Kay 1985:124-25). The critical element seems to be whether hunters believed their increased killing for trade to constitute disrespect for animals. Sporadically, religious leaders among the Algonquians would assert a connection between declining game populations and irresponsible fur hunting. The Shawnee Tenskwatawa made such arguments in the early nineteenth century. His followers appear to have reduced their hunting for trade, but such religiously inspired conservation appears to have been both unusual and temporary. In most areas it could not overcome dependence on the trade (National Archives of Canada 1807).

A second example of Indian responses to overhunting can be found in Sioux actions during the late nineteenth century. These show that Indian beliefs about animals could actually make conservation in the twentieth-century sense more difficult in situations where animal populations were declining. Like the Algonquians, the Sioux believed that the abundance of animals was a function of the way they were treated and of ritual relations with them. For them, the disappearance of the buffalo was a sign that buffalo were not being treated with the proper respect; in response, the animals were withdrawing underground. But the Sioux could also see that it was not they but the Americans who were mistreating buffalo. When the Ghost Dance religion promised to restock the plains with buffalo, it was thus being perfectly consistent with Sioux ecology and environmental beliefs (DeMallie 1982:390-91).

DOMESTICATED ANIMALS

Association with Euro-American settlers led to a rise in domesticated animals — cattle, sheep, horses, and pigs. The northward dispersal of the horse enabled numerous tribes on the margins of the Plains to move out into the grasslands to exploit the bison herds. Tribes such as the Comanches are better understood as horse pastoralists who happened to exploit the buffalo, as opposed to buffalo hunters who happened to use horses. For the Comanches, horses were sources of food as well as vehicles for hunting, transportation, and war (Downs 1964). In the Great Lakes region, the movement of the Potawatomi, Sauk, and Fox onto prairie lands was accompanied by adoption of the horse at about the same time that Choctaws were beginning to raise small ponies for transportation and food (Clifton 1984). In the central valley of California, horses stolen from Spanish and Mexican rancheros became a basic food item in Indian diets (G. Phillips 1983). And on the Northwest Coast even tribes living in the western foothills of the Cascades became herders, receiving horses from the much larger herds of the Plateau and northern Great Basin. Everywhere in North America south of the Subarctic, the horse gradually became an essential part of Indian subsistence practices.

19

Cattle too became regionally important. The Nez Perce and their neighbors built up large cattle herds, as did the Papagos of the Southwest (Josephy 1965; Manuel, Ramon, and Fontana 1978:522–25). So too did many Southeast Indians, such as the Choctaw and Chickasaw. Virtually everywhere in the East, cattle eventually ranged throughout prairies and open woodlands where deer had once thrived. In the Southeast, Indians also kept pigs in the frontier manner, allowing them to range freely in the woods. Finally, in the Southwest, the Navajo and to a lesser degree the Pueblos became accomplished shepherds. Sheep and horses initially complemented agriculture among the Navajo and gave them increased security in facing the irregular subsistence cycles of a harsh and arid land.

As an example of the divergent ways that peoples living in similar environments might choose to utilize the horse, both the Pawnee and the Teton Sioux benefited from the northward spread of horses. Both groups at the time they acquired the horse lived on lands bordering the Plains. For the Teton Sioux, the acquisition of horses meant more effective buffalo hunting, greater security of subsistence, and a general movement away from dependence on the fur trade.

For tribes like the Sioux, maintaining horse herds through the rigors of the Plains winter became one of their most important environmental challenges. Because the short bunch grasses of the High Plains remain nutritious even after their topgrowth has dried and withered, horses could graze until snow covered the ground. After that, horses often depended on the young growth of cottonwoods and on cottonwood bark harvested by their Indian owners. Even with the widespread cutting of these trees, which grew only on narrow stream margins and hence could easily become depleted across wide areas, many horses still died in bad winters. Replacing them meant raiding, usually directed against tribes living in more southern areas where milder winter weather meant greater survival of the horse herds. This pattern of horse starvation and Indian raiding appears to have been among the most important reasons for the longstanding tendency of many Plains nomads to migrate gradually south and west, but this is a matter of controversy. They sought to move not only toward the original source of horses but toward the milder southern lands where the animals could better survive the winter (R. White 1978, 1983; Osborn 1983; Albers and James 1985).

In contrast the Pawnee were horticulturalists, and although horses certainly increased the efficiency of their seasonal buffalo hunting on the plains, the animals, unless carefully watched, also threatened the unfenced crops Pawnee women planted along the tributary streams of the Platte and Loup rivers. There were also problems in trying to feed them during the late fall before departure on the winter hunt, during the hunt itself, and in the early spring when the Pawnee returned to their villages to plant. Paradoxically, in a land of abundant grass the horses could nonetheless starve because the tall grasses of the eastern plains store their nutrients in their rhizomes and their dried stalks thus have little food value. In the fall, Pawnees fed the horses corn nubbins or grazed them in sheltered areas such as Grand Island, where fresh grass was available. During the winter, the Pawnees, like the nomads, cut and fed them the bark and small branches of cottonwood trees.

The real danger came in the early spring, when the horses, already weakened by a harsh winter, had to carry the Pawnees and their dried meat and equipment back to the earth lodge villages at a time when new grass had not yet normally appeared. The Pawnee could not wait for the grass to appear, or they would arrive home too late to plant; however, if they left too early they would lose their horses, along with the stores of dried meat they carried. The Pawnees' eventual solution was to manipulate the environment to produce earlier growth of grasses. They methodically burned the lands around their villages and along the routes to their Plains hunting grounds. By removing dead top growth and debris, the Pawnees made sure that the soil warmed more quickly and the grass sprouted sooner. They thus managed to fit the horse into an existing subsistence cycle at the same time that the Teton Sioux used the animal to create a subsistence cycle that was largely new (R. White 1983:180–86).

Outside of the horse on the Plains, probably no animal was integrated more fully into an Indian way of life than sheep were among the Navajos. The Navajos were horticulturalists, hunters, and raiders before they obtained the herds and remained so afterwards; but the addition of herds of sheep did give them a prosperity and environmental security they had lacked. Rather than depending on a single food or activity to produce a surplus that hedged against famine, the Navajo relied on a mixed subsistence base. A group that hunted, farmed, and grazed sheep was more secure than a group that relied on only one such activity. The herds thus became a critical link in Navajo subsistence. Particularly after the Navajo return from the Bosque Redondo in the 1860s, during a period when they came close to hunting out their newly constricted lands, sheep alone often stood between them and famine (R. White 1983).

Among the different Indian peoples who adopted them, domesticated animals undoubtedly had some of the same environmental effects among Indian communities as they did among European ones, though in general Indian pastoralism probably had less concentrated effects because of the lower population densities involved. Weed species were undoubtedly encouraged in places where animals were kept in large numbers. New concepts of animal ownership encouraged patterns of raiding and theft that, *21* if not entirely new, took on new meaning for Indian cultures, especially among peoples in the trans-Mississippi West, where the horse herds were so regularly threatened with starvation. Among horticulturalists, greater attention had to be paid to protecting crops in places where animals were kept. The problem of feeding animals during scarce seasons of the year could encourage deforestation and erosion alike. Despite these potential problems, the adoption of domesticated animals appears to have been a very viable response for Indian peoples who found themselves confronted with declining populations of the native species on which they had formerly depended for food.

Just as Indians were quick to incorporate European tools into their earlier patterns of subsistence, so too were they willing to become pastoralists relying on the introduced animals for a substantial portion of their social and economic life.

WORKS CITED

Albers, Patricia C., and William R. James. 1985. Historical Materialism vs. Evolutionary Ecology: A Methodological Note on Horse Distribution and American Plains Indians. *Critique of Anthropology* 6:87-100. London.

Alcoze, Thomas M. 1981. Presettlement Beaver Population Density in the Upper Great Lakes Region. (Unpublished Ph.D. Dissertation in Zoology, Michigan State University, East Lansing.)

Anderson, Gary C. 1984. Kinsmen of Another Kind: Dakota-White Relations in the Upper Mississippi Valley, 1650-1862. Lincoln: University of Nebraska Press.

Arno, Stephen F. 1985. Ecological Effects and Management Implications of Indian Fires. Pp. 81-86 in Proceedings — Symposium and Workshop on Wilderness Fire; Missoula, Mont., November 15-18, 1983. *U.S. Department of Agriculture, Forest Service, Intermountain Forest and Range Experiment Station, Ogden, Utah. General Technical Report* INT-182. Washington: U.S. Government Printing Office.

Bacqueville de la Potherie, Claude C. Le Roy. 1722. Histoire de l'Amérique septentrionale. 4 vols. Paris: J.L. Nion and F. Didot.

Bean, Lowell J., and Harry W. Lawton. 1973. Some Explanations for the Rise of Cultural Complexity in Native California with Comments on Proto-agriculture and Agriculture. Pp. v-xlvii in Patterns of Indian Burning in California: Ecology and Ethnohistory. Henry T. Lewis, ed. *Ballena Press Anthropological Papers* 1. Ramona, Calif.

Beauharnois, Claude de la Boische de Beauharnois et de Villechauve, and Gilles Hocquart. 1737. Mémoire au Ministre. *Archives Nationales, Colonies IIA*, Vol. 67, folio 100-101. Paris.

Bishop, Charles A. 1974. The Northern Ojibwa and the Fur Trade: An Historical and Ecological Study. Toronto: Holt, Rinehart and Winston of Canada.

Black, Mary B. 1977. Ojibwa Power Belief System. Pp. 141-151 in The Anthropology of Power: Ethnographic Studies from Asia, Oceania, and the New World. Raymond D. Fogelson and Richard Adams, eds. New York: Academic Press.

————. 1977a. Ojibwa Taxonomy and Percept Ambiguity. *Ethos* 5(1):90-118.

Bradfield, Maitland. 1971. The Changing Pattern of Hopi Agriculture. *Occasional Papers of the Royai Anthropological Institute* 30. London.

Ceci, Lynn. 1977. The Effect of European Settlement and Trade on the Settlement Pattern of Indians in Coastal New York, 1524-1665: The Archaeological and Documentary Evidence. (Unpublished Ph.D. Dissertation in Anthropology, City University of New York.)

Chapman, H.H. 1932. Is the Longleaf Type a Climax? *Ecology* 13(4):328-334.

Charlevoix, Pierre F.X. de. 1744. Histoire et description générale de la Nouvelle-France, avec le journal historique d'un voyage fait par ordre du roi dans l'Amérique Septentrionale. 6 vols. Paris: Rollin Fils.

Clifton, James. 1984. From Bark Canoe to Pony Herds: The Lake Michigan Transportation Revolution, 1750-1755. (Paper presented at the Chicago Maritime Conference, 1984.)

Cronon, William. 1983. Changes in the Land: Indians, Colonists, and the Ecology of New England. New York: Hill and Wang.

Crosby, Alfred W. 1972. The Columbian Exchange: Biological and Cultural Consequences of 1492. Westport, Conn.: Greenwood Press.

————. 1976. Virgin Soil Epidemics as a Factor in the Aboriginal Depopulation of America. *William and Mary Quarterly, 3d ser., Vol.* 33(2):289-299. Williamsburg, Va.

Day, Gordon M. 1953. The Indian as an Ecological Factor in the Northeastern Forest. *Ecology* 34(2):329-346.

Deloria, Vine, Jr. 1970. We Talk, You Listen: New Tribes, New Turf. New York: Macmillan.

DeMallie, Raymond J. 1982. The Lakota Ghost Dance: An Ethnohistorical Account. *Pacific Historical Review* 51(4):385-405.

Dobyns, Henry F. 1981. From Fire to Flood: Historic Human Destruction of Sonoran Desert Riverine Oases. *Ballena Press Anthropological Papers* 20. Socorro, N.M.

————. 1983. Their Number Become Thinned: Native American Population Dynamics in Eastern North America. Knoxville: University of Tennessee Press.

Downs, James F. 1964. Comments on Plains Indian Cultural Development. *American Anthropologist* 66(2):421-422.

————. 1966. The Two Worlds of the Washo: An Indian Tribe of California and Nevada. New York: Holt, Rinehart and Winston.

Driver, Harold. 1969. Indians of North America. 2d ed. Chicago: University of Chicago Press.

Drucker, Philip, and Robert F. Heizer. 1967. To Make My Name Good: A Reexamination of the Southern Kwakiutl Potlatch. Berkeley: University of California Press.

Flannery, Regina. 1939. An Analysis of Coastal Algonquian Culture. *Catholic University of America Anthropological Series* 7. Washington. (Reprinted: AMS Press, New York, 1983.)

Flores, Dan L. 1983. Zion in Eden: Phases of the Environmental History of Utah. *Environmental Review* 7(4):325-344.

Gruell, George E. 1985. Indian Fires in the Interior West: A Widespread Influence. Pp. 68-74 in Proceedings — Symposium and Workshop on Wilderness Fire; Missoula, Mont., Nov. 15-18, 1983. *U.S. Department of Agriculture, Forest Service. Intermountain Forest and Range Experiment Station, Ogden, Utah. General Technical Report* INT-182. Washington: U.S. Government Printing Office.

Hallowell, A. Irving. 1949. The Size of Algonkian Hunting Territories: A Function of Ecological Adjustments. *American Anthropologist* 51(1):35-45.

————. 1976. Contributions to Anthropology: Selected Papers of A. Irving Hallowell. Chicago: University of Chicago Press.

Hatley, Marvin T., III. 1977. The Dividing Path: The Direction of Cherokee Life in the Eighteenth Century. (Unpublished M.A. Thesis in Anthropology, University of North Carolina, Chapel Hill.)

Hickerson, Harold. 1965. The Virginia Deer and Intertribal Buffer Zones in the Upper Mississippi Valley. Pp. 43-65 in Man, Culture and Animals: The Role of Animals in Human Ecological Adjustments. Anthony Leeds and Andrew P. Vayda, eds. *American Association for the Advancement of Science Publication* 78. Washington.

Hill, W.W. 1938. The Agricultural and Hunting Methods of the Navaho Indians. *Yale University Publications in Anthropology* 18. New Haven. (Reprinted: AMS Press, New York, 1978.)

Hudson, Charles M. 1976. The Southeastern Indians. Knoxville: University of Tennessee Press.

JR=Thwaites, Reuben G., ed. 1896-1901. The Jesuit Relations and Allied Documents: Travel and Explorations of the Jesuit Missionaries in New France, 1610-1791. The Original French, Latin and Italian Texts, with English Translations and Notes. 73 vols. Cleveland, Ohio: Burrows Brothers. (Reprinted: Pageant, New York, 1959.)

Jacobs, Wilbur R. 1972. Dispossessing the American Indian: Indians and Whites on the Colonial Frontier. New York: Scribner.

22

Jorgenson, Joseph G. 1980. Western Indians: Comparative Environments, Languages, and Cultures of 172 Western American Indian Tribes. San Francisco: W.H. Freeman.

Josephy, Alvin M., Jr. 1965. The Nez Perce Indians and the Opening of the Northwest. New Haven, Conn.: Yale University Press.

Kay, Jeanne. 1977. The Land of La Baye: The Ecological Impact of the Green Bay Fur Trade, 1634–1836. (Unpublished Ph.D. Dissertation in Geography, University of Wisconsin, Madison.)

————. 1979. Wisconsin Indian Hunting Patterns, 1634–1836. Annals of the Association of American Geographers 66:402–418. Washington.

————. 1985. Native Americans in the Fur Trade and Wildlife Depletion. Environmental Review 9(2):118–130.

Krech, Shepard, III. 1978. Disease, Starvation, and Northern Athapaskan Social Organization. American Ethnologist 5(4):710–32.

————. 1981. Indians, Animals and the Fur Trade: A Critique of Keepers of the Game. Athens: University of Georgia Press.

Lahontan, Louis Armand de Lom d'Arce de. 1905. New Voyages to North America by the Baron de Lahontan [1703]. Reuben G. Thwaites, ed. 2 vols. Chicago: A.C. McClurg.

Lewis, Henry T., ed. 1973. Patterns of Indian Burning in California: Ecology and Ethnohistory. Ballena Press Anthropological Papers 1. Ramona, Calif.

MacLeod, William C. 1936. Conservation Among Primitive Hunting Peoples. Scientific Monthly 43(December):562–566.

McNeill, William H. 1976. Plagues and Peoples. Garden City, N.Y.: Anchor Press/Doubleday.

Manuel, Henry F., Juiliann Ramon, and Bernard L. Fontana. 1978. Dressing for the Window: Papago Indians and Economic Development. Pp. 511–577 in American Indian Economic Development. Sam Stanley, ed. The Hague: Mouton.

Martin, Calvin. 1978. Keepers of the Game: Indian–Animal Relationships and the Fur Trade. Berkeley: University of California Press.

Matthiessen, Peter. 1959. Wildlife in America. New York: Viking Press.

Miller, Christopher L., and George R. Hamell. 1986. A New Perspective on Indian–White Contact: Cultural Symbols and Colonial Trade. Journal of American History 73(2):311–328.

Mooney, James. 1890. Cherokee Theory and Practice of Medicine. Journal of American Folk-Lore 3(1):44–50.

NYCD=O'Callaghan, Edmund B., ed. 1853–1887. Documents Relative to the Colonial History of the State of New York; Procured in Holland, England and France, by John R. Brodhead. 15 vols. Albany, N.Y.: Weed, Parsons.

Oritz, Alfonso. 1969. The Tewa World: Space, Time, Being, and Becoming in a Pueblo Society. Chicago: University of Chicago Press.

Osborn, Alan J. 1983. Ecological Aspects of Equestrian Adaptations in Aboriginal North America. American Anthropologist 85(3):563–591.

Pearce, Roy H. 1953. The Savages of America: A Study of the Indian and the Idea of Civilization. Baltimore, Md.: Johns Hopkins University Press.

Phillips, George. 1983. Commerce in the Valley: Indian–White Trade in Mexican California. (Paper presented at the American Historical Association Meeting, Dec. 1983.)

Pyne, Stephen J. 1982. Fire in America: A Cultural History of Wildland and Rural Fire. Princeton, N.J.: Princeton University Press.

Radin, Paul. 1924. Primitive Man as Philosopher. New York: D. Appleton.

Ray, Arthur J. 1974. Indians in the Fur Trade: Their Role as Trappers, Hunters, and Middlemen in the Lands Southwest of Hudson's Bay 1660–1870. Toronto: University of Toronto Press.

————. 1980. Indians as Consumers in the Eighteenth Century. Pp. 255–271 in Old Trails and New Directions: Papers of the Third North American Fur Trade Conference. Carol M. Judd and Arthur J. Ray, eds. Toronto: University of Toronto Press.

Rostlund, Erhard. 1960. The Geographic Range of the Historic Bison in the Southeast. Annals of the Association of American Geographers 50(4):395–407. Washington.

Salisbury, Neal E. 1982. Manitou and Providence: Indians, Europeans, and the Making of New England, 1500–1643. New York: Oxford University Press.

Sauer, Carl O. 1971. Sixteenth Century North America: The Land and the People as Seen by the Europeans. Berkeley: University of California Press.

Sheehan, Bernard W. 1973. Seeds of Extinction: Jeffersonian Philanthropy and the American Indian. Chapel Hill: University of North Carolina Press.

Slotkin, Richard. 1973. Regeneration Through Violence: The Mythology of the American Frontier, 1600–1860. Middletown, Conn.: Wesleyan University Press.

Smith, Henry N. 1950. Virgin Land: The American West as Symbol and Myth. Cambridge, Mass.: Harvard University Press.

Speck, Frank G. 1938. Aboriginal Conservators. Bird-lore 40(4):258–261. New York.

Stanley, George F.G. 1953. The Indians and the Brandy Trade During the Ancien Régime. Revue d'Histoire de l'Amérique Française 6(4):489–505. Montreal.

Steward, Julian H. 1933. Ethnography of the Owens Valley Paiute. University of California Publications in American Archaeology and Ethnology 33(3):233–350. Berkeley.

23

————. 1941. Culture Element Distributions, XIII: Nevada Shoshone. *University of California Anthropological Records* 4(2):209–359. Berkeley.

Sturtevant, William, series ed. 1989. Handbook of North American Indians. Washington: Smithsonian Institution Press.

Tanner, Adrian. 1979. Bringing Home Animals: Religious Ideology and Mode of Production of the Mistassini Cree Hunters. New York: St. Martins Press.

Vachon, André. 1960. L'Eau-de-vie dans la société indienne. Pp. 23–32 in *Canadian Historical Association Report for 1960*. John P. Heisler and Paul E. Dumas, eds. Ottawa.

Wallace, Anthony F.C. 1970. Death and Rebirth of the Seneca. New York: Knopf.

Wells, Philip V. 1970. Historical Factors Controlling Vegetation Patterns and Floristic Distributions in the Central Plains Region of North America. Pp. 211–221 in Pleistocene and Recent Environments of the Central Great Plains. Wakefield Dort and J. Knox Jones, Jr., eds. *University of Kansas, Department of Geology, Special Publication* 3. Lawrence.

Weltfish, Gene. 1965. The Lost Universe: The Way of Life of the Pawnee. New York: Basic Books.

White, Richard. 1978. The Winning of the West: The Expansion of the Western Sioux in the Eighteenth and Nineteenth Centuries. *Journal of American History* 65(2):319–343.

————. 1980. Land Use, Environment, and Social Change: The Shaping of Island County, Washington. Seattle: University of Washington Press.

————. 1983. The Roots of Dependency: Subsistence, Environment and Social Change Among the Choctaws, Pawnees, and Navajos. Lincoln: University of Nebraska Press.

Will, George F., and George E. Hyde. 1964. Corn Among the Indians of the Upper Missouri [1917]. Lincoln: University of Nebraska Press.

Wishart, David J. 1979. The Fur Trade of the American West, 1807–1840: A Geographical Synthesis. Lincoln: University of Nebraska Press.

The French Presence in Huronia: The Structure of Franco-Huron Relations in the First Half of the Seventeenth Century

BRUCE G. TRIGGER

Few studies of Canadian history in the first half of the seventeenth century credit sufficiently the decisive role played at that time by the country's native peoples. The success of European colonizers, traders, and missionaries depended to a greater degree than most of them cared to admit on their ability to understand and accommodate themselves not only to native customs but also to a network of political and economic relationships that was not of their own making. Traders and missionaries often were forced to treat Algonkians and Iroquoians as their equals and sometimes they had to acknowledge that the Indians had the upper hand. If the Europeans were astonished and revolted by many of the customs of these Indians (often, however, no more barbarous than their own), they also admired their political and economic sagacity.[1] Indeed, one Jesuit was of the opinion that the Huron were more intelligent than the rural inhabitants of his own country.[2] If the missionary or fur trader

From *Canadian Historical Review* 49 (1968): 107–141. Reprinted with the permission of University of Toronto Press Incorporated.

felt compelled to understand the customs of the Indians, the modern historian should feel no less obliged to do so.

In order to appreciate the role that the Indians played in the history of Canada in the first half of the seventeenth century, it is necessary to study their customs and behaviour and the things they valued. Because their way of life differed from that of the Europeans, the fur traders and missionaries who interacted with them frequently became amateur anthropologists, and some of them became very good ones. For some tribes the documentation amassed by these early contacts is extensive and of high quality. For no tribe is this truer than for the Huron.[3] From the detailed picture of Huronia that emerges from these studies, it is possible to ascertain the motives that prompted the behaviour of particular Indians, or groups of Indians, in a manner no less detailed than our explanations of those which governed the behaviour of their European contemporaries. I might add, parenthetically, that historians are not alone to blame for the failure to utilize anthropological insights in the study of early Canadian history. Iroquoian ethnologists and archaeologists have tended to avoid historical or historiographic problems. Only a few individuals, such as George T. Hunt, have attempted to work in the no man's land between history and anthropology.

Two explanations have been used by anthropologists and historians to justify the existing cleavage between their respective studies. One of these maintains that when the Europeans arrived in eastern North America, the native tribes were engaged in a struggle, the origins and significance of which are lost in the mists of time and therefore wholly the concern of ethnohistorians. Because of this, there is no reason for the historian to try to work out in detail the causes of the conflicts and alliances that existed at that time.[4] Very often, however, the struggle between different groups is painted in crude, almost racist, terms (and in complete contradiction to the facts) as one between Algonkian- and Iroquoian-speaking peoples, the former being an indigenous population, mainly hunters, the latter a series of invading tribes growing corn and living in large villages. It should be noted that such a simplistic explanation of European history, even for the earliest periods, would now be laughed out of court by any competent historian. The alternative hypothesis suggests that European contact altered the life of the Indian, and above all the relationships among the different tribes, so quickly and completely that a knowledge of aboriginal conditions is not necessary to understand events after 1600.[5] From an *a priori* point of view, this theory seems most unlikely. Old relationships have a habit of influencing events, even when economic and political conditions are being rapidly altered. Future studies must describe in detail how aboriginal cultures were disrupted or altered by their contact with the Europeans, rather than assume that interaction between Indians and Europeans can be

25

explained as a set of relationships that has little or no reference to the native culture.

We will begin by considering developments in Huronia prior to the start of the fur trade.

The Huron

When the Huron tribes were described for the first time in 1615,[6] they were living in the Penetanguishene Peninsula and the part of Simcoe County that runs along Matchedash Bay between Wasaga Beach and Lake Simcoe. The Huron probably numbered twenty to thirty thousand, and, according to the most reliable of the descriptions from the Jesuit missionaries,[7] they were divided into four tribes that formed a confederacy similar in its structure to the league of the Iroquois.[8] The Attignaouantan or Bear tribe, which included about half of the people in the confederacy, lived on the western extremity of Huronia. Next to them lived the Attingueenougnahak, or Cord tribe, and the Tahontaenrat or Deer tribe. Farthest east, near Lake Simcoe, were the Ahrendarrhonon or Rock nation. The Tionnontate, or Petun, who spoke the same language as the Huron and were very similar to them, inhabited the country west of Huronia near the Blue Mountain. The Petun, however, were not members of the Huron confederacy and prior to the arrival of the French, they and the Huron had been at war. Another Iroquoian confederacy, the Neutral, lived farther south between the Grand River and the Niagara frontier. Except for a few Algonkian bands that lived west of the Petun, there do not appear to have been any other Indians living in southern Ontario, except in the Ottawa Valley. The uninhabited portions of the province were the hunting territories of the Huron, Neutral, and Petun and also served as a buffer zone between these tribes and the Iroquois who lived south of Lake Ontario.

The Huron, like other Iroquoian tribes, grew corn, beans, and squash. These crops were planted and looked after by the women, who also gathered the firewood used for cooking and heating the houses. Contrary to popular notions, the men also made an important contribution to the tribal economy, inasmuch as it was they who cleared the fields for planting (no small task when only stone axes were available) and who caught the fish which were an important source of nutrition. Because of the high population density, the areas close to Huronia appear to have been depleted of game, and expeditions in search of deer had to travel far to the south and east.[9] In general, hunting appears to have been of little economic importance among the Huron.

Huron villages had up to several thousand inhabitants and the main ones were protected by palisades made of posts woven together with smaller branches. Inside large villages there were fifty or more long-

26

houses, often 100 feet or more in length, made of bark attached to a light wooden frame. These houses were inhabited by eight to ten very closely related families. Families that traced themselves back to a common female ancestor formed a clan, which was a political unit having its own civil chief and war leader. Each tribe in turn was made up of a number of such clans and the clan leaders served on the tribal and confederal councils.[10]

The events that led to the formation of the Huron confederacy are not well understood. The Huron themselves said that it began around AD 1400, with the union of the Bear and Cord tribes, and grew thereafter through the addition of further lineages and tribes. Archaeologically it appears that, although one or more of the Huron tribes was indigenous to Simcoe County, other groups moved into historic Huronia from as far away as the Trent Valley, the Toronto region, and Huron and Grey counties to the west.[11] Two tribes, the Rock and the Deer, had been admitted to the confederacy not long before the arrival of the French.

27

Historians frequently have asserted that it was fear of the Iroquois that prompted the Huron to seek refuge in this remote and sheltered portion of Ontario.[12] While this may be why some groups moved into Huronia, it is clear that in prehistoric times the Huron outnumbered the Iroquois and probably were not at any military disadvantage. For this reason ethnologists have begun to seek other explanations to account for the heavy concentration of population in Huronia in historic times. An abundance of light, easily workable soil may be part of the answer. Since the Huron lacked the tools to work heavier soils, this advantage may have outweighed the tendency towards drought and the absence of certain trace minerals in the soil which now trouble farmers in that area.[13] Huronia also lay at the south end of the main canoe route that ran along the shores of Georgian Bay. North of there the soil was poor and the growing season short, so that none of the tribes depended on agriculture. They engaged mainly in hunting and fishing, and tribes from at least as far away as Lake Nipissing traded surplus skins, dried fish, and meat with the Huron in return for corn, which they ate in the winter when other food was scarce.[14]

As early as 1615 the French noted that Huronia was the centre of a well-developed system of trade. Hunt, however, seems to have seriously overestimated both the extent of this network and the degree to which the Huron were dependent on it.[15] The main trade appears to have been with the hunting peoples to the north, who happened to be Algonkian-speaking. The other Iroquoian tribes had economies similar to that of the Huron, so that with the exception of a few items, such as black squirrel skins, which came from the Neutral country, and tobacco from the Petun, trade with the other Iroquoian tribes was of little importance. Trade with the north, however, brought in supplies of dried meat, fish, skins, clothing, native copper, and "luxury items" such as charms, which were obtained in exchange for corn, tobacco, fishing nets, Indian hemp, wampum, and squirrel skins.[16] Although manufactured goods, as well as natural products, flowed in both directions, the most important item the Huron had for export undoubtedly was corn. In 1635 Father Le Jeune described Huronia as the "granary of most of the Algonkians."[17]

Whole bands of northerners spent the winters living outside Huron villages, trading furs and dried meat with their hosts in return for corn. The Huron assumed a dominant position in these trading relationships and the Jesuits record that when the Algonkians had dealings with them, they did so in the Huron language since the latter did not bother to learn Algonkian.[18] The social implications of such linguistic behaviour cannot be lost on anyone living in present-day Quebec. In the French accounts the Algonkians appear to have been better friends of the Rock tribe than they were of the Bear.[19]

Considerable quantities of European trade goods that are believed to date between 1550 and 1575 have been found in Seneca sites in New York State.[20] Since both archaeological and historical evidence suggests that there was contact between the Huron and the tribes that lived along the St. Lawrence River in the sixteenth century,[21] it is possible that trade goods were arriving in Huronia in limited quantities at this time as well. In any such trade the Algonkin tribes along the Ottawa River would almost certainly have been intermediaries. It is thus necessary to consider the possibility that trade between the Huron and the northern Algonkians originally developed as a result of the Huron desire to obtain European trade goods.

There are a number of reasons for doubting that trade with the northern tribes had a recent origin. For one thing, the rules governing trade were exceedingly elaborate. A particular trade route was recognized as the property of the Huron tribe or family that had pioneered it, and other people were authorized to trade along this route only if they had obtained permission from the group to which it belonged.[22] Thus, since the Rock were the first Huron tribe to establish relations with the French on the St. Lawrence, they alone were entitled by Huron law to trade with them.[23] Because of the importance of this trade, however, the Rock soon "shared" it with the more numerous and influential Bear, and with the other tribes of Huronia.[24] The control of trade was vested in a small number of chiefs, and other men had to have their permission before they were allowed to engage in it.[25] An even more important indication of the antiquity of Huron contact with the north is the archaeological evidence of the Huron influence on the native cultures of that region, which can be dated as early as AD 900 and is especially evident in pottery styles.[26] Taken together, these two lines of evidence provide considerable support for the hypothesis of an early trade.

In the historic period the Huron men left their villages to visit other tribes in the summers, while their women were working in the fields. Profit was not the only reason for undertaking long voyages. The Jesuits

28

report that many travelled into distant regions to gamble or to see new sights — in short, for adventure. Trading expeditions, like war, were a challenge for young men.[27] Trading between different tribes was not always a safe and uncomplicated business and, for all they had to gain from trade during the historic period, the Huron frequently were hesitant to initiate trade with tribes of whom they had only slight acquaintance.

The dangers that beset intertribal contacts were largely products of another institution, as old, if not older than trade — the blood feud. If a man was slain by someone who was not his kinsman, his family, clan, or tribe (depending on how far removed the murderer was) felt obliged to avenge his death by slaying the killer or one of the killer's relatives. Such action could be averted only by reparations in the form of gifts paid by the group to which the murderer belonged to that of the murdered man. When an act of blood revenge actually was carried out, the injured group usually regarded it as a fresh injury; thus any killing, even an accidental one, might generate feuds that would go on for generations. This was especially true of intertribal feuds.[28]

The Huron and Five Nations had both suppressed blood feuds within their respective confederacies, but only with great difficulty. When quarrels arose between individuals from tribes not so united, they frequently gave rise to bloodshed and war. The chances of war were also increased because skill in raiding was a source of prestige for young men who therefore desired to pursue this activity.[29] If it were possible, prisoners captured in war were taken back to their captors' villages to be tortured to death, partly as an act of revenge, but also as a sacrifice to the sun or "god of war."[30] These three motives — revenge, individual prestige, and sacrifice — were common to all the Iroquoian-speaking peoples of the northeast and to many of their neighbours, and generated and sustained intertribal wars over long periods of time. Indeed, where no close political ties existed, such as those within the Huron confederacy, and where there were no mutually profitable trading relationships, war between tribes appears to have been the rule. The Huron were almost invariably at war with one or more of the Five Nations, and prior to the development of the fur trade (when they started to carry French goods to the south and west) they appear to have been at war with the Neutral and Petun as well.[31]

On the other hand, when a trading relationship developed between the Huron and some neighbouring tribe, every effort was made to control feuds that might lead to war between them. The payment that was made to settle a blood feud with the Algonkians was greater than that made to settle a feud inside the confederacy,[32] and the dearest payment on record was made to the French in 1648 to compensate them for a Jesuit *donné* murdered by some Huron chiefs.[33]

A second method of promoting stable relations between tribes that wished to be trading partners appears to have been the exchange of a few people both as a token of friendship and to assure each group that

29

the other intended to behave properly. Very often, these hostages appear to have been children. Although this custom is never explicitly described by the early French writers, the evidence for its existence is clear-cut. A Huron, whose sons or nephews (sister's sons and therefore close relatives) were sent to the Jesuit seminary in Quebec, boasted that they were relatives of the French and for this reason hoped for preferential treatment when they went to trade on the St. Lawrence.[34] Others said they had "relatives" among the Neutral and Petun and one man is reported as leaving his daughter with these relatives.[35] The priests and lay visitors who came to Huronia in early times were treated as kinsmen by the Huron, and families and individuals were anxious to have them live with them,[36] no doubt because the Huron regarded these visitors as pledges of good faith whose association with a particular family would establish good relations between that family and the French officials and traders downriver. The presentation of young children to Jacques Cartier at a number of villages along the St. Lawrence suggests, moreover, that this custom may have been an old one.[37]

30

The Huron thus not only traded with other tribes prior to the start of the fur trade, but also, in common with other tribes in the northeast, had developed a code or set of conventions that governed the manner in which this trade was conducted. Being a product of Indian culture, this code was designed to deal with specifically Indian problems. We will now turn to the French attempts to adapt themselves to the native trading patterns after Champlain's first encounter with the Indians in 1608.

Early Franco-Huron Relations

In 1608, the year Champlain established a trading post at Quebec, he was visited by the representatives of some Algonkin tribes from the Ottawa Valley and, in order to win their respect for him as a warrior and to secure their goodwill, he agreed to accompany them the following year on a raid against their chief enemy, the Iroquois.[38] The regions to the north gave promise of more pelts and ones of better quality than did the Iroquois country to the south, and fighting with a tribe alongside its enemies was an effective way of confirming an alliance.[39] Thus Champlain's actions seem to have been almost inevitable. At the same time he probably also hoped to drive Iroquois raiders from the St. Lawrence Valley and to open the river as a valuable trade artery.[40]

When the Ottawa River Algonkin returned the next year, they were accompanied by a party of Huron warriors from the Rock tribe. In later times the Huron informed the Jesuits that they had first heard of the French from the Algonkians early in the seventeenth century, and as a result of this had decided to go downriver to meet these newcomers for themselves.[41] Very likely, Champlain's account and the Huron one refer to the same event. Some of the Ottawa River Algonkin, who were already probably in the habit of wintering in Huronia, may have tried to recruit Huron warriors for their forthcoming expedition against the Iroquois, and the Huron, prompted by curiosity and a desire for adventure, may have agreed to accompany them to Quebec.

Champlain was keenly interested at this time both in exploring the interior and in making contacts with the people who lived there. Learning the size of the Huron confederacy and their good relations with the hunting (and potentially trapping) peoples to the north, Champlain realized their importance for the development of the fur trade and set out to win their friendship. The Huron, on the contrary, were at first extremely hesitant in their dealings with the French,[42] in part because they had no treaty with them and also because they regarded the French as allies of the Algonkin, who might become hostile if they saw the Hurons trying to establish an independent relationship with them.

31

The ambiguity of the Huron position can be seen in the exchange of children that was arranged in 1610. At that time the Huron gave Champlain custody of a boy, who was to go to France with him, and in exchange they received a young Frenchman. When the Huron departed, however, the French boy (probably Étienne Brûlé) did not leave with them, but stayed with Iroquet, an Algonkin chief from the lower Ottawa.[43] Iroquet, however, seems to have been one of the Algonkin who was in the habit of wintering in Huronia. Thus a three-sided exchange seems to have been arranged in which the Huron laid the basis for a friendly relationship with the French, but one that was subordinate to, and dependent upon, their relationship with the Algonkin.

As trade with the French increased, the Huron began to appreciate French goods and to want more of them. Metal awls and needles were superior to native bone ones, and iron arrowheads could penetrate the traditional shields and body armour of their enemies. Metal kettles were easier to cook in than clay pots and metal knives were much more efficient than stone ones. Clearing fields and cutting wood was easier when stone axes were replaced by iron hatchets. Luxury items, such as cloth and European beads, were soon sought after as well.[44]

The growing demand for these products in a population that numbered between twenty and thirty thousand no doubt made the Huron anxious to establish closer relations with the French, without, if possible, having to recognize the Ottawa River Algonkin as middlemen or to pay them tolls to pass through their lands.[45] Since the principal item that the French wanted was beaver pelts,[46] the Huron probably also began to expand their trade with the north at this time in order to secure these furs in larger quantities. In return for these furs, they carried not only corn and tobacco but also French trade goods to their northern trading partners. The tribes north of Lake Huron seem to have continued to trade exclusively with the Huron rather than seeking to obtain goods from the French. No doubt this was in part because Huronia was nearby and reaching it did not require a long and hazardous journey down the Ottawa River. Such a journey would have been time-consuming, if not impossible, for a small tribe. More importantly, however, they wanted corn for winter consumption, which the Huron, but not the French, were able to provide. Although there is no documentary evidence to support this suggestion, it seems likely that increasing supplies of corn permitted these hunters to devote more time to trapping and relieved them of some of their day-to-day worries about survival.[47] Thus the growth of the fur trade may have led the northern groups to concentrate on trapping and the Huron to devote more of their energy to producing agricultural surpluses to trade with the north.[48] On at least one occasion, the Huron were providing even the French at Quebec with needed supplies of food.[49] In the 1640s their close friends and trading partners, the Nipissing, were travelling as far north as James Bay each year in order to collect the furs which they passed on to the Huron.[50]

In spite of the Huron desire for French goods and their ability to gather furs from the interior, the development of direct trade between Huronia and the St. Lawrence required the formation of a partnership that was expressed in terms the Indian could understand. Without continual assurances of goodwill passing between Huron and French leaders and without the exchange of gifts and people, no Huron would have travelled to Quebec without fear and trepidation. Even after many years of trade, Hurons going to Quebec felt safer if they were travelling with a Frenchman whom they knew and who could be trusted to protect their interests while they were trading.[51] Champlain understood clearly that treaties of friendship were necessary for successful trading partnerships with the Indians. For this reason he had been willing to support the Algonkin and Montagnais in their wars with the Mohawk and, since it was impossible to be friendly with both sides, had maintained his alliance with these northern tribes in spite of Iroquois overtures for peace.[52] The cementing of a treaty with the various Huron tribes was clearly the main reason he visited Huronia in 1615, a visit made in the face of considerable opposition from the Ottawa River Algonkin.[53]

Quite properly in Huron eyes, Champlain spent most of his time in Huronia with the Rock tribe. This had been the first of the Huron tribes to contact him on the St. Lawrence and therefore had a special relationship with the French according to Huron law. When he accompanied a Huron war party on a traditional, and what appeared to him as an ill-fated raid against the central Iroquois, Champlain was resorting to a now-familiar technique for winning the friendship of particular tribes.[54] What Champlain apparently still did not realize was that the aim of these expeditions was adventure and taking prisoners, rather than the destruction of enemy villages.[55] The Huron were undoubtedly far more pleased with the results of the expedition than Champlain was.

From 1615 on, a number of Frenchmen were living in Huronia; their main purpose in being there was to encourage the Huron to trade.[56] Many of these young men, like the coureurs de bois of later times, enjoyed their life among the Indians and, to the horror of the Catholic clergy, made love to Huron women and probably married them according to local custom. The rough and tumble ways of individuals like Étienne Brûlé endeared them to their Huron hosts and this, in turn, allowed them to inspire confidence in the Indians who came to trade. It has been suggested that the main reason these men remained in Huronia was to persuade the Huron to trade in New France rather than to take their furs south to the Dutch who had begun to trade in the Hudson Valley after 1609.[57] This explanation seems unlikely, however. Until 1629 most of the Dutch trade appears to have been confined to the Mahican.[58] Although the Dutch were apparently anxious to trade with the "French Indians" as early as 1633, the Mohawk were not willing to allow them to do so unless they were in some way able to profit from the trade themselves.[59] This the Huron, who had a long-standing feud with the Iroquois, were unwilling to let them do.

The main job of the early coureurs de bois appears to have been to live in Huronia as visible evidence of French goodwill and as exchanges for the Huron youths who were sent to live with the French.[60] In this capacity they were able to encourage the Indians to engage in trade. Each year some of them travelled downriver with the Huron to see that the Algonkin did not prevent the passage of their canoes or scare the Huron off with stories of disasters or plots against them in Quebec.[61] They also acted as interpreters for the Huron and aided them in their dealings with the traders.[62] Except for the years when the Mohawk blockaded the Ottawa River, the Huron sent an annual "fleet" or series of fleets to Quebec bearing the furs they had collected.[63] It is unfortunate that the records do not supply more information on these fleets, particularly about who organized them and what was their tribal composition. The fleets left Huronia in the spring and returned several months later. When the St. Lawrence was blocked by the Iroquois, the Hurons made their way to Quebec over the smaller waterways that led through the Laurentians.[64]

The Recollet and Jesuit missionaries who worked in Huronia between 1615 and 1629 were accepted by the Huron as part of the Franco-Huron trading alliance and as individuals whose goodwill was potentially advantageous in dealing with the traders and authorities in Quebec. That they lacked interest except as shamans is evident from Gabriel Sagard's statement that it was hard to work among any tribe that was not engaged in trade (i.e., bound by the Franco-Huron alliance).[65] The priests appear to have restricted their missionary activities to caring for the needs of the French traders in Huronia and trying to make some converts among the Indians. Their preaching, as far as it was understood, did not appear to present a challenge or affront to the Huron way of life, although the customs of the priests were strange to the Indians, who found these men austere and far less appealing than the easy-going coureurs de bois.[66] For obvious reasons, relations between the priests and local traders were not good and Sagard claims that among other things the latter often refused to help the missionaries learn native languages.[67] The most serious charge that the priests levelled at these traders was that their behaviour sowed confusion and doubt among the Huron and impeded the spread of the Christian faith among them.[68] These early experiences convinced the Jesuits that to run a mission in Huronia properly the priests must control those Europeans who were allowed to enter the country.

In the early part of the seventeenth century the colony of New France was nothing more than a trading post and its day-to-day existence depended upon securing an annual supply of furs.[69] Not understanding the long-standing hostility between the Huron and the Iroquois, the French were apprehensive of any move that seemed likely to divert furs from the St. Lawrence to the Hudson Valley. The French made peace with the Mohawk in 1624 and French traders did business with them, an arrangement that no doubt pleased the Mohawk as it made them for a time less dependent on the Dutch and therefore gave them more bargaining power in their dealings with Albany.[70] Nevertheless, the French became extremely alarmed about a peace treaty that the Huron negotiated with the Seneca in 1623. This appears to have been one of the periodic treaties that the Huron and Iroquois negotiated in order to get back members of their respective tribes who had been taken prisoner, but not yet killed, by the enemy.[71] As such, it was probably perfectly harmless to French interest. Nevertheless the situation was judged sufficiently serious for a delegation of eleven Frenchmen, including three clerics, to be sent to the Huron country.[72] Various writers have followed Jean Charlevoix in saying that this delegation was instructed to disrupt the new treaty. Charlevoix, however, wrote long after the event took place and is not an unbiased witness.[73] It seems more likely that the expedition had as its main purpose simply the reaffirming of the alliances made between Champlain and the various Huron chiefs in 1615. In actual fact the Huron probably had no thought of trading with the Iroquois at this time. To the chagrin of the Dutch, the Mohawk were firm in their refusal to allow the northern tribes to pass through their country to trade on the Hudson. The Huron undoubtedly felt that direct trade with the French, even if they were farther from Huronia than the Dutch,[74] was preferable to trade via the Mohawk with the Europeans in New York State.

The very great importance that the Huron attached to their trade with the French even at this time is shown by their efforts to prevent potential rivals, such as the Petun or Neutral, from concluding any sort of formal alliance with the French. Neither group seems to have constituted much of a threat, since the Petun had to pass through Huron territory in order to paddle north along the shore of Georgian Bay[75] and the Neutral, who do not seem to have had adequate boats, would have had to travel down the St. Lawrence River to Quebec — en route the Mohawk would have either stolen their furs or forced them to divert most of the trade to the south.[76] The Huron do not seem to have minded well-known coureurs de bois occasionally visiting the Neutral or other tribes with whom they traded, but when, on his visit to the Neutral in 1626, Father de La Roche Daillon proposed an alliance between them and the French, the Huron spread rumours about the French that brought an end to the proposed treaty.[77] The ease with which the Huron did this, and repeated the manoeuvre in 1640–41,[78] is an indication both of the insecurity that tribes felt in the absence of a proper treaty with foreigners and of the importance that the Huron placed on their privileged relationship with the French. These observations reinforce our conclusion that coureurs de bois did not live in Huronia simply to dissuade the Huron from going to trade with either the Mohawk or the Dutch, but instead were a vital link in the Franco-Huron alliance and necessary intermediaries between the Huron and the French fur traders in Quebec. Such were the services for which Brûlé received a hundred pistoles each year from his employers.[79]

Franco-Huron trade increased in the years prior to 1629. Undoubtedly the Huron were growing increasing reliant on European goods, but it is unlikely that they were ever completely dependent on trade during this period. There is no evidence that the British occupation of Quebec led them to trade with New Holland or with the Iroquois. Several renegade Frenchmen, including Brûlé, remained in Huronia and probably encouraged the Huron to trade with the British.[80] It was during this period that Brûlé was murdered by the Huron living in Toanché. Since he was given a proper burial it is unlikely that he was tortured to death and eaten as Sagard reports.[81] More likely, he was killed in a brawl with the Huron among whom he lived. That he was killed during the British occupation of New France does not, however, seem to be without significance. Until the French withdrawal he had been protected not only by his popularity but more importantly by the Franco-Huron alliance. Once the French had departed, he was on his own.

The Jesuits Take Control

The Compagnie des Cent-Associés, which took effective control of the affairs of New France after the colony was retroceded to France in 1632, was different from earlier trading companies in that its members were more interested in missionary work than their predecessors had been. At this time the Society of Jesus also managed to obtain the *de facto* monopoly over missionary activities in New France that it was to hold for many years.[82] The Jesuits brought about a number of changes in policy with regard to Huronia. In particular, they were much more anxious to evangelize the Huron *as a people* than the Recollets had been.[83] As their prime goal they sought to lead the entire confederacy toward the Christian religion, rather than to convert individuals. Moreover, as a result of the strong influence they wielded at the French court, they were in a better position to command the support of officials and fur traders.[84] For the first while after they returned to the Huron country, the Jesuits continued many of the mission practices that had been current prior to 1629, such as sending Indian children to their seminary at Quebec.[85] As their knowledge of the Huron language and of the country improved (in both cases as a result of systematic study), they gradually began to modify their work along lines that were more in keeping with their general policy.[86]

A major *bête noire* of the missionaries prior to 1629 was the French traders who lived in Huronia and set a bad example for the natives. In order to assure unity of purpose for their work, the duties that formerly had been carried out by these coureurs de bois were taken over by lay brothers, workmen, and *donnés* directly subject to Jesuit supervision.[87] Later accusations that the Jesuits were engaged in the fur trade seem to have sprung largely from this action. The oft-repeated claim that priests were vital to the fur trade in Huronia is obviously without foundation. The coureurs de bois, who had lived in Huronia for many years, not only had functioned effectively during this period without missionary support but also appear to have been substantially more popular and more effective in their dealings with the Huron than the priests had been. The Jesuits wished to be rid of this group principally to assure that the French living in Huronia would not be working at cross-purposes. The trading companies apparently were willing to allow the Jesuits to have their own way in this matter, but in return it was necessary that the laymen attached to the Jesuit mission discharge at least the most vital functions of organizing the annual trade which the coureurs de bois had done heretofore.[88] The reasons that the Jesuits had for wanting to be rid of the coureurs de bois were clearly religious, not economic.

The Jesuits' connections with the fur trade did not arise, however, simply from their desire to be rid of the coureurs de bois; they also depended on it not only to get into Huronia but also for their personal safety so long as they remained there. The Huron were obviously not at all interested in what the Jesuits had to teach, and on several occasions after 1634 they made it clear that they preferred the former coureurs de bois to the Jesuits and their assistants.[89] In 1633, and again in 1634, they offered a whole series of excuses, including the hostility of the Algonkin from Allumette Island, as reasons for not taking the Jesuits home with them.[90] Moreover, fearing revenge for the death of Brûlé, they were unwilling to allow their children to remain as seminarians at Quebec.[91]

In 1634 Champlain made the official French position clear when he informed the Huron that he regarded the Jesuits' presence in their country as a vital part of a renewed Franco-Huron alliance, at the same time expressing the hope that they would someday agree to become Christians.[92] Since the Huron wanted to renew their former trading relationship with the French, they agreed to accept the priests as a token of this alliance. Henceforth they were bound by treaty to allow the Jesuits to live among them and to protect the priests from harm. The thought of having these individuals who were so respected by the French in Huronia and under their control must also have given the Huron confidence in their dealings with the French who remained in Quebec.

Although the Jesuits travelled to Huronia in 1635 in canoes that belonged to members of the Cord and Rock tribes, they were put ashore rather unceremoniously in the territory of the Bear tribe, where Brébeuf had worked previously and where Brûlé had been murdered.[93] It is not clear whether the Jesuits had wanted to go to this region or were left there by their Rock and Cord hosts who did not want to take them to their own villages. It is possible that the Bear, who were the most powerful of the Huron tribes, exerted their influence to have the Jesuits left among them. In this regard it is perhaps not without meaning that the Jesuits previously had discussed with the Indians the possibility of their settling in Ossossané, the chief town of the Bear nation.[94] Brébeuf was welcomed by the villagers of Ihonitiria, among whom he had lived before, and the Jesuits decided to settle in that village both because it was close to the canoe route to New France and also in order to persuade the villagers that they bore them no ill will for having murdered Brûlé. The latter, the Jesuits said, was regarded by the French as a traitor and debauched renegade.[95] Nevertheless, his murder haunted the Huron, and even some neighbouring tribes,[96] who feared that it might lead to war with the French. Such fears may have been responsible for the dispute that the Jesuits observed between certain villages of the Bear tribe shortly after their arrival in Huronia.[97]

It would appear that according to native custom the Jesuits coming to Huronia had a right to expect they would receive free food and lodgings. This would have been in return for similar care given by the French to the young seminarists in Quebec.[98] In Huron eyes the latter had been exchanged as tokens of good faith in return for the Jesuits and their assistants.[99] In fact, the Huron provided food and shelter for the Jesuits only rarely. The missionaries had to purchase or provide these things for themselves and found the Huron demanding payment of some sort for most of their services.[100]

For a time after their return to Huronia the Jesuits were the objects of friendly public interest and their presence and goodwill were sought after, in part because individual Hurons sought to obtain favours in Quebec through their commendation, in part because the services people

37

performed for the Jesuits, and even attendance at religious instruction, were rewarded with presents of trade goods and tobacco. The latter, although a native product, was scarce in Huronia at the time.[101] Since all of the priests (except perhaps Brébeuf) were struggling to learn the Huron language, most of the missionary activities during the first few years were confined to the Bear country. Only a few trips were made into more distant areas of Huronia.[102]

The Epidemics of 1635 to 1640

The first serious trial for the Jesuits, and for the Franco-Huron alliance, occurred between the years 1635 and 1640. An unspecified disease, either measles or smallpox, was present in Quebec the year the Jesuits returned to Huronia, and it followed the Huron fleet upriver. This was the beginning of a series of epidemics which swept away more than half the Huron population in the next six years.[103] These new maladies were especially fatal to children and old people. Because they were fatal to the latter group, many of the most skilful Huron leaders and craftsmen, as well as the people most familiar with native religious lore, perished.[104] The loss of children may well have meant that the proportion of men of fighting age in the Huron population was below normal by the end of the next decade.

The Jesuits, who wished to save the souls of dying children, frequently baptized them, both with and without their parents' permission. The Huron, being unclear about the Jesuits' intention in doing this, observed that children tended to die soon after baptism and came to suspect that the Jesuits were practising a deadly form of witchcraft.[105] The rumour revived that the Jesuits had been sent to Huronia to seek revenge for Brûlé's murder,[106] a rumour which gained credence from pictures of the torments of hell that the Jesuits displayed in their chapel and from the ritual of the mass (which the Huron understood had something to do with eating a corpse).[107] According to Huron law, sorcerers could be killed without a trial, and in times of crisis extensive pogroms appear to have been unleashed against persons suspected of this crime.[108] Nevertheless, while individuals threatened to murder the Jesuits and on one occasion a council of the confederacy met to try the Jesuits on a charge of witchcraft,[109] none of the Frenchmen in Huronia was killed.

Although the majority of the people were frightened of the Jesuits and believed that they were working to destroy the country, their leaders repeatedly stressed that they could not afford to rupture the Franco-Huron alliance by killing the French priests.[110] One well-placed chief said that if the Huron did not go downriver to trade with the French for even two years, they would be lucky if they found themselves as well off as the [despised] Algonkians.[111] While this statement was a bit of rhetoric, it stresses the importance of the fur trade to the Huron at this time and their growing reliance on French trade goods. During the entire course of the epidemics only one village, apparently a small one, was willing to give up the use of trade goods, and hence presumably to sever relations with the French.[112] Instead, the Huron resorted to indirect means to persuade the Jesuits to leave Huronia *voluntarily*. Children were encouraged to annoy them, their religious objects were befouled, and occasionally they were personally threatened or mistreated.[113] The Jesuits noted, rather significantly, that these persecutions diminished before the annual trip downriver or after the return of a successful fleet.[114] The French officials in Quebec were aware of the dangerous situation in which the Jesuits found themselves, but as long as feelings ran high in Huronia, these authorities could do no more than to try to spare them from the worst excesses of Huron anger. They did this by threatening to cut off trade if the Jesuits were killed.

By 1640 the serious epidemics in Huronia were over. That summer, the new governor of Canada, Charles Huault de Montmagny, took action to "punish" the Huron who came to Quebec for their bad treatment of the Jesuits.[115] It is not clear what form this punishment took, but it appears that in the course of his dealings with them he made it clear that he considered their bad treatment of the Jesuits had terminated the existing alliance. At the same time he offered to renew the alliance, but only on the clear understanding that the Jesuits would continue to live in Huronia and work there unmolested. This is the first time, to our knowledge, that French officials had injected a positive element of threat into their dealings with the Huron. Presumably, the great losses in manpower and skills that the Huron had suffered and their consequent increasing dependence on trade and French support made such action possible. The Huron were in good health and expecting an abundant harvest; hence, many of the anxieties that had plagued them in recent years were dispelled. Because of this they were once more in a good mood and, hence, under the protection of a renewed Franco-Huron alliance the Jesuits found themselves free not only to continue the mission work among them but also to intensify their efforts.[116]

Already during the final crisis of 1639, the Jesuits had decided to establish a permanent centre for their missionary work in the Huron area. This centre was foreseen as serving various functions. Not only would it provide a refuge in time of danger (such as they lacked in 1639), but it also would allow them to put up buildings of European design. It had not been economical to construct these in the Huron villages which shifted their location about once every decade. The Jesuits' centre was thus designed to be a further example of European culture in the heart of Huronia, a focus from which new ideas could diffuse to the local population. Gradually, pigs, fowl, and young cattle were brought upriver from Quebec and European crops were grown in the fields nearby.[117] The residence of Ste Marie acquired a hospital and a burial ground and became a place where Christian Indians could come for spiritual retreats and assembly on feast days.[118] Being located apart from any one village, and near the geographical centre of the confederacy, it was better able, both from a political and a geographical point of view, to serve as a mission centre for all Huronia. (During the worst years of the epidemics the Jesuits had remained for the most part in the northwest corner of Huronia.) In 1639 the Jesuits also made a survey and census of the country prior to setting up a system of missions that would carry the Christian message to all of the Huron tribes and, as far as possible, to other tribes as well.[119]

The Jesuits had thus weathered a difficult period. It is clear that they had been allowed to enter Huronia and to continue there only because of the Franco-Huron alliance. That they were not killed or expelled from Huronia at the height of the epidemics is an indication of how dependent the Hurons were becoming on the fur trade and how much the alliance with the French meant to them. It also indicates that the Huron leaders were able to restrain their unruly followers in order to preserve good relations with New France.[120] Evidence of lingering malice towards the priests can be seen in the events that came to light on the visit of Fathers Brébeuf and Chaumonot to the Neutral country in the winter of 1640–41. There the priests learned that the Huron had offered the Neutral rich presents, if they would kill the missionaries.[121] In this way the Huron hoped to destroy two of the "sorcerers" who had been tormenting their nation without endangering the French alliance. They also had other motives, however. The proposed murder, so long as it was not traced back to the Huron, would put the Neutral in a bad light and would prevent Brébeuf from pursuing any dealings with the Seneca. Although there is no evidence that Brébeuf planned to visit the Seneca, a rumour had spread that having failed to kill the Huron with witchcraft he now was seeking to turn their enemies loose upon them.[122]

A Crisis in Huron–Iroquois Relations

If the year 1640 marked the end of the persecution of the Jesuits in Huronia, unknown to them and to their Huron hosts, it also marked the beginning of a crisis that was to destroy Huronia. Beaver had become rare in the Huron country and most of the skins they traded with the French came from neighbouring tribes to the north.[123] A similar decline in the beaver population of New York State seems to have reached a point of crisis by 1640. That year the number of pelts traded at Fort Orange is reported to have dropped sharply.[124] While it is possible that at least part of the decline was the result of clandestine traders cutting into official trade, most commentators agree that it was basically related to the exhaustion of the supply of beaver in the Iroquois' home territory.[125]

While this hypothesis is not well enough documented that it can be regarded as certain, it seems a useful one for explaining Iroquois behaviour during the next few years. There is little doubt that after 1640 the Iroquois were preoccupied with securing new sources of pelts. The main controversy concerning their relations with their neighbours during this period centres on whether they were seeking to obtain furs by forcing the Huron to share their trade with them[126] or were attacking their neighbours in order to secure new hunting territories. Although Trelease[127] supports the latter theory, the data he uses apply for the most part to a later period and come mainly from sources in New York State and New England. Contemporary Canadian evidence definitely seems to rule out his claims; indeed if his hypothesis were true, the events leading to the destruction of Huronia would make little sense at all.

Trelease's theory finds its main support in claims made by the Iroquois in the early part of the eighteenth century that they had conquered Ontario and adjacent regions as beaver hunting grounds. In the treaty of 1701, in which the Iroquois placed their "Beaver ground" under the protection of the King of England, the Iroquois said explicitly that they had driven the indigenous tribes from this area in order to hunt there.[128] Trelease errs, however, in assuming that the reasons the Iroquois gave for conquering this territory in 1701 were the same as those they actually had for doing so half a century earlier. There is no doubt that in 1701 the Iroquois (mainly the Seneca) were hunting beaver in Ontario, but since the Huron country was reported in the 1630s to be as hunted out as their own it is illogical to assume that they attacked this region in 1649 in order to secure more hunting territory. The Huron beaver supplies they sought to capture were those coming by trade from the north. Only after their attacks failed to capture the western fur trade and after Ontario was deserted for a time allowing the restoration of the local beaver population did the Iroquois begin to hunt there. Since they lacked historical records, it is not surprising that by 1701 the Iroquois believed the use that they were making of Ontario at the present time was the same reason they had for attacking the tribes there long before. The attacks the Iroquois launched against the Petun and Neutral, following their attack on the Huron, offer no opposition to this theory. Although these groups had not participated in the fur trade prior to 1649, there was considerable danger that with the Huron gone they would attempt to do so. Hence, their dispersal was also necessary.

Trelease's theory thus fails to provide an acceptable explanation of events in Canada in the middle of the seventeenth century. It seems much more likely that the Iroquois, and mainly the Mohawk, began by trying to force the Huron to trade with them and that only latterly, when their efforts in this direction were unsuccessful, did they decide

41

The Iroquoian Groups of the Lower Great Lakes, at the Beginning of the Seventeenth Century

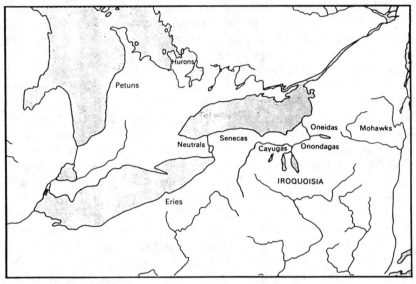

Marcel Trudel, *Introduction to New France* (Toronto: Holt, Rinehart and Winston, 1978), 28.

to destroy the Huron (and their neighbours) as an intermediary group.

The Mohawk began to intimidate the Huron by harassing those travelling along the Ottawa River — a tactic that had the additional advantage of providing a supply of captured furs. In 1642 Iroquois raiders spread fear and terror throughout all of the Huron villages,[129] and in 1644 they succeeded in preventing contact between Quebec and Huronia.[130] The increasing number of guns that the Iroquois were acquiring from the Dutch, English, and Swedish colonies along the Atlantic seaboard gradually gave them military superiority over the Huron, among whom the French had limited and controlled the sale of guns.[131] In 1644 the French despatched more than twenty soldiers to Huronia to protect the Huron over the winter and assure the arrival of their furs in Quebec the next spring.[132] The Mohawk were also harassing the French in the St. Lawrence Valley, who were moved the next spring to discuss peace, both to assure their own safety and to re-open the river to trade. Although the subsequent treaty of 1645 was with the French, the Mohawk seem to have interpreted it as involving a commitment that in the future the Huron would trade with them as well as with the French.[133] The Huron, however, had no intention of doing this, and the French, who may not have perceived clearly what the Mohawk wanted, did not want to encourage them to divert trade. The main French reason for the treaty with the Mohawk was the short-term one of opening the river. The

French had little to offer the Iroquois in return and refused to sell them guns, the one item they wanted.[134] When it became clear to the Mohawk that the Huron did not intend to trade with them, they renewed their attack on Huronia and on the Huron fleet.

The Development of a Christian Faction

While this dangerous crisis in intertribal relations was boiling up, a situation was developing in Huronia that put a new strain on the Franco-Huron alliance.

Prior to 1640, most Christian converts were Hurons on the point of death, many of whom knew nothing about Christian theology but hoped that baptism would save their lives.[135] At one point during the epidemics a Huron version of the rite of baptism became part of a native healing cult that was said to be inspired by a native deity who had revealed himself as the real Jesus.[136] In these rites the sick were sprinkled with water as part of an orgiastic ceremony typical of traditional Huron healing rituals. After 1640, however, the Jesuits began to convert increasing numbers of people who were in good health. Many were men of importance, whose conversions made that of their families, friends, and tribesmen easier.[137] In order to prevent backsliding, the Jesuits at first made it a policy to baptise (except in cases of extreme ill health) only adults who had provided substantial proof of their devotion to Christianity and whose family life seemed to be stable.[138]

Many factors seem to have induced people to convert: some admired the bravery of the Jesuits, others wished to be able to follow a Christian friend to heaven, still others noted in their names a theological term that the Jesuits were using.[139]

Although economic motives were not the only ones involved in conversion, it is noteworthy that at least a few Huron became Christians to avoid participation in pagan feasts, which required them to give away considerable amounts of property in the form of presents and entertainment.[140] A far larger number of people hoped through conversion to receive preferential treatment in their dealings with traders and officials in New France.[141] In 1648, when only 15 per cent of the Huron were Christian, half of the men in the Huron fleet were either converts or were preparing for baptism.[142] Those who traded with the French in Quebec not only were more exposed to French culture and to Christianity than were those who remained at home but also had more to gain from good relations with the French. Commercial considerations may also explain why the Jesuits generally found it easier to convert men than women.

While stressing the practical economic motives that certainly motivated many conversions, personal and cultural factors should not be ignored. The Huron were increasingly dependent on French culture and in the eyes of many, but (as we shall see) certainly not all, of the Huron the priest was coming to replace the native sorcerer as an object of awe and respect. This did not, however, lead the Huron to lose faith in themselves or in their culture, as it did in many other tribes.[143] Supported by the respect shown by the Jesuits for the Huron people and for much of their culture, many Huron converts appear to have been imbued with a sincere zeal to change and reform their own culture. No doubt the size of the Huron confederacy and its isolation from unsupervised contact with the Europeans did much to prevent the deterioration in self-confidence that is obvious among many weaker tribes. Had other circumstances not been adverse, I think it would have been possible for the Jesuits to have transformed Huronia successfully into a nation that was both Christian and Indian.

44

For a time the growing number of Huron converts posed no serious problems for the rest of society, although individual converts were frequently taunted and sometimes expelled from their longhouses with much resulting personal hardship.[144] (A woman who had been a member of a pagan healing society was threatened with death when after conversion she refused to perform in the society.[145]) Threats and assassination no doubt were the fate of other converts. The Jesuits and their assistants, however, were no longer attacked or molested in any way.[146] It appears that at least some headmen surrendered their political office on becoming Christians, since they felt that the obligation to participate in Huron festivals which these offices entailed was contrary to their new faith.[147] In this and in other ways the nascent Christian community avoided for a time the possibility of an open clash with the large pagan majority.

Gradually, however, a rift began. Some Christians refused, for example, to be buried in their tribal ossuaries, which in effect was to deny membership in their village or tribe.[148] They also refused to fight alongside pagans in the war parties but instead formed their own detachments, no doubt because of the religious implications of traditional Iroquoian warfare.[149] As the number of converts grew, men retained their political offices after conversion, but appointed deputies to handle the religious functions traditionally associated with them.[150] As the number of Christians who held these important offices continued to grow, the split between pagans and Christians became increasingly a political issue.

The Jesuits, for their part, now set as their immediate goal the Christianizing of an entire village.[151] Significantly the most promising town was Ossossané where the Jesuits had been working for a long time. This town, belonging to the Bear tribe, was also the political centre of the Huron confederacy.[152] In 1648 they achieved their objective. By then the majority of people in Ossossané were converts. And that winter the chiefs of the village refused to allow the people who remained pagan to celebrate the traditional festivals, and they appointed a Jesuit as the chief headman of the village, with the right to act as a censor of public morals.[153]

The Pagan Reaction and the Destruction of Huronia

Although in 1645 such social revolutions were still several years in the future, many of the pagans had already begun to fear for the survival of their traditional customs and beliefs.[154] Undoubtedly a large number of these people were genuinely attached to the old ways and for this reason alone resented the growth of Christianity. It is also possible that many chiefs who wished to remain pagan began to fear a decline in their own influence as Christians began to play a stronger role in the life of the country. They probably resented the closer contacts that Christian chiefs had with the French and feared that these contacts would be used as a source of power. As a result of these fears and rivalries, pagan and Christian factions began to develop within the various tribes and villages throughout Huronia.[155]

45

Although the documentation in the Jesuit Relations is scanty, there appears to have been a considerable variation in attitude towards the Jesuits and Christianity among the different Huron tribes. The Bear, among whom the Jesuits had lived for the longest time and whose main town, Ossossané, had a large and rapidly growing Christian community, seem to have been the most pro-Christian and pro-French.[156] The Cord probably had much the same sort of attitude.[157] The Rock and Deer tribes, however, seem to have been considerably less friendly. The Jesuits report that the former tribe, being the easternmost, had suffered most from the attacks of the Iroquois and was therefore the most inclined to seek peace with their traditional enemies. The Rock were also described, however, as a tribe with a strong aversion to the faith, who never had been converted.[158] The Deer had a reputation among the Jesuits for being sorcerers,[159] and one assumes from this that they gave the missionaries a bad time. Both of these tribes joined the Iroquois of their own free will after the break-up of Huronia in 1649.[160] Despite this variation, however, there were people in all the Huron tribes who were starting to have misgivings about the future of Huronia and who resented the changes that the French alliance was bringing about.

After 1645 these sentiments seem to have led to the formation of a sizable anti-French party, which apparently found a certain amount of support everywhere in Huronia, except perhaps in Ossossané. This marked a new development in French–Huron relations, all previous opposition having been to the priests resident in Huronia rather than to the French in general. Supporters of this party seem to have reasoned that Christianity was a threat to Huronia, that Christianity flourished because the Jesuits were able to work there under the terms of the Franco-

Huron alliance, and that the best way to save the country (and enhance the power of the pagan chiefs at the expense of their Christian rivals) was therefore to expel the Jesuits, break off the alliance, and begin trading with the Iroquois. In this way, not only would the traditional culture of Huronia be saved, but the attacks of the Iroquois, which had been growing in intensity,[161] could be brought to an end. Thus for the first time a respectable body of opinion in Huronia came to believe that an alliance with enemies who shared similar beliefs and culture was preferable to one with strangers seeking to change the Huron way of life. The threat that was facing the traditionalists made the thought of trading with their old enemies and rivals seem much less unpleasant than it had been a few years previously.

The first plan for a rapprochement with the Iroquois was well conceived and sought to exploit internal differences within the Iroquois confederacy for the Hurons' own advantage. Since the treaty of 1645 had failed to obtain the furs they wanted, the Mohawk were likely to be suspicious of, if not hostile to, further Huron blandishments. The Seneca likewise were unfriendly because of recent Huron attacks on them.[162] The Onondaga, however, had long enjoyed the position of being the chief tribe in the confederacy and were increasingly jealous of the Mohawk, who were exploiting their close contacts with the Dutch and the English in an effort to dominate the league.[163] It is therefore no surprise that it was through the Onondaga that the Huron attempted to make peace with the Iroquois.

The Jesuits did not record, and may not have known, the exact nature of the treaty that the Huron were trying to negotiate. The presence of a clause promising that the Huron would trade furs with the Iroquois is suggested by a remark, attributed to the Andaste or Susquehannock (who were allies of the Huron and sent ambassadors to the Onondaga to argue on their behalf), that such a treaty would promote the trade of all these tribes with one another.[164] It is also significant that among the Huron the Bear tribe was the one most opposed to this treaty.[165] The Jesuits said this was because the Bear had suffered less from Iroquois raids than had the other Huron tribes, but a second reason could be that the Christians, who were more numerous in this tribe than in the others, saw in these negotiations a clear threat to the Franco-Huron alliance and to their own power and well-being. Negotiations continued for some time, but were terminated in January 1648, when a party of Mohawk warriors slew a Huron embassy on its way to the chief Onondaga town to arrange the final terms of the treaty.[166] A distinguished Onondaga chief, who had remained in Huronia as a hostage, committed suicide when he learned what the Mohawk had done.[167]

There seems little reason to doubt the honesty of the Onondaga in these negotiations. The Mohawk probably attacked the Huron embassy because they were angry that negotiations were being conducted with the Onondaga rather than with them. The Mohawk may also have believed that the Huron were trying to deceive the Onondaga and that the only way of dealing with the Huron confederacy was to destroy it. In any case, the Mohawk managed to bring the first major political offensive of the anti-French faction in Huronia to an ignominious conclusion.

Even though this first effort had failed, at least some Huron apparently believed that a rapprochement with the Iroquois still was possible. Indeed, either because they were totally convinced of the necessity of appeasing the Iroquois or because of their extreme hatred of the Christians, a minority seems to have become convinced that a break with the French was a precondition for further negotiation. The group responsible for the next move was led by six, apparently distinguished, chiefs from three villages.[168] Unfortunately, these village are unnamed. The chiefs decided to make a public issue of the question of a continued Franco-Huron alliance through the simple expedient of killing a Frenchman. They do not appear to have designated any particular victim, and their henchmen slew Jacques Douart, a *donné* whom they encountered not far from Ste Marie. Once Douart was slain, the conspirators issued a proclamation calling for the banishment from Huronia of the French and all of the Huron who insisted on remaining Christian.[169] An emergency council was convened (apparently from all over the country) and for several days these proposals were debated. On the one side were the Christians and those pagans who felt that the Franco-Huron alliance should continue; on the other the traditionalists who had stirred up the trouble and no doubt some other Hurons who hated neither Christianity nor the French, but who felt that a peace treaty with the Iroquois was important enough to be worth the termination of the French alliance. Among the latter must have been many refugees from the Rock tribe, which had been forced to abandon its villages as a result of Iroquois attacks only a short time before.[170] The pro-French party finally won the debate and the Jesuits in turn agreed to accept the traditional Huron compensation for a murder, in this case one hundred beaver skins.[171] The ritual presentation of this settlement made clear that it was designed to reaffirm and protect the Franco-Huron alliance, which the unprecedented actions of these chiefs had endangered. Thus ended what appears to have been the last attempt to rupture the Franco-Huron alliance.

During the summer of 1648 the Seneca attacked and destroyed the large town of St. Joseph. As the situation grew more serious the Huron turned increasingly to the French for help and the number of conversions increased sharply.[172] As in 1644, a few French soldiers were sent to winter in Huronia. These soldiers, so long as they remained in Huronia, were believed sufficient to hold off the Iroquois, but they had been instructed to return to Quebec with the Huron fleet in the spring.[173] As the military situation in Huronia grew more desperate, the French in Quebec became

47

increasingly anxious to profit as much as possible while they still could. In the summer of 1649, a party of over thirty coureurs de bois made a flying trip to Huronia and returned to Quebec bringing with them 5000 pounds of beaver.[174]

In the spring of 1649 the Iroquois unleashed the attack that resulted in the death of Fathers Lalemant and Brébeuf and brought about the dispersal of the Huron confederacy. Many factors contributed to the Iroquois victory, but their superior number of guns was undoubtedly the most important.[175] Hunt has suggested that the Huron were so given over to trading by 1649 that virtually all of their food was imported from the Neutral and Petun tribes and that the main factor in their defeat was therefore the cutting of their supply routes.[176] This suggestion is entirely without foundation. Agriculture was a woman's occupation and little affected by increasing trade. While men may have spent more time trading, the importation of iron axes made it easier to cut trees and hence there was no problem clearing the forests for agriculture. There are frequent references to the Huron as engaged in agricultural activities in the years prior to 1649, and one of the reasons the Iroquois returned to Huronia in the spring of 1650 was to prevent the planting of crops.[177] Driven from their homes and deprived of food, the Hurons scattered, and their trading monopoly came to an end. It is interesting that large numbers of Huron, particularly from the Rock and Deer tribes, migrated to the Iroquois country and settled there. The latter tribe settled *en masse* among the Seneca, where they lived in their own village and retained their separate customs for a long time.[178] Their tribal affiliations suggest that these refugees were for the most part traditionalists and probably among them were many of the people who had been the most hostile to the French during the last years of the Jesuit mission. This hostility explains how these groups were so easily adopted by the people who had destroyed their homeland.

For the Jesuits the destruction of Huronia was the end of their first dream of leading a nation to Christianity in the heart of the Canadian forest. At least once in the Relations they mentioned the work their colleagues were accomplishing in Paraguay and compared this work with their own.[179] The chance had been lost of converting a people to Christianity while allowing them to retain their language and those institutions and customs that were not incompatible with their new faith. Because they were writing for a patriotic French audience, the Jesuits have little to say about the constitutional status of the Huronia they wished to create. Nevertheless, it seems clear that what they aimed at was not so much a French colony as an Indian state, which under Jesuit leadership could blend the good things of Europe with those already in the native culture. A Catholic Huronia would of necessity have been allied with France, the only Catholic power in eastern North America. Years later Louis de Buade de Frontenac probably came closer to a basic truth than he realized when he accused the Jesuits at Quebec of disloyalty because they kept the Indians apart from the French and taught them in their own language.[180]

The fur trade was the one means by which the Jesuits could gain admittance to Huronia and the only protection they had while working there. Ties with fur traders and government officials in Quebec were thus vital for the success of the Huron mission, but these ties do not seem to have prevented the Jesuits from seeking to serve the best interests of their Huron converts and Huronia at large — as they perceived these interests. To reverse the equation and say that the Jesuits were in Huronia mainly *for the purpose* of serving either the fur trade or the French government does not accord with anything we know about their activities.

In the short run the destruction of Huronia was a serious setback for New France. For a time the fur trade, on which the well-being of the colony depended, was cut to practically nothing. The Iroquois, on the other hand, seem to have achieved less than they hoped for from the destruction of Huronia. The western tribes soon became involved in a protracted war with the Erie,[181] and tribal jealousies rent the confederacy. As a result of these jealousies the four western tribes began to trade with the French to avoid travelling through Mohawk towns to reach the Dutch.[182] By 1654 the French were starting to put together the rudiments of a new trading network north of the Great Lakes.[183] The remnants of the Huron and Petun who had remained in this area, and more importantly the Ottawa, an Algonkian tribe, played a major role in pushing this trading network to the west in the years that followed.[184] As the population of New France increased, the young men of the colony, with or without official permission, joined in this trade. Thus the destruction of Huronia was neither a total nor a permanent disaster for New France and certainly it did not help to save North America for Protestantism and the Anglo-Saxons, as at least one eminent historian has suggested.[185]

A more serious question is what would have happened had the anti-French party in Huronia been successful. Had they been able to organize an effective resistance to the Huron Christians and conclude a treaty with the Iroquois, the trade from the north might have been diverted permanently from the St. Lawrence into the Hudson Valley. Had that happened (and as Sagard and Le Clercq indicate the people in Quebec knew it well[186]) the chances of the infant French colony surviving even for a short time would have been slim. Instead of the destruction of Huronia tipping the balance of power in favour of the English, its survival might well have led to a Huron–Iroquois alliance that would have resulted in the destruction of New France and the end of the French presence in North America.

NOTES

This paper is based in part on research carried out with the assistance of Miss A. Elaine Clark during the academic year 1965–66. Miss Clark's assistance was made possible through a research grant provided by the French Canada Studies Programme of McGill University.

[1] See, e.g., Samuel de Champlain's comment on the sagacity of the Indians in trade (H.P. Biggar, ed., *The Works of Samuel de Champlain* (6 vols.; Toronto, 1922–36), 2: 171), and Jean de Brébeuf, Gabriel Lalemant, and Francesco Bressani on the efficacy of Huron law (R.G. Thwaites, ed., *The Jesuit Relations and Allied Documents* (73 vols.; Cleveland, 1896–1901), 10: 215; 28: 49–51; 38: 277).

[2] Thwaites, ed., *Relations* 18: 21. A similar statement is made by Paul Ragueneau (29: 281).

[3] Invariably, however, these early witnesses of Indian culture were interested in rather limited aspects of Indian life and tended to interpret Indian culture in terms of their own. Because of this, a valid assessment of these early records requires a comparative knowledge of Indian culture in later times. The groundwork for our understanding of seventeenth-century Huron culture is thus the work of several generations of ethnologists and ethnohistorians in Canada and the United States. The best résumé of Huron culture is Elisabeth Tooker, *An Ethnography of the Huron Indians, 1615–1649* (Washington, 1964). For a shorter and less complete synopsis see W.V. Kinietz, *The Indians of the Western Great Lakes, 1615–1760* (Ann Arbor, 1940).

[4] F. Parkman, *The Jesuits in North America in the Seventeenth Century* (Centenary Edition, Boston, 1927), 3, 4, 435, 436; G.E. Ellis, "Indians of North America," in J. Winsor, ed., *Narrative and Critical History of America* (8 vols.; Boston and New York, 1884–89), 1: 283.

[5] G.T. Hunt, *The Wars of the Iroquois: A Study in Intertribal Relations* (Madison, 1940), 4, 19.

[6] Biggar, ed., *Works of Champlain* 3: 49–51; 4: 238–44.

[7] Thwaites, ed., *Relations* 16: 227.

[8] L.H. Morgan, *League of the Ho-de-no-sau-nee, or Iroquois* (Rochester, 1851; reprinted New Haven, 1954). For a briefer description, see Morgan's *Houses and House-life of the Indian Aborigines* (Washington, 1881; reprinted with original pagination Chicago, 1965), 23–41.

[9] Meat remained largely a festive dish, commonest in winter and spring (G.M. Wrong, ed., *Sagard's Long Journey to the Country of the Hurons* [Toronto, 1939], 82; Thwaites, ed., *Relations* 17: 141–43).

[10] Thwaites, ed., *Relations* 16: 227–29. See also Elisabeth Tooker, "The Iroquois Defeat of the Huron: A Review of Causes," *Pennsylvania Archaeologist* 33 (1963): 115–23, especially 119, 120.

[11] J.V. Wright, *The Ontario Iroquois Tradition* (Ottawa, 1966), 68–83. For information concerning the movements from the west I am indebted to a personal communication from Dr. Wright.

[12] See, for example, D. Jenness, *The Indians of Canada* (5th ed.; Ottawa, 1960), 280.

[13] B.G. Trigger, "The Historic Location of the Hurons," *Ontario History* 54 (1962): 137–48. For physiographic conditions, see L.J. Chapman and D.F. Putnam, *The Physiography of Southern Ontario* (2nd ed.; Toronto, 1966), 299–312.

[14] Biggar, ed., *Works of Champlain* 3: 52, 53. On the importance of corn meal among the northern hunters see Wrong, ed., *Sagard's Long Journey*, 268.

[15] Hunt, *Wars of the Iroquois*, 53–65.

[16] For the reference to squirrel skins see Thwaites, ed., *Relations* 7: 13; to nets, 6: 309.

[17] Thwaites, ed., *Relations* 8: 15.

[18] Wrong, ed., *Sagard's Long Journey*, 86.

[19] For a hostile statement about the Bear by the Algonkins, see Thwaites, ed., *Relations* 10: 145.

[20] C.F. Wray and H.L. Schoff, "A Preliminary Report on the Seneca Sequence in Western New York State, 1550–1687," *Pennsylvania Archaeologist* 23 (1953): 53–63.

[21] Colonel James F. Pendergast (personal communication) reports finding considerable evidence of Huron influence in late Iroquoian sites along the St. Lawrence River. These probably date from the sixteenth century or only a little earlier. For the historical evidence of contacts between the St. Lawrence Iroquoians and the interior of Ontario, see H.P. Biggar, ed., *The Voyages of Jacques Cartier* (Ottawa, 1924), 170–71, 200–202.

[22] Thwaites, ed., *Relations* 10: 225.

[23] Thwaites, ed., *Relations* 20: 19.

[24] Thwaites, ed., *Relations* 20: 19. In 1640 Lalemant reported that the Rock still considered themselves the special allies of the French and were inclined to protect them. This attitude changed after the Jesuits became more active in the interior of Huronia.

[25] Wrong, ed., *Sagard's Long Journey*, 99. Sagard says that a special council decided each year the number of men who could go out from each village. For more on the control of trade by old and influential men, see Thwaites, ed., *Relations* 14: 39.

[26] J.V. Wright, "A Regional Examination of Ojibwa Culture History," *Anthropologica* N.S. 7 (1965): 189–227.

[27] Thwaites, ed., *Relations* 5: 241.

[28] The Huron claimed that their feud with the Iroquois had been going on fifty years prior to 1615 (Biggar, ed., *Works of Champlain* 5: 78).

[29] Thwaites, ed., *Relations* 23: 91.

[30] Wrong, ed., *Sagard's Long Journey*, 159-61. For comparative discussions of Iroquoian warfare see Nathaniel Knowles, "The Torture of Captives by the Indians of Eastern North America," *Proceedings of the American Philosophical Society* 82 (1940): 151-225; R.L. Rands and C.L. Riley, "Diffusion and Discontinuous Distribution," *American Anthropologist* 58 (1958): 274-97.

[31] For the wars with the Petun, see Thwaites, ed., *Relations* 20: 43. Even at the time of Sagard's visit, there was a threat of war with the Neutral (Wrong, ed., *Sagard's Long Journey*, 151, 156, 157).

[32] Thwaites, ed., *Relations* 33: 243.

[33] Thwaites, ed., *Relations* 33: 239-49.

[34] Thwaites, ed., *Relations* 13: 125. The Bear Tribe wanted the French to participate in their Feast of the Dead so that they could thereby claim them as relatives (10: 311).

[35] Thwaites, ed., *Relations* 27: 25; 20: 59.

[36] Chretien Le Clercq, *First Establishment of the Faith in New France*, trans. J.G. Shea, 2 vols. (New York, 1881), 1: 97; Wrong, ed., *Sagard's Long Journey*, 71.

[37] Biggar, ed., *Voyages of Cartier*, 132-3, 143. The custom of giving children to Cartier may have arisen, on the other hand, as a result of the Indians observing Cartier's predilection for kidnapping Indians. In 1534 he had seized the two sons of Donnaconna, the chief of Stadacona.

[38] The fact that the Huron and Algonkians both were at war with the Five Nations naturally pitted the French against these latter tribes. Presumably Champlain's decision to side with the Huron and Algonkians was based on his conviction that it was impossible to maintain satisfactory relations with both sides, as well as on the economic factors mentioned in the text. For a discussion of the origins of the hostility between the Algonkians and Five Nations, see B.G. Trigger, "Trade and Tribal Warfare on the St. Lawrence in the Sixteenth Century," *Ethnohistory* 9 (1962): 240-56.

[39] For Champlain's own comment on Indian expectations in this regard, see Biggar, ed., *Works of Champlain* 2: 70, 71, 110.

[40] H.A. Innis, *The Fur Trade in Canada* (2nd ed.; Toronto, 1956), 23-26.

[41] Thwaites, ed., *Relations* 15: 229. The first Huron chief to have dealings with the French was Atironta of the Rock tribe.

[42] Biggar, ed., *Works of Champlain* 2: 188, 189, 193. For a more general reference see 2: 254.

[43] Biggar, ed., *Works of Champlain* 2: 141; 4: 118, 119. This interpretation is reinforced by Champlain's statement that the boy was brought back by 200 Huron on June 13, 1611 (2: 186; 4: 136).

[44] For comments on the Indians' desire for European manufactured goods, see Innis, *Fur Trade*, 16-19; Hunt, *Wars of the Iroquois*, 4, 5.

[45] For examples of Algonkin harassment of Huron trade along the Ottawa River and various Algonkin attempts to imperil French-Huron relations (particularly by the Algonkin from Allumette Island) see Biggar, ed., *Works of Champlain* 5: 102; Wrong, ed., *Sagard's Long Journey*, 262; Thwaites, ed., *Relations* 5: 239; 7: 213; 8: 83, 99; 9: 271; 10: 77; 14: 53. The Montagnais also tried to intimidate the Huron, mainly to get free corn (Wrong, ed., *Sagard's Long Journey*, 265-68).

[46] Innis, *Fur Trade*, 3-6, 11-15.

[47] This is essentially the kind of relationship that existed between trading companies and Indian trappers in the north in more recent times.

[48] Champlain reports that the Huron produced large food surpluses which he says were meant to carry them over years of poor crops (Biggar, ed., *Works of Champlain* 3: 155-56). At least a part of these surpluses was used for trade.

[49] Le Clercq, *Establishment* 1: 298.

[50] Thwaites, ed., *Relations* 35: 201. There is good evidence, however, that the Nipissing were travelling north even earlier (Biggar, ed., *Works of Champlain* 2: 255-56).

[51] Le Clercq, *Establishment* 1: 211; Wrong, ed., *Sagard's Long Journey*, 244.

[52] Biggar, ed., *Works of Champlain* 5: 73-80; Hunt, *Wars of the Iroquois*, 69.

[53] The Huron had invited Champlain to visit their country as early as 1609 (Biggar, ed., *Works of Champlain* 2: 105). His attempt to travel up the Ottawa River in 1613 was brought to an end by the opposition of the Algonkin, among other things. Marcel Trudel (*Histoire de la Nouvelle-France*, vol. 2, *Le Comptoir, 1604-1627* [Montréal, 1966], 198-201) may be correct when he suggests that the Algonkin stirred up trouble between Champlain and Vignau in order to protect their trading interests in the interior.

[54] Although Champlain visited all the major Huron villages, he returned repeatedly to Cahiague, a Rock village. He also spent more time there than anywhere else. Lalemant reports that in 1640 his reputation was still very much alive among the Rock (Thwaites, ed., *Relations* 20: 19).

[55] Biggar, ed., *Works of Champlain* 3: 66, 69,73; 4: 254-66; also Hunt, *Wars of the Iroquois*, 20.

[56] Since most of the available data about this period was recorded by priests, we have little information about these men, and practically none from a friendly source. For what there is see, Biggar, ed., *Works of Champlain* 5: 101, 108, 129, 131, 132, 207; Le Clercq, *Establishment* 1: 205; Wrong, ed., *Sagard's Long Journey*, 194-95; Thwaites, ed., *Relations* 5: 133; 6: 83; 14: 17, 19; 18: 45; 20: 19; 25: 85.

[57] A.W. Trelease, *Indian Affairs in Colonial New York: The Seventeenth Century* (Ithaca, 1960), 30.

[58] Trelease, *Indian Affairs*, 46. Intermittent hostilities between the Mahican and Mohawk kept the latter from Fort Orange prior to the stunning defeat of the Mahican in 1628 or 1629 (48).

[59] Trelease, *Indian Affairs*, 52-54; Thwaites, ed., *Relations* 8: 59-61; Hunt, *Wars of the Iroquois*, 34.

51

In 1638 the Huron told the Jesuits that "Englishmen" had come as far as Montreal telling the Indians that the Jesuits were the cause of sickness in Huronia (and no doubt attempting to trade with them or divert trade to the south) (Thwaites, ed., *Relations* 15: 31.)

[60] See, e.g., Biggar, ed., *Works of Champlain* 5: 101, 207.

[61] Biggar, ed., *Works of Champlain* 5: 108. On the usefulness of having Frenchmen accompany the fleet see Wrong, ed., *Sagard's Long Journey*, 262. Sagard reports that in the 1620s the Iroquois refrained from attacking Huron flotillas when they knew Frenchmen were travelling with the Indians (261).

[62] These were at least the functions that the Huron expected Frenchmen who had lived in Huronia would perform. The *coureurs de bois* are frequently referred to as interpreters (Biggar, ed., *Works of Champlain* 3: 168–72).

[63] Wrong, ed., *Sagard's Long Journey*, 249–56.

[64] This route apparently had been used in prehistoric times as well (Biggar, ed., *Voyages of Cartier*, 200–201, as interpreted by Innis, *Fur Trade*, 22).

[65] Edwin Tross, ed., *Histoire du Canada et voyages que les Frères mineurs Recollets y ont faicts pour la conversion des infidèles depuis l'an 1615 . . .* , by G. Sagard (4 vols.; Paris, 1866), 1: 42. This statement refers to the visit Le Caron made with Champlain. On the Huron desire to have the priests act as go-betweens in their trade with the French see Wrong, ed., *Sagard's Long Journey*, 244; Le Clercq, *Establishment* 1: 211.

[66] The Indians often were reluctant to take missionaries back to Huronia with them (Thwaites, ed., *Relations* 4: 221). Some priests, however, became personally popular with the Huron. The popularity of Father Brébeuf during his initial stay in Huronia is evident from the welcome he received when he returned in 1634.

[67] This claim appears in the *Dictionary of Canadian Biography*, vol. 1, *1000 to 1700* (Toronto, 1966), 133. It appears to be based on Sagard's comments on the behaviour of an interpreter named Nicolas Marsolet. Although Marsolet refused to teach the Montagnais language to the Recollets, he later agreed to instruct the Jesuits (Tross, ed., Histoire du Canada 2: 333).

[68] It is perhaps significant that the main complaint was about the sexual behaviour of these men rather than the sale of alcohol to the Indians (cf. André Vachon, "L'Eau-de-vie dans la société indienne," Canadian Historical Association, *Report*, 1960, 22–32). Alcohol does not appear to have been a serious problem in Huronia, no doubt because the Huron did not at this time feel their culture threatened by European contacts. The Jesuits' distaste for these men is reiterated in the Jesuit Relations, particularly when they are compared with the *donnés* and other men who served in Huronia under Jesuit supervision after 1634. See Thwaites, ed., *Relations* 6: 83; 14: 19; 15: 85; 17: 45.

[69] Trudel, *Histoire de la Nouvelle-France* 2: 405–434.

[70] Trelease, *Indian Affairs*, 52; Hunt, *Wars of the Iroquois*, 69–70.

[71] Thwaites, ed., *Relations* 33: 121.

[72] Le Clercq, *Establishment* 1: 204; Tross, ed., *Histoire du Canada*.

[73] There is nothing in Sagard or Le Clercq that implies that the priests were instructed to disrupt this treaty, as Hunt implies. Trudel (*Histoire de la Nouvelle-France* 2: 370) says that it was necessary to send Father Le Caron and the other Frenchmen to Huronia to prevent a commercial treaty between the Huron and the Iroquois. It is my opinion that the prospect of this treaty was a figment of the imagination of the French in Quebec and never a real possibility (see text below).

[74] On the Mohawk refusal to let the French Indians pass through their country to trade with the Dutch see Trelease, *Indian Affairs*, 52–53; Hunt, *Wars of the Iroquois*, 34. Trudel's (*Histoire de la Nouvelle-France* 2: 364–66) suggestion that the Huron were about to trade with the Dutch and that the French who stayed in Huronia did so to prevent this seems unlikely in view of the traditional enmity between the Huron and the Iroquois. To reach Albany the latter would have had to travel through the tribal territory of the three eastern Iroquois tribes. Mohawk opposition to this seems to have effectively discouraged the Huron from attempting such trade.

[75] Sagard says that the Huron did not permit other tribes to pass through their territory without special permission (Wrong, ed., *Sagard's Long Journey*, 99). The Jesuits say categorically that the Huron did not permit the Petun to trade with the French (Thwaites, ed., *Relations* 21: 177).

[76] For a reference about canoes see Hunt, *Wars of the Iroquois*, 51.

[77] Le Clercq, *Establishment* 1: 267. The Huron spread evil rumours about the Jesuits among the Petun when the Jesuits tried to do mission work there in 1640 (Thwaites, ed., *Relations* 20: 47–51).

[78] Thwaites, ed., *Relations* 21: 207-15. At first the priests pretended to be traders. This pretence, however, failed.

[79] Biggar, ed., *Works of Champlain* 5: 131.

[80] The French later describe him as a traitor (Thwaites, ed., *Relations* 5: 241).

[81] Tross, ed., *Histoire du Canada* 2: 431. For a description of his proposed reburial see Thwaites, ed., *Relations* 10: 307–309.

[82] G. Lanctot, *A History of Canada*, vol. 1 (Toronto, 1963), 148-9.

[83] It appears that one reason the Recollets received little support from the trading companies was that their policy of settling migratory Indians and of wanting Huron converts to settle in Quebec conflicted with the traders' own interests (Le Clercq, *Establishment* 1: 111).

[84] The support of Governor Montmagny appears to have been particularly effective (Thwaites, ed., *Relations* 21: 143; 22: 309, 311).

52

85 Thwaites, ed., *Relations* 10: 33; 11: 97, 109, 111, 113; 13: 9; 14: 125 161, 231, 235, 255. On the discontinuation of the seminary, see 24: 103. During the first two years the Jesuits were back in Huronia they were struggling to orient themselves and to understand the nature of Huron society better. At first they tended to be rather patronizing. They gave advice on military matters (10: 53) and, failing to understand the nature of Huron politics, felt that their intervention was needed to mediate disputes among the different tribes (9: 273; 14: 17, 21). Later, when they realized how the Huron did things and that intervention was unnecessary, these efforts ceased.

86 One example is the decision to seek to baptize older men — and especially influential ones (Thwaites, ed., *Relations* 15: 109).

87 For Jesuit policy regarding lay assistants in Huronia, see Thwaites, ed., *Relations* 21: 293-303. See also 6: 81, 83; 15: 157; 17: 45; 20: 99; 25: 85; 27: 91.

88 Parkman, *Jesuits in North America*, 465-67. Concerning early charges of Jesuit participation in the fur trade and a declaration by the directors of the Company of New France concerning their innocence, see Thwaites, ed., *Relations* 25: 75.

89 Thwaites, ed., *Relations* 14: 17-19. For a clear statement that the Jesuits were aware that their presence in Huronia depended on the traders' ability to coerce the Huron to let them stay, see 34: 205. Soon after the Jesuits returned to Huronia, Brébeuf wrote that they won the esteem of the Indians by giving them arrowheads and helping them to defend their forts (34: 53). He hoped that the confidence won by these actions would permit the Jesuits eventually to "advance the glory of God."

90 The main reason seems to have been that the French had detained a Huron who was implicated in killing a Frenchman in Huronia (Thwaites, ed., *Relations* 6: 19). It is interesting to note that the Huron also made it clear they wanted Frenchmen with guns instead of, or at least alongside, the priests (7: 217).

91 Thwaites, ed., *Relations* 9: 287.

53

92 Thwaites, ed., *Relations* 7: 47. The officials in Quebec continued to exhort the Huron to become Christians (17: 171).

93 Thwaites, ed., *Relations* 8: 71, 91, 99.

94 That was in July 1633 (Thwaites, ed., *Relations* 5: 259). The people of Ossossané continued to press the Jesuits to move there.

95 Thwaites, ed., *Relations* 8: 99, 103-105. They also stayed at Ihonitiria because they felt it better to start work in a small village rather than a large and important one (8: 103). Ossossané was also unsatisfactory as its inhabitants were planning to relocate the village the next spring (8: 101).

96 Thwaites, ed., *Relations* 5: 239; 8: 99; 10: 309; 14: 99-103.

97 For an account of this dispute and the Jesuits' attempts to resolve it, see Thwaites, ed., *Relations* 10: 279-81, 307; 14: 21. No mention is made of the dispute after 1637, so presumably it was patched up. Brébeuf mentions elsewhere that, as a result of Brûlé's murder, other Huron were threatening the people of Toanché (the village where he was killed) with death (8: 99). The bad relations between Ossossané and the village of Ihonitiria (which was inhabited by Toanchéans) were exacerbated in 1633 when the latter became angry at the efforts of the chiefs of Ossossané to persuade all the Jesuits to settle in their village (5: 263).

98 Presents were also given to the Huron both as tokens of goodwill and to ensure the good treatment of the Jesuits.

99 For a discussion of the financial help the Jesuits expected to receive from the trading company see Thwaites, ed., *Relations* 6: 81-83. The financial support of the mission is discussed in Parkman, *Jesuits in North America*, 465-67.

100 Thwaites, ed., *Relations* 10: 249; 13: 141; 17: 95; 18: 19, 97.

101 Thwaites, ed., *Relations* 10: 301.

102 One of these trips was to visit the father of a young convert named Amantacha who lived at St. Joseph (Thwaites, ed., *Relations* 8: 139). A careful tabulation by Miss Clark of the places the Jesuits mention visiting each year and the amount of attention given to each village in Huronia shows clearly that prior to 1640 their activities were confined to the Bear nation and particularly to the Penetang Peninsula. After that time their mission work spread into all parts of Huronia.

103 To less than twelve thousand.

104 Thwaites, ed., *Relations* 19: 123, 127; 8: 145-47. The high mortality rate among children is an overall impression gained from reading the relations of the years 1636-40. It also corresponds with what is known about similar epidemics among other Indian groups.

105 Thwaites, ed., *Relations* 19: 223.

106 Thwaites, ed., *Relations* 14: 17, 53, 99-103.

107 Thwaites, ed., *Relations* 39: 129.

108 Thwaites, ed., *Relations* 19: 179.

109 Thwaites, ed., *Relations* 15: 59-67.

110 At all times the Huron leaders appear to have been convinced that killing a priest or one of their assistants would terminate the Franco-Huron alliance.

111 Thwaites, ed., *Relations* 13: 215, 217. For a French statement emphasizing the Huron dependence on trade goods see 32: 179 (1647-48).

112 Thwaites, ed., *Relations* 15: 21.

113 Thwaites, ed., *Relations* 15: 51.

[114] Thwaites, ed., *Relations* 15: 55; 17: 115.

[115] Thwaites, ed., *Relations* 21: 143; 22: 310.

[116] Thwaites, ed., *Relations* 21: 131.

[117] One heifer and a small cannon arrived in 1648 (Thwaites, ed., *Relations* 32: 99).

[118] Thwaites, ed., *Relations* 26: 201.

[119] Concerning the establishment of Ste Marie and the mission system see Thwaites, ed., *Relations* 19: 123–65.

[120] There is a considerable amount of other evidence concerning the coercive power of Huron chiefs. See B.G. Trigger, "Order and Freedom in Huron Society," *Anthropologica* N.S. 5 (1963): 151–69.

[121] Thwaites, ed., *Relations* 21: 213. About the same time the Huron were spreading bad reports concerning the Jesuits among the Petun (20: 54) with whom they had recently made a new treaty of friendship (20: 43). These rumours were spread by Huron traders.

[122] Thwaites, ed., *Relations* 30: 75–77. So bitter was the Huron opposition to Brébeuf after he returned to Huronia that the Huron mission was compelled to send him down to Quebec until the situation quieted down (23: 35).

[123] The Jesuit Relation of 1635 records that the beaver was already totally extinct in the Huron country and that all the skins they traded with the French were obtained elsewhere (Thwaites, ed., *Relations* 8: 57).

[124] Trelease, *Indian Affairs*, 118–20; Hunt, *Wars of the Iroquois*, 32–34. For a later source see Jean Talon cited in Hunt, *Wars of the Iroquois*, 137.

[125] Hunt, *Wars of the Iroquois*, 32–34; Trelease, *Indian Affairs*, 118.

[126] This theory was first advanced by C.H. McIlwain in 1915. It was taken up in Innis, *Fur Trade*, 34–36 and Hunt, *Wars of the Iroquois*, 32–37, 74.

[127] Trelease, *Indian Affairs*, 120.

[128] E.B. O'Callaghan, ed., *Documents Relative to the Colonial History of the State of New York* . . . (15 vols.; Albany, 1853–87), 4: 908.

[129] Thwaites, ed., *Relations* 23: 105.

[130] Hunt, *Wars of the Iroquois*, 76.

[131] Tooker, "Defeat of the Huron," 117–18.

[132] Thwaites, ed., *Relations* 26: 71; 27: 89, 277. Brébeuf returned to Huronia at this time.

[133] Hunt, *Wars of the Iroquois*, 77–78.

[134] For the Iroquois desire to obtain French guns, see the evidence presented in Hunt, *Wars of the Iroquois*, 74.

[135] Thwaites, ed., *Relations* 10: 13; 13: 171.

[136] Thwaites, ed., *Relations* 20: 27–31.

[137] Thwaites, ed., *Relations* 20: 225; 26: 275.

[138] Thwaites, ed., *Relations* 15: 109. For the later relaxation of these requirements see 33: 145–47.

[139] Thwaites, ed., *Relations* 19: 191.

[140] Thwaites, ed., *Relations* 17: 111; 23: 129.

[141] Concerning this preferential treatment see Thwaites, ed., *Relations* 20: 225, 227.

[142] Thwaites, ed., *Relations* 32: 179.

[143] Vachon, "L'Eau-de-vie."

[144] Thwaites, ed., *Relations* 23: 67, 127; 26: 229. Pagan women also attempted to seduce Christian men to persuade them to give up their faith (30: 33). The Relation of 1643 mentions that some converts lived for six months at Quebec to avoid facing temptation in their homeland (24: 121).

[145] Thwaites, ed., *Relations* 30: 23.

[146] Thwaites, ed., *Relations* 21: 131.

[147] Thwaites, ed., *Relations* 23: 185.

[148] Thwaites, ed., *Relations* 23: 31.

[149] For another reference to the Huron–pagan rift see Thwaites, ed., *Relations* 23: 267.

[150] Thwaites, ed., *Relations* 28: 89. For other acts of Christian assertiveness around this time see 29: 263–69; 30: 63.

[151] Thwaites, ed., *Relations* 25: 85.

[152] Tross, ed., *Histoire du Canada* 1: 200; Thwaites, ed., *Relations* 5: 259.

[153] Thwaites, ed., *Relations* 34: 105, 217.

[154] For one incident see Thwaites, ed., *Relations* 30: 61–63. Various cults also arose that appear to have been aimed at organizing ideological resistance to Christianity. One was the cult of a forest monster (30: 27); the second was more explicitly anti-Christian (30: 29–31).

[155] As one Huron put it, "I am more attached to the church than to my country or relatives" (Thwaites, ed., *Relations* 23: 137). The Jesuits also observed that it was hard to be a good Christian and a good Huron (28: 53).

[156] Thwaites, ed., *Relations* 26: 217. The Jesuits had noted the special inclination of the Bear tribe to receive Christianity as early as 1636 (10: 31).

[157] After the destruction of Huronia the Cord were very loyal to the French. They were the only Huron tribe that refused to leave Quebec to go and live with the Iroquois (Thwaites, ed., *Relations* 43: 191). Prior to 1640, the Cord were not at all friendly with the Jesuits (17: 59); their change in attitude seems to have come about soon after (21: 285; 23: 151; 26: 265).

[158] Thwaites, ed., *Relations* 42: 73. Concerning their early desire for peace with the Iroquois see 33: 119-121.

[159] Thwaites, ed., *Relations* 17: 89.

[160] Thwaites, ed., *Relations* 36: 179. The Deer lived among the Seneca in their own village and on good terms with their hosts (44: 21). Many Rock people including the Indians of Contarea, lived among the Onondaga (42: 73).

[161] For evidence of incipient deterioration in morale and the beginning of the abandonment of Huronia in the face of Iroquois attack, see Thwaites, ed., *Relations* 30: 87; 33: 83-89.

[162] Thwaites, ed., *Relations* 33: 125. Hunt (*Wars of the Iroquois*, 72) notes that in 1637 the Huron had broken a peace treaty with the Seneca.

[163] Thwaites, ed., *Relations* 33: 71, 123.

[164] Thwaites, ed., *Relations* 33: 131.

[165] Thwaites, ed., *Relations* 33: 119-21.

[166] Thwaites, ed., *Relations* 33: 125.

[167] Thwaites, ed., *Relations* 33: 125-27. He probably did this through anger at his allies and to show the innocence of the Onondaga. He might also have committed suicide to avoid Huron vengeance directed against his person, but this would have been construed as an act of cowardice. It is unlikely that the Onondaga would have exposed an important chief to almost certain death had they not been negotiating in good faith.

[168] Thwaites, ed., *Relations* 33: 229.

[169] Thwaites, ed., *Relations* 33: 231.

[170] Thwaites, ed., *Relations* 33: 81.

[171] Thwaites, ed., *Relations* 33: 233-49.

[172] Thwaites, ed., *Relations* 34: 227.

[173] Thwaites, ed., *Relations* 34: 83.

[174] Lanctot, *History of Canada* 1: 194, based on Thwaites, ed., *Relations* 34: 59-61.

[175] Tooker, "Defeat of the Hurons," 117-18; Innis, *Fur Trade*, 35-36. For the effective use of firearms by the Iroquois see Thwaites, ed., *Relations* 22: 307. The Jesuits saw the danger of growing Iroquois firepower as early as 1642 (22: 307) but the French officials in Quebec never developed a policy to counteract it. The restiveness of the Huron pagans may be one reason why the French did not want too many guns in Huron hands, even if they were being sold only to Christians.

[176] Hunt, *Wars of the Iroquois*, 59.

[177] Thwaites, ed., *Relations* 35: 191.

[178] Thwaites, ed., *Relations* 36: 179; 44: 21; 45: 243. Many of the Rock nation, particularly from Contarea, were later found living with the Onondaga (42: 73).

[179] Thwaites, ed., *Relations* 12: 221. The work in Paraguay is also mentioned in 15: 127.

[180] G. Lanctot, *A History of Canada* 2 (Toronto, 1964), 63.

[181] Hunt, *Wars of the Iroquois*, 100-102.

[182] Thwaites, ed., *Relations* 41: 201-203, and 44: 151; Hunt, *Wars of the Iroquois*, 99, 100.

[183] Thwaites, ed., *Relations* 40: 215; Lanctot, *History of Canada* 1: 212-13. On the lack of furs in Montreal in 1652-53 see Thwaites, ed., *Relations* 40: 211.

[184] Hunt, *Wars of the Iroquois*, 102-103.

[185] Parkman, *Jesuits in North America*, 550-53.

[186] Tross, ed., *Histoire du Canada* 3: 811; Le Clercq, *Establishment* 1: 204.

55

Employees of the Hudson's Bay Company with their stock and canoes, 1882.

Until relatively recently the Indian peoples have not figured prominently in works dealing with the fur trade. Rather, they generally appear only as shadowy figures who are always present, but never central characters, in the unfolding events.

Arthur J. Ray, "Fur Trade History as an Aspect of Native History"

The Nature and Impact of the Fur Trade

French fur traders preceded the English within the boundaries of present-day Canada by nearly a century. In 1670, Charles II granted a royal charter to the "Company of Adventurers of England trading into Hudson Bay." The Hudson's Bay Company, as it became known, gained an exclusive monopoly, among English subjects, over the fur trade in "Rupert's Land" — all the territory whose rivers drained into Hudson Bay. Rupert's Land, named after Prince Rupert, the Hudson's Bay Company's first governor, comprised almost half of present-day Canada.

Until the Conquest, in 1760, French traders operating out of Montreal opposed the Hudson's Bay Company's monopoly. Afterward, a new challenge arose, when British traders working out of Montreal allied with the French to form the North West Company. Only after the forced union of the two companies in 1821 did the Hudson's Bay Company have a practical monopoly of the northern fur trade, and only then did it truly enjoy the rights and privileges granted to it in 1670.

The Woodland Indians welcomed the French and English traders with their iron manufactured goods — axes, knives, spears, and kettles. These durable items made hunting, cooking, and warfare easier and more efficient than they had been when only stone, wood, and bone implements were available. As a result of the trade, however, the Cree Indians living near the Hudson's Bay Company's posts on Hudson and James bays came to rely on the newcomers. Did the European fur traders, and in particular the Hudson's Bay Company, exploit the Native peoples? Arthur Ray examines the Indians' role in the exchange in his essay "Fur Trade History as an Aspect of Native History."

An important consequence of the fur traders' arrival was the rise of a mixed-blood, or Métis, population, the result of intermarriage between the white fur traders and Indian women. Traditionally, historians of the fur trade ignored the role of these Indian wives. Sylvia Van Kirk analyzes their contribution in "'Women in Between': Indian Women in Fur Trade Society in Western Canada."

E.E. Rich has written the standard account of the Hudson's Bay Company and its rivals in *The Fur Trade and the Northwest to 1857* (Toronto: McClelland and Stewart, 1967). Also of interest is W.J. Eccles's "The Fur Trade and Eighteenth-Century Imperialism," *William and Mary*

Quarterly, 3rd series, 40 (1983): 341–62. The first notable study of the fur trade is H.A. Innis, *The Fur Trade in Canada* (1930; reprint edition, Toronto: University of Toronto Press, 1962). A.J. Ray provides a more recent study in his *Indians in the Fur Trade* (Toronto: University of Toronto Press, 1974). Dan Francis has written a popular account of the personalities of the fur trade in Western Canada, *Battle for the West: Fur Traders and the Birth of Western Canada* (Edmonton: Hurtig, 1982). Three scholarly analyses that focus on the fur trade in a specific region are Dan Francis and Toby Morantz's *Partners in Furs: A History of the Fur Trade in Eastern James Bay, 1600–1870* (Kingston: McGill-Queen's University Press, 1983); Paul C. Thistle's *Indian–European Trade Relations in the Lower Saskatchewan River Region to 1840* (Winnipeg: University of Manitoba Press, 1986); and J.C. Yerbury's *The Subarctic Indians and the Fur Trade, 1680–1860* (Vancouver: University of British Columbia Press, 1986).

A survey of recent literature dealing with the Indians' involvement in the fur trade is found in "The Indian and the Fur Trade: A Review of Recent Literature," by Jacqueline Peterson with John Afinson, *Manitoba History* 10 (1985): 10–18. An excellent popular summary of the fur trade is the illustrated *Where Two Worlds Meet: The Great Lakes Fur Trade* (St. Paul: Minnesota Historical Society, 1982), by Carolyn Gilman. For a short overview consult the chapters entitled "The First Businessmen: Indians and the Fur Trade" and "'A Mere Business of Fur Trading,' 1670–1821," in Michael Bliss, *Northern Enterprise: Five Centuries of Canadian Business* (Toronto: McClelland and Stewart, 1987), 33–54, 79–108. Toby Morantz stresses the continuity of Amerindian culture throughout the early fur trade in "Old Texts, Old Questions: Another Look at the Issue of Continuity and the Early Fur-Trade Period," *Canadian Historical Review* 73, 2 (1992): 166–93.

Sylvia Van Kirk, in *"Many Tender Ties": Women in Fur-Trade Society, 1670–1870* (Winnipeg: Watson and Dwyer, 1980), and Jennifer S.H. Brown, in *Strangers in Blood: The Fur Trade Company Families in Indian Country* (Vancouver: University of British Columbia Press, 1980), have written two excellent accounts of women in the fur trade. Olive Patricia Dickason takes a pan-Canadian view of the rise of a mixed-blood population in her "From 'One Nation' in the Northwest to 'New Nation' in the Northwest: A Look at the Emergence of the Metis," *American Indian Culture and Research Journal* 6, 2 (1982): 1–21. For a survey of the history of the Métis, see D. Bruce Sealey and Antoine S. Lussier, *The Métis: Canada's Forgotten People* (Winnipeg: Manitoba Métis Federation Press, 1975).

The history of the Indians' involvement in the fur trade on the Pacific Coast is covered in Wilson Duff's *The Indian History of British Columbia* (Victoria: Provincial Museum of British Columbia, 1964). More recent studies include Robin Fisher's *Contact and Conflict: Indian–European Re-*

lations in British Columbia, 1774–1890, 2nd ed. (Vancouver: University of British Columbia Press, 1992), and Theodore J. Karamanski's *Fur Trade and Exploration: Opening the Far Northwest, 1821–1852* (Vancouver: University of British Columbia Press, 1983).

Fur Trade History as an Aspect of Native History

ARTHUR J. RAY

Howard Adams, among others, has made the point that the dominant white Euro-Canadian culture has projected racist images of the Indians that "are so distorted that they portray natives as little more than savages without intelligence or beauty."[1] He argued further that the Indians "must endure a history that shames them, destroys their confidence, and causes them to reject their heritage.[2] There is a great deal of truth in Adams's statements, and clearly a considerable amount of historical research needs to be done to correct these distorted images. One important aspect of any new meaningful Indian history necessarily will be concerned with the involvement of the Indian peoples in the fur trade and with the impact of that participation upon their traditional cultures as well as those of the European intruders. Work in this area will be important not only because it holds a potential for giving us new insights into Indian history, but also because it should serve to help establish Indian history in its rightful place in the mainstream of Canadian historiography. As some of Canada's most prominent historians have emphasized, the fur trade was a molding force in the economic, political, and social development of Canada,[3] and the Indian peoples played a central role in this enterprise. For these reasons Indian history should not simply be devoted to recounting the manner in which the aboriginal peoples of Canada were subjugated and exploited, but it must also consider the positive contribution that the Indian peoples made to the fur trade and, hence, to the development of Canada. If this positive contribution is recognized, it should help destroy some of the distorted images that many Canadians have of Indians and their history.

Given that fur trade history and Indian history are inextricably bound together, several questions immediately arise. How much attention have historians devoted to the roles that the Indians played in the fur trade in the considerable body of fur trade literature that already exists?

59

From *One Century Later: Western Canadian Reserve Indians since Treaty 7*, ed. Ian A.L. Getty and Donald B. Smith (Vancouver: University of British Columbia Press, 1978), 7–19. Copyright © University of British Columbia Press, 1978. All rights reserved. Reprinted with permission.

What images of the Indian peoples emerge from this literature? What aspects of Indian involvement have yet to be explored fully?

Until relatively recently the Indian peoples have not figured prominently in works dealing with the fur trade.[4] Rather, they generally appear only as shadowy figures who are always present, but never central characters, in the unfolding events.[5] In part, this neglect appears related to the fact that historians have been primarily concerned with studying the fur trade as an aspect of European imperial history or of Canadian business and economic history.[6] And, reflecting these basic interests, the considerable biographical literature that fur trade research has generated deals almost exclusively with Euro-Canadian personalities.[7] Relatively few Indian leaders have been studied to date.[8]

Although the tendency to consider the fur trade primarily as an aspect of Euro-Canadian history has been partly responsible for the failure of scholars to focus on the Indians' role in the enterprise, other factors have been influential as well. One of the basic problems with most studies of Indian–white relations has been that ethno-historians and historians have taken a retrospective view. They see the subjugation of the Indian peoples and the destruction of their lifestyles as inevitable consequences of the technological gap that existed between European and Indian cultures at the time of contact.[9] From this technological-determinist perspective, the Indian has been rendered as an essentially powerless figure who was swept along by the tide of European expansion without any real hope of channeling its direction or of influencing the character of the contact situation. The dominance of this outlook has meant that in most fur trade studies the Indian has been cast in a reflexive role. Reflecting this perspective, until recently most ethno-historical research has been approached from an acculturation-assimilation point of view. The questions asked are generally concerned with determining how Indian groups incorporated European technology as well as social, political, economic, and religious customs into their traditional cultures.

While also interested in these issues, historians have devoted a considerable amount of attention toward outlining the manner and extent to which Euro-Canadian groups, particularly missionaries and government officials, helped the Indians to adjust to the new socio-economic conditions that resulted from the expansion of Western cultures into the new world.[10] Often historical research has taken a certain moralistic tone, assuming that members of the dominant white society had an obligation to help the Indians adopt agriculture and European socio-economic practices and moral codes, so that the Indian peoples could fit into the newly emerging social order.[11] Thus, historians who undertake these types of studies are frequently seeking to determine whether or not the traders, missionaries, and government officials had fulfilled their obligations to help "civilize" the Indian.

Granting that much good work has been done in the above areas, it is my opinion that many new insights into Indian history can be ob-

60

tained if we abandon the retrospective, technological-determinist outlook and devote more attention to an examination of Indian involvement in the fur trade in the context of contemporary conditions. Such an approach would necessarily recognize that the nature of the trading partnerships that existed between Indian groups and various European interests changed substantially over time and place, making it difficult, frequently misleading, and certainly premature, given the amount of research that still needs to be done, to make any sweeping statements at this time about the nature of Indian–white relations in the context of the Canadian fur trade.

In order to pursue this work effectively, two courses of action need to be followed — one is not currently popular, and the other is extremely tedious. First, students of Indian history need to abandon the assumption that the Indians were ruthlessly exploited and cheated in all areas and periods by white traders. At present this is a very popular theme for both Indian and liberal white historians. All of us have heard the story many times of how the Indians sold Manhattan Island for a few pounds of beads, and we have been informed of the many instances when Indians parted with valuable furs for trinkets and a drink. But why are we never informed of what the Indians' perceptions of trade were? It may well be that they too thought they were taking advantage of the Europeans. For example, in 1634, when commenting on Montagnais beaver trapping in eastern Canada, Father Le Jeune wrote:

61

> The Castor or Beaver is taken in several ways. The Savages say it is the animal well-beloved by the French, English and Basques, — in a word, by the Europeans. I heard my [Indian] host say one day, jokingly, *Missi picoutau amiscou*, "The Beaver does everything perfectly well, it makes kettles, hatchets, swords, knives, bread; and in short, it makes everything." He was making sport of us Europeans, who have such a fondness for the skin of this animal and who fight to see who will get it; they carry this to such an extent that my host said to me one day, showing me a beautiful knife, "The English have no sense; they give us twenty knives like this for one Beaver skin."[12]

While there is no denying that European abuses of Indians were all too common, there are several things wrong with continually stressing this aspect of the fur trade and Indian history. As the previous quote suggests, it gives us only half the story. Of greater importance, by continually focusing only on this dimension of the trade, we run the serious risk of simply perpetuating one of the images in Indian historiography that Adams, among others, most strongly objects to, namely, the view that the Indians were little more than "savages without intelligence." It also glosses over a fundamental point that must be recognized if the Indian is to be cast in an active and creative role. We must not forget that the Indians became involved in the fur trade by their own choice. Bearing that in mind, an objective and thorough examination of the archival records of the leading trading companies, admittedly a wearisome task, gives considerable evidence that the Indians were sophisticated traders, who had their own clearly defined sets of objectives and conventions for carrying on exchange with the Europeans.

This can be demonstrated by following several lines of inquiry. One of these involves attempting to determine the kind of consumers the Indians were at the time of initial contact and how their buying habits changed over time. Probably one of the most striking pictures that emerges from an examination of the early correspondence books of the Hudson's Bay Company is that, contrary to the popular image, the Indians had a sharp eye for quality merchandise and a well-defined shopping list. In short, they were astute consumers and not people who were easily hoodwinked.

If this is doubted, the early letters that the traders on Hudson Bay sent to the governor and committee of the Hudson's Bay Company in London should be read carefully. A substantial portion of almost every letter deals with the subject of the quality of the company's trade goods and with the Indians' reactions to it. Not only do these letters reveal that the Indians could readily recognize superior merchandise, but they also indicate that the Indians knew how to take advantage of the prevailing economic situation to improve the quality of the goods being offered to them. The following quote, typical of those that were written in the period before 1763, demonstrates the point and at the same time indicates one of the problems that is associated with carrying on research of this type. On 8 August 1728, Thomas McCliesh sent a letter from York Factory to the governor and committee in London informing them:

62

> I have sent home two bath rings as samples, for of late most of the rings [which] are sent are too small, having now upon remains 216 that none of the Indians will Trade. I have likewise sent home 59 ivory combs that will not be traded, they having no great teeth, and 3900 large musket flints and small pistol flints, likewise one hatchet, finding at least 150 such in three casks that we opened this summer which causes great grumbling amongst the natives. We have likewise Sent home 18 barrels of powder that came over in 1727, for badness I never saw the like, for it will not kill fowl nor beast at thirty yards distance: and as for kettles in general they are not fit to put into a Indian's hand being all of them thin, and eared with tender old brass that will not bear their weight when full of liquid, and soldered in several places. Never was any man so upbraided with our powder, kettles and hatchets, than we have been this summer by all the natives, especially by those that borders near the French. Our cloth likewise is so stretched with the tenter-hooks, so as the selvedge is almost tore from one end of the pieces to the other. I hope that such care will be taken so as will prevent the like for the future, for the natives are grown so politic in their way of trade, so as they are not to be dealt by as formerly . . . and I affirm that man is not fit to be entrusted with the Company's interest here or in any of their factories that does not make more profit to the Company in dealing in a good commodity than in a bad. For now is the time to oblidge [sic] the natives before the French draws them to their settlement.[13]

From McCliesh's letter one gets the impression that few of the goods on hand were satisfactory as far as the Indians were concerned. Taken out of context, comments of this type, which are common in the correspondence from the posts, could be construed to indicate that the governor and committee of the Hudson's Bay Company hoped to enhance their profits by dealing in cheap, poor quality merchandise whenever possible. However, such a conclusion would distort the reality of the situation and overlook important developments that were under way in the eighteenth century. If one examines the letters that the governor and committee sent to the Bay during the same period, as well as the minutes of their meetings in London and correspondence with British manufacturers and purchasing agents, other important facts emerge.

These other documents reveal that from the outset the governor and committee were concerned with having an array of the types and quality of goods that would appeal to the Indians. From the minute books of the company we learn that in the earliest years of operations the London directors relied heavily upon the experience and judgement of Pierre-Esprit Radisson to provide them with guidance in developing an inventory of merchandise that would be suitable for their posts in Canada. Radisson helped choose the patterns for knives, hatchets, guns, and so forth that manufacturers were to use, and he was expected to evaluate the quality of items that were produced for the company.[14] The governor and committee also sought the expertise of others in their efforts to maintain some quality control. For instance, in 1674 they attempted to enlist the services of the gunsmith who inspected and approved the trade guns of the East India Company.[15] They wanted him to evaluate the firearms that the Hudson's Bay Company was purchasing.

In their annual letters to the posts on the Bay, the governor and committee generally asked the traders to comment on the goods that they received and to indicate which, if any, manufacturer's merchandise was substandard. When new items were introduced, the directors wanted to know what the Indians' reactions to them were.

The question that no doubt arises is, if the governor and committee were as concerned with the quality of the products they sold, as suggested above, then why was there a steady stream of complaints back to London about their goods? Before a completely satisfactory answer to this question can be given, a great deal more research needs to be done in these records. However, several working hypotheses may be put forth at this time for the sake of discussion and research orientation. In developing its inventory of trade goods, the Hudson's Bay Company, as well as other European groups, had to deal with several problems. One of these was environmental in character. Goods that may have been satisfactory for trade in Europe, Africa, or Asia often proved to be unsuitable in the harsh, subarctic environment. This was especially true of any items that were manufactured of iron. For example, one of the problems with the early flintlocks was that the locks froze in the winter.[16]

The extremely cold temperatures of the winter also meant that metal became brittle. Hence, if there were any flaws or cracks in the metal

63

used to make mainsprings for guns, gun barrels, knives, hatchets, or kettles, these goods would break during the winter. In this way the severe environment of the subarctic necessitated very rigid standards of quality if the goods that were offered to the Indians were going to be satisfactory. These standards surely tested the skills of the company's suppliers and forced the company to monitor closely how the various manufacturers' goods held up under use.

Besides having to respond to environmental conditions, the traders also had to contend with a group of consumers who were becoming increasingly sophisticated and demanding. As the Indians substituted more and more European manufactures for traditional items, their livelihood and well-being became more dependent upon the quality of the articles that they were acquiring at the trading posts. This growing reliance meant that the Indians could no longer afford to accept goods that experience taught them would fail under the stress of hard usage and the environment, since such failures could threaten their survival. It was partly for these reasons that the Indians developed a critical eye for quality and could readily perceive the most minute defects in trade merchandise.

Indian groups were also quick to take advantage of competitive conditions. They became good comparison shoppers and until 1821 used European trading rivalries to force the improvement of quality and range of goods that were made available to them. For example, during the first century of trade on Hudson Bay, the Indians frequently brought to Hudson's Bay Company posts French goods that they judged to be superior to those of English manufacture. The Indians then demanded that the Hudson's Bay Company traders match or exceed the quality of these items or risk the loss of their trade to the French. Similar tactics were used by the Indians in later years whenever competition was strong between Euro-Canadian groups. Clearly such actions were not those of "dumb savages," but rather were those of astute traders and consumers, who knew how to respond to changing economic conditions to further their own best interests. The impact that these actions had on the overall profitability of the trade for Euro-Canadian traders has yet to be determined.

The issue of profits raises another whole area of concern that is poorly understood and should be studied in depth. To date we know little about how the economic motivations of the Europeans and the Indians influenced the rates of exchange that were used at the posts. In fact, there is still a great deal of confusion about the complicated system of pricing goods and furs that was used in Canada. We know that the Hudson's Bay Company traders used two sets of standards. There was an official rate of exchange that was set by the governor and committee in London which differed from the actual rate that was used at the posts. Of importance, the traders advanced the prices of their merchandise above the stated tariff by resorting to the use of short measures. Contemporary critics of the Hudson's Bay Company and modern native historians have attacked the company for using such business practices, charging that the Indians were thereby being systematically cheated, or to use the modern expression, "ripped off."[17] But was this the case? Could the company traders have duped the Indians over long periods of time without the latter having caught on? Again, common sense and the record suggest that this was not the case.

The traders have left accounts of what they claimed were typical speeches of Indian trading leaders. One central element of all of these addresses was the request by these leaders that the traders give the Indians "full measure and a little over."[18] Also, the Indians usually asked to see the old measures or standards. Significantly, the Indians do not appear to have ever challenged the official standards, while at the same time they knew that they never received "full measure." What can we conclude from these facts?

In reality, the official standards of trade of the Hudson's Bay Company, and perhaps those of other companies as well, served only as a language of trade, or point of reference, that enabled the Indians and the traders to come to terms relatively quickly. The traders would not sell goods at prices below those set in the official standard. The Indian goal, on the other hand, was to try to obtain terms that approximated the official rate of exchange. An analysis of the Hudson's Bay Company post account books for the period before 1770 reveals that the company traders always managed to advance prices above the standard, but the margin of the advance diminished as the intensity of French opposition increased.[19] And even under monopoly conditions such as existed in Western Canada before the 1730's, the Hudson's Bay Company traders were not able to achieve an across-the-board increase that exceeded 50 per cent for any length of time.[20] This suggests strongly that the Indians successfully used competitive situations to improve the terms of trade and that they had their limits. If prices were advanced beyond a certain level, the Indians must have perceived that their economic reward was no longer worth the effort expended, and they broke off trade even if there was no alternative European group to turn to.

These remarks about the *overplus* system apply to the period before 1770. What we need to know is the extent to which the Indians were able to influence the rates of exchange during the time of bitter Hudson's Bay Company and North West Company rivalry. A preliminary sample of data from that period suggests their impact was much greater and that range of price variation was much more extreme than in the earlier years. Similarly, it would be helpful to have some idea what effect the re-establishment of the Hudson's Bay Company's monopoly after 1821 had on trade good prices and fur values in Western Canada. Being able to monitor prices under these contrasting conditions would enable us to obtain some idea of how the Indians were coping with the changing

65

economic situation and how their responses influenced the material well-being of the different tribal groups.

Although this sample of the early accounting records shows that the Indians were economic men in the sense that they sought to maximize the return they obtained for their efforts, the same documents also indicate that, unlike their European counterparts, the Indians did not trade to accumulate wealth for status purposes. Rather, the Indians seem to have engaged in trade primarily to satisfy their own immediate requirement for goods. On a short-term basis their consumer demand was inelastic. In the early years this type of response was important in two respects. It was disconcerting to the European traders in that when they were offered better prices for their furs, the Indians typically responded by offering fewer pelts on a per capita basis. This type of a supply response was reinforced by gift-giving practices. Following the Indian custom, prior to trade, tribal groups and the Europeans exchanged gifts. As rivalries for the allegiance of the Indians intensified, the lavishness of the gifts that the traders offered increased.

The ramifications that Indian supply responses to rising fur prices and to European gift-giving practices had for the overall conduct of the fur trade have yet to be fully explored. Clearly the costs that the Europeans would have had to absorb would have risen substantially during the periods when competition was strong, but to date no one has attempted to obtain even a rough idea of the magnitude by which these costs rose during the time of English–French or Hudson's Bay Company–North West Company rivalry. Nor has serious consideration been given to the manner in which such economic pressures may have favoured the use and abuse of certain trade articles such as alcohol and tobacco.

Concerning the use of alcohol, the excessive consumption of this drug was an inevitable consequence of the manner in which the economies of the Indian and European were linked together in the fur trade and of the contrasting economic motives of the two groups. As rivalries intensified, the European traders sought some means of retaining their contacts with the Indians, while at the same time keeping the per capita supply of furs that were obtained at as high a level as was possible. However, in attempting to accomplish the latter objective, the Europeans faced a number of problems. The mobile life of the Indians meant that their ability to accumulate material wealth was limited, especially in the early years when the trading posts were distant from the Indians' homelands. And, there were social sanctions against the accumulation of wealth by individual Indians.[21] To combat these problems, the traders needed to find commodities that could be transported easily or, even better, consumed at the trading post.

Unfortunately, alcohol was ideal when viewed from this coldly economic perspective. It offered one of the best means of absorbing the excess purchasing power of the Indians during periods of intensive com-

66

petition. Furthermore, alcohol could be obtained relatively cheaply and diluted with water prior to trade.[22] Hence, it was a high profit trade item, an article that helped the traders hold down their gift-giving expenses, and it could be consumed at the forts. Given these characteristics, the only way that the abusive use of alcohol in trade could have been prevented in the absence of a strong European or native system of government was through monopoly control.

The traditional Indian consumer habits and responses to rising fur prices were important in another way. They were basically conservationist in nature although not intentionally so. By trapping only enough furs to buy the goods they needed in the early years, the pressures that the Indians exerted on the environment by their trapping activities were far less than they would have been had the objective been one of accumulating wealth for status purposes. If the latter had been the primary goal, then the Indians would have been tempted to increase their per capita supply of peltry as fur prices rose, since their purchasing power was greater.

In light of the above, the period between 1763 and 1821 is particularly interesting and warrants close study. During that period Euro-Canadian trading rivalries reached a peak, and one of the consequences of the cutthroat competition that characterized the time was that large territories were over-hunted and trapped by the Indians to the point that the economies of the latter were threatened.[23] The question is, had the basic economic behaviour of the Indians changed to such an extent that it facilitated their over-killing fur and game animals? Or, was the heavy use of addictive consumables such as alcohol and tobacco a major factor in the destruction of the environment?

Yet another aspect of the fur trade that has received too little attention is the connection that existed between the European and eastern North American markets and the Western Canadian operations of the trading companies. It needs to be determined how prices for trade goods and furs in these markets, as well as transportation costs, influenced rates of exchange at the posts. For instance, it has become popular to cite cases where European traders advanced the prices of certain articles by as much as 1000 per cent over what it cost the companies to buy them in Europe. Similarly, accounts of occasions when the Indians received a mere pittance for valuable furs[24] are common. But, it is rarely reported, and indeed it is generally not known, what percentage of the total gross revenues of a company were made by buying and selling such items. Nor is it known if losses were sustained on the sales of other commodities. Equally important, there is not even a rough idea of what the total overhead costs of the companies were at various times. Hence, their net profit margins remain a mystery, and what was considered to be a reasonable profit margin by European standards in the seventeenth, eighteenth, and early nineteenth centuries is not known. Answers to all of these questions must be found before any conclusions can be reached about whether or not the Indian or the European trader was being "ripped off."

And indeed, the Indian side must be considered when dealing with this question and when attempting to understand how the trading system responded to changing economic conditions. Even though Harold Innis pointed out that Indian trading specialists played a crucial role in the development and expansion of the fur trade, a common view of the Indians in the enterprise is still one that portrays them basically as simple trappers who hunted their own furs and accepted whatever prices for these commodities the traders were willing to give them. The fact of the matter is that the records show that in the period before 1770, probably 80 per cent of all of the furs the Europeans received in central Canada came from Indian middlemen who acquired their peltry through their own trading networks.

68   Furthermore, these middlemen charged the Europeans substantially more for these furs than they had paid to obtain them from the trapping bands with whom they dealt. In turn, the middlemen advanced the prices for their trade goods well above the levels they had been charged by the Europeans, sometimes by margins of almost 1000 per cent.

These practices of the Indian middlemen raise a difficult question. If the Indians were not engaged in the trade to accumulate wealth, as suggested earlier, then why did the middlemen advance their prices to the extent that they did? Did their price levels simply enable them to maintain a material standard that they had become accustomed to? Before this question can be answered, a great deal more needs to be known about the problems that the Indian middlemen had to cope with in their efforts to acquire and transport goods and furs. A clearer understanding of their motives for engaging in the trade is also required. For example, why did some Indian groups quickly assume the middleman role while others were apparently content to continue as trappers? How did middlemen groups fare, economically, in comparison with trapping groups?

The Indians played a variety of other roles in the fur trade. They served as provision suppliers, canoe builders, canoe and boat men, and farm labourers around the posts, to name only a few. The Indians quickly assumed these roles as economic conditions changed, rendering old positions obsolete and opening up new opportunities.

This brings to mind another broad research area that should be explored more fully than it has been to date. It deals with determining how the various Indian groups perceived and responded to changing economic situations. Work in this area would serve to destroy another distorted image that many Euro-Canadians have of Indian societies, namely, the view that these societies are rigid and incapable of responding to change. Historically there is little evidence to support such a notion for the period before 1870. While the fur trade was a going concern and the Indians were not tied to the reserves and shackled with bureaucratic red tape, they made many successful adaptations to new circumstances. More needs to be written about this aspect of Indian history. If this work is done, perhaps a picture will emerge that shows the Indians to be innovative, dynamic, and responsive people, whose creativity and initiative have been thwarted in the post-treaty period.

In conclusion, this paper has focused upon the early phases of the Western Canadian fur trade, and the discussion has been restricted primarily to the economic dimension of trade. However, this restriction is justified because many of the problems of Indian–white relations are rooted in the past. Also, many of the distorted images that Euro-Canadians currently hold regarding Indians, thereby causing problems in the relationships between the two groups, have been generated and perpetuated by the manner in which the fur trade history has been written. Correcting these images requires starting at the beginning, and it is not simply a matter of rewriting what has already been done. New research has to be conducted in the various archival collections across the country and records that have received little attention to date, such as accounting records, need to be exhaustively explored. In conducting this research and presenting our results, the urge to overcompensate for past wrongs and inaccuracies by placing the Indian on a pedestal must be resisted. If the latter course of action is taken, a new mythology that will not stand the test of time will be created. Even more serious, it would probably serve only to perpetuate the warped images that such research set out to destroy, because it would fail to treat the Indians as equals with their own cultures and sets of values. Finally, if one of the objectives of studying the fur trade is to attempt to obtain a better understanding of Indian–white relations, it must be based on solid objective historical research.

69

NOTES

I would like to thank Charles A. Bishop, SUNY-Oswego, James R. Gibson and Conrad Heidenrich, York University, and Carol Judd, Ottawa, for commenting on earlier drafts of this paper. The author, of course, is responsible for this paper.

[1] Howard Adams, *Prison of Grass* (Toronto: New Press, 1975), 41.

[2] Adams, *Prison of Grass*, 43.

[3] The most notable example was probably Harold Innis. See H.A. Innis, *The Fur Trade in Canada* (1930; reprint ed., New Haven: Yale University Press, 1962), 386–92.

[4] See, for example, Innis, *The Fur Trade*; A.S. Morton, *The History of the Canadian West to 1870–71*, 2nd ed. (Toronto: University of Toronto Press, 1973); and E.E. Rich, *The Fur Trade and the Northwest to 1857* (Toronto: McClelland and Stewart, 1967).

[5] C. Jaenen, *Friend and Foe* (Toronto: McClelland and Stewart, 1976), 1–11.

[6] Innis and Rich deal extensively with the fur trade as an aspect of imperial history. See Innis, *The Fur Trade*, 383; and Rich, *Fur Trade and Northwest*, xi and 296. Several corporate histories have been written. See as examples, L.R. Masson, *Les Bourgeois de la Compagnie du Nord-Ouest*, 2 vols. (1889–90; reprint ed., New York: Antiquarian Press, 1960); E.E. Rich, *The History of Hudson's Bay Company, 1670–1870*, 2 vols. (London: Hudson's Bay Record Society, 1958–59); and W.S. Wallace, *Documents Relating to the North West Company* (Toronto: Champlain Society, 1934).

7 One of the problems, of course, is that biographical details regarding Indian personalities are few. The historical record often does not provide information regarding births, deaths, and family relationships of Indian leaders.

8 There are some notable exceptions such as Dempsey's study of Crowfoot and Sluman's of Poundmaker. See H. Dempsey, *Crowfoot: Chief of the Blackfoot* (Edmonton: Hurtig, 1972); and N. Sluman, *Poundmaker* (Toronto: McGraw-Hill Ryerson, 1967).

9 This point of view was perhaps most strongly expressed by Diamond Jenness. See Diamond Jenness, "The Indian Background of Canadian History," Canada, Department of Mines and Resources, National Museum of Canada Bulletin No. 86 (Ottawa, 1937), 1–2; and Diamond Jenness, *Indians of Canada*, 6th ed. (Ottawa: National Museum of Canada, 1963), 249. See also George F. Stanley, "The Indian Background of Canadian History," Canadian Historical Association, *Papers* (1952), 14.

10 A notable example of this interest as it pertains to Western Canada is the early work of Frits Pannekoek. See Frits Pannekoek, "Protestant Agricultural Missions in the Canadian West in 1870" (M.A. thesis, University of Alberta, 1970). More recently, Pannekoek has begun to consider the divisive role these groups played in terms of race relations in Western Canada. See Frits Pannekoek, "The Rev. Griffiths Owen Corbett and the Red River Civil War of 1869–70," *Canadian Historical Review* 57 (1976): 133–49.

11 A notable exception to this viewpoint is that expressed by Stanley in 1952. He pointed out that programmes oriented towards assimilating the Indians into the dominant white society lead to cultural extinction of the former group. This is offensive to any people having a strong sense of identity. See Stanley, 21.

12 R.G. Thwaites, ed., *The Jesuit Relations and Allied Documents*, vol. 6 (New York: Pagent Book Company, 1959), 297–99.

13 K.G. Davies, ed., *Letters from Hudson Bay*, 1703–40 (London: Hudson's Bay Record Society, 1965), 136.

14 E.E. Rich, ed., *Minutes of the Hudson's Bay Company*, 1671–74 (Toronto: Champlain Society, 1942), 26–27, 58–59.

15 Rich, *Minutes*, 91.

16 A.J. Ray, *Indians in the Fur Trade* (Toronto: University of Toronto Press, 1974), 75.

17 For example, in the eighteenth century Arthur Dobbs charged that the company advanced the prices of its goods above the Standards of Trade to such an extent that it discouraged the Indians from trading. Arthur Dobbs, *An Account of the Countries Adjoining to Hudson's Bay in the Northwest Part of America* (London, 1744), 43. More recently the company has been attacked for its pricing policy by Adams, *Prison of Grass*, 24.

18 C.E. Heidenreich and A.J. Ray, *The Early Fur Trades: A Study in Cultural Interaction* (Toronto: McClelland and Stewart, 1976), 82–83.

19 A.J. Ray, "The Hudson's Bay Company Account Books as Sources for Comparative Economic Analyses of the Fur Trade: An Examination of Exchange Rate Data," *Western Canadian Journal of Anthropology* 6, 1 (1976): 44–50.

20 The principal exception was at Eastmain where the prevailing rates exceeded the 50 per cent markup level from the late 1690's until about 1720. However, it should be pointed out that French opposition was relatively weak in this area. See Ray, "Hudson's Bay Company Account Books," 45–50.

21 For example, one of the virtues of Indian leaders was generosity. And, generalized reciprocity or sharing was practised amongst band members. These values and practices served to discourage any individual, regardless of his position, from accumulating wealth in excess of that of his kinsmen.

22 Generally, alcohol was diluted with water by a ratio of one-quarter to one-third at the Hudson's Bay Company posts in the eighteenth century. See Davies, *Letters from Hudson Bay*, 268.

23 Ray, *Indians in the Fur Trade*, 117–24.

24 Adams, *Prison of Grass*, 51; and Susan Hurlich, "Up Against the Bay: Resource Imperialism and Native Resistance," *This Magazine* 9, 4 (1975): 4.

"Women in Between": Indian Women in Fur Trade Society in Western Canada

SYLVIA VAN KIRK

In attempting to analyse the life of the Indian woman in fur trade society in Western Canada, especially from her own point of view, one is immediately confronted by a challenging historiographical problem. Can the Indian woman's perspective be constructed from historical sources that were almost exclusively written by European men? Coming from a non-literate society, no Indian women have left us, for example, their views on the fur trade or their reasons for becoming traders' wives.[1] Yet if one amasses the sources available for fur trade social history, such as contemporary narratives, journals, correspondence, and wills, a surprisingly rich store of information on Indian women emerges. One must, of course, be wary of the traders' cultural and sexual bias, but then even modern anthropologists have difficulty maintaining complete objectivity. Furthermore, the fur traders had the advantage of knowing Indian women intimately — these women became their wives, the mothers of their children. Narratives such as that of Andrew Graham in the late eighteenth century and David Thompson in the nineteenth, both of whom had native wives, comment perceptively on the implications of Indian–white social contact.[2] The key to constructing the Indian woman's perspective must lie in the kinds of questions applied to data;[3] regrettably the picture will not be complete, but it is hoped that a careful reading of the traders' observations can result in a useful and illuminating account of the Indian women's life in fur trade society.

The fur trade was based on the complex interaction between two different racial groups. On the one hand are the various Indian tribes, most importantly the Ojibway, the Cree, and the Chipewyan. These Indians may be designated the "host" group in that they remain within their traditional environment. On the other hand are the European traders, the "visiting" group, who enter the Northwest by both the Hudson's Bay and St. Lawrence–Great Lakes routes. They are significantly different from the Indians in that they constitute only a small, all-male fragment of their own society. For a variety of factors to be discussed, this created a unique situation for the Indian women. They became the "women in between" two groups of males. Because of their sex, Indian women were able to become an integral part of fur trade society in a

71

From *Historical Papers* (1977), 30–47. Reprinted with the permission of the Canadian Historical Association.

sense that Indian men never could. As country wives[4] of the traders, Indian women lived substantially different lives when they moved within the forts. Even within the tribes, women who acted as allies of the whites can also be observed; certain circumstances permitted individual women to gain positions of influence and act as "social brokers" between the two groups.

It is a major contention of this study that Indian women themselves were active agents in the development of Indian–white relations.[5] A major concern then must be to determine what motivated their actions. Some themes to be discussed are the extent to which the Indian woman was able to utilize her position as "woman in between" to increase her influence and status, and the extent to which the Indian woman valued the economic advantage brought by the traders. It must be emphasized, however, that Indian–white relations were by no means static during the fur trade period.[6] After assessing the positive and negative aspects of the Indian woman's life in fur trade society, the paper will conclude by discussing the reasons for the demise of her position.

72

I

Miscegenation was the basic social fact of the western Canadian fur trade. That this was so indicates active cooperation on both sides. From the male perspective, both white and Indian, the formation of marital alliances between Indian women and the traders had its advantages. The European traders had both social and economic reasons for taking Indian mates. Not only did they fill the sexual void created by the absence of white women,[7] but they performed such valuable economic tasks as making moccasins and netting snowshoes that they became an integral if unofficial part of the fur trade work force.[8] The traders also realized that these alliances were useful in cementing trade ties; officers in both the Hudson's Bay and North West companies often married daughters of trading captains or chiefs.[9] From the Indian point of view, the marital alliance created a reciprocal social bond which served to consolidate his economic relationship with the trader. The exchange of women was common in Indian society, where it was viewed as "a reciprocal alliance and series of good offices . . . between the friends of both parties; each is ready to assist and protect the other."[10] It was not loose morality or even hospitality which prompted the Indians to be so generous with their offers of women. This was their way of drawing the traders into their kinship circle, and in return for giving the traders sexual and domestic rights to their women, the Indians expected equitable privileges such as free access to the posts and provisions.[11] It is evident that the traders often did not understand the Indian concept of these alliances and a flagrant violation of Indian sensibilities could lead to retaliation such as the Henley House massacre in 1755.[12]

But what of the women themselves? Were they just pawns in this exchange, passive, exploited victims? Fur trade sources do not support this view; there are numerous examples of Indian women actively seeking to become connected with the traders. According to an early Nor'Wester, Cree women considered it an honour to be selected as wives by the voyageurs, and any husband who refused to lend his wife would be subject to the general condemnation of the women.[13] Alexander Ross observed that Chinook women on the Pacific coast showed a preference for living with a white man. If deserted by one husband, they would return to their tribe in a state of widowhood to await the opportunity of marrying another fur trader.[14] Nor'Wester Daniel Harmon voiced the widely held opinion that most of the Indian women were "better pleased to remain with the White People than with their own Relations," while his contemporary George Nelson affirmed "some too would even desert to live with the white."[15] Although Alexander Henry the Younger may have exaggerated his difficulties in fending off young Indian women, his personal experiences underline the fact that the women often took the initiative. On one occasion when travelling with his brigade in the summer of 1800, Henry was confronted in his tent by a handsome woman, dressed in her best finery, who told him boldly that she had come to live with him as she did not care for her husband or any other Indian. But Henry, anxious to avoid this entanglement partly because it was not sanctioned by the husband whom he knew to be insatiably jealous, forced the woman to return to her Indian partner.[16] A year or so later in the lower Red River district, the daughter of an Ojibway chief had more luck. Henry returned from New Year's festivities to find that "Liard's daughter" had taken possession of his room and the devil could not have got her out."[17] This time, having become more acculturated to fur trade life, Henry acquiesced and "Liard's daughter" became his country wife. The trader, however, resisted his father-in-law's argument that he should also take his second daughter because all great men should have a plurality of wives.[18]

The fur traders also comment extensively on the assistance and loyalty of Indian women who remained within the tribes. An outstanding example is the young Chipewyan Thanadelthur, known to the traders as the "Slave Woman."[19] In the early eighteenth century, after being captured by the Cree, Thanadelthur managed to escape to York Factory. Her knowledge of Chipewyan made her valuable to the traders, and in 1715–16, she led an H.B.C. [Hudson's Bay Company] expedition to establish peace between the Cree and the Chipewyan, a necessary prelude to the founding of Fort Churchill. Governor James Knight's journals give us a vivid picture of this woman, of whom he declared: "She was one of a Very high Spirit and of the Firmest Resolution that ever I see any Body in my Days."[20]

Post journals contain numerous references to Indian women warning the traders of impending treachery. In 1797, Charles Chaboillez, having been warned by an old woman that the Indians intended to pillage his

73

post, was able to nip this intrigue in the bud.[21] George Nelson and one of his men escaped an attack by some Indians in 1805 only by being "clandestinely assisted by the women."[22] It appears that women were particularly instrumental in saving the lives of the whites among the turbulent tribes of the Lower Columbia.[23] One of the traders' most notable allies was the well-connected Chinook princess known as Lady Calpo, the wife of a Clatsop chief. In 1814, she helped restore peaceful relations after the Nor'Westers had suffered a raid on their canoes by giving them important information about Indian custom in settling disputes. Handsome rewards cemented her attachment to the traders with the result that Lady Calpo reputedly saved Fort George from several attacks by warning of the hostile plans of the Indians.[24]

The reasons for the Indian women's actions are hinted at in the traders' observations. It was the generally held opinion of the traders that the status of women in Indian society was deplorably low. As Nor-'Wester Gabriel Franchère summed it up:

> Some Indian tribes think that women have no souls, but die altogether like the brutes; others assign them a different paradise from that of men, which indeed they might have reason to prefer . . . unless their relative condition were to be ameliorated in the next world.[25]

Whether as "social brokers" or as wives, Indian women attempted to manipulate their position as "women in between" to increase their influence and status. Certainly women such as Thanadelthur and Lady Calpo were able to work themselves into positions of real power. It is rather paradoxical that in Thanadelthur's case it was her escape from captivity that brought her into contact with the traders in the first place; if she had not been a woman, she would never have been carried off by the Cree as a prize of war. Once inside the H.B.C. fort, she was able to use her position as the only Chipewyan to advantage by acting as guide and consultant to the Governor. The protection and regard she was given by the whites enabled Thanadelthur to dictate to Indian men, both Cree and Chipewyan, in a manner they would not previously have tolerated. Anxious to promote the traders' interests, she assaulted an old Chipewyan on one occasion when he attempted to trade less than prime furs; she "ketcht him by the nose Push'd him backwards & call'd him fool and told him if they brought any but Such as they ware directed they would not be traded."[26] Thanadelthur did take a Chipewyan husband but was quite prepared to leave him if he would not accompany her on the arduous second journey she was planning to undertake for the Governor.[27] It is possible that the role played by Thanadelthur and subsequent "slave women" in establishing trade relations with the whites may have enhanced the status of Chipewyan women. Nearly a century later, Alexander Mackenzie noted that, in spite of their burdensome existence, Chipewyan women possessed "a very considerable influence in the traffic with Europeans."[28]

74

Lady Calpo retained a position of influence for a long time. When Governor Simpson visited Fort George in 1824, he found she had to be treated with respect because she was "the best News Monger in the Parish"; from her he learned "More of the Scandal, Secrets and politics both of the out & inside of the Fort than from Any other source."[29] Significantly, Lady Calpo endeavoured to further improve her rank by arranging a marriage alliance between the Governor and her carefully raised daughter. Although Simpson declared he wished "to keep clear of the Daughter," he succumbed in order "to continue on good terms with the Mother."[30] Many years later, a friend visiting the Columbia wrote to Simpson that Lady Calpo, that "'fast friend' of the Whites" was still thriving.[31]

As wives of the traders, Indian women could also manoeuver themselves into positions of influence. In fact, a somewhat perturbed discussion emerges in fur trade literature over the excessive influence some Indian women exerted over their fur trader husbands. The young N.W.C. [North West Company] clerk George Nelson appears to have spent long hours contemplating the insolvable perplexities of womankind. Nelson claimed that initially Cree women when married to whites were incredibly attentive and submissive, but this did not last long. Once they had gained a little footing, they knew well "how to take advantage & what use they ought to make of it."[32] On one of his first trips into the interior, Nelson was considerably annoyed by the shenanigans of the Indian wife of Brunet, one of his voyageurs. A jealous, headstrong woman, she completely dominated her husband by a mixture of "caresses, promises & menaces." Not only did this woman render her husband a most unreliable servant, but Nelson also caught her helping herself to the Company's rum. Brunet's wife, Nelson fumed, was as great "a vixen & hussy" as the tinsmith's wife at the market place in Montreal: "I now began to think that women were women not only in civilized countries but elsewhere also."[33]

Another fur trader observed a paradoxical situation among the Chipewyan women. In their own society, they seemed condemned to a most servile existence, but upon becoming wives of the French-Canadian voyageurs, they assumed "an importance to themselves and instead of serving as formerly they exact submission from the descendants of the Gauls."[34] One of the most remarkable examples of a Chipewyan wife rising to prominence was the case of Madam Lamallice, the wife of the brigade guide at the H.B.C. post on Lake Athabasca. During the difficult winter of 1821–22, Madam Lamallice was accorded a favoured position because she was the post's only interpreter and possessed considerable influence with the Indians.[35] George Simpson, then experiencing his first winter in the Indian Country, felt obliged to give in to her demands for extra rations and preferred treatment in order to prevent her defection. He had observed that the Nor'Westers' strong position was partly due to the fact that " . . . their Women are faithful

75

to their cause and good Interpreters whereas we have but one in the Fort that can talk Chipewyan."[36] Madam Lamallice exploited her position to such an extent that she even defied fort regulations by carrying on a private trade in provisions.[37] A few years later on a trip to the Columbia, Governor Simpson was annoyed to discover that Chinook women when married to the whites often gained such an ascendancy "that they give law to their Lords."[38] In fact, he expressed general concern about the influence of these "petticoat politicians," whose demands were "more injurious to the Companys interests than I am well able to describe."[39] The Governor deplored Chief Factor James Bird's management of Red River in the early 1820s because of his habit of discussing every matter "however trifling or important" with "his Copper Cold Mate," who then spread the news freely around the colony.[40] Too many of his officers, Simpson declared, tended to sacrifice business for private interests. Particular expense and delay were occasioned in providing transport for families. Simpson never forgave Chief Factor John Clarke for abandoning some of the goods destined for Athabasca in 1820 to make a light canoe for his native wife and her servant.[41]

76

It is likely that Simpson's single-minded concern for business efficiency caused him to exaggerate the extent of the Indian women's influence. Nevertheless, they do seem to have attempted to take advantage of their unique position as women "in between" two groups of men. This fact is supported by the traders' observation that the choice of a husband, Indian or white, gave the Indian woman leverage to improve her lot. Now she could threaten to desert to the whites or vice versa if she felt she were not being well-treated:

> She has always enough of policy to insinuate how well off she was while living with the white people and in like manner when with the latter she drops some hints to the same purpose.[42]

Although Chipewyan women who had lived with the voyageurs had to resume their former domestic tasks when they returned to their own people, they reputedly evinced a greater spirit of independence.[43] Considerable prestige accrued to Chinook women who had lived with the traders; upon rejoining the tribes, they remained "very friendly" to the whites and "never fail to influence their connections to the same effect."[44]

From the Indian woman's point of view, material advantage was closely tied to the question of improved influence or status. The women within the tribes had a vested interest in promoting cordial relations with the whites. While George Nelson mused that it was a universal maternal instinct which prompted the women to try to prevent clashes between Indian and white,[45] they were more likely motivated by practical, economic considerations. If the traders were driven from the country, the Indian woman would lose the source of European goods, which had revolutionized her life just as much as if not more than that of the Indian man. It was much easier to boil water in a metal kettle than to have to laboriously heat it by means of dropping hot stones into a bark container. Cotton and woolen goods saved long hours of tanning hides. "Show them an awl or a strong needle," declared David Thompson, "and they will gladly give the finest Beaver or Wolf skin they have to purchase it."[46]

Furthermore, it can be argued that the tendency of the Indians to regard the fur trade post as a kind of welfare centre was of more relevance to the women than to the men. In times of scarcity, which were not infrequent in Indian society, the women were usually the first to suffer.[47] Whereas before they would often have perished, many now sought relief at the companies' posts. To cite but one of many examples: at Albany during the winter of 1706, Governor Beale gave shelter to three starving Cree women whose husband had sent them away as he could only provide for his two children.[48] The post was also a source of medical aid and succour. The story is told of a young Carrier woman in New Caledonia, who having been severely beaten by her husband managed to struggle to the nearest N.W.C. post. Being nearly starved, she was slowly nursed back to health and allowed to remain at the post when it became apparent that her relatives had abandoned her.[49] The desire for European goods, coupled with the assistance to be found at the fur trade posts, helps to explain why Indian women often became devoted allies of the traders.

In becoming the actual wife of a fur trader, the Indian woman was offered even greater relief from the burdens of her traditional existence. In fact, marriage to a trader offered an alternative lifestyle. The fur traders themselves had no doubt that an Indian woman was much better off with a white man. The literature presents a dreary recital of their abhorrence of the degraded, slave-like position of the Indian women. The life of a Cree woman, declared Alexander Mackenzie, was "an uninterrupted success of toil and pain."[50] Nor'Wester Duncan McGillivray decided that the rather singular lack of affection evinced by Plains Indian women for their mates arose from the barbarous treatment the women received.[51] Although David Thompson found the Chipewyan a good people in many ways, he considered their attitudes toward women a disgrace; he had known Chipewyan women to kill female infants as "an act of kindness" to spare them the hardships they would have to face.[52]

The extent to which the fur traders' observations represent an accurate reflection of the actual status of Indian women in their own societies presents a complex dilemma which requires deeper investigation. The cultural and class biases of the traders are obvious. Their horror at the toilsome burdens imposed upon Indian women stems from their narrow, chivalrous view of women as the "frail, weaker sex." This is scarcely an appropriate description of Indian women, particularly the Chipewyan who were acknowledged to be twice as strong as their male counterparts.[53] Furthermore, while the sharp sexual division of labour

77

inflicted a burdensome role upon the women, their duties were essential and the women possessed considerable autonomy within their own sphere.[54] Some traders did think it curious that the women seemed to possess a degree of influence in spite of their degraded situation; indeed, some of the bolder ones occasionally succeeded in making themselves quite independent and "wore the breeches."[55]

A possible way of explaining the discrepancy between the women's perceived and actual status is suggested in a recent anthropological study of the Mundurucú of Amazonian Brazil. In this society, the authors discovered that while the official (male) ideology relegates women to an inferior, subservient position, in the reality of daily life, the women are able to assume considerable autonomy and influence.[56] Most significantly, however, Mundurucú women, in order to alleviate their onerous domestic duties, have actively championed the erosion of traditional village life and the concomitant blurring of economic sex roles which have come with the introduction of the rubber trade. According to the authors, the Mundurucú woman "has seen another way of life, and she has opted for it."[57]

This statement could well be applied to the Indian woman who was attracted to the easier life of the fur trade post. In the first place, she now became involved in a much more sedentary routine. With a stationary home, the Indian woman was no longer required to act as a beast of burden, hauling or carrying the accoutrements of camp from place to place. The traders often expressed astonishment and pity at the heavy loads which Indian women were obliged to transport.[58] In fur trade society, the unenviable role of carrier was assumed by the voyageur. The male servants at the fort were now responsible for providing firewood and water, although the women might help. In contrast to Indian practice, the women of the fort were not sent to fetch home the produce of the hunt.[59] The wife of an officer, benefiting from her husband's rank, enjoyed a privileged status. She herself was carried in and out of the canoe[60] and could expect to have all her baggage portaged by a voyageur. At Fond du Lac in 1804, when the wife of N.W.C. *bourgeois* John Sayer decided to go on a sugar-making expedition, four men went with her to carry her baggage and provisions and later returned to fetch home her things.[61]

While the Indian woman performed a variety of valuable economic tasks around the post, her domestic duties were relatively lighter than they had traditionally been. Now her energies were concentrated on making moccasins and snowshoes. As one Nor'Wester declared, with the whites, Indian women could lead "a comparatively easy and free life" in contrast to the "servile slavish mode" of their own.[62] The prospect of superior comforts reputedly motivated some Spokan women to marry voyageurs.[63] The ready supply of both finery and trinkets which *bourgeois* and voyageurs were seen to lavish on their women may also have had an appeal.[64] Rival traders noted that luxury items such as lace, ribbons, rings, and vermilion, which "greatly gain the Love of the Women," were important in attracting the Indians to trade.[65] The private orders placed by H.B.C. officers and servants in the 1790s and later include a wide range of cloth goods, shawls, gartering, earrings, and brooches for the women.[66] When taken by a trader, *à la façon du pays*, it became common for an Indian woman to go through a ritual performed by the other women of the fort; she was scoured of grease and paint and exchanged her native garments for those of a more civilized fashion. At the N.W.C. posts, wives were clothed in "Canadian fashion," which consisted of a shirt, short gown, petticoat, and leggings.[67]

The traders further thought that Indian women benefited by being freed from certain taboos and customs which they had to bear in Indian society. Among the Ojibway and other tribes, for example, the choicest part of an animal was always reserved for the men; death, it was believed, would come to any woman who dared to eat such sacred portions. The Nor'Westers paid little heed to such observances. As Duncan Cameron sarcastically wrote: "I have often seen several women living with the white men eat of those forbidden morsels without the least inconvenience."[68] The traders were also convinced that Indian women welcomed a monogamous as opposed to a polygamous state. Polygamy, several H.B.C. officers observed, often gave rise to jealous and sometimes murderous quarrels.[69] It is possible, however, that the traders' own cultural abhorrence of polygamy[70] made them exaggerate the women's antipathy toward it. As a practical scheme for the sharing of heavy domestic tasks, polygamy may in fact have been welcomed by the women.

79

II

Thus far the advantages which the fur trade brought to Indian women have been emphasized in order to help explain Indian women's reactions to it. It would be erroneous, however, to paint the life of an Indian wife as idyllic. In spite of the traders' belief in the superior benefits they offered, there is evidence that fur trade life had an adverse effect on Indian women. Certainly, a deterioration in her position over time can be detected.

First there is the paradox that the supposedly superior material culture of the fur trade had a deleterious effect on Indian women. It was as if, mused Reverend John West, the first Anglican missionary, "the habits of civilized life" exerted an injurious influence over their general constitutions.[71] Apart from being more exposed to European diseases, the Indian wives of traders suffered more in childbirth than they had in the primitive state.[72] Dr. John Richardson, who accompanied the Franklin Expedition of the 1820s, noted that not only did Indian women now have children more frequently and for longer periods, but that they were more susceptible to the disorders and diseases connected with pregnancy and childbirth.[73] It was not uncommon for fur traders' wives to give birth to from eight to twelve children, whereas four children were the average in Cree society.[74]

The reasons for this dramatic rise in the birth rate deserve further investigation, but several reasons can be advanced. As recent medical research had suggested, the less fatiguing lifestyle and more regular diet offered the Indian wife could have resulted in great fecundity.[75] The daily ration for the women of the forts was four pounds of meat or fish (one half that for the men);[76] when Governor Simpson jokingly remarked that the whitefish diet at Fort Chipewyan seemed conducive to procreation he may have hit upon a medical truth.[77] Furthermore, sexual activity in Indian society was circumscribed by a variety of taboos, and evidence suggests that Indian men regarded their European counterparts as very licentious.[78] Not only did Indian women now have sex more often, but the attitudes of European husbands also may have interfered with traditional modes of restricting family size. The practice of infanticide was, of course, condemned by the whites, but the Europeans may also have discouraged the traditional long nursing periods of from two to four years for each child.[79] In their view this custom resulted in the premature aging of the mothers,[80] but the fact that Indian children were born at intervals of approximately three years tends to support the recent theory that lactation depresses fertility.[81]

The cultural conflict resulting over the upbringing of the children must have caused the Indian women considerable anguish. An extreme example of the tragedy which could result related to the Chinook practice of head-flattening. In Chinook society, a flat forehead, achieved by strapping a board against the baby's head when in its cradle, was a mark of class; only slaves were not so distinguished. Thus it was only natural that a Chinook woman, though married to a fur trader, would desire to bind her baby's head, but white fathers found this custom abhorrent. The insistence of some fathers that their infants' heads not be flattened resulted in the mothers murdering their babies rather than have them suffer the ignominy of looking like slaves. Gradually European preference prevailed. When Governor Simpson visited the Columbia in the early 1820s, he reported that Chinook wives were abiding by their husbands' wishes and no cases of infanticide had been reported for some years.[82]

In Indian society, children were the virtual "property" of the women who were responsible for their upbringing;[83] in fur trade society, Indian women could find themselves divested of these rights. While the traders acknowledged that Indian women were devoted and affectionate mothers, this did not prevent them from exercising patriarchal authority, particularly in sending young children to Britain or Canada so that they might receive a "civilized" education.[84] It must have been nearly impossible to explain the rationale for such a decision to the Indian mothers;

80

their grief at being separated from their children was compounded by the fact that the children, who were especially vulnerable to respiratory diseases, often died.[85]

It is difficult to know if the general treatment accorded Indian women by European traders met with the women's acceptance. How much significance should be attached to the views of outside observers in the early 1800s who did not think the Indian woman's status had been much improved? Some of the officers of the Franklin Expedition felt the fur traders had been corrupted by Indian attitudes toward women; Indian wives were not treated with "the tenderness and attention due to every female" because the Indians would despise the traders for such unmanly action.[86] The first missionaries were even stronger in denouncing fur trade marital relations. John West considered the traders' treatment of their women disgraceful: "They do not admit them as their companions, nor do they allow them to eat at their tables, but degrade them *merely* as slaves to their arbitrary inclinations."[87] Such statements invite skepticism because of the writers' limited contact with fur trade society, and, in the case of the missionaries, because of their avowedly hostile view of fur trade customs. Furthermore, the above statements project a European ideal about the way women should be treated, which, apart from being widely violated in their own society, would have had little relevance for Indian women. It is doubtful, for example, that the Indian women themselves would have viewed the fact that they did not come to table, a custom partly dictated by the quasi-military organization of the posts, as proof of their debased position.[88] The segregation of the sexes at meals was common in Indian society, but now, at least, the women did not have to suffice with the leftovers of the men.[89]

81

Nevertheless, there is evidence to suggest that Indian women were misused by the traders. In Indian society, women were accustomed to greater freedom of action with regard to marital relationships than the traders were prepared to accord them. It was quite within a woman's rights, for example, to institute a divorce if her marriage proved unsatisfactory.[90] In fur trade society, Indian women were more subject to arbitrary arrangements devised by the men. Upon retiring from the Indian Country, it became customary for a trader to place his country wife and family with another, a practice known as "turning off." Although there was often little they could do about it, a few cases were cited of women who tried to resist. At a post in the Peace River district in 1798, the Indian wife of an *engagé*, who was growing tired of wintering *en derouine*, absolutely rejected her husband's attempt to pass her to the man who agreed to take his place.[91] At Fort Chipewyan in 1800, the estranged wife of the voyageur Morin foiled the attempt of his *bourgeois* to find her a temporary "protector"; she stoutly refused three different prospects.[92] Indian women also did not take kindly to the long separations which fur trade life imposed on them and their European mates. Although the Indian wife of Chief Factor Joseph Colen was to receive every attention during his absence in England in the late 1790s, Colen's successor could not dissuade her from taking an Indian lover and leaving York Factory.[93]

Indian wives seem to have been particularly victimized during the violent days of the trade war when rivals went so far as to debauch and intimidate each other's women. In 1819 at Pelican Lake, for example, H.B.C. servant Deshau took furs from a N.W.C. servant and raped his wife in retaliation for having had his own wife debauched by a Nor'Wester earlier in the season.[94] A notorious instance involved the Indian wife of H.B.C. servant Andrew Kirkness at Isle à la Crosse in 1810-11. In the late summer, this woman in a fit of pique had deserted her husband and sought refuge at the Nor'Westers' post. She soon regretted her action, however, for she was kept a virtual prisoner by the Canadians, and all efforts of the H.B.C. men to get her back failed. The upshot was that Kirkness himself deserted to the rival post, leaving the English in dire straits since he was their only fisherman. Kirkness was intimidated into remaining with the Nor'Westers until the spring with the threat that, should he try to leave, "every Canadian in the House would ravish his woman before his eyes." Eventually Kirkness was released, but only after his wife had been coerced into saying that she did not want to accompany him. As the H.B.C. party were evacuating their post, the woman tried to escape but was forcibly dragged back by the Nor'Westers and ultimately became the "property" of an *engagé*.[95]

Such abusive tactics were also applied to the Indians. By the turn of the century, relations between the Indians and the Nor'Westers in particular showed a marked deterioration. In what seems to have been a classic case of "familiarity breeding contempt," the Nor'Westers now retained their mastery through coercion and brute force and frequently transgressed the bounds of Indian morality. An especially flagrant case was the Nor'Westers' exploitation of Chipewyan women at its posts in the Athabasca district. By the end of the eighteenth century, they had apparently built up a nefarious traffic in these women; the *bourgeois* did not scruple at seizing Chipewyan women by force, ostensibly in lieu of trade debts, and then selling them to the men for large sums.[96] The situation became so bad that the Chipewyan began leaving their women behind when they came to trade, and when Hudson's Bay traders appeared on Lake Athabasca in 1792, the Indians hoped to secure their support and drive out their rivals. The English, however, were too weak to offer any effective check to the Nor'Westers, who continued to assault both fathers and husbands if they tried to resist the seizure of their women. Since they were not powerful enough to mount an attack, the Chipewyan connived at the escape of their women during the summer months when most of the traders were away. Resentful of their treatment, many of the women welcomed the chance to slip back to their own people, so that the summer master at Fort Chipewyan was almost solely pre-occupied with keeping watch over the *engagés* women.[97] By 1800 at least one voyageur had been killed by irate Chipewyan, and the *bourgeois* contemplated offering a reward for the hunting down of "any d—nd rascal" who caused a Frenchman's woman to desert.[98]

The Indians appear to have become openly contemptuous of the white man and his so-called morality. A northern tribe called the Beaver Indians took a particularly strong stand. At first they had welcomed the Canadians but, having rapidly lost respect for them, now forbade any intercourse between their women and the traders.[99] Elsewhere individual hunters boycotted the traders owing to the maltreatment of their women.[100] Sporadic reprisals became more frequent. Whereas Indian women had previously played a positive role as a liaison between Indian and white, they were now becoming an increasing source of friction between the two groups. Governor Simpson summed up the deteriorating situation:

83

> It is a lamentable fact that almost every difficulty we have had with Indians throughout the country may be traced to our interference with the Women of the Forts in short 9 murders out of 10 Committed on Whites by Indians have arisen through Women.[101]

Although there is little direct evidence available, it is possible that the Indian women themselves were becoming increasingly dissatisfied with their treatment from the whites. In spite of the initiative which the women have been seen to exercise in forming and terminating relationships with the traders, there were undoubtedly times when they were the unwilling objects of a transaction between Indians and white men. Certainly not all Indian women looked upon the whites as desirable husbands, a view that was probably reinforced with experience. George Nelson did observe in 1811 that there were some Indian women who showed "an extraordinary predilection" for their own people and could not be prevailed upon to live with the traders.[102]

The increasing hostility of the Indians, coupled with the fact that in well-established areas marriage alliances were no longer a significant factor in trade relations, led to a decline in the practice of taking an Indian wife. In fact in 1806, the North West Company passed a ruling prohibiting any of its employees from taking a country wife from among the tribes.[103] One of the significant factors which changed the traders' attitudes toward Indian women, however, was that they were now no longer "women in between." By the turn of the century a sizeable group of mixed-blood women had emerged and for social and economic reasons, fur traders preferred mixed-blood women as wives. In this way the Indian women lost their important place in fur trade society.

The introduction of the Indian woman's perspective on Indian–white relations serves to underscore the tremendous complexity of inter-cultural contact. It is argued that Indian women saw definite advantages to be gained from the fur trade, and in their unique position as "women in between," they endeavoured to manipulate the situation to improve their existence. That the limits of their influence were certainly circumscribed, and that the ultimate benefits brought by the traders were questionable does not negate the fact that the Indian women played a much more active and important role in the fur trade than has previously been acknowledged.

NOTES

[1] The lack of written Indian history is, of course, a general problem for the ethnohistorian. Indeed, all social scientists must rely heavily on the historical observations of the agents of white contact such as fur traders, explorers, and missionaries. Little seems to have been done to determine if the oral tradition of the Indians is a viable source of information on Indian–white relations in the fur trade period.

[2] Glyndwr Williams, ed., *Andrew Graham's Observations on Hudson's Bay, 1769–91* (London: Hudson's Bay Record Society, vol. 27, 1969); Richard Glover, ed., *David Thompson's Narrative, 1784–1812* (Toronto: Champlain Society, vol. 40, 1962).

[3] A fascinating study which indicates how the application of a different perspective to the same data can produce new insights is *Women of the Forest* by Yolanda and Robert Murphy (New York, 1974). Based on field work conducted twenty years earlier in Amazonian Brazil, the authors found that by looking at the life of the Mundurucú tribe from the woman's point of view, their understanding of the actual as opposed to the official functioning of that society was much enlarged.

[4] Marriages between European traders and Indian women were contracted according to indigenous rites derived from the Indian custom. For a detailed explanation, see Sylvia Van Kirk, "'The Custom of the Country': An Examination of Fur Trade Marriage Practices," in L.H. Thomas, ed., *Essays in Western History* (Edmonton, 1976), 49–70.

[5] See Murphy, *Women of the Forest*, Ch. 6, for a useful comparison. Mundurucú women actively welcomed the social change brought about by the introduction of the rubber trade into their traditional economy.

[6] An instructive study of the Indians' economic role in the fur trade is provided by Arthur Ray in *Indians in the Fur Trade* (Toronto, 1974). He shows that the Indian played a much more active, although changing, role in the dynamics of the fur trade than had previously been acknowledged.

[7] H.B.C. men were prohibited from bringing women to Hudson Bay. It was not until the early nineteenth century that the first white women came to the Northwest.

[8] In 1802 H.B.C. men defended their practice of keeping Indian women in the posts by informing the London Committee that they were "Virtually your Honors Servants," H.B.C. Arch., B.239/ b/79, fos. 40d–41. For a discussion of the important economic role played by native women in the fur trade, see Sylvia Van Kirk, "The Role of Women in the Fur Trade Society of the Canadian West, 1700–1850," unpublished Ph.D. thesis, University of London, 1975.

[9] H.B.C. Arch., Albany Journal, 24 Jan. 1771, B.3/a/63, f. 18d; "Connolly vs. Woolrich, Superior Court, 9 July 1867, *Lower Canada Jurist* 11: 234.

[10] Charles Bishop, "The Henley House Massacres," *The Beaver* (Autumn 1976): 40.

[11] Bishop, "The Henley House Massacres," 39. For a more technical look at the socio-economic relationship between the Indians and the traders, see the discussion of "balanced reciprocity" in Marshall Sahlins, *Stone Age Economics* (Chicago, 1972), Ch. 5.

[12] In this instance the Indian captain Woudby attacked Henley House because the master was keeping two of his female relatives but denying him access to the post and its provisions.

[13] Alexander Henry, *Travels and Adventures in Canada and the Indian Territories, 1760–1776*, ed. Jas. Bain. (Boston, 1901), 248.

[14] Alexander Ross, *The Fur Hunters of the Far West*, vol. 1 (London, 1855), 296–97.

[15] W. Kaye Lamb, ed., *Sixteen Years in the Indian Country: The Journal of Daniel Williams Harmon, 1800–1816* (Toronto, 1957), 29; Toronto Public Library, George Nelson Papers, Journal 1810–11, 24 April 1811, 42.

[16] Elliot Coues, ed., *New Light on the Early History of the Greater North West: The Manuscript Journals of Alexander Henry and David Thompson, 1799–1814*, (Minneapolis, 1965), 71–73.

[17] Coues, *New Light*, 163.

[18] Coues, *New Light*, 211.

[19] For a detailed account of the story of this woman, see Sylvia Van Kirk, "Thanadelthur," *The Beaver* (Spring 1974): 40–45.

[20] Van Kirk, "Thanadelthur," 45.

[21] Public Archives of Canada (P.A.C.), Masson Collection, Journal of Charles Chaboillez, 13 Dec. 1797, 24.

[22] Nelson Papers, Journal and Reminiscences 1825–26, 66.

[23] Ross, *Fur Hunters* 1: 296.

[24] Coues, *New Light*, 793; Frederick Merk, ed., *Fur Trade and Empire: George Simpson's Journal, 1824–25* (Cambridge, Mass., 1931), 104.

[25] Gabriel Franchère, *Narrative of a Voyage to the Northwest Coast of America, 1811–14*, ed. R.G. Thwaites (Cleveland, Ohio, 1904), 327.

[26] Van Kirk, "Thanadelthur," 44.

[27] Van Kirk, "Thanadelthur," 45.

[28] W. Kaye Lamb, ed., *The Journals and Letters of Sir Alexander Mackenzie* (Cambridge, Eng., 1970) 152.

[29] Merk, *Fur Trade and Empire*, 104.

[30] Merk, *Fur Trade and Empire*, 104–105.

[31] H.B.C. Arch., R. Crooks to G. Simpson, 15 March 1843, D. 5/8, f. 147.

[32] Nelson Papers, Journal 1810–11, pp. 41–42.

[33] Nelson Papers, Journal 1803–04, 10–28 *passim*.

[34] Masson Collection, "An Account of the Chipwean Indians," 23.

[35] E.E. Rich, ed., *Simpson's Athabasca Journal and Report, 1820–21* (London, H.B.R.S., vol. 1, 1938), 74.

[36] Rich, *Athabasca Journal*, 231.

[37] H.B.C. Arch., Fort Chipewyan Journal 1820–21, B.39/a/16, fos. 6–21d. *passim*.

[38] Merk, *Fur Trade and Empire*, 99.

[39] Merk, *Fur Trade and Empire*, 11–12, 58.

[40] H.B.C. Arch., George Simpson's Journal, 1821–22. D.3/3, f.52.

[41] Rich, *Athabasca Journal*, 23–24; see also Merk, *Fur Trade and Empire*, 131.

[42] "Account of Chipwean Indians," 23–24.

[43] "Account of Chipwean Indians," 23.

[44] Ross, *Fur Hunters* 1: 297.

[45] Nelson Papers, Journal and Reminiscences 1825–26, 66. Nelson claimed that around 1780 some Indian women had warned the Canadian pedlars of impending attack because in their "tender & affectionate breast (for women are lovely all the world over) still lurked compassion for the mothers of those destined to be sacrificed."

[46] Glover, *Thompson's Narrative*, 45. Cf. with the Mundurucú women's desire for European goods, Murphy, *Women of the Forest*, 182.

[47] Samuel Hearne, *A Journey to the Northern Ocean*, ed. Richard Glover (Toronto, 1958), 190.

[48] H.B.C. Arch., Albany Journal, 23 Feb. 1706, B.3/a/1, f. 28.

[49] Ross Cox, *The Columbia River*, ed. Jane and Edgar Stewart (Norman, Okla., 1957), 377.

[50] Lamb, *Journals of Mackenzie*, 135.

[51] A. S. Morton, *The Journal of Duncan McGillivray . . . at Fort George on the Saskatchewan, 1794–95* (Toronto, 1929), 60.

[52] Glover, *Thompson's Narrative*, 106.

[53] Hearne, *Journey to Northern Ocean*, 35: "Women," declared the Chipewyan chief Matonabee, "were made for labour; one of them can carry, or haul, as much as two men can do."

[54] There has been a trend in recent literature to exalt the Indian woman's status by pointing out that in spite of her labour she had more independence that the pioneer farm wife. See Nancy O. Lurie, "Indian Women: A Legacy of Freedom," *The American Way* 5 (April 1972): 28–35.

[55] Morton, *McGillivray's Journal*, 34; L.R.F. Masson, *Les Bourgeois de la Compagnie du Nord-Ouest* 1: 256.

[56] Murphy, *Women of the Forest*, 87, 112.

[57] Murphy, *Women of the Forest*, 202.

[58] Lamb, *Journals of Mackenzie*, 254; Glover, *Thompson's Narrative*, 125.

[59] Masson Collection, Journal of John Thomson, 15 Oct. 1798, p. 10.

[60] J.B. Tyrrell, *Journals of Samuel Hearne and Philip Turnor, 1774–92* (Toronto, Champlain Society, vol. 21, 1934), 252.

[61] Michel Curot, "A Wisconsin Fur Trader's Journal, 1803–04," *Wisconsin Historical Collections* 20: 449, 453.

[62] Nelson Papers, Journal 1810–11, 41: Reminiscences, Part 5, 225.

[63] Cox, *Columbia River*, 148.

[64] Coues, *New Light*, 914; Ross, *Fur Hunters* 2: 236.

[65] Tyrrell, *Journals of Hearne and Turnor*, 273.

[66] H.B.C. Arch., Book of Servants Commissions, A.16/111 and 112 *passim*.

[67] Lamb, *Sixteen Years*, 28–29.

[68] Masson, *Les Bourgeois* 2: 263.

[69] Hearne, *Journey to Northern Ocean*, 80; Williams, *Graham's Observations*, 158.

[70] Alexander Ross, *Adventures of the First Settlers on the Oregon or Columbia River* (London, 1849) 280–81; Glover, *Thompson's Narrative*, 251.

[71] John West, *The Substance of a Journal during a residence at the Red River Colony, 1820–23* (London, 1827), 54.

85

72 The traders were astonished at the little concern shown for pregnancy and childbirth in Indian society, see for example Lamb, *Journals of Mackenzie*, 250, and Williams, *Graham's Observations*, 177.
73 John Franklin, *Narrative of a Journey to the Shores of the Polar Sea, 1819-22* (London, 1824), 86.
74 Franklin, *Narrative of a Journey*, 60. The Indian wives of Alexander Ross and Peter Filder, for example, had thirteen and fourteen children respectively.
75 Jennifer Brown, "A Demographic Transition in the Fur Trade Country," *Western Canadian Journal of Anthropology* 6, 1: 68.
76 Cox, *Columbia River*, 354.
77 J.S. Galbraith, *The Little Emperor* (Toronto, 1976), 68.
78 Nelson Papers, Reminiscences, Part 5, p. 155.
79 Brown, "A Demographic Transition," 67.
80 Margaret MacLeod, ed. *The Letters of Letitia Hargrave* (Toronto, Champlain Society, vol. 28, 1947), 94-95; Alexander Ross, *The Red River Settlement* (Minneapolis, 1957), 95, 192.
81 Brown, "A Demographic Transition," 65.
82 Merk, *Fur Trade and Empire*, 101.
83 Williams, *Graham's Observations*, 176, 178.
84 Ross, *Adventures on the Columbia*, 280; W.J. Healy, *Women of Red River* (Winnipeg, 1923), 163-66.
85 Lamb, *Sixteen Years*, 138, 186.
86 Franklin, *Narrative of a Journey*, 101, 106.
87 West, *Red River Journal*, 16.
88 Cox, *Columbia River*, 360.
89 Hearne, *Journey to the Northern Ocean*, 57.
90 Williams, *Graham's Observations*, 176.
91 Thomson's Journal, 19 Nov. 1798, p. 20.
92 Masson, *Les Bourgeois* 2: 384-85. We are not told whether she also escaped being sold when the brigades arrived in the spring as the *bourgeois* intended.
93 H.B.C. Arch., York Journal, 2 Dec. 1798, B.239/a/103, f. 14d.
94 H.B.C. Arch., Pelican Lake Journal, 18 Jan. 1819, D.158/a/1, f. 7d.
95 This account is derived from the Isle à la Crosse Journal, H.B.C. Arch., B.89/a/2, fos. 5-36d *passim*.
96 Tyrrell, *Journals of Hearne and Turnor*, 446n, 449.
97 Tyrrell, *Journals*, 449-50.
98 Masson, *Les Bourgeois* 2: 387-88.
99 Lamb, *Journals of Mackenzie*, 255; Rich, *Athabasca Journal*, 388.
100 Masson Collection, Journal of Ferdinand Wentzel, 13 Jan. 1805, p. 41.
101 Merk, *Fur Trade and Empire*, 127.
102 Nelson Papers, Journal 1810-11, 41-42.
103 W.S. Wallace, *Documents relating to the North West Company* (Toronto, Champlain Society, vol. 22, 1934), 211. This ruling was not enforced in outlying districts such as the Columbia. Even after the union in 1821, Governor Simpson continued to favour the formation of marital alliances in remote regions as the best way to secure friendly relations with the Indians. See Rich, *Athabasca Journal*, 392.
104 For a discussion of the role played by mixed-blood women in fur trade society, see Van Kirk, "Role of Women in Fur Trade Society."

The venerable Mère Marie de l'Incarnation, the first Mother Superior of the Ursuline Order of Nuns in New France (1600–72). Engraving by Jean Edelinck.

The praises of Marie de l'Incarnation, Jeanne Mance, and Marguerite Bourgeoys have been sung so often as to be tiresome. Perhaps, though, a useful vantage point is gained if one assesses them as neither saints nor heroines, but simply as leaders. In this capacity, the nuns supplied money, publicity, skills, and settlers, all of which were needed in the colony.

Jan Noel, "New France: Les femmes favorisées"

Topic Three

The Society of New France

The population of New France grew extremely slowly because of the dominance of the fur trade, which required only a small work force. In the autumn of 1608, only twenty-eight people lived at Quebec, and, more than thirty years later, the population of all of New France had not reached three hundred. Only after the establishment of direct royal government in 1663 did the colony begin to expand.

Royal government helped the colony's growth in three specific ways. First, the Crown established an effective political system. Second, the dispatch of a sizable military force against the Iroquois led to an effective truce with the Confederacy, securing twenty years of peaceful development for the colony. Third, the French government sponsored the immigration of several thousand settlers, men and women, who helped to build a more diversified economy in New France. From 1663 to 1700, the colony's population grew from 2500 to 15 000. By the late seventeenth century, the society of New France had taken on a definite form.

Who were these French Canadians of the New World? What was the nature of this new North American society? In what respects, if any, did New France differ from France? W.J. Eccles outlines the general characteristics of the French Canadians in New France in "Society and the Frontier," a chapter from his book *The Canadian Frontier, 1534–1760*. In "New France: Les femmes favorisées," Jan Noel provides an in-depth study of the role of women in the colony.

There are a number of excellent surveys of the society of New France. One of the best is Louise Dechêne's study of Montreal in the late seventeenth century, *Habitants and Merchants in Seventeenth Century Montreal*, translated by Liana Vardi (Montreal and Kingston: McGill-Queen's University Press, 1992). In *The Beginnings of New France, 1524–1663* (Toronto: McClelland and Stewart, 1973), Marcel Trudel reviews several aspects of the society of New France in its early years. W.J. Eccles, in *Canada under Louis XIV, 1663–1701* (Toronto: McClelland and Stewart, 1964), and Dale Miquelon, in *New France, 1701–1744: "A Supplement to Europe"* (Toronto: McClelland and Stewart, 1987), examine later periods. The most recent survey of New France is Jacques Mathieu's *La Nouvelle-France: Les Français en Amérique du Nord, XVIe–XVIIIe Siècle* (Sainte-Foy, Québec: Presses de l'Université Laval, 1991).

Recently, several important studies on the history of women in New France have appeared. Chapter 2 in Alison Prentice et al., *Canadian Women: A History* (Toronto: Harcourt Brace Jovanovich, 1988), 41–64, entitled "French Women in the New World," and the opening chapter of Micheline Dumont et al., *Quebec Women: A History*, trans. R. Gannon and R. Gill (Toronto: Women's Press, 1987) survey the position of women in the French colony. Lilianne Plamondon has written about a commercially minded woman in "A Businesswoman in New France: Marie-Anne Barbel, The Widow Fornel," in *Rethinking Canada: The Promise of Women's History*, ed. Veronica Strong-Boag and Anita Clair Fellman (Toronto: Copp Clark Pitman, 1986), 45–59. In *Orphelines en France pionnières au Canada: Les filles du roi au XVIIe siècle* (Montréal: Leméac Éditeur, 1992), Yves Landry provides a collective biography of the 770 female immigrants to New France between 1663 and 1673. Karen Anderson's *Chain Her by One Foot: The Subjugation of Women in Seventeenth-Century New France* (London: Routledge, 1991) examines the treatment of Amerindian women by the French.

90

Other important studies of various aspects of the society of New France include Cornelius Jaenen's *The Role of the Church in New France* (Toronto: McGraw-Hill Ryerson, 1976), a review of an important institution in the colony. W.J. Eccles writes about early Canadian society in his *France in America*, rev. ed. (New York: Harper and Row, 1990); *Essays on New France* (Toronto: Oxford University Press, 1987); and *The Canadian Frontier, 1534–1760* (from which one of the readings for this topic has been taken). Three important articles, by G. Frégault, J. Hamelin, and W.J. Eccles, are reprinted in *Society and Conquest*, ed. Dale Miquelon (Toronto: Copp Clark, 1977), 85–131. A good summary of economic life in New France appears in "Doing Business in New France," a chapter in Michael Bliss's *Northern Enterprise: Five Centuries of Canadian Business* (Toronto: McClelland and Stewart, 1987), 55–77. Peter Moogk's "*Les Petits Sauvages*: The Children of Eighteenth-Century New France," in *Childhood and Family in Canadian History*, ed. Joy Parr (Toronto: McClelland and Stewart, 1982), 17–43, 192–95 deals with a subject that had previously been neglected in the literature. Also of value is Moogk's "Reluctant Exiles: The Problem of Colonization in French North America," *William and Mary Quarterly* 46, 3 (July 1989); 463–505. R. Cole Harris's *The Seigneurial System in Early Canada* (Madison: University of Wisconsin Press, 1966) provides a useful overview. Because there were no newspapers in New France, there is a dearth of information on popular events and opinions; consequently, historians have often underestimated the extent of popular discontent under the French regime. Terence Crowley presents the surviving evidence in "'Thunder Gusts': Popular Disturbances in Early French Canada," Canadian Historical Association, *Historical Papers* (1982): 11–32.

For a first-hand account of New France in 1750, students should consult the English translation of Peter Kalm's *Travels in North America*, 2 vols. (New York: Dover Publications, 1964).

Society and the Frontier

W.J. ECCLES

Of the more tangible factors that influenced Canadian society there can be no doubt that geography was very important. The St. Lawrence River and certain of its tributaries dominated life in the colony. The land suitable for agricultural settlement stretched in a narrow band along the St. Lawrence, wider on the south shore than on the north. Near Quebec the Laurentian Shield, scraped nearly bare long ago by an advancing ice age, meets the river. Below this point only small pockets of land at river mouths were suitable for agriculture. Above Quebec, on the north shore, the Shield draws away from the river to a distance of some forty miles at Montreal. On the south shore the belt of fertile land is quite wide between Quebec and Montreal but becomes a narrow ribbon along the river toward Gaspé. West of Montreal there is also good land but on both the St. Lawrence and Ottawa rivers, rapids make communications difficult. Consequently throughout the French regime land settlement was concentrated in the St. Lawrence Valley from a point a few miles west of Montreal to a little below Quebec, with pockets of settlement on both sides lower down the river.

Prior to 1663 the number of settlers and the amount of land cleared grew very slowly. In 1634 the first seigneurial grant was made to Robert Giffard by Richelieu's Company of New France. During the ensuing thirty years some seventy other seigneuries were granted. The company sent a few settlers to the colony but in the main let this responsibility fall to the seigneurs who, for the most part, lacked the means to engage in a large-scale immigration program. The religious orders did bring out a goodly number of servants, laborers, and settlers; and the crown from time to time sent detachments of soldiers to aid in the colony's defense. By these means the population slowly grew, and stretches of forest near the three areas of settlement, Quebec, Trois-Rivières, and Montreal, were cleared back from the shores of the river. In 1640 the total French population in the colony — settlers, soldiers, clergy, fur trade company employees — numbered only about 240; by 1663, largely as a result of the efforts of the religious orders, this number had increased

From *The Canadian Frontier, 1534–1760*, by W.J. Eccles (Albuquerque, N.M.: University of New Mexico Press, 1965). Reprinted with permission.

to some 2500. After the latter date, under the stimulus of the crown, settlement increased very rapidly; by 1669 the population had increased by two-thirds, and by the end of the century it was at approximately the 15,000 mark, doubling thereafter each generation to a total of some 70,000 at the Conquest.[1]

The St. Lawrence dictated the pattern of settlement in another way. It was the main means of communication in the colony, in summer by canoe or sailing barque, in winter by sleigh on the ice. The need for roads was thus obviated until the eighteenth century. Every settler desired land on the river, and the land holdings early took on the peculiar pattern that has endured to the present day, that of narrow strips running back from the river. Survey lines separating seigneuries ran at right angles to the river and as the generations succeeded each other the individual holdings became increasingly narrow. According to the law of the land, the *Coutume de Paris,* a seigneur's eldest son inherited the manor house and half the domain land; the rest was divided among the remaining children. The children of the humbler settlers, the *censitaires,* inherited equal parts of the parental land. After a few generations many of the individual holdings became too narrow to be worked efficiently, and in 1745 the intendant forbade anyone to build a house or barn on land narrower than one and a half arpents (approximately 100 yards) by thirty or forty linear arpents in depth. Those who contravened the *ordonnance* were fined 100 *livres* and their buildings were torn down at their expense.

By the eighteenth century the pattern was well established. Along both banks of the St. Lawrence from Quebec to Montreal the farms stretched back from the river, the houses and barns on the river bank spaced a few hundred yards apart. Every few miles there was a seigneurial manor house and a mill, and eventually a steep-roofed stone church. Later in the century concessions were taken up in the second range and another row of narrow strip farms stretched back from the rear of the first, with a roadway between the two. To anyone traveling by river up to Montreal nearly all of New France passed in review.

This pattern of land settlement was not without its disadvantages. Until the end of the seventeenth century the Iroquois were an almost constant menace, and with the homes spaced in this fashion mutual aid in times of attack was almost impossible. Individual farms and their occupants could be destroyed all too easily before aid could be mustered. While the Iroquois assaults were at their height stockaded forts had to be built in the exposed seigneuries where the people could take refuge with their livestock, abandoning their homes to the depredations of the enemy. Attempts by some of the royal officials to have the settlers live in villages, with their concessions radiating out like spokes of a wheel, were not very successful. The Canadians insisted on having river frontage and living apart, lords of their own little domains, with access to the wider world beyond by way of the river.

National Gallery of Canada, Ottawa/No. 6275.

Château-Richer. This painting by Thomas Davies (c. 1737–1812), completed in 1787, portrays typical habitant farm buildings on the shores of the St. Lawrence east of Quebec City.

By the mid-eighteenth century the farm houses in the first range and the churches were nearly all of stone, thick-walled, substantial; steep Norman roofs were modified by a graceful curving wide eave, to afford shade in the hot Canadian summers. Peter Kalm, a Swedish professor of natural history who visited Canada in 1749, going by boat from Montreal to Quebec, remarked:

> The country on both sides was very delightful to-day, and the fine state of its cultivation added to the beauty of the scene. It could really be called a village, beginning at Montreal and ending at Quebec, which is a distance of more than one hundred and eighty miles, for the farmhouses are never above five arpents and sometimes but three apart, a few places excepted. The prospect is exceedingly beautiful when the river flows on for several miles in a straight line, because it then shortens the distance between the houses, and makes them form one continued village. . . . We sometimes saw *windmills* near the farms. They were generally built of stone, with a roof of boards, which together with its wings could be turned to the wind.[2]

The principal crop grown was wheat but the climate of the St. Lawrence Valley was not particularly suitable for this cereal. Heavy rains sometimes caused serious loss from smut; early frosts were a constant menace; and plagues of caterpillars occasionally destroyed everything growing. Yet crop failures appear to have been no more frequent than in France, where they were anticipated, on an average, once in five years.³ In the early years the yield was high, the natural result of rich virgin soil. By the mid-eighteenth century it had declined considerably, despite the increase in the number of cattle and the consequent increased use of manure.

Peter Kalm was very critical of the inefficient agricultural methods he had observed in the English colonies. He was not less critical of those in New France; they both compared unfavorably with farming methods that he had studied in England, which he stated were the most advanced in Europe. One factor that militated against efficient agricultural production, in New France as in the English colonies, was the chronic shortage of labor. When able-bodied men could obtain land very cheaply, they were not inclined to work for others, except at excessively high wages. The wages paid skilled tradesmen were also high, resulting in a drift from the country to the three towns, which contained 25 percent of the colonial population. A much more important factor, however, was the large number of men, of necessity the young and physically fit, who were continually out of the colony on voyages to the west.

All the evidence indicates that the Canadian *habitants* and the laboring class in the towns enjoyed a higher standing of living and much more personal freedom than did their counterparts in Europe. This undoubtedly accounts, to some degree, for the difference in their attitudes and character that visitors from Europe all remarked on. But what seems to have had an even greater influence was their frequent contact, on terms of equality, with the Indian nations. Nor did they have to voyage far for this contact. Within the confines of the colony, or close by, were several resident Indian bands. Near Quebec, at Lorette, resided a band of Huron, survivors of the 1649 diaspora. A few miles south of Quebec was the Abenaki village of St. François, removed from Acadia to protect the colony's southern approaches from Anglo-American incursions up the Connecticut River. Near Montreal were two Indian settlements: the Mission Iroquois at Sault St. Louis and the Sulpician mission that had first been established on the lower slopes of Mount Royal, then, as the town grew, had been moved first to the north side of the island, later to the western tip, and finally across the Lake of Two Mountains to Oka. The Mission Iroquois at Sault St. Louis (Caugnawaga to the Iroquois) were originally Mohawks who had been converted to Christianity by the Jesuits and had then removed to New France the better to preserve their new faith.⁴ Members of other of the Iroquois nations, after conversion, subsequently moved to Caugnawaga to spare themselves the constant taunts of their fellow tribesmen who had remained pagan.

Another reason for this Iroquois defection to Canada was the desire to avoid the Albany rum traders. Not all the Indians were incapable of resisting the temporary delights that intoxication brought; the authorities of both New France and New York were frequently asked by the chiefs of Iroquois and Algonkin nations to keep liquor away from their villages. The governors of New France, for the most part, did their best to comply and managed to curb the abuse to a considerable degree. The same could not be said of the authorities at Albany. There, rum and whiskey of such appalling quality that it was little better than poison was the main item of trade, used to get the Indians drunk before they traded their furs, in order to defraud them. This practice was so common that the Dutch traders at Albany were little more than Canada's secret weapon, for although many of the western Indians would bypass the French posts to go to Albany where they were given all the liquor they could drink,[5] they were not so besotted that they did not later realize the consequences. This is not to say that there were no Canadian traders willing to use liquor in the same way in their commercial dealings with the Indians. The Jesuit missionaries at Sault St. Louis waged a constant struggle to keep such traders away from their charges, and the Oka mission had removed to this site largely to keep the converts away from the taverns and unscrupulous purveyors.

The members of this latter mission were a mixture of Iroquois and northern Algonkin; the common factor was their conversion to Christianity. During the colonial wars these warriors, particularly those of Sault St. Louis, performed valiant service; indeed, the authorities at Albany were greatly concerned lest most of the Five Nations should remove to Canada. Had this occurred Albany and all the northern settlements would have had to be abandoned. Although in expeditions against the villages of the Five Nations the Mission Iroquois could not be depended on — they frequently gave their kinsmen warning — the devastating raids on the settlements of New England were carried out by war parties composed largely of these domiciled tribesmen, combined with Canadian militia, and led by officers in the colonial regulars, the Troupes de la Marine. Thus the Canadians were closely associated with the Indians, waging war after their fashion, using their techniques and becoming as adept in the harsh, cruel methods as any Iroquois or Abenaki. There was therefore a demonstrable degree of truth in the opinion of the Canadians expressed by one French officer: "They make war only by swift attacks and almost always with success against the English, who are not as vigorous nor as adroit in the use of fire arms as they, nor as practiced in forest warfare."[6]

In peacetime, too, the Canadians were in constant association with the Indians. The Indians were frequent visitors to Montreal, and to prevent constant blood baths, the intendant had to set aside certain taverns for the Indian trade, allocated by nation, and strictly regulated. It is, therefore, hardly surprising that the Canadians early adopted much of the Indian way of life and became imbued with some of their character traits. Native foods such as corn, squash, and pumpkins found ready acceptance. Indian means of travel — the snowshoe, toboggan, and canoe — were quickly mastered. Many of the Canadians, who were inveterate pipe smokers, preferred to mix their locally grown tobacco with the inner bark of the cherry or dogwood tree, a custom borrowed from the Indians. In their mode of dress the *habitants* copied the Indians, with an effect rather startling to European eyes. The women, except when dressed up fine for Sunday mass, wore a short jacket or blouse and a short skirt which, Peter Kalm several times observed, "does not reach to the middle of their legs."

It was during their frequent trips to the west that the Canadians were most exposed to the Indian way of life. Immediately following the establishment of royal government in 1663 the population of the colony expanded rapidly, from approximately 2500 to an estimated 15,000 by the end of the century. Of the latter number as many as five hundred of the active males were always off in the west on trading expeditions. It was during these years that senior officials, newly arrived from France, began to comment on the striking difference between the Canadians and their peers in France. Inevitably, these officials were first struck by what seemed to them the deleterious social and economic effects of the metamorphosis.

The Marquis de Denonville, governor general from 1685 to 1689, was appalled by certain attitudes and habits of the Canadians. Instead of laboring on the land, they preferred to spend their lives in the bush, trading with the Indians, where their parents, the *curés*, and the officials could not govern them, and where they lived like savages. Even when they returned to the colony these youths showed a shocking proclivity for going about half naked in the hot weather, as did the Indians. "I cannot emphasize enough, my lord, the attraction that this Indian way of life has for all these youths," Denonville wrote to the minister. But he then went on to say, "The Canadians are all big, well built, and firmly planted on their legs, accustomed when necessary to live on little, robust and vigorous, very self willed and inclined to dissoluteness; but they are witty and vivacious."[7] The intendant Jean Bochart de Champigny in 1691 wrote in much the same vein, stating, "It is most unfortunate that Canadian youths, who are vigorous and tough, have no inclination for anything but these voyages where they live in the forest like Indians for two or three years at a time, without benefit of any of the sacraments."[8] Peter Kalm in 1749 was also much impressed by the martial qualities of the Canadians, acquired through their frequent sojourns in the west. He noted that they were exceptional marksmen: "I have seldom seen any people shoot with such dexterity as these. . . . There was scarcely one of them who was not a clever marksman and who did not own a rifle." He then went on:

> It is inconceivable what hardships the people of Canada must undergo on their hunting journeys. Sometimes they must carry their goods a great way by land. Frequently they are abused by the Indians, and sometimes they are killed by them. They often suffer hunger, thirst, heat, and cold, and are bitten by gnats,

and exposed to the bites of snakes and other dangerous animals and insects. These (hunting expeditions) [*sic*] destroy a great part of the youth in Canada, and prevent the people from growing old. By this means, however, they become such brave soldiers, and so inured to fatigue that none of them fears danger or hardships. Many of them settle among the Indians far from Canada, marry Indian women, and never come back again.[9]

Some of the Jesuit missionaries in the west took a much more jaundiced view of the effects of the close relations between the Canadians and the Indians. Fathers St. Cosme and Carheil at Michilimackinac made that post appear, from their description, a veritable Sodom or Gomorrah, where the only occupations of the Canadians, apart from trading furs, were drinking, gambling, and lechery. Things had come to such a pass that the *coureurs de bois* took Indian women with them rather than men on their trading expeditions. The men claimed that these women worked for lower wages than men demanded, and were willing to perform such chores as cutting firewood and cooking. The missionaries refused to be persuaded that other fringe benefits were not involved.[10] The governor general Vaudreuil, although he did not support the Jesuit proposal to keep the Canadians and Indians as far apart as possible, was strongly opposed to mixed marriages. He claimed that the children of mixed blood incorporated the worst character traits of both races and were a constant source of trouble. He therefore issued orders forbidding such marriages at Detroit, the main French post in the west at that time (1709).[11]

These complaints on the part of the missionaries have to be taken with a pinch of salt. To them chastity, or failing this monogamy with the benefit of the marriage sacrament, was the ideal. They expected these *voyageurs* who, if married, had left their wives in the colony, to live like monks while in the west. The Indians had different moral values and chastity was not among them. Father Charlevoix, who was not a missionary, took a more tolerant view of Canadian society in the 1740s. He commented:

> Our Creoles are accused of great avidity in amassing, and indeed they do things with this in view, which could hardly be believed if they were not seen. The journeys they undertake; the fatigues they undergo; the dangers to which they expose themselves, and the efforts they make surpass all imagination. There are, however, few less interested, who dissipate with greater facility what has cost them so much pains to acquire, or who testify less regret at having lost it. Thus there is some room to imagine that they commonly undertake such painful and dangerous journeys out of a taste they have contracted for them. They love to breathe a free air, they are early accustomed to a wandering life; it has charms for them, which make them forget past dangers and fatigues, and they place their glory in encountering them often. . . . I know not whether I ought to reckon amongst the defects of our Canadians the good opinion they entertain of themselves. It is at least certain that it inspires them with confidence, which leads them to undertake and execute what would appear impossible to many others. . . . It is alleged they make bad servants, which is owing to their

great haughtiness of spirit, and to their loving liberty too much to subject themselves willingly to servitude.[12]

These observations on the cupidity of the Canadians, coupled with their
spendthrift attitude, are significant for these same traits were quite pronounced among the Indians. Like the Indian, the Canadian did not see
any merit in storing up worldly goods; both looked down on those who
did, and up to those who spent their money ostentiously on good living. The
Canadians, too, became proud, independent, and improvident, glorying
in their physical strength, their hardihood, and their contempt for danger,
caring little for the morrow. One French officer commented, in 1757:

> "They are not thrifty and take no care for the future, being too fond of their
> freedom and their independence. They want to be well thought of and they
> know how to make the most of themselves. They endure hunger and thirst pa-
> tiently, many of them having been trained from infancy to imitate the Indians,
> whom, with reason, they hold in high regard. They strive to gain their esteem
> and to please them. Many of them speak their language, having passed part
> of their life amongst them at the trading posts."[13]

It would seem an obvious conclusion that the Canadians had acquired
this attitude from the Indians, and were able to do so because the necessities of life were relatively easily come by in Canada. In other words,
this character trait was a product of relative affluence and the frontier
environment. It was to no small degree the fact that the Canadians did
come to share this attitude with the Indians that their individual relations
with them were usually better than were those of the Anglo-Americans.
Ruette D'Auteuil, the attorney general at Quebec, spoke the truth for
his day when he claimed that, the price of trade goods being equal,
the Indians preferred to have dealings with the French rather than with
the English.[14] This view was later corroborated by a British commentator
who stated that, "the French have found some secret of conciliating the
affections of the savages, which our traders seem stranger to, or at least
take no care to put it in practice."[15] Not only did the Canadians travel
to the far west, they also voyaged northeastward, serving as crews on
fishing boats in the Gulf and in the seal- and whale-hunting expeditions
along the coast of Labrador. There, too, they came in frequent contact
with Indians, and also with the Eskimo. In wartime they served on privateers, preying on shipping along the New England coast. French pri-
vateer captains frequently called at Quebec to take on crews, Canadians
being very highly regarded for their toughness and bellicosity.

Canadians in all sections of the colony were accustomed to make
trips to distant parts of the continent and to live among peoples of an
entirely different culture. The whole continent from Labrador and Hudson Bay to the Rocky Mountains and the Gulf of Mexico was their world.
Unlike their counterparts in Europe who rarely moved beyond the confines of their native parish, there was nothing parochial about them;

they were men of broad horizons and a continental outlook able to accommodate themselves to almost any conditions anywhere. Were life to become too restrictive in the settlements along the St. Lawrence or were a wife to nag too constantly, some of them at least could hire out as *voyageurs* for the west or as crew on a voyage to Labrador, France, or the West Indies. Even those who never made such a trip could feel that the opportunity was there, and this must have given them a sense of freedom. They could not help but hear the tales of those who had voyaged far afield, of the strange peoples with stranger customs in these distant lands. They, too, shared the experience, vicariously.

Royal officials in the eighteenth century, upon first arriving in the colony, were quick to remark that the Canadians had become a distinct people with values and manners markedly at variance with those of the same class in the mother country. Usually they were quite taken aback by the attitudes and way of life of the Canadians. Only after they had been in the colony for a few years did they come to appreciate the positive side of what had at first seemed a society and people sadly in need of discipline and reform. It was the free and easy, seemingly dissolute, ways of the Canadians, their independent attitude, their insistence on being led not driven, that irked the officials, both civil and military. Other observers were struck by their profligacy, their feast or famine attitude, their recklessness. A Sulpician priest upon arrival in the colony in 1737 remarked that the bulk of the people — military officers, merchants, artisans, and *habitants* alike — were "as poor as artists and as vain as peacocks" and spent every sou they had on ostentatious living. He was shaken to see country girls who tended cows during the week, on Sundays bedecked in lace and hoop skirts, wearing their hair in the very elaborate, high-piled style known then as *à la Fontange*.[16]

Despite these shortcomings, all observers agreed that the Canadians were tough and hardy, gloried in feats of endurance that made Europeans blanch, could travel from one end of the continent to another while living off the land, and had no equal in forest warfare. It was also noted that these same men, when in their homes, were uncommonly courteous, with a natural air of gentility more usual among the nobility than the lower classes.[17] In this respect they compared very favorably with their counterparts, the peasants of France and the settlers in the English colonies. Peter Kalm was particularly struck by this and in his journal he noted that:

99

> The inhabitant of Canada, even the ordinary man, surpasses in politeness by far those people who live in these English provinces. . . .
>
> On entering one of the peasant's houses, no matter where, and on beginning to talk with the men or women, one is quite amazed at the good breeding and courteous answers which are received, no matter what the question is. . . . Frenchmen who were born in Paris said themselves that one never finds in France among country people the courtesy and good breeding which one observes everywhere in this land. I heard many native Frenchmen assert this.[18]

It would, of course, be very easy to ascribe these peculiarities to the frontier environment of New France. There can be no doubt that the frontier had a good deal to do with this, but the changes that took place in Canadian society were very complex. It is therefore necessary to examine conditions in the colony closely to discover the various elements that differed from those of France and then decide which ones were occasioned by the frontier.

Perhaps the basic factor was the abundance of free, fertile land, and the peculiar terms of land tenure under the seigneurial regime. This meant that the Canadian *habitants* were assured of as much land as they could cultivate, and they paid for it only very modest seigneurial dues, if they paid any at all, amounting to less than 10 percent of their annual income from the land.[19] Apart from this obligation, and the tithe for the church, fixed by royal decree at one twenty-sixth of the wheat grown, the *habitants* paid no other taxes. Labor service for the seigneurs, in the form of *corvées*, was very rarely imposed and was, in fact, a violation of the *Coutume de Paris*. In the few seigneuries where it was imposed it consisted of one day's labor in March or an exemption payment of two *livres*. Parish and royal *corvées* for work on the seigneurial common land, roads, bridges, or fortifications were a form of taxation but they usually amounted to not more than three or four days of labor a year, and the seigneur was supposed to do his share, under the supervision of the militia captain.

Unlike the peasant in France who spent his life sweating, scrimping, cheating, and saving to put aside enough money to buy a small piece of land or to purchase exemption from manorial obligations, and who had to keep his little hoard well hidden, wearing rags, living in a hovel, giving every appearance of near starvation to prevent the tax collectors from seizing his savings, the Canadian could spend what he had earned without a care. He could buy land for his sons so as to have them near him and spare them the necessity of clearing virgin forest on a new seigneury, or he could spend his earnings on consumer goods and entertainment. Whereas the economics of the situation would tend to make the French peasant mean and grasping, the Canadian could afford to be openhanded, with little care for the morrow.

In 1699 the intendant Jean Bochart de Champigny commented that for the most part the *habitants* lived well, enjoying the right to hunt and fish, privileges that were stringently denied their European counterparts. In that age wood and leather were vital commodities; the Canadians had ample supplies of both. Canadians who moved to France complained bitterly of the shortage and high cost of firewood, and declared that they suffered far more from the damp winter cold there than they ever had in Canada. In the eighteenth century the intendant Gilles Hocquart remarked that no one starved in Canada. Of few lands in Europe could this have been said. The normal consumption of meat was half a pound per person a day, and of white wheat bread, two French pounds a day. Moreover, the climate allowed the Canadians to keep plentiful supplies of meat, fish, and game frozen hard for use throughout the winter; but a mid-winter thaw that lasted too long could be calamitous. At the town markets fish were sold frozen and cut with a saw. Eels, taken at Quebec by the thousand, were a staple food; smoked or salted, they were described by Frontenac as the *"habitants'* manna." They were also a major export item to France, being considered far better than the European variety. Ice houses were common, making possible iced drinks and desserts all summer, not just for the wealthy as in France, but for the majority of the population. The colored ices served by the French in hot weather were a source of wonderment to visiting Indians when entertained by the governor, and their effect on the decayed teeth of certain elderly chiefs was electric.

The vitamin content of the Canadian diet, being much richer in protein, was considerably higher than that of the peasants and urban working class in France, who had to exist on coarse bread and vegetable stews with meat only on very rare occasions.[20] In Europe the bulk of the population went to bed hungry most nights. Such was rarely the case in Canada. Mme. Marie-Isabelle Bégon, widow of the governor of Trois-Rivières, who in 1749 moved from Montreal to the family estate near Rochefort, querulously asked, "Where are those good partridges we left for the servants? I would gladly eat them now."[21] It is not surprising that the fine physical stature of the Canadians occasioned frequent comment from persons recently come from France. In fact, the Canadians were better fed then than a sizable percentage of North Americans are today.

101

If the Canadians had been willing to work hard, they could all have been very prosperous. Some of the royal officials, charged with improving the colonial economy, declared that the men showed a marked distaste for hard work and that the unbridled vanity of their womenfolk kept them poor. In 1699 Champigny noted: "The men are all strong and vigorous but have no liking for work of any duration; the women love display and are excessively lazy."[22] Denonville, thirteen years earlier, had also remarked that the indolence of the men and the desire of the women to live like gentle ladies kept the people poor and the colony's economy backward. Such comments have to be considered in context.

The Canadian *habitant* could provide for his basic needs without too much effort, and he preferred to devote his extra time, not to produce an agricultural surplus to please the intendant or to add to his own store of worldly goods, but to the relaxed enjoyment of his leisure hours. He would grow enough flax or hemp to supply his own needs, but frequently declined to raise a surplus for export. Rather than raise more cattle, he raised horses; by the early eighteenth century all but the poorer families had a carriage and sleigh for social occasions, and every youth had his own horse, used not for the plow but for racing, or to pay calls on the neighborhood girls. During the War of the Spanish Succession the governor and intendant became concerned over this, claiming that in winter the men no longer used snowshoes because they always traveled by horse and sleigh. It was difficult, they stated, to find enough men who could use snowshoes when they were needed for war parties against New England. The question might well be asked; how many peasants in Europe owned horses and carriages, let alone used them for mere social purposes. The average horse cost forty *livres* (roughly $80.00 in today's money) and a good one a hundred *livres* or more,[23] thus the Canadian *habitants* were relatively affluent, and this could not help but have influenced their social attitudes.

Given these conditions it is hardly surprising that the Canadians were by no means as submissive or even respectful, on occasion, toward their social superiors as was thought fitting. As early as 1675 the members of the Sovereign Council were incensed by derogatory graffiti on walls in Quebec, and several years later the intendant had to threaten stern action against those who composed, distributed, or sang songs that he regarded as libelous and defamatory of certain prominent persons in the colony. This last, however, might be regarded as merely the continuance of an old French tradition that had flourished in the days of the *Mazarinades*. Thus, rather than the frontier environment, economic affluence and the French temperament were the more significant factors here.

Much is made of the prevalence of lawlessness on the Anglo-American frontier. To a limited degree this was also true of New France, and it is significant that it was at Montreal, the fur trade and military base, the main point of contact between European and Indian cultures, more than at Quebec, that respect for law and order was sometimes lacking. In 1711 the governor and intendant had to establish a police force in Montreal, consisting of one lieutenant and three archers, to make the citizens keep the peace and to control drunken Indians. An educated soldier in the colonial troops, newly arrived in Canada, remarked that the citizens of Montreal called those of Quebec "sheep," and that the character of the latter was gentler and less proud. The Quebecers reciprocated by calling the men of Montreal "wolves," a label that the soldier thought apt since the Montrealers spent much of their time in the forest among the Indians. In 1754 an officer recommended that Quebec men be employed to transport supplies to the Ohio forts because they were much "gentler" and almost as vigorous as those from the Montreal area.

Despite the frequent tavern brawls and duels, the incidence of crimes of violence was not great. But what is much more significant is that, given the nature of the populace, accustomed to the relatively unrestrained, wild, free life that the fur trade afforded, very rarely was there any overt resistance to authority. On the few occasions when the people protested openly and vigorously something done, or not done, the authorities were able to subdue them quickly without recourse to punitive measures. Most of these manifestations — some five in all — were occasioned by high prices charged for certain commodities, leading the people to believe that the merchants were profiteering and that the authorities were delinquent in not taking steps to stop them. The heaviest penalty inflicted on the leaders of these "seditious gatherings" appears to have been less than two months in jail.[24] The conclusion to be drawn from all this is that the Canadian people had little to complain about, but when they did complain too vigorously, order was maintained without the overt use of force.

The attitude of the Canadians toward the religious authorities makes it plain that their opinions had to be taken into account. When it was decided, immediately after the inauguration of royal government in 1663, to impose tithes on the people for the support of a secular clergy, the bishop stipulated that it be at the rate of one thirteenth of the produce of the land, payable in wheat. The people protested vigorously, claiming this to be more than they could afford. The bishop reduced his demand to one twentieth, but the *habitants* and seigneurs would agree to pay only one twenty-sixth of their wheat, not of all their produce, with a five year exemption for newly settled concessions. With this the clergy had to be satisfied. That it was not enough is made plain by the fact that the crown had to provide the clergy with an annual subsidy to make up the difference between what the tithe produced and what the *curés* needed. By the 1730s, however, as more land came into production, many of the parish priests were relatively well off.

Further evidence that the Canadians were anything but subservient to clerical authority is provided by the frequent *ordonnances* of the intendant ordering the *habitants* of this or that parish to behave with more respect toward the cloth, to cease their practice of walking out of church as soon as the *curé* began his sermon; of standing in the lobby arguing, even brawling, during the service; of slipping out to a nearby tavern; of bringing their dogs into church and expostulating with the beadle who tried to chase them out. Frequently the bishop thundered from the pulpit against the women who attended mass wearing elaborate coiffures and low-cut gowns. But all to no avail; décolletage remained that of the Paris salons. When Bishop St. Vallier somehow learned that the female members of his flock wore nothing but petticoats under their gowns he was horrified. In a curiously phrased pastoral letter he demanded that they immediately cease to imperil their immortal souls in this manner.[25] What the response was is not known. And a practice that might be advanced in support of the thesis that the frontier bred initiative was the Canadian custom of *mariage à la gaumine,* a form of "do it your-self" marriage ceremony which both the clergy and the civil authorities frowned on severely.[26]

At the upper end of the social scale, the most significant feature of this Canadian society was the aristocratic and military ethos that dom-inated it. This was not unique to Canada; it was part of the French old régime heritage. In the seventeenth century the aim of the rising, powerful bourgeois class was to gain entry into the ranks of the nobility, or at least to emulate the way of life of the aristocracy. Molière made this plain in *Le Bourgeois Gentilhomme.* Despite the fact that the Canadian economy was basically commercial and dependent largely on the fur trade, bourgeois commercial values did not dominate society; indeed, they were scorned. The ambitious Canadian merchant wished to be some-thing more than prosperous. That was merely one rung on the ladder. The ultimate goal was entry into the ranks of the *noblesse* and receipt of the coveted Order of St. Louis for distinguished service. More than wealth, men wished to bequeath to their sons a higher social status and a name distinguished for military valor, some great achievement, or the holding of high office. The proverb *"Bon renom vaut mieux que ceinture dorée"* summed up the Canadian philosophy at all levels of society.[27]

Wealth was, of course, desired, and ethics frequently went by the board in its pursuit. Men who might well have been ennobled for valiant service were denied if they lacked the means to live in a fitting manner. Wealth was sought, not for itself, but to enable men to live in the style of the class they sought to enter. Father Charlevoix, the Jesuit historian, writing in the 1740s commented on one aspect of this proclivity: "There is a great fondness for keeping up one's position, and nearly no one amuses himself by thrift. Good cheer is supplied, if its provision leaves means enough to be well clothed; if not, one cuts down on the table in order to be well dressed." He then went on to compare the Canadians with the English colonists to the south: "The English colonist amasses means and makes no superfluous expense; the French enjoys what he has and often parades what he has not. The former works for his heirs; the latter leaves his in the need in which he is himself to get along as best he can."[28]

In Canada it was in some ways much easier than in France for am-bitious men to adopt the values and attitudes of the nobility and even to become ennobled. Despite the fact that society was very much status ordered, it was relatively easy for a talented, ambitious man or woman to move up the social scale. Four factors help account for this: the avail-ability of free land, the economic opportunities presented by the fur trade, the Royal edict of 1685 which permitted members of the nobility resident in Canada to engage directly in commerce and industry, something that, with a few notable exceptions such as the manufacture of glass and paper, was not permitted in France, and the presence of a large corps of regular troops in the colony in which Canadians could obtain commissions as officers.

It is rather ironic that when the king issued the edict of 1685 allowing nobles in Canada to engage in trade, he intended merely to stimulate the colonial economy.[29] It quickly came, however, to function in a way not anticipated by Louis XIV, for if those who were of noble status could engage in trade, there was nothing to prevent merchants and entrepreneurs who were not noble from aspiring to become so, provided they fulfilled the other requirements. Thus a Canadian of humble origin could make his fortune in the fur trade, acquire a seigneury, have his sons, if not himself, commissioned in the Troupes de la Marine, and hope that one day he, or his sons, would be ennobled for valiant service. Enough Canadians accomplished this feat to encourage a much larger number to govern their lives accordingly. It was the old story, few are chosen but many hear the call.

To be a seigneur, the first rung up the social ladder, was a distinct mark of social superiority, made manifest in a variety of ways; hence there was never any lack of applicants,[30] but it necessitated accepting rather onerous responsibilities and in the seventeenth century most seigneurs had a hard time making ends meet. Yet so eager were the Canadians to attach the coveted particle *de* to their names that by 1760 there were nearly 250 seigneuries in the colony. Even more significant, it is estimated that there were some 200 *arrière fiefs*, or sub-seigneuries, that is, small seigneuries granted by a seigneur within his own seigneury to a friend or relative whom he wished to see get on in the world. Another significant point is that many seigneurs, the majority of whom lived in the towns and not on their lands, did not bother to collect the stipulated dues, the *cens et rentes*, from their *censitaires*. Clearly, many seigneurs were not interested in the economic aspect of land holding. The only other motive would appear to be the social prestige attached to the title. In other words, Joseph Blondeau was undoubtedly a good name, but Joseph Blondeau de Grandarpents, or even de Petitarpents, was much better.

There were some who sought to gain entry into the *noblesse* through the back door, by simply assuming a title and claiming its privileges. In 1684 a royal edict was enacted levying a fine of 500 *livres* on any Canadian who falsely claimed noble status. A few years later the intendant Champigny stated that there were many such in the colony, but in time of war he thought it unwise to initiate an enquiry lest it cool their ardor for military campaigns. He also declared that several officers had requested to be ennobled, and although some of them merited it, he could not support their requests because they lacked the means to live as members of the *noblesse* should.[31] Although gaining entry into the ranks of the nobility was by no means easy, it was remarked in the mid-eighteenth century that there was a greater number of nobles in New France than in all the other French colonies combined. It was not the

105

actual number of nobles that was important; rather it was the scale of values that they imparted to the whole of society, the tone that was set, and the influence it had on the way of life of the Canadian people.

Inextricably mingled with, and greatly strengthening, this aristocratic ethos was the military tradition of New France. In Europe wars were fought by professional armies, and civilians were not directly involved unless they happened to get in the way while a battle was being fought. This was more true of France and Britain than of other countries, since they both had sense enough to wage their wars on other nations' territory. In Canada when war came, all the settled areas were a battlefield and everyone was obliged to be a combatant. The administration of the colony was organized along military lines. The entire male population was formed into militia companies, given military training, and employed in campaigns. In 1665 the Carignan Salières regiment arrived in the colony to quell the Iroquois; it comprised over a thousand officers and men, and many of them stayed on as settlers. This greatly enhanced the influence of the military, for at that time the total population was less than 3000. Twenty years later the Troupes de la Marine were permanently stationed in the colony, some 1300 men and 400 officers by the end of the century among a total population of 15,000.

In the campaigns against the Iroquois and the English colonies it was quickly discovered that Canadians made better officers in forest warfare than did regulars from France. Consequently this career was opened to the seigneurs and their sons. They seized on it eagerly. Youths in their teens were enrolled as cadets and served on campaigns with their fathers or elder brothers to gain experience, then were sent out in command of scouting and small raiding parties to capture prisoners for intelligence purposes. The minister, however, thought they were being enrolled at far too early an age, while still mere children, and suspected the practice was merely a means for their families to draw military pay and allowances. Mme. de Vaudreuil, wife of the governor general, declared, "It would be advantageous for the well-being of the colony to accept youths of good families as cadets in the troops at fifteen or sixteen; that would form their characters early, render them capable of serving well and becoming good officers." The minister and Louis XIV were not convinced; they ordered that cadets had to be seventeen before they could be enrolled.[32] The dominant values of Canadian society were clearly those of the soldier and the noble, the military virtues those held in highest regard.

The social circles of Montreal and Quebec, comprising the senior officials, the army officers, and seigneurs, were undoubtedly very urbane, reflecting the polish and social graces of the French *noblesse*. Certainly Peter Kalm found this society much more civilized than that which he encountered in the English colonies where few people thought of anything but making money and not spending it.[33] Some of the senior officials who came from France in the eighteenth century, men like the intendant Claude Thomas Dupuy and the Comte de la Galissonière, took a keen interest in natural science, as had earlier the doctor and surgeon Michel Sarrazan who was a corresponding member of the Académie Royale des Sciences, but few Canadians showed much interest in intellectual pursuits.

The parish schools provided a basic education for those who wished it, and the Jesuit college at Quebec offered facilities as good as those in the larger French provincial cities. The letters and dispatches of Canadian-born officers and merchant traders in the mid-eighteenth century demonstrate that, with the rare exception of an officer such as Claude-Pierre Pécaudy de Contrecoeur who although a competent commandant had obviously had little schooling, they were all well-educated men. They expressed themselves succinctly and quite often felicitously: their syntax was good, the subjunctive employed where required; the literary style as well as the contents of their letters make them a pleasure to read. In fact, these men appear to have been as well educated as their counterparts in the French and British armies.

107

Yet the colony did not develop a literary tradition; the published journals depicting life in the colony were written by men from France and were intended for a metropolitan audience. But then, Canadians would see little merit in describing what was familiar to all their compatriots. Several Canadians had large private libraries, but there was no public library. Nor was there a printing press in the colony, hence no newspaper, not because of any sinister repression of thought by the clergy, but because there was no great need therefore no demand for one. In these realms of activity Canada lagged far behind the English colonies. In short, New France was the Sparta, not the Athens of North America.

NOTES

[1] *Chronological List of Canadian Censuses*, Bureau of Statistics, Demography Branch, Ottawa.

[2] Adolph B. Benson, ed., *Peter Kalm's Travels in North America*, 2 vols. (New York, 1966), 2: 416–17.

[3] Le Roi à Vaudreuil et Raudot, Versailles, 6 juillet 1709, *Rapport de l'Archiviste de la Province de Québec* (1942–43) (hereafter cited as *RAPQ*), 408.

[4] E.B. O'Callaghan and J.R. Brodhead, *Documents Relating to the Colonial History of New York*, 15 vols. (Albany, 1856–1883), 4: 693.

[5] Benson, ed., *Peter Kalm's Travels in North America*, 2: 600.

[6] Papiers La Pause. *RAPQ* (1931–32): 66–67.

[7] Denonville au Ministre, Que., 13 nov. 1685, Archives Nationales, Colonies, Series C11A, 7: 89–95.

[8] Memoire instructif sur le Canada, 10 mai 1691, *ibid.*, 11: 262–68.

[9] Benson, ed., *Peter Kalm's Travels in North America*, 2: 522, 563.

[10] Étienne de Carheil, S.J. à Champigny, Michilimackinac, 30 d'auest 1702, Public Archives of Canada, Series M, vol. 204, part 1, pp. 177–79; Fr. J.-F. St. Cosme, Michilimackinac, 13 sept. 1689, *RAPQ* (1965): 37.

[11] In a dispatch to the minister, Vaudreuil stated, "tous les françois qui ont épousé des sauvagesses sont devenus libertins feneans, et d'une independence insuportable, et que les enfans qu'ils ont esté d'une feneantise aussy grande que les sauvages mesmes, doit empecher qu'on ne permette ces sortes de mariages." Vaudreuil et Raudot au Ministre, Que., 14 nov. 1709, *RAPQ* (1942–43): 420.

[12] Charlevoix, *Histoire de la Nouvelle France*, vol.2, *Journal d'un voyage fait par order du Roi dans l'Amérique septentrionale addressé à Madame la Duchesse de Lesdiguières* (Paris, 1744), 247–49.

[13] Papiers La Pause, *RAPQ* (1931–32): 67. See also Fernand Ouellet, "La mentalité et l'outillage économique de l'habitant canadien 1760 . . ." *Bulletin des Recherches Historiques* (1956): 131–36.

[14] Memoire sur les affaires au Canada, Avril 1689, *RAPQ* (1922–23): 7.

[15] *The American Gazetteer*, 3 vols.(London, 1762), vol. 2, entry under Montreal.

[16] Relation d'un voyage de Paris à Montréal en Canadas en 1737. *RAPQ* (1947–48): 16–17.

[17] See Benson, ed., *Peter Kalm's Travels in North America*, 2: 446–47, 558; H.R. Casgrain, ed., *Voyage au Canada dans le nord de l'Amérique septentrionale fait depuis l'an 1751 à 1761 par J.C.B.* (Quebec, 1887), 169.

[18] Benson, ed., *Peter Kalm's Travels in North America*, 2: 558, 626.

[19] Richard Colebrook Harris, *The Seigneurial System in Early Canada* (Madison, Wis., 1966), 81.

[20] Robert Mandrou, *Introduction à la France moderne. Essai de psychologie historique 1500-1640* (Paris, 1961), 17–39.

[21] Mme Bégon à son gendre, Rochefort, 8 déc. 1750. *RAPQ* (1934–35): 129.

[22] Champigny au Ministre, Que., 20 oct. 1699. Archives Nationales, Colonies, Series C11A, 17: 106–110.

[23] Benson, ed., *Peter Kalm's Travels in North America*, 2: 536.

[24] For a revealing account of one such protestation, which could have become dangerous, and the cool way it was subdued without the *habitants* concerned being treated at all harshly, see Vaudreuil au Conseil de la Marine, 17 oct. 1717, Archives Nationales, Colonies, Series C11A, 38: 123–24. It is interesting to note that in this dispatch Vaudreuil is justifying his having had the ten ringleaders summarily arrested and kept in cells for nearly two months without trial. He considered that the circumstances had warranted the use of his exceptional powers, which permitted arrest and imprisonment without trial only in cases of sedition and treason. The Council of Marine subsequently approved his action in this instance. The common sense attitude of the government toward the governed is illustrated in another incident, which at first appeared to be a seditious assembly but was treated as being much less serious. See Raudot au Ministre, Que, 11 nov. 1707, *ibid.*, 26: 202–203.

[25] Mandement de Jean éveque de Québec, 26 avril 1719 ("Trivia," Cameron Nish), *William and Mary Quarterly*, 3rd series, 23 (July 1966): 477–78.

[26] See Les Mariages à la Gaumine, *RAPQ* (1920–21): 366–407.

[27] Mme de Contrecoeur à son Mari, Montreal, 23 mai 1755. Fernand Grenier, ed., *Papiers Contrecoeur et autres documents concernant le conflit Anglo-Français sur l'Ohio de 1745 à 1756* (Quebec, 1952), 349. The context in which the proverb is cited is quite revealing.

[28] Pierre-François-Xavier de Charlevoix, S.J., *Histoire de la Nouvelle France*, vol. 3, *Journal d'un voyage fait par ordre du Roi dans l'Amérique septentrionale addressé à Madame la Duchesse de Lesdiguières* (Paris, 1744), 79.

[29] Arrest du Conseil d'Estat qui permet aux Gentilshommes de Canada de faire Commerce, du 10 mars 1685, Archives Nationales, Colonies, Series F3, 7: 214; Le Roy au Sr. de Meulles, Versailles, 10 mars 1685, *ibid.*, Series B, 11: 99

[30] Roland Mousnier, "L'évolution des institutions monarchiques en France et ses relations avec l'état social," *XVIIe Siècle*, 1963, nos. 58–59.

[31] Extrait des Registres du Conseil d'Estat, 10 avril 1684, Bibliothèque Nationale, Collection Clairambault, vol. 448, p. 369; Champigny au Ministre, Que., 10 mai 1691. Archives Nationales, Colonies, Series C11A, 11: 255; Memoire Instructif sur le Canada, *ibid.*, 265–67.

[32] Le Ministre à M. de Vaudreuil, Versailles, 30 juin 1707, *RAPQ* (1939–40): 375; Résumé d'une lettre de Mme de Vaudreuil au Ministre, Paris, 1709. *RAPQ* (1942–43): 416; Mémoire du Roy à MM de Vaudreuil et Raudot, à Marly, 10 mai 1710, *RAPQ* (1946–47): 376; Archives du Seminaire de Quebec, Fonds Verreau, carton 5, no. 62.

[33] Benson, ed., *Peter Kalm's Travels in North America*, 1: 343–46, 375–76, 392–93; 2: 446–47, 558, 626, 628.

New France: Les femmes favorisées

JAN NOEL

You constantly behold, with renewed astonishment, women in the very depths of indigence and want, perfectly instructed in their religion, ignorant of nothing that they should know to employ themselves usefully in their families and who,

From *Atlantis: A Women's Studies Journal* 6, 2 (Spring 1981): 80–98. Revised and printed with the permission of the Institute for the Study of Women, Mount Saint Vincent University.
For translations of all the French passages in this article, please see pages 131-32.

by their manners, their manner of expressing themselves and their politeness, are not inferior to the most carefully educated among us.[1]

Les femmes l'emportent sur les hommes par la beauté, la vivacité, la gaité [sic] et l'enjouement; elles sont coquettes et galantes, préfèrent les Européens aux gens du pays. Les manières douces et polies sont communes, même dans les campagnes.[2]

. . . les femmes y sont fort aimables, mais extrêmement fières.[3]

. . . elles sont spirituelles, ce qui leur donne de la supériorité sur les hommes dans presque tous les états.[4]

Many a man, observing the women of New France, was struck by the advantages they possessed in education, cultivation, and that quality called *esprit* or wit. Even an unsympathetic observer of colonial society, such as the French military officer Franquet, who visited New France in 1752-53, admitted that its women "l'emportent sur les hommes pour l'esprit, généralement elles en ont toutes beaucoup, parlant un français épuré, n'ont pas le moindre accent, aiment aussi la parure, sont jolies, généreuses et même maniérées."[5] He notes, albeit with disapproval, that women very commonly aspired to stations above those to which they were born.[6] The Swedish naturalist Peter Kalm, who deplored the inadequate housekeeping of Canadian women, nevertheless admired their refinement.[7]

109

Those for whom history is an exercise in statistics have taught us caution in accepting the accounts of travellers, which are often highly subjective. However, the consensus (particularly that of seasoned observers such as Charlevoix and Kalm) on the superior education and wit of women in New France suggests that their views are founded on something more than natural male proclivity toward *la différence*. Moreover, historians' accounts of society in New France offer considerable evidence that women did indeed enjoy an unusually privileged position in that colony. It is difficult to think of another colony or country in which women founders showed such important leadership — not just in the usual tending of families and farms but in arranging financing, immigration, and defences that played a major role in the colony's survival. It is unusual for girls to receive a primary education better than that of the boys — as many evidently did in New France. One is also struck by the initiative of Canadiennes in business and commerce. In sum, with respect to their education, their range and freedom of action, women in New France seem in many ways to compare favourably with their contemporaries in France and New England, and certainly with the Victorians who came after them.

Two cautions are in order. First, to arrive at a full appreciation of the position of women in New France would require detailed comparisons with their contemporaries in other Western countries and colonies. The study of *ancien régime* businesswomen, in particular, is a nascent enterprise. In this paper some twenty outstanding figures in business and politics will be examined and hypotheses put forward about what facilitated their rise to positions of influence. To what degree these women were outstanding in the context of their times one cannot yet say with precision. Second, it is not intended to portray New France as some sort of utopia for women. Women, like men, suffered from disease, privation, class inequalities, and the perennial scourge of war. There were also women's particular hardships, such as the dangers of childbirth and the difficulties of assuming double duty when the men were away. A definitive study of women in New France, which will plumb the primary sources and range the continents for useful comparisons, remains to be made. The purpose of this paper is to marshal the fairly extensive evidence that can be found in published works on New France in support of the thesis that women there enjoyed a relatively privileged position, and to discuss why they might have done so.

110

Why did the women of New France assume leadership positions? How did they acquire a superior education? How did they come to be involved in commerce? There is no single answer. Three separate elements help account for the situation. First, as studies of Western Europe under the *ancien régime* have indicated, ideas about women's roles were surprisingly flexible and varied at the time New France was founded. Second, the particular demographic configuration of the colony gave female immigrants a number of advantages not available to their counterparts in Europe. Third, the colonial economy, with its heavy emphasis on war and the fur trade, seems to have presented women with a special set of opportunities. Thus, as we shall see, the French cultural heritage and demographic and economic conditions in the colony combined to create the situation that so impressed contemporary observers.

Women and the Family under the *Ancien Régime*

The notion of "woman's place" or "women's role," popular with nineteenth-century commentators, suggests a degree of homogeneity inappropriate to the seventeenth century. It is true that on a formal ideological level men enjoyed the dominant position. This can be seen in the marriage laws, which everywhere made it a wife's duty to follow her husband to whatever dwelling place he chose.[8] In 1650, the men of Montreal were advised by Governor Maisonneuve that they were in fact responsible for the misdemeanours of their wives since "la loi les établit seigneurs de leurs femmes."[9] Under ordinary circumstances the father was captain of the family hierarchy.[10] Yet, it is clear that this formal male authority in both economic and domestic life was not always exercised. Of early seventeenth-century France we are told that

si la prééminence masculine n'a rien perdu de son prestige, si elle n'a eu à
se défendre contre aucune revendication théorique . . . elle a dû . . . souvent
se contenter des apparences et abandonner devant les convenances et les exigences
du public l'intérêt positif qu'elle défendait.[11]

The idea of separate male and female spheres lacked the clear definition it later acquired. This is in part related to the lack of communication and standardization characteristic of the *ancien régime* — along
sexual lines or any other. Generalizations about women are riddled with
exceptions. Contradicting the idea of female inferiority, for example, were
the semi-matriarchal system in the Basque country and the linen workers'
guild, in which a 1645 statute prevented a worker's husband from engaging in occupations unrelated to his wife's business, for which he often
served as salesman or partner. More important, because it affected a
larger group, was the fact that noblewomen were frequently exempt from
legal handicaps affecting other women.[12]

One generalization, however, applies to all women of the *ancien
régime*. They were not relegated to the private, domestic sphere of human
activity because that sphere did not exist. Western Europeans had not
yet learned to separate public and private life. As Philippe Ariès points
out in his study of childhood, the private home, in which parents and
children constitute a distinct unit, is a relatively recent development.
In early modern Europe most of domestic life was lived in the company
of all sorts of outsiders. Manor houses, where all the rooms interconnect
with one another, show the lack of emphasis placed on privacy. Here,
as in peasant dwellings, there were often no specialized rooms for sleeping, eating, working, or receiving visitors; all were more or less public
activities performed with a throng of servants, children, relatives, clerics,
apprentices, and clients in attendance. Molière's comedies illustrate the
familiarity of servants with their masters. Masters, maids, and valets
slept in the same room and servants discussed their masters' lives quite
openly.[13]

Though familiar with their servants, people were less so with their
children. They did not dote on infants to the extent that parents do
today. It may have been, as some writers have suggested, that there was
little point in growing attached to a fragile being so very apt, in those
centuries, to be borne away by accident or disease. These unsentimental
families of all ranks sent their children out to apprentice or serve in
other people's homes. This was considered important as a basic education.[14] It has been estimated that the majority of Western European
children passed part of their childhood living in some household other
than their natal one.[15] Mothers of these children — reaching down, in
the town, as far as the artisan class — might send their infants out to
nursemaids and have very little to do with their physical maintenance.[16]

This lack of a clearly defined "private" realm relates vitally to the
history of women, since this was precisely the sphere they later were

111

to inhabit.[17] Therefore it is important to focus on their place in the pre-private world. To understand women in New France one first must pass through that antechamber which Peter Laslett appropriately calls "the world we have lost." Its notions of sexuality and of the family apply to France and New France alike.

In this public world people had not yet learned to be private about their bodily functions, especially about their sexuality. For aid with their toilette, noblewomen did not blush to employ *hommes de chambre* rather than maids. The door of the bedchamber stood ajar, if not absolutely open. Its inhabitants, proud of their fecundity, grinned out from under the bedclothes at their visitors. Newlyweds customarily received bedside guests.[18] The mother of Louis XIV held court and chatted with visitors while labouring to bring *le Roi Soleil* into light of day. Humbler village women kept lesser court among the little crowd of neighbours who attended the midwife's efforts.[19] On the other side of the ocean, Franquet, arriving at Trois-Rivières in 1753, enjoyed the hospitality of Madame Rigaud de Vaudreuil who, feeling poorly, apparently received her visitors at bedside; farther west, he shared a bedroom with a married couple at Fort St. Jean.[20] From the seventeenth century to the colony's last days, clerics thundered more or less futilely against the *décolletage* of the *élite*.[21] Lesser folk leaned toward short skirts[22] and boisterous public discussion of impotent husbands.[23] Rape cases also reveal a rather matter-of-fact attitude. Courts stressed monetary compensation for the victim (as if for trespass on private property) rather than wreaking vengeance on the lustful villain.[24] There was not the same uneasiness in relations between the sexes which later, more puritanical, centuries saw, and which, judging by the withdrawal of women from public life in many of these societies, probably worked to their detriment.

112

Part of the reason these unsqueamish, rather public people were not possessive about their bodies was that they did not see themselves so much as individuals but as part of a larger, more important unit — the family. In this world the family was the basic organization for most social and economic purposes.[25] As such it claimed the individual's first loyalty.[26] A much higher proportion of the population married than does today.[27] Studies of peasant societies suggest that, for most, marriage was an economic necessity:

> Le travail, particulièrement en milieu rural, était alors fondé sur une répartition des tâches entre les sexes: les marins et colporteurs sont absents plusieurs mois, leurs femmes font valoir les terres; les pêcheurs des marais vont au marché, les femmes à la pêche; le laboureur travaille aux champs, sa femme à la maison, c'est elle qui va au marché; dans le pays d'Auge, "les hommes s'occupent des bestiaux et les femmes aux fromages." Pour vivre il fallait donc être deux, un homme et une femme.[28]

The family was able to serve as the basic economic unit in pre-industrial societies because the business of earning a living generally occurred at home. Just as public and private life were undifferentiated, so too were home and workplace. Agricultural and commercial pursuits were all generally "domestic" industries. We see this both in France and in New France. Removal of the man from home for most of the working day, an event that Laslett describes as the single most important event in the history of the modern European family,[29] was only beginning. The idea of man as breadwinner and woman as homemaker was not clearly developed. Women's range of economic activity was still nearly as wide as that of their husbands. Seventeenth-century France saw women working as bonesetters, goldbeaters, bookbinders, doubletmakers, burnishers, laundresses, woolfullers, and wigmakers. Aside from their familiar role in the textile and clothing industries, women also entered heavy trades such as stoneworking and bricklaying. A master plumber, Barbe Legueux, maintained the drainage system for the fountains of Paris. In the commercial world, women worked as fishmongers, pedlars, greengrocers, publicans, money-lenders, and auctioneers.[30] In New France, wives of artisans took advantage of their urban situation to attract customers into the taverns they set up alongside the workshop.[31] It was in farm work, which occupied most of the population, that male and female tasks differed the least of all. *Habitantes* in New France toiled in the fields alongside the men, and they almost certainly — being better educated than their French sisters — took up the farm wife's customary role of keeping accounts and managing purchases and sales.[32] Studies of Bordeaux commercial families have revealed that women also took a large role in business operations.[33] Marie de l'Incarnation's background as manager of one of France's largest transport companies[34] shows that the phenomenon existed in other parts of France as well.

113

Given the economic importance of both spouses, it is not surprising to see marriage taking on some aspects of a business deal, with numerous relatives affixing their signatures to the contract. We see this in the provisions of the law that protected the property rights of both parties contracting a match. The fact that wives often brought considerable family property to the marriage, and retained rights to it, placed them in a better position than their nineteenth-century descendants were to enjoy.[35]

In New France the family's importance was intensified even beyond its usual economic importance in *ancien régime* societies. In the colony's early days, "all roads led to matrimony. The scarcity of women, the economic difficulties of existence, the danger, all tended to produce the same result: all girls became wives, all widows remarried."[36] Throughout the colony's history there was an exceptionally high annual marriage rate of eighteen to twenty-four per thousand.[37] The buildup of the family as a social institution perhaps came about because other social institutions, such as guilds and villages, were underdeveloped.[38] This heightened importance of the family probably enhanced women's position. In the family women tended to serve as equal partners with their husbands, whereas women were gradually losing their position in European guilds and professions.[39] We see this importance of the family in the government's great concern to regulate it. At that time, the state *did* have a place in Canadian bedrooms (whose inhabitants we have already seen to be rather unconcerned about their privacy). Public intervention in domestic life took two major forms: the operation of the legal system and governmental attempts at family planning.

The outstanding characteristic of the legal system in New France — the Coutume de Paris — is its concern to protect the rights of all members of the family. The Coutume de Paris is considered to have been a particularly benevolent regional variation of French law.[40] It was more egalitarian and less patriarchal than the laws of southern France, which were based on Roman tradition. The Coutume reinforced the family, for example, by the penalties it levied on those transferring family property to non-kin.[41] It took care to protect the property of children of a first marriage when a widow or widower remarried.[42] It protected a woman's rights by assuring that the husband did not have power to alienate the family property (in contrast to eighteenth-century British law).[43] The Canadians not only adopted the Parisian Coutume in preference to the Norman *coutume*, which was harsher;[44] they also implemented the law in a way that maximized protection of all family members. Louise Dechêne, after examining the operation of the marriage and inheritance system, concludes that the Canadian application of the law was generous and egalitarian:

> Ces conventions matrimoniales ne nous apparaissent pas comme un marché, un affrontement entre deux lignées, mais comme un accord désintéressé entre les familles, visant à créer une nouvelle communauté, à l'assister si possible, à dresser quelques barrières à l'entour pour la protéger. . . . [45]

The criminal law, too, served to buttress family life with its harsh punishments for mistreatment of children.[46]

The royal administration, as well as the law, treated the family as a matter of vital public concern. The state often intervened in matters that later generations left to the individual or to the operations of private charity. Most famous, of course, is the policy of encouraging a high birth rate with financial incentives. There were also attempts to withdraw trading privileges from voyageurs who showed reluctance to take immigrant women to wife.[47] Particularly in the seventeenth century, we see the state regulating what modern societies would consider intimate matters. However, in a colony starved for manpower, reproduction was considered a matter of particularly vital public concern — a concern well demonstrated in the extremely harsh punishments meted out to women who concealed pregnancy.[48] We see a more positive side of this intervention in the care the Crown took of foundlings, employing nurses at a handsome salary to care for them and making attempts to prevent children from bearing any stigma because of questionable origins.[49]

114

State regulation of the family was balanced by family regulation of the state. Families had an input into the political system, playing an important role in the running of the state. Indeed, it might be argued that the family was the basic political unit in New France. In an age when some members of the *noblesse* prided themselves on their illiteracy, attending the right college was hardly the key to political success. Marrying into the right family was much more important. Nepotism, or rewarding one's kin with emoluments, seemed a most acceptable and natural form of patronage for those in power.[50] In this sense, a good marriage was considered a step upward for the whole family, which helps to explain why choice of spouse was so often a family decision.[51] These family lines were particularly tightly drawn among the military élite in New France. Franquet remarked that "tous les gens d'un certain ordre sont liés de parenté et d'amitié dans ce pays."[52] In fact, with top military positions passing down from generation to generation, by the eighteenth century this élite became a caste.[53]

In this situation, where the *nom de famille* was vastly more important than that of the individual, it was apparently almost as good for political (though not military) purposes to be an Agathe de Repentigny as a Le-Gardeur de Repentigny. Moreover, women's political participation was favoured by the large role of entertaining in political life. For the courtier's role, women were as well trained as men, and there seems to have been no stigma attached to the woman who participated independently of her husband. Six women, Mesdames Daine, Pean, Lotbinière, de Repentigny, Marin, and St. Simon, along with six male officers, were chosen by the Intendant to accompany him to Montreal in 1753.[54] Of the twelve only the de Repentignys were a couple. It is surprising to see women from the colony's first families also getting down to what we would today consider the "business" end of politics. Madame de la Forest, a member of the Juchereau family, took an active role in the political cliques that Guy Frégault describes.[55] Mme. de la Forest's trip to France to plead the cause of Governor de Ramezay was inconsequential, though, in comparison with that of Mme. de Vaudreuil to further Governor Vaudreuil's cause in 1709. "Douée d'un sens politique très fin,"[56] she soon gained the ear of the Minister of Marine. Not only did she secure the Governor's victory in the long conflict with the Intendants Raudot (father and son) and win promotion for his patrons; she appears to have gone on to upstage her husband by becoming the virtual director of colonial policy at Versailles for a few years. Vaudreuil's biographer discusses the influence Madame de Vaudreuil exerted with the Minister Pontchartrain who so regularly sought her comments on colonial patronage that supplicants began to apply directly to her rather than to the minister.[57] Contemporaries agreed that her influence was vast:

115

Pontchartrain, rapporte Ruette d'Auteuil, ne lui refuse rien, "elle dispose de tous les emplois du Canada, elle écrit de toutes parts dans les ports de mer

des lettres magnifiques du bien et du mal qu'elle peut faire après de lui," et
le ministre "fait tout ce qu'il faut pour l'autoriser et justifier ses discours." Riverin confirme que . . . "ce n'est plus qu'une femme qui règne tant présente
qu'absente."[58]

Governor Frontenac's wife (though not a Canadienne) also played an
important role at court, dispelling some of the thunderclouds that threatened her husband's stormy career.[59]

As for the common folk, we know less about the political activity
of women than that of men. That women participated in a form of popular
assembly is hinted at in a report of a meeting held in 1713 (in present-
day Boucherville), in which Catherine Guertin was sworn in as midwife
after having been elected "dans l'assemblée des femmes de cette paroisse,
à la pluralité des suffrages, pour exercer l'office de sagefemme."[60] Were
these women's assemblies a general practice? If so, what other matters
did they decide? This aspect of habitant politics remains a mystery. It
is clear, though, that women were part of what historians have called
the "pre-industrial crowd."[61] Along with their menfolk, they were full-
fledged members of the old "moral economy" whose members rioted
and took what was traditionally their rightful share (and no more) when
prices were too high or when speculators were hoarding grain.[62] The
women of Quebec and Montreal, who rioted against the horsemeat rations
and the general hunger of 1757–58, illustrate this aspect of the old
polity.[63]

In sum, women's position during the *ancien régime* was open-ended.
Although conditions varied, a wide range of roles were available to
women, to be taken up or not. This was so because the separate spheres
of men and women in *ancien régime* societies were not so clearly developed
as they later became. There was as yet no sharp distinction between
public and private life: families were for most purposes the basic social,
economic, and political unit. This situation was intensified in New France
due to the underdevelopment of other institutions, such as the guild,
the seigneurie, and the village. The activities of breadwinner and homemaker were not yet widely recognized as separate functions belonging
to one sex or the other. All members of the family also often shared
the same economic functions, or at least roles were interchangeable. Nor
had the symbolic honorific aspects of government yet been separated
from the business end of politics and administration. These conditions,
typical of most of pre-industrial France, were also found in New France,
where particular demographic and economic conditions would enable the
colony's women to develop the freedoms and opportunities that this fluid
situation allowed.

116

Demographic Advantages

Demography favoured the women of New France in two ways. First, the women who went there were a highly select group of immigrants. Second, women were in short supply in the early years of the colony's development, a situation that worked in their favour.

The bulk of the female immigrants to New France fall into one of two categories. The first was a group of extremely well-born, well-endowed, and highly dedicated religious figures. They began to arrive in 1639, and a trickle of French nuns continued to cross the ocean over the course of the next century. The second distinct group was *filles du roi*, government-sponsored female migrants who arrived between 1663 and 1673. These immigrants, though not as outstanding as the *dévotes*, were nevertheless privileged compared to the average immigrant to New France, who arrived more or less threadbare.[64] The vast majority of the women (and the men) came from the Île-de-France and the northwestern parts of France. The women of northern France enjoyed fuller legal rights and were better educated and more involved in commerce than those in southern France.[65] When they set foot on colonial soil with all this auspicious baggage, the immigrants found that they had yet another advantage. Women constituted a small percentage of the population. As a scarce resource they were highly prized and therefore in an excellent position to gain further advantages.

The first *religieuses* to arrive in New France were the Ursulines and Hospitallers, who landed at Quebec in 1639. These were soon followed by women who helped establish Montreal in 1642. Their emigration was inspired by a religious revival in France, which is thought to have arisen in response to the widespread pauperism following the French civil wars of the sixteenth century. The seventeenth-century revival distinguished itself by tapping the energies of women in an unprecedented way.[66] Among its leaders were Anne of Austria and a number of the leading ladies at court.[67] In other parts of France, women of the provincial élite implemented the charity work inspired by Saint Vincent de Paul.[68] Occurring between 1600 and 1660, this religious revival coincided almost exactly with the period when the fledgling Canadian colony, besieged by English privateers and by the Iroquois, was most desperately in need of an injection of immigrants, money, and enthusiasm.[69] It was at this moment that the Jesuits in Quebec appealed to the French public for aid. Much to their surprise, they received not a donation but a half-dozen religious zealots, in person. Abandoning the centuries-old cloistered role of female religious figures these nuns undertook missionary work that gave them an active role in the life of the colony.[70] Thus the great religious revival of the seventeenth century endowed New France with several exceptionally capable, well-funded, determined leaders

117

imbued with an activist approach to charity and with that particular mixture of spiritual ardour and worldly *savoir-faire* that typified the mystics of that period.[71] The praises of Marie de l'Incarnation, Jeanne Mance, and Marguerite Bourgeoys have been sung so often as to be tiresome. Perhaps, though, a useful vantage point is gained if one assesses them as neither saints nor heroines, but simply as leaders. In this capacity, the nuns supplied money, publicity, skills, and settlers, all of which were needed in the colony.

Marie de l'Incarnation, a competent businesswoman from Tours, founded the Ursuline Monastery at Quebec in 1639. Turning to the study of Indian languages, she and her colleagues helped implement the policy of assimilating the young Indians. Then, gradually abandoning that futile policy, they turned to the education of the French colonists. Marie de l'Incarnation developed the farm on the Ursuline seigneurie and served as an unofficial adviser to the colonial administrators. She also helped draw attention and money to the colony by writing some 12,000 letters between 1639 and her death in 1672.[72]

An even more prodigious fund-raiser in those straitened times was Jeanne Mance, who had a remarkable knack for making friends in high places.[73] They enabled her to supply money and colonists for the original French settlement on the island of Montreal, and to take a place beside Maisonneuve as co-founder of the town.[74] The hospital she established there had the legendary wealth of the de Bullion family — and the revenues of three Norman domains — behind it. From this endowment she made the crucial grant to Governor Maisonneuve in 1651 that secured vitally needed troops from France, thus saving Montreal.[75] Mance and her Montreal colleague Margeurite Bourgeoys both made several voyages to France to recruit settlers. They were particularly successful in securing the female immigrants necessary to establish a permanent colony, recruiting sizable groups in 1650, 1653, and 1659.[76]

Besides contributing to the colony's sheer physical survival, the nuns raised the living standards of the population materially. They conducted the schools attended by girls of all classes and from both of the colony's races. Bourgeoys provided housing for newly arrived immigrants and served in a capacity perhaps best described as an early social worker.[77] Other nuns established hospitals in each of the three towns. The colonists reaped fringe benefits in the institutions established by this exceptionally dedicated personnel. The hospitals, for example, provided high-quality care to both rich and poor, care that compared favourably with that of similar institutions in France.[78] Thus, the *dévotes* played an important role in supplying leadership, funding, publicity, recruits, and social services. They may even have tipped the balance toward survival in the 1650s, when retention of the colony was still in doubt.

In the longer run, they endowed the colony with an educational heritage, which survived and shaped social life long after the initial heroic piety had grown cold. The schools that the *dévotes* founded created a situation very different from that in France, where education of women in the seventeenth century lagged behind that of men.[79] The opinion-setters in France sought to justify this neglect in the eighteenth century and a controversy began over whether girls should be educated outside the home at all.[80] Girls in Montreal escaped all this. Indeed, in 1663 Montrealers had a school for their girls but none for their boys. The result was that for a time Montreal women surpassed men in literacy, a reversal of the usual *ancien régime* pattern.[81] The superior education of women that Charlevoix extolled in 1744 continued until the fall of New France (and beyond) — a tendency heightened by the large per-centage of soldiers, generally illiterate, among the male population.[82] The Ursulines conducted schools for the élite at Quebec and Trois-Rivières. This order was traditionally rather weak in teaching housekeeping (which perhaps accounts for Kalm's famous castigation of Canadian housewif-ery). Nevertheless they specialized in needlework, an important skill since articles of clothing were a major trade good sought by the Indians. More-over, the Ursulines taught the daughters of the élite the requisite skills for administering a house and a fortune — skills which, as we shall see later, many were to exercise.[83]

119

More remarkable than the Ursuline education, however, was that of the Soeurs de la Congrégation, which reached the popular classes in the countryside.[84] Franquet was apparently shocked by the effect of this exceptional education on the colonial girls. He recommended that the Soeurs' schools be suppressed because they made it difficult to keep girls down on the farm:

> Ces Soeurs sont répandues le long des côtes, dans des seigneuries où elles ont été attirées pour l'éducation des jeunes filles; leur utilité semble être démontrée, mais le mal qu'en résulte est comme un poison lent qui tend à dépeupler les campagnes, d'autant qu'une fille instruite fait la demoiselle, qu'elle est maniérée, qu'elle veut prendre un établissement à la ville, qu'il lui faut un négociant et qu'elle regarde au dessous d'elle l'état dans lequel elle est née.[85]

The second distinct group of female immigrants to New France was the famous *filles du roi*, women sent out by the French government as brides in order to boost the colony's permanent settlement. Over 900 arrived between 1663 and 1673.[86] If less impressive than the *dévotes*, they, too, appear to have arrived with more than the average immigrant's store of education and capital. Like the nuns, they were the product of a particular historical moment that thrust them across the sea. The relevant event here is that brief interlude in the 1660s and 1670s when the King, his Minister Colbert, and the Intendant Talon applied an active hand to colonial development.[87]

There has been much historical controversy about whether the *filles du roi* were pure or not.[88] More relevant to our discussion than their morality are their money and their skills. On both these counts, this was a very selective immigration. First of all, the majority of the *filles du roi* (and for that matter, of seventeenth-century female immigrants generally) were urban dwellers, a group that enjoyed better access to education than the peasantry did.[89] Moreover, the *filles du roi* were particularly privileged urbanites. Over one-third, some 340 of them, were educated at the Paris Hôpital Général. Students at this institution learned writing and such a wide variety of skills that in France they were much sought after for service in the homes of the wealthy. Six per cent were of noble or bourgeois origin. Many of the *filles* brought with them a 50–100 *livres* dowry provided by the King;[90] some supplemented this with personal funds in the order of 200–300 *livres*. Sixty-five of the *filles* brought considerably larger holdings, in the range of 400 to 450 *livres*, to their marriages.[91] The Parisian origins of many *filles du roi*, and of the nuns who taught their children, probably account for the pure French accent that a number of travellers attributed to the colony's women.[92]

These two major immigrant groups, then, the nuns and the *filles du roi*, largely account for the superior education and "cultivation" attributed to the colony's women. Another demographic consideration also favoured the women of New France. As a result of light female emigration, men heavily outnumbered women in the colony's early days.[93] It might be expected that, as a scarce commodity, women would receive favoured treatment. The facility of marriage and remarriage, as well as the leniency of the courts and the administrators toward women, suggests that this hypothesis is correct.

Women had a wider choice in marriage than did men in the colony's early days. There were, for example, eight marriageable men for every marriageable woman in Montreal in 1663. Widows grieved, briefly, then remarried within an average of 8.8 months after their bereavement. In those early days the laws of supply and demand operated to women's economic advantage, as well. Rarely did these first Montreal women bother to match their husband's wedding present by offering a dowry.[94] The colony distinguished itself as "the country of the *douaire* not of the *dot*."[95]

In the social and legal realm we also find privileges that may have been attributable to the shortage of women. Perhaps it is due to the difficulties of replacing battered wives that jealous husbands in New France were willing to forgo the luxury of uncontrolled rage. Some of the intendants even charged that there were libertine wives in the colony who got away with taking a second husband while the first was away trading furs.[96] Recent indications that New France conformed rather closely to French traditions make it unlikely that this was common.[97] But the judgements of the Sovereign Council do offer evidence of peaceful reconciliations such as that of Marguerite Leboeuf, charged with adultery in 1667. The charge was dismissed when her husband pleaded before the Sovereign Council on her behalf. Also leaving vengeance largely to the Lord was Antoine Antorche, who withdrew his accusation against his wife even after the Council found her doubly guilty.[98] In this regard the men of New France differed from their Portuguese brothers in Brazil, who perpetrated a number of amorous murders each year; also from their English brethren in Massachusetts, who branded or otherwise mutilated their errant wives and daughters.[99] When such cases reached the courts in New France the judges, too, appear to have been lenient. Their punishments for adulterous women were considerably lighter than those imposed in New England. A further peculiarity of the legal system in New France, which suggests that women were closer to being on an equal footing with men than in other times and places, was the unusual attempt to arrest not only prostitutes but their clients as well.[100]

Another indication of the lenient treatment Canadian women enjoyed is the level of insubordination the authorities were willing to accept from them. There was a distinct absence of timidity vis-à-vis the political authorities. In 1714, for example, the inhabitants of Côte St. Leonard violently objected to the Bishop's decision to cancel their membership in the familiar church and enrol them in the newly erected parish of Rivière-des-Prairies. A fracas ensued in which the consecrated altar breads were captured by the rebellious parishioners. An officer sent to restore order was assailed by angry women:

> L'huissier chargé d'aller assigner les séditieux, raconte que toutes les femmes l'attendaient "avec des roches et des perches dans leurs mains pour m'assassiner," qu'elles le poursuivirent en jurant: "arrête voleur, nous te voulons tuer et jeter dans le marais."[101]

Other women hurled insults at the Governor himself in the 1670s.[102] An even more outrageous case of insubordination was that of the two Desaulniers sisters, who by dint of various appeals, deceits, and stalling tactics continued to run an illegal trading post at Caughnawaga for some twenty-five years despite repeated orders from governors, intendants, and the ministry itself to close it down.[103]

A further indication of women's privileged position is the absence of witchcraft persecution in New France. The colony was founded in the seventeenth century when this persecution was at its peak in Western Europe. The New Englanders, too, were burning witches at Salem. Not a single Canadienne died for this offence.[104] It is not — as Marie de l'Incarnation's account of the 1663 earthquake makes clear[105] — that the Canadians were not a superstitious people. A scholar of crime in New France suggests that this surprising absence of witchcraft hysteria relates to the fact that "depuis le début de la colonie une femme était une rareté très estimée et de ce fait, protégée de la persécution en masse."[106]

Thus, on the marriage market, and in their protection from physical violence, women seem to have achieved a favourable position because of their small numbers. Their relatively high wages and lighter court sentences may also have related to the demographic imbalance. Moreover, the original female immigrants arrived in the colony with better than average education and capital, attributes that undoubtedly helped them to establish their privileged status.

Economic Opportunities

Even more than demographic forces, the colonial economy served to enhance the position of women. In relation to the varied activities found in many regions of France, New France possessed a primitive economy. Other than subsistence farming, the habitants engaged in two major pursuits. The first was military activity, which included not only actual fighting but building and maintaining the imperial forts and provisioning the troops. The second activity was the fur trade. Fighting and fur trading channelled men's ambitions and at times removed them physically from the colony. This helped open up the full range of opportunities to women, whom we have already seen to have had the possibility of assuming a wide variety of economic roles in *ancien régime* society. Many adapted themselves to life in a military society. A few actually fought. Others made a good living by providing goods and services to the ever-present armies. Still others left military activity aside and concentrated on civilian economic pursuits — pursuits that were often neglected by men. For many this simply meant managing the family farm as best as one could during the trading season, when husbands were away. Other women assumed direction of commercial enterprises, a neglected area in this society that preferred military honours to commercial prizes. Others acted as sort of home-office partners for fur-trading husbands working far afield. Still others, having lost husbands to raids, rapids, or other hazards of forest life, assumed a widow's position at the helm of the family business.

New France has been convincingly presented as a military society. The argument is based on the fact that a very large proportion of its population was under arms, its government had a semi-military character, its economy relied heavily on military expenditure and manpower, and a military ethos prevailed among the élite.[107] In some cases, women joined their menfolk in these martial pursuits. The seventeenth century sometimes saw them in direct combat. A number of Montrealers perished during an Iroquois raid in 1661 in which, Charlevoix tells us, "even the women fought to the death, and not one of them surrendered."[108] In Acadia, Madame de la Tour took command of the fort's forty-five soldiers and warded off her husband's arch-enemy, Menou D'Aulnay, for three days before finally capitulating.[109]

The most famous of these seventeenth-century *guerrières* was, of course, Madeleine de Verchères. At the age of fourteen she escaped from a band of Iroquois attackers, rushed back to the fort on her parents'

122

seigneurie, and fired a cannon shot in time to warn all the surrounding settlers of the danger.[110] Legend and history have portrayed Madeleine as a lamb who was able, under siege, to summon up a lion's heart. Powdered and demure in a pink dress, she smiles very sweetly out at the world in a charming vignette in Arthur Doughty's *A Daughter of New France, being a story of the life and times of Magdelaine de Verchères*, published in 1916. Perhaps the late twentieth century is ready for her as she was: a swashbuckling, musket-toting braggart who extended the magnitude of her deeds with each successive telling, who boasted that she never in her life shed a tear, a contentious thorn in the side of the local curé (whom she slandered) and of her *censitaires* (whom she constantly battled in the courts).[111] She strutted through life for all the world like the boorish male officers of the *campagnard* nobility to which her family belonged.[112] One wonders how many more there were like her. Perhaps all trace of them has vanished into the wastebaskets of subsequent generations of historians who, with immovable ideas of female propriety, did not know what on earth to do with them — particularly after what must have been the exhausting effort of pinching Verchères' muscled frame into a corset and getting her to wear the pink dress.

123

By the eighteenth century, women had withdrawn from hand-to-hand combat, but many remained an integral part of the military élite as it closed in to become a caste. In this system, both sexes shared the responsibility of marrying properly and of maintaining those cohesive family ties which, Corvisier tells us, lay at the heart of military society. Both also appealed to the ministry for their sons' promotions.[113]

What is more surprising is that a number of women accompanied their husbands to military posts in the wilderness. Wives of officers, particularly of corporals, traditionally helped manage the canteens in the French armies.[114] Almost all Canadian officers were involved in some sort of trading activity, and a wife at the post could mind the store when the husband had to mind the war. Some were overzealous. When Franquet rode into Fort Saint Frédéric in 1752 he discovered a terrific row among its inhabitants. The post was in a virtual state of mutiny because a Madame Lusignan was monopolizing all the trade, both wholesale and retail, at the fort; and her husband, the Commandant, was enforcing the monopoly.[115] In fact, Franquet's inspection tour of the Canadian posts is remarkable for the number of women who greeted him at the military posts, which one might have expected to be a male preserve. Arriving at Fort Sault Saint Louis he was received very politely by M. de Merceau and his two daughters. He noted that Fort Saint Frédéric housed not only the redoubtable Madame Lusignan but also another officer's widow. At Fort Chambly he "spent the whole day with the ladies, and visited Madame de Beaulac, an officer's widow who has been given lodging in this fort."[116]

The nuns, too, marched in step with this military society. They were, quite literally, one of its lifelines, since they cared for its wounded. A majority of the invalids at the Montreal Hôtel-Dieu were soldiers, and the Ursuline institution at Trois-Rivières was referred to simply as a *hôpital militaire*.[117] Hospital service was so vital to the army that Frontenac personally intervened to speed construction of the Montreal Hôtel-Dieu in 1695, when he was planning a campaign against the Iroquois.[118] In the colony's first days, the Ursulines also made great efforts to help the Governor seal Indian alliances by attempting to secure Iroquois students who would serve as hostages, and by giving receptions for Iroquois chiefs.[119]

Humbler folk also played a part in military society. In the towns female publicans conducted a booming business with the thirsty troops. Other women served as laundresses, adjuncts so vital that they accompanied armies even on the campaigns where wives and other camp followers were ordered to stay home.[120] Seemingly indispensable, too, wherever armies march, are prostitutes. At Quebec City they plied their trade as early as 1667. Indian women at the missions also served in this capacity.[121] All told, women had more connections with the military economy than is generally noted.

While warfare provided a number of women with a living, it was in commerce that the Canadiennes really flourished. Here a number of women moved beyond supporting roles to occupy centre stage. This happened for several reasons. The first was that the military ethos diverted men from commercial activity. Second, many men who entered the woods to fight or trade were gone for years. Others, drowned or killed in battle, never returned.[122] This left many widows who had to earn a livelihood. This happened so often, in fact, that when women, around the turn of the eighteenth century, overcame their early numerical disadvantage, the tables turned quickly. They soon outnumbered the men and remained a majority through to the Conquest.[123] Generally speaking, life was more hazardous for men than for women[124] — so much so that the next revolution of the historiographic wheel may turn up the men of New France (at least in relation to its women) as an oppressed group.

At any rate, women often stepped in to take the place of their absent husbands or brothers. A surprising number of women traders emerge in the secondary literature on New France. In the colony's earliest days, the mere handful of women included two merchants at Trois-Rivières: Jeanne Enard (mother-in-law of Pierre Boucher), who "by her husband's own admission" was the head of the family as far as fur-trading was concerned; and Mathurine Poisson, who sold imported goods to the colonists.[125] At Montreal there was the wife of Artus de Sully, whose unspecified (but presumably commercial) activities won her the distinction of being Montreal's biggest debtor.[126] In Quebec City, Eleonore de Grandmaison was a member of a company formed to trade in the Ottawa country. She added to her wealth by renting her lands on the Île d'Orleans to Huron refugees after Huronia had been destroyed. Farther east,

124

Madame de la Tour involved herself in shipping pelts to France. Another Acadian, Madame Joybert, traded furs on the Saint John River.[127]

With the onset of the less pious eighteenth century, we find several women at the centre of the illegal fur trade. Indian women, including "a cross-eyed squaw named Marie-Magdelaine," regularly carried contraband goods from the Caughnawaga reserve to Albany.[128] A Madame Couagne received Albany contraband at the other end, in Montreal.[129] But at the heart of this illegal trade were the Desaulniers sisters, who used their trading post on the Caughnawaga reserve as an *entrepôt* for the forbidden English strouds, fine textiles, pipes, boots, lace, gloves, silver tableware, chocolate, sugar, and oysters that the Indians brought regularly from Albany.[130] Franquet remarked on the power of these *marchandes*, who were able to persuade the Indians to refuse the government's request to build fortifications around their village.[131] The Desaulniers did not want the comings and goings of their employees too closely scrutinized.

These *commerçants*, honest and otherwise, continued to play their part until the Conquest. Marie-Anne Barbel (*Veuve* Fornel) farmed the Tadoussac fur trade and was involved in diverse enterprises including retail sales, brickmaking, and real estate.[132] On Franquet's tour in the 1750s he encountered other *marchandes* besides the controversial "Madame la Commandante" who had usurped the Fort Saint Frédéric trade. He enjoyed a restful night at the home of Madame de Lemothe, a *marchande* who had prospered so well that she was able to put up her guests in splendid beds that Franquet proclaimed "fit for a duchess."[133]

A number of writers have remarked on the shortage of entrepreneurial talent in New France.[134] This perhaps helps to account for the activities of Agathe de St. Père, who established the textile industry in Canada. She did so after the colonial administrators had repeatedly called for development of spinning and weaving, with no result.[135] Coming from the illustrious Le Moyne family, Agathe St. Père married the ensign Pierre Legardeur de Repentigny, a man who, we are told, had "an easygoing nature." St. Père, of another temperament, pursued the family business interests, investing in fur trade partnerships, real estate, and lending operations. Then in 1705, when the vessel bringing the yearly supply of French cloth to the colony was shipwrecked, she saw an opportunity to develop the textile industry in Montreal. She ransomed nine English weavers who had been captured by the Indians and arranged for apprentices to study the trade. Subsequently these apprentices taught the trade to other Montrealers on home looms that Madame de Repentigny built and distributed. Besides developing the manufacture of linen, drugget, and serge, she discovered new chemicals that made use of the native plants to dye and process them.[136]

Upon this foundation Madame Benoist built. Around the time of the Conquest, she was directing an operation in Montreal in which women turned out, among other things, shirts and petticoats for the fur trade.[137] This is a case of woman doing business while man did battle, for Madame Benoist's husband was commanding officer at Lac des Deux Montagnes.

The absence of male entrepreneurs may also explain the operation of a large Richelieu lumbering operation by Louise de Ramezay, the daughter of the Governor of Montreal. Louise, who remained single, lost her father in 1724. Her mother continued to operate the sawmill on the family's Chambly seigneury but suffered a disastrous reverse due to a combination of flooding, theft, and shipwreck in 1725. The daughter, however, went into partnership with the Seigneuress de Rouville in 1745 and successfully developed the sawmill. She then opened a flour mill, a Montreal tannery, and another sawmill. By the 1750s the trade was flourishing: Louise de Ramezay was shipping 20,000-*livre* loads, and one merchant alone owed her 60,000 *livres*. In 1753 she began to expand her leather business, associating with a group of Montreal tanners to open new workships.[138]

Louise de Ramezay's case is very clearly related to the fact that she lived in a military society. As Louise was growing up, one by one her brothers perished. Claude, an ensign in the French navy, died during an attack on Rio de Janeiro in 1711. Louis died during the 1715 campaign against the Fox Indians. La Gesse died ten years later in a shipwreck off Île Royale. That left only one son, Jean-Baptiste-Roch; and, almost inevitably, he chose a military career over management of the family business affairs.[139] It may be that similar situations accounted for the female entrepreneurs in ironforging, tilemaking, sturgeon-fishing, sealing, and contract building, all of whom operated in New France.[140]

The society's military preoccupations presented business opportunities to some women; for others, the stress on family ties was probably more important. Madame Benoist belonged to the Baby family, whose male members were out cultivating the western fur trade. Her production of shirts made to the Indians' specifications was the perfect complement. The secret of the Desaulniers' successful trade network may well be that they were related to so many of Montreal's leading merchants.[141] The fur trade generally required two or more bases of operation. We saw earlier in our discussion that this society not only placed great value on family connections but also accepted female commercial activity. It was therefore quite natural that female relatives would be recruited into business to cover one of the bases. Men who were heading for the west would delegate their powers of attorney and various business responsibilities to their wives, who were remaining in the colony.[142]

We find these husband-wife fur trade partnerships not only among "Les Grandes Familles" but permeating all classes of society. At Trois-Rivières women and girls manufactured the canoes that carried the fur trade provisions westward each summer. This was a large-scale operation that profited from fat government contracts.[143] In Montreal, wives kept the account-books while their husbands traded. Other women spent the winters sewing shirts and petticoats that would be bartered the following summer.[144]

The final reason for women's extensive business activity was the direct result of the hazards men faced in fighting and fur-trading. A high proportion of women were widowed; and as widows, they enjoyed special commercial privileges. In traditional French society, these privileges were so extensive that craftsmen's widows sometimes inherited full guildmaster's rights. More generally, widows acquired the right to manage the family assets until the children reached the age of twenty-five (and sometimes beyond that time). In some instances they also received the right to choose which child would receive the succession.[145] In New France these rights frequently came into operation, and they had a major impact on the distribution of wealth and power in the society. In 1663, for example, women held the majority of the colony's seigneurial land. The *Veuve* Le Moyne numbered among the twelve Montreal merchants who, between 1642 and 1725, controlled assets of 50,000 *livres*. The *Veuve* Fornel acquired a similar importance later on in the regime. Some of the leading merchants at Louisbourg were also widows. The humbler commerce of tavernkeeping was also frequently a widow's lot.[146]

127

Thus, in New France, both military and commercial activities that required a great deal of travelling over vast distances were usually carried out by men. In their absence, their wives played a large role in the day-to-day economic direction of the colony. Even when the men remained in the colony, military ambitions often absorbed their energies, particularly among the upper class. In these situations, it was not uncommon for a wife to assume direction of the family interests.[147] Others waited to do so until their widowhood, which — given the fact that the average wife was considerably younger than her husband and that his activities were often more dangerous — frequently came early.[148]

Conclusion

New France had been founded at a time in Europe's history in which the roles of women were neither clearly nor rigidly defined. In this fluid situation, the colony received an exceptionally well-endowed group of female immigrants during its formative stage. There, where they long remained in short supply, they secured a number of special privileges at home, at school, in the courts, and in social and political life. They consolidated this favourable position by attaining a major role in the colonial economy, at both the popular and the directive levels. These circumstances enabled the women of New France to play many parts. *Dévotes* and traders, warriors and landowners, smugglers and politicians, industrialists and financiers: they thronged the stage in such numbers that they distinguish themselves as *femmes favorisées*.

NOTES

[1] F.-X. Charlevoix, *History and General Description of New France* (New York, 1900), 23: 28.

[2] Cited in R.-L. Séguin, "La Canadienne aux XVIIe et XVIIIe siècles," *Revue d'histoire de l'Amérique français* (hereafter *RHAF*), 13 (mars, 1960): 492.

[3] Séguin, "La Canadienne," 500.

[4] Séguin, "La Canadienne," 500.

[5] L. Franquet, *Voyages et mémoires sur le Canada* (Montréal, 1974), 57, recording a tour in 1752-53.

[6] Franquet, *Voyages*, 31.

[7] Séguin, "La Canadienne," 492, 505.

[8] G. Fagniez, *La Femme et la société française dans la première moitié du XVIIe siècle* (Paris, 1929), p.154.

[9] Marcel Trudel, *Montréal, la formation d'une société* (Montréal, 1976): 216-17.

[10] John F. Bosher, "The Family in New France," in Barry Gough, ed., *In Search of the Visible Past* (Waterloo, Ont., 1976), 7.

[11] Fagniez, *Femme et société française*, 121.

[12] Fagniez, *Femme et société française*, 149, 104, 193.

[13] Philippe Ariès, *Centuries of Childhood* (New York, 1962), 392-406.

[14] Ariès, *Centuries of Childhood*, 365-66.

[15] Peter Laslett, "Characteristics of the Western Family Considered over Time," *Journal of Family History* 2 (Summer 1977): 89-115.

[16] Richard Vann, "Women in Preindustrial Capitalism," in R. Bridenthal, ed., *Becoming Visible: Women in European History* (Boston, 1977), 206.

[17] Vann, "Women in Preindustrial Capitalism," 206-08; Ariès, *Centuries of Childhood*, 397-406.

[18] Fagniez, *Femme et société française*, 122-23, 179.

[19] Vann, "Women in Preindustrial Capitalism," 206.

[20] Franquet, *Voyages*, 135, 61.

[21] Séguin, "La Canadienne," 499; R. Boyer, *Les Crimes et châtiments au Canada française du XVIIIe au XXe siècle* (Montréal, 1966), p.391.

[22] Séguin, "La Canadienne," 506.

[23] Boyer, *Crimes et châtiments*, 351.

[24] Boyer, *Crimes et châtiments*, 344-46.

[25] Laslett, "Western Family," 95.

[26] I. Foulché-Delbosc, "Women of Three Rivers, 1651-1663," in A. Prentice and S. Trofimenkoff, eds., *The Neglected Majority* (Toronto, 1977), 26.

[27] Bosher ("The Family," 3) found the marriage rate in New France to be about three times that of modern-day Quebec.

[28] This information is taken from a study of Normandy, which was the birthplace of many of the Canadian colonists. J.M. Gouesse, "La Formation du couple en Basse-Normandie," *XVIIe Siècle* 102-3 (1974): 56.

[29] Laslett, "Western Family," 106.

[30] Fagniez, *Femme et société française*, 99-104, 108, 111, 114-16.

[31] Louise Dechêne, *Habitants et marchands de Montréal au XVIIe siècle* (Paris, 1974), 393.

[32] Fagniez, *Femme et société française* 101; Séguin, "La Canadienne," 503; also G. Lanctôt, *Filles de joie ou filles du roi* (Montréal, 1952), 210-13.

[33] Cf. Paul Butel, "Comportements familiaux dans le négoce bordelais au XVIIIe siècle," *Annales du Midi* 88 (1976): 139-57.

[34] M.E. Chabot, "Marie Guyart de l'Incarnation, 1599-1672," in M. Innis, ed., *The Clear Spirit* (Toronto, 1966), 28.

[35] Bosher, "The Family," 7; H. Neatby, *Quebec, The Revolutionary Age* (Toronto, 1966), 46.

[36] Foulché-Delbosc. "Women of Three Rivers," 15.

[37] Bosher, "The Family," 3. I have rounded his figures.

[38] Dechêne, *Habitants et marchands*, 434; Bosher, "The Family," 5.

[39] Vann, "Women in Preindustrial Capitalism," 205; cf. also Alice Clark, *Working Life of Women in the Seventeenth Century* (London, 1919), Chs. 5,6; and Fagniez, *Femme et société française*, for the scarcity of women's guilds by the seventeenth century.

[40] Fagniez, *Femme et société française*, 168ff.

[41] Y. Zoltvany, "Esquisse de la Coutume de Paris," *RHAF* (décembre, 1971).

[42] Foulché-Delbosc, "Women of Three Rivers," 19.

[43] Neatby, *Quebec*, 46.

[44] Fagniez, *Femme et société française*, 147.

[45] Dechêne, *Habitants et marchands*, 423-24.

[46] A. Morel, "Réflexions sur la justice criminelle canadienne au 18e siècle," *RHAF* 29 (septembre, 1975), 241-53.

[47] Lanctôt, *Filles de joie*, 219.

[48] Boyer, *Crimes et Châtiments*, 128-29.

[49] W.J. Eccles, Social Welfare Measures and Policies in New France," *Congreso Internacional de Americanistas* 4 (1966), Seville, 9-19.

[50] J. Bosher, "Government and Private Interests in New France," in J.M. Bumsted, ed., *Canadian History before Confederation* (Georgetown, Ontario, 1972), 122.

[51] Bosher, "The Family," 5-7; Fagniez, *Femme et société française*, 182.

[52] Franquet, *Voyages*, 148; cf. also Frégault, *Le XVIIIᵉ siècle canadien* (Montréal, 1968), 292-93.

[53] W.J. Eccles, "The Social, Economic and Political Significance of the Military Establishment in New France," *Canadian Historical Review* 52 (March 1971): 8-10.

[54] Franquet, *Voyages*, 129-30. For another similar trip, see 140-42.

[55] Frégault, *Le XVIIIᵉ siècle*, 208-09, 216-21.

[56] Frégault, *Le XVIIIᵉ siècle*, 229-30.

[57] Y. Zoltvany, *Philippe de Rigaud de Vaudreuil* (Toronto, 1974) 110, 217.

[58] Frégault, *Le XVIIIᵉ siècle*, 228-30.

[59] W.J. Eccles, *Frontenac: The Courtier Governor* (Toronto, 1959), 29.

[60] *Rapport de l'archiviste de la province de Québec* (1922-23): 151.

[61] For example, George Rudé, *The Crowd in the French Revolution* (New York, 1959).

[62] Superbly described in E.P. Thompson, *The Making of the English Working Class* (London, 1976), Ch. 3.

[63] Cited in T. Crowley, " 'Thunder Gusts': Popular Disturbances in Early French Canada," *CHAR* (1979): 19-20.

[64] Jean Hamelin, "What Middle Class?" *Society and Conquest*, Miquelon, ed. (Toronto, 1977), 109-10; and Dechêne, *Habitants et marchands*, 44, who concludes that the largest contingents of male immigrants arriving in seventeenth-century Montreal were *engagés* and soldiers.

[65] H. Charbonneau, *Vie et mort de nos ancêtres* (Montréal, 1975), 38; A. Burguière, "Le Rituel du mariage en France: Pratiques ecclésiastiques et pratiques populaires, (XVIᵉ-XVIIIᵉ siècle)," *Annales E.S.C.*, 33ᵉ année (mai-juin, 1978): 640; R. Mousnier, *La famille, l'enfant et l'éducation en France et en Grande-Bretagne du XVIᵉ au XVIIIᵉ siècle* (Paris, 1975); Fagniez, *Femme et société française*, 97. Commercial activities, however, also prevailed among the women of Bordeaux, an important port in the Canada trade. Fagniez, *Femme et société française*, 196.

[66] Fagniez, *Femme et société française*, 267, 273-74, 311-12, 360-61.

[67] Claude Lessard, "L'Aide financière de l'Eglise de France à l'Eglise naissante du Canada," in Pierre Savard, ed., *Mélanges d'histoire du Canada français offerts au professeur Marcel Trudel* (Ottawa, 1978), 175.

[68] Fagniez, *Femme et société française*, 311-21.

[69] Marcel Trudel, *The Beginnings of New France* (Toronto, 1973), for a gloomy assessment of the neglected colony during this period.

[70] G. Brown et al., eds., *Dictionary of Canadian Biography* (herafter *DCB*) (Toronto, 1966-   ), 1: 118; J. Marshall, ed., *Word from New France* (Toronto, 1967), 2.

[71] Fagniez, *Femme et société française*, 320-33, 358. Of course, not all *religieuses* were competent as leaders. Madame de la Peltrie, for example, patron of the Ursuline convent, appears to have been a rather unreliable benefactress. Despite her first-hand knowledge of the difficulties under which the Ursulines laboured, her "charity" was quixotic. In 1642, she suddenly withdrew her support from the Ursulines in order to join the colonists setting off to found Montreal. Later she again held back her funds in favour of a cherished chapel project, even though the Ursulines' lodgings had just burned to the ground.

[72] Chabot, "Marie Guyart de l'Incarnation," 27, 37; *DCB* 1: 353; Lessard, "Aide financière," 169-70.

[73] *DCB* 1: 483-87; also Lessard, "Aide financière," 175.

[74] This is the interpretation given by G. Lanctôt in *Montreal under Maisonneuve* (Toronto, 1969), 20-24, 170.

[75] Lanctôt, *Montreal under Maisonneuve*, 188.

[76] Lanctôt, *Filles de joie*, 81; Trudel, *Montréal*, 21. The Hôtel-Dieu de Montréal also sponsored immigrants from 1655 to 1662 (Lanctôt, *Filles de joie*, 81.).

[77] Trudel, *Montréal*, 84.

[78] Eccles, "Social Welfare Measures," 19; F. Rousseau, "Hôpital et société en Nouvelle-France: l'Hôtel-Dieu de Québec à la fin du XVIIᵉ siècle," *RHAF* 31 (juin, 1977): 47.

[79] Mousnier, *La famille, l'enfant et l'éducation*, 319-31.

[80] Vann, "Women in Preindustrial Capitalism," 208.

[81] Trudel, *Montréal*, 276, 87; P. Goubert, *The Ancien Régime* (New York, 1974), 262.

[82] Neatby, *Quebec*, 237; French soldiers had a literacy rate of 3 to 4 per cent. A Corvisier, *L'Armée française de la fin du XVIIᵉ siècle ou ministère de Choiseul* (Paris, 1964), 862.

[83] Fagniez, *Femme et société canadienne*, 191.

[84] Séguin, "La Canadienne," 501, lists nine of these schools in addition to the original one in Montreal.

[85] Franquet, *Voyages*, 31-32.

[86] According to Lanctôt (*Filles de joie*, 121-30), there were 961. Silvio Dumas counts only 774 (*Les Filles du roi en Nouvelle France* [Québec, 1972], 164). Other estimates have ranged between 713 and 857.

[87] J.-N. Fauteux, *Essai sur l'industrie au Canada sous le Régime Français* (Québec, 1927), "Introduction."

129

[88] For the record, it now seems fairly well established that the females sent to New France, unlike those sent to the West Indies, were carefully screened, and any of questionable morality were returned by the authorities to France. Lanctôt (*Filles de joie*) and Dumas (*Filles du roi*) agree on this. See also Foulché-Delbosc, "Women of Three Rivers," 22-23.

[89] Dechêne finds a majority of *Parisiennes* among the Montréal filles (*Habitants et marchands*, 96). Lanctôt states that one-half of the 1634-63 emigrants were urbanites and that two-thirds of the *filles* were from Île-de-France (*Filles de joie*, 76-79, 124). On education in France, see Mousnier, *La famille, l'enfant et l'éducation*, 319-25.

[90] Lanctôt, *Filles de joie*, 110-30, 202.

[91] Dumas, *Filles du roi*, 39, 41, 51-54, 56, 59.

[92] Séguin, "La Canadienne," 492; Franquet, *Voyages*, 57.

[93] J. Henripin, *La population canadienne au début du XVIIIe siècle* (Paris, 1954), 120. The overall population was 63 per cent male in 1663 (Trudel, *Beginnings*, 261), an imbalance that gradually declined.

[94] Trudel, *Montréal*, 45-47, 108, 113.

[95] Foulché-Delbosc, "Women of Three Rivers," 19.

[96] Cole Harris, *The Seigneurial System in Early Canada* (Québec, 1968), 163.

[97] The richest single source for evidence along these lines is Dechêne's *Habitants et marchands*.

[98] Boyer, *Crimes et châtiments*, 326.

[99] Toronto *Globe and Mail*, 29 October 1979, p. 1; Boyer, *Crimes et châtiments*, 329, 340. Cf. also N. Hawthorne's novel, *The Scarlet Letter*, based on an actual occurrence.

[100] Boyer, *Crimes et châtiments*, 329, 350, 361-62; also Morel, "Justice criminelle canadienne." See also the more recent discussions of women and crime by A. LaChance, "Women and Crime in Canada in the Early Eighteenth Century," in L. Knafla, ed., *Crime and Criminal Justice in Canada* (Calgary, 1981), 157-78.

[101] Dechêne, *Habitants et marchands*, 464.

[102] Séguin, "La Canadienne," 497-99.

[103] Jean Lunn, "The Illegal Fur Trade Out of New France, 1713-60," Canadian Historial Association, *Report* (1939), 61-62.

[104] Boyer, *Crimes et châtiments*, 286-87.

[105] Marshall, *Word from New France*, 287-95.

[106] Boyer, *Crimes et châtiments*, 306.

[107] Eccles, "The Social, Economic and Political Significance of the Military."

[108] Charlevoix, *New France*, 3: 35.

[109] Ethel Bennett, "Madame de la Tour, 1602-1645," in M. Innis, ed., *The Clear Spirit* (Toronto, 1966), 21.

[110] *DCB* 3: 308-13.

[111] *DCB* 3: 308-13 Boyer, *Crimes et châtiments*, 338-39.

[112] For a splendid description of the attitudes and lifestyle of this class in France, see P. de Vaissière, *Gentilshommes campagnards de l'ancienne France* (Paris, 1903).

[113] G. Frégault, *Le Grand Marquis* (Montréal, 1952), 74-75; Corvisier, *L'Armée française*, 777.

[114] Corvisier, *L'Armée française*, 762-63, 826.

[115] Franquet, *Voyages* 56, 67-68, 200.

[116] Franquet, *Voyages*, 35, 76, 88.

[117] Dechêne, *Habitants et marchands*, 398; Franquet, *Voyages*, 16.

[118] *DCB* 2: 491.

[119] Marshall, *Word from New France*, 27, 213, 222-23, 233.

[120] Dechêne, *Habitants et marchands*, 393; Franquet, *Voyages*, 199; Foulché-Delbosc, "Women of Three Rivers," 25; Corvisier, *L'Armée française*, 760.

[121] Boyer, *Crimes et châtiments*, 349-51; Dechêne, *Habitants et marchands*, 41. Dechêne concludes that, considering Montreal was a garrison town with a shortage of marriageable women, the degree of prostitution was normal or, to use her term, *conformiste* (437-38).

[122] Eccles, "The Social, Economic and Political Significance of the Military," 11-17; Dechêne, *Habitants et marchands*, 121.

[123] J. Henripin, *Trends and Factors of Fertility in Canada* (Ottawa, 1972), 2; Séguin, "La Canadienne," 495, 503.

[124] Trudel, *Montréal*, 30-33; Charbonneau, *Vie et mort*, 135.

[125] Foulché-Delbosc, "Women of Three Rivers," 25.

[126] Trudel, *Montréal*, 163.

[127] Bennett, "Madame de la Tour," 16; Madame Joybert was the mother of the future Madame de Vaudreuil. *DCB* 1:399. For E. de Grandmaison, see *DCB* 1:345.

[128] Lunn, "Illegal Fur Trade," 62.

[129] Eccles, *Canadian Society*, 61.

[130] Lunn, "Illegal Fur Trade," 61-75.

[131] Franquet, *Voyages*, 120-21.

[132] Lilianne Plamondon, "Une femme d'affaires en Nouvelle-France: Marie-Anne Barbel, Veuve Fornel," *RHAF* 31 (septembre, 1977).

[133] Franquet, *Voyages*, 156-58.

[134] For example, Hamelin in "What Middle Class?" The absence of an indigenous bourgeoisie is also central to the interpretation of Dechêne in *Habitants et marchands*.

[135] Séguin, "La Canadienne," 494.

[136] For accounts of Agathe de Saint-Père, see *DCB* 3: 580–81; Fauteux, *Industrie au Canada*, 464–69; Massicote, *Bulletin des Recherches historiques* (hereafter *BRH*) (1944): 202–07.

[137] Neatby refers to this activity in the early post-Conquest era (*Quebec*, 72–73); Franquet encountered Madame Benoist in 1753 (*Voyages* 150).

[138] For discussion of the De Ramezay's business affairs, see Massicote, *BRH* (1931): 530; Fauteux, *Industrie au Canada*, 158–59, 204–15, 442.

[139] *DCB* 2: 548.

[140] Fauteux, *Industrie au Canada*, 158, 297, 420–21, 522; P. Moogk, *Building a House in New France* (Toronto, 1977), 60–64.

[141] Lunn, *Illegal Fur Trade*, 61.

[142] See Moogk (*Building a House*, 8) for one case of a husband's transfer of these powers.

[143] Franquet, *Voyages*, 17.

[144] Dechêne, *Habitants et marchands*, 151–53, 187, 391; Séguin, "La Canadienne," 494.

[145] Charbonneau, *Vie et mort*, 184; Fagniez, *Femme et société française*, 111, 182–84. A recent study by Butel ("Comportements familiaux") has documented the phenomenon of widows taking over the family business in eighteenth-century Bordeaux.

[146] Trudel, *Beginnings*, 250. This was largely due to the enormous holdings of Jean Lauzon's widow. Dechêne, *Habitants et marchands*, 209, 204–05, 393; Plamandon, "Femme d'affaires." W.S. MacNutt, *The Atlantic Provinces* (Toronto, 1965), 25.

[147] This happened on seigneuries as well as in town, as in the case M. de Lanouguère, "a soldier by preference," whose wife, Marguerite-Renée Denys, directed their seigneury (*DCB* 1: 418).

[148] The original version of this paper was written as the result of a stimulating graduate seminar conducted by Professor William J. Eccles at the University of Toronto. My thanks to him, and to others who have offered helpful comments and criticisms, particularly Professors Sylvia Van Kirk and Allan Greer at the University of Toronto. The revised version printed here has benefited from the detailed response of Professor Micheline Dumont to the original version published in the Spring 1981 volume of *Atlantis*. For Professor Dumont's critique of the article, and my reply, see *Atlantis*, 8, 1 (Spring 1982): 118–30.

131

TRANSLATIONS OF FRENCH PASSAGES

Page 109

[2] Women surpass men in beauty, vivaciousness, cheerfulness and sprightliness; they are coquettish and elegant and prefer Europeans to the local folk. Gentle and polite manners are common, even in the countryside.

[3] . . . the women there are very pleasant but extremely proud.

[4] . . . they are witty, which affords them superiority over men in almost all circumstances.

[5] "surpass men in wit; generally they all have a great deal of it and speak in refined French, without the least accent. They also like finery, are pretty, generous and even genteel."

Page 110

[9] "the law establishes their dominion over their wives."

Page 111

[11] if the masculine pre-eminence has lost none of its prestige, if it has not had to defend itself against any theoretical claim . . . it has often had to . . . be content with appearances and abandon, in the fact of expediency and public opinion, the substance of its claims.

Page 112

[28] Work, particularly in rural areas, was at that time based on a division of labour between the sexes: sailors and pedlars were absent for several months, their wives worked the land; the fishermen of the marsh-lands went to the market, the women went fishing; the labourer worked in the fields, his wife worked in the home but it was she who went to market; in the Auge region "the men looked after the livestock and the women attended to the cheese." In order to live, therefore, they had to be a couple, a man and a woman.

Page 114

[45] These matrimonial conventions do not resemble a "marriage market" in which two groups confront each other, but rather an unbiased agreement between the families aiming to create a new community, to help it, if possible, to erect some barriers around it in order to protect it. . . .

Page 115

[52] "all those of a certain class are linked by kinship and friendship in this country."

[56] "Gifted with a very shrewd political sense,"

Pages 115–16

[58] Pontchartrain, Ruette d'Auteuil reports, refuses her nothing, "she has all the jobs in Canada at her disposal; she writes splendid letters from ports of call everywhere, about the good and the bad that

she can do by using her influence with him," and the minister "does everything necessary to support her claims." Riverin confirms that . . . "there is no longer anyone but a woman in charge and she reigns whether she is present or absent."

Page 116

[60] "in the assembly of the women in this parish, by a majority of votes, to practice as a midwife."

Page 119

[85] These sisters are spread out across the countryside, in seigneuries where they have gone to educate the girls; their usefulness seems to be evident, but the harm which results is like a slow poison which leads to a depopulation of the countryside, given that an educated girl becomes a young lady, puts on airs, wants to set herself up in the city, sets her sights on a merchant and looks upon the circumstances of her birth as beneath her.

Page 121

[101] The officer who was sent to put down the rebellion relates that all the women were waiting for him "with rocks and sticks in their hands to kill me" and that they chased him yelling "stop, thief, we want to kill you and throw you in the swamp."

[106] "in the early days of the colony, women were scarce, prized, protected from mass persecution."

Louisbourg harbour, as it would have appeared, from the clock tower, in 1744. The painting is by Lewis Parker.

All in all, French stronghold that Louisbourg was, the seaport community was also home to a wide range of minority populations. Some differed from the majority in terms of ethnicity, others in terms of religion, and still others in terms of the language they spoke.

A.J.B. Johnston, "The People of Eighteenth-Century Louisbourg"

Topic Four

The Early Societies of Atlantic Canada

During the fifteenth century, Europe entered an age of expansion, marked by the development of overseas commerce and the establishment of colonies. The English, the Portuguese, the Basques, and the French were among the earliest Europeans to harvest the rich Newfoundland fishery, and to travel to northeastern North America. Only one European group, as far as we know, had previously visited North America — the Norse, around 1000 A.D. Five centuries after the Norse voyages, European fishermen established a number of seasonal settlements on the Atlantic coast to prepare and dry their fish. The Basques, from what is now the border country on the Bay of Biscay between Spain and France, arrived in the 1520s and 1530s. The origins of English-speaking Canada date back to 1583, when Sir Humphrey Gilbert laid claim to Newfoundland. England's fishery off the island soon grew to rival that of France, Spain, and Portugal. Keith Matthews summarizes the first two centuries of English and French settlement in Newfoundland, and the struggle between these groups to control the fishery, in his two lectures "The Nature of Newfoundland History" and "The Framework of Newfoundland History."

The French established their first permanent settlement on the Atlantic coast in 1604, naming it Acadia (later to become Nova Scotia). Its strategic location near the Gulf of St. Lawrence meant that England and France fought continually for its possession. The region changed hands frequently until 1713, when France ceded Acadia to England in the Treaty of Utrecht. For the next half-century, Britain ruled over the colony with its predominantly French-speaking and Roman Catholic population.

The Acadians sought to remain neutral in conflicts between England and France. Initially this was possible, but with the construction of the large French fortress of Louisbourg on Cape Breton Island during the 1720s and the founding of Halifax in 1749, the situation changed. In "The People of Eighteenth-Century Louisbourg," A.J.B. Johnston takes a close look at the important French port. With the revival of hostility between France and England in 1755, Charles Lawrence, Nova Scotia's Lieutenant-Governor, and his council at Halifax insisted that the Acadians take an unconditional oath of allegiance to the British Crown. When they refused, Lawrence expelled approximately ten thousand French Acadians. In "The Golden Age: Acadian Life, 1713–1748," Naomi Griffiths reviews Acadian society before the expulsion.

For an overview of European exploration in the North Atlantic, consult Samuel Eliot Morison, *The European Discovery of America: The Northern Voyages, A.D. 500–1600* (New York: Oxford University Press, 1971), and Robert McGhee, *Canada Rediscovered* (Ottawa: Canadian Museum of Civilization, 1991). An illustrated account of the Norse and their arrival in northeastern North America is *The Vikings and Their Predecessors*, by Kate Gordon, with a contribution by Robert McGhee (Ottawa: National Museum of Man, 1981). Three popular accounts of the Basques on the southern Labrador coast are James A. Tuck and Robert Grenier, "A 16th Century Basque Whaling Station in Labrador," *Scientific American* 245, 5 (November 1981): 180–90; Selma Barkham, "From Biscay to the Grand Bay," *Horizon Canada* 1, 1 (1984): 14–19; and the series of articles in the *National Geographic* 168, 1 (July 1985): 40–71, entitled "Discovery in Labrador: A 16th Century Basque Whaling Port and Its Sunken Fleet," with contributions by archaeologists James A. Tuck and Robert Grenier.

D.W. Prowse, in *A History of Newfoundland* (London: Macmillan, 1895), and Frederick W. Rowe, in *A History of Newfoundland and Labrador* (Toronto: McGraw-Hill, 1980), deal with early settlement in Newfoundland. Several specialized articles on the early history of Newfoundland appear in *Early European Settlement and Exploration in Atlantic Canada*, ed. G.M. Story (St. John's: Memorial University, 1982). A short summary of Newfoundland's history is given by Gordon Rothney in his booklet *Newfoundland: A History*, Canadian Historical Association, Historical Booklet no. 10 (Ottawa: CHA, 1964).

An abundant literature exists on the Acadians; in fact, by the end of the nineteenth century, two hundred books and pamphlets had been written on the subject of the Acadian expulsion alone, many of them of a controversial and partisan nature. A short review of the historical debate appears in Thomas Garde Barnes's "Historiography of the Acadians' *Grand Dérangement* (1755)," *Québec Studies* 7 (1988): 74–86. Good introductions to Acadian society include Naomi Griffiths' *The Acadians: Creation of a People* (Toronto: McGraw-Hill Ryerson, 1973) and her more recent book, *The Contexts of Acadian History, 1686–1784* (Montreal and Kingston: McGill-Queen's University Press, 1992); J.B. Brebner's earlier *New England's Outpost: Acadia before the British Conquest of Canada* (New York: Columbia University Press, 1927); and Andrew H. Clark's *Acadia: The Geography of Early Nova Scotia to 1760* (Madison: University of Wisconsin Press, 1968). For an award-winning account of life at Louisbourg, consult Christopher Moore's *Louisbourg Portraits: Five Dramatic True*

Tales of People Who Lived in an Eighteenth Century Garrison Town (Toronto: Macmillan, 1982). Terry Crowley provides a short history of this important port in *Louisbourg: Atlantic Fortress and Seaport*, Canadian Historical Association, Historical Booklet no. 48 (Ottawa: CHA, 1990). Valuable maps of early Atlantic Canada appear in the *Historical Atlas of Canada*, vol. 1, *From the Beginning to 1800*, ed. R. Cole Harris (Toronto: University of Toronto Press, 1987).

The Nature and the Framework of Newfoundland History

KEITH MATTHEWS

The Nature of Newfoundland History

137

The basic factor in Newfoundland history is that which underlies many events in modern times — the expansion of Western Europe, which in the fifteenth century began to emerge from self-containment and comparative isolation to seek out and eventually to dominate vast areas in other parts of the world. This expansion took the form of overseas commerce and the establishment of colonies beyond the seas. From the very earliest days the Newfoundland fishery formed an important element in the development of European trans-oceanic commerce, and while the establishment of a settlement upon the Island occurred comparatively late when compared with those of the Spanish and Portuguese in South America, it was one of the first settlements to be attempted by the English who eventually possessed Newfoundland. Even more, it was through the "migratory" fishery wherein men from the west of England came annually to fish here that the English first acquired the seamanship interest in and knowledge of the North American world which enabled them to develop what eventually became a world-wide empire.

This brings us to a seeming paradox. This was the first part of North America to be visited by Englishmen and amongst the first areas to receive English settlers, and yet the Island's economic, social, and political development was painfully slow when compared to the West Indian colonies, or the thirteen British colonies in what is now the United States of America. This is one of the greatest puzzles of Newfoundland history, and in the lectures following we will try to find answers to it. We know that Newfoundland was not neglected because it was thought unimportant, for the Newfoundland fishery, the Grand Cod Fishery of the Universe as Pitt the Elder described it, was considered to be one of the

From *Lectures on the History of Newfoundland: 1500–1830*, Newfoundland History Series, vol. 4 (St. John's: Breakwater Press, 1988). Copyright © M. Kathleen Matthews. Reprinted with permission.

most important foreign trades carried on from Western Europe. As early as 1620 it was said that without Newfoundland dried cod, Spain and Italy could hardly live, while France and England quarrelled, competed, and often fought over the right to control the fishery. If one thinks of the importance of the Grand Bank fishery to the fleets of many nations today, it is hardly surprising that ever since the discovery of the New World, it has been eagerly sought after by Europeans.

We can say therefore that the history of Newfoundland has been shaped by its fishery and by the international competition which arose around it.

The fishery alone attracted men to Newfoundland and in the competition for the fishery, the Island fell almost as a by-product into the hands of the English who won the struggle. The old west country fishermen of the seventeenth century had a rhyme; "If it were not for wood, water, and fish, Newfoundland were not worth a rush," and for the fishermen and for the nations they came from, that saying expressed almost all that was valued here. As can be seen today, the fishery could be carried on without necessarily occupying the land, but if you wanted to make the light salted "shore" fish for which Newfoundland became famous, then you needed "fishing rooms" in the harbours along the coast, and the first struggles over the Island, as distinct from the fishery, occurred as men quarrelled about who should take possession of the best fishing rooms. Yet the fact remained, the hopes and dreams of the first settlers notwithstanding, Newfoundland was valued only as a fishery and the Island as a great ship moored near the banks.

We know that the English won control over the Island of Newfoundland, but we should not assume that this was inevitable. Indeed until the last twenty years of the sixteenth century, her fishery at Newfoundland was puny when compared to that of France, Spain, or even Portugal. Why then did she emerge as the dominant nation? We will discuss this question quite often during the course of the series.

Newfoundland depended upon the fishery for its very life and that was established long before the first settlers came out to plant. The international fishery had developed its own rough laws and customs which took no account of the possibility of permanent settlement. In the rest of the New World, European settlers came out to virgin territory, unpopulated and unvisited by other Europeans, so that, able to ignore the native peoples as savages, they could do what they pleased. This was not true of Newfoundland for the first English settlers arrived to find thousands of English fishermen and many more of France, Portugal, and Spain who also claimed the right to use the Island for making fish. England claimed to own Newfoundland but France also laid claim to it and Spain could at least claim that she had anciently used the land for her fishing. Thus from the outset, colonisation in Newfoundland was radically different from that of the rest of the New World. Four nations claimed rights, thousands of men from different countries were established here, and settlement had to take account of this.

The experiences of the first settlers soon showed that they, as much as the visiting fishermen, must go a-fishing if they wanted to make a living for the land was infertile and our mining industry did not develop until the nineteenth century. Thus the settlers became completely dependent upon an uncertain industry which not even the merchants who bought their fish could control, for the fish had to be sold in foreign countries in Southern Europe. Unlike the settlers of the English mainland colonies, those in Newfoundland could not even hope to become self-sufficient, for the infertility of the soil, the shortness of the growing season, and (until the mid-eighteenth century) the lack of a hardy crop like the potato meant that almost all of the food they consumed had to be imported from abroad. If you kept a cow here in the seventeenth century, you might have to import hay from Boston to keep it alive during the winter. The fishing season lasted only during the summer, so that a settler had to make enough money in three or four months to buy all that he needed to live for twelve, and almost everything that he ate, wore, or used had to be imported and paid for with fish. It was a hard life and not many people wanted to emigrate here. However, for anyone who knew how to fish, a good living could be made, so that most of the early settlers were men from the west of England who, bred up to the trade by coming here annually to fish, decided for various reasons to settle down for a while at least and try the life of a "planter."

139

The origins of these early colonists made Newfoundland rather different from the English mainland colonies. There, men had come out from many different regions of Europe and for many different reasons, but most of them expected to "make a new life" and to leave the Old World behind forever. Those who came to Newfoundland, however, came out to fish and having relatives and friends back in the west of England (or later in Southern Ireland), could always return to their homes on a fishing ship anytime they wanted to. Many of our settlers were indeed indentured servants hired to come out and work here for two or three years before returning to Britain. This was in marked contrast to the rest of North America.

By 1800 the mainland colonies contained settlers from many different regions of Europe for the need to develop the land created a great demand for labour and called for skills which were widespread through much of Western Europe. In Newfoundland the demand was for skilled fishermen only — no one came to Newfoundland to go farming, and commerce and industry were only just beginning to develop. Only the French and the English knew anything about fishing in Newfoundland, and the French, after 1713, were not allowed to live here. This left the English and Irish as the only possible colonisers of our Province. In England, only the people living in the "West Country" counties of Devonshire,

Dorset, Somerset, and Hampshire knew anything about the fishery, and most of the Irishmen came out via Waterford and Cork; two ports on the south coast of Ireland which had much contact with Newfoundland. They were drawn mainly from four counties around those cities. Thus our population was remarkably homogeneous compared with North America as a whole, and of course it has largely remained so.

The fishery first drew men to Newfoundland; the fishery shaped the policies of the nations concerned in it; the fishery both created and limited the way of life of the colonists; and the fishery, through its fluctuating prosperity, its assumed value to Europe, and the conflicts it caused, determined when, where, in what numbers, and under what conditions the colonists should settle. By 1670 English settlement in Newfoundland had become firmly established, but England did not possess the entire Island. France had established settlements in Placentia Bay and at St. Mary's, and she and the Spanish monopolised the fishery north of Bonavista Bay. The English fishery in Newfoundland was confined to what is in some places still referred to as the "Old English Shore," a region stretching from Trepassey to Greenspond. Only in this area could English colonists find protection and here English settlement was confined until 1713. This was not a great handicap at the time for the area contained excellent fishing grounds and harbours for shipping and for making fish, but as the first region of English settlement, it continued to be the major region of population on the Island until the present century and contains the oldest settler families here. Expansion of settlement to the rest of Newfoundland had to await the evacuation of other nations and a growth in the population and fishery of Newfoundland which would make men want to exploit the other fishing areas, while the development of inland communities had to await this present century, for the population lived only by fishing. As a result, Newfoundland lacked a natural "centre" which could link together the many communities and regions into one whole "community." All communications were by sea, and each bay had its own major commercial centres which were independent of the others, importing and exporting goods and people directly from and to the outside world. The towns of the west of England which controlled the fishery at Newfoundland "divided up" the English shore, with particular parts of the west of England fishing only along particular parts of the Newfoundland coast. Thus the settlers who came to the various communities and bays chose their place of residence from the ports which their ship came to. Since the merchants of Poole, for example, controlled all the trade of Trinity and Bonavista bays, most of the English settlers there came from the counties of Dorset, Hampshire, and Somerset. The "Southern Shore" from Torbay to Trepassey was fished by the fishermen and merchants of South Devon, so that most of the English settlers there came from the same region. It might be said that until the nineteenth century there was no "community" of Newfoundland, but a series of separate cultural and economic bays independent of and relatively indifferent to each other. This feeling exists even today in some forms. Only with the rise of St. John's as the commercial and political capital of the Island did the feeling of distinctness and independence between the bays begin to decline, and this did not begin to happen until late in the eighteenth century.

These are some of the themes in Newfoundland history. Beginning as an international fishery, the Island became a largely British fishery carried on by a mixture of settlers and visiting fishermen, then an English colony, and finally a distinctive "community" with an identity and culture of its own.

The Framework of Newfoundland History

In the last lecture I mentioned that the main theme of our history was the manner in which Newfoundland changed from an international fishery to a largely British fishery and finally to a distinctive community on its own. This change took over 300 years and was caused by the ever changing pressures of events and the decisions and conflicts of men. To enable you to understand how these changes occurred I am devoting this lecture to a breakdown of that long period of time into seven distinct periods. With this chronology in mind the lectures which follow can be more easily understood.

The first period we will call the period of anarchy. It begins with the rediscovery of the Island by Europeans in the fifteenth century and ends in 1610 with the establishment of an English colony in Newfoundland. John Cabot claimed the Island for England by right of discovery, but this meant little, for England at this time was weak and backward, her naval and commercial strength were undeveloped and she was absorbed in the aftermath of the Wars of the Roses. Although English fishermen soon followed Cabot, they were few in number and the French and Portuguese nations soon outstripped the English in the Newfoundland fishery. By 1640 Spain, with her enormous wealth and power, had also become important in the fishery and all nations were soon competing to develop their interests at the expense of their neighbours. In Europe the shifting alliances of nations saw many wars and the fighting inevitably spread to the Newfoundland fishing fleets. Obsessed with these conflicts no nation attempted to establish a colony on the Island, although in the second half of the sixteenth century individuals in both France and England began to think of doing so. While Europe quarrelled, the international fishery in Newfoundland grew chaotically with no one to keep the peace either between the national groups or even within them. To solve this problem the fishermen gradually evolved a code of customs which, unrecognised by any government, at least attempted to control

141

the anarchy and violence amongst the fishing fleets. As late as 1570 the English still lagged far behind their competitors in the size of their fishery, yet the complex changes which occurred in Western Europe between then and 1600 created conditions in the Newfoundland trade which by 1700 had made England equal in importance to France while the fisheries of Spain and Portugal were in irreversible decline.

The next period in Newfoundland's history lasted between 1610 and 1660 and may be called the era of English settlement. With the end of the European conflict in 1604 nations turned to trade and colonisation, and both the French and English fisheries prospered well. By 1620 a de facto division of the land was taking place, each nation gradually confining its fishing operations to separate parts of the coast. The English fished along what became known as the "Old English Shore" stretching from Trepassey to Greenspond, while the French used the south coast and the area North of Bonavista Bay. This process was not the result of any international agreement and occurred only gradually and for a time; the Spanish and Portuguese continued to fish wherever they could find harbour room. England laid claim to most of Newfoundland but France too claimed sovereignty, and in practice each contented itself with what it could control. The English domination of the Avalon Peninsula turned men's thoughts towards the possibility of establishing colonies here which, paying their way by fishing, logging, agriculture, mining and even manufacturing, might become profitable to their promoters and help to secure the fishery for England. However, repeated attempts ended in failure for the settlements could not be made to return a profit. There was also conflict between the proprietors of some colonies and the already established English migratory fishery. The English Civil War brought chaos and ruin to the fishery, but although the Proprietary Colonies failed, groups of settlers had become firmly established on the Island.

The third period lasted from 1660 to 1713 and was the period of Anglo-French rivalry within the Island itself. Until 1659 France claimed sovereignty over parts of Newfoundland but, developing her colonies on the mainland and in the West Indies, did not formally plant here. In 1662 however she established a settlement in her main fishing area at Placentia and for a few years energetically promoted schemes to increase settlement. Simultaneously, the end of war in Europe saw a great revival in the French fishery which by 1675 was seriously affecting the fortunes of that of the English. The latter were in a state of decline, for the long wars and a series of disastrous fishing seasons in the 1660s had ruined the west of England merchants and captains. The old methods of fishing no longer sufficed and new ones were required. Both the settlers and visiting fishermen were ruined by the declining fishery and the latter attempted to have the settlers removed. The British government alone could decide upon this, and at first they agreed that settlement should

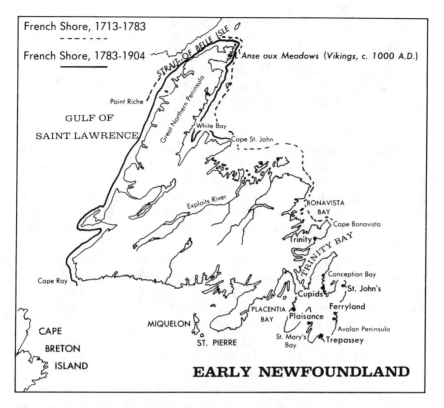

French Shore, 1713-1783

French Shore, 1783-1904

STRAIT OF BELLE ISLE

Point Riche

GULF OF
SAINT LAWRENCE

Great Northern Peninsula

White Bay

Cape St. John

L'Anse aux Meadows (Vikings, c. 1000 A.D.)

Exploits River

BONAVISTA
BAY

Cape Bonavista

Trinity

TRINITY BAY

Cape Ray

Conception Bay

Cupids

St. John's

Ferryland

PLACENTIA
BAY

MIQUELON

Plaisance

Avalon Peninsula

CAPE

BRETON

ISLAND

ST. PIERRE

St. Mary's
Bay

Trepassey

EARLY NEWFOUNDLAND

143

Adapted from Paul Cornell, Jean Hamelin, Fernand Ouellet, and Marcel Trudel, eds., *Canada: Unity in Diversity* (Toronto: Holt, Rinehart and Winston, 1967), 111.

be ended. However, they quickly changed their mind, but were unable to decide whether the Island should be formally recognised as a colony. For twenty years after 1680 the government followed a policy of having no policy and the Island was left to develop as best it could. In 1689 King William's War broke out and with an intermission between 1697 and 1701 the conflict lasted until 1713. The fighting both here and in Europe had drastic effects upon Newfoundland, and the government was forced to formulate some kind of policy towards her. That policy was unworkable, but the war obscured this to some degree. In 1713 by the Treaty of Utrecht France ceded her colony on the south coast to England and admitted English sovereignty over the entire Island. However, she obtained certain fishing rights along parts of the coast, and the "French shore" problem began its wearying course. The war had also obscured fundamental changes within the fishery which were changing the old division between "settlers" and "migratory" fishermen, bringing them together under the west country merchants.

Newfoundland underwent a new series of adaptations in what I will call the era of integration within the English fishery between 1713 and 1763. English settlement expanded into the south coast and as far up as Fogo and Twillingate. The fishery continued to be poor until the late 1720s but the need for men to move into the newly ceded south coast resulted in the beginnings of large-scale Irish emigration to Newfoundland, with enormous effects upon its future history. Men found that the attempt to divide the Island into an area monopolised by the English and another shared between them and the French created much friction, but the French had lost their best fishing grounds, their competition in Europe gradually diminished and from 1730 onwards the English fishery began to prosper well. The English soon developed a thriving bank fishery which together with the bye boat keepers formed the backbone of the migratory English fishery, causing not only its revival but a steady expansion by 1750.

It was an era when the merchants of London withdrew from the fishery, which was now almost monopolised by merchants and fishermen of the west of England. After 1748 the population began to rise steadily and during the Seven Years' War (1756–1763) English fishermen for the first time learned of the rich fishing grounds along the Northern Peninsula and even more important on the Labrador. The British government was forced by increasing population to introduce a rudimentary civil government, and there was an end to discord between the settlers and the visiting fishermen. The Seven Years' War resulted in the English conquest of Canada and laid the conditions for an even larger expansion in Newfoundland after 1763.

Period five was short, lasting only from 1763 until 1775, when the outbreak of the American Revolution portended great changes for Newfoundland. However, it was a period of great prosperity and growth both in settlement and in the fortunes of the fishery. The Treaty of Paris in 1763, amongst other things, ceded the French possessions in Canada to Britain, and the English government decided to attach Labrador and the Magdalen Islands to Newfoundland. Thus began the Labrador fishery. In Europe the markets for Newfoundland fish continued to grow and for almost the entire period the fishery proved unusually successful. This created a great demand for ships, seamen, and fishermen, so that both the migratory and the sedentary fishery grew quickly and the population rose. However, after a long period of neglect the British government again looked at the question of how Newfoundland should be governed. Their first thought was to create a formal colony, but a change of government and the advent of Governor Palliser caused an abrupt change of mind. Alarmed by the growth of settlement the government sought to discourage it and to promote the migratory fishery. This policy was first adapted for the new fishery at Labrador, where it failed. The government persisted and in 1775 Palliser's Act was passed. It signalled a renewal of official hostility towards the settlers, but was viewed with intense hostility by the merchants, and the outbreak of the American Revolution delayed its enforcement.

The sixth period lasted from the beginning of the American Revolution in 1775 to the outbreak of the French Revolutionary Wars in 1793. Before 1775 America had been a great competitor to Newfoundland in the fishery, but it had also become almost the only supplier of shipping, foodstuffs, and rum, without which the settlers could not live. The outbreak of war abruptly severed the supply routes between America and Newfoundland and caused great but temporary problems. The war itself had great effects on the fishery but even more important was the result. American independence took the United States out of the British Empire and her vessels could no longer bring supplies. Neither could fishermen and merchants buy American shipping and America could no longer supply the British West Indies with fish. In the years before 1775 anyone who wanted to leave Newfoundland during a time of depression could easily find a ship to take him to Boston. Now this was no longer possible and he would be forced to remain on the Island if he could not return to England or Ireland. The supply links with the American colonies were slowly replaced by links with the Maritimes of Canada and with Quebec. Newfoundland built its own ships and took over the West Indian markets for fish. From 1783 to 1789 there was a great post-war boom in the fishery, which again caused a rapid increase in settlement. In 1789 the boom collapsed, but the population did not decline greatly, as had been the case in past depressions. The migratory fishery began to decline and by 1793 it was becoming clear that Newfoundland now had a population which was too large to be moved, which could not even be discouraged from growing, and which was in desperate need of better government and laws. The British government was forced to abandon its policy of discouraging settlement and the future of the Island was assured.

Our last period commences with the outbreak of war in 1793 and lasts until 1832. It may be called the "era of Newfoundland's emergence as an independent community." The long and difficult wars killed the migratory fishery and made all dependent upon the resident fishermen. Until 1810 it was difficult to obtain labour from England or Ireland, but natural increase amongst the Newfoundland population kept it growing and restricted wartime markets meant that no more labour was required. From 1811 to 1815 the gradual re-opening of the European markets together with the temporary extinction of every fishing competitor with the exception of Canada created one of the greatest booms that Newfoundland had ever known. In response thousands of men poured into Newfoundland, especially from Southern Ireland. The Labrador seal and cod fisheries gave additional sources of employment, and there was a great boom in shipbuilding for the Labrador and the coastal trades. St. John's became truly the capital of Newfoundland, and the growth of a large, more or less resident middle class led to the development of social and political consciousness, which led to the formation of groups and institutions devoted to charitable, social, and eventually political ends. This middle class became the ruling elite of the Island and took the lead in the definition of a distinct Newfoundland consciousness, first expressed in the desire for internal self-government.

The People of Eighteenth-Century Louisbourg

A.J.B. JOHNSTON

One of the truisms about history — that is, history as the study of the past — is that it always reflects the present. Whatever interests a given society at a fixed point in time — be it a constitutional, religious, social, or political question — there are usually historians around who can find some precedent or background information to shed light on the particular question. Thus, in recent decades, to cite just one example, we have witnessed the birth and growth of the field of women's history, as a direct response to the feminist movement.

Today, as we move into the 1990s, one of the questions facing Canadian society is the ethnic composition of the nation. With each passing year, the country moves further and further away from a vision of itself as simply an English–French duality. Accordingly, historians now find themselves going back to examine 200- and 300-year-old documents to determine just how diverse the country's population might have been in previous eras. Some of their findings will come as a surprise to more than a few readers.

For instance, how many Nova Scotians know that there was a Black man, possibly Mathieu da Costa, serving as a translator, travelling with the Sieur de Monts and Samuel de Champlain on their voyages along the Atlantic coast back in 1604–05? And how many ever learned that there were perhaps as many as 5,000 Blacks among the Loyalists who came to Nova Scotia after the American Revolution? Or that in 1788 there were approximately 200 "robust able black men" — slaves from Bermuda — working as fishermen on the Grand Banks?[1] What other ethnic "surprises" are there in our history from other parts of the region?

The time and place in Nova Scotian history that we focus on in this article is that of Louisbourg during the period 1713–58, when the fishing port and strategic stronghold was a major French colonial set-

From *Nova Scotia Historical Review* 11, 2 (December 1991): 75–86. Reprinted with the permission of the Public Archives of Nova Scotia.

tlement in North America. The question we ask is simply the following: Who were the people of eighteenth-century Louisbourg?

The short answer — they were French, Roman Catholic, and worked in the fishery or trade, or served in the military or laboured in someone's kitchen — has long been sufficient. In light of the detailed questions people are now asking about ethnic origin and related matters, however, it is time for a more in-depth response. The intention of this article is to provide information on the following: (1) Louisbourg's population and gender ratio; (2) the origins of its inhabitants; (3) the religions they professed; and (4) the languages they spoke.

Throughout Louisbourg's forty-five-year history, there was always an imbalance between the sexes, with males greatly outnumbering females. This is as one would expect, for Louisbourg began as a pioneer settlement — typically with few women — and then developed into a garrison town and busy seaport, both of which functions called for large numbers of unmarried men: "In the 1720s, adult males outnumbered adult females eight or ten to one. The gap decreased somewhat as the years went by, but even leaving out the military population, the ratio of adult males to females was never lower than three to one."[2] One of the effects of this imbalance in the sexes was that Louisbourg brides married younger (average age at time of first marriage was 19.9 years) and men older (average age was 29.2 years) than was the case elsewhere in New France. In Canada, the eighteenth-century name for the French settlements along the St. Lawrence River, the average ages for first-time brides and grooms were 22.0 and 27.7, respectively.[3]

147

As for actual population totals, Table 1 summarizes some of the available data.

TABLE 1   Population of Louisbourg, Selected Years

	1720	1724	1737	1752
Men (heads of household)	69	113	163	274
Fishermen	372	377	250	674
Servants (men and women)	—	—	229	—
domestiques (males)	—	—	—	366
servantes (females)	—	—	—	71
Women (heads/wives)	50	84	157	299
Children	142	239	664	776
Habitants newly arrived	—	—	—	200
Households of governor and *commissaire-ordonnateur*	—	—	—	30
Civilian Total	**633**	**813**	**1,463**	**2,690**
Soldiers	317	430	543	1,250
Total Population	**950**	**1,243**	**2,006**	**3,940**

Source: Archives Nationales (Paris), Outre Mer, G1, 467 (1720), part 3A; ibid., 466, pièce 67 (1724); ibid., no. 71 suite (1737); Archives du Séminaire de Québec, Poly 55-49 (1752). J.S. McLennan, *Louisbourg from Its Foundation to Its Fall, 1713-1758* (London, 1918), 371, also provides population totals.

There is no single document that describes where the people of Louisbourg came from. There are many census returns, but only three of them list places of origin, and even then the birthplace is given only for those individuals who are identified as *habitants*, or heads of household. No such information is provided on the origins of the vast majority of the population: the hundreds of servants, fishermen, and soldiers. Nor does the census data tell us about the birthplace of wives. Widows and single women who were heads of household are identified, but not ordinary married women.

The first Louisbourg census to include a "Place of Birth" column was that of 1724.[4] In that year, the census-takers recorded that the town had a permanent civilian population of 813 persons. Of that total, 113 were identified by name and place of origin. On the census of 1726, Louisbourg's civilian population was given as 963, of which 153 were listed as *habitants* with an identifiable place of origin.[5] Eleven years later, in 1737, the town's population had grown to 1,463, of whom 163 were listed by name.[6] What the town's population was during the 1740s is not known, but it was probably around 2,000 civilian men, women, and children. That estimate is roughly half way between the recorded population of 1,463 for the year 1737 and the total of 2,690 for the year 1752.[7] Keep in mind, however, that none of these figures includes totals for the garrison, or for fishermen and others who might have been in town only on a seasonal basis.

In spite of their limitations, three Louisbourg census returns — 1724, 1726, and 1734 — are of interest in that they provide data on the origins of the town's principal inhabitants during one ten-year period. In particular, the data underline that, as Louisbourg steadily grew over that decade, it attracted fishing proprietors, merchants, artisans, cabaret owners, and so on, from a wide variety of regions in France, from New France, and even from foreign countries.

Though the graphs of Figure 1 are largely self-explanatory, there are a few points worth making about the data they summarize. First, nearly everyone within the "Southwest France" category came from the largely Basque, coastal region near the Spanish border. These individuals tended to be from Saint-Jean-de-Luz, Hendaye, Bayonne, and Bidart. Second, about half of the people from "Midwest France" were from major urban centres such as Bordeaux, Nates, La Rochelle, and Rochefort. The rest were from smaller towns and villages in Poitou and in the Saintonge, Armagnac, and Perigord regions. Third — not surprisingly — nearly everyone in the "Île de France" category came from Paris. Fourth, almost everyone from "Normandy/Brittany" was from a coastal settlement; Saint-Malo was the predominant place of origin.

Fifth, within the "New France" category, in 1734 there were ten heads of household in Louisbourg who had been born in Acadia: eight from Placentia, and two born on Île Royale itself. Sixth, the "Other

FIGURE 1 Places of Origin of Louisbourg's *Habitants*, 1724, 1726, and 1734

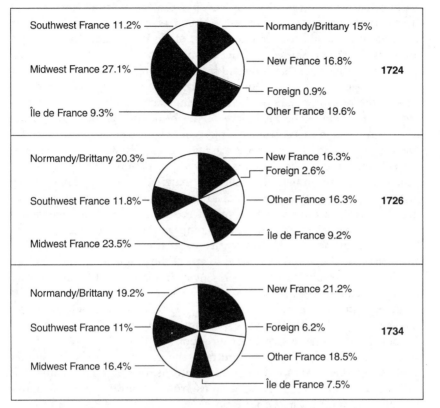

Source: Archives Nationales (Paris), Outre Mer, G1, 466, pièce 67 (1724); ibid., 466, pièce 67, Recensement . . . 1924; ibid., pièce 68, Recensement . . . 1726; Barbara Schmeisser, *The Population of Louisbourg, 1713-1758*, Manuscript Report no. 303 (Ottawa, 1976).

France" category included individuals from all over the rest of France, from Picardy to Lyon and from Toulon to Champagne. One town that stood out, on each of the three census returns, was Limoges; there were never any fewer than six *habitants* in Louisbourg who hailed originally from that city. Last, the "Foreign" category in 1734 included three people from Switzerland and two each from Belgium, Flanders, and German states. It is important to remember, however, that this list of "foreigners" was only for individuals who were heads of household; there were many other outsiders serving as soldiers, working as servants, or employed in some other capacity.

Keeping in mind that the three census documents analysed above reveal the birthplaces of members of the *habitants* category only, it is important to use other sources to obtain an image of the rest of the Louisbourg population. On a 1752 listing of 199 ordinary fishermen in Île

Royale, 48.7 per cent of the *pêcheurs* came from the southwest (largely Basque) corner of France, while 37.6 per cent were from Norman and Breton ports along the Gulf of Saint-Malo.[8] If one can assume that these two relatively small areas produced most of Île Royale and Louisbourg's ordinary fishermen throughout the colony's history, then we get a quite different picture than that provided by the *habitants* on the census.

Marriage records are another source that must be considered. As part of the priest's notations accompanying each wedding entry, he was required to include the birthplace of the bride and groom. One virtue of such records is that a woman's place of origin is not subsumed under her husband's, as is usually the case in an eighteenth-century census. A weakness, on the other hand, is that wedding data reveal nothing about people who were unmarried or already married when they came to live in Louisbourg. Another flaw is that a roll-up of marriage data over several decades does not offer a "snapshot" of the town at any particular point in time. Nonetheless, it is useful to compare the origins of Louisbourg brides and grooms with the census data already presented. Barbara Schmeisser's tabulations were used to create the graphs in Figure 2.

The two graphs for brides present a dramatically different picture from that obtained from the census data concerning Louisbourg's heads of households (compare with Figure 1). Unlike the men of the town, the women of Louisbourg were predominantly from the New World. Demographic pressures led most girls born in the colony to wed while still in their teens. By way of contrast, the grooms' graphs are similar to those for the *habitants* of the census returns, one exception being that there is a lower percentage of grooms from "Midwest France" and a higher percentage from "Other France."

The evidence examined thus far gives us the following picture of eighteenth-century Louisbourg: the ordinary fishermen were overwhelmingly from the Norman/Breton coastline along the Gulf of Saint-Malo and the Basque region of southwest France; about 80 per cent of the household heads were from France (see graphs for details); and a clear majority of the brides were colonial-born (Placentia, Canada, Acadia, or Île Royale).

A close look at all available parish records (marriages, baptisms, and burials) for the periods 1722–45 and 1749–58 yields further insight into the origins and ethnic background of Louisbourg's civilian population. The limitation with parish records as a source is their "hit-or-miss" quality. Practising Roman Catholics who married, had a child baptized, or died while at Louisbourg are mentioned in this source, but there is no way of knowing how many other inhabitants or transients went unrecorded. Nonetheless, the parish records do provide us with an indication of the minimum number of individuals in Louisbourg from non-French backgrounds.

There are, for instance, references to a handful of Protestants from English, Irish, or Scottish backgrounds who converted to Catholicism

FIGURE 2 Places of Origin of Louisbourg's Brides and Grooms, 1722–45 and 1749–58

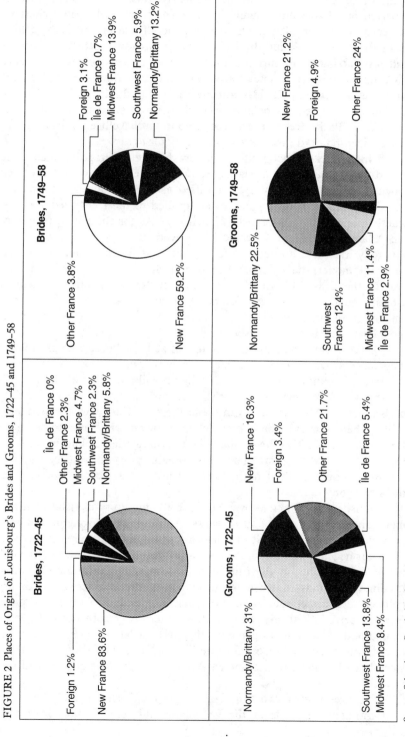

Source: Schmeisser, *Population of Louisbourg*.

while in the capital of Île Royale. Similarly, there is also mention, over a period of decades and usually in the form of an adolescent's baptism, of nearly two dozen Blacks. These were generally slaves sent to the colony from the Antilles. Adult Blacks who were already practising Catholics had less likelihood to turn up in the parish records, unless they gave birth or married. It is noteworthy, however, that there were a few free Blacks in Louisbourg, at least during the 1750s. In 1753, Jean-Baptiste Cupidon purchased his beloved's freedom in order to marry her.[9] The number of Blacks, freed or enslaved, who might have been in Louisbourg at any fixed point in time, however, is difficult to say.

While Blacks predominated, a few North American Indians also ended up in Louisbourg as slaves. Some of these may have actually been Pawnee Indians, for they are identified as "Panis" in the documents, but then again that term came to be applied to most enslaved Indians, whether or not they were really Pawnees.[10] As for the native people of the Atlantic region, the Micmacs, they were rarely seen in town. They generally lived and hunted in the southern part of the island, in the vicinity of modern-day Chapel Island and St. Peters, as well as inland around the Bras d'Or Lakes. Nonetheless, "the occasional baptism of a native child, the entry into domestic service of a young Micmac girl, and the infrequent visits of their scouts or chiefs" testifies that Micmacs did sometimes come to Louisbourg.[11]

Of the various non-French minorities at Louisbourg, the group that may have proved the most compatible with the French was probably the Irish Catholics. They had both religion and a distrust of the English in common. Some forty to fifty Irish surnames turn up in the Louisbourg parish records. Most were servants, but there were a few with craftsmen's skills. There was even an occasional Irish priest who came to serve on Île Royale. In 1750, no fewer than eight Irish families sailing from Newfoundland to Halifax jumped ship and sought refuge in Louisbourg. The freedom to practise their faith, Roman Catholicism, seems to have been the attraction.[12]

Louisbourg, of course, was not just a community of fishermen and merchants, tradespeople and servants. As a fortified stronghold and an important garrison town, it also had a sizeable military population. Soldiers formed anywhere from one-quarter to one-half of the total population, depending on the time period examined. Unfortunately, when it comes to origins, it is usually difficult to ascertain where the ordinary enlisted men came from, other than that they were recruited in France. For the period 1720–45, years in which there may have been well over a thousand soldiers in Louisbourg, historian Allan Greer has been able to determine the birthplaces for only seventy-five.[13] Of those, only three were born outside France: one in Acadia, one in Switzerland, and one in Ireland.

The presence of two "foreigners" — the Irishman and the Swiss — fighting on the side of the French should come as no surprise. It was common in the eighteenth century for armies to recruit and accept troops from wherever they could get them, provided they met certain height and health standards. There were many Irishmen and Scots in French regiments, and even more Germans in British ones. The word "mercenary" was then a descriptive term, not a pejorative one.

One foreign mercenary regiment even found itself at Louisbourg. This was the Swiss-based Karrer Regiment, which served in the fortress between 1722 and 1745. With up to as many as 150 men, or about 20 per cent of the entire garrison at that time,[14] the Karrer troops were known collectively as *les Suisses*, though many, perhaps even a majority, were actually from German-speaking areas outside Switzerland. Many, if not most, were also Protestant. This made for an interesting irony: here was Louisbourg — a French Catholic stronghold — defended in part by a good many German and Swiss Protestants.[15]

The Karrer Regiment did not return to Louisbourg in 1749, when Île Royale reverted to French jurisdiction according to the terms of the Treaty of Aix-la-Chapelle (1748). Yet that did not mean there were no more non-French soldiers in the town. According to a detailed troop roll drawn up in 1752 that listed the approximately one thousand Compagnies Franches soldiers in the garrison at that time,[16] there were fifty-three foreigners serving in the garrison, or about 5 per cent of the total military population. The origin of those men was as follows:

Spanish	21	Savoyard	3
Catalan	1	Saxon	12
Portuguese	1	Italian	1
German	7	Piedmontese	2
Prussian	2	Neapolitan	1
Austrian	2	Genoese	1
Brabant	3	Hungarian	1
Flemish	1	Luxemburger	1
Dutch	1	Berber	1
Swiss	1	Irish	1

The Spaniards would seem to have been numerous enough to form something of a sub-culture within the garrison. Similarly, the different Germanic-speaking individuals may also have used their language among themselves and similarly kept alive other aspects of their original culture.

The impression of Louisbourg's military population would therefore be the following: it was always predominantly French-born, but in the period up to 1745 there was a large Swiss and German minority, as high as about 20 per cent. During the early 1750s, there was still a 5 per cent scattering of non-French soldiers.

There is no doubt that Louisbourg was officially and overwhelmingly Roman Catholic. Overwhelmingly, because the vast majority of the town's inhabitants were of that persuasion. Officially, because the context of the time was one in which the French state lent its full support to its national church (known as the Gallican Church), just as the church gave the same support back to the monarchy. The king named all French bishops, including the one for New France, paid their salaries, and had them take an oath of loyalty. The only religious ceremonies and celebrations that were permitted to be held in public were those associated with Roman Catholicism. Furthermore, only practising Catholics could hold public posts. The partnership between church and state has been succinctly expressed by historian Guy Frégault: "The men of the State were Catholics, the men of the Church served the State."[17]

While most of Louisbourg was thus Roman Catholic — nominally if not devoutly — there were exceptions. Most noticeably, there were the German and Swiss soldiers of the Karrer Regiment. We have no way of knowing exactly how many of these were Protestants, but there were enough to cause occasional difficulties within a town that was supposed to be exclusively Catholic: "In 1724, Governor Saint-Ovide warned the minister of marine that France's Micmac allies regarded the Protestant troops 'as suspects.' Three years later, the governor complained that the Karrer officers refused to lead their soldiers in the Fête-Dieu (Corpus Christi) procession in the town.[18]

There were a few other Protestants in Louisbourg as well, beside the soldiers in the Karrer Regiment. The names of several individuals originally from England, Scotland, or New England turn up in baptismal records when they converted to Catholicism. There is even a reference to a Jewish conversion.[19]

Aside from French, which was obviously the dominant language, Basque, Breton, German, Swiss German, Spanish, English, and perhaps Irish, Provençal, and occasionally Micmac were sometimes spoken in Louisbourg.[20] There were also a few people, notably the foreign-born soldiers listed above, who on occasion might have spoken Dutch, Italian, and Portuguese.

The largest single non-French-language community consisted of the several hundred fishermen and few merchants who spoke Basque. The Récollet priests who served the parish were repeatedly asked to bring over a Basque-speaking priest from southwest France, but this they never did.[21] When unilingual Basques had to give evidence in court cases, interpreters were used to translate their testimony.

How many of the people from Brittany spoke Breton, a Celtic language said to be more akin to Welsh than to any other, is unknown, because there is no record of Bretons demanding to have their language spoken. This is likely because most of them spoke French in addition to Breton, and also because the parish priests were all initially from Brittany, and some of them at least would have been able to speak their ancient Celtic tongue.

The German- and Swiss German–language communities were comprised of soldiers and, in some cases, their wives. German-speakers were most numerous during the 1740s, when the Karrer Regiment was present. While much smaller, there continued to be a German presence on the island in the 1750s, even after the departure of the Karrer Regiment. This presence was localized in the Village des Allemands, established on the Mira River in the 1750s. Its inhabitants were mostly German Catholics who had abandoned the new settlement at Lunenburg on mainland Nova Scotia.[22]

In conclusion, the people of Louisbourg, aside from being predominantly French and Roman Catholic, were a mix of men, women, and children, with males largely outnumbering females. There were a few hundred Basques and Germans, a few dozen Blacks and Irish, and a scattering of Spanish, English, and Scottish. There were more than a few Protestants, especially during the 1730s and 1740s, and perhaps even a few Jews. There were many in the fishery who spoke Basque — and perhaps others who used Breton — while in the military there were a lot of German- and Swiss German–speakers in the 1740s. Spanish was probably the most common "second" language in the garrison during the 1750s.

155

All in all, French stronghold that Louisbourg was, the seaport community was also home to a wide range of minority populations. Some differed from the majority in terms of ethnicity, others in terms of religion, and still others in terms of the language they spoke.

NOTES

[1] Hilary Russell, "Opportunities to Introduce the History of People of African Descent at Existing National Historic Sites," unpublished paper, National Historic Sites Directorate (Ottawa, 1990). For details, see Robin Winks, *The Blacks in Canada: A History* (Montreal, 1971) and James W. St. G. Walker, *The Black Loyalists: The Search for a Promised Land in Nova Scotia and Sierra Leone, 1783–1870* (New York, 1976).

[2] A.J.B. Johnston, *Religion in Life at Louisbourg, 1713–1758* (Kingston and Montreal, 1984), 5.

[3] Ibid., 122–44; for figures on other regions in New France, see Hubert Charbonneau, *Vie et mort de nos ancêtres: Étude démographique* (Montreal, 1975), 158–64; Gisa Hynes, "Some Aspects of the Demography of Port Royal, 1650-1755," *Acadiensis* 3, 1 (Autumn 1973): 3–17.

[4] Archives Nationales (Paris), Outre Mer, G1, 466, pièce 67, Recensement . . . 1724.

[5] Ibid., pièce 68, Recensement . . . 1726.

[6] Ibid., pièce 71-suite, "Dénombrement de L'Isle Royalle," 1737.

[7] Barbara Schmeisser, *The Population of Louisbourg, 1713-1758*, Manuscript Report no. 303 (Ottawa, 1976), 10.

[8] B.A. Balcom, *The Cod Fishery of Isle Royale, 1713-1758* (Ottawa, 1984), 55–56; A.J.B. Johnston, "The Fishermen of Eighteenth-Century Cape Breton: Numbers and Origins," *Nova Scotia Historical Review* 9, 1 (1989): 62–72.

[9] A.N., Outre Mer, G3, 2041-suite, pièce 78, 1 mars 1753.

[10] Cornelius J. Jaenen, *Friend and Foe: Aspects of French–Amerindian Cultural Contact in the Sixteenth and Seventeenth Centuries* (Toronto, 1976), 139.

[11] Johnston, *Religion in Life*, 8–9.

[12] Ibid., 8; A.A. MacKenzie, *The Irish in Cape Breton* (Antigonish, 1979).

[13] Allan Greer, "The Soldiers of Isle Royale, 1720-1745," *History and Archaeology*, no. 28 (Ottawa, 1979), 30–31.

[14] Ibid., 13–23; see also Margaret Fortier, "The Ile Royale Garrison, 1713-45," Microfiche Report (Ottawa, 1981).

[15] Johnston, *Religion in Life*, 7–8.

[16] The troop roll in question is the "Signalement général des troupes . . . ," drawn up by Michel Le Courtois de Surlaville: National Archives of Canada, MG 18, F30, Dossier 1.

[17] Guy Frégault, *Le XVIIIe siècle canadien: Études* (Montreal, 1968), 148.

[18] Johnston, *Religion in Life*, 8.

[19] Gaston Du Boscq de Beaumont, ed., *Les derniers jours de l'Acadie (1748-1758): Correspondances et mémoires* (Geneva, 1975), 63.

[20] Christopher Moore, "Harbour Life and Quay Activities," in *Street Life and Public Activities in Louisbourg: Four Studies for Animators*, Manuscript Report no. 317 (Ottawa, 1977).

[21] Johnston, *Religion in Life*, 47–48.

[22] W.P. Bell, *The "Foreign Protestants" and the Settlement of Nova Scotia: The History of a Piece of Arrested British Colonial Policy in the Eighteenth Century* (Toronto, 1961), 375–77.

The Golden Age: Acadian Life, 1713–1748

NAOMI GRIFFITHS

156

Until the 1950s Acadian history was most frequently written either as epic or as case study — as the drama of a people or as an example of the political and diplomatic struggles between great powers. The tragic nature of the deportation in 1755 seemed the obvious and fundamental starting point for all that the Acadians experienced since, and equally the culmination of everything that had occurred in their previous history. In the last thirty years, however, an ever-increasing number of scholarly works have been devoted to the examination of Acadian history from much more complex perspectives. These include attempts to analyze not merely 1755 as an event of major importance in the war between English and French for North America, but also works centred upon Acadian language,[1] folklore,[2] geography,[3] sociology,[4] as well as upon Acadian history as the history of a developing community.

Acadian studies have, in fact, come to an impressive maturity over the past thirty years. This maturity is magnificently documented in the work edited by Jean Daigle, *Les Acadians des Maritimes*, where some twenty scholars present complex essays outlining the problems, the work done, and the work to be done in every area of Acadian studies from history to folklore, from political science to material culture.[5] The result of all this publication is, of course, the temptation, if not the necessity, for present scholars to look at past syntheses of Acadian history, to discover where the new information demands new theories, and to build, if not entirely new interpretations of the Acadian past, at least interpretations which are more richly decorated and more densely structured.

This challenge is as dangerous as it is irresistible, for the amount of material is considerable indeed. As a result, this paper is a cautious

From *Social History* 17, 33 (May 1984): 21–34. Reprinted with permission.

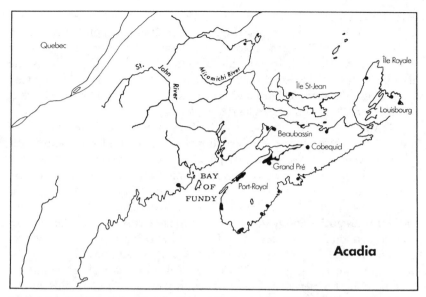

Adapted from Paul Cornell, Jean Hamelin, Fernand Ouellet, and Marcel Trudel, eds., *Canada: Unity in Diversity* (Toronto: Holt, Rinehart and Winston, 1967), 121.

one. Its main aim is to paint Acadian life between 1713 and 1748 in such a way that the reader may sense the complex nature of the Acadian community during these years. This was the period to be remembered by the community in exile after 1755. All those over the age of ten or eleven in 1755 would have had some knowledge of these years. It was the time that would be recalled in exile and the time which would form the basis for the stories of past life as the Acadians once more established themselves in the Maritimes. It spanned the decades from the Treaty of Utrecht to that of Aix-la-Chapelle, during which years the lands on which the Acadians lived turned from being the border between two empires to the frontier between enemies.

The political geography of "Nova Scotia or Acadia," as the lands were called in the contemporary international treaties, had meant turmoil for its inhabitants from the outset of European colonization. As J.B. Brebner wrote, these lands were "the eastern outpost and flank for both French and English in North America." They made, in his words, a "continental cornice." Throughout the seventeenth century this cornice frequently changed hands between English and French. It became a true border, for whatever name it was given and whatever limits were claimed, it lay "inside the angle between the St. Lawrence route to French Canada and the northern route to New England which branched off from it south of Newfoundland."[6] Those who settled there in the seventeenth century would quickly find their situation akin to that of such people as the Basques, caught between France and Spain; the Alsatians, moulded by French and German designs; and those who lived on the borders between England and Scotland or England and Wales.

It was the French who began the first permanent settlement in the area in 1604. Whatever the international designation of the colony over the next century, its non-Indian people would be called the Acadians. While predominantly French-speaking and Catholic, they were nevertheless a people who also absorbed English-speaking migrants such as the Melansons[7] and the Caisseys.[8] They also had a considerable knowledge of the Protestant religion, and it is very probable that some of the families who joined them from near Loudun in the 1630s were of the reform church.[9] By the end of the century the Acadians had known one lengthy and legitimate period of English rule, 1654–1668, as well as a number of much shorter periods of English control as a result of raids out of Massachusetts. By 1700 the Acadians were, as the detailed work of Professors Daigle and Reid has shown,[10] almost as accustomed to dealing with the officials of England as those of France. Thus the defeat of Subercase in 1710 and the subsequent transfer of the colony once more to English control by the treaty of Utrecht was for the Acadians yet one more step in a complicated ritual, an exchange of control over them from France to England, something which had happened before and would most probably be reversed in the not too distant future.

This fundamental belief in the mutability of power, this dominant sense of the probability of alternate French and English control of the colony, became the cornerstone of Acadian politics during the years 1713 to 1748. It was the basis for the Acadian action over requests made by the English officials that they swear an oath of allegiance to the King of England. From the Acadian viewpoint, it would have been folly indeed to engage in any action which would bind them irrevocably to one Great Power when the other was still not only obviously in the neighbourhood, but even more obviously still interested in the future status of the colony and its inhabitants. Thus the Acadians built a policy compounded of delay and compromise. The oath to George I was first rejected outright; among other reasons they presented for the refusal, the Acadians of Minas remarked that "pendant que nos ancetres ont étés sous la domination angloise on ne leur a jamais exigé de pareille Sermente. . . . "[11] Later on, oaths were taken to George II, but in such circumstances as to enable the Acadians to believe that they had been granted the right to remain neutral. In fact, as Brebner pointed out, the practice of both English and French of referring to them from 1730 on as either "les français neutres" or "the Neutral French" indicates that this accommodation was generally tolerated, if not accepted, by those in power during these years.[12]

However it might have looked to outsiders, the question of neutrality was serious enough to the Acadians. It was in fact a consistent policy that was first enunciated in 1717 by the Acadians of Annapolis Royal and later adhered to by them, and others in time of war. On being asked for an oath of allegiance to George I, the response of Annapolis Royal Acadians was a refusal, the reasons given being that matters of religious freedom were not yet clarified and danger from Indians, who were bound to disapprove friendship between Acadian and English, led to fears for Acadian security. Nevertheless, the response continued, "we are ready to take an oath that we will take up arms neither against his Britannic Majesty, nor against France, nor against any of their subjects or allies."[13] In 1744 when hostilities broke out between English and French in North America, Mascerene, then the lieutenant-governor of the colony, wrote to his masters in London: "These latter [i.e., the French inhabitants] have given me assurances of their resolutions to keep in their fidelity to his Majesty."[14] Mascerene was convinced that had the Acadians not remained neutral during the hostilities, the colony would have fallen to the French.[15] Certainly there is more than enough evidence to show the Acadian dislike of the war, including a most strongly worded letter from those of Grand-Pré to the French, pointing out forcibly that the village preferred peace to war, tranquility and food to soldiers fighting across their farmlands.[16]

159

There is no doubt that between 1713 and 1748 the majority of the Acadians strove to live on their land truly as neutrals, giving loyalty to neither French nor English. This policy procured for their communities nearly thirty-five years of peace, but its final failure in 1755 has overshadowed its earlier success. It is worth emphasizing that it was a policy, not merely a series of inconsistent, unconnected reactions to the demands made by English and French. It was transmitted by delegates from the several Acadian communities to the English officials on a number of separate occasions and, as has been suggested, adhered to during a time of considerable pressure in the 1740s. It was a policy that produced peace and quiet for the Acadian communities, however catastrophic it finally proved to be. Its evolution and development gave the Acadians a knowledge of political action and a sense of their independent reality that would prove invaluable to them when they confronted the vicissitudes of the deportation.[17] Above all, it was the framework for the expansion and development of the Acadian communities between 1713 and 1748.

The demographic expansion of the Acadians during these years is a commonplace in one sense; in another it is something acknowledged rather than fully understood. As Gysa Hynes wrote in 1973, "the rapid natural increase of the population of the Acadians during the period from 1650 to 1750 . . . has long been recognised, but no historian has explored the demography of Acadia before the Dispersion."[18] As a result, while it is generally agreed that the Acadian population probably doubled every twenty years between 1713 and the early 1750s without the aid of any considerable immigration, there has been little real analysis of this development.[19] Gisa Hynes's excellent article was a pioneer study relating above all to Port Royal/Annapolis Royal and has not been followed by much else. Enough raw material does exist, however, to outline the tantalizing landscape waiting to be fully explored, a demographic territory which differs significantly from contemporary Europe and also, in some considerable measure, from that of other colonial settlements in North America.

It is a debatable point whether the longevity of the Acadians or their fertility should receive most comment. At a time when only 50 percent of the population reached the age of 21 in France, 75 percent reached adulthood in Port Royal.[20] Further, while mortality did take its toll during the middle years, death coming through accident and injury rather than epidemic, old age was a common enough phenomenon. In fact at the time of the Treaty of Utrecht, when the French were making every effort to withdraw the Acadians from land ceded to the English and to establish them on Isle Royal (Cape Breton), one of the priests noted that the Acadians refused to go because

> It would be to expose us manifestly [they say] to die of hunger burthened as we are with large families, to quit the dwelling places and clearances from which we derive our usual subsistence, without any other resource, to take rough, new lands, from which the standing wood must be removed. One fourth of our population consists of aged persons, unfit for the labour of breaking up new lands, and who, with great exertion, are able to cultivate the cleared ground which supplied subsistence for them and their families.[21]

The presence of an older generation in the community meant a rich heritage of memories of past politics. Any Acadian over forty-two in 1713 would have been born when the colony was controlled by the English, for the terms of the Treaty of Breda were not honoured by Temple until 10 January 1671. Any Acadian over twenty-five would have personal memories of the stormy raids by New Englanders on their villages and of the French counter-measures. The reality of life on a border would be a commonplace for Acadian reminiscences in a community whose people lived long enough to remember.

If Acadians could see relatively long life as a possibility, they could also see life itself as abundant. From the travelling French surgeon-poet Dièreville to the almost equally travelling English official, Governor Philipps, the observations were the same. In 1699 the Frenchman wrote that "the swarming of Brats is a sight to behold."[22] The Englishman commented in 1730 on the Acadians' ability to increase and spread "themselves over the face of the province . . . like Noah's progeny."[23] Present-day research has confirmed the accuracy of these impressions. Gisa Hynes discovered in her analysis of Port Royal that four out of five marriages were complete, that is "were not disrupted by the death of husband or wife before the onset of menopause."[24] In these marriages, if the women were under 20 on their wedding day, they had some ten or eleven children; those wedded between 20 and 24, nine children; and those married in their late 20s, seven or eight children.[25] For the population as a whole, it is probable that the average family in the colony had six or seven children.[26]

These bare statistical bones of Acadian family life can now be covered first with the skin of individual family genealogy and then clothed with the fabric of community life. As an example of the first, there is the life of Claude Landry, born in 1663, the youngest of some ten children of René Landry of Port Royal, who himself had arrived in the colony sometime in the 1640s from Loudun.[27] When he was about eighteen, Claude married Catherine Thibodeau, whose father had been an associate of Emmanuel LeBorgne and come to the colony from around Poitiers in the 1650s.[28] She was the fifth child in a family of sixteen, eleven of whom reached adulthood.[29] Catherine was apparently fifteen when married and bore her first child within the year. She had some ten children in all, eight of whom lived to maturity.

161

The young couple moved very early in their marriage to Grand-Pré, where they brought up their family and watched their children's children flourish. When Claude Landry died in 1747, aged eighty-six, his grandchildren through the male line numbered forty-six and his great-grandchildren, also through the male line, eleven. Claude's last child, a son, had been born in 1708; his first grandson was born in 1710. Between 1717 and 1747 there was only one year in which no birth is recorded for his sons, and it is not unlikely that one of Claude's two daughters might have had a child that year. The year 1735 saw the birth of the first great-grandchild within the male line.[30]

The growth of such extended families was supported by a healthy mixed economy, based upon farming, hunting, and fishing with enough trade, both legal and illegal, to make life interesting. In Grand-Pré the Landry family was part of the flourishing development which Mascerene had described in 1730 as "a platt of Meadow, which stretches near four leagues, part of which is damn'd [*sic*] in from the tide, and produced very good wheat and pease."[31] Westward this great marsh is edged by the massive presence of Cape Blomidon, the tides of the Bay of Fundy curve across its northern shore, and wooded uplands circumscribe its other boundaries. Between 1710, when the first grandson was born, and 1747, when Claude died, the population of the area grew from well under a thousand to something more than four thousand.[32] The community lived in houses scattered across the landscape, not grouped close together in a village. Charles Morris, who was commissioned by Governor Shirley of Massachusetts to make a survey of the Bay of Fundy area in 1747, reported that the dwellings were "low Houses fram'd of timber and their Chimney framed with the Building of wood and lined with Clay except the fireplace below. . . . "[33] Very often the houses sheltered a mixture of families, and the sheer work required to provide them necessities of life must have been considerable.[34]

The daily life of both men and women would be governed by the seasons, for the frame of the economy was what was grown and raised for food and clothing. Fishing, hunting, and trade could and did provide important additions to this base, but the standard of living of the majority of the Acadians depended upon the produce of their land-holdings. At the very least a household would possess a garden, and from the seventeenth century on travellers had noticed the variety and abundance of vegetables grown. Dièreville, whose evidence is of the close of the seventeenth century, remarked upon the wealth of cabbages and turnips,[35] and another report of the same period lists the gardens as including "choux, betteraves, oignons, carottes, cives, eschalottes, navets, panets et touttes sortes de salades."[36] Most families would have also an amount of land varying in size between that of a smallholding and a farm, depending on where the community was in the colony and what level of resources the family in question could command. A.H. Clark considered that the households of Grand-Pré and the surrounding area usually had five to ten acres of dyked and tilled farmland within the marsh, supplemented with an orchard situated on the upland slopes. Morris reported the marshlands to be "Naturally of a Fertile Soil . . . and . . . of so strong and lasting a Nature that their Crops are not Diminished in ten or twenty years Constant Tillage."[37] The crops sown included most of the grain crops common to western Europe: wheat, oats, rye, and barley, as well as peas, hemp, and flax. Writing in 1757 another traveller remarked on the abundance of fruit trees, apples, pears, "cherry and plumb trees," and noted that "finer flavoured apples and greater variety, cannot in any other country be produced."[38]

Working with the land, whether garden or farm, did not only imply digging and ploughing, weeding and gathering. There was also the care of livestock. Poultry was everywhere about, as much for feathers as for the eggs and meat. Down-filled mattresses and coverlets were a noted Acadian possession, and the export of feathers to Louisbourg a common item of trade.[39] Pigs rooting around the houses were so common that few surveyors interested in estimating Acadian wealth even bothered to count them. A number of observers, however, remarked on the Acadian liking for fat-back (le lard), which could be cooked with cabbage or fried and added to whatever vegetables were available.[40] Sheep were also numerous, raised for wool rather than for meat. Most households would also possess cows and a horse. The estimation of the total livestock in the colony varies widely since the Acadians, like most peasant populations, had no great wish to inform any official of the true extent of their possessions. Life must have been sustained at considerably more than bare subsistence, however, since extant records show that in the 1740s the Acadians, particularly those of Grand-Pré and of the Minas basin in general, were able to export cattle, sheep, pigs, and poultry to Louisbourg.[41] While the authorities at Annapolis Royal thundered against such trade, they also admitted that the Acadians were no worse than others, noting that "there is so great an illicit Trade carried on by the People of Massachusetts Bay and New Hampshire."[42] As has been suggested, the trade that existed was enough to make life for the Acadians interesting, and the goods imported included not only necessities such as "Spanish Iron, French Linnens, Sail Cloth Wollen cloths," but also "Rum, Molasses, Wine and Brandy."[43]

The sum of this evidence suggests an excellent standard of living among the Acadians, something which showed, of course, in the population increase of the first half of the eighteenth century. While there is little evidence of luxury, there is less of poverty. The staples of life, food, shelter, and clothing were abundant, even if the abundance was available only after hard work. Further, the absence of conspicuous consumption and the lack of development of towns and industry in no way meant an absence of specie. It is clear from the records of the deportation itself that Acadians took coinage with them into exile.[44] The Acadian community did not have the rate of economic growth that the New Englanders possessed, but it provided amply for the totality of individuals. Fishing and hunting added to the resources of the households. Charles Morris remarked that the population around Grand-Pré "had some shallops, in which they employed themselves in the catching of Fish just upon their Harbours, being out but a few days at a Time; This was rather for their Home Consumption than the foreign Market. . . . "[45] Clark remarked that the Acadians were "particularly interested in salmon, shad, gaspereau, and the like during their spring runs up the rivers and creeks. . . . "[46] As for hunting, it was less the meat that was immediately valued than the furs. Game was sought in order to sell it in Annapolis Royal,[47] but "avec les fourrures d'ours, de castor, de renard, de loutre, et de martre," they had material which gave them "non seulement le comfort, mais bien souvent de jolis vêtements."[48] Dièreville had also commented on the way in which the Acadians made shoes from sealskin and the hides of moose.[49]

Given the considerable work necessary to turn the resources of their environment into food and clothing for the family, it is extraordinary that the Acadians should have been criticized for being idle.[50] The tools they worked with were scarcely labour-saving devices and were basically of their own manufacture. Clark has listed the main implements available to them as "pickaxes, axes, hoes, sickles, scythes, flails, and wooden forks and rakes," as well, of course, as spades, essential for dyke-building.[51] They were known as competent carpenters and joiners, and the census made by the French during the seventeenth century reported the existence of blacksmiths, locksmiths, and nailmakers among them.[52] Working basically in wood, the Acadians built their own houses, barns, and the oc-

163

casional church, made their own furniture, including enclosed beds which must have provided considerable privacy in the crowded households, tables, chairs, chests, kegs, and barrels, as well as looms and spinning-wheels.[53] There was a remarkably fluid, though not entirely egalitarian social structure. Considerable importance was attached to the actual possession of land, and the recognition of proper boundaries.[54]

Specie did not serve as a major regulator of the internal economy. The available evidence shows that it was rare indeed for Acadian communities to pay one another, except in kind, for goods and services rendered. The gold gained through trade, or through wages from French and English officials, was kept for trade and most reluctantly handed over for any other purposes, especially rents and taxes.[55] Labour relations among the Acadians tended to be either barter-based (perhaps two days' digging or ploughing in exchange for some quantity of seed grain), co-operative (three or four people engaged in quilt-making or fishing, the resultant produce being divided equitably), or communal (several households joined together to build another dwelling and ready to be reconvened for such a purpose whenever the occasion warranted). The social ambiance produced by such labour relations encouraged the development of a community where family connections were as important as the particular attainments of an individual. Marriage would be seen as the connection between kin rather than the limited engagement of two individuals of particular social status. As Dièreville remarked, to his considerable surprise social barriers seemed to have no part to play in the regulation of marriage.[56]

In sum, Acadian life between 1713 and 1748 centred around the demands and rewards of family and land, although this did not mean isolation from a wider environment. During these decades the care and nurture of children must have been the dominating factor in the lives of most Acadians, male or female. A child born every two or three years on average in individual families meant the arrival of a child almost every year in multi-family households. Even with the importation of some yard goods, the provision of clothes and coverings for the children demanded continuous thought and activity. Records emphasize the extent to which the Acadians were self-sufficient in this area. Dièreville remarked on the way in which they made their own outfits, including caps and stockings.[57] Raynal, writing for Diderot's *Encyclopaedia* with information supplemented by the memorials of those Acadians exiled to France, asserted that they depended for their daily clothing on "leur lin, leur chanvre, la toison de leurs brebis."[58] From diapers to shawls, from shirts to shifts, with considerable liking for mixing black with red for ornament, and binding their skirts with ribbons,[59] the Acadians spun, wove, knitted, and sewed their garments. Even with every economy between one generation and the next, even with children fully accustomed to hand-me-downs, the sheer number of bonnets and mittens, stockings and shoes, cloaks, coats, and trousers, shirts, blouses, and jackets that would be needed is difficult to envisage.

Organizing the clothing was probably as much a year-round occupation for the women as the provision of meals was their daily chore. Grains were usually ground at grist-mills rather than within each household, although there is a tradition that most families possessed pestles and mortars capable of making coarse flour for porridge.[60] Bread would be baked in each household and was considered by Isaac Deschamps to have been the staple of Acadian diets.[61] Linguistic studies by Massignon show that doughnuts and pancakes were also common. She discovered references to documents dated 1744 referring to *croxsignoles*, a form of doughnut, as part of the Acadian diet.[62] It is also probable that those who came to the community from Normandy and Ile-et-Vilaine brought with them a taste for buckwheat pancakes, something that was certainly common among Acadians in northern New Brunswick at the close of the eighteenth century.[63] There is a strange debate about whether the Acadians grew potatoes before 1755, since a number of popular guides such as the *Guide Bleu de Bretagne* refer to them introducing the vegetable to France.[64] Again, it is certainly true that the potato was a staple of Acadian diets by the opening of the nineteenth century,[65] but more evidence is needed before one can accept that it was a common food for the Acadians fifty years earlier. Milk was abundant[66] and the Acadians found in exile that they had been particularly fortunate in this respect.[67] Its plenteousness must have been a great help in coping with what was known as the *pourginés d'enfants*.[68]

This charming word for a numerous family invites consideration of the emotional climate in which families grew and developed. The evidence here is, at present, somewhat sketchy. The extent to which the Acadians cared for one another during their exile, seeking news of brothers and sisters as well as advertising for husbands and wives, suggests the importance of family relations.[69] As to the actual treatment of children during these decades, one has very few concrete details. It is possible that the reputation the Acadians had for long and faithful marriages was not coupled with a bitterness against those whose lives followed other patterns. One of the few cases relating to children that reached the English officials at Annapolis Royal between 1720 and 1739 was one where grandparents fought for the privilege of raising an illegitimate child.[70] The folklore research of Jean-Claude Dupont reveals a considerable amount about children's toys and games current in the nineteenth century, and it is probable that some of these, at least, were also part of Acadian life during the eighteenth century. Certainly the early mobile-rattle, a dried pig's bladder filled with peas and hung so an infant could bat it about and watch it swing, listening to its noise, which Dupont has reported for the nineteenth century, would have been a useful toy to have in the house in the eighteenth century.[71]

There were, of course, the usual arguments and quarrels among the Acadians, the kinds of disputes common to any group of people. The court records of Annapolis show not only debates over landholdings and boundaries, but also slander actions, particularly between women, and at least one appeal for aid to control a nagging wife.[72] But the tenor of life was undoubtedly rendered easier by the ready supply of necessities, a supply which might depend on continuous hard work but one that was available. There was no major shortage of food for the Acadians between 1713 and 1748; shelter was readily available; clothing was adequate; and, above all, there were no major epidemics. Even when plague did reach the colony its ravages were confined, both in 1709 and 1751, almost exclusively to the garrisons.[73]

Quite how the Acadians escaped the general epidemics of the eighteenth century has yet to be fully determined. It is obvious from the mortality rates they suffered during the early years of exile that during the first half of the eighteenth century they had acquired no community levels of immunity to smallpox, yellow fever, or typhoid. When those diseases struck as the exiles reached Boston, Philadelphia, South Carolina, or the British seaports, a third or more of the Acadians died.[74] Yet the idea that this vulnerability developed because of the more or less complete isolation of the communities from outside contact is a theory which demands a great deal more examination. The Acadian tradition of trading-cum-smuggling which was established in the seventeenth century took at least some of the men regularly enough to Boston and probably to points south.[75] In the eighteenth century this activity was continued and Acadian connections with Louisbourg were also developed. The fact that between 1713 and 1748 no large body of immigrants came to the area has tended to overshadow both the trickle of newcomers to the settlements and the continuous nature of the relationships between this "continental cornice" and the wider world. The parish records of Grand-Pré examined by Clark show that of the 174 marriages for which detailed information is available almost exactly one-third involved partners either from elsewhere in the colony or from abroad, sixteen coming from France, eight from Quebec, and three from Cape Breton.[76] As for travellers, most of the settlements encountered them in the form of soldiers and traders as well as government and church officials. Given the normal rate of the spread of infections during these decades, it is extraordinary that no epidemics seem to have come to the settlements via contact with Boston or Quebec, Annapolis Royal, or Louisbourg.

If the life of the Acadian settlements was much more open to outside influences than has been generally thought, it was also much less controlled by religious devotion than has been generally supposed. There is no question that the Acadians cherished the Catholic faith. There is also no doubt that they were as much trouble to their priests as any other group of humanity might be. The immense political importance of the Catholic religion to the community has overshadowed questions about its social importance. Acadians' delight in litigation was not their only cross-grained trait. Quarrels that sprung up through their drinking were also matters that concerned their pastors. A report of the archdiocese of Quebec of 1742, which drew particular attention to this flaw, also inferred that bars (*cabarets*) were not only open on Sundays and feast-days, but also kept open during the celebration of Mass.[77] This same report also went on to condemn some of the Acadian communities that allowed men and women not only to dance together after sunset but even permitted the singing of "des chansons lascives." The lack of detail in the report is frustrating: was the alcohol spruce beer? Cider? Rum? Were the *cabarets* found in the front room of the local smuggler, or did Grand-Pré have something close to a village hostelry? Was the dancing anything more than square-dancing? Was the music played on flutes, whistles, and triangles only? Or were there also violins? And the songs — which of the presently known folklore airs might they have been: "Le petit Capucin"? "Le chevalier de la Tour ronde"?

167

Considerably more work needs to be done in the relevant archives before the nature of Acadian beliefs before 1755 can be fully described. The document just cited suggests only that the Acadian interpretation of Catholicism before 1755 owed very little to Jansenism. This would be scarcely surprising. There is little indication, even with the present evidence, that the Acadians indulged in major projects of ostensible devotion, either public or private. There are no stone churches built by them before 1755 nor are there any records of vocations among them before that date, either to the priesthood or to the religious life. Religion among the Acadians seems to have been a matter of necessity but not a question of sainthood, an important and vital ingredient in life, but not the sole shaping force of the social and cultural life of their communities.[78]

For, in sum, the life of the Acadians between 1713 and 1755 was above all the life of a people in fortunate circumstances, the very real foundation for the later myth of a "Golden Age." The ravages of the Four Horsemen of the Apocalypse were remarkably absent, for famine, disease, and war barely touched the Acadians during these years. There was sufficient food for the growing families and apparently enough land for the growing population. One's nearest and dearest might have been as aggravating as one's kin can often be, but circumstances not only did not add the burdens of scarcity to emotional life but in fact provided a fair abundance of the necessities. Certainly the daily round for both men and women must have been exhaustingly busy; but work did have its obvious rewards and, for both sexes, it would be varied enough and carried out with companionship and sociability. While the season would often have imposed harsh demands for immediate labour, for seeds must be sown, crops gathered, fish caught and fuel cut as and when the weather dictates, the year's turning would also have brought its own festivities and holidays. Massignon's work suggests that the Acadians kept the twelve days of Christmas, the customs of Candelmas as well as the celebrations common to Easter.[79] The long winter evenings knew card-playing, dancing, and pipe-smoking, as well as story-telling and sing-songs. The spring and summer months would see the celebrations of weddings and the most frequent new-births. Quarrels, scandals, politics, the visits of priests, the presence of Indians, people whose children occasionally married with the Acadians and who instructed the settlers in the use of local foods,[80] the presence of the English, now and again also marrying with the Acadians[81] — there is no doubt that Acadian life before 1755 was neither crisis-ridden nor lapped in the tranquility of a back-water. It was instead a life of considerable distinctiveness. It was a life rich enough to provide the sustenance for a continuing Acadian identity, based not only upon a complex social and cultural life, but also upon the development of a coherent political stance, maintained throughout the settlements over a considerable period of years. It is not surprising that, fragmented in exile, the Acadians remembered these years and that this remembrance would be built into their future lives.

NOTES

[1] For example, Geneviève Massignon, *Les Parlers français d'Acadie*, 2 vols. (Paris: C. Klincksieck, n.d.).

[2] For example, Antonine Maillet, *Rabelais et les traditions populaires en Acadie* (Québec: Presses de l'université Laval, 1971); Anselme Chiasson, *Chéticamp, histoire et traditions acadiennes* (Moncton: Éditions des Aboiteaux, 1962); Catherine Jolicoeur, *Les plus belles légendes acadiennes* (Montréal: Stanké, 1981).

[3] A.H. Clark, *Acadia: The Geography of Early Nova Scotia to 1760* (Madison: University of Wisconsin Press, 1968), and J.C. Vernex, *Les Acadiens* (Paris: Éditions Entente, 1979).

[4] Jean-Paul Hautecoeur, *L'Acadie du Discours* (Québec: Presses de l'université Laval, 1976).

[5] Jean Daigle, ed., *Les Acadiens des Maritimes: Études thématiques* (Moncton: Centre d'Études Acadiennes, 1980). See my review in *Histoire social — Social History* 16 (May 1983): 192–94.

[6] J.B. Brebner, *New England's Outpost* (New York: Columbia University Press, 1927), 15–16.

[7] While there has been considerable debate about whether this family had Anglophone roots (for example, see Clark, *Acadia*, 101), there now seems no doubt of their origins. For details of their ancestry as recorded in declarations made by their descendants in Belle-Île-en-Mer after the deportation, see M.P. and N.P. Rieder, *The Acadians in France*, 3 vols. (Metairie, La.: M.P. & N. Rieder, 1972), 2, *passim*.

[8] Bona Arsenault, *Histoire et Généalogie des Acadiens*, 2 vols. (Québec: Le Conseil de la vie française en Amérique, 1965), 2: 550.

[9] This is suggested, in particular, in the reports of discussions with the second Mme La Tour, in Candide de Nantes, *Pages glorieuses de l'épopée Canadienne: une mission capucine en Acadie* (Montréal: Le Devoir, 1927), 150f.

[10] Jean Daigle, "Nos amis les ennemis: relations commerciales de l'Acadie avec le Massachusetts, 1670–1711" (Ph.D. dissertation, University of Maine, 1975); and John Reid, *Acadia, Maine and New Scotland: Marginal Colonies in the Seventeenth Century* (Toronto: University of Toronto Press, 1981).

[11] This document, headed "answer of several French inhabitants, 10 February 1717," is printed in the *Collection de documents inédits sur le Canada et l'Amérique publiés par le Canada français*, 3 vols. (Québec: Le Canada français, 1888–90), 2: 171. The collection was published anonymously, but its editor is known to be the abbé Casgrain. The original of the document is in the Public Records Office, London (hereafter PRO), CO/NS 2, as part of the Nova Scotia government documents.

[12] Brebner, *New England's Outpost*, 97.

[13] T.B. Akins, ed., *Selections from the Public Documents of the Province of Nova Scotia* (Halifax, 1869), 15–16.

[14] Mascerene to the Lords of Trade, 9 June 1744, printed in *Collection de Documents inédits* 2: 80.

[15] This was also the opinion of the French officer in charge of the attack on Grand-Pré, Duvivier. He defended himself at his court-martial on the charge of failure, by protesting that Acadian neutrality had rendered his task impossible. Robert Rumilly, *Histoire des Acadiens*, 2 vols. (Montréal: Fides, 1955), 1: 304.

[16] Letter from the inhabitants of Minas, Rivière aux Canards, and Piziquid to Duvivier and de Gannes, 13 October 1744, printed in Rumilly, *Histoire des Acadiens* 1: 304-5.

[17] The full story of the Acadian years in exile remains to be told, but some indication of the strength of the community is given in Naomi Griffiths, "Acadians in Exile: The Experience of the Acadians in the British Seaports," *Acadiensis* 4 (Autumn 1974): 67-84.

[18] Gisa I. Hynes, "Some Aspects of the Demography of Port Royal, 1650-1755," *Acadiensis* 3 (Autumn 1973): 7-8.

[19] For a good overview of what is available, see Muriel K. Roy, "Peuplement et croissance démographique en Acadie", in Daigle, *Acadiens des Maritimes*, 135-208.

[20] Hynes, "Demography of Port Royal", pp. 10-11. In recent years scholarship about demography has been prolific. One of the most readable accounts of the French reality during the late seventeenth century is that of Pierre Goubert: "In 1969 the average expectation of life is something over seventy years. In 1661 it was probably under twenty-five. . . . Out of every hundred children born, twenty-five died before they were one year old, another twenty-five never reached twenty and a further twenty-five perished between the ages of twenty and forty-five. Only about ten ever made her sixties." Pierre Goubert, *Louis XIV and Twenty Million Frenchmen* (New York Random House, 1972), 21. On the demography of New England, see esp. James H. Cassedy, *Demography in Early America: Beginnings of the Statistical Mind, 1600-1800* (Cambridge, Mass.: Harvard University Press, 1969). Cassedy points out that the demographic scale was at first weighted towards mortality, but at a different time for each colony, "this precarious balance righted itself." The incidence of disease, malnutrition, and frontier warfare were demonstrably greater for New England than they were for Acadia. The conditions of life along the St. Lawrence were much closer to those along the Bay of Fundy. In the eighteenth century the population of Canada doubled every thirty years. In Acadia, however, the increase was even higher: it doubled every fifteen years between 1671 and 1714, and every twenty years between 1714 and 1755. Furthermore, migration was a minimal factor in Acadian demography after 1740. On Canada, see Jacques Henripin, *La population canadienne au début du XVIIIᵉ siècle* (Paris: Institut national d'études démographiques, 1954); on Acadia, see Roy, "Peuplement," 152.

[21] Father Felix Pain to the governor of Isle Royale, September 1713, printed in Clark, *Acadia*, 187.

[22] Sieur de Dièreville, *Relation of the Voyage to Port Royal in Acadia or New France*, ed. J.C. Webster (Toronto: Champlain Society, 1933), 93.

[23] Public Archives of Canada (hereafter PAC), MG 11, CO 217, vol. 5, Phillipps to the Board of Trade, 2 September 1730 (PAC reel C-9120).

[24] Hynes, "Demography of Port Royal," 10.

[25] Hynes, "Demography of Port Royal," 10-11.

[26] Clark, *Acadia*, 200f, arrived at somewhat different statistics, concluding that the average family size was closer to four or five.

[27] Massignon, *Parlers français* 1:45; Arsenault, *Généalogie* 1: 432, 433; 2: 666.

[28] Arsenault, *Généologie* 1: 518.

[29] This calculation rests partly upon the assumption that the Acadians followed a common contemporary practice of using the name of a child that died for the next-born of the same sex.

[30] Arsenault, *Généalogie* 1: 518; 2: 666, 667f.

[31] PAC, MG 11, CO 217, vol. 2 (PAC reel C-9119).

[32] These figures are my own estimations, based upon the work of Clark, *Acadia*, 216, and the overview by Roy, "Peuplement," 134-207.

[33] "A Brief Survey of Nova Scotia" (MS in Library of the Royal Artillery Regiment, Woolwich, n.d.), 2: 25-26, cited in Clark, *Acadia*, 217.

[34] There is considerable debate about the kin system of these households. Grandparents can only have lived in one home, and there is still debate on how siblings linked house-keeping arrangements.

[35] Dièreville, *Relation*, 256.

[36] PAC, MG 1, Series C 11 D, 3: 199-203, Villebon to the Minister, 27 October 1694.

[37] Cited in Clark, *Acadia*, 237.

[38] Captain John Knox, *An Historical Journal of the Campaigns in North America for the Years 1757, 1758, 1759 and 1760*, ed. A.B. Doughty, 3 vols. (Toronto, 1914-18), 1: 105.

[39] PAC, AC 2B, 12, "Supplied from Acadia entering Louisbourg, 1740," printed in Clark, *Acadia*, 259.

[40] L.U. Fontaine, *Voyage de Sieur de Dièreville en Acadia* (Québec, 1885), 56.

[41] "Supplies from Acadia", in Clark, *Acadia*, 259; and "Report of custom collector Newton" (PAC, AC, NSA-26, 29-33), printed in A. Shortt, V.K. Johnston and F. Lanctot, eds. *Currency, Exchange and Finance in Nova Scotia, with Prefatory Documents, 1675-1758* (Ottawa, 1933), 223-24.

[42] PAC, AC, NSA-26, 52, cited in Clark, *Acadia*, 258. See also the chart of Louisbourg trade on (324-25).

[43] PAC, AC, NSA-26, 51, cited in Clark, *Acadia*, 258.

[44] For example, the Acadians sent to Maryland and South Carolina were able to purchase ships. See PAC, NS A/60, "Circular to the governors on the continent, July 1st, 1756, Halifax."

[45] Morris, "A Brief Survey," 2: 4, quoted in Clark, *Acadia*, 244.

169

[46] Quoted in Clark, *Acadia*, 246.

[47] Fontaine, *Voyage*, 56.

[48] Observations made by Moise de Les Derniers shortly after 1755 and printed in Casgrain, *Un pèlerinage au pays d'Évangéline* (Paris, 1889), App. III, 115.

[49] Dièreville, *Relations*, 96.

[50] It was Perrot who first commented upon this in 1686 (PAC, AC, C11D-2[1], 119, mémoires généraux); and many later observers, such as Dièreville and Phillipps, insinuated similar flaws.

[51] Clark, *Acadia*, 232.

[52] PAC, MG1, series C11D, 2: 96-106, report on Menneval, 10 September 1688.

[53] R. Hale, "Journal of a Voyage to Nova Scotia Made in 1731 by Robert Hale of Beverley," *The Essex Institute Historical Collections* 42 (July 1906): 233.

[54] Comments on the litigious nature of the Acadians span all regimes. See Clark, *Acadia*, 198, and Brebner, *New England Outpost*, 140.

[55] In particular, note the trouble that Subercase faced collecting taxes, in Shortt et al., *Currency*, 16.

[56] Dièreville, *Relation*, 93.

[57] Dièreville, *Relation*, 96.

[58] Guillaume Thomas François Raynal, *Histoire philosophique et politique des établissements et du commerce des Européens dans les deux Indes* (Paris, 1778), 6: 309.

[59] Moise de les Derniers, cited in Casgrain, *Un pèlerinage*, 155.

[60] Massignon, *Parlers français* 2: 548, 1316. The *bûche à pilon* is illustrated in Paul Doucet, *Vie de nos ancêtres en Acadie — l'alimentation* (Moncton: Éditions d'Acadie, 1980), 17.

[61] Deschamps, cited in Clark, *Acadia*, 237.

[62] Massignon, *Parlers français* 2: 550, 1320.

[63] Massignon, *Parlers français* 2: 551, 1322; Ph.F. Bourgeois, *Vie de l'Abbé François-Xavier LaFrance* (Montréal, 1925), 83.

[64] *Les Guides Bleus de Bretagne* (Paris, 1967), 662.

[65] Bourgeois, *Vie de l'abbé LaFrance*, 83.

[66] Dièreville, *Relation*, 266, 110.

[67] Records of the complaints of Acadians exiled to Brittany, described by Naomi Griffiths, "Petitions of Acadian Exiles, 1755-1785: A Neglected Source," *Histoire sociale — Social History* 11 (May 1978): 215-23.

[68] Massignon, *Parlers français* 2: 648, 1702.

[69] Griffiths, "Petitions of Acadian Exile," 218f.

[70] A.M. MacMechan, ed., *Nova Scotia Archives*, vol. 3, *Original Minutes of H.M. Council at Annapolis Royal, 1720-1739* (Halifax, 1908), 112, 122.

[71] Jean-Claude Dupont, *Héritage d'Acadie* (Québec: Leméac, 1977), 172, and *Histoire populaire de l'Acadie* (Montréal: Leméac, 1979).

[72] MacMechan, *Nova Scotia Archives* 3: 3, 17.

[73] W.P. Bell, *The "Foreign Protestants" and the Settlement of Nova Scotia: The History of a Piece of Arrested British Colonial Policy in the Eighteenth Century* (Toronto: University of Toronto Press, 1961), 44-45, 64-85, 328-35.

[74] Griffiths, "Petitions of Acadian Exiles," 216f.

[75] Jean Daigle, "Les Relations commerciales de l'Acadie avec le Massachusetts: le cas de Charles-Amador de Saint-Étienne de la Tour, 1695-1697", *Revue de l'Université de Moncton* 9 (1976): 353-61.

[76] Clark, *Acadia*, 203-4.

[77] Têtu et Gagnon, *Mandements, lettres pastorales et circulaires des évêques de Quebec, 1888*, 15-16, reprinted in E. de Grace, G. Desjardins, R.-A. Mallet, *Histoire d'Acadie par les Textes*, 4 fascicules (Fredericton: Ministère de l'éducation du Nouveau-Brunswick, 1976), 1 (1604-1760): 19.

[78] A most interesting question which needs further investigation and which reinforces the theory of Acadian respect for, but not subservience to, the Catholic church, is the matter of dispensations for marriage between second cousins accorded at Annapolis Royal between 1727 and 1755, the usual reason for such dispensations being pre-marital pregnancy. Cf. Clark, *Acadia*, 203-4, *passim*.

[79] Massignon, *Parlers français* 2: 691-99.

[80] Not only fiddle-heads but also *titines de souris (salicornia Europaia)* and *passe-pierre (saxifraga Virginiensis)*. See Massignon, *Parlers français* 1: 183.

[81] Knox, *Historical Journal* 1:94-96, quoted in A.G. Doughty, *The Acadian Exiles* (Toronto: Glasgow, Brook and Company, 1916), 40.

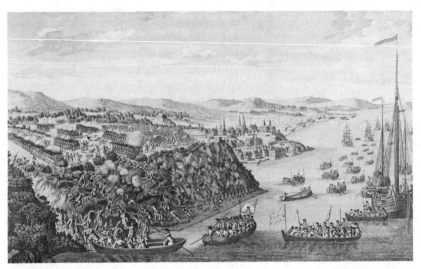

An anonymous British engraving of the Battle of the Plains of Abraham, September 13, 1759.

The actual battle had lasted only fifteen minutes. Half of North America was lost and won in that short engagement.

W.J. Eccles, "The Preemptive Conquest, 1749–1763"

Topic Five

Imperial Conflict

The Seven Years' War in Europe, which set France, Austria, Sweden, and a few small German states against Britain and Prussia, might well be viewed as the first "world war." Hostilities were waged from 1756 to 1763 over as large a portion of the world as was the case in 1914–18. Britain engaged in naval campaigns against France (and later Spain) in the Atlantic, the Caribbean, the Mediterranean, and the Indian Ocean.

In North America, the struggle between Britain and France had begun in 1754 with a clash between French troops and Virginia militia in the Ohio country, the result of an attempt by the American colonists to expel the French from the area immediately west of the Allegheny Mountains. The following year, the British, under General Braddock, experienced a disastrous defeat at Monongahela (present-day Pittsburgh, Pennsylvania). In 1756, this North American struggle merged into the Seven Years' War. Until 1757, New France, although outnumbered in population twenty to one by the American colonies, continued to hold the upper hand.

The whole character of the war changed in 1758, when William Pitt became England's prime minister. Pitt regarded the North American campaign as a primary, not secondary, theatre of the war, and consequently redirected the emphasis of Britain's war effort to North America. The British fleet, which had twice as many ships as its French counterpart, blockaded the French navy and kept it to its home ports, thus cutting off supplies and troop reinforcements to New France. Yet despite the extent of the British commitment, New France held out for another two years, until 1760. W.J. Eccles chronicles the final round of conflict for control of northeastern North America in "The Preemptive Conquest, 1749–1763," a chapter from his *France in America*. Military historian C.P. Stacey reviews the final two years of conflict in his "Generals and Generalship before Quebec, 1759–1760."

For a review of the nearly one-half century of armed conflict between the French and English in the New World, students should consult I.K. Steele's *Guerillas and Grenadiers* (Toronto: The Ryerson Press, 1969). For a more detailed examination of New France's final years, see George F.G. Stanley's *New France: The Last Phase, 1744–1760* (Toronto: McClelland and Stewart, 1968); Guy Frégault's *La Guerre de la conquête* (1955), translated by Margaret Cameron as *Canada: The War of the Conquest* (Toronto: Oxford University Press, 1969); and Martin L. Nicolai's "A Different Kind of Courage: The French Military and the Canadian Irregular Soldier during the Seven Years' War," *Canadian Historical Review* 70 (1989): 53–75. C.P. Stacey's *Quebec, 1759: The Siege and the Battle* (Toronto: Macmillan, 1959) examines that crucial year in the struggle. W.J. Eccles's "The French Forces in North America during the Seven Years' War" and C.P. Stacey's "The British Forces in North America during the Seven Years' War," in the *Dictionary of Canadian Biography*, vol. 3, *1741–1770*, xv–xxiii and xxiv–xxx, respectively, review the military strengths of the two opponents. Peter MacLeod provides a useful account of the Native peoples' support for New France in his "Microbes and Muskets: Smallpox and the Participation of the Amerindian Allies of New France in the Seven Years' War," *Ethnohistory* 39, 1 (Winter 1992): 42–64.

174   For a thorough discussion of the various interpretations of the Conquest, see Ramsay Cook's "The Historian and Nationalism," in *Canada and the French-Canadian Question* (Toronto: Macmillan, 1966), 119–42, and his essay "Conquêtisme," in *The Maple Leaf Forever* (Toronto: Macmillan, 1971), 99–113.

The Preemptive Conquest, 1749–1763

W.J. ECCLES

In the Americas the War of the Austrian Succession had changed nothing and settled nothing. After 1748 France wanted an enduring peace to rebuild and restore, but the British commercial community wanted a renewal of the war at the earliest opportunity. The latter powerful group, with Newcastle and Pitt as its political agents, was convinced that peace was good for France, but bad for England. The struggle just ended had achieved sufficient success to demonstrate that were Britain to concentrate her resources on a commercial war, France as a competitor in world markets could be destroyed and British merchants could then pick up the pieces.[1] This aggressive policy found a counterpart in North America where the planters and land speculators of Virginia and Pennsylvania were now eyeing the rich lands of the Ohio Valley. Land companies were formed in both provinces to seize and parcel out these lands for settlement. Meanwhile, fur traders, who in some instances were also agents of the land companies, had established trading posts in the region and drawn the local tribes into a commercial alliance.[2]

From *France in America*, by W.J. Eccles. Copyright © 1972 by W.J. Eccles. Reprinted with the permission of HarperCollins Publishers Inc.

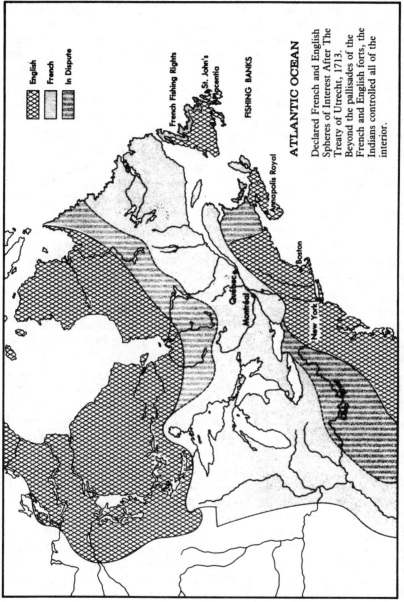

ATLANTIC OCEAN

Declared French and English Spheres of Interest After The Treaty of Utrecht, 1713. Beyond the pallisades of the French and English forts, the Indians controlled all of the interior.

English
French
In Dispute

French Fishing Rights

St. John's
Placentia

FISHING BANKS

Annapolis Royal

Boston

Quebec

Montreal

New York

175

Paul Cornell, Jean Hamelin, Fernand Ouellet, and Marcel Trudel, eds., *Canada: Unity in Diversity* (Toronto: Holt, Rinehart and Winston, 1967), 38.

The French in Canada were acutely aware of the danger posed by this encroachment on lands they claimed. Were it to go unchallenged the English colonials would not only threaten their hold on the northwest fur trade but, by expanding down the Ohio to the Mississippi, would eventually sever communications between Canada and Louisiana. Looking even further ahead, were the English to seize and settle the lands between the Alleghenies and the Mississippi, their rapidly expanding population would grow immeasurably in numbers and wealth, and with that, England's commerce. Since military power was determined to a considerable degree by the size of a country's population, by the number of trained men with muskets that could be put in the field, the much larger population of France compared to England's would eventually be offset by that of the English colonies. In America, therefore, English expansion had to be checked.

At Quebec the governor general, the comte de La Galissonière, took note of these dangers and recommended measures to circumvent them. He proposed that garrisoned forts be established in the Ohio Valley and the Indian tribes brought into the French alliance. In this way English expansion would be blocked. But more than that, from Canada and the proposed Ohio bases, the English colonies could be threatened by Canadian and Indian war parties. All that would be needed was a small force of French regulars to garrison the bases. In the previous wars the Canadians had more than held their own against the English colonials. In Britain's balance of trade those colonies were such an important item the English would have to respond to such a threat. They would have to send troops to aid the ineffectual colonial militia, and this would require the support of sizable elements of the Royal Navy which would then not be available for attacks on the French West Indies, or French maritime commerce, or to blockade the French ports as they had done so successfully in the past war. In other words, the role of the French in North America was to be that of a fortress, with a small garrison to tie down a much larger force of the enemy.[3]

With the approval of the Ministry of Marine, La Galissonière lost no time initiating this policy. In 1749 he dispatched an expedition, led by the veteran western commander Pierre-Joseph de Céloron de Blainville, to the Ohio to show the flag, claim the region for France, and drive out the Anglo-American traders. Céloron discovered that British infiltration of the region and influence over the Indian nations was far more serious than had been imagined. La Galissonière's successor, Pierre-Jacques de Taffanel, marquis de la Jonquière, strengthened the French forts in the Great Lakes area, but did little more. The governor of Louisiana, however, Canadian-born Pierre de Rigaud, marquis de Vaudreuil, showed a greater awareness of the need for action. He strengthened the garrisons at the posts in the Illinois country and began the construction of Fort Chartres, near Kaskaskia; but even after receiving reinforcements in 1751, he had only some two thousand indifferent regulars to hold the Mississippi Valley from New Orleans to the Illinois River. The French hold on this region had to depend on retaining the active allegiance of the Indian nations.[4]

On the Atlantic coast the French greatly strengthened the defenses of Louisbourg and sent out fifteen hundred garrison troops under officers who this time maintained discipline. Some of the Acadians of Nova Scotia were enticed to remove to Île Royale (Cape Breton); merchants and fishermen, with their families, reestablished themselves there until by 1752 the population stood at 5,845.[5] Other Acadians were persuaded to settle on Île St. Jean (Prince Edward Island), and at Beaubassin where the French had a fort. The swift economic recovery of Louisbourg fully justified the sacrifices made to regain it at the peace table. The fishery expanded rapidly, and the old trade with Canada, the West Indies, and New England throve. Yet in this region too the French had to count on the Indian tribes, the Micmacs and Abenaquis, and, hopefully, on the Acadians still resident in Nova Scotia. The English, however, were fully conscious of this revival of French power that threatened their North Atlantic trade. In 1749 they began the construction of a naval base and fortress at Halifax, which not only countered the menace to English shipping but precluded the possibility of the Acadians liberating Nova Scotia.

In the west the French seized the initiative.[6] Unlike the Anglo-Americans, the governor general of New France was able to mobilize the colony's entire military resources with no regard for cost. In 1753 he dispatched two thousand men to Lake Erie to construct a road from southeast of that lake to the headwaters of the Ohio and build a chain of forts at strategic points. The Indian nations, impressed by this show of strength, began to sever their trade connections with the Anglo-Americans. All that the latter could do to counter this erosion of their position was to send a major of militia, George Washington, with an escort of seven men and a letter from Governor Robert Dinwiddie of Virginia, protesting the French invasion of lands claimed by Great Britain and demanding their immediate withdrawal. Jacques Legardeur de Saint-Pierre, commandant at Fort Le Boeuf, a tough veteran of the west, received Washington politely, but contemptuously rejected his blustering ultimatum.

The following year a small force of Virginia militia attempted to establish a fort at the junction of the Ohio and the Monongahela. Before they were well begun a French force, five hundred strong, swept down the upper Ohio and forced them to retire over the crest of the Alleghenies, which the French claimed to be the border between their territory and that of the English colonies. The French now built Fort Duquesne on the site and thereby dominated the whole region. The Anglo-American response was to send George Washington back, at the head of a motley collection of militia, to drive the French out. They ambushed a small

French party sent to order them to retire. The officer in command, Ensign Joseph Coulon de Villiers de Jumonville, and nine of his men were killed, twenty-one taken prisoner. This was the first clash of arms in what was to become a global war. Significantly, it began while both powers were at peace. It also began under very dubious circumstances.[7]

The French reacted swiftly. Washington, with some 350 undisciplined colonial militia, made a stand at Great Meadows, where 500 French, after a short engagement, compelled them to surrender. Washington signed the capitulation terms without taking the trouble to inquire too closely into their meaning and subsequently dishonored them, then fled precipitately with his men back to Virginia. In his haste he abandoned his baggage containing his journal. The contents of that journal were to be used by the French government to brand the English as perfidious throughout Europe.[8] Washington's ignominious defeat brought the last of the wavering Indian nations to the French cause. From that point on, the English had not a single Indian ally in the west, while the strength of the French was enhanced immeasurably. At every turn of events the French had overreached the Anglo-Americans. They were securely in possession of the Ohio country, from its upper reaches to the Mississippi, and from their advanced forts war parties could fall on the rear of the English colonies at any time. For the time being, however, they kept their Indian allies securely on leash, determined on no account to give the enemy an excuse for attack.

The English colonies, with the exception of New York, which had no desire to have its profitable contraband trade with the French colonies disrupted, clamored for war to drive the French out of North America once and for all. In the previous wars England had furnished scant aid to her American subjects. This time the war party, led by Cumberland, Henry Fox, and William Pitt, forced Newcastle to agree to full-scale hostilities against the French in America and on the seas without bothering with the formality of declaring war.[9]

In October, 1754, Major General Edward Braddock, commanding two battalions, eight hundred men, was ordered to North America with orders to capture Fort Duquesne, while the colonial forces attacked Fort Niagara, the French forts on Lake Champlain, and those on the Nova Scotia border. This force could not sail until the following April, and on the eve of its departure the French obtained a copy of Braddock's orders. Immediately, they raised six battalions, three thousand men from the better regiments of the *troupes de terre*.[10] In April they too were ready to sail. When the British cabinet learned of this they issued secret orders to Admiral Edward Boscawen with two squadrons composed of nineteen ships of the line and two frigates to intercept the French convoy, seize the ships, and if resistance were offered, give battle. A few days after he sailed, on April 27, the French ambassador to the Court of St. James's received word that Boscawen had orders to attack the French squadron. On May 10, however, two cabinet ministers dined at his house and cheerfully reassured him that such rumors were completely false, that no such orders had been issued.[11]

Off Newfoundland Boscawen succeeded in intercepting only three ships of the French convoy. When Captain Toussaint Hocquart hailed Captain Richard Howe, asking if they were at peace or war, the reply came, "At peace, at peace," followed by shattering broadsides.[12] Two of the French ships were captured; the third escaped to Louisbourg. The rest of the convoy, with all but eight companies of troops, and with the newly appointed governor general of New France, Pierre de Rigaud, marquis de Vaudreuil, on board, reached Louisbourg and Quebec safely.[13] Elsewhere the Royal Navy had better luck. More than three hundred French ships and eight thousand sailors were seized in English ports or on the high seas.[14] This was a serious blow to French maritime strength. Needless to say, the French lost no time proclaiming the English to have been guilty of the blackest treachery.[15]

On land in North America, now that hostilities had begun in earnest, but still without a declaration of war, the British did not fare so well. Braddock, at the head of 2,200 men, British regulars and colonial troops, got his army over the mountains and within a few miles of Fort Duquesne — by itself no mean feat. In an almost forlorn hope Captain Daniel de Beaujeu led 108 Troupes de la Marine, 146 Canadian militia, and 600 Indians to oppose him. The ensuing clash was a disaster for the British. The Canadian and Indian forces took cover on the forested flank of the enemy, encumbered by siege artillery and a vast wagon train. The measured British volleys had little effect against the concealed foe. The Canadians and Indians advanced close. Noting that the British ranks reloaded to ordered drumbeats, they picked off the officers and drummers.[16] Confusion, then panic, spread through the British ranks. The battle became a slaughter. The troops broke and fled. More than two-thirds of the British force were killed or captured, along with the cannon and a vast store of supplies. This, at a cost to the French and their allies of twenty-three killed and twenty wounded.[17]

In the mortally wounded Braddock's captured baggage the plans for the attacks on the other fronts were found. Thus, by the time the ill-organized colonial forces had mustered for an attack on Niagara, the French had moved reinforcements to oppose them. The acting commander in chief of the Anglo-Americans, William Shirley, governor of Massachusetts, after his 2,400 colonial troops had been reduced to 1,400 by sickness and desertion, abandoned the campaign. On the Lake Champlain front the Anglo-Americans failed to reach the lake, being forestalled by the French, led by the commander of the regular troops Jean-Armand, baron de Dieskau, who had the misfortune to be wounded and captured in the brief and inconclusive engagement that both sides claimed as a victory.

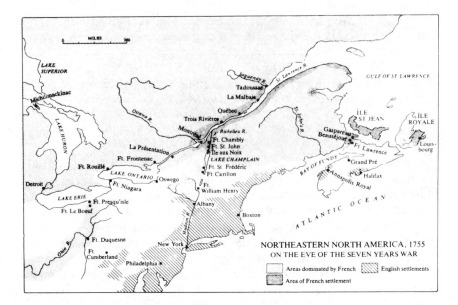

NORTHEASTERN NORTH AMERICA, 1755
ON THE EVE OF THE SEVEN YEARS WAR

Areas dominated by French   English settlements
Area of French settlement

Only on the Acadian frontier did the British enjoy any success. Fort Beauséjour, at the foot of the Bay of Fundy, was captured and the threat to the English in Nova Scotia effectively removed. Then followed one of the most controversial acts of the war, the expulsion of the Acadians.[18] Not only were the Acadians, both those captured in arms and those who had sworn the oath to His Britannic Majesty, expelled in brutal fashion, but the Indians were likewise driven off their land to make way for New England settlers. Many of the Acadians managed to elude the New England troops sent to seize them, and made their way to Quebec. They constituted a warning to the Canadians of what they could expect should they be conquered. Nothing could have been better calculated to make them fight with a ferocity born of despair. The French authorities at Quebec made the most of this.

Although war had not been declared, and would not be until May, 1756, the British assaults on New France permitted Vaudreuil to take the offensive. Indian war parties led by Canadian officers ravaged the frontiers of Virginia and Pennsylvania; but Vaudreuil's strategy was defensive. His purpose was to use the advanced French bases in the west to hold the Indian nations in the French alliance, thereby offsetting the Anglo-American superiority in numbers. Thus small Canadian and Indian guerrilla detachments could force the British to maintain large defensive forces on their frontier. To take the offensive against these bases the British would require an army, have to build roads through the wilderness to move and supply it, and employ large bodies of men to maintain their supply lines. With their command of the rivers the French could move men and supplies much more easily than could the British. Moreover, the Anglo-American militia usually fled at the mere rumored approach of the enemy.[19]

On the New York frontier Vaudreuil's strategy was to block the Lake Champlain invasion route by maintaining a strong garrison at Fort St. Fréderic and by building an advanced fort at the head of the lake, Fort Carillon, later known as Ticonderoga. When the enemy attempted to attack Canada by this route, a relatively small force could delay them at Carillon and hold them at the narrows by Fort St. Fréderic while the Canadians and Indians harassed their supply lines. Carillon would also serve as an advance base to threaten Albany and the American frontier settlements, thereby containing sizable enemy forces. The main dangers to Canada were the threat of invasion from Lake Champlain, from Lake Ontario down the St. Lawrence, and a maritime assault up the river against Quebec. On the Lake Ontario front, the English fort at Oswego was the major threat, and Vaudreuil made plans in 1755 to destroy it. As for an assault on Quebec, the best that could be done there was to harass an invading fleet as it came up river, then rely on the natural defenses of the town to prevent its capture.

If necessary, the extended defense lines could be pulled back to Niagara, Fort Frontenac, and Fort St. Fréderic. The enemy's communications and supply lines would then be lengthened and more vulnerable to attack by the French irregulars. Thus the British would have to employ vastly superior forces, and their need to build roads through the forest to supply their armies on the periphery of New France, growing ever longer, would limit the number of troops they could bring into action.[20] The British could, of course, transport whole armies to America without much danger of attack from the smaller French fleet.[21] Moreover, Britain could use ports from Halifax to Charleston; Canada had only one. An English fleet in the St. Lawrence could isolate Canada completely. Without reinforcements and supplies from France, the colony could be starved into surrender. Yet, not until 1760 did the Royal Navy succeed in blocking the St. Lawrence. French supply ships reached Quebec every year until the city fell. Much, however, depended on the food the colony could itself provide, and this became crucial with all the additional mouths to feed, the army, the Acadians, and the allied Indians who had to be fed and provided with military supplies before they would take the field. When the crops failed in 1758 famine threatened, and inadequate food supplies, to some degree, dictated military tactics; yet food was never the major factor that it has sometimes been claimed. The people went hungry at times, but they did not starve. It was not a food shortage that caused the eventual fall of New France.

In 1756 a replacement for Dieskau arrived in the person of Louis-Joseph, marquis de Montcalm-Gozon de Saint-Véran, a battle-tried regimental commander. He had the rank of *maréchal de camp*, equivalent

181

to major-general, and command over the *troupes de terre* only. He was subordinate to the governor general, Vaudreuil, who had overall command of all the military forces, *troupes de terre*, Troupes de la Marine, the naval detachments, and the Canadian militia; all told, some 16,000 men. In addition there were the Indian allies. One reason for Vaudreuil's appointment as governor general was his intimate knowledge of, and ability to control, these proud, independent, and unpredictable warriors. Although he had served in the Troupes de la Marine from childhood and in 1738 had been recommended by Governor General Beauharnais for the post of commander of the companies stationed in Canada, he had served only briefly in one campaign in the west. Most of his experience had been administrative, lately as governor of Louisiana, where he had performed very creditably.[22]

Unfortunately, Montcalm and Vaudreuil quickly came to detest each other. Both were vain, each very jealous of his authority, each convinced of the other's incompetence and his own superior judgment. Vaudreuil did, however, know the country and what warfare in it entailed. He could, as much as anyone could, handle the Indians; and he was respected by both the Canadian militia and the Troupes de la Marine. He had contrived the strategy of extended defense lines and wanted to take full advantage of the differing capabilities of his motley forces. Montcalm rejected this strategic concept. He recommended that the French abandon the Ohio Valley and Lake Champlain, then concentrate the forces at the colony's inner defense line.[23] He wished the war to be conducted on European lines, sieges and set battles, in which superior discipline, training, and his leadership would bring victory. The sort of warfare that the Canadians excelled at he regarded with contempt, as accomplishing no worthwhile purpose. As for the Indian allies, he had no use for them at all.[24] But his greatest weakness was his confirmed defeatism. He quickly convinced himself that the French position was hopeless and devoted much of his time and energy to casting blame on Vaudreuil for the disasters he was sure would ensue. Nor did he make any attempt to hide his opinion of the governor general. He criticized Vaudreuil and all things Canadian before his officers, thereby fanning the latent hostility between the Canadian officers of the Troupes de la Marine and those newly come from France with the *troupes de terre* who looked down on the colonials. Naturally, the Canadian officers, with their much greater experience in forest warfare and their unblemished record of victory, resented the attitude of Montcalm and his staff. Montcalm's defeatism, and his attitude toward the Canadians, could not fail to sap the morale of both troops and militia.

Another factor that helped to lower morale, and to some degree to hinder the French war effort — although not to the extent that has been claimed — was the malversation of the intendant François Bigot. By a series of clever devices he and his associates mulcted the Crown of millions of livres. Supplies sent to the colony, or produced in the colony, were bought at low prices by Bigot's agents, then sold at upwards of thirty times as much to the Crown. That Bigot was able to organize this very lucrative looting operation and get away with it for so long was a measure of his cleverness and ability.[25] He was an extremely efficient administrator, and although a scoundrel, he did keep the army and the colony supplied. To what degree military operations were hindered by his activities is extremely difficult to discern.

Despite these internal problems, the French forces won a succession of victories during the first two years of hostilities. Before Montcalm's arrival Vaudreuil had made plans to destroy Oswego and remove that threat to French communications with the west. In February, 1756, he sent a war party which, by destroying Fort Bull, cut Oswego's supply route to Schenectady. Other detachments hovered about Oswego, cutting down the supply columns, keeping it blockaded. In July Montcalm, with many misgivings, took command of a three-thousand-man assault force which captured Oswego after a four-day siege. Thirty Americans were killed, seventeen hundred taken prisoner, and a vast store of boats, cannon, and supplies captured, with only thirty casualties among the French. This was stunning blow to the Anglo-Americans, opening up the northwest frontier of New York to invasion. The entire western frontier of the English colonies was now ravaged by Canadian and Indian war parties. The early confidence that Canada would quickly be destroyed was replaced by fear that the French would soon invade the English colonies in force. Pleas for aid, recriminations, fears of conquest were voiced in the middle colonies. Far from winning the war, they were losing it.

The following year Vaudreuil continued this strategy of forcing the Anglo-Americans onto the defensive in the west with his raiding parties, supplied and sent out from Fort Duquesne.[26] On the central front Vaudreuil had to expect the British to mass their forces for an assault on Lake Champlain to drive the French back and open the invasion route into Canada. To forfend this he sent Montcalm with 3,600 men and 1,500 Indian allies to destroy the advanced British fort, William Henry, and then press south to threaten Albany. Arriving at the fort on August 3, Montcalm went through all the motions of a siege in the accepted European style and mounted his batteries. On the ninth the garrison commander, Colonel George Monro, asked for terms. He, with his 2,331-man garrison, was granted the honors of war and freedom to withdraw on condition they did not serve in operations against the French for eighteen months. After they had surrendered and were marching off, Montcalm's Indian allies, enraged at seeing their hated foe walk away unharmed, and inflamed by the liquor with which the Americans had foolishly tried to appease them, fell on the straggling columns. The French then did everything they could to stop the massacre, but twenty-nine were killed, over a hundred taken prisoner.

Regardless of this nasty episode, which afforded the British an opportunity to brand the French as war criminals, Montcalm had dealt the Anglo-Americans a severe blow. Their forward base was destroyed, they were deprived of a large body of troops and large stores of arms and cannon, and some three thousand barrels of pork and other valuable food supplies were added to the French stores. All this at a cost of thirteen killed and forty wounded. The Anglo-American troops defending the northern front were completely demoralized; Montcalm's were ready for anything. At New York the Provincial Council waited to hear that the French had taken the next strongpoint, Fort Edward, and fully expected Albany to fall. They wrote to Lord Loudoun, the commander in chief, who was at Halifax, "We may fear New York also."[27] Yet although Montcalm knew the dispirited and disorganized state of the enemy, that Fort Edward was only sixteen miles away, that its capture would have created panic in Albany and further reduced the offensive spirit of the Anglo-Americans, he refused to follow up his victory. He claimed the road was bad, his men worn out, and the militia needed back on their farms for the harvest. Since the harvest in Canada did not usually begin until September, even if the militia could not have been kept in the field beyond the first week of that month, it still allowed the French more than a fortnight to take Fort Edward, and that would have been enough time as things stood. Montcalm here betrayed his grave weakness as a commander. He was not aggressive; he could not seize the initiative when the opportunity presented itself. He preferred to react to the enemy's moves rather than make the enemy react to his.

184

Vaudreuil, of course, was infuriated by Montcalm's failure to execute his orders to march on Fort Edward. Their latent animosity now surfaced, and they quarreled openly. Their dispatches to the minister made their attitude all too plain. For his part, Vaudreuil infuriated Montcalm by taking credit for the victories; first at Oswego, then at Fort William Henry, as though he had commanded the troops during the actions, from his desk at Quebec.

Despite these victories, Canada had to have continued support from France to withstand the assaults that had been delayed but were sure to come.[28] Vaudreuil sent one of his Canadian officers to Versailles to explain the strategic and tactical situation and outline the additional forces needed to defend New France. He also allowed Montcalm to send two of his officers, Colonel Louis-Antoine de Bougainville and the commissary Doreil, to add their pleas. They were listened to much more attentively than was Vaudreuil's emissary. The dispute between the governor general and Montcalm was resolved in the latter's favor. Montcalm was promoted to lieutenant-general and given overall command of all the military forces in the colony. Vaudreuil now had to defer to Montcalm's decisions in all military matters. In addition, the government ordered that Vaudreuil's extended lines defensive strategy be abandoned and Montcalm's instituted. The French forces were to fall back on the settlements in the St. Lawrence Valley as the enemy advanced and strive only to hold them on the doorstep of the colony proper. This meant that the enemy would be allowed to advance almost unopposed through the wilderness and consolidate their supply lines for a massed assault. Everything, therefore, would depend on the ability of the French forces to hold Quebec and defeat much larger enemy armies south and west of Montreal. The French were, in short, to conduct the war in Canada on European lines and strive to hold the rump of New France in the hope that some part of the territory could be retained until hostilities ceased. If France still had a foot-hold in North America it would be in a much stronger position when the bargaining began at the peace table. Montcalm, through his emissaries, had painted such a bleak picture of the military position that the King's council apparently decided it would be folly to commit large forces in a forlorn hope. Thus fewer than five hundred replacements for the army in Canada accompanied Bougainville on his return to Quebec, raising the effective strength of the regular troops to less than six thousand.

185

Ironically, the French government, although its armies in the field had won startling victories, reducing the authorities in some of the English colonies to plead for peace on any terms before further defeats rendered even those terms unobtainable, had adopted the defeatist attitude of Montcalm, whereas the British government, now dominated by Pitt, took determined measures to drive the French, not just out of the territory claimed by Britain but out of North America. More British regiments were shipped to the colonies until more than 20,000 regulars of an army now totaling 140,000 soldiers and marines were in the theater and one-quarter of the Royal Navy, in addition to 22,000 colonial troops and militia. The French army, on the other hand, had only twelve of its 395 battalions serving in Canada and Louisbourg plus 2,000 Troupes de la Marine.[29] To that degree, fortress Canada was fulfilling its intended role in French imperial strategy; with a handful of troops it was tying down a much larger enemy force, preventing its being employed in some other theater.

In 1758 Pitt, who dictated military strategy, planned three concerted campaigns against Louisbourg, Quebec, and Fort Duquesne. Louisbourg, without a strong naval detachment, withstood a sixty-day siege by 8,000 troops under Jeffrey Amherst, but under fierce bombardment had finally to capitulate. It had, however, held out long enough to force the abandonment of the intended maritime assault on Quebec for that year. Brigadier James Wolfe acidly commented: "If this force had been properly manag'd, there was an end of the French colony in North America in one Campaign."[30] The fall of Louisbourg, by removing that potential threat to British shipping in the North Atlantic, allowed Pitt to transfer a large naval force to the West Indies. The object there was to capture

Martinique to exchange at the peace table for Minorca, taken by the French in June, 1756, and so avoid the necessity to give back Louisbourg. The French defenses of Martinique proving too strong, the assault was transferred to Guadeloupe. Not, however, until May 1, 1759, were that island's defenders forced to capitulate, but Pitt now had the gage his strategy required. The war had taken a new direction. Previously it had been waged for commercial aims. Now territorial conquest was the chief end.[31]

On the central Canadian front Major General James Abercromby massed an army of 15,000, 6,000 of them British regulars, to drive down Lake Champlain to the Richelieu and the heart of Canada. He got no farther than Ticonderoga, where Montcalm and 3,500 regulars and militia had hastily entrenched themselves behind a wall of logs and felled trees. Cannon would have blasted this breast-work asunder. Abercromby, however, chose to send his regulars against it in a frontal column attack. They suffered heavy losses, but returned again and again until even these disciplined troops could take no more. The British withdrew to Fort William Henry, their losses nearly 2,000 men. The French had lost only 527 killed and wounded. The demoralized British had suffered another stunning defeat. Their retreat was almost a rout. They abandoned boats, arms, and supplies, as though the devil had been after them. Although a large contingent of Canadians reached Montcalm immediately after his victory, he made no attempt to follow it up by pursuing the beaten foe. Vaudreuil pleaded with him to send raiding parties to harass the enemy and their supply lines, and hammer it home to them that the route to Canada was impregnable. Montcalm, however, appeared satisfied with what he had already accomplished. And certainly, he had put a stop to the drive on the colony for that year. But that was not enough.

In the west the British had better success. In August Lieutenant Colonel Bradstreet with nearly 3,000 men caught the French at Fort Frontenac off guard.[32] Although the fort was very poorly sited, its walls no protection against cannon fire, the commandant, Pierre-Jacques Payen de Noyan, conducted the defense very ineptly. With his armed sloops he could have intercepted the attackers in their bateaux and shot them out of the water. Instead they were allowed to land and bring up their cannon. Three days later the fort surrendered. After destroying the store of provisions, the small French fleet, and the fort itself, Bradstreet swiftly retired across the lake. It was not the destruction of the fort but the loss of the stores, and the boats to transport them to Niagara and the Ohio, that hurt the French.

Farther west the British slowly mounted a campaign to drive the French out of the Ohio Valley. Montcalm convinced himself that this was merely a feint to draw troops away from Lake Champlain. Unfortunately for the French, they were now deprived of their Indian allies in the midwest. In October the authorities of Pennsylvania had met with delegates of the war-weary Ohio tribes at Easton and there negotiated a peace, a principal condition of which was a renunciation by Pennsylvania of all claims to lands beyond the crest of the mountains. The Indians guilelessly assumed that the Americans would honor the treaty; thus having achieved their main objective, they withdrew from the war. When Brigadier-General John Forbes, whose forces had been badly mauled by small Canadian war parties, learned from a French prisoner that the garrison at Fort Duquesne was far less than the reputed thousand, and with the Indian menace removed, he pressed on against the fort. The commandant, François Le Marchand de Ligneris, his supplies almost exhausted, his men in like condition, stripped the fort of its cannon, blew it up, and retreated to Fort Machault, there to await reinforcements and supplies from Montreal. He fully intended, when they were received, to counterattack and drive the Anglo-Americans back over the mountains.

In Canada that winter of 1758-1759, food supplies were again short. The mass of the population was reduced to bare subsistence rations. Not so their leaders. Bigot and his entourage wanted for nothing. Gambling for desperately high stakes was the principal amusement. Vaudreuil remained aloof. He knew that Bigot was protected by senior officials in the Ministry of Marine, and this likely explains why he did not use his authority to curb the excesses. Montcalm, in his journal and his correspondence, was bitterly critical, but felt that his presence was required at the constant round of dinners and balls with which the senior officials and his officers beguiled themselves during the long winter nights.

Another scourge, inflation, hit the junior officers hard.

They were no longer paid in specie, but in postdated letters of credit to be redeemed three years hence. The merchants in the colony accepted them at a mere quarter of their face value. Lieutenants were paid 1,330 to 1,500 livres a year, and it cost them more than 7,500 to live. Fortunately, the ordinary soldiers who were billeted on the *habitants* when not on campaign did not suffer. They received their rations and worked for inflated wages, earning up to a pistole a day sawing firewood. Many of them married Canadian girls and were determined to remain in Canada when hostilities ended.

With the regular troops dispersed among the civilian population in this fashion, discipline suffered and training proved impossible. The battalion commanders did not know how many men they had on strength, except at the beginning of the campaigns in the spring and again in the autumn when muster parades were held. The lack of regular training exercises was to prove fatal. The reinforcements sent from France in 1757 had been a particularly poor lot; as casualties thinned the ranks of the regulars, Montcalm pressed Canadian militia into the battalions to maintain them at full strength. For the type of set battle that he wished to fight, it required eighteen months of training on the drill ground

187

to turn a civilian into a soldier, capable of maneuvering en masse, marching up to the enemy and firing in volleys on command, and standing fast in the face of the enemy's volley or bayonet charge. By 1759 Montcalm's troops were no longer capable of that style of warfare. Although he and his staff officers in their letters and dispatches expressed nothing but defeatism and the belief that the colony was doomed — indeed, Montcalm eventually proposed retiring to Louisiana with the army should the British break through his lines — yet his second in command, the Chevalier de Lévis, and some at least of the junior officers were more sanguine about the outcome.[33]

Fortunately for the French, twenty-two supply ships reached Quebec in May, 1759, bringing enough food to keep the army in the field until the harvest. Hard on their heels, however, came the Royal Navy, bringing an army of 8,000 seasoned troops commanded by Major General James Wolfe, for an assault on the bastion of New France. On the Lake Champlain front Jeffrey Amherst, the commander in chief of the British forces in America, had massed an army of 6,236 regulars and provincials to dislodge the French from their forts. It took him a month to get his army in motion. The French officers had orders to fight delaying actions only at Carillon and St. Fréderic, then retire on Fort Île aux Noix to make a stand. After Amherst had spent several days preparing trenches and gun emplacements at Carillon the French mined the fort, lighted the fuses, and slipped away. They did the same at Fort St. Fréderic, but Amherst made no move to pursue them. Instead he devoted the remainder of the summer to repairing the fort at Ticonderoga and building a massive new fort near where Fort St. Fréderic had stood. The only purpose these forts could serve was to block an army advancing south from Canada. Were Quebec to be taken there was no danger whatsoever of that. Obviously, Amherst did not expect Quebec to fall. This was a view shared by others in the British forces.

In the west, de Ligneris renewed his raids on the British supply lines to Fort Pitt, constructed near the ruins of Fort Duquesne. He was, however, forced to desist and rush to the aid of the small garrison at Niagara, under siege by an American provincial army 2,500 strong. De Ligneris never got there. His force was ambushed and cut to pieces by the Americans. On July 26 Fort Niagara capitulated. The Americans had finally achieved their original war aims. Their hold on the Ohio Valley and Lake Ontario was now secure. Moreover, the St. Lawrence was, at last, open for a descent on Montreal.

At Quebec, however, things were not going so well for the British. Although Montcalm had proposed siting batteries downriver at three spots which dominated the river channel and could have made the passage very costly for a fleet at the mercy of wind, current, and tide, nothing had been done. Admiral Charles Saunders was able to bring up the army and land it unopposed on Île d'Orléans on June 27. Only when the British fleet was in the river were measures taken to fortify the immediate approaches to Quebec. Entrenchments were dug on the Beauport flats, across the St. Charles River from Quebec. On the insistence of the Chevalier de Lévis they were extended to the Montmorency River, but, incredibly, Montcalm made no attempt to fortify the cliffs across the river from Quebec. To oppose the British, Montcalm had a total of nearly 16,000 men, regulars, militia, and Indians at his disposal, double the number that Wolfe commanded.

The French had prepared a flotilla of fire ships. On the night of June 28 they were sent down on the British fleet. The operation was a fiasco. Set alight too soon, British sailors in longboats were able to tow all seven clear before they reached their objective. The next day, on the insistence of Admiral Saunders, the British occupied Point Lévis and French attempts to drive them out failed miserably. The British were now able to mount heavy mortars to bombard the town across the mile-wide river. They were also able to get their ships upriver above Quebec and to threaten a landing on either side of the town. A landing above Quebec was particularly to be feared since Montcalm had established his main supply depot at Batiscan, some sixty miles upriver. Wolfe, however, stuck resolutely to his original plan to break the Beauport lines, but every assault was beaten back.[34]

189

Still convinced that if he could only force Montcalm to give battle on open ground he could defeat his foe, Wolfe, in his last letter to his mother, remarked, "The Marquis de Montcalm is at the head of a great number of bad soldiers, and I am at the head of a small number of good ones, that wish for nothing so much as to fight him — but the wary old fellow avoids an action doubtful of the behavior of his army." There was more than a little truth in his judgment, as events were to prove. Although Wolfe was a poor strategist, he had always been an excellent regimental officer, a great admirer of Prussian military methods.[35] The training, discipline, and morale of his troops was now vastly superior to that of Montcalm's regulars. The Canadians, however, could be counted on to fight with savage desperation to protect their homeland and avoid the fate meted out earlier to the Acadians.

As July became August, Wolfe, frustrated at every turn and suffering from poor health, quarreled with his brigadiers. They regarded his tactics to date inept and resented his secretive, arrogant manner. Unable to force the enemy to come out of his lines, Wolfe gave orders for the systematic destruction of the colony. The Canadian settlements were to receive the same treatment as had the Scottish Highlands after Culloden, in which Wolfe had played an active part. Upon first landing on the Île d'Orléans he had issued a manifesto ordering the Canadian people not to assist the "enemy," warning them that if they took up arms in defense of their homeland they would be punished with fire and sword, treated as Indians, who Wolfe had earlier declared merited extermination.[36] He took no account of the fact that every Canadian male between fifteen and sixty was a member of the militia, and thus had to obey the orders of his officers and fight the invader. To Wolfe war was the prerogative of regular uniformed troops; the civilian population had to stand aside and accept the outcome, regardless of its consequences for their lives and the lives of their descendants. At the end of July Wolfe repeated his proclamation, then turned loose the American Rangers, whom he had labeled "the worst soldiers in the universe," to burn the houses, buildings, and crops in all the parishes up and down the river. When any resistance was met, and prisoners taken, they were shot and scalped. At least fourteen hundred farms were destroyed, most of them fine stone buildings in the earlier-settled and more prosperous part of the colony. Bigot tersely commented: "M. Wolfe est cruel."

Wolfe claimed that this devastation was intended to force Montcalm to emerge and give battle. In this it failed. At the same time he increased the number of cannon bombarding Quebec from the Lévis side to forty pieces. Hardly a building in the city was left undamaged; 80 percent of Quebec was destroyed. It was the civilian population, not the army, that suffered. The bombardment served no useful military purpose. This whole policy of calculated destruction of Quebec and of the seigneuries about it made no military sense whatsoever, unless it had been concluded that Quebec could not be taken, and Canada not conquered. In his journal, under date of August 13, Major Patrick Mackellar noted that the bombardment of Quebec had been stepped up, and commented, "This was thought to be done either to favor a storm by water, or to do the town all possible damage if it could not be taken, which was now becoming doubtful, as there was little or no appearance of making good a landing upon that coast, it being so well fortified and defended by such Superior Numbers."[37] Wolfe himself, in his dispatch of September 2 to Pitt, in which he reviewed the course of the campaign, expressed profound pessimism as to the outcome, declaring: "In this situation, there is such a choice of difficulties, that I own myself at the loss how to determine." At that late date only a few weeks remained before the fleet would be forced to withdraw, taking the army with it. Of his original troop strength of 8,500 barely half were fit for duty. Casualties had been heavy. The men were now on short rations, reduced to eating horse flesh. More than a thousand men were in sick bay. Dysentery and scurvy were taking a heavy toll. At the end of August, in a letter to Admiral Saunders, Wolfe stated, "Beyond the month of September I conclude our operations cannot go." He then made the revealing comment that Barré had prepared a list of where the troops would be quartered, "supposing (as I have very little hope of) they do not quarter here."[38] But Wolfe could not give up without making one last attempt to conquer Quebec.

He wanted to launch another attack on the Beauport lines below Quebec, but when he proposed three variants of this plan to his brigadiers they rejected the concept of any attack there. Instead they proposed a landing above Quebec between the city and the supply depot at Batiscan. Such a landing would, they pointed out, cut the road to Montreal. The brigadiers argued that there a landing in strength would force Montcalm to emerge from behind his defense works and give battle in the open. Ever since the fleet had forced a passage above Quebec, British raiding parties had landed above the town periodically. This had forced Montcalm to detach 3,000 of his better troops under Bougainville to march up and down abreast of the British ships to counter the threat.

Wolfe accepted the brigadiers' suggestion for a landing above Quebec; but whereas they had intended the landing to be made well above the city, he chose the Anse au Foulon, at the foot of the 175-foot cliff, less than two miles from Quebec. The operation required the troops to be transported above the city by the fleet, then, during the night, to embark in the landing craft, drift down with the tide, land, make their way up the steep path to the top of the cliff, overpower the French outpost stationed there, then assemble on the heights before the city walls and wait for the French reaction. It was a most desperate gamble, requiring the complete cooperation of the elements — and also of the French. Rear Admiral Charles Holmes, who was in charge of the operation, afterward described it: "The most hazardous and difficult task I was ever engaged in: For the distance of the landing place; the darkness of the night; and the chance of exactly hitting the very spot intended, without discovery or alarm; made the whole extremely difficult."[39]

Everything depended on surprise. Were the French to have had a battalion of troops on the heights above the Anse au Foulon, the landing could never have succeeded. Montcalm was convinced that Wolfe would not lift the siege without one last assault, and reading his adversary's mind, he anticipated an attack on the right of the Beauport lines.[40] The fleet movements above Quebec he regarded as a diversion. He had moved a battalion to the heights near the Anse au Foulon on September 5 but recalled it the following day to the Beauport lines.[41] As it was, the small French detachment on top of the cliff was taken completely by surprise, routed by the first British troops to scale the heights. The way was open for the army to follow. When Wolfe himself landed, the situation still looked desperate. His comment reveals that he regarded the enterprise as a forlorn hope: "I don't think we can by any possible means get up here; but, however, we must use our best endeavour."[42] This they did, and the surprise of the French was complete. By daybreak Wolfe had more than 4,400 men on the Plains of Abraham, a thousand yards from the city walls. But they were in an extremely vulnerable position. Before them was Quebec, poorly fortified, but still protected by a wall that would have to be breached by heavy guns, brought up the cliff, before an assault could be made. In Quebec and the Beauport lines Montcalm had some 6,000 troops, and a few miles above Quebec was Bougainville with 3,000 more. Wolfe's army was between the two. Moreover, he had to win a complete victory. Few generals have burned their bridges more successfully than did Wolfe. Retreat was virtually impossible. The army would have had to withdraw down the steep cliff path, then wait to be taken off the narrow beach by the ships' long boats. Such an operation would have invited slaughter. The alternatives for the British would have been: be shot, be drowned, or surrender. It is doubtful that many would have escaped. The army most likely would have been destroyed, and the fleet would have had to sail back to England with the shattered remnants. But none of this happened. Yet the possibility must have been in the minds of the soldiers as they climbed the cliff. It speaks volumes for their morale and discipline.

Upon finding the British army on the heights, Montcalm had several courses of action open to him, and ample time to carry them out. He could have sent word immediately to Bougainville, ten miles away, to bring his forces up to attack the British in the rear while he launched a frontal assault. He could have marched his army around the British and joined up with Bougainville for a consolidated attack. He could have withdrawn his main force into the city and forced Wolfe to launch an assault while Bougainville and the Canadian militia harassed the British rear. Montcalm could afford to wait; Wolfe could not. Bringing up supplies for his army from the fleet would have been difficult, to say the least. A siege was out of the question. The British had only two or three weeks left in which to take Quebec or be forced to withdraw. In short, Montcalm could have forced Wolfe to fight on his terms. Instead, he chose to throw away all these advantages and fight on the ground and at the time chosen by the British, employing only half his available forces.

By nine o'clock he had some 4,500 men mustered on the plain in front of the walled city, facing the British. The Canadian militia, fighting from cover on the flanks in their traditional manner, had engaged the enemy and were inflicting casualties. Then Montcalm gave the order for a frontal attack. The French regiments, bolstered by untrained Canadian militia, advanced at a run, fired volleys at long range, then dropped to the ground to reload. Their lines quickly became ragged. The disciplined British lines held their fire until the French were close, fired measured volleys, reloaded, advanced out of the gunsmoke, then fired again. When the lines were thirty yards apart, volleys all down the British line shattered the reeling French ranks. The French turned and fled toward the city, the British in pursuit. All that saved the remnants of the army was the withering fire of the Canadian militia on the flanks that forced the British to turn and regroup. By noon Wolfe's men were in command of the field. The actual battle had lasted only fifteen minutes. Half of North America was lost and won in that short engagement.

When it was over, Vaudreuil, who had never thought Montcalm would attack so precipitately, arrived on the field with reinforcements.

Bougainville appeared later still, then quickly retired. The British still held only the Plains of Abraham.[43] The French had more than twice as many effectives and held the town. Casualties on both sides had been very heavy: 658 for the British,[44] almost as many for the French. Among the killed was Wolfe, and among the dying, Montcalm. For the generals on both sides to be killed in a battle was indeed remarkable. True to form, Montcalm's last action before expiring was to address a letter to Brigadier General George Townshend, who had succeeded Wolfe in command, yielding up Quebec.

Vaudreuil, meanwhile, was struggling to rally the French forces to attack the British the following day, but the colonels of the *troupes de terre* had no stomach for it. Vaudreuil, therefore, gathered up all the troops and militia, then withdrew around the British to join Bougainville and regroup above the Jacques Cartier River, thirty-two miles from the city. In Quebec he had left the Chevalier de Ramesay with a token force and ill-conceived instructions to hold out as long as possible but not necessarily to wait for a British assault before surrendering. The Chevalier de Lévis, come posthaste from Montreal, now took command of the French army and prepared to counterattack. Before he could do so Ramesay surrendered Quebec and the British marched in. The French then fell back and established their forward outpost at Jacques Cartier, while the main forces retired to Montreal.

193

In Quebec, when the fleet finally sailed in October, Brigadier James Murray was left in command with the bulk of the army. He likely did not receive a letter until the following year written by Thomas Ainslie at Louisbourg and dated October 28: "I now congratulate you on your success at Quebec a thing little expected by any here, and posterity will hardly give credit to it, that such a handful of men should carry a point against such numbers, and with such advantages, thank God you have escaped, it is a miracle that you have."[45] After the British ships had sailed, the French got some of their ships past Quebec with dispatches for France pleading for a strong naval squadron to be sent early to block the St. Lawrence and prevent the British garrison at Quebec from being reinforced. Ten thousand troops, artillery, and supplies were also demanded to repel the British assaults that were sure to come the following year.

Murray's troops suffered cruelly during that winter in the city they had shattered. Sentries froze to death. Wood-cutting parties were savaged by the Canadians. Scurvy took a heavy toll.[46] In April Lévis gathered up his forces, 7,000 men, and marched back to try to retake Quebec. On the twenty-seventh he was at Ste. Foy, five miles from the city. Ironically, Murray committed the same tactical error as Montcalm had done. He marched his troops out, 3,866 strong, to give battle.[47] Lévis had 3,800 on the battlefield. Again the armies were evenly matched. But this time the British were routed. Abandoning their guns, they were pursued right to the city gates. Lévis then laid siege to the town while awaiting the relief ships from France. Those ships never came. Versailles had decided that Canada was irretrievably lost. The Duc de Choiseul sagely concluded that the British, by conquering New France, would merely strengthen their American colonies and their latent urge to strike out for independence. There was, therefore, no point in risking France's remaining naval strength, thousands of troops, and adding to the nation's hideous load of debt to achieve an end that the loss of Canada would achieve in due course at no cost to France. A token force was sent to Canada — five ships escorted by one frigate, bearing four hundred soldiers and some supplies. They sailed late. When they arrived in the Gulf of St. Lawrence a powerful British fleet was already in the Gulf. After putting up a gallant fight the French ships were sunk in Restigouche Bay.

By mid-May the British ships of the line were at Quebec. Lévis had to raise the siege and retire on Montreal, where he intended to make a last stand — not to save the colony, for that was clearly impossible, but to save the honor of the French army and his own reputation. Three British armies now moved in to crush what remained of Canada. Murray moved upriver, by-passing the French defense points, and pressed on toward Montreal. To quell the resistance of the Canadians the homes at Sorel along a four-mile stretch were put to the torch. Even though their situation was hopeless, the consequences of further resistance cruel, many of the Canadians kept on fighting. Many, however, gave up.

On the Lake Champlain front the French had to fall back before Brigadier William Haviland's army, abandoning the chain of forts on the Richelieu after a heavy artillery bombardment. To the west Amherst at long last put in an appearance, moving down the St. Lawrence from Oswego. On September 6 he landed at Lachine. Seventeen thousand British troops now confronted Lévis. His forces had shrunk to two thousand. More than fifteen hundred of his regulars had deserted.[48] On the seventh Vaudreuil asked Amherst for terms. With a conspicuous lack of gallantry Amherst refused to grant the honors of war. Lévis protested violently. He demanded that the regulars be allowed to make a final stand rather than accept such shameful conditions. Vaudreuil, fearing savage reprisals on the Canadian people and recognizing the futility of further resistance, ordered that Amherst's terms be accepted. That night Lévis ordered his regiments to burn their colors to avoid the dishonor and anguish of spirit of handing them over to Amherst. On September 9 the British marched into Montreal. What remained of the French and Canadian regulars stacked their arms on the Champ de Mars. Before the month was out, they and the administrative officials were transported to France.[49] According to the terms of the capitulation the troops could not serve again during the continuance of the war.

Canada had finally been conquered. Yet that conquest had, by no means, been inevitable. Had no regular troops been involved on either

194

National Archives of Canada/C11043.

The capitulation of the French to the British, Montreal, September 1760. Canadian artist A.S. Scott has re-created the scene as it might have looked as the French turned their arms over to the British, and surrendered New France.

side it is highly unlikely that the Anglo-Americans could have conquered New France. Fifteen years later, on the eve of the American Revolution, Chief Justice Hey at Quebec remarked: "I believe it to be as true as anything can be that has not been reduced to absolute proof that the Colonies, without the assistance of England, would have been reduced from North to south by this province in the last war. They thought so themselves. . . . "[50] And against Louisiana, where no British troops were engaged, the Indian allies of the French punished the American frontier so severely that no attempts were made to invade that province. Had Montcalm not employed such disastrous tactics at Quebec on September 13, 1759, the fortress city would not have fallen; instead the British army might well have been destroyed. Then, the wavering, war-weary British government would have been more inclined to seek an end to the war. Ineptitude in the French military command and government at home, and the fortunes of war, gave Britain dominion over the vast French territory. But what might have been was now of no account. All that mattered to the conquered Canadians was to restore their destroyed homes before the onset of winter. Beyond that their main concern was what their ultimate fate would be. They were all disarmed and obliged to swear an oath of allegiance to the British monarch. Over them all hung the terrible fear of deportation, not to be dispelled for three generations. Yet the war still raged in Europe. They could still hope that France might win victories elsewhere with which to purchase their liberation. Meanwhile they had to make the best they could of life under the military rule of their conquerors.

NOTES

[1] See Paul Vaucher, *Robert Walpole et la Politique de Fleury (1731-1742)* (Paris, 1924), 298-302; Sir Julian S. Corbett, *England in the Seven Years' War*, 2 vols. (London, 1918), 1: 23-29; E.E. Rich, ed., *The Cambridge Economic History of Europe* (Cambridge Univ. Press, 1967), 4: 536-37.

[2] It is not without significance that the furs of the Ohio Valley were considered by the Canadians to be of very little value. See the informed comments by D'Aigremont; Paris, Archives Nationales, Colonies, C11A, 29: 61. On Anglo-American aims and activities in the Ohio Valley see John Mitchell, *The Contest in America Between Great Britain and France with Its Consequences and Importance* (London, 1757), iii-xlix, 17-38; Alfred P. James, *The Ohio Company: Its Inner History* (Univ. of Pittsburgh Press, 1959).

[3] See W.J. Eccles, *The Canadian Frontier, 1534-1760* (New York, 1969), 157-60.

[4] Guy Frégault, *Le Grand Marquis: Pierre de Rigaud de Vaudreuil et la Louisiane* (Montréal, 1952), 163-77.

[5] George F.G. Stanley, *New France: The Last Phase, 1744-1760* (Toronto, 1968), 60.

[6] On the events, strategy, and tactics of the war see Stanley, *New France: The Last Phase*; Eccles, *The Canadian Frontier*, 157-85; Guy Frégault, *Canada: The War of the Conquest* (Toronto, 1969); Corbett, *England in the Seven Years' War;* Lawrence Henry Gipson, *The British Empire before the American Revolution*, vols. 4-8 (New York, 1939-54); Gerald S. Graham, *Empire of the North Atlantic: The Maritime Struggle for North America* (Toronto, 1950).

[7] This incident has long been a subject of controversy, American historians seeking to excuse Washington, while French and French-Canadian historians, for the most part, declare his act to have been that of a common assassin. See Stanley, *New France: The Last Phase*, 54-55.

[8] The journal was sent to Governor General Duquesne at Quebec, who predictably commented: "Rien de plus indigne et de plus bas Et meme de plus noir que les sentimens Et la facon de penser de ce Washington, Il y auroit eu plaisir de luy Lire Sous le nez Son outrageant journal." He had a translation made, a copy of which is in the Archives du Séminaire de Québec. See Fernand Grenier, ed., *Papiers Contrecoeur et autres documents concernant le conflit anglo-français sur l'Ohio de 1745 à 1756* (Québec, 1952), 133-81, 251.

[9] Walter L. Dorn, *Competition for Empire, 1740-1763* (New York, 1963), 287-89.

[10] *Troupes de terre* were the regiments of the regular army, so designated because many of them took their nomenclature from the provinces where they were raised, e.g., Régiment de Languedoc, Régiment de Béarn.

[11] See Corbett, *England in the Seven Years' War* 1: 45-46; Richard Waddington, *Louis XV et le renversement des alliances* (Paris, 1896), 96-97.

[12] Waddington, *Louis XV et le renversement des alliances,* 104-110.

[13] The strength of the four battalions sent to Quebec, on arrival, was 108 officers, 1,693 other ranks. See Paris, Archives Nationales, Colonies, D2C, 46: 254.

[14] See A.T. Mahan, *The Influence of Seapower upon History* (New York, 1890; paperback ed., New York, 1957), 1957 ed., p. 251. The strength of the French navy was depleted further by an epidemic of typhus that swept through the fleet and naval ports in 1757. It was this, rather than the greater strength or efficiency of the Royal Navy, that allowed the latter eventually to blockade the French ports and dominate the Atlantic. Seamen and dockyard workers fled the ports; ships could not be manned for lack of crews and sometimes had to go into action with a handful of seamen amid impressed landsmen. See Ruddock F. Mackay, *Admiral Hawke* (Oxford 1965), 204, 213, 227, 234, 249.

[15] For an example of the use made of these incidents by French diplomats abroad on instructions of the foreign minister see *Rapport de l'Archiviste de la Province de Québec RAPQ* (1949-51): 5, M. Durand d'Aubigny, Résident du Roi à Liège, au Ministre, Liège, 27 juillet 1755; *RAPQ* (1949-51): 9, D'Aubigny au Ministre, à Liège le 11 oct. 1755.

[16] See *RAPQ* (1931-32): 19, Mémoire du Chevalier de la Pause.

[17] The most detailed and frequently cited study of this action is Stanley M. Pargellis, "Braddock's Defeat," *American Historical Review* 41 (1936): 253-69. It is, however, dated; the limitations of the musket were not taken sufficiently into account, and the effectiveness of guerrilla tactics against regular troops untrained for such warfare had not been as clearly demonstrated in 1936 as it was to be in subsequent years.

[18] On this issue many historians have allowed national sentiment to weight their judgment. This is particularly true of Francis Parkman, *Montcalm and Wolfe* (London, 1964 ed.), 175-208, and Gipson, *The British Empire before the American Revolution* 6: 212-344. Waddington, *Louis XV et le renversement*

des alliances, 372–417, gives a detailed account of events and roundly condemns the British. For a judicious view see Guy Frégault, *Canada: The War of the Conquest*, 164–200; "La déportation des Acadiens," *Revue d'Histoire de l'Amérique Française* 8, 3 (1954-55): 309–358.

[19] A contemporary American observer put the situation very succinctly: "Our colonies are all open and exposed, without any manner of security or defense. Theirs are protected and secured by numbers of forts and fortresses. Our men in America are scattered up and down the woods, upon their plantations, in remote and distant provinces. Theirs are collected together in forts and garrisons. Our people are nothing but a set of farmers and planters, used only to the axe or hoe. Theirs are not only well trained and disciplined but they are used to arms from their infancy among the Indians; and are reckoned equal, if not superior in that part of the world to veteran troops. Our people are not to be drawn together from so many different governments, views, and interests; are unable, unwilling, or remiss to march against an enemy, or dare not stir, for fear of being attacked at home. They are all under one government, subject to command like a military people. While we mind nothing but trade and planting. With these the French maintain numbers of Indians — We have none, — These are troops that fight without pay — maintain themselves in the woods without charges — march without baggage — and support themselves without stores and magazines — we are at immense charges for those purposes. By these means a few Indians do more execution, as we see, than four or five times their number of our men, and they have almost all the Indians of that continent to join them." Mitchell, *The Contest in America Between Great Britain and France*, 137-38. See also pp. 118–19, 125-26, and Charles Henry Lincoln, ed., *The Correspondence of William Shirley*, 2 vols. (New York, 1912), 2: 133–34, Shirley to James Delancey, Boston, Feb. 24, 1755.

[20] See Henri-Raymond Casgrain, ed., *Collection des manuscripts du maréchal de Lévis*, 12 vols. (Montréal and Québec, 1889–95), vol. 4, *Lettres et pièces militaires, instructions, ordres, mémoires, plans de campagne et de défense, 1756–1760* (Québec, 1891), 153.

197

[21] In 1756 France had 45 ships of the line ready for sea, 15 in dock being readied, several under construction (Waddington, *Louis XV et le renversement des alliances*, 246). England had 130 ships of the line, but they were inferior to the French; the reverse was true of the officers of the two navies. (Dorn, *Competition for Empire*, 105–121). In 1756, with war declared, the French government decided on an invasion of England. The American theater tied down a sizable part of the Royal Navy; a diversionary assault on Minorca would tie down more. Diversionary assaults were to be made on Scotland and Ireland, then the main invasion launched against England. It was anticipated that all the ships and troops in the latter assault would be lost, but not before they had caused worse panic than the Jacobite march on London in 1745, the collapse of the country's financial structure, and a consequent willingness of the ruling class to accept reasonable peace terms to avert worse losses. See Corbett, *England in the Seven Years' War* 1: 83–95; Dorn, *Competition for Empire*, 355.

[22] See Frégault, *Le grand marquis*.

[23] See Frégault, *Canada: The War of the Conquest*, 241–43.

[24] His attitude is revealed by a comment in his journal: "A quoi donc sont bons les sauvages? A ne pas les avoir contre soi." Casgrain, *Collection des manuscrits* 7: 591.

[25] Bigot's activities were regarded as criminal, and he later paid for them; but to a degree, he appears to have been used as a scapegoat. It is interesting to note the difference in attitude toward his malversations and the bland acceptance in England of Henry Fox's amassing of a fortune, perhaps as large as that acquired by Bigot, while serving as paymaster-general. See Lucy S. Sutherland and J. Binney, "Henry Fox as Paymaster-General of the Forces," *English Historical Review* 70 (Apr. 1955). For Bigot's checkered career see Guy Frégault, *François Bigot: Administrateur français*, 2 vols. (Montréal, 1948).

[26] For a brief contemporary description of the nature of this guerrilla warfare see *RAPQ* (1931-32): 43, Mémoire et observations sur mon voyage en Canada, Chevalier de la Pause.

[27] New York State Archives, Albany, Colonial Documents, 84: 149.

[28] Historians who accept — usually as an unstated, and likely unconscious, premise — that what happened had to happen, and therefore regard the conquest of New France as inevitable, always advance as a main argument the dependence of Canada on France for support. They thereby ignore that the English colonies were more dependent on England for military aid than Canada was on France.

[29] In 1758 the British army and marines numbered 140,000. Rex Whitworth, *Field Marshall Lord Ligonier: A Study of the British Army, 1702-1770* (Oxford, 1958), 208, 246. The French army at maximum strength, 1757-1762, was slightly under 330,000 men in line units. Lee Kennet, *The French Armies in the Seven Years' War* (Duke Univ. Press, 1967), 75–78.

[30] McCord Museum, McGill University, Wolfe Papers, No. 1288.

[31] On the West Indies campaign and Pitt's strategy see Corbett, *England in the Seven Years' War* 1: 371–95; Gipson, *The British Empire before the American Revolution*, vols. 5 and 8.

[32] Mr. James Turnbull, presently preparing a Ph.D. thesis on the role of Governor General Vaudreuil during the war, has advanced the proposition, on good evidence, that the French suffered a breakdown in the intelligence service provided them by the Five Nations. Previously the Iroquois had kept Vaudreuil well informed of English plans and preparations. On this occasion they conspicuously did not. It may be that they regarded it as in their interests to have the British destroy Fort Frontenac, located as it was on lands they claimed as theirs. When the French destroyed Oswego in 1756 the

Iroquois pointedly thanked Vaudreuil for having thus "reestablished the Five Nations in possession of lands that belonged to them." See *RAPQ* (1932-33): 327.

33 See Archives de la Guerre, Series A1, Vol. 3540, pt. 1, pp. 115, 138-39.

34 On August 11 he wryly remarked: "We had a lively skirmish this morning — we are as usual victorious and yet I am afraid we lost more than the enemy owing to our original disposition and partly to the irregularity and folly of our men. . . . " Public Archives of Canada, James Murray Papers, Wolfe to Brig.-Gen. Murray, Aboard Sterling Castle, 11 Aug. 1759.

35 See Wolfe to Captain Maitland, August 5, 1757: "I have ever entertained a profound admiration for the King of Prussia as the first soldier of this Age and our Master in the Art of War. . . . Some of H.M.'s manouvres are curious and the Deployments display uncommon ingenuity. They doubtless will be adopted by us if Occasion arises." McCord Museum, McGill University, Wolfe Papers, M1385. On Wolfe's generalship see E.R. Adair, "The Military Reputation of Major-General James Wolfe," Canadian Historical Association, *Report* (1936); C.P. Stacey, *Quebec, 1759* (Toronto, 1959), 170-78.

36 For Wolfe's views on the Indians, see McCord Museum, McGill University, Wolfe Papers, No. 1288. His manifesto is printed in Casgrain, *Collection des manuscrits* 4: 273-76.

37 Public Archives of Canada, MG23, GII-1, Series 2-7, P. Mackellar's short account of the expedition against Quebec, p. 20.

38 Christopher Hibbert, *Wolfe at Quebec* (London, 1959), 165; Stacey, *Quebec, 1759*, 102.

39 Stacey, *Quebec, 1759*, 132-33.

40 C.P. Stacey, *Quebec, 1759*, 111-12, 168, opines that Montcalm lacked one essential quality of a good general, the ability to divine his antagonist's intentions, citing his failure to anticipate the landing above Quebec as an example. Montcalm gave abundant evidence of poor generalship, but in this particular case he cannot be faulted, for he had read Wolfe's mind very accurately. What he failed to divine was that Wolfe would defer to the tactics proposed by his brigadiers. He could not have been expected to know that this had transpired.

41 For the confusion that this incident occasioned in the minds of Canadian historians see the intriguing critique by C.P. Stacey, "The Anse au Foulon, 1759: Montcalm and Vaudreuil," *Canadian Historical Review* 40, 4 (Mar. 1959): 27-37.

42 See C.P. Stacey, "Quebec, 1759: Some New Documents;' *Canadian Historical Review* 47, 4 (Dec. 1966): 344-55; Frégault, *Canada: The War of the Conquest*, 253.

43 In 1711 Governor General Philippe de Rigaud de Vaudreuil, father of the governor general of 1759, had prepared to repel an English seaborne assault on Quebec. He had entrenchments made and cut all the roads everywhere the enemy could effect a landing on both sides of the city, from Beauport to Cape Rouge. He stated that even should the enemy break through these defenses, which they could not do without suffering heavy losses, "they would still hold nothing." *RAPQ* (1946-47): 433-34.

44 The total British casualties in the Quebec campaign were 21 officers killed, 93 wounded, 1,384 other ranks killed, wounded, and missing. McCord Museum, McGill University, No. 824, A Return of the Kill'd & Wounded etc. of H.M. Forces up the River St. Lawrence from the 27th June to the Reduction of Quebec 10 [*sic*] Sept. 1759.

45 Public Archives of Canada, James Murray Papers, vol. 1, pt. 3, pp. 8-9.

46 Vaudreuil proposed to detach 1,500 to 1,800 men to harass the British garrison continually and by preventing their obtaining firewood force Murray to surrender. The proposal was rejected owing to the shortage of food supplies for such a detachment and also because the French were sure that Murray would retaliate by burning the homes of all the Canadians within his reach. This might indicate that the British policy of *schrechlichkeit* had served a purpose. See *RAPQ* (1938-39): 7.

47 The best brief account of this battle to date is G.F.G. Stanley, *New France: The Last Phase*, 242-50.

48 Their officers reported that the majority of the regulars were resolved not to return to France. Many of them had married Canadian girls, with the consent of Montcalm, who had promised them that they could take their discharge and remain in the colony at the war's end. See Eccles, *The Canadian Frontier*, 176, 184. For a graphic contemporary account of the collapse of French resistance see *RAPQ* (1931-32): 120, Relation de M. Poularies.

49 A handful of officers in the Troupes de la Marine, six captains, three lieutenants, four *enseignes*, were granted permission in 1760 to remain in the colony either to recuperate from serious wounds or to attend to urgent family affairs. Only three Canadian merchants returned to France at the capitulation: Guillaume-Michel Perrault, d'Étienne Charest, Louis Charly de Saint Ange. See Claude Bonnault de Méry, "Les Canadiens en France et aux colonies après la cession (1760-1815)," *Revue de l'Histoire des Colonies Françaises* 17 (1924): 495-550.

50 Shortt and Doughty, *Documents Relating to the Constitutional History of Canada, 1759-1791* 2: 669.

Generals and Generalship before Quebec, 1759–1760

C.P. STACEY

I

The two hundredth anniversary of the fall of Quebec is a good time for Canadian historians to take stock of the most famous series of events in Canadian history. After two centuries, these events are still, apparently, interesting to the public. At any rate, publishers seem to think so; for about half a dozen new books about them are being published in 1959.[1]

There is an enormous literature about the Seven Years' War in America, and the Quebec campaign of 1759 in particular. In spite of this, many aspects of the period remain controversial. I shall today attempt a review of some of the controversies. But as a preliminary it seems desirable to review also the work of the historians who have contributed to them. Both things I propose to do in the light of a re-examination of the primary sources of information.

199

If I may begin with a personal explanation, some time ago I set out to write a short book on the events at Quebec in 1759. With what seems to me now considerable simplicity, I assumed that so much work had been done on these events that I could avoid doing much tiresome research and concentrate on producing a leisured and gentlemanly commentary on the well-established facts. Before I had done much reading I discovered that I had been too optimistic. I found myself driven on to start digging into the primary sources — a process rendered fatally easy by the fact that I was living in Ottawa, which possesses the greatest existing collection of such sources on the subject. In the end, I wrote, not the essay I had hoped for, but a documented history of the campaign, an attempt, however inadequate, at a new interpretation based on a new study of the contemporary evidence. I had come to feel, rightly or wrongly, that this was needed.

II

As a result of my reading I arrived at two disturbing conclusions. The first was that the history of the siege of Quebec had been, on the whole, rather badly written. The second, I am sorry to say, was that the worst of the bad writing had been done in Canada.

From Canadian Historical Association, *Report* (1959): 1–15. Reprinted with the permission of the author and the Canadian Historical Association.

Whatever the political, social, or economic historian may say, military operations are not the easiest stuff of which to make history. The fog of war has a way of drifting into the historian's study and getting into his eyes; and when to the grey fog of war is added the golden haze of romance, visibility tends to fall close to zero. The haze of romance settled over the Quebec area within a few weeks of the Battle of the Plains of Abraham, and it has not lifted yet. A good deal of what has been scribbled in the resulting murk seems to me not much better than romantic nonsense.

Prejudice, of course, has played a great part in the result. The influence of national prejudice is obvious. But there has been much personal prejudice too. Historians have become devoted adherents or bitter opponents of the leading personalities of the time. Moreover, some of them have suffered woefully from lack of military knowledge. Finally, there has been a considerable amount of just plain inadequate investigation. Writers of high reputation have been guilty of surprising lapses. I offer one example.

200

Sir Julian Corbett's book *England in the Seven Years' War* is regarded, not without some reason, as a standard military study of the war. In discussing the appointment of Wolfe to command the Quebec expedition, Corbett asserts that the Army in America had asked for him. There is in the Record Office, he says, a "curious paper" in which three colonels (Monckton, Murray, and Burton) recommended to Pitt that he appoint Wolfe. This seemed decidedly "curious," even in the eighteenth century, and with the aid of Mr. Ormsby of the Public Archives I checked the source cited by Corbett. It turned out to be a document sent, not from America to England, but in the opposite direction; it is in fact the "Proposals for the Expedition to Quebec" sent by Pitt to General Amherst for his guidance.[2] It begins by noting that Colonel Wolfe is to command, with the rank of major general "for and during the Expedition to Quebec only"; it then goes on to list as "Brigadiers to Act under the same Restrictions" the names of Monckton, Murray, and Burton. Incredible as it may seem, there appears to be no doubt that Corbett read these three names as *signatures* to the document. This led him, not only to perpetrate an historical absurdity, but to miss a point of much interest. This is the fact that Ralph Burton was originally slated to be the third brigadier, but was displaced, in circumstances which remain rather obscure, by the better-connected George Townshend. Townshend was evidently forced upon Wolfe.[3] Here we have, one suspects, part of the background for the serious rift that developed between Wolfe and Townshend before Quebec.

This example at least serves to indicate that not all the historiographical crimes in connection with the 1759 campaign have been committed by Canadians. The Canadians, however, have been responsible for more than their fair share. It is particularly astonishing that they have failed to make better use of the plans of Quebec available in the Ottawa archives. Nothing of the slightest value has ever been done on the state of the Quebec fortifications in 1759, though ample material lies ready to hand. The late Sir Arthur Doughty gave currency to the legend that there are no defensive works at Quebec today which antedate 1820 — though a mere glance at the plans immediately establishes the fact that, basically, the city walls today are the same that stood there in 1759. Sir Arthur also accepted as an accurate account of the fortifications the plan drawn by Patrick Mackellar (Wolfe's Chief Engineer) after his captivity at Quebec in 1757. Yet the defences on the land side in Mackellar's plan are those shown on Charlevoix's map of 1744. These were in fact wholly altered beginning in 1745. Mackellar's plan was thus fourteen years out of date in 1759.[4] It was lucky for Wolfe that, thanks to the inefficiency of the engineers and administrators of New France, the new fortifications were about as bad as the old ones; and Mackellar's basic conclusion, that the best way to take the city was to attack its weak land side, remained sound, even though the information on which it was based was entirely inaccurate.

201

Of the individual historians who have written about the events of 1759 one could speak endlessly. Leaving earlier writers aside, we may begin with Parkman. It seems to me that *Montcalm and Wolfe*, published in 1884, has worn remarkably well. There is not much that his successors can teach the Bostonian; on the contrary, many of them could learn from him. It is true that he tells some stories (which incidentally have been repeated by virtually every writer since his time) which are probably unfounded. It is true that he takes liberties with documents[5] — though never, so far as I have seen, to the extent of altering the sense. Also, his account of the Quebec campaign is relatively brief, and much is left out. But on balance one can only salute him for his achievement.

Among the other writers who have dealt broadly with the Seven Years' War, and more incidentally with the Quebec campaign, Richard Waddington is an eminent figure. *La Guerre de sept ans*, so far as I can judge it, is a book impressive in research as well as monumental in scope. And it is pleasant to be able to say that North American scholarship in our own day has produced a work worthy to stand beside these triumphs of the past. Professor Gipson's book *The Great War for the Empire*, a part of his larger work, *The British Empire before the American Revolution*, is fine in its sweep and most admirable in its investigation of the sources. I would not agree with everything in it, but it is a splendid achievement of the historian's craft.

I turn now to the more specialized studies, and first to the group of Canadian historians who laboured in the field in the late Victorian period and early in the present century. Among the French-speaking scholars of this period the dominant figure was the Abbé H.-R. Casgrain. Following in the footsteps of Garneau, he interpreted the war of the conquest in terms of French-Canadian nationalism. This appears particularly in his championship of Vaudreuil, who, it may be recalled, was Canada's first native-born Governor General. The eighteenth-century division between the French of France and the French of Canada is reflected and paralleled in the nineteenth-century bickering between Casgrain and René de Kerallain, the biographer of Bougainville. De Kerallain observed, "L'abbé Casgrain appartient à la catégorie des écrivains patriotes; et, quand le patriote se double d'un Canadien, son patriotisme est deux fois plus nerveux."[6]

Casgrain's great achievement is, of course, his edition of the Lévis Papers, a vastly important group of documents.[7] Since the original manuscripts are now in the Public Archives of Canada, it is possible to assess the value of the published version. It is certainly a most useful contribution. The documents which Casgrain did not publish are relatively few and unimportant. The transcription does not meet the meticulous standards of modern scholarship, but it is broadly accurate. Occasionally, it is true, Casgrain's transcriber made a real howler. Again one example, from the account of the Battle of the Plains in the journal called Montcalm's. The author of this part of the journal, apparently the artillery officer Montbeillard, describes a conversation with Montcalm just before the fatal attack. The Casgrain version makes the general say, "If we give him time to establish himself, we shall never be able to attack him with the few troops we have (*le peu de troupes que nous avons*)." But the phrase in the manuscript is clearly not "le peu de troupes" but "L'Espèce de troupes" — *the kind of troops* we have.[8] Fortunately, errors as bad as this are not frequent, and I must say that I should hate to have to pick my way through the Lévis manuscripts without the guidance of Casgrain's printed edition.

The most famous monument of English-Canadian scholarship in this field is the six volumes of Doughty's *The Siege of Quebec and the Battle of the Plains of Abraham*, published in collaboration with G.W. Parmelee in 1901. This book is partly a history, partly a collection of documents. The documents are — with some reservations — invaluable. The history belongs in a lower category. Doughty was one of those whose vision was seriously affected by the golden haze. He had a romantic regard for both Wolfe and Montcalm, and even for that versatile but inefficient soldier Bougainville. His knowledge of the Casgrain documents — a comparatively recent publication in his time — seems to have been imperfect. He devotes some indignation to the purblind people who insist on suggesting that Bougainville was at Cap Rouge on the eventful night of the 12th–13th September 1759, and produces some second-hand evidence to indicate that he was not there.[9] Yet Casgrain had published the only letter by Bougainville himself describing that night. Bougainville wrote to Bourlamaque, "Un homme se laisse surprendre à l'anse des Mères; je suis au cap Rouge."[10] Doughty, like some other partisans of Wolfe, convinced himself, in spite of the absence of any real evidence whatever, that Wolfe had in mind from the beginning the landing at the Anse au Foulon which was finally executed on 13 September.[11]

Even the documents Doughty presents, invaluable as they are, have to be treated with some reserve. I was surprised to discover that two paragraphs which the British government censored out of Wolfe's famous dispatch to Pitt when it was first published in 1759 are still missing from Doughty's version, as they are from almost every version in print. I found also that part of Wolfe's almost equally famous and informative letter to Admiral Saunders written on 31 August 1759 is missing from Doughty's text.[12]

A writer at least as influential in Canada as Doughty was Colonel William Wood, author of *The Fight for Canada* and several volumes in the "Chronicles of Canada" series. Wood was a devoted worker in Canadian military history, and it is not pleasant to have to depreciate his writings; but his influence, so far as the Seven Years' War is concerned, has been most unfortunate. He was an amateur soldier and an amateur historian, but he has been regarded by the authors of general histories of Canada as a reliable guide through the complexities of the Quebec campaigns. The results have been regrettable. Wood's predilections and prejudices were much the same as Doughty's: a romantic regard for both Wolfe and Montcalm, a deep hostility to Vaudreuil. How far his interpretation was really based on documents can be judged from the fact that he changed it late in life and published an account of Wolfe far less favourable to the general than the eulogistic one presented in *The Fight for Canada* some twenty years before.[13]

203

The fact is that Wood's work abounds in errors, major and minor. It would be no trick to compile a very long list of them. Perhaps the most egregious was his attribution to Vaudreuil of the phrase, "There is no need to believe that the English have wings," which was actually written to Vaudreuil by Montcalm on 29 July.[14] In *The Passing of New France*[15] Wood dramatically represents Vaudreuil as making this remark to Montcalm on 12 September, "Raising his voice so that the staff could hear him." An author who is capable of this is capable of practically anything. Wood popularized the story of Vaudreuil's countermanding Montcalm's order moving the Guyenne battalion to the site of Wolfe's landing the night before the Battle of the Plains, though as I have tried to show elsewhere the evidence for this is extraordinarily slight.[16] He did not even know Wolfe's actual rank in the Army — having apparently not discovered the *Army List*.[17] He asserts that books contain statements which, on inspection, turn out to be not there.[18]

Wood's works are less well known outside than inside Canada — and the writing done outside is none the worse for this, though it is worth remarking that British and American writers have neglected his useful compilation *The Logs of the Conquest of Canada* as much as his less valuable works. But Canadian writers have tended to swallow him whole. Evidence of his prestige is the fact that even so thorough and reliable an historian as Professor Creighton clearly relied on Wood as a basis for the pages on the 1759 campaign in *Dominion of the North.* The result is that he repeated a succession of unfounded tales, including the inherently impossible one (also in Parkman and many other books) of the Highland officer who answered the sentry's question about his regiment with the words "De La Reine,"[19] and the oft-printed detail of the Royal-Roussillon battalion marching on to the battlefield "in its distinctive blue" (Royal-Roussillon, like all the other French regiments in Canada, wore white.)[20]

Two Canadian biographies, both old books now, may be mentioned. Sir Thomas Chapais was devoted to his subject, as biographers tend to be; yet his life of Montcalm is distinguished by considerable objectivity as well as by careful research. W.T. Waugh's *James Wolfe, Man and Soldier*, on the other hand, is one of the romantic works, ready to take leave of the documents at any time to achieve an interpretation favourable to his hero. (Read his account of the correspondence between Wolfe and the brigadiers at the end of August 1759.)

A quite different approach to Wolfe, however, was that of Waugh's McGill colleague, Professor Adair, in his presidential address to this association in 1936.[21] This was a realistic re-interpretation based on careful examination of a wide range of sources. It may be called, in fact, the most thorough account that could be compiled within the city limits of Montreal. I find myself of the opinion that Mr. Adair somewhat overdid his onslaught on Wolfe's reputation; he was not without prejudice against Vaudreuil; but his paper was certainly the most significant Canadian contribution to the subject and, in spite of its exaggerations, possibly the best thing on Wolfe ever written anywhere. More recently an eminent French-Canadian scholar, Mr. Frégault, has given us a full-length book on the Seven Years' War in America.[22] Like so many earlier works written in Quebec, it presents a nationalistic view favourable to Vaudreuil. It is distinguished, however, by its careful use of primary sources in both French and English. On matters of fact, Professor Frégault's narrative is almost always firmly grounded; as to his interpretation of the facts, there is almost always room for discussion. Unfortunately, although he goes into great detail about the operations at Oswego in 1756, he has comparatively little to say about the much more important ones at Quebec three years later.

Finally, a general word about document collections. My initial assumption that everything important was in print turned out to be unjustified. I have spoken of Casgrain and Doughty. The other basic collection is that of Gertrude S. Kimball, *Correspondence of William Pitt . . . with Colonial Governors and Military and Naval Commanders in America.*[23] This has the virtue that the text of the letters is accurately transcribed from the original manuscripts. But unfortunately none of the enclosures is printed; and often they are more important than the letter itself. The Kimball notes, moreover, have very little value.

Even at this late date, there are still significant documents that are not in print at all. A particularly striking example is Vaudreuil's long dispatch dated 5 October 1759 which is his description of the campaign and his *apologia* for the loss of Quebec.[24] A large number of very valuable papers are attached to it as appendices. I can only attribute the failure to print this document to the hostility to Vaudreuil, which has been so evident among certain historians, including Doughty. Apparently it was considered that the governor was so prejudiced that it was unnecessary or undesirable to allow his views to go before the court.

III

With this background, we may pass on to discuss the much-controverted campaign of 1759.

205

To me, after a long period spent studying the documents, it seems that there was no really first-class military figure among the men present at Quebec on that famous occasion. The claims to genius made on behalf of both Wolfe and Montcalm have been advanced by writers unduly influenced by the romantic circumstances in which they fought and died. Both possessed military talents. Neither deserves to rank among the great captains of history. Montcalm's reputation has been gilded by a glorious failure and a gallant death, while Wolfe's has reflected the splendour of a famous victory which he apparently did not expect and probably did not deserve.

Pitt took a considerable chance when he appointed Wolfe to the Quebec expedition, for the young general had had no experience in independent command. And the campaign which he conducted during the summer of 1759, in spite of the success which finally crowned it, suggests that Wolfe was in fact unfitted for such command. Our knowledge of the development of his plans, though incomplete, is considerably improved by his letters to Monckton in the Northcliffe Collection at Ottawa,[25] which have not been used by his biographers or by any historian of the campaign. They serve further to document Wolfe's vacillations and uncertainties, which are already familiar to students and were emphasized by Adair. According to my calculation — and another person would probably arrive at another figure — Wolfe adopted and rejected seven different operational plans before finally settling upon the one which gave him his victory. To drag this audience through all the detail would be extreme cruelty; but I feel that I must at least attempt an outline.

Knowing before he reached Quebec that his basic problem was to get at the weak land side of the fortress, Wolfe's main idea was to seize and fortify the Beauport shore below the city, with a view to advancing thence across the St. Charles.[26] But when he landed on the Isle of Orleans on 27 June he at once discovered that Montcalm had anticipated him and had himself fortified that area. Wolfe's first plan was thus defeated. His second one, adopted on 3 July after consultation with Admiral Saunders, was to "get ashore if possible above the town."[27] To assist this scheme he proposed to bombard Quebec from the south shore of the St. Lawrence, and to make a landing below the Montmorency as a diversion. But by the 10th he had clearly abandoned this plan — probably partly because the Navy did not yet fully control the waters about Quebec, partly because of French military counter-moves — and had converted the Montmorency diversion into his main operation. On 16 July he outlined to Monckton in some detail a scheme for a frontal attack on the French entrenchments here.[28] This was his third plan. But on the night of 18–19 July a division of the fleet for the first time passed Quebec and got into upper river. Wolfe now, probably very wisely, switched back to that flank, abandoning the Montmorency scheme in favour of an enterprise above the town.

Early on the morning of 20 July he wrote Monckton[29] at Point Lévis ordering him to cooperate in an attack that evening which was apparently to be directed at St. Michel, a short distance above the Anse au Foulon. Preparations went forward actively; but at 1 p.m. the same day Wolfe postponed the operation, apparently because the French, alarmed by the movement of the ships, were moving men and guns. He kept this hopeful fourth plan alive for some days, but by 25–6 July he had abandoned it and was back to the eastern flank, reconnoitring the crossings of the Montmorency. Getting no encouragement here, on the 28th he announced that he had decided on an attack on an outwork of the French Beauport position. A small redoubt on the beach, which Wolfe calculated was out of musket-shot of the French entrenchments, was to be captured and strengthened. The hope was that Montcalm would attack it and allow the British to fight a defensive action. Wolfe wrote, "I take it to be better that the Marquis shou'd attack a firm Corps of ours w^h superiority of numbers, than that we should attack his whole Army entrenched, w^h what we can put on shoar at one landing. . . . "[30]

This was his fifth plan. He tried to carry it out on the eventful 31st of July. The first stage was to run a couple of armed vessels ashore close to the redoubt. Wolfe boarded one of them to reconnoitre, and at once saw that his calculations had been at fault. The redoubt was closer to the entrenchments than he had believed, and would not be tenable under their fire. With the French shot flying about him, Wolfe made a reappraisal. He decided to go on with the operation; but now it took the form he had rejected a couple of days before — a frontal attack on the French army in its entrenchments, the circumstances in which the Canadian militia were most formidable. This was so fundamental a change that it deserves to be called his sixth plan. And the attack was a bloody failure.

A pause followed, during which Wolfe continued his incendiary bombardment of Quebec, and began systematically devastating the farming communities above and below the city. He hoped that this might goad Montcalm into coming out of his inaccessible entrenchments and attacking him; but "the Marquis" refused to be drawn. Then Wolfe fell ill; and in a famous memorandum he sought, belatedly, the advice of his three able brigadiers. He asked them to consider three possible plans of operations, all simply variants of the Montmorency attack that had failed on 31 July. In their forceful reply the brigadiers politely rejected all three and put their collective finger on the dominant fact of the strategic situation — the fact that there was virtually no food in Quebec, and that the garrison and the inhabitants were entirely dependent upon supplies brought in from the west. Cut that line of communication, and Montcalm would have to come out and fight. Their advice accordingly was, abandon the Montmorency position and concentrate the hitherto divided army for action above the town. It was excellent advice, and Wolfe took it.

207

By 7 September, accordingly, the main body of the army was embarked in the ships above Quebec. The brigadiers recommended a landing above Cap Rouge, in the St. Augustin–Pointe-aux-Trembles area, a dozen or more miles west of the city. Orders were issued for this operation, which we may term the seventh plan; and it came close to being executed on 8 September. But the weather broke; and before the rain stopped Wolfe changed his mind again. He had adopted, and kept to, the most vital features of the brigadiers' plan (a point which Doughty did not understand or appreciate); but on the important matter of choice of a landing-place he now took leave of it. What drew his attention to the Anse au Foulon we simply do not know;[31] but he decided to land there, less than three miles from Quebec, at a point where the steepness of the cliffs would make an opposed landing impossible, and where the main French force was close at hand. The brigadiers' scheme offered the same strategic advantage — the cutting of the supply line from the west — with much less risk and better hope of a decisive result; for an army defeated near Pointe-aux-Trembles would have had fewer facilities for a withdrawal towards Montreal than one defeated on the Plains of Abraham. But fortune, which is said to favour the brave, favoured Wolfe; every break went his way; a plan whose success depended entirely upon luck was blessed with that commodity in unlimited quantities. To the last, indeed, Wolfe himself seems to have found it difficult to believe in his own good fortune. There is a fairly well authenticated story that after reaching the top of the cliff he sent Isaac Barré back to stop the landing until he could be quite certain that the French were not in the area in strength. Barré, finding that the "second flight" of troops were already offshore ready to land, simply refrained from delivering the order and allowed the landing to proceed.[32]

These are not the actions of a great commander. As a strategist — a big word for such small operations, but it seems to be the only one — Wolfe was painfully inadequate. There is no military figure so ineffective as a general who cannot make up his mind. Wolfe was the last man who should have been trusted with an independent command. Moreover, he had defects of personality which made it difficult for him to work effectively with his senior subordinates. Two of his brigadiers came to detest him, and while we know little about his relations with the third, Monckton, we do know that the general wrote Monckton two letters apologizing for some slight and begging him not to turn against him.[33] Wolfe's journal contains strictures on the Navy which suggest that he was a difficult colleague; Admiral Saunders' opinion of him unfortunately seems not to have been recorded. Add to this the policy of deliberate terror which Wolfe applied against the city of Quebec and the neighbouring parishes, a policy which did little or nothing to advance his campaign, and we get a total picture which is not impressive.

Nevertheless, Wolfe was not without valuable military qualities. He was an uncommonly fine fighting officer, at his best under fire; and this accounts for his great reputation among the junior ranks of his army, who knew nothing of his deficiencies as a planner. Once the army was ashore at the Anse au Foulon no mistakes were made. Wolfe was as decisive on the battlefield as he had been indecisive through the long weeks when he was fumbling with his strategic problem. To say that he was no more than "a good regimental officer" is I think to underrate him. It would be truer to say that he had it in him to be a good tactician, capable of vigorous and effective leadership and control in action. Working under a higher commander who could prescribe his tasks, he would have been a very valuable officer. He could win a battle, though he could not plan a campaign.

IV

Let us turn to Montcalm. As a strategist be seems to me to have been superior to Wolfe. French-Canadian writers, including Professor Frégault, have criticized him for adopting so exclusively a defensive a policy; but this was the policy suited to his means and his circumstances, and therefore it was right. He had more men than Wolfe, but they were largely amateurs, confronting an army of professionals. Under these conditions, it was in Wolfe's interest to bring on a battle in the open field, and in Montcalm's to avoid one. And time was on Montcalm's side. If he could only hold his position and avoid a disaster, the approach of winter would drive the British out of the St. Lawrence. The best tribute to the soundness of Montcalm's policy is Wolfe's letters and dispatches, which testify repeatedly to the manner in which he was frustrated by the French defences and Montcalm's determination to remain within them. Yet Montcalm had made a fundamental strategic error in keeping the French food supplies in depots up the river, and thereby rendering his force dependent from day to day on an exposed line of communication. The object was to enable the field army to retire westward, and still be fed, in case of the loss of Quebec; and it is apparent that it was almost an article of belief among the French that major units of the British fleet could not get past the city. But when this happened, and the British cut the line of communication, Montcalm's whole defensive policy fell to the ground and he had to risk a battle.

Montcalm lacked one invaluable ability which some fortunate generals have possessed. He had no flair for penetrating his adversary's intentions. To him, as apparently to everybody else in authority on the French side, the landing at the Foulon was a thunderbolt out of a clear sky. All the evidence indicates that to the last he thought Wolfe's most probable course was a blow at Beauport, with a landing far up the river as second choice. And it is not to Montcalm's credit as a commander that he failed to observe the possibilities of the Foulon track — which offered a perfectly good means of moving cannon up from the river to the heights west of the city.

Montcalm, as has often been recognized, committed a serious tactical error on the battlefield. He certainly had to attack, to clear his line of communication; but he did not have to attack at ten o'clock in the morning instead of a few hours later. As I already mentioned, he feared that the British would soon establish themselves too firmly to be evicted; and with what seems to have been characteristic impulsiveness he launched his assault without waiting for Colonel de Bougainville, who was only a few miles away and had the best troops in the French army with him. He thus threw away his best hope of victory.

Like Wolfe, Montcalm had defects of temperament which affected his military usefulness. His feud with Vaudreuil is well known. The pompous Governor undoubtedly gave him provocation, but Montcalm's own journal provides evidence that the general had a rather low boiling-point. I suspect that the same nervous impatience that drove him on to the premature attack on 13 September made it difficult for him to bear with Vaudreuil. The discord between the two men was a misfortune for New France, though its military effects have probably been somewhat exaggerated. The French Court ought to have removed one or the other. A proposal was in fact made at the end of 1758 to relieve Montcalm, replacing him with the Chevalier de Lévis; but the King seems to have decided against it. The decision was probably unfortunate, for it was important to restore concord to the colony, and Lévis, certainly a soldier of ability, would doubtless have conducted the defence as well as Montcalm did.

V

The more one considers the campaign of 1759, the more the conclusion emerges that the decisive factor in the result was not superior British generalship but the superior efficiency of the British forces. The professionals beat the amateurs, as they usually do. British sea power was of course the basic strategic determinant, but in addition the presence of a large and efficient British fleet before Quebec had enormous influence on the tactical operations. As for the military forces, the British superiority in quality, evident throughout the campaign, appears with special clarity in the final crisis of 13 September. The British tactical plan for the approach and landing at the Anse au Foulon, excellent in itself, was executed by the Navy with a skill which it requires some study of combined operations to appreciate. The same boats landed three flights of troops in rapid succession. The one hitch — the fact that the tide carried the first flight some distance below the intended point of landing — was offset by the resourcefulness of Lt.-Col. William Howe, who led his light infantrymen straight up the cliff before them, an athletic feat which was I believe no part of Wolfe's plan.

210

By comparison, the picture on the French side is one of extreme disorganization, beginning with the extraordinary fact that after ordering a movement of provision boats, and warning their posts to pass them through, the French authorities cancelled the movement without informing the posts. Everything else was of a piece with this. Control, communication, and vigilance were all lacking, with the result that at dawn, when the British army was pouring ashore at the Foulon, the French army, having manned its Beauport entrenchments much of the night, was retiring to its tents. In the actual encounter on the Plains, the result was clearly due to superior British discipline and training. The weak French regular battalions had been heavily diluted with militia, and the attackers were falling into hopeless disorder long before the British fired a musket-shot at them.[34] Wolfe had assumed with the utmost confidence that his highly trained professional soldiers would have an easy victory if the French could only be brought to action in the open; and the result justified his calculations.

VI

The Battle of the Plains was only half a victory: partly because of the plan Wolfe had adopted, which gave the French the chance of retiring behind the St. Charles River and getting away to the west by way of Charlesbourg and the Lorettes, and partly perhaps because of Wolfe's own death, which deprived the British of effective higher leading at a moment when a skilful and energetic tactician might possibly have made the triumph really complete. The result was that the British got Quebec, but the French field army remained in being, and another year's campaign was needed to destroy that army and end the war in Canada. About the 1760 campaign I propose to say only a few words.

The French position this year was hopeless, first because the Court of Versailles sent inadequate assistance, and secondly because the assistance it sent never reached its destination — since in 1760 the British fleet got into the St. Lawrence first. But the campaign conducted by Lévis and Vaudreuil in the hope of large-scale help from France was both a valiant adventure and a skilful strategic performance. The popular French-Canadian legend of this campaign and in particular of its chief incident, the defeat of Murray in the so-called Battle of Ste. Foy on 28 April, seems to be that it was an improvised effort carried out with inadequate means largely by the Canadian militia. The material means available to Lévis were certainly pitifully inadequate, but it would be an error to assume that at Ste. Foy the British regulars were defeated by the Canadian amateurs. In this battle, as in the one in the previous September, the professional soldier was the essential figure. Montcalm in the Battle of the Plains had five battalions of the *troupes de terre*. Lévis at Ste. Foy had eight (less detachments spared for Lake Champlain), three of them having been virtually unengaged in 1759. The total force collected for his expedition was just under 7,000 men, including 3,889 regulars, while Murray reports that he himself had 3,866 officers and men in the battle.[35] Thus Lévis had almost exactly the same number of regulars as Murray, plus his 3000 militiamen as a bonus. Taking a "calculated risk" with respect to other fronts, he had effected a powerful concentration before Quebec.

Murray has been criticized for abandoning his excellent defensive position outside the walls of Quebec in order to attack Lévis. The criticism is probably just, for in the presence of so superior an enemy a defensive battle was Murray's best chance for a victory. Nevertheless, he came closer to winning than has been generally recognized. He explains that, reconnoitring the French, he "preceiv'd their Van busy throwing up Redoubts while their Main body was yet on their march"; and he attempted "to attack them before they could have time to Form."[36] Snow and mud hindered the movement of his guns. Yet it was a very near thing — so near that Lévis momentarily lost his nerve, decided that his troops were not going to succeed in forming and ordered the abandonment of a vital position on the left flank. The day was saved for the French by Lt.-Col. Dalquier, commanding the La Sarre brigade in this sector. Estimating the situation more accurately than Lévis, he took it on himself to countermand the general's order and led his men to the attack. Subsequently Lévis thanked him for this timely disobedience.[37] Since both the opposing commanders made serious miscalculations, the level of generalship at Ste. Foy cannot be said to have been particularly high.

211

* * *

What can one say in conclusion? Reviewing these great events of two centuries ago, and what has been written about them, it is hard to take much pride in our historiography. To a large extent, the chief actors have been interpreted in the light of prejudice and sentimentality. They have been made romantic heroes or villains rather than human beings to be studied on the basis of the records. Historians have approached the men and events of the time with their minds already made up, and have looked to the documents for evidence to bolster up their preconceptions rather than for facts to enable them to arrive at an objective appraisal. In his presidential address last year Dr. Lamb quietly made the devasting remark, "Real accuracy in Canadian historical writing is rare." Many of the histories of the conquest of Canada illustrate this observation only too forcibly. Much remains to be done in Canadian history. Unfortunately also, it appears that a good deal is going to have to be done over again.

212

NOTES

[1] This paper is a by-product of a book by the author entitled *Quebec, 1759: The Siege and the Battle*, published in September 1959 by The Macmillan Company of Canada Limited. Since the book is fully documented, some documentation which would otherwise have been necessary has been dispensed with here.

[2] Corbett, *England in the Seven Years' War*, 2 vols. (London, 1907), 1: 398. Public Record Office, London, C.O. 5/213 (transcript, Public Archives of Canada [PAC]).

[3] See Wolfe to Townshend, 6 Jan. 1759, in Beckles Willson, *The Life and Letters of James Wolfe* (London, 1909), 414. Cf. Rex Whitworth, *Field-Marshal Lord Ligonier* (London, 1958), 278-80. Von Ruville in his *William Pitt, Earl of Chatham*, 3 vols. (London, 1907) notes that Burton was passed over; but his comment is not perceptive (2: 262n.).

[4] It is reproduced in A.G. Doughty's edition of Knox's *Historical Journal of the Campaigns in North America*, 3 vols. (Toronto, 1914-16), vol. 3, opposite p. 150. It should be compared with the subsequent *Plan of the Town of Quebec . . .* , also signed by Mackellar (PAC).

[5] *Eg.*, the version of Vaudreuil's letter to Bourlamaque, 6 Aug. 1759 (Bourlamaque Papers, PAC) printed in *Montcalm and Wolfe* (ed. 1910, 3: 75) in inverted commas, is not a quotation but a very free paraphrase.

[6] See De Kerallain's *La Jeunesse de Bougainville et la guerre de sept ans* (Paris, 1896), 7.

[7] *Collection des Manuscrits du Maréchal de Lévis*, 12 vols. (Montreal and Quebec, 1889-95).

[8] *Collections des Manuscrits du Maréchal de Lévis* 7: 612. MS of Montcalm journal, Lévis Papers, PAC.

[9] *The Siege of Quebec* 3: 107.

[10] *Collection des Manuscrits du Maréchal de Lévis* 5: 357 (18 Sept. 1759).

[11] *The Siege of Quebec* 3: 301.

[12] The dispatch to Pitt is published in full in Kimball. The letter to Saunders was published in *Gentleman's Magazine*, June 1801. For Doughty's version, published he says "in full," see *The Siege of Quebec* 2: 151-54.

[13] *Unique Quebec* (Literary and Historical Society of Quebec, 1924).

[14] Letter of 29 July 1759, appended to Vaudreuil to the Minister, 5 Oct. 1759, PAC, F3, vol. 15.

[15] Toronto, 1920 (Chronicles of Canada), 128.

[16] "The Anse au Foulon, 1759: Montcalm and Vaudreuil," *Canadian Historical Review* (March 1959).

[17] *The Fight for Canada* (ed. Boston, 1906), 142-43, 145. Wood calls Wolfe "a regimental lieutenant-colonel," but he had been Colonel of the 67th Foot since 1757.

[18] *The Fight for Canada*, 334, re Robert Stobo's *Memoirs*.

[19] This battalion was with Bourlamaque on Lake Champlain. And no French sentry would have asked such a question. Transport was no task for regular troops.

[20] *Etat Militaire de France, pour l'année 1759 . . .* (Paris, 1759), 228.

[21] "The Military Reputation of Major-General James Wolfe," Canadian Historical Association, *Report* (1936).

[22] *La Guerre de la conquête* (Montréal, 1955).

[23] 2 vols., New York, 1906.

[24] Above, note 14.

[25] Monckton Papers, vol. 22.

[26] Letter to Major Walter Wolfe, 19 May 1759, Willson, 427–29. This letter also refers to the possibility of entrenching a detachment *above* the town.

[27] Wolfe's Journal, McGill University version.

[28] Monckton Papers, vol. 22.

[29] Monckton Papers, vol. 22.

[30] To Monckton, n.d. (29 July ?), Monckton Papers, vol. 22.

[31] The statements of Doughty and Wood that Robert Stobo cannot have suggested it because he left Quebec on 7 September with dispatches for Amherst have no validity — for it was on the very next day that Wolfe (according to Townshend) "went a reconoitring down the river" and may have first observed the Foulon path. Stobo might well have made the suggestion in a final interview. But there is no evidence for this.

[32] Henry Caldwell to James Murray, 1 Nov. 1772, Amherst Papers, Packet 28 (transcript, PAC).

[33] 15 and 16 Aug. 1759, Monckton Papers, vol. 22.

[34] See, eg., Malartic to Bourlamaque, 28 Sept. 1759, Bourlamaque Papers, *Variarum*, PAC.

[35] Lévis' Journal, April 1760, *Collection des Manuscrits*, vol. 1; strength return, *Collection des Monuscrits* 1: 257. Murray's dispatch to Pitt, 25 May 1760, C.O. 5/64.

[36] Murray's Journal, 28 Apr. 1760 (photostat, PAC).

[37] Lt.-Gen. le Comte de Maurès de Malartic, *Journal des Campagnes au Canada de 1755 à 1760* (Paris, 1890), 317. Cf. Bourlamaque to Bougainville, 3 May 1760, de Kerallain, *La Jeunesse de Bougainville*, 167.

Tory Refugees on Their Way to Canada, *by H. Pyle.*

> **The Revolution had deprived them of their rightful place in the world, the aftermath had thrown them into an unwelcome dependence on the British patronage system, and finally the northern frontier threatened to sap their energies and their talents without yielding any commensurate sense of achievement.**
>
> **Ann Gorman Condon, *The Envy of the American States: The Loyalist Dream for New Brunswick***

The Impact of the American Revolution on the Maritime Colonies

Ironically, Britain's success in expelling France from North America contributed to its own expulsion from the Thirteen Colonies only fifteen years later. The removal of the French threat from Quebec and Louisbourg had, in the minds of many American colonists, ended the need for Britain in North America. This realization, along with a growing sense of nationalism among the Thirteen Colonies, led to the demand for greater self-government. Britain's attempt to tax the colonies finally led to open rebellion. The first armed clash at Lexington, Massachusetts, in mid-April 1775, officially began the American Revolution.

The Nova Scotians had to make a difficult decision: to support Britain, join the American cause, or remain neutral. Three-quarters of Nova Scotia's roughly 20 000 settlers in 1775 were New Englanders with strong economic and family ties with the New England colonies. This being the case, why did they choose to remain loyal to the Crown? George Rawlyk offers an explanation for their loyalty in "The American Revolution and Nova Scotia Reconsidered."

During the Revolutionary War, thousands of American farmers, craftsmen, and small merchants, as well as large landowners and government officials, had sided with the Crown. After Britain's defeat, about 80 000 of these United Empire Loyalists chose, or were forced, to depart with the British garrisons, and more than half of them settled in two of the remaining British colonies to the north, Nova Scotia and Quebec. Approximately 30 000 went to Nova Scotia, almost doubling the size of the existing population; about 5000 came to the St. Lawrence Valley, doubling, perhaps even tripling, the English-speaking population there, from 4 or 5 percent to 10 or 15 percent of the total population; and nearly 10 000 settled in the western portion of the Province of Quebec, which became Upper Canada in 1791. The Loyalist migration led to the founding of two new colonies, New Brunswick and Upper Canada. In "The Envy of the American States," Ann Gorman Condon discusses the Loyalists' dreams for New Brunswick on the basis of letters, diaries, and accounts written by members of the Loyalist elite.

The classic account of Nova Scotia's response to the revolutionary struggle in the Thirteen Colonies is John Bartlet Brebner's *Neutral Yankees of Nova Scotia* (Toronto: McClelland and Stewart, 1969; first published in 1937). For a history of Nova Scotia–New England relations, see George Rawlyk, *Nova Scotia's Massachusetts: A Study of Massachusetts–Nova Scotia Relations, 1630 to 1784* (Montreal: McGill-Queen's University Press, 1973). Also useful are *Revolution Rejected, 1775–1776*, ed. George Rawlyk (Scarborough, Ontario: Prentice-Hall, 1968); the essays in *They Planted Well: New England Planters in Maritime Canada*, ed. Margaret Conrad (Fredericton: Acadiensis Press, 1988); and Margaret Conrad's *Making Adjustments: Change and Continuity in Planter Nova Scotia, 1759–1800* (Fredericton: Acadiensis Press, 1991). J.M. Bumsted's *Henry Alline* (Toronto: University of Toronto Press, 1971) reviews the career of the leader of an important religious revival in Nova Scotia during the years of the American Revolution.

The anthology *The United Empire Loyalists,* ed. L.S.F. Upton (Toronto: Copp Clark, 1967) provides a general overview. Neil MacKinnon reviews the impact of the Loyalists on Nova Scotia in *The Unfriendly Soil: The Loyalist Experience in Nova Scotia, 1783–1791* (Kingston and Montreal: McGill-Queen's University Press, 1986). On the background of the American Loyalists, see W.H. Nelson, *The American Tory* (Toronto: Oxford, 1961). For information on black Loyalists who came to Nova Scotia after the American Revolution, see James W. St. G. Walker's *The Black Loyalists: The Search for a Promised Land in Nova Scotia and Sierra Leone, 1783–1870* (Toronto: University of Toronto Press, 1992; first published in 1976 by Longman Group and Dalhousie University Press).

Three general studies of the Loyalists are Wallace Brown and Hereward Senior, *Victorious in Defeat: The Loyalists in Canada* (Toronto: Methuen, 1984); Christopher Moore, *The Loyalists: Revolution, Exile, Settlement* (Toronto: Macmillan, 1984); and Ann Gorman Condon, *The Envy of the American States: The Loyalist Dream for New Brunswick* (Fredericton: New Ireland Press, 1984), from which the reading in this section has been taken.

Robert S. Allen has compiled a useful bibliography, *Loyalist Literature: An Annotated Bibliographical Guide to the Writings on the Loyalists of the American Revolution* (Toronto: Dundurn Press, 1982). For books and articles produced after 1981, consult Bruce Bowden, "The Bicentennial Legacy — A Second Loyalist Revival," *Ontario History* 77 (1985): 65–74.

The American Revolution and Nova Scotia Reconsidered

GEORGE A. RAWLYK

On the eve of the American Revolution, Nova Scotia was little more than a political expression for a number of widely scattered and isolated communities. These stretched from Halifax to Maugerville on the St. John River and to the tiny outpost of Passamaquoddy on the St. Croix. At the end of the Seven Years' War many land-hungry settlers from Rhode Island, New Hampshire, Massachusetts, and Connecticut pushed up into the fertile regions bordering the Bay of Fundy which had been abandoned by the Acadians when they were expelled from the peninsula in 1755. In 1775 Nova Scotia had a population of only approximately 20,000 inhabitants,[1] three-quarters of whom were New Englanders with strong economic, cultural, and family ties with their former homeland.[2]

In spite of the fact that Nova Scotia was virtually New England's north-eastern frontier and was peopled by a majority of recently arrived New Englanders,[3] the colony refused in 1775 and 1776 to join in attempting to shatter the framework of the British colonial system. Instead, most of the inhabitants, especially the New Englanders, endeavoured to pursue a policy of neutrality, even though their moral support was firmly behind the "rebels." It is interesting to note that this policy of neutrality was exactly the same policy that the New Englanders severely condemned when it had been adopted by the Acadians two decades earlier. However, toward the end of the Revolution, the sympathies of the neutral New Englanders, largely as the result of serious depredations committed by American privateers throughout Nova Scotia from 1777 to 1782, shifted towards Great Britain.[4]

Why did Nova Scotia not join the Thirteen Colonies in attempting to break away from Britain in 1775 and 1776? Three distinct schools of thought have emerged in the effort to answer this question. First, the proponents of the "Halifax-merchant" school have stressed that the influential Halifax merchants were directly responsible for keeping Nova Scotia loyal to the Crown.[5] The merchants, believing that the Revolution was a Heaven-sent opportunity to supplant the New England colonies in the West Indian trade, and also that in the long run their colony would gain more than it would lose in retaining political and economic ties with Britain, were able to impose their will upon the other inhabitants. This is indeed an interesting interpretation, but one without any

217

From *Dalhousie Review* 43, 3 (Autumn 1963): 379–94. Reprinted with permission.

real foundation, since in 1775 the population of Halifax was only 1800 and the influence of the Halifax merchants was largely confined chiefly to the area of the Bedford Basin.[6] It is clear that their economic ties with Britain were strong, but it is just as clear that they were in no effective position to impose their will upon the other Nova Scotians, who in actual fact reacted violently to the merchant clique that was attempting to manipulate the economic and political life of the colony.

Second, W.B. Kerr, who has written far more about Nova Scotia during the Revolutionary period than any other historian, has strongly argued that as early as 1765 it was inevitable that Nova Scotia would remain loyal to George III. Kerr maintains that there was an almost total absence of "national sentiment"[7] among the New Englanders of Nova Scotia and that, because of this lack of "nationalism,"[8] there was very little popular support for the Revolutionary cause in Nova Scotia.[9] It appears that Kerr has clearly underestimated the general significance of the widespread sympathy for Revolutionary principles. This feeling was prevalent throughout Nova Scotia, with the notable exception of Halifax, in 1775 and 1776. Moreover, he has failed to draw sufficient attention to the profound impact that the isolation of most of the Nova Scotian settlements and the British control of the North Atlantic had upon seriously weakening the indigenous Revolutionary movement.

Third, J.B. Brebner, in his excellent work, *The Neutral Yankees of Nova Scotia*, has asserted that the Revolutionary movement failed in Nova Scotia because "the sympathizers with rebellion among the outlying populace could make no headway because their friends in the rebellious Colonies had no navy and because they themselves could not assemble from the scattered settlements an effective force for unassisted revolt."[10] Brebner's is certainly the most satisfactory answer to the original question regarding Nova Scotia and the Revolution. A careful and critical examination of events in the Chignecto region of Nova Scotia in the years 1775 and 1776 will not only serve to prove the validity of Brebner's thesis, but will also cast a considerable amount of light upon the relations between Nova Scotia and the colonies to the south during a most critical period.

The Isthmus of Chignecto provided the stage upon which a somewhat inconsequential scene from the American Revolutionary drama was played. The Eddy Rebellion of 1776 had most of the characteristics of a tragic comedy; a glorious failure, it was nevertheless accompanied by death and destruction.

The Chignecto Isthmus is a narrow neck of land joining the peninsula of Nova Scotia to the North American mainland. Roughly ten miles in width and twenty in length, the Isthmus is bordered on the north-east by Baie Verte, on the south-west by the Cumberland Basin, and on the north-west and south-east by the Sackville and Amherst Ridges, respectively. J.C. Webster, one of New Brunswick's outstanding historians, has

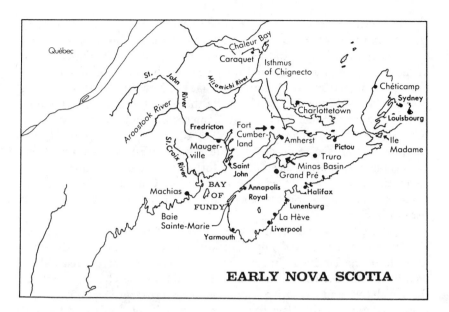

EARLY NOVA SCOTIA

Paul Cornell, Jean Hamelin, Fernand Ouellet, and Marcel Trudel, eds., *Canada: Unity in Diversity* (Toronto: Holt, Rinehart and Winston, 1967), 121.

asserted that "no area of its [Chignecto's] size anywhere in America has a greater or more varied wealth of historical memories and traditions."[11] There is much evidence to support Webster's sweeping generalization.

The vacuum created by the expulsion of the majority of the Acadians from the fertile Isthmus in 1755 was quickly filled at the end of the Seven Years' War by settlers from New England.[12] Unlike the Acadians, these men energetically began to clear and to cultivate the ridge lands, which had a heavy forest cover.[13] Only after many frustrating failures were the New Englanders able to master marsh agriculture.[14] From 1772 to 1775 they sullenly observed the arrival of over 500 Yorkshire immigrants seeking "a better livelihood"[15] in the New World. These newcomers had been recruited by the aggressive Lieutenant-Governor of Nova Scotia, Michael Francklin.[16]

Thus in 1775 the general Chignecto Isthmus region contained three important elements within its population. The New Englanders were the most numerous, but the Yorkshiremen were not too far behind. Together these two groups numbered 220 families.[17] The third element was the Acadian; there were thirty Acadian families, most of the members of which worked on the land belonging to the English-speaking farmers.[18]

There was considerable friction and ill-feeling between the New Englanders and the newcomers from the north of England on the one hand, and between the former and the Halifax government on the other. Most of the New Englanders detested their new neighbours, not only because the Yorkshiremen had settled on land that the New Englanders had long coveted and considered to be rightfully theirs, but also because the outlook of the Englishmen was almost diametrically opposite to that of the Americans. The Yorkshiremen were Methodists closely tied to the Mother Country and all she represented, while the New Englanders were Congregationalists who had been greatly influenced by the North American environment and whose ties with the Mother Country were extremely tenuous. The Old World was in conflict with the New on this narrow neck of land.

The New Englanders, moreover, were greatly dissatisfied with the Halifax government. Had not Francklin encouraged the Yorkshiremen to settle in the Isthmus? Furthermore, the New Englanders reacted violently to the fact that a small clique of Halifax merchants controlled the legislative and executive functions of government,[19] stubbornly refusing to grant to the New Englanders the right of "township form of government," which Governor Lawrence had promised them in 1758 and 1759.[20]

A spark was needed to set the kindling discontent ablaze. The American Revolution provided the spark, but the fire was quickly and easily extinguished before it could spread and result in any serious damage.

The centre of organized activity against Nova Scotia during the first years of the Revolution was the tiny lumbering outpost of Machias, a few miles west of the St. Croix River.[21] Most of the inhabitants wanted to grow rich by sacking the prosperous Nova Scotian settlements, particularly Halifax. These freebooters, these eighteenth-century filibusters, unsuccessfully endeavoured to hide their real, selfish motive beneath a veneer of concern for Revolutionary principles.

In the summer of 1775 they proposed to General Washington to invade Nova Scotia if supported by a force of 1000 soldiers and four armed vessels.[22] When Washington was asked to act upon this bold plan in August, he tactfully refused; all available men and supplies were needed for the proposed Quebec invasion. His reasoned arguments justifying his refusal are of considerable consequence since they explain why Washington refused to mount any kind of offensive against Nova Scotia in 1775 and 1776:

> As to the Expedition proposed against Nova Scotia by the Inhabitants of Machias, I cannot but applaud their Spirit and Zeal; but, after considering the Reasons offered for it, there are Several objections . . . which seem to me unanswerable. I apprehend such an Enterprise inconsistent with the General Principal upon which the Colonies have proceeded. That Province has not acceeded, it is true, to the Measures of Congress; and therefore, they have been excluded from all

220

Commercial Intercourse with the other Colonies; But they have not Commenced Hostilities against them, nor are any to be apprehended. To attack *them*, therefore, is a Measure of Conquest, rather than Defence, and may be attended with very dangerous consequences. It might, perhaps, be easy, with the force proposed, to make an Incursion into the Province and overawe those of the Inhabitants who are Inimical to our cause; and, for a short time prevent the Supplying the Enemy with Provisions; but the same Force must continue to produce any lasting Effects. As to the furnishing Vessels of Force, you, Gentlemen, will anticipate me, in pointing out our weakness and the Enemy's Strength at Sea. There would be great Danger that, with the best preparation we could make, they would fall an easy prey either to the Men of War of that Station [Halifax] or some who would be detach'd from Boston.[23]

Washington was no doubt right in the long run, but the inhabitants of Machias almost intuitively realized that in the summer of 1775 Nova Scotia was ripe for plucking from the British colonial tree. American economic pressure had resulted in a serious recession,[24] Governor Legge was alienating leading elements of the population, and the exploits of the Revolution had captured the imagination of the New Englanders.[25] In addition, there were only thirty-six British regulars guarding Halifax,[26] and Legge, who seriously believed that the New Englanders "were rebels to the man," sadly observed that "the fortifications [of Halifax] were in a dilapidated state, the batteries . . . dismantled, the gun-carriages decayed, the guns on the ground."[27] If the men from Machias had had their way, the invading force would have been enthusiastically welcomed and openly supported by the vast majority of "Yankees" and would have easily gained control of the colony. However, the lack of suitable land communications between the various settlements in Nova Scotia, as well as between Nova Scotia and the other colonies, together with the British control of the Atlantic, would have probably forced the American troops to abandon Nova Scotia after a brief occupation. Washington's refusal to attack Nova Scotia when it was ripe for conquest and the arrival of military reinforcements in Halifax in October[28] virtually made certain that the Colony would remain within the framework of the British colonial system during the war years.

In the summer months an indigenous revolutionary movement came into being in the Chignecto region.[29] It was led by John Allan, a Scot who had been won over to the American revolutionary cause, and Jonathan Eddy, who had left Massachusetts to settle in the Isthmus after the Seven Years' War. Sam Rogers, Zebulon Rowe, Obadiah Ayer, and William Howe, among others, all respected and prosperous New Englanders, supported Allan and Eddy. These men were greatly encouraged by the successful sacking in August of Fort Frederick, a tiny British military outpost at the mouth of the Saint John River, by a small Machias force,[30] and also by the bold pronouncement of the inhabitants of Maugerville in favour of the Revolution. The Maugerville settlers declared

221

that they were willing "to submit ourselves to the government of the Massachusetts Bay and that we are ready with our lives and fortunes to share with them the event of the present struggle for liberty, however, God in his providence may order it."[31]

Towards the end of November, Allan, Eddy, and their not insignificant following were given an excellent opportunity to precipitate a crisis that could have conceivably led to a successful rebellion. The long-simmering discontent with the government authorities finally boiled over when the assembly, controlled by the small Halifax merchant clique with strong commercial ties with Britain, passed two acts, one to call out a fifth of the militia, the other to impose a tax for its support.[32] Almost immediately the two bills were loudly denounced throughout the colony, but especially in the Chignecto region. Allan and Eddy, instead of quickly harnessing the deep dissatisfaction within the framework of armed rebellion, decided to widen first the popular basis of their support by sending a rather mildly worded yet firm protest against the two bills to Governor Legge. In the protest, which was eventually signed by almost 250 inhabitants including many Yorkshiremen, the Chignecto settlers objected to the new tax and to the possibility of being forced to "march into different parts in arms against their friends and relations."[33] Allan and Eddy had succeeded in gaining much popular support for their attack upon the Halifax government, but at the moment when they attempted to use this support to emulate the example of the colonies in revolt, Legge suddenly pulled the rug from under their unsuspecting feet. Realizing the seriousness of the discontent as reflected in the Chignecto petition, the governor promptly suspended the two contentious acts. In so doing, Legge had removed the catalyst from the potential revolutionary situation not only in the Isthmus but throughout Nova Scotia.

Failing to grasp the significance of Legge's clever manoeuvre, Allan and Eddy decided during the first weeks of January, 1776, that the time was propitious for fomenting an insurrection. Nothing could have been further from the truth. Having won the support of the Acadians, but the equally enthusiastic disapprobation of the Yorkshiremen, Allan and Eddy decided that before taking any further steps on the road to rebellion it was first imperative to sound out carefully the general feeling of the mass of New Englanders towards the proposed vague plan. The two leaders were genuinely shocked to discover that the vast majority of New Englanders, even though they "would have welcomed an army of invasion,"[34] stubbornly refused to support the planned insurrection. Ground between the millstones of contending forces, most of the Chignecto New Englanders, as well as those throughout the colony, had decided to walk the tightrope of neutrality until it was clear that a strong rebel invading force would be able to gain effective control of Nova Scotia. Allan and Eddy were forced to alter drastically their proposed policy;

they decided to petition General Washington and the Continental Congress to send an "army of liberation" to Nova Scotia. The Machias plan of August 1775 had been resurrected.

Jonathan Eddy, with a band of fourteen men, had set out in February from Chignecto to persuade Washington and the Continental Congress to invade Nova Scotia. On March 27, Eddy met with the American general at Cambridge.[35] Washington carefully considered Eddy's often illogical arguments, but believing that the British forces that had abandoned Boston[36] ten days earlier were now in Halifax, the General informed the ambassador that "in the present uncertain state of things . . . a much more considerable force [than Eddy had even requested] would be of no avail."[37] Washington reaffirmed the policy he had first enunciated on hearing of the Machias plan in August of the preceding year.[38] The disillusioned Eddy next went to the Continental Congress in Philadelphia, but as he expected, here too his urgent appeal fell on unresponsive ears.[39] After his return to the Isthmus in May it was decided that, as a last resort, the government of Massachusetts should be approached for military aid. The persistent Eddy, accompanied by Howe, Rogers, and Rowe, immediately set sail for Boston.

During the months of January and February the Halifax government had been strangely indifferent to developments in the Chignecto Isthmus. The loyalist leaders, Charles Dixon and the Rev. John Eagleson, had bombarded the Governor and his Executive Council with frantic letters.[40] A delegation had been sent to General Washington by the New Englanders;[41] and on hearing a rumour that the American army had captured Bunker Hill, the supporters of Allan and Eddy had procured "a chaise and six horses, postillion and a flag of liberty, and drove about the isthmus, proclaiming the news and blessings of liberty."[42] Dixon and Eagleson demanded immediate government action. In March the Executive Council resolved "that the lieutenant-governor [Francklin] be desired to proceed, as soon as possible to [Chignecto] . . . and there make a strict inquiry into the behavior and conduct of the inhabitants, and to make report thereof to the governor; also, that he will apprehend all persons, who, on due proof, shall be found guilty of any rebellious and treasonable transactions."[43] Francklin, however, was able to accomplish absolutely nothing. It was not until June that the government exerted some semblance of authority on the troubled Isthmus. This delay was at least partly the result of the recall of Legge in May and his replacement by Lieutenant-Colonel Arbuthnot.[44] In June, 200 Royal Fencibles[45] under the command of Lieutenant-Colonel Joseph Gorham were sent to occupy Fort Cumberland, which had been abandoned by the British eight years earlier.[46] Fort Cumberland, the reconstructed French Fort Beauséjour, was strategically located at the extreme southern tip of the Fort Cumberland Ridge which, together with the Fort Lawrence Ridge, cuts through the Chignecto marshlands until it almost touches the waters

223

of the Bay of Fundy. Gorham found the fort in a state of serious disrepair. He reported that "the face of the Bastions, Curtains, etc., by being so long exposed to the heavy rains and frost were bent down to such a slope that one might with ease ascend any part of the fort."[47] Gorham set about repairing the fort, and he went out of his way to overlook what he considered to be the harmless activities of the energetic American sympathizers. He hoped that a simple show of strength would completely undermine the position held by the Eddy-Allan faction.

It was not until July that the Halifax authorities, at last convinced of the seriousness of the revolutionary movement in the Isthmus, considered it necessary to strike against the leaders of the "American Party." A proclamation was issued offering a reward of 200 for the capture of Eddy and 100 for Allan, Howe, and Rogers.[48] On hearing that he was a man with a price on his head, Allan decided to join his friends in Massachusetts and left a committee in charge of "the revolutionary interests."[49]

Eddy was unsuccessful in his attempt to persuade the General Court of Massachusetts to send a military expedition "supplied with some necessaries, as provisions and ammunition . . . [to] destroy those [Nova Scotian] forts and relieve our brethren and friends."[50] Nevertheless, he had not entirely failed. He was promised sufficient ammunition and supplies to equip properly whatever force he himself could muster. Eddy immediately rushed off to Machias, where he knew there was a group of men still vitally interested in attacking Nova Scotia. By carefully playing upon their cupidity Eddy was able to recruit twenty-eight men from Machias.[51] On August 11, just as the invading army was embarking, Allan arrived. Fully aware of the weakness of the revolutionary movement on the Isthmus, Allan endeavoured in vain to dissuade Eddy from carrying out his rash and hopeless plan. Eddy refused to come to grips with the hard facts of reality; he hoped that his force would build up like a giant snowball at Passamaquoddy and Maugerville and that the Chignecto New Englanders would eagerly rally to his banner. He seemed to believe that it would be only a matter of time before his liberating army would force the British to abandon "New England's Outpost."[52]

At Passamaquoddy, a few miles to the east of Machias, Eddy added seven new recruits and then sailed to Maugerville in three whale boats.[53] At the settlement on the upper Saint John River he found the inhabitants "almost universally to be hearty in the cause,"[54] but was able to enlist only twenty-seven settlers and sixteen Indians.[55] Eddy's liberating army, now numbering some eighty men, returned to the mouth of the Saint John River to await the arrival of the promised ammunition and supplies from Boston.[56] There was an unexpected prolonged delay, and the force was unable to move eastwards until the last week of October. On October 29, Eddy's men easily captured fourteen of Gorham's troops who were stationed at the military outpost of Shepody, to the south of present-day Moncton.[57] The invaders[58] then swung sharply to the north and made their way up the Petitcodiac and Memramcook rivers to the Acadian settlement of Memramcook, where Eddy had no trouble whatsoever in persuading a number of Acadians to support him.[59] From Memramcook, on November 5, Eddy and his men marched eastwards towards their immediate objective — Fort Cumberland.[60]

The supporters of Allan and Eddy on the Isthmus loudly "expressed their Uneasiness at seeing so few [invaders] . . . and those unprovided with Artillery."[61] They vehemently argued that, taking everything into consideration, there was no possible chance of success. Even if Fort Cumberland were captured, and this was highly unlikely, British reinforcements would readily rout Eddy's motley collection of undisciplined freebooters, Indians, and Acadians. Eddy was forced to resort to outright intimidation and to false promises in order to win the unenthusiastic support of his friends. His policy was objectively described by his associate Allan:

225

> That they [Chignecto New Englanders] had supply'd the Enemys of America which had much displeased the States. That the Congress doubted their integrity, that if they would not rouse themselves and oppose the British power in that province [Nova Scotia] they would be looked upon as enemys and should the country be reduced by the States they would be treated as conquered people and that if they did not Incline to do something he [Eddy] would return and report them to the States. But if they would now assert their rights publickly against the King's Govt, he was then Come to help them and in Fifteen days Expected a reinforcement of a large body of men.[62]

These reinforcements existed only in Eddy's active imagination.

Only fifty New Englanders, against their better judgment, rallied to Eddy's banner, and they were joined a short time later by twenty-seven men from the Cobequid region of Nova Scotia.[63] The invading army now numbered roughly 180 men.[64] Eddy must be given a considerable amount of credit for using his relatively small force to gain virtual control of the entire Chignecto Isthmus, except, of course, for Fort Cumberland. Most of the Yorkshiremen, fearing the destruction of their property if they supported Gorham, quickly surrendered their guns and ammunition to the invaders.[65] It should be noted that well over half of the New Englanders supported neither Eddy nor Gorham, but instead carefully pursued a policy of neutrality.

Eddy was not a demagogue, nor was he a megalomaniac. He was convinced that all ties with Britain should be severed, and his fanatical enthusiasm for the Revolutionary cause seriously dulled his already undeveloped sense of military strategy. In spite of fantastic rumours regarding the size of Eddy's invading force which spread like wildfire throughout Nova Scotia during the months of October and November, the inhabitants could not be aroused from their lethargic neutrality.

As early as August, Gorham had heard of Eddy's invasion plans, but it was not until the beginning of November that he learned that

Eddy was in the Chignecto region.[66] With fewer than 200 troops at his command[67] and believing that Eddy had at least 500 men,[68] Gorham was of the opinion that he was in no position to attack the invaders.[69] Therefore he felt that the only alternative was to adopt a defensive policy and to wait for reinforcements from Halifax. This was the right policy at the right time.[70]

During the early morning hours of November 7, Eddy's forces experienced their only real victory in the futile Chignecto campaign. Taking advantage of a thick fog which had settled over the coastal region, Zebulon Rowe and a handful of men thirsting for excitement and possible loot set out to capture a sloop filled with supplies for the Fort Cumberland troops.[71] Because of the low tide the sloop lay on the broad mud flats to the south-west of the fort. Eddy's description of this most humorous incident of the rebellion makes fascinating reading:

226

> After a Difficult March, they arrived opposite the Sloop; on board of which was a Guard of 1 Sergt and 12 men, who had they fir'd at our People, must have alarmed the Garrison in such a Manner as to have brought them on their Backs. However, our men rushed Resolutely towards the sloop up to their Knees in Mud, which made such a Noise as to alarm the Centry, who hailed them and immediately called the Sergt of the Guard. The Sergt on coming up, Ordered his Men to fire, but was immediately told by Mr. Row[e] that if they fired one Gun, Every Man of Them should be put to Death; which so frightened the poor Devils that they surrendered without firing a Shot, although our People Could not board her without the Assistance of the Conquered, who let down Ropes to our Men to get up by.[72]

As the working parties from the fort arrived to unload the sloop, they too were easily captured.[73] Altogether thirty-four of Gorham's troops, including Captain Barron, Engineer of the Garrison, and the Chaplain, the bibulous Rev. Eagleson, were seized by Rowe's detachment.[74] The captured sloop was sailed away at high tide in the direction of the Missiquash River, but not before the Royal Fencibles "fired several cannon shots"[75] at the brazen enemy.

Only two attempts were made to capture Fort Cumberland, one on November 13[76] and the other nine days later.[77] Both were miserable failures. Before Eddy could organize a third attempt, British reinforcements arrived.

On November 27 and November 28, the British relieving force, consisting of two companies of Marines and one company of the Royal Highlanders, finally landed at Fort Cumberland.[78] The relieving force had sailed from Halifax and Windsor.[79] On the 28th Gorham ordered Major Batt, an officer who had accompanied the reinforcements, to lead an attack on Eddy's camp, one mile north of the fort.[80] At five-thirty in the morning of the 29th, Batt marched out of Fort Cumberland with 170 troops, hoping to surprise the "rebels."[81] If it had not been for an alert young Negro drummer who furiously beat the alarm when he sighted the enemy,[82] Eddy's men would have been slaughtered in their sleep. Wiping sleep from their eyes, Eddy's confused followers ran into the neighbouring woods in search of cover.[83] In the skirmish that followed only seven "rebels" and four British soldiers were killed.[84] Seeing the hopelessness of the situation, Eddy ordered his men to retreat westwards "to the St. John River . . . and there make a stand."[85] Batt refused to pursue the "rebels"; instead he had his men put to the torch every home and barn belonging to those inhabitants of the Isthmus who had openly supported Eddy.[86] The billowing dark clouds of smoke could be seen by the defeated invaders as they fled in panic towards Memramcook.[87]

Eddy's rash attempt to capture Fort Cumberland failed not only because he lacked artillery, but also because his men were poorly trained, undisciplined, and badly led. With British control of the North Atlantic firmly established, with Washington's refusal to support the invasion, and with the great majority of Nova Scotians desperately trying to be neutral, Eddy's task was hopeless. Even though the Eddy Rebellion, by any broad strategic standards, was quite insignificant in the larger Revolutionary context, it is of some importance as an illustration of the fact that in 1775 and 1776, under their superficial neutrality, the New Englanders tacitly supported the Revolutionary movement. Moreover, the Eddy Rebellion helps to indicate how effectively British naval power and the isolated nature of the settlements of Nova Scotia had "neutralized the New England migrants."[88]

227

From 1777 to 1782 almost every Nova Scotian coastal settlement (with the notable exception of Halifax) from Tatamagouche on Northumberland Strait to the Saint John River was ravaged by American privateers.[89] As a result of these freebooting forays many New Englanders in Nova Scotia, who had originally been rather sympathetic to the Revolution, became increasingly hostile to their brethren to the south. In 1775 and 1776 most of the Nova Scotians "divided betwixt natural affection to our nearest relations, and good Faith and Friendship to our King and Country,"[90] had decided to walk the tightrope of neutrality even though they appeared to lean precariously in the direction of their "nearest relations." By the closing years of the conflict, however, as the "Neutral Yankees" reached the end of their hazardous journey, they had begun to lean towards the opposite extreme, towards the King.

What real impact did the Revolution have upon the inhabitants of Nova Scotia? Of course most of them resolved to adopt a policy of neutrality; many suffered because of the depredations of the American privateers; while a few, especially the Halifax merchants, grew rich from the usual profits of war. But was there nothing else? M.W. Armstrong has convincingly argued that probably the most important impact of the

Revolution upon Nova Scotia was in precipitating the "Great Awakening of Nova Scotia."[91] In addition, Armstrong has emphasized that the "Great Awakening" encouraged the development of neutrality:

> Indeed, the Great Awakening itself may be considered to have been a retreat from the grim realities of the world to the safety and pleasantly exciting warmth of the revival meeting, and to profits and rewards of another character . . . an escape from fear and divided loyalties . . . an assertion of democratic ideals and a determination to maintain them, the Great Awakening gave self-respect and satisfaction to people whose economic and political position was both humiliating and distressing.[92]

228

The prophet and evangelist of the spiritual awakening was Henry Alline who, when he was twelve, had moved from Rhode Island to Falmouth, Nova Scotia.[93] An uneducated farmer, Alline had experienced an unusual "Conversion,"[94] and in 1776 he began to preach an emotional Christian message that has been described as being a combination of "Calvinism, Antinomianism, and Enthusiasm."[95] The flames of religious revival[96] swept up the Minas Basin in 1777, across the Bay of Fundy in 1779, and to the South Shore in 1781.[97] All Protestant Churches in Nova Scotia were in one way or another affected by the "Great Awakening," and largely as a direct result the evangelical wing of the various Protestant Churches was able to dominate Maritime religious life throughout the nineteenth century.

British sea power, the isolated nature of the settlements, the refusal of Washington to mount an offensive against Nova Scotia, and perhaps the religious revival, all combined to keep the "Yankees" neutral during the Revolution.

NOTES

[1] W.B. Kerr, "Nova Scotia in the Critical Years, 1775-6", *Dalhousie Review* (April 1932), 97.

[2] S.D. Clarke, *Movements of Political Protest in Canada, 1640-1840* (Toronto, 1959), 63.

[3] It should be borne in mind that there was a significant German-speaking population in the Lunenburg region and that there were pockets of Highland Scots, Yorkshiremen, Acadians, and Scots-Irish scattered throughout the peninsula of Nova Scotia. Most of these settlers (a few Acadians and Scots-Irish are the exception to the rule) also remained neutral during the Revolution even though their sympathies lay with the Crown.

[4] J.B. Brebner, *The Neutral Yankees of Nova Scotia* (New York, 1937), 329-37.

[5] V. Barnes, "Francis Legge, Governor of Loyalist Nova Scotia, 1773-1776," *New England Quarterly* (July 1931), 420-47. See also a convincing criticism of this view in W.B. Kerr, "The Merchants of Nova Scotia and the American Revolution," *Canadian Historical Review* (March 1932), 21-34.

[6] A.L. Burt, *The United States, Great Britain, and British North America* (Toronto, 1940), 13.

[7] W.B. Kerr, *The Maritime Provinces of British North America and the American Revolution* (Sackville, n.d.), 59.

[8] Kerr, *The Maritime Provinces*, 60.

[9] Kerr, *The Maritime Provinces*, 53-60.

[10] Brebner, *Neutral Yankees of Nova Scotia*, 352.

[11] J.C. Webster, *The Forts of Chignecto* (Sackville, 1930), 5.

[12] W.C. Milner, *History of Sackville, New Brunswick* (Sackville, 1955), 14-21.

[13] B.J. Bird, "Settlement Patterns in Maritime Canada, 1687-1876," *The Geographic Review* (July 1955), 398-99.

[14] Bird, "Settlement Patterns," 398-99.

[15] W.C. Milner, "Records of Chignecto," *Collections of the Nova Scotia Historical Society*, vol. 15 (Halifax, 1911), 41-45.

[16] Milner, "Records of Chignecto," 40.
[17] Kerr, *The Maritime Provinces*, 68.
[18] Kerr, *The Maritime Provinces*, 68.
[19] J.M. Beck, *The Government of Nova Scotia* (Toronto, 1957), 22–25.
[20] D.C. Harvey, "The Struggle for the New England Form of Township Government in Nova Scotia," Canadian Historical Association, *Report* (1933), 18 [hereafter *CHAR*].
[21] D.C. Harvey, "Machias and the Invasion of Nova Scotia," *CHAR* (1932), 17.
[22] J.C. Fitzpatrick, ed., *The Writings of George Washington* (Washington, 1931), 3: 415.
[23] Fitzpatrick, ed., *Writings of George Washington* 3: 415–16.
[24] The Petition of the Chignecto Inhabitants, December 23, 1775, *Nova Scotia Archives*, A94, 330–38.
[25] Kerr, "Nova Scotia in the Critical Years 1775-6," 98.
[26] Governor Legge to the Secretary of State, July 31, 1775, *Canadian Archives Report for 1894* (Ottawa, 1895), 334 [hereafter *CAR, 1894*].
[27] E.P. Weaver, "Nova Scotia and New England during the Revolution," *American Historical Review* (October 1904), 63.
[28] B. Murdoch, *A History of Nova Scotia* (Halifax, 1860), 2: 554.
[29] Kerr, *The Maritime Provinces*, 69.
[30] Kerr, *The Maritime Provinces*, 63.
[31] Quoted in F. Kidder, *Military Operations in Eastern Maine and Nova Scotia During the Revolution* (Albany, 1867), 64.
[32] Kerr, *The Maritime Provinces*, 70.
[33] The Petition of Chignecto Inhabitants, *Nova Scotia Archives*, A94, 330–38.
[34] Quoted in Kerr, *The Maritime Provinces*, 73.
[35] Fitzpatrick, ed., *Writings of George Washington* 4: 437.
[36] H. Peckham, *The War for Independence* (Chicago, 1959), 32.
[37] Fitzpatrick, ed., *Writings of George Washington* 4: 438.
[38] Fitzpatrick, ed., *Writings of George Washington* 4: 438.
[39] Kerr, *The Maritime Provinces*, 73.
[40] See *CAR, 1894*, 345.
[41] *CAR, 1894*, 345.
[42] Kerr, *The Maritime Provinces*, 74.
[43] Quoted in Murdoch, *History of Nova Scotia* 2: 568.
[44] In the administrative shuffle Francklin was demoted to Indian Agent.
[45] The Royal Fencibles were mostly recruited from the Loyalists in the Thirteen Colonies.
[46] W.B. Kerr, "The American Invasion of Nova Scotia, 1776-7," *Canadian Defense Quarterly* (July 1936), 434.
[47] Gorham's Journal, *CAR, 1894*, 360.
[48] Kerr, *The Maritime Provinces*, 78.
[49] Kidder, *Military Operations*, 12.
[50] Petition of Jonathan Eddy, Aug. 28, 1776, in P. Force, ed., *American Archives*, 5th series (Washington, 1851), 2: 734.
[51] *American Archives* 2: 734
[52] Kidder, *Military Operations*, 12.
[53] Gorham's Journal, 355.
[54] Quoted in Harvey, "Machias and the Invasion of Nova Scotia," 21.
[55] Kerr, "The American Invasion," 434.
[56] Kerr, "The American Invasion," 435.
[57] Kerr, "The American Invasion," 435.
[58] The description of the Rebellion is to be found in Gorham's Journal, *CAR, 1894*, 355-57, 359-65, and in Eddy's Journal, in Harvey, "Machias and the Invasion of Nova Scotia," 22–24.
[59] Eddy's Journal, 22.
[60] Eddy's Journal, 22.
[61] Eddy's Journal, 22.
[62] Allan's Journal, in Harvey, "Machias and the Invasion of Nova Scotia," 24.
[63] Kerr, "The American Invasion," 435.
[64] Eddy's Journal, 23.
[65] Kerr, "The American Invasion," 436.
[66] Gorham's Journal, 355.
[67] Gorham's Journal, 360.
[68] Gorham's Journal, 356.
[69] Gorham's Journal, 360.
[70] For the opposite point of view see Kerr, "The American Invasion," 441: "A well-directed sortie could at any time have broken up Eddy's camp."
[71] Eddy's Journal, 22.
[72] Eddy's Journal, 22.
[73] Eddy's Journal, 22–23.
[74] Eddy's Journal, 22–23.
[75] Eddy's Journal, 23; Gorham's Journal, 356.

[76] Gorham's Journal, 361–62.

[77] Gorham's Journal, 361–62.

[78] Gorham's Journal, 362.

[79] Gorham's Journal, 362. This point must be emphasized especially, after examining Stanley's inaccurate reference to an overland march. See G.F.G. Stanley, *Canada's Soldiers, 1605-1954* (Toronto, 1954), 118.

[80] Gorham's Journal, 362.

[81] Gorham's Journal, 362.

[82] C.E. Kemp, "Folk-Lore About Old Fort Beauséjour", *Acadiensis* (October 1908), 301–302. Also see Kerr, "The American Invasion," 440.

[83] Gorham's Journal, 362.

[84] Kerr, "The American Invasion," 441.

[85] Eddy's Journal, 23.

[86] Gorham's Journal, 362.

[87] The contest for present-day western New Brunswick continued until the end of the Revolutionary War. In the summer of 1777 Allan's invading force of some 100 men from Machias was compelled to retreat overland from the St. John Valley towards the St. Croix when confronted by a strong British military expedition led by Major Gilford Studholme and Francklin. For the remainder of the war Allan unsuccessfully attempted to persuade the St. John River Indians to join the Revolutionary cause.

[88] Brebner, *The Neutral Yankees*, 353.

[89] Brebner, *The Neutral Yankees*, 324-35.

[90] Petition of the Inhabitants of Yarmouth, Dec. 8, 1775. Quoted in Brebner, *The Neutral Yankees*, 291.

[91] M.W. Armstrong, "Neutrality and Religion in Revolutionary Nova Scotia," *New England Quarterly* (Mar. 1946), 50-61.

[92] Armstrong, "Neutrality and Religion," 57, 58, 60.

[93] Armstrong, "Neutrality and Religion," 55.

[94] See W. James, *The Varieties of Religious Experience* (New York, 1958), 134-35: "My sins seemed to be laid open; so that I thought that every one I saw knew them, and sometimes I was almost ready to acknowledge many things, which I thought they knew; yea sometimes it seemed to me as if every one was pointing me out as the most guilty wretch upon earth."

[95] Quoted in Armstrong, "Neutrality and Religion," 58.

[96] The following is Alline's description of the Liverpool revival of 1776: "We had blessed days, the Lord was reviving his work of grace. Many under a load of sin cried out, what shall we do to be saved? and the saints seemed much revived, came out and witnessed for God. In a short time some more souls were born to Christ, they came out and declared what God had done for their souls and what a blessed change had taken place in that town." Quoted in Armstrong, "Neutrality and Religion," 55-56.

[97] Armstrong, "Neutrality and Religion," 55.

230

The Envy of the American States

ANN GORMAN CONDON

> If I was to be transformed into an instrument of musick and to make choice for myself I wou'd chuse to be a fiddle, because it wou'd require some skill & taste to play upon me, and if I sounded well some little credit wou'd redound to myself. But if I was a band-organ and turn'd with a Wench — its a mere mechanical operation and neither the musician or the instrument gain much credit.

> Edward Winslow[1]

The original Loyalist leaders of New Brunswick were intensely proud, self-conscious men. Although born in an apparently safe, secure world where the path to distinction was illuminated by a series of well-placed markers, their lives had in fact been characterized by flux, by a series of abrupt reversals and successes, over which they themselves had little control. Chance, caprice, bad luck, good fortune had played a far larger role in determining their fate than the anticipated tests of ability, hard work, good taste, and good connections. Instead of being able to exercise their talents in a satisfying and socially constructive manner, these men were haunted by the conviction that their "prime of life" had been spent fighting a fruitless war, coping with an unfamiliar wilderness, and striving to provide the rudiments of a decent existence for themselves and their families.

In short, the Loyalist leaders feared their lives might prove a waste. All the bright promises of their youth, the high standards they had set for themselves, the skills they had mastered, and the dreams they harbored of being prominent, productive members of their community were repeatedly subjected to frustration and failure. The Revolution had deprived them of their rightful place in the world, the aftermath had thrown them into an unwelcome dependence on the British patronage system, and finally the northern frontier threatened to sap their energies and their talents without yielding any commensurate sense of achievement.

231

In establishing the society of New Brunswick, these Loyalist leaders strove to reverse the downward course of their lives. With an impetuosity that sometimes bordered on frenzy, they tried to reproduce the social customs and the set of religious and educational institutions which they had known before the war. These extensive cultural efforts can only be understood in terms of the Loyalist leaders' determination to defy fate, to retrieve the world they had lost, and to pass on to their children the social standards, the educational advantages, and the political and moral values which they esteemed so highly.

The goal of the Loyalist leaders was summed up by the phrase, "the envy of the American states." By envy was not just meant simply spite, although there certainly was an element of that in their motives. But even more importantly, the Loyalist leaders were determined to set up a society which would be envied because it was in fact better, finer — or, to use their favorite term, more respectable — than the rival republic to the south. Their goal was not merely to establish a viable community, but one that was characterized by dignity and cultural achievement as well. It must be a society that conformed to the elitist standards of their Tory background and that was a worthy home for themselves and their families.

The efforts of the Loyalist leaders to establish such a highly civilized society in New Brunswick were inspired by a profound sense of mission. For, if their province did in fact become "the envy of the American states," its distinguished character would justify the Loyalists' choices during the American Revolution — both to themselves and to posterity.

Given the importance of this goal, the Loyalist leaders naturally placed an extremely high value on the internal social development of New Brunswick. They also tended to be quite exclusive and self-righteous in choosing which social and cultural institutions should be encouraged. And the standards which they set for the new province had a rigid quality which often did not make sufficient allowance for the character of the general population or the ruggedness of the northern frontier.

Finally, and perhaps most significantly, the Loyalists' sense of cultural mission was reflected in their relationships with their children. Much of their zealous haste to establish rich cultural institutions in New Brunswick, and to maintain a dignified style of life there, grew out of their determination that their children should not suffer from the effects of the American Revolution, that they should receive all the advantages which the Loyalist leaders had themselves enjoyed in their youth, and that they should have access to respectable, rewarding careers. With enormous love, and often at great personal cost, these men gave their children the best educations they could afford, they exposed them to the graces of civilized life, and they exerted all their influence to launch them upon profitable careers and suitable marriages. As the infirmities of age began to take their toll, the Loyalist leaders became increasingly anxious to pass on the torch, to transfer to their children both their personal and their political hopes. In the process, they imbued these children with their own civil and moral code, with their distinctive standards of public duty and private conduct, and with an unforgettable sense of the sacrifices their fathers had made to preserve the empire and to uphold a community ideal which permitted law, culture, and personal liberty to flourish together.

232

Style of Life

As the Loyalist leaders took up residence in the province of New Brunswick, they did so in a style befitting their status as members of the gentry and as public officials. Ward Chipman built an architectural gem of a town house in Saint John, which he decorated with English wallpaper and furniture. George Leonard's farm in Sussex was described by Bishop Charles Inglis as "exceedingly neat and in good taste, and resembles a gentleman's villa in Europe." Many travellers commented favorably on the "elegant pile" of private and public buildings which dotted Fredericton, although Inglis himself felt the Loyalists had gone too far when they designed the Anglican Church there: "Portland Chapel in London was absurdly taken for a model to build this Church," and the cost of construction proved excessive. Many of the Loyalist leaders lived on spacious farms overlooking the St. John River, in houses of "noble appearance," which were stocked with mahogany furniture that had either been brought up from their former homes or purchased from England. The hard-headed Scottish traveller, Patrick Campbell, deplored the Loyalists' preference for mahogany imports, and he noted approvingly that Chief Justice George Ludlow's tastes ran to the beautiful native woods: "I have not seen a bit of mahogony in his elegant and commodious new house, but he is a man of very enlightened understanding. . . . " For most of the Loyalist leaders, however, furnishings and clothes from England were considered marks of gentility. When Jonathan Bliss wished to buy a present for his wife, he wrote away to London and asked Mrs. Benedict Arnold to "once more display her elegant Taste in a Bonnet or Hat, or whichever is fashionable, for *Mrs.* Bliss."[2]

The high points of social intercourse in the province were the numerous balls. These were launched even before the province was founded and provided the main focal point for exchanging gossip, for matchmaking, and for displaying the prized ball gowns and military dress uniforms of the assemblage. The pride which the Loyalist gentry took in these moments of elegance was evidenced by Edward Winslow's whimsical challenge to Sir John Wentworth of Nova Scotia: "I am determined to figure at the Assemblies . . . 'tis say'd they are already very brilliant. — You men of Halifax must look out — We shall so far exceed you in our Society & our amusements will probably be so much more rational that those of your Ladies who have great sensibility and true taste must incline to our side of the Bay." In 1802, the American visitor Charles Turner was amazed and amused to discover how faithfully the social customs of New England had been preserved in the backwoods of New Brunswick. While travelling in a remote, northeastern corner of the province, Turner encountered "a collection of young folks, — nine young ladies and one widow, and six young gentlemen, who were prepared to spend the evening in dancing, after quilting. The ladies all dressed in white, and all performed their parts in the style and taste of Boston, where eighteen years ago, Satan's seat was. . . . "[3] Col. Joseph Gubbins, a senior British military officer had a more acid reaction to the social airs of the Saint John elite:

> The amusements at this place, like those at Fredericton, are same and tiresome. At evening parties, which are here denominated Gregories from the name of the person who first introduced them, the ladies sit round the room and entertain one another with whispers. . . . This is succeeded by a substantial supper, an hour after which is generally devoted to songs too bad to even laugh at. The ridiculous delicacy of their expressions are very diverting. A New Brunswick lady conceives it indecorous to call a male bird a cock, for which they substitute rooster, even to the weather rooster; knees they denominate benders, and so on.[4]

The frequent mustering of the troops provided another chance for color and conviviality, as did Governor Carleton's visits to various parts of the province. The governor's entry into the City of Saint John was

233

marked with great formality: "On his arrival at the Kennebeckasis ferry, he was met and escorted thence by the Company of Light-Horse . . . to the Government House. — Many of the most respectable inhabitants went out on horseback to receive his EXCELLENCY; and he was welcomed to this City under a discharge of cannon from the Artillery Park. . . ." News of British military victories against either the French or the Americans occasioned elaborate displays of fireworks and celebratory balls. A special poem entitled "On the shore of the Potomack in Washington City" was sung at the ball after Hull's invasion of the American capital. Similar "rejoicing and mirth were 'the order of the day'" each time the British navy triumphed over the French fleets. Prominent citizens would illuminate their houses to demonstrate their patriotism. And the Loyalist ladies frequently chose blue as the predominant color in their ball gowns in order to honor the British navy.[5]

234   The moment of greatest pomp and circumstance in early New Brunswick history occurred in 1794 when Prince Edward, the Duke of Kent, visited the province. Mayor Gabriel G. Ludlow delivered the welcoming address for the citizens of Saint John, and he stressed the peculiar significance which they, as Loyalists, attached to this royal visit:

> We contemplate with Admiration and heartfelt Pleasure an event so little to be expected in this remote corner of His Majesty's Dominion, as the presence of one of the Sons of our Most Gracious Sovereign . . . our Loyalty and attachment to whose Person and Government induced us with chearfulness to sacrifice the Comforts of our former Situations, and seek an Asylum under the British constitution in this lately uncultivated wilderness. . . . [6]

Ward Chipman served as the Prince's host during his stay, and the experience was easily the most gratifying public moment in Chipman's long career. Although not normally given to hyperbole, Chipman was simply transported by the demeanor of his royal guest: "He is without exception the most accomplished character I have ever seen, his manners are so dignified & at the same time marked with so much affability & condescension, he discovers so much good sense, sound understanding & so improved a mind, that I can find no bounds to my admiration for him. . . . " On a more personal level, Chipman was profoundly moved by "the enjoyment of so distinguished an honor as that of entertaining a Son of our beloved Sovereign. I confess the circumstance has been peculiarly flattering to my feelings . . . his Royal Highness was pleased to express himself in very obliging terms respecting his accommodations while with us." Chipman's Loyalist friends congratulated him on this unique privilege, but his Yankee sister, who never relented in her campaign to lure her brother back to the land of his birth, was decidedly less impressed: "I congratulate Mrs. C. and yourself on the departure of your Royal guest — you would be freed from these cares if you would dwell in our Country where all are Princes alike."[7]

Two weekly newspapers helped to keep this isolated Loyalist community in contact with the world at large. The principal items of interest were news from England and from the United States, though provincial politics were given due attention in moments of dispute. The health of the King and the progress of British military efforts were the principal subjects reported from London, although occasionally New Brunswickers were treated to more gossipy matters, such as the mounting debts of the Prince of Wales or the political trials of Warren Hastings and George Gordon. American news consisted primarily of political reports, garnered almost exclusively from New York and Boston papers of a decidedly pro-Federalist, pro-British line. Ordinarily the New Brunswick papers simply reprinted items of interest published in the American journals. In 1801, however, *The Royal Gazette* broke its traditional silence in order to lament the political defeat of President John Adams: " . . . there is every reason to apprehend that a new administration will produce very different measures from those pursued under the mild and equitable system for which Mr. Adams has been so highly and justly distinguished. . . . "[8]

The more lurid events of the French Revolution were also noted by the two papers. Judging from the frequency of articles on the "'Crimes committed during the French Revolution,'" replete with details of blood-letting, the Loyalists must have derived a certain morbid satisfaction from the collapse of that experiment in republicanism.[9] Equally popular was the work of the great Tory satirist, William Cobbett. As an outspoken champion of the pastoral, semi-feudal life of the English countryside and an implacable foe of republicanism, Cobbett's views were obviously very congenial to the New Brunswick Loyalists — for both provincial newspapers carried his "Letters of Peter Porcupine." Cobbett had actually served as a British soldier in New Brunswick, and he may have acquired some of his prejudices against republicanism from the Loyalists. He certainly enjoyed his years there, albeit he seemed astonished by the inflated titles and pretensions of the Loyalist gentry: "Thousands of captains . . . without soldiers, and of squires without shares." This phenomenon would persist well into the nineteenth century, as Col. Gubbins noted:

235

> Militia titles do not convey great ideas of rank or respectability in this quarter of the world. . . . General Coffin on the British halfpay was fined for selling rum without a license and was in the act of retailing cabbages at St. John's market slip when he received the information of his promotion.[10]

New Brunswickers followed Cobbett's subsequent misadventures in the United States through their newspapers, and Jonathan Odell, for one, expressed great resentment at "the Wanton cruelty and democratic oppression" which the Americans inflicted on the "Poor Fellow."[11]

At least one New Brunswicker sought to maintain a more personal relationship with the English literary world. This was Jonathan Odell, the poet-intellectual among the Loyalist leaders, who continued to write verses of a heavily religious and royalist slant during his years in New Brunswick. He also contributed occasional articles on syntax and Hebrew punctuation to English literary journals and sought desperately to maintain some toehold in the world of ideas. Odell particularly mourned the death of Jonathan Boucher in 1804: "Thus I have lost the only friend of literary eminence that was remaining in the Circle of Friends in England," he confided to his main intellectual companion in the province, Ward Chipman.[12] The only other Loyalist leader to have a literary turn of mind was Edward Winslow, who occasionally wrote political satires for the amusement of his friends. Although Winslow's light pieces were far earthier and less formal than Odell's, they possessed a flair and an ironic, warmhearted acceptance of the human condition that was notably lacking in Odell's highly fragile, obsequious efforts. Unfortunately Winslow's straitened financial circumstances, as well as the lack of a large reading public in New Brunswick, prevented him from developing his satirical talents more extensively. For one can well imagine that, under more encouraging conditions, Winslow's "Tammany" might have joined company with T.C. Haliburton's "Sam Slick" to provide the world with two distinctive examples of Tory wit in the Maritimes.[13]

236

* * *

Travellers to New Brunswick confirmed the success of the Loyalists in taming the wilderness. All early accounts of the province portray a society blessed with fertility, affluence, and refinement. For some, the highly stylized manners of the Loyalist leaders seemed a bit excessive. The American Charles Turner noted that Gabriel Ludlow, the "Lord Mayor" of Saint John greeted his party "with as much Politeness as we could expect from a Provincial official aping the hauteur of the British." And even Winslow felt compelled to protest against the elegant incompetence of Jonathan Odell: "His Habits and manners are such as in the days of superstition might have suited a High priest of the order of Melchisedec, but are ill calculated for a civil department. His hauteur is so disgusting that he has become completely obnoxious. . . . " Yet for all their pretensions, the Loyalist leaders did establish a high standard for public service. Education, involvement in the community, and dignified personal behavior were held up as prerequisites for public leadership.[14]

This standard was difficult, if not impossible to maintain in a frontier community. As time passed the Loyalist leaders themselves grew old and increasingly weary of their missionary task. The hardships of the circuit ride on horseback, the rigors of attending Council meetings in wintertime, the time-consuming effort needed to manage a farm or maintain even a small law practice, the afflictions of the gout — all sapped their energies for public service until the records of these men in performing their duties became a matter of public concern. They were accused of clinging to their offices beyond their time, just to keep the title and the salary.

There was in fact a dark side to the Loyalist leaders' record of public service. For these men brought to New Brunswick many of the poorer political practices of the eighteenth century, such as nepotism and multiple-office holding, as well as many of the good ones. Jonathan Bliss, for example, sought to be mayor of the city of Saint John as well as attorney general of the province — despite the fact that his duties as attorney general required him to be in Fredericton, while the mayor was, of course, expected to be seventy miles away in Saint John. And Jonathan Odell was accused in the public prints of manipulating public offices so as to reserve a clerkship for "his Billy."[15] The most relentless office-seeker of them all, however, was Edward Winslow. During his years in New Brunswick, Winslow sought, or was appointed to, the following public posts: secretary of the province, member of the Council, surrogate general of the province, commanding officer of a regiment of New Brunswick Fencibles, justice of the peace, deputy paymaster of His Majesty's Troops in New Brunswick, secretary to the Boundary Commission, receiver general of the quit rents, deputy surveyor of the King's Woods, collector of the customs, justice of the Supreme Court, and president of the Council.

237

The most egregious display of Winslow's ambition occurred in connection with the quit rents. When the Loyalists were given their original land grants, they were excused from paying quit rents for a period of ten years in recognition of their wartime services. When these fees finally became due in the 1790s, neither the provincial nor the imperial government regarded them of sufficient importance to press for payment. Suddenly, however, in 1800 Winslow sent an impassioned letter to Edward G. Lutwyche, an influential Loyalist living in London, urging that the quit-rent provision should be enforced in New Brunswick in order to support the British war effort. He claimed that the system of voluntary contributions to the Patriotic Fund was not working fairly: "The loyal and ambitious were making sacrifices beyond their means and . . . the factious and mercenary part of the community avoided all connection with the subscriptions." By contrast, a quit rent would, Winslow maintained, tax people according to the extent of their property holdings and would thus be much more equitable. Winslow reinforced this argument by suggesting to Lutwyche that "the instability and ill-timed indulgences of the Mother Country — contributed more to the establishment of American independence than all their severities and restrictions . . . It appears to me essential to the tranquility and happiness of this province That the inhabitants of it should realize and (on all occasions) acknowledge their *dependence upon Great Britain.*" The quit rent, he concluded, was the most "rational" means for citizens to demonstrate their allegiance.[16]

Although he emphatically denied that "any consideration of personal benefit" prompted him to make this proposal, Winslow did allow that he would be willing to serve as receiver general of the quit rents. His proposal was seconded by his close friend, George Leonard, who explicitly nominated Winslow to be receiver general. At first, the British authorities reacted negatively to the proposal on the grounds that "the amount is too trifling in their estimation to risque exciting any discontent." Prompted, however, by the urgings of Governor Carleton and other provincial officials, Great Britain finally agreed to let New Brunswick collect her quit rents — provided the House of Assembly formally approved of the measure. This proviso completely unravelled Winslow's grand design — for both he and the governor well knew the Assembly would never willingly establish a fund over which it had no control. The New Brunswick leaders had, therefore, to reverse their position completely and work to dissuade Great Britain from insisting upon quit rent collection — a measure which might provoke a new political confrontation with the Assembly. Winslow was actually in England in 1806 when the new land regulations for New Brunswick were finally settled, and he proudly reported home that he had been "instrumental" in relieving New Brunswick "from the shameful oppression of Quit-rents. . . . " This last phrase leaves little doubt that Winslow's original arguments in favor of patriotism and equity were simply an elaborate device to get himself a good job.[17]

238

In the end, Winslow did get the well-paying post he had courted so assiduously for twenty years, but the particular appointment seemed to mock the Loyalists' high standards of public service. For through his English connections, particularly Lord Sheffield and the Duke of Northumberland, Winslow managed to get himself appointed to the Supreme Court of New Brunswick in 1806 — despite the fact that he was not a lawyer. Governor Carleton protested that "nothing can be more absurd or more injurious to the King's Service" than to appoint a non-professional man to such a high legal post, and the lawyers of New Brunswick wholly agreed. Even Ward Chipman, Winslow's dearest friend, felt mortified by this affront to the profession. Chipman had served as solicitor general of New Brunswick for twenty years without pay, and had in numerous other ways exerted himself to establish high standards for the provincial Bar. All these efforts seemed worthless, he confessed in a despondent letter to Jonathan Sewell, Jr., "when men, without any professional education, as in the late instance of our friend Winslow, are thrust in." Winslow, however, dismissed these criticisms out of hand. He felt his long record of service to the province had earned him the right to any post which opened up. As for the lawyers' professional quibbles, he refused to take them seriously, noting that this was "An objection which has never been considered of much weight in the appointment of puisne Judges in the colonies. . . . "[18]

Not only were the Loyalist leaders greedy in seeking public office, but they could on occasion be faulted for failure to perform their duties conscientiously. Governor Carleton's constant complaints about the difficulties of getting a quorum to attend Council meetings were one evidence of this neglect — particularly in view of the fact that only five of the twelve members were needed to make a quorum. At one point Carleton became so exasperated that he requested permission to reduce the quorum number to three. The depth of his difficulties may be illustrated by the fact that some of the Council members never attended even one meeting of the Board. Beverley Robinson, Sr., was the most flagrant example. For although Robinson accepted an appointment to the Council and held on to it until 1790, he never in fact left England to go to New Brunswick, and only gave up his post when he could safely pass it on to his son.[19] Jonathan Sewell, Sr., did come out to New Brunswick and strove desperately to cling to his remaining appointments as judge of the Vice-Admiralty Court and member of the Council. Yet Sewell spent his final days in New Brunswick as a virtual recluse and never participated in any public business.[20] Even Christopher Billopp, a much younger, more active man, attended the Council meetings only six times during his entire term of twenty-seven years.[21]

239

The record of the Supreme Court was vulnerable to similar criticism. . . . [T]here was deep public resentment of the Court's unwillingness to sit anywhere but in Fredericton — a refusal which was criticized regularly in the press for being self-serving and detrimental to the public interest. John Saunders provided another insight into the Court when he applied for the chief justiceship in 1808. Although he was the most junior member of the Court, Saunders maintained that he should be preferred over his colleagues because the other judges were all too ill or too feeble to perform their duties.[22]

At the level of the House of Assembly, the Loyalist leaders' professed standards for public service also proved difficult to maintain in practice. Although members of the Loyalist gentry stood for election to the first Assembly, the duties were apparently so arduous and inconvenient that they declined to run again. As a result, the qualifications of the members dropped sharply, and it soon became apparent that many members sought Assembly seats only in order to get their hands on some ready cash. This, of course, was completely inconsistent with the Loyalists' ideals of public service. An anonymous letter writer was shocked in 1795 to find "That men destitute of Talents, without even the advantage of a common School Education, should aspire to a Trust of this Nature. . . ." And Edward Winslow as well lamented that "Our gentlemen have all become potato farmers — & our Shoemakers are preparing to legislate." Yet it was clear that this deterioration in the public service was due as much to the withdrawal of the gentlemen as it was to the ambition of the shoemakers.[23]

* * *

How can the Loyalist leaders' high standards of public service be reconciled with these obvious lapses? In the first place, it should be stressed that the Loyalist leaders regarded nepotism and plural officeholding as legitimate rewards for public service, rather than as corrupt practices. Thus Edward Winslow fought vigorously to retain his office of surrogate general after he was named to the Supreme Court on the grounds that both Mr. Cushing and Mr. Hutchinson had held the two posts simultaneously in colonial Massachusetts. Likewise, Jonathan Odell considered it part of his parental duty to facilitate the entry of his son — and many of his friends' sons — into the public service, and he simply ignored criticism to the contrary. In the second place, it can be said that the failures of the Loyalist leaders to live up to their own standards of public service were due much more to human frailty than to any lack of commitment on their part. The burdens of increasing age afflicted them all. And many had to bear heavy financial burdens as well. Edward Winslow, for example, never extricated himself from the debts he had accumulated during the American Revolution. His frantic office-seeking was, therefore, amply justified in his own eyes by the demands of his creditors and the needs of his large family.[24] Joshua Upham was nearly as badly off. In fact, both men died heavily in debt. And the New Brunswick House of Assembly, in a wholly unprecedented action, made substantial grants of money to the distressed families in recognition of the many meritorious services the two men had contributed to the province.[25] Even those who brought capital to New Brunswick found it difficult to live up to their own personal standards. Ward Chipman, who had made money during the Revolution and who received a substantial fee for his work as the British agent to the Boundary Commission, confessed in 1804 that he never dreamed life in New Brunswick would be so arduous and so unrewarding. "If I could have anticipated that so little advantage and emolument would have been reaped from a continuance in it, I should most certainly have quitted it many years ago, for after toiling here nearly twenty years, I find my circumstances in no degree bettered, and am now not only without an income sufficient to support me tho living in the most frugal manner consistent with a decent appearance, but have no prospect of any alterations for the better."[26]

*   *   *

Whatever their failure in performance, the Loyalist leaders never gave up their ideal of creating a respectable society in New Brunswick. When Gabriel Ludlow succeeded to the presidency of the province after Carleton's departure, he recommended to the Assembly that a heavy tax should be placed on rum, so as to raise the moral fibre of the community. Similarly, when Ward Chipman was raised to the Council Board in 1806, he viewed his appointment as an opportunity to revitalize the original Loyalist standards. "I think there is an Augean Stable to be cleaned . . . as our lot is cast here, at least while it so remains, it behooves us all to make the community as respectable as we can."[27]

Religion

The efforts to root the Church of England in New Brunswick's soil exhibited the same combination of interest and ennui which characterized other Loyalist undertakings. All the Loyalist leaders were members of the established Church, and they were theoretically eager to see it flourish in the province. In addition to the religious succour it offered, the leadership regarded the Church as a primary agent for inculcating habits of respect and obedience, and they welcomed the well-educated Anglican ministers as cultural assets. They even hoped and worked for the appointment of a bishop of New Brunswick, who would help kindle religious devotion and who, by his mere presence, would add to the dignity of the province.[28]

Despite this high level of theoretical commitment, the Anglican Church was an ineffective institution in the early history of New Brunswick. Several factors contributed to its weakness, which can only be fully understood in terms of the specific spiritual environment of the province. Despite the Loyalists' efforts at cultivation and civilization, New Brunswick remained a rugged frontier area until well after 1815. The pockets of settlement were small in comparison with the vast stretches of forest and the large amounts of uncultivated wilderness. There was, of course, an abundance of natural resources which men could exploit. Yet long, harsh winters and the lack of any transportation system other than the rivers created a sense of isolation among the inhabitants. Whether they were engaged in fishing, farming, lumbering, or commerce, most of the people spent their lives in a lonely, physically exhausting struggle with this tough natural environment. And whether their efforts were ultimately successful or not, they all soon became acquainted with the particular perils posed by the northern wilderness. The dread effects of getting lost in wintertime or in the forest, the havoc which a sudden Spring freshet could cause, the destructive fury of the winds and the tides in the Bay of Fundy — such were the commonplace experiences of the people of New Brunswick. Given this intimate, awesome contact with the powers of the physical universe, many of these people sought in religion a form of solace or reassurance or justification that matched their brutal encounters with nature. These early New Brunswickers wanted religion to provide them with a spiritual experience which corresponded in intensity to the physical and emotional rigors of their daily lives, so that it could calm their fears and make their efforts meaningful.

The longing for a highly emotional form of religious worship was, of course, a familiar phenomenon in the various frontier communities of North America. Unfortunately, however, the Anglican Church in New Brunswick was singularly unsuited to meet the spiritual cravings of many in its supposed "flock." The personal qualifications of its ministers, its institutional arrangements, and its operating philosophy were scarcely adequate for the needs of the population at large. Its first ministers, for example, were the aged, infirm survivors of the American Revolution. Although often men of eminence, they were physically ill equipped to spread the Gospel in the wilderness. Many of them had spent the years between their exile from New York and their appointment to parishes in New Brunswick in a "destitute Situation," without financial support, and they tended as a result to be excessively concerned with salary matters and physically comfortable accommodations at the expense of their spiritual responsibilities.[29]

The organization of the Church in New Brunswick further tended to dissociate it from the general population. The Church of England was formally established by law in 1786. At the same time, religious toleration was extended to all dissenting Protestant sects, although both the Loyalist leadership and the British imperial government hoped the Church of England would become the primary religious force in the province. In support of this goal, the British government agreed to finance the construction of the first Anglican churches in New Brunswick and to pay the ministers' salaries during the initial settlement period. Britain clearly meant this financial aid to be only temporary, but in fact the Anglican clergy remained financially dependent on British grants until well after 1815. At first this aid was continued because both Governor Carleton and Bishop Charles Inglis convinced the government that the province was too poor to support the Church. Later, it remained a habit. Inglis himself grew increasingly acid in his complaints about the "backwardness of the people in contributing to their support . . . now when their circumstances have become easy and comfortable. . . ." Although this British aid unquestionably enabled the Church to develop physically at an accelerated rate, at the same time it tended to isolate the clergy psychologically from the daily concerns of the New Brunswick population. The sense of community which might have sprung up from a common effort to build a church and support a minister did not develop among the members of the Church in New Brunswick. For example, in 1814, a year of high wartime inflation in New Brunswick, the vestry of the Anglican Church in Saint John wrote Inglis begging for financial assistance because their own funds were "so much embarrassed" that they would have difficulty paying the salary of their new minister and could by no means afford to support an assistant. Yet in the very next sentence of their letter, they admitted that both the Methodist and Baptist societies were expanding their congregations, and the Kirk of Scotland was building a new church in the city — all without outside aid. It was clear that the dissenting churches, which depended on their members for support and spoke to them out of a common frame of reference, were much more effective in stirring the zeal and devotion of the New Brunswickers.[30]

A final obstacle which tended to separate the Church from the people was the highly formal, materialistic policies of the Anglican hierarchy.

The New Brunswick clergy was under the jurisdiction of two church authorities — Charles Inglis, the first Bishop of Nova Scotia, and William Morice, the British Secretary of the Society for the Propagation of the Gospel in Foreign Parts (S.P.G.). Both men were rigidly conservative in their outlook, distrustful particularly of innovation in matters of ritual, and prone to equate religious enthusiasm with fanaticism or (in the case of Inglis) republicanism. As a result, both Inglis and Morice sought to extend the influence of the Church through building programs rather than through the development of more meaningful rituals. During the first twenty years of the Church's activity in New Brunswick, primary attention was given to such matters as the erection of churches, the acquisition of glebe lands, the definition of the respective powers of the governor, the bishop, and the vestry in Church government, the establishment of proper Anglican rituals, and the assignment of pew spaces. In 1809, for example, Inglis was distressed to learn that the pews in the Church at Kingston, New Brunswick, were held in common rather than being assigned individually, and he severely reprimanded the local vestry:

> I never knew an instance before this, in Europe or America, where pews were thus held . . . and where men — perhaps of the worst character — might come and set themselves down by the most religious and respectable characters in the parish. This must ultimately produce disorder and confusion. . . . What could occasion such an innovation — such a departure from the usage of the Church of England I am unable to conceive.[31]

Such preoccupations were far removed from the needs of the population at large. Although there has not been sufficient study of religion in early New Brunswick to permit quantitative comparisons, it does appear that the Anglican Church drew its members from the more static elements in New Brunswick society: the official and propertied classes plus the more stable agricultural communities. A larger percentage of the population preferred the more humanitarian, meliorist approach to life and to God which the dissenting churches, particularly the Baptists and Methodists, offered. And a growing number turned for comfort to the highly emotional "New Light" preachers, who were not necessarily attached to any congregation or rule, and whom Inglis denounced in 1809 as "Fanatical Itinerant Preachers who obtrude themselves in every district. The People," he fulminated, " . . . are insensibly alienated from the national Church and its worship."[32] Col. Gubbins reached the same conclusions about the power of the sects and the "pernicious" nature of their doctrines:

> The most importantly mischievous of their tenets is that a thorough convert to their faith can never sin in what they call spirit. After this spiritual regeneration, the soul they affirm is no longer accountable for the actions of the body even though it was to violate every law of the Decalogue.

Or, as Gubbins was to put it more humorously on another occasion, the New Light preachers held "that there is no sin in man below his heart."[33]

243

On the whole, the Loyalist leaders accepted the limited effectiveness of the Anglican Church with a curious indifference. Jonathan Odell was really the only member of the leadership group to take strong exception to the rising influence of evangelical religion in New Brunswick. Odell was, of course, an ordained Anglican minister, and although he never held a clerical post in New Brunswick, he did feel compelled periodically to go into the pulpit and protest against "the self appointed teachers" who were leading the Christians of the province away "from the Voice of Truth and that ancient apostolical form of worship which remain in primitive purity in the National Church." Yet most of the Loyalist leaders were at heart good eighteenth-century gentlemen: philosophical in their own religious outlook and quite tolerant of dissent. Although they personally disdained the more extreme forms of religious enthusiasm, most would have agreed with Edward Winslow that no legal sanctions should be invoked against the itinerant preachers — because persecution would simply increase their popularity. Winslow himself condemned the itinerants as unscrupulous "harpies," but he felt that only time and the example of a correct, righteous clergy could redeem the common people from such extravagances.[34]

The lukewarm attitude of the Loyalist leaders was particularly evident in their policy regarding marriage. The only real privilege of the "established church" in New Brunswick was that its clergy had the exclusive right to perform the marriage ceremony, although justices of the peace were permitted to marry people according to the Anglican rite when no minister was available. This privilege was a definite grievance for many devout New Brunswickers, who resented the fact that they could not be married by their own ministers according to their own forms of worship. At virtually every session of the Assembly a bill would be passed enabling dissenting ministers to perform the marriage ceremony — a bill which the Council invariably rejected because it violated the royal instructions as well as the firm policy of Bishop Inglis. In 1795 resentment over the marriage restrictions ran so deep that James Glenie was able to get through the House a "Declaratory Act" which effectively disestablished the Anglican Church. The Loyalist leadership managed to patch over this highly divisive issue by means of a compromise which reflected their basic apathy. On the one hand, they regularly rejected the Assembly's attempts to invade the privileges of the established Church, and they never even suggested to the imperial government that some change in the marriage regulations would relieve a source of deep distress in New Brunswick. On the other hand, they made it known that they were willing to bend the law a bit in practice, by offering the more respectable dissenting ministers commissions as justices of the peace, which would at least enable them to marry according to the Anglican rite. For better or for worse, the Loyalist leaders were simply not zealots on religious matters. They would not impose their religious convictions on the general population, nor were they willing to wave

244

the flag of religious liberty in order to serve these people more effectively.[35]

New England Company

The lack of religious zeal among the Loyalist leaders also contributed to the tragic failure of the New England Company in New Brunswick. The New England Company was an English missionary society, dedicated to converting the North American Indians to both the Christian religion and the more sedentary Christian way of life. It was founded in 1649, under the inspiration of the powerful Puritan missionary, John Eliot of Massachusetts, and until the American Revolution its work among the Indians was confined to the New England area. When the thirteen American colonies achieved their political independence, the British directors of the Company decided to transfer its operations to British territory so as to insure adequate control. Thus in 1786, the New England Company appeared, much like manna from heaven, on New Brunswick's doorstep. As might be expected, the provincial government was delighted to welcome such a well endowed, highly distinguished British charitable institution, and a blue-ribbon committee of Loyalist leaders was appointed to the local Board of Commissioners: Isaac Allen, George Ludlow, Jonathan Odell, George Leonard, Jonathan Bliss, Ward Chipman, John Coffin, and Edward Winslow.[36]

245

Despite this warm official reception, the Company's program for Indian education never really found a home in the hearts or plans of the New Brunswick population. Over the course of the next thirty years a series of educational experiments were undertaken in order to find some means of assimilating the Indians into the provincial way of life. Roving schools, consolidated schools, agricultural programs, apprentice systems were all tried and then discarded. In support of these endeavors, the Company expended over $140,000, and some of the Loyalist leaders — particularly George Leonard — also made generous contributions of time and money.[37] Yet the project was a failure from start to finish. When two S.P.G. missionaries inspected the Indian School at Sussex Vale during the 1820s, they were appalled to find that the few Indians enrolled in the program were being ruthlessly exploited by local white farmers and that a great deal of the Company's money was being used to educate white children. An unseemly amount was also being pocketed by the director of the school, the Rev. Oliver Arnold. Both missionaries recommended that the Company should close down its operations in New Brunswick, and this judgment was confirmed by the findings of the new governor of the province, Sir Howard Douglas.[38]

The reasons for the failure of this extensive effort to convert the Indians were many. Certainly the most fundamental problems arose from the Indians' deep distrust of Protestant missionaries and the equally strong hostility of the average white settler toward the native people. The Indians much preferred the ministrations of Roman Catholic priests, who were willing to learn their language and adapt themselves to the native way of life — instead of insisting that the Indians conform to the white pattern.[39] As for the attitude of the New Brunswickers in general, this was well expressed in a letter to the local Board of Commissioners urging them to use their funds to provide schools for white children rather than the Indians: " . . . as we are . . . poor families in this new settlement, low in Circumstances, unable to help one another — as much in need of the means of Useful Knowledge as the aboriginal Natives of these Provinces (For these are already . . . Converted to Roman Catholicism)."[40]

It has also been argued that the failure of the Company's efforts in New Brunswick was due in large measure to "the board's composition of prominent, rapacious American Loyalists," whose "indifference to the aims of the New England Company" was matched by "their superabundance of interest in its funds." The charge has some validity, particularly in the case of the superintendent of the school, John Coffin, who did divert Company funds to his own uses. Yet Coffin's behavior was censured by other Loyalist leaders, and the group as a whole was demonstrably scrupulous in handling Company money, as well as occasionally generous in their own contributions. The problem was not that the Loyalist leaders were "rapacious," but that they were "lukewarm" (to use Inglis's favorite pejorative). They did not merely lack the spiritual commitment of a John Eliot — they positively disdained that kind of religious zeal. The Loyalist leaders did, of course, have their own special missionary goal, which they pursued assiduously. This goal was to create a civilized, respectable society in New Brunswick. If the Indian population could be integrated into this society, well and good. But the Loyalist leaders were not willing to abandon their goal and accept the Indians' way of life simply because the New England Company decided to move to New Brunswick. Indeed Ward Chipman candidly told the S.P.G. missionary, John West, that the Indian schools had never worked effectively in New Brunswick and that, in his opinion, the only feasible way to civilize the Indians was to give them land in remote areas and then get missionaries to live among them and train them. It was clear, however, that none of the Loyalist leaders ever saw themselves performing such a task. The fact that they were willing to arrange for "a French royalist priest to come as a missionary to the Indians" while the New England Company was trying to counteract such Catholic influence demonstrates their very limited involvement in the proselytizing side of the Company's program. It seems dubious, therefore, to judge these men by Eliot's standards — when they did not share his ambitions. Surely the record of the Loyalist leaders can only be legitimately assessed in terms of their professed goals. It would seem much more meaningful, for example, to compare the efforts of Ward Chipman to establish a respectable legal profession in New Brunswick with Eliot's work among the Indians. In pursuing his objective, the Loyalist lawyer displayed an intensity, a personal dedication, and a certain self-righteous idealism that was reminiscent of the Puritan missionary.[41]

Black Loyalists

The treatment accorded the Black Loyalists by the New Brunswick leaders — and indeed by the overwhelming majority of white Loyalists — underlines even more dramatically the limits which historical circumstances placed on the Loyalists' social outlook. The Black Loyalists were the very special offspring of the American Revolution. They originally were slaves who had been encouraged by the British military to run away from their masters and enlist in the British Army in return for their personal freedom. During the war they had served in various paramilitary capacities, and at war's end nearly 3000 free Blacks were dispatched by Sir Guy Carleton to the Maritimes, including about 300 who eventually settled in New Brunswick. They had been promised equal treatment with the white Loyalists in terms of land grants, food, and provisions.[42]

247

Theoretically the Loyalist leaders should have felt some special sense of obligation towards these comrades in arms. Both the wartime commitments of the British government and the Loyalists' own Anglican faith and their aristocratic code of *noblesse oblige* should have produced a paternalistic, protective policy toward such peculiarly vulnerable members of their community. And indeed, in dealing with the similarly placed Acadian population, Governor Carleton and his Loyalist Council proved admirably sensitive to the religious and material needs of a defenceless minority.[43] With the Black Loyalists, however, the case was quite the reverse.

The problem was, of course, the Black's historic position as slaves. The Loyalists had known them in this status in the American colonies and had brought over 500 Black slaves with them to New Brunswick. A majority of the Loyalist Council were themselves slaveowners: Edward Winslow, Isaac Allen, Joshua Upham, Jonathan Odell, Beverley Robinson, Jr., and both Gabriel C. and George Duncan Ludlow. As well, at least two ministers of the established Church, Odell and Rev. James Scovil, owned slaves, and the local newspapers carried frequent advertisements announcing slave auctions or seeking runaways.[44]

Given this clear acceptance by most white Loyalists of slavery and of the Black man as an inferior being, destined to serve whites, discriminatory treatment of the free Black Loyalists was probably inevitable.

At no time were these Loyalists treated as gallant comrades in arms. Instead they were given smaller land grants, fewer provisions, and subjected to conditions not demanded of their white counterparts. In the political sphere, they were not eligible to vote for representatives in the House of Assembly, or to enjoy the important privileges of freedom of the City of Saint John, or to fish in the Saint John River. Even in the religious sphere, while they were welcomed as members of the Anglican Church, they were assigned separate seating places. The Baptists too split off the Blacks into separate congregations. Only the Quakers and the Wesleyan Methodists accepted them fully as human beings.[45]

The Blacks of New Brunswick were, of course, profoundly discouraged by this kind of life. Not only was white discrimination the rule, but their own lack of inner resources drove them further into dependency and degradation. They had, after all, been born and raised in slavery. They were conditioned to accept dependence, to take direction, and look to others for necessities. Now they were suddenly expected to find the self-reliance and initiative systematically denied them for generations, to fend for themselves in a forbidding climate on wilderness lands. To have made this transition successfully, the Black Loyalists would have needed sustained special assistance from outside. Instead they got discrimination and commercial exploitation from a white community too preoccupied with its own problems of survival to lend anyone else a hand.

Many Blacks gave up. Some 200 completely lost faith in the promise of the New World and emigrated with British assistance to Sierra Leone, to begin their lives all over again on what they hoped would be more hospitable African soil.[46] Others formed their own separate Churches, where they received consolation from charismatic preachers like David George and Boston King, and baptised themselves exhuberantly in the Saint John River to the utter alarm of local authorities. George reported that on visits to Saint John and Fredericton, he was greeted by slaves "'so full of joy that they ran out from waiting at table on their masters, with knives and forks in their hands, to meet me at the water side.'"[47] Others retreated into the bottle, to dull the pain of their existence with New Brunswick's ubiquitous rum. Virtually all who remained slipped into a state of semi-dependency as servants or day labourers. This status would remain their fate long after slavery disappeared from New Brunswick.

Among the New Brunswick leadership, only Ward Chipman was conspicuous for his efforts to improve the condition of these people. In 1800 Chipman volunteered his services to the slave Nancy in order to test the legality of slavery in the New Brunswick Supreme Court. The Court's verdict was inconclusive but Chipman's action did induce several slaveholders to manumit their charges voluntarily. This trend continued until the New Brunswick government could report to Whitehall in 1822 that slavery no longer existed in the province. In part this rapid disappearance of slavery was inspired by the humanitarian impulses emanating from the Abolitionist movement in Great Britain, but in large part it must be attributed to the economy and topography of New Brunswick, which did not lend itself to large-scale, slave-based agriculture. Great Britain sent a new group of some 3000 Black refugees to New Brunswick in 1815. Chipman again took up their cause and sought to locate them "within a convenient distance from the city for them to carry home the earnings of their labour at such seasons as they find useful employment here." By this time, the importance of giving Blacks viable economic circumstances and preventing their becoming a "nuisance" was recognized by the Loyalist establishment.[48]

Among the Churches, only the local Quaker congregation in Beaver Harbor rejected slavery on principle, although in England such philanthropic groups as the Associates of Dr. Bray and the Wesleyan Methodists made practical efforts to raise Black levels of literacy. One school financed by the Associates of Dr. Bray was operated in Fredericton from 1798 to 1814 by the Rev. George Pidgeon, an Anglican. It proved discouraging work according to Pidgeon. For although the Blacks were "'exceedingly importunate'" to get the school, afterwards they proved "'negligent and indifferent'" about actually attending and applying themselves.[49]

249

* * *

The history of the Blacks and the Indians in New Brunswick was poignantly sad. It also seems intractable. Every modern historian who has studied the problem has absolved the Loyalist leadership of any violent prejudice, any conspiratorial purpose, any systematic exploitation. Rather their conclusions center on the deep-rooted nature of the cultural attitudes held by both the ethnic majority and the ethnic minorities, and the limited effectiveness of either political principles or religious ideals in counteracting them.[50] The white Loyalists felt they were fighting for their political and cultural survival, and they demanded every member of their community should accept and assimilate their goals. For their part, the Blacks and Indians simply could not follow the white way or accept white goals. So they either dropped out entirely or became peripheral. The Loyalist record towards both Blacks and Indians, in fact, compares favorably with other communities in North America. Yet one feels certain that if any of the bewildered Blacks, Micmacs, or Maliseets had learned the King's English well enough to comment on the Loyalists' record of stewardship, they would have condemned it unequivocally.

Education

In contrast to their attitude toward religion, there was no ambivalence whatsoever among the Loyalist leaders concerning the importance of educational institutions in New Brunswick. The need to pass on to their children the benefits of their cultural heritage and to protect them from the unrefined impulses of the frontier was given the highest possible priority. The original educational programs of the Loyalist leaders were designed primarily "for their own children, the leaders to be," and the responsibility for educating "plain folk" was delegated to "the traditional agencies of the Church and private initiative." Thus the Loyalist leaders effectively pursued a class policy in the educational area and worked to establish institutions which would serve the needs of the governing elite, rather than trying to develop a more comprehensive program which would benefit the entire population. Very soon after their arrival in New Brunswick, the Loyalist leaders tried to set up grammar schools, libraries, and even a college — academic institutions which would provide the necessary background for a professional or managerial career. No comparable effort was made on behalf of popular education. In fact, in 1793, the Council blocked the only early attempt by the House of Assembly to establish a parish school system.[51]

250

This narrow, exclusive educational policy was doubtless forced upon the Loyalist leaders by financial necessity. The letters of Charles Inglis demonstrate that the governing elite was quite sympathetic to the desire of "many poor families" to educate their children, and they hoped the S.P.G. would provide the necessary funds. The ability of the province itself to support any educational endeavor was, however, extremely limited, and the government leaders reserved the funds available for the education of the children of the more respectable classes. Even so, the minimal effort undertaken could not be sustained by the public purse. A high tuition fee and funds from the New England Company were needed to supplement the provincial grants, and the Loyalist leaders also tried, though without success, to get the imperial government to support their educational efforts. When the province's financial resources began to improve after the turn of the century, a local school system was begun — with the full support of the Council. In subsequent years, this system was extended as rapidly as public funds permitted. It would seem, therefore, that although the early educational efforts of the Loyalist leaders were definitely self-serving, they were more the product of necessity than of choice.[52]

The actual educational institutions established in New Brunswick before 1815 were few in number and inferior in quality. Although the Loyalist leaders aspired to a much better system, New Brunswick was simply too young, too remote, and too poor to meet their standards. As early as 1785, the Council approved a charter for a provincial college, but the British government declined to grant the necessary articles of incorporation. This refusal reflected British uncertainty as to how best to provide for higher education in the colonies — given the obvious limits of local support. Finally, in 1790, the Pitt government informed Governor Carleton that the King had decided to endow a college in Nova Scotia, which would serve students from all the North American colonies, and that in addition a fund would be set up at Oxford and Cambridge "for the maintenance of a certain Number of Young men, being natives of His North American Dominions. . . . " The scholarship fund was never actually established, so that in effect this policy decreed that New Brunswick was not to have her own college, but was to use King's College in Nova Scotia to educate her sons. In an eloquent letter describing the importance of a college to the New Brunswick Loyalists, Carleton pleaded with the British government to reconsider this decision:

> The inhabitants of this province are, with very few exceptions, in circumstances that cannot afford the expences of an Education at a distance from home; Yet many of the inhabitants have themselves had liberal Educations and covet the like advantages for their children; and it would be a great consolation to them to see this Institution cherished and encouraged by Government. . . . It would also be to them a pleasing proof that, in this respect, no preference has been given to the Elder province of Nova Scotia.[53]

Despite Carleton's strong advocacy, the British government was not willing to underwrite a second college in North America, and the New Brunswickers were forced to fend for themselves. A grammar school in Fredericton was the most they were able to establish before 1800. The council granted this "provincial seminary" a tract of 6000 acres, which produced a rental income of about £100 a year. The Assembly also made one grant of £100 to the school in 1792, but it specifically refused Governor Carleton's request to establish an annual allowance for the school, on the grounds that the revenues of "this infant province" were still too unstable to permit such long-term commitments. Tuition fees were another source of income for the school. Yet it evidently still had difficulty meeting its expenses, for in 1798 the Trustees of the Fredericton Academy "'found it necessary to annex the duties of Indian Missionary to the appointment of their president, of whose Salary a considerable part was paid by the Commissioners for Indian Schools. . . . '"[54] In 1800 this Academy was granted a provincial charter of incorporation as the College of New Brunswick. As the economic fortunes of the province improved, the House of Assembly was able to grant an annual allowance to this college, beginning with £100 per annum in 1805 and increasing periodically thereafter. Nonetheless, the college continued to be plagued by financial problems and the difficulty of inducing competent professors and administrators (who were required by the charter to be members of the Anglican Church) to accept appointments at this remote, frontier institution. It was not until 1828 that the college granted its first two degrees — a full forty-three years after the Loyalist leaders had begun their efforts to establish higher education in New Brunswick.[55]

The Loyalist leaders were truly distressed by the difficulties they encountered in trying to establish a respectable college in New Brunswick. Although many sent their own children out of the province to complete their schooling, this did not lessen the desire of the leadership for good local educational institutions. George Leonard was a particularly active supporter of this cause. After it became clear that Great Britain would do nothing for education in New Brunswick, Leonard tried to persuade some private English philanthropists to become patrons of the Academy and to endow a provincial library. He feared, he confessed to Chipman, that unless such facilities soon became available, "the girls" would have no choice but to marry the "Common peasantry of the Country." When his English friends failed to provide any support, Leonard became despondent about the prospects for New Brunswick: "I begin to think that [Jonathan] Bliss is right respecting my madness about formal education in New Brunswick . . . and that it is more sense to give the Superiority to the women, leaving the rising tribe of men to be fools." Despite their profound commitment, the Loyalist leaders were unable to establish more than the rudiments of an educational system during their lifetime.[56]

252

Fathers and Sons

The narrow range of opportunities which New Brunswick offered to men of talent proved particularly frustrating to the Loyalist leaders as they contemplated the future of their sons. Loyalist life in New Brunswick centered around strong, affectionate family relations, and as the Loyalist leaders were forced to accept the limited possibilities of their own careers, they often transferred their ambitions to their sons. Considering the education offered by the college at Fredericton inadequate, many of them sent their sons out of the province for higher learning. Most of the boys went to King's College in Nova Scotia, although some fathers reached higher: Chipman and Upham sent their sons to Harvard, William Botsford, Jr., went to Yale, and the eldest Winslow boy and both Saunders children received their education in England. In addition, at least three Loyalist leaders — Ward Chipman, Munson Jarvis, and John Saunders — enabled their sons to read law at the English Inns of Court.

Even more difficult than the problem of education was the decision regarding a career. Perhaps New Brunswick offered a comfortable, peaceful area for the average settler, but was it good enough for the sons of the Loyalist leaders? Some, like Jonathan Odell and George Leonard, thought it was, and they proceeded to use every ounce of their political influence to insure that their sons would inherit their offices.[57] But many thought not. Jonathan Bliss, who never altered his opinion that New Brunswick was a "wretched country," trained one son to practice law in Nova Scotia, where he ultimately sat on the Supreme Court, and sent the other to England, where he became the New Brunswick agent. Winslow encouraged two of his boys to join the British Army and a third to pursue a merchant career with the East India Company.[58] Sometimes the young men made the choice for themselves. Gabriel V. Ludlow and Jonathan and Stephen Sewell all studied law under Ward Chipman and considered a New Brunswick career. But a short period of practice led to the acute observation (*circa* 1795) that all the profitable offices and clients in the province were taken up by the original Loyalist leaders, men still comparatively young in years, and that it would be decades before the second generation could expect to fill their shoes. Thus Ludlow took off for New York and the Sewell boys for their unusually distinguished careers in Lower Canada.[59]

Perhaps the two most revealing instances of father–son relationships among the Loyalist leaders occurred in the cases of Ward Chipman and John Saunders. Both men had but one son, and each had tender feelings for his heir. Chipman, the less affluent of the two, sent his son to grammar school in New England and then to Harvard College with the help of his brother-in-law, the wealthy merchant William Gray. Ward Chipman, Jr., proved to be such an outstanding student that he was asked to deliver the "English Oration" at his Commencement exercises, and his proud father informed Edward Winslow that "the great lawyer Sam Dexter pronounced it 'the best performance for matter & manner that he had ever heard in Cambridge.'" William Gray agreed that his nephew was a most impressive young man, and he offered either to take him into his merchant firm or to finance his legal education in the United States. But Chipman was adamant that his son should seek a career within the British empire, and Gray's largesse apparently did not extend to an English education.[60]

253

Since his own family could not afford to send him abroad for study, Ward, Jr., returned to New Brunswick after finishing Harvard and read law under his father's direction. While he pursued his studies, the elder Chipman wrote to such old Loyalist friends as Chief Justice Sampson Salter Blowers of Nova Scotia and Jonathan Sewell, Jr., then attorney general of Lower Canada, in order to ascertain the state of the legal profession in their provinces. "I see but little prospect," Chipman informed Blowers, "of his having sufficient business for his support in this Province in which I have so unprofitably sacrificed so great a part of my life. . . . I most certainly should prefer his living where I may have the best chance of sometimes seeing him and most frequently and easily hearing from him."[61]

After much deliberation, Chipman decided in 1808 to send his son to Quebec to begin his career under Sewell's guardianship. Although Chipman regarded Sewell "as dear to me as a Son or brother," the prospect of parting permanently with their only child filled both parents with intense agony. "Indeed," Chipman wrote, "when I think of his leaving me my heart fails me, but these feelings I must subdue and endeavour to reconcile his mother to the event. . . . " As the time of leave-taking drew near, Chipman declared that it was "one of the severest trials I have ever experienced. . . . But on the other hand when I consider how cruelly my own time has been sacrificed and the prime of my life thrown away in a place, where to this hour I am not able to obtain sufficient to *support me*, I start at the thought of being hereafter upbraided by him, for subjecting him to scenes of similar mortification if I should detain him here." In a final, desperate act of parental love, the Chipmans actively considered moving with their son to Montreal, and they begged Sewell for precise information on the cost of living in that city and the prospect of the elder Chipman's obtaining an official post there.[62]

One can only imagine the joy which filled the Chipman household when suddenly at this dark moment in their family life, Ward Chipman, Sr., was appointed to the Supreme Court of New Brunswick. The appointment opened up an entirely new, incomparably brighter prospect. For it meant that Ward, Sr., would have a secure, salaried post for the first time in his entire career, that Ward, Jr., could take over his father's law practice, and that money could be laid aside for further education. In 1810, enough had been saved to send young Ward to the Middle Temple. He spent three years there, rubbing off, as he informed his uncle William Ward, "a little of the college rust." Although he claimed to fear that "my fond father is probably expecting a second *Lord Mansfield*," the young man returned to New Brunswick with obvious joy. In succeeding years, he would chart the same course of public service which his father had pursued: recorder of the city of Saint John, solicitor general, attorney general, member of the Council, agent to the Boundary Commission, and Supreme Court justice. In 1834 Ward Chipman, Jr., was named Chief Justice of the New Brunswick Supreme Court, and two years later Harvard gave an honorary Doctor of Laws to its distinguished son. Unfortunately for the province, the Chipman tradition came to an end with his death in 1851, for Ward, Jr., was childless. Both father and son established in New Brunswick a record of public service that was marked by unusually high professional qualifications and a deep, sustained interest in the welfare of the province.[63]

Whereas the Chipmans found money to be the prime obstacle to their freedom of choice, John Saunders almost lost the company of his son through too lavish an education. John Simcoe Saunders was sent as a young lad to "one of the best public schools in England," according to his grandfather, James Chalmers. His classmates were the sons of "Admirals, Generals and Dignataries of Church & state," and his education included, in addition to the traditional academic subjects, instruction in dancing and fencing. He then went to Oxford and, after taking his degree in 1815, informed his father that he wished to study law under a special pleader in London. Although John Saunders had deliberately given his son this first-class English education, he had always intended that the young man should eventually return to New Brunswick to practice law and manage the baronial estate he was trying to develop north of Fredericton. For young Saunders, however, the thought of returning to New Brunswick after living for ten years among the English upper classes was repugnant: "I can never bring down my own mind to the narrow sphere of prejudice and ignorance to which everyone there must accommodate himself . . . the society of New Brunswick is quite insulated. . . . Indeed after the exertions I have made I could never submit [to] lavish them on the woods & 'desert air.'"[64]

In fact, the younger Saunders was "astonished" that his father expected him to return to New Brunswick. "For I have always turned my thoughts either to the East or West Indies — Canada or Nova Scotia or the English bar; never allowing myself for a moment to degrade my prospect by thinking of the possibility of throwing away my views in life by practising in such a miserable place as New Brunswick." To drive his point home, the young man then compared his father's career with that of Jonathan Sewell, Jr., who was by then chief justice of the province of Lower Canada:

255

> At the time of your appointment to the [New Brunswick] bench Sewall set out a needy adventurer for the Canadian bar with a few shillings in his pocket and a few introductions to different gentlemen in Quebec. At that time you set out too — superior in talents, education, experience, friends & resources — but how wide is the difference at this moment — he after an active career retires to the highest post of honor with more than two thousand a year — you with four hundred & fifty still obliged to "bow the knee and bend the neck to Smyth" [the Lieutenant Governor of New Brunswick].[65]

The elder Saunders could be just as determined as his son, and the young man was apparently forced to come home because his father refused to underwrite his life in England any longer. From 1816 until 1822, young Saunders practiced law in New Brunswick, but it was not a happy experience, and he yearned to return to England and continue his legal studies. His father found it difficult to understand his son's feelings, for the elder Saunders himself frankly preferred "to be of some importance in the society where I might live." But rather than see his son unhappy, Saunders finally capitulated in 1823 and agreed to help the young man establish himself at the English Bar. He had concluded, in a moment of excruciating candor, that it was "through my want of judgment you were placed where you acquired habits perhaps impossible for you to overcome." Over the next six years, John Simcoe Saunders studied at Lincoln's Inn, was admitted to the English Bar, clerked under the distinguished London lawyer, Joseph Chitty, married an English bride, and published a legal text on "Pleading and Evidence" which would go through several editions. His father, true to his word, gave his son every possible support in these ventures. He not only supplied young Saunders with an annual income of £400, but offered to sell off part of the lands at his beloved "Barony" in order to provide him with a marriage settlement. He also informed him that he would be willing to resign his post as Chief Justice of New Brunswick in favor of his son — if this appeared desirable.[66]

Despite this solid parental support, young Saunders terminated his English career in 1830, and returned to New Brunswick, where, like Ward Chipman, Jr., he became one of the government's most distinguished leaders. Although he never achieved his ambition to become chief justice of the province, he did hold many important posts, including provincial secretary, member of both the Executive and the Legislative Councils, surveyor general, and president of the Executive Council. The records do not reveal whether this second generation of Loyalist leaders (like their fathers) found that their early hopes and ambitions cast a shadow over the sense of fulfillment they derived from their service to the province.

*   *   *

The Loyalist leaders were determined to develop in New Brunswick a style of life which would make their province "the envy of the American states" and an "asylum of loyalty" within the empire. Yet these internal goals represent only one-half of the challenge facing these pioneer community builders. Always confronting them from the outside was the unfolding example of the new republic to the south and the unpredictable, almost equally uncontrollable policies of the imperial politicians in London. To understand fully the challenge and accomplishment of New Brunswick under the Loyalist leadership, it is necessary to look at its external relations, both material and ideological, with the two great powers which impinged on its destiny.

NOTES

[1] Winslow to Chipman, 7 January 1784, Lawrence Collection of Chipman Papers, *Public Archives of Canada.*

[2] James Hannay, "The Loyalists," *The New England Magazine*, New Series, vol. 4, no. 3, 297–315; Diary of Bishop Charles Inglis, entries for 20 July 1792 and 9 August 1792, Inglis Papers, *Public Archives of Nova Scotia*, Charles Turner, "New Brunswick in 1802," in William O. Raymond, ed., *Acadiensis* 7 (1907): 132; Patrick Campbell, *Travels in the Interior Inhabited Parts of North America in the Years 1791 and 1792*, 40–42, 252; Jonathan Bliss to Benedict Arnold, 3 December 1798, Benedict Arnold Papers, *New Brunswick Museum.*

[3] Winslow to Wentworth, 27 November 1784,, Winslow Papers, *University of New Brunswick*. Charles Turner, "New Brunswick in 1802," 135.

[4] Howard Temperley, ed., *Gubbins' New Brunswick Journals 1811 and 1813* (Fredericton, 1980), 60.

[5] "New Brunswick," *Royal Gazette*, 26 August 1800; "Hull's Invasion," *Royal Gazette*, 21 September 1812; "St. Andrews," *Royal Gazette*, 30 October 1799; "Saint John," *Saint John Gazette*, 14 December 1798.

[6] "St. John," *Royal Gazette*, 24 June 1794.

[7] Chipman to Jonathan Sewell, Jr., 15 July 1794, Sewell Papers, *Public Archives of Canada*; Eliza Gray to Ward Chipman, n.d. [*circa* 1794], Chipman Papers.

[8] "New Brunswick . . . American Politics," *Royal Gazette*, 17 February 1801. George A. Rawlyk describes the remarkable congruence of political views held by the New England Federalists and the New Brunswick leaders in "The Federalist-Loyalist Alliance in New Brunswick, 1784–1815," *Humanities Association Review* 27 (1976): 147. Rawlyk's information is illuminating, although I find the New Brunswick leaders less arbitrary and conspiratorial than he (142–46).

[9] "New York. Further Translations from the 'History of Crimes committed during the French Rev-

olution,'" *Saint John Gazette*, 10 November 1797; "Important Documents," *Royal Gazette*, 30 July 1799.

[10] Wallace Brown, "William Cobbett in the Maritimes," *Dalhousie Review* 56 (1976-77): 452; Temperley, *Gubbins' Journals*, 84.

[11] "Porcupine's Farewell to the People of the United States," *Royal Gazette*, 10 June 1800; Odell to Chipman, 20 March 1800, Chipman Papers.

[12] Odell to Chipman, 10 May 1802, Papers of Jonathan Odell, *New Brunswick Museum*; Odell to Chipman, 8 November 1804, Lawrence Collection. Jonathan Odell, "The Agonizing Dilemma," in Thomas B. Vincent, ed., *Narrative Verse Satire in Maritime Canada, 1799-1814* (Ottawa, 1978), 173-86. For a description of the interest in lexicography shared by Odell and Boucher, see Anne Y. Zimmer, *Jonathan Boucher, Loyalist in Exile* (Detroit, 1978), 313-26.

[13] The two most complete pieces written by Winslow were: (1) a satirical play written during the 1795 election, recently reprinted as Condon, "New Brunswick's First Political Play" and (2) the newspaper series by "Tammany" which he published in the *Royal Gazette* during 1802 to satirize the Loyalist half-pay officers who were returning to the United States (see Ch. 9 [in Condon, *The Envy of the American States*]). In addition his letters were filled with the vivid metaphors and similes which he fashioned to entertain his friends.

[14] Turner, "New Brunswick in 1802," 131; Winslow to Daniel Lyman, 12 March 1800, Winslow Papers.

[15] George Leonard to Ward Chipman, 11 March 1795, Chipman Papers; "Vth Letter of Alfred," *Saint John Gazette*, 16 October 1805.

[16] Winslow to Lutwyche, 4 March 1800, Winslow Papers.

[17] George Leonard to John King, 29 March 1799, C.O. 188/10; Carleton to Hobart, 21 June 1802, C.O. 188/11; Lutwyche to Winslow, 17 May 1800, Winslow Papers; Hobart to Carleton, 6 March 1802, C.O. 189/1; Winslow to James Fraser, 12 October 1806, Winslow Papers.

[18] Lutwyche to Winslow, 5 January 1807, Winslow Papers; Thomas Carleton to John Saunders, 6 July 1809, Saunders Papers, *University of New Brunswick*; Chipman to Jonathan Sewell, Jr., 28 October 1808, Sewell Correspondence; Winslow to Lutwyche, 12 October 1806, Winslow Papers.

[19] Carleton to Sydney, 5 December 1787, C.O. 188/4; Beverley Robinson, Sr., to Beverley Robinson, Jr., 15 March 1790, Robinson Papers, *New Brunswick Museum*.

[20] Winslow to Jonathan Sewell, Jr., 14 January 1797, Sewell Papers.

[21] Chipman to Lord Bathurst, 9 September 1823, C.O. 189/1.

[22] Draft of letter, John Saunders to [Thomas Carleton], n.d., [*circa* 1808], Saunders Papers.

[23] "To the FREEHOLDERS of the PROVINCE of NEW BRUNSWICK," from "A Friend to the Province," 21 August 1795, *Saint John Gazette*.

[24] Winslow to Chief Justice Ludlow, 22 July 1807, Winslow Papers.

[25] *Journal of the House of Assembly* 2: 58 and 88.

[26] Chipman to Stephen Kemble, 26 March 1806, Lawrence Collection of Chipman Papers.

[27] *Journal of the House of Assembly* 2: 99 (30 January 1807); Chipman to Winslow, 29 July 1806, Winslow Papers.

[28] George Leonard to Jonathan Odell, 24 October 1794, Papers relating to Church Matters (NBM); John S. Moir, *The Church in the British Era: From the British Conquest to Confederation* (Toronto, 1972), 22-23.

[29] Rev. Samuel Cooke to Rev. Jacob Bailey, 6 May 1786, Papers of Jacob Bailey, *Public Archives of Nova Scotia*.

[30] Inglis to William Morice, 25 August 1804, Inglis Papers; "W.S." and "A.T.," Church Wardens to Bishop Inglis, 24 May 1784, Chipman Papers.

[31] Judith Fingard, *The Anglican Design in Loyalist Nova Scotia, 1783-1816* (London, 1972), 27-38, 182-83; Walter Bates, *Kingston and the Loyalists of the 'Spring Fleet'*, W.O. Raymond, ed. (Saint John, 1889), 17.

[32] Samuel D. Clark, *Church and Sect in Canada* (Toronto, 1948), ch. 2; Goldwin French, *Parsons and Politics: The Role of the Methodists in Upper Canada and the Maritimes* (Toronto, 1962), 32-39; Inglis to Sir George Prevost; 22 June 1809, Inglis Papers. Lively sympathetic accounts of early Baptist congregations are given in articles by George A. Rawlyk and Esther Clark Wright in Barry Moody, ed., *Repent and Believe: The Baptist Experience in Maritime Canada* (Hantsport, N.S., 1980), 1-26, 66-74. See also Thomas William Acheson, "Denominationalism in a Loyalist County: A Social History of Charlotte County, 1763-1940" (Unpublished M.A. thesis, UNB, 1964), 3-4, 16-17, 25, 29-31.

[33] Temperley, *Gubbins' Journals*, 15-16, 83, 17.

[34] Jonathan Odell, Sermon Preached in Fredericton, 9 August and 10 September, 1801, Odell Papers; Undated remarks of Edward Winslow on the Old Inhabitants and Itinerant Preachers [c. 1803], Winslow Papers, vol. 18.

[35] Carleton to Inglis, 9 March 1791, Papers relating to Church Matters; "A Bill Declaratory of What Acts of Parliament are binding in this Province," C.O. 188/6; Hugh Mackay to Robert Watson, 26 April, 1803, Winslow Papers. Moir, *Church in the British Era*, 25.

[36] William Kellaway, *The New England Company, 1649-1776* (London, 1961), 280; "Petition of the Company for the Propagation of the Gospel in New England and Parts Adjacent in North America," C.O. 188/2.

[37] Leslie Francis S. Upton, *Micmacs and Colonists: Indian-White Relations in the Maritimes 1713-1867* (Vancouver, 1979) 160-63; Judith Fingard, "The New England Company and the New Brunswick

257

Indians, 1786–1826: A Comment on the Colonial Perversion of British Benevolence," *Acadiensis* 1 (Spring 1972): 28–43.

38 "Report to New England Company by the Reverend Walter Bromley," 22 September 1822, Lawrence Collection; Report of John West on the Indian Academy at Sussex Vale to the New England Company, 20 September 1826, Lawrence Collection; Sir Howard Douglas to William Vaughan, 13 December 1824, Lawrence Collection.

39 Upton, *Micmacs and Colonists*, xv, 101, 155–59.

40 George Gillmore to George Leonard & Board, 22 January 1789, Lawrence Collection.

41 Fingard, "The New England Company," 41; Extract of a letter from Governor Carleton to Henry Dundas, 14 June 1794, Papers of the New Brunswick House of Assembly. Col. Gubbins was as despairing as Chipman: "The Indians are so fond of a wandering life that I know of only one instance where an individual was weaned from it. (*Gubbins' Journals*, 11). The destructive impact of Loyalist culture on the Micmac way of life is described in Upton, *Micmacs and Colonists*, 127–41.

42 Robin Winks, *The Blacks in Canada: A History* (Montreal, 1971), 29–31; William A. Spray, *The Blacks in New Brunswick* (Fredericton, 1972), 31.

43 See Ch. 5 [in Condon, *The Envy of the American States*]. For a description of the contented, law-abiding state of the Acadians under Loyalist rule, see Temperley, *Gubbins' Journals*, 21–22, 72–74.

44 Winks, *Blacks in Canada*, 44; Spray, *Blacks in New Brunswick*, 16–17, 20–21.

45 James W. St. Gême Walker, *The Black Loyalists: The Search for a Promised Land in Nova Scotia and Sierra Leone, 1783–1870* (New York, 1976), 67–72.

46 Winks, *Blacks in Canada*, 44; Walker, *Black Loyalists*, Ch. 5 ff.

47 Walker, *Black Loyalists*, 71–79.

48 Spray, *Blacks in New Brunswick*, 24; Chipman to William F. Odell, 2 November 1816, Lawrence Collection of Chipman Papers.

49 Spray, *Blacks in New Brunswick*, 53; Winks, *Blacks in Canada*, 59.

50 For examples, see Walker, *Black Loyalists*, 39, 45–46.

51 Katherine B. MacNaughton, *The Development of the Theory and Practice of Education in New Brunswick, 1784–1900* (Fredericton, 1947), 41–42.

52 Inglis to Dr. Morice, 28 September 1798, Inglis Papers.

53 William Wyndham Grenville to Carleton, 3 June 1790, C.O. 188/4; Carleton to Grenville, 9 March 1793, Thomas Carleton Papers, *Public Archives of Canada*.

54 Carleton to Grenville, 20 August 1790, C.O. 188/4; *Journal of the House of Assembly* 1:288; Inglis to Jonathan Odell, 18 October 1798, Papers relating to Church Matters.

55 Carleton to Portland, 4 August 1800, C.O. 188/10; MacNaughton, *History of Education in New Brunswick*, 52; Thomas J. Condon, "Similar Origins: Effects of Isolation on the Early Development of the University of New Brunswick and Harvard University," *Atlantic Advocate* 55 (May 1965): 35–41.

56 Leonard to Chipman, 28 October 1794, 6 November 1794, 13 November 1794, Hazen Collection of Chipman Papers, *New Brunswick Museum*.

57 Memorial of Jonathan Odell to Lord Castlereagh, 5 September 1808, C.O. 188/14; George Leonard to J. Chapman in Lord Camden's Office, 30 November 1804, C.O. 188/12.

58 Jonathan Bliss to Benedict Arnold, 12 July 1796, Benedict Arnold Papers (NBM); Joseph W. Lawrence, *The Judges of New Brunswick and Their Times* (Saint John, 1907), 180–84.

59 Jonathan Sewell, Jr., successfully occupied every legal post in Lower Canada, until his career was capped by his appointment as Chief Justice of the Provincial Supreme Court in 1808. His brother Stephen confined himself mainly to private practice in Montreal, although he did serve for a brief period as Solicitor General of Lower Canada.

60 Chipman to Winslow, 24 November 1804 and 5 October 1805, Winslow Papers; Chipman to Jonathan Sewell, Jr., 18 July 1800, Sewell Correspondence.

61 Chipman to Blowers, 6 August 1808, Chipman Papers; Chipman to Jonathan Sewell, Jr., 16 November 1805, Sewell Correspondence.

62 Chipman to Jonathan Sewell, Jr., 8 July 1808 and 28 October 1808, Sewell Correspondence.

63 Ward Chipman, Jr., to William Ward, 1 August 1813, Thomas W. Ward Papers, *Massachusetts Historical Society*, Box No. 1; Lawrence, *Judges of New Brunswick*, 301–38.

64 James Chalmers to John Saunders, 4 June 1806, Saunders Papers; G.H. Storie to John Saunders, 16 June 1815, Saunders Papers; John Simcoe Saunders to John Saunders, 4 September 1815, Saunders Papers.

65 John Simcoe Saunders to John Saunders, 4 November 1814, Saunders Papers.

66 John Saunders to his son, 27 June 1828 and 14 September 1824, Saunders Papers; Lawrence, *Judges of New Brunswick*, 274–75.

A late-eighteenth-century watercolour of a scene near the settlement of Lévis, opposite Quebec, by James Peachey, ca. 1785.

The British newcomers, few though they were, had to be reckoned with. By 1765 they were powerful enough to have Governor Murray recalled and by 1777 they would be strong enough to command the majority of investments in the fur trade.

José Igartua, "A Change in Climate: The Conquest and the *Marchands* of Montreal"

Topic Seven

The Economy and Society of Quebec, 1760–1791

In the Treaty of Paris of 1763, France ceded New France to England. The British now faced the difficult task of formulating a policy to govern a colony whose population was different in language, culture, and religion from their own. That policy, as outlined in the Proclamation of 1763, limited New France, now renamed the Province of Quebec, to the St. Lawrence Valley. It was designed to transform the former French colony into a British one through the establishment of British institutions and laws — in short, to assimilate the French-Canadian population.

The policy failed, however. Very few English-speaking immigrants came to Quebec, preferring to settle in the warmer, more fertile Ohio Valley, amid a familiar, English-speaking population. Furthermore, James Murray and Guy Carleton, the first two governors of Quebec, sided with the French-speaking seigneurs against the aggressive, English-speaking merchants in the colony. Realizing that there was little likelihood of the colony becoming Anglicized, Governor Carleton recommended the reinstatement of French civil law, the seigneurial system of holding land, and the right of the Roman Catholic Church to collect the tithe. London accepted his proposals and, in the Quebec Act of 1774, completely reversed its earlier policy of 1763.

By that time, however, the basic economic structure of the colony had changed. The few English-speaking colonists who had settled in Quebec had taken a prominent role in the economic life of the colony. Although it was small, this Anglo-American commercial class had gained enormous influence — enough to secure the recall of James Murray, the first governor, in 1766. In terms of economic power, by 1777, this group even commanded a majority of the investments in the fur trade. How had this tiny English-speaking group prospered so? Was it because of the return to France of the commercial class of New France, the superior abilities of the English-speaking merchants, or the favouritism of the British administrators? Dale Standen reviews the major interpretations in "The Debate on the Social and Economic Consequences of the Conquest: A Summary." One of the most satisfactory of these interpretations is provided by José Igartua in his article "A Change in Climate: The Conquest and the *Marchands* of Montreal." It examines the rise of the English-speaking merchants in the fur trade.

For an overview of the period, see A.L. Burt's *The Old Province of Quebec*, 2 vols. (Toronto: McClelland and Stewart, 1968; first published in 1933); Pierre Tousignant's "The Integration of the Province of Quebec into the British Empire, 1763–91. Part 1: From the Royal Proclamation to the Quebec Act," in *Dictionary of Canadian Biography*, vol. 4, *1771–1800*, xxxii–xlix; Hilda Neatby's *Quebec: The Revolutionary Age, 1760–1791* (Toronto: McClelland and Stewart, 1966); and Philip Lawson's *The Imperial Challenge: Quebec and Britain in the Age of the American Revolution* (Montreal and Kingston: McGill-Queen's University Press, 1989). Fernand Ouellet's *Histoire économique et sociale du Québec, 1760–1850* (Montréal: Fides, 1966), translated as *Economic and Social History of Quebec, 1760–1850* (Toronto: Macmillan, 1980), is an important study. Recently, a number of Ouellet's essays, edited and translated by Jacques A. Barbier, were published in the collection *Economy, Class, and Nation in Quebec: Interpretive Essays* (Toronto: Copp Clark Pitman, 1991). Michel Brunet presents an alternative view to Ouellet's in *Les Canadiens après la Conquête, 1759–1775* (Montréal: Fides, 1969). Dale Miquelon's *Society and Conquest* (Toronto: Copp Clark, 1977) is a valuable collection on the effect of the Conquest on French-Canadian society. An important local study is Allan Greer, *Peasant, Lord, and Merchant: Rural Society in Three Quebec Parishes, 1740–1840* (Toronto: University of Toronto Press, 1985). On the history of the early English-speaking population in the Province of Quebec, see Ronald Rudin's *The Forgotten Quebecers: A History of English-Speaking Quebec, 1759–1980* (Québec: Institut québécois de la recherche sur la culture, 1985).

262

The Debate on the Social and Economic Consequences of the Conquest: A Summary

S. DALE STANDEN

The debate over the Conquest of Canada in 1760 began with its consequences, then widened into a debate over the nature of society in New France and into a controversy over crisis in Lower Canada in the early nineteenth century. In its primitive stages the debate focussed upon the magnitude of immediate consequences, and whether or not these did irrevocable damage to the long-term social, political, and economic development of French Canada. The controversy acquired sophistication as further research raised more complex questions about the historical

From *Proceedings of the Tenth Meeting of the French Colonial Historical Society*, April 12–14, 1984, ed. Phillip P. Boucher. Copyright © 1985 by the University Press of America. Reprinted with permission.

process at work in the St. Lawrence Valley from the seventeenth to the nineteenth centuries. Interest in the single event of the Conquest, however important, yielded to interest in the longer historical continuum in which the Conquest, like other events, was situated.

Even with this expansion, however, one pre-occupation dominates: it is to demonstrate one way or the other whether the economic development of Quebec and Lower Canada, and in particular French Canadian participation in that development, was retarded on the one hand by some circumstantial *force majeure* — the Conquest, imperial subjugation, geography, markets — or on the other hand by rooted social and cultural traits that led French Canadians to eschew business and material progress. It is notable that many participants in the debate on both sides assume Quebec's economic development to have been backward to some extent. Recently this notion has been seriously challenged. Cultural mentality or irresistible circumstance: these are the poles that inform the largest part of Quebec historiography.

263

Debate over the effects of the Conquest dates from shortly after the event itself, and for long concentrated on the issue of whether Canadian society was deprived of its leadership by an exodus following the Conquest. In 1899 Louis Baby demonstrated from his research that emigration had not deprived Canadians of their social leadership, or at least nowhere near the degree that historians like F.-X. Garneau had claimed. The recent debate over the effects of the Conquest developed in the generation following the Second World War. Industrial and urban expansion since the end of the nineteenth century was accompanied as elsewhere by increased secularization. It was among the new, secular, Quebecois nationalists that the idea of the Conquest as the prime impediment to French Canadian development found its warmest adherents. By the 1950s in Quebec the ethnic division among occupations and corporate ownership was stark: Anglophones monopolized financial services and the managerial echelons of large corporations; and Anglophones, domestic or foreign, owned the lion's share of these corporations. How did this come to be?

In seeking an explanation the new nationalists were understandably reluctant to accept the notion that values inherent in their nationality might be responsible. This was quite unlike their clerical nationalist forebears who glorified the myth that the French Canadian's vocation was spiritual and moral, not mundane and material. The new nationalists, having embraced modernity and materialism, were drawn to explanations of their so-called "economic backwardness" that did not compromise their secular national self-image. If French Canadians were absent from the ranks of big business, it could not be due to a cultural deficiency in entrepreneurship or capitalist spirit. The Conquest, which for generations of nationalists had been a dark event in their history, became the object of reinterpretation. The result was to darken it even more.

The Province of Quebec, 1763–1791

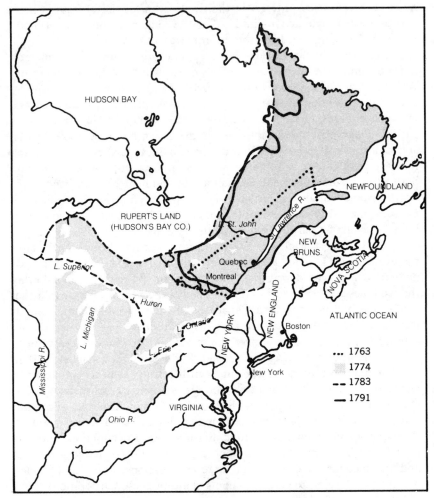

HUDSON BAY

RUPERT'S LAND
(HUDSON'S BAY CO.)

NEWFOUNDLAND

St. John

St. Lawrence R.

NEW
BRUNS.

NOVA SCOTIA

L. Superior

Quebec

Montreal

L. Huron

L. Michigan

L. Ontario

L. Erie

NEW YORK

NEW ENGLAND

ATLANTIC OCEAN

Boston

Mississippi R.

New York

VIRGINIA

Ohio R.

```
···  1763
▒▒   1774
- -  1783
—    1791
```

Edgar McInnis, *Canada: A Political and Social History*, 4th ed. (Toronto: Holt, Rinehart and Winston, 1982), 161.

Three historians of the University of Montreal — Maurice Séguin, Guy Frégault, and Michel Brunet — are associated most closely with developing the hypothesis that the Conquest was responsible for the inferior economic position of French Canadians. Séguin originated the new hypothesis, and Brunet was the most enthusiastic of its developers. Reflecting a current sociological interest in the roots of modern capitalism and the role of the bourgeoisie, the Montreal historians predicated their hypothesis upon the assumption that for a colonial society to develop "normally" it required the achievements of a capitalist bourgeoisie. Prior to the Conquest, New France was developing as a normal French colony, replete with capitalist bourgeoisie that controlled wealth, power, and politics in the colony. Into this group were lumped seigneurs, nobles, military officers, administrators, as well as their entrepreneurial agents. By precipitating the exodus of this capitalist elite, the Conquest deprived *Canadien* society of its vital bourgeoisie and hence normal development in future. Into the vacuum jumped British entrepreneurs so that the French Canadian collectivity never recovered its place. Thus, the new nationalists accepted in modified form the decapitation hypothesis that had been challenged half a century earlier.

Brunet found the effects of decapitation compounded by other consequences of the Conquest. British governors from Murray to Dorchester excluded French Canadians from their councils, except for a handful of cyphers chosen from among seigneurs hungry for favours, and for the clergy who collaborated to protect the interests of the Church. In the realm of commerce and military contracts, it was British merchants who benefited from patronage and favouritism. The small-scale *Canadien* merchants who did remain were greatly disadvantaged by having lost their familiar suppliers in France and suffered heavy war losses for which they had only worthless or discounted government promissory notes to show. The only vocations left for *Canadiens* were the Church, the professions, and most of all, agriculture. Thus began the clerical domination of French Canadian national ideology, planting the myth that the destiny of French Canadians was to perfect a Catholic, agricultural society. The Conquest had set in place conditions which, through an inexorable historical process, quickly led to social and economic distortion within the French Canadian community.

265

This so-called "bourgeoisie hypothesis" left little hope for "normal" development of French Canadian society in Quebec, particularly French Canadian participation in the highest echelons of business, unless the Conquest could be undone. Many could not accept this conclusion and challenged the hypothesis' basic assumptions. It was from among the Social Science Faculty at Laval University that the strongest criticism came, notably from Fernand Ouellet and Jean Hamelin.

In his thesis presented to l'École Pratique des Hautes Études in Paris, published in 1960 as *Economie et Société en Nouvelle-France*, Jean Hamelin questioned the existence of a *grande bourgeoisie capitaliste* in New France. If there was no entrepreneurial bourgeoisie to be decapitated or otherwise destroyed, then there would have to be some other explanation than the Conquest for the disproportionately small number of French Canadians in large-scale business over the years. By employing quantitative methods, though only in part and to incomplete data, Hamelin examined aspects of the economy of New France, in particular skilled labour, agriculture, and the fur trade. He concluded that the colony had inadequate skilled labour to sustain any but small-scale manufactures; that agriculture was essentially subsistance; and that only the fur trade generated a respectable return on capital. However, since the returns from the fur trade went largely to investors in France, little profit was left to create a colonial *grande bourgeoisie capitaliste*. His conclusion is consistent with what intendants had been writing all along.

In the course of his work Hamelin offered as one explanation for the shortage of skilled labour the habitant's psychological disinclination for occupations that tied him down for lengthy periods. The source of this attitude he attributed to the quality of immigrants to New France, reinforced by their experience of seasonal labour in the colony, usually in the fur trade. Here we are offered as partial explanation for the weaknesses in the economy of New France a factor of mentality, culture, social value.

Professor Fernand Ouellet was particularly forthright in his dismissal of the bourgeoisie hypothesis and has rested his case more explicitly upon arguments of social mentality. In an article written in 1956 to answer Michel Brunet, Ouellet denied the existence of a Golden Age of bourgeois enterprise in New France. Furthermore, he rejected Brunet's description of a capitalist bourgeoisie as simplistic and meaningless because of its inclusiveness of numerous social groups. Citing the work of Werner Sombart and the *Annales*, he noted that pluralism within social groupings made broad definitions virtually impossible. There are, however, certain attributes and values necessary for successful entrepreneurship: dynamism, productivity, precision, calculation, foresight, opportunism, orderliness, frugality, and a penchant for reinvestment. Although there were some in New France who possessed these attributes, their efforts for the most part were frustrated, if not overwhelmed, by a dominant contrary mentality, that of the *noblesse*. The values of the nobility included recklessness, haughtiness, lack of system or diligence, improvidence, and a taste for consumption and lavish display that bore no relationship to income. That many colonial bourgeois and members of the lower orders assumed the values of the *noblesse*, rather than the other way around, is supported by the work of Professor William Eccles on the aristocratic ethos which pervaded colonial society and which was reinforced by its military establishment.

It is worth noting that Eccles in no way implied, as did other critics of the bourgeoisie hypothesis, that the values of society in New France inhibited its economic development. On the contrary, a peculiar combination of bureaucratic enterprise, paternalistic order, and military ingenuity served to develop the colony's resources more than they might otherwise have been. With the Conquest, new laissez-faire rules of economic exploitation introduced by the British were completely alien to the ordered, state-regulated environment of New France. The implication is that one ought not to be surprised if following the Conquest those accustomed to the new, though by no means superior, values should eventually supplant the *Canadiens* in directing the economic life of the colony.

266

The fundamental debate, however, was enjoined between the advocates of a deterministic Conquest and the advocates of a hostile social mentality, with their opposing explanations of subsequent failures in the Quebec economy and failures of French Canadians to participate proportionately in the business life of the colony.

Much research has been done on eighteenth century Canada, some directly inspired by the controversy over the Conquest and bourgeoisie hypotheses, but much in pursuit of answers to other questions, which nevertheless have illuminated the debate. Attempts to reconcile bourgeois and aristocratic characteristics by defining a new social class unique to the elite of New France were not long pursued. The synthetic *bourgeois-gentilhomme*, proposed by Cameron Nish as typical of such a class, was in the final analysis an exceptional case: that of François-Étienne Cugnet. The attempt at synthesis through sociological redefinition of class foundered in the sea of social particularities. One study by José Igartua of the immediate effects of the Conquest upon the community of Montreal merchants was more successful at clarifying some issues. We learn that British speculators may have been disadvantaged as much as *Canadien* merchants by holding discounted French government promissory notes. Where there was a will, *Canadiens* found financial backing and suppliers in London with little difficulty. There is evidence of British officials and military officers discriminating for security reasons in favour of British merchants in some military contracts, and in the issuing of licences to trade in the far west. At the same time there were ways, notably through partnerships, that *Canadiens* could and did neutralize this discrimination. Their expertise in local markets was a notable advantage in their favour. *Canadien* merchants did tend to withdraw from investing in the fur trade, but the question is whether this was by preference or necessity. Accustomed to a well-regulated trade environment during the French Regime, where the volume of business was in balance with the number of merchants engaged in it, the *Canadiens* were, Igartua suggests, disinclined to enter the murderous, unethical competition which accompanied the laissez-faire trade policy of the British. The "change in climate" to which Igartua alludes might be seen as a variant of the contrasting social values observed by William Eccles between the French and British regimes. Here the question of "mentality" once again comes into play.

Numerous articles and monographs on business, economic, and social history betray an increasing interest in understanding how things worked. The work of historians such as Dale Miquelon, Louise Dechêne, and Peter Moogk, to mention only three, show that the tendency has been to qualify many generalizations made from scanty evidence. By exploring sources that are more likely to give answers to particular questions — notarial and business records — we are learning a great deal about how businesses were organized and managed, how colonial trade was financed,

267

how investments were patterned, how colonial merchants made their livings, how farmers and tradesmen made theirs. The hundreds of case studies recently provided by the *Dictionary of Canadian Biography* have also contributed to our understanding of complexity in colonial society and economy.

The result of this research is probably to discredit the more exaggerated claims of the new nationalists concerning the disastrous effects of the Conquest on French Canadian society. If there was no *grande bourgeoisie capitaliste* in New France to be decapitated, there was nevertheless a viable colonial economy with adequate communities of businessmen and skilled labourers. But it is also true that these continued on in Canada after the Conquest, making their livings as before. If there were some disadvantages faced by *Canadien* merchants after 1763 in the fur trade and import-export sector, they also had the advantage of expertise and situation in the local market, and many demonstrated that their problems were not insurmountable. The inclination of many not to lose their shirts in the cut-throat fur trade may be seen as lack of enterprise, or just as easily as good business sense. I have yet to see a tally of the number of British merchants who went bankrupt in the fur trade in these years, or the number who responded, as did apparently the French Canadians, by leaving it to the hands of those more ruthless than they. The jury is still out on the issue of whether cultural mentality is the independent variable, or the dependent variable, in determining the course of the Quebec economy and the participation of French Canadians in it immediately following the Conquest.

The fact that the Conquest and its effects have receded lately in the historiography of early French Canada, and that attention has focussed upon long-term developments converging in Lower Canada, is perhaps evidence that the initiative passed to the critics of the bourgeoisie hypothesis. If so, the force of Fernand Ouellet's work is largely responsible.

Employing quantitative methods of social and economic history Ouellet, by scrutinizing price trends, demographic trends, commodity production, and other basic economic structures, found widespread continuities throughout the eighteenth century. These continuities were momentarily disrupted by the Seven Years' War but otherwise little affected by the Conquest. It was to structural changes in the early nineteenth century, coinciding with and in some cases responding to events in the larger Atlantic world, that Ouellet pointed as having significant consequences. In a series of articles he propounded his thesis that agricultural production in Lower Canada entered a phase of chronic crisis in the first decade of the nineteenth century. The thesis was elaborated upon and placed in the context of *histoire totale* in 1966 with the publication of his *Histoire économique et sociale du Québec, 1760–1850*. It was a powerful argument that the watershed in French Canadian history was not 1760, but 1802.

Although Ouellet's work undertook to integrate economic development with social change, political response, and ideological development in Lower Canada, the major controversy has focussed upon whether or not the condition of the agricultural economy can properly be described as a crisis. It is probably fair to say that the "crisis" hypothesis has been increasingly challenged, largely by economic historians — two notable ones sitting on this panel, Gilles Paquet and Marvin McInnis. Their criticism aims to cast doubt upon claims that cultural factors had a notable effect upon the development of the agricultural economy in Lower Canada.

The belief that the agricultural economy of Lower Canada was unhealthy has existed since contemporary observers condemned it as such. It became widely accepted that the cultural attributes of the French Canadian farmer were largely responsible for this state of affairs — he was portrayed as being backward, unproductive, inefficient, and tenaciously clinging to ruinous, primitive, extensive farming techniques and technology. Even by mid-twentieth century when Lower Canadian agriculture fell beneath the scrutiny of scholarship, earlier impressions persisted. R.L. Jones, although he noted important circumstantial factors such as the absence of proximate markets and a series of natural disasters — wheat midge and potato failure in the 1830s and 1840s — still attributed the backwardness of agriculture to the French Canadian farmer's peculiar culture. Maurice Séguin, though he ascribed the primary cause to a lack of strong markets to which the French Canadian farmer would have responded by modernizing (as farmers elsewhere did), nevertheless accepted the "backwardness" assumption. He ultimately blamed the failure to modernize on the Conquest, since the exterior market for Lower Canadian wheat was Britain where producers from Upper Canada and elsewhere somehow had an advantage, and squeezed out the Lower Canadian producer.

The thesis of Fernand Ouellet sustains most vigorously the cultural argument for the failure of Lower Canadian agriculture to modernize, which produced a crisis condition. Although the *paysan* after 1760 showed some signs of responding positively to the opening of an imperial market for his wheat, the structural changes at the beginning of the nineteenth century proved too great a challenge for him. Ouellet contends that there was no shortage of markets: the same external markets were available to the Lower Canadian farmer as to the Upper Canadian, and there were local markets — Montreal, Quebec, and the lumber industry — which the Lower Canadian producer proved unable to take advantage of. The problem was supply, not demand. It was not the wheat midge in the 1830s that forced Lower Canadian farmers to abandon wheat as a crop: production began to fail seriously twenty years earlier, due largely to soil exhaustion from poor farming methods. A high rural birth rate and the unavailability of new cultivable land by the early nineteenth century led to rural overpopulation. Since little high-yield virgin land came into production, per capita agricultural output declined.

269

Thus, we have in the agricultural sector an apparent cultural deficiency that prevented French Canadian farmers from getting ahead, similar to the cultural deficiency among other orders of society that prevented French Canadians from assuming a role in business and many trades proportionate to their overall numbers in the province.

Every element of the "Agricultural Crisis" thesis has been assailed. Gilles Paquet and Jean-Pierre Wallot denied that a production problem occurred as early in the century as Ouellet located it. The methodology they applied to the scarce statistical evidence available embroiled them in a secondary argument with Terry LeGoff, which served at least to underscore the ambiguity of evidence in this matter. However, the timing of production difficulties is important, for if there was no faltering of production until the 1830s, then insects and disease might be sufficient explanation. Paquet and Wallot drew attention to the significant point raised by Séguin and credited by most other critics as well, that the farming methods of Lower Canadians were similar to those elsewhere in North America until at least the 1840s. If this is so then it would make little sense to brand the Lower Canadian farmer as inefficient: what is the standard of efficiency? Paquet and Wallot further argue that there was no reliable external demand for wheat, and therefore the farmer was making a rational choice to avoid the risks of the wheat export market by diversifying into other products for which a growing market existed in Lower Canada. In other words, he was responding within the constraints imposed upon him as one would expect.

In a comparison of economic development in Ontario and Quebec before 1870, John McCallum reinforces and extends the argument that Lower Canadian agriculture did not lag behind other regions in North America. Extensive farming was common everywhere and he found no evidence of differences due to cultural factors. If there was a difference from New England, it was that Lower Canada lacked nearby markets for alternate crops such that substituting them for wheat gave less relief. McCallum judged the markets of Montreal, Quebec, and the lumber camps to be of insufficient size to invite large-scale modernization or specialization of agricultural production. Again, given the constraints facing the Lower Canadian farmer, there was no profit in intensive farming methods, and to expect him to have adjusted more rapidly than he did is to demand of him a higher efficiency than demonstrated by other North American farmers at the time. The Quebec farmer, McCallum concludes, "lived in the worst of all worlds," flooded by western produce from frontier areas and without large internal markets as substitutes. If there was evidence of any unique cultural response, it might be sought in the failure of Lower Canadian farmers to emigrate in larger numbers than they did.

The most recent and probably inclusive critique of the cultural-influence argument is that of Marvin McInnis. In fact, McInnis spares no one in his determination to expose the lack of empirical evidence behind most historians' assumptions about the nature of Lower Canadian agriculture — like the skeptic Pierre Bayle ferreting out the errors and inconsistencies in the Old Testament upon which Christian theology in his day depended. Nothing is sacred: the backwardness of the peasant farmer; the exhausted state of the soil; over-population; the shortage of cultivable land; the deficiency of markets; among others. All are scrutinized in light of new evidence and reinterpretation. He concludes that the case for the occurrence of an "agricultural crisis," "of a longer-term fall in the level of material well-being in Lower Canada," is not proven.

It should be noted that these issues are very much alive and that the adherents of the cultural argument have not been persuaded by their critics, though revisions have been made on several sides as is to be expected in the best of serious scholarly debates. The finality of statistical data lies in the interpretation put on it and there is clearly room for debate. One should keep in mind that the agricultural economy is only one element in the history of Lower Canada and that no matter what was happening to agriculture — crisis or healthy modernization — the social and political leaders within the colony could be expected to read events according to their own script in any case. The same might be said of contemporary perceptions of emerging ethnic divisions among occupations.

271

Thus, political, social, and ethnic tensions, such as those which Ouellet finds exacerbated, if not caused, in the early nineteenth century by the agricultural "crisis," and which he sees as precipitating the first French Canadian nationalist reaction, can arguably be anticipated in a period of severe structural change. Did agricultural crisis have to take place in order for a political elite to prey upon the imagined fears of the peasantry? If they had the *impression* that they were stagnating compared with outsiders, Lower Canadian farmers might have been susceptible to a nationalist adventure even if the impression were wrong.

The attractiveness of the circumstantial argument is that it relegates culture to the status of a dependent variable where it can be easily ignored. Perhaps too easily. One then need not deal with historical forces that are often obscure and always difficult to measure. Only the most rigid materialist would argue that wars and revolutions are an inevitable and direct consequence of particular economic circumstances. Political and social structures with their attendant ideologies play some role in constraining, or not, the fears, ambitions, and other responses of people confronted with social stress. These must be cultural atavisms. If they are in some way connected with material circumstances, they are not wholly dependent upon them. Or at least, over time, they have gained some independence. And if we are to understand the relationships between all variables, then some attempt must be made to assign weights to them all.

Of course, the economic historian may not be interested in undertaking this task, content to limit himself, as most of us do, to examining the particular historical processes that interest him. Skepticism is essential in a discipline where theology often passes for history. The debate over the consequences of the Conquest is, like all historical debates, an exercise in identifying what is theology and what is history. Along the way, one hopes, we have learned something about the historical process.

SELECTED BIBLIOGRAPHY

Baby, L.F.G. *L'Exode des classes dirigeantes à la cession du Canada*. Montréal, 1899.

Brunet, Michel. *French Canada and the Early Decades of British Rule 1760-1791*. Ottawa: Canadian Historical Association, 1963.

Brunet, Michel. "La Conquête anglaise et la déchéance de la bourgeoisie canadienne (1760-1793)." In *La Présence anglaise et les Canadiens*, 49-109. Montréal: Beauchemin, 1958.

Dechêne, Louise. *Habitants et Marchands de Montréal au XVIIe siècle*. Montréal, Paris: Plon, 1974.

Eccles, W.J. *The Canadian Frontier, 1534-1760*. New York: Holt, Rinehart and Winston, 1969.

Eccles, W.J. *Canadian Society during the French Regime*. Montreal: Harvest House, 1968.

Frégault, G. *Canadian Society in the French Regime*. Ottawa: Canadian Historical Association, 1956.

Hamelin, Jean. *Economie et société en Nouvelle-France*. Québec: Presses de l'Université Laval, 1961.

Igartua, José. "A Change in Climate: The Conquest and the *Marchands* of Montreal." *Historical Papers*, Canadian Historical Association, 1974.

Jones, R.L. "French Canadian Agriculture in the St. Lawrence Valley, 1815-1851." *Agricultural History* 16 (1942): 137-48.

Jones, R.L. "The Agricultural Development of Lower Canada, 1850-67." *Agricultural History* 19 (1945): 212-24.

Jones R.L. "Agriculture in Lower Canada, 1792-1815," *Canadian Historical Review* 27 (1946): 33-51.

LeGoff, T.J.A. "The Agricultural Crisis in Lower Canada, 1802-12: A Review of a Controversy." *Canadian Historical Review* 55 (March 1974): 1-31.

LeGoff, T.J.A. "A Reply." *Canadian Historical Review* 56 (June 1975): 162-68.

McCallum, John. *Unequal Beginnings: Agriculture and Economic Development in Quebec and Ontario until 1870*. Toronto: University of Toronto Press, 1980.

McInnis, R.M. "A Reconsideration of the State of Agriculture in Lower Canada in the First Half of the Nineteenth Century." In D.H. Akenson, ed. *Canadian Papers in Rural History*, vol. 3. Gananoque: Langdale Press, 1982.

Miquelon, D., ed. *Society and Conquest: The Debate on the Bourgeoisie and Social Change in French Canada, 1700-1850*. Toronto: Copp Clark, 1977.

Miquelon, D. "Havy and Lefebvre of Quebec: A Case Study of Metropolitan Participation in Canadian Trade, 1730-60." *Canadian Historical Review* 56 (March 1975): 1-24.

Moogk, P.N. "Rank in New France: Reconstructing a Society from Notarial Documents." *Histoire Sociale/Social History* 8 (mai/May 1975): 34-53.

Nish, C. *Les Bourgeois-Gentilshommes de la Nouvelle-France*. Montréal: Fides, 1968.

Ouellet, Fernand. "M. Michel Brunet et la problème de la Conquête," *Bulletin de Recherches Historiques* 62 (1956): 92-101.

Ouellet, Fernand. *Histoire économique et sociale du Québec, 1760-1850: Structures et conjonctures*. Montréal: Fides, 1966.

Ouellet, Fernand. "Le Mythe de L'Habitant sensible au marché" *Recherches Sociographiques* 17 (1976): 115-32.

Paquet, Gilles, and J.-P. Wallot. "The Agricultural Crisis in Lower Canada, 1802-1812: *mise au point*. A Response to T.J.A. LeGoff." *Canadian Historical Review* 56 (June 1975): 133-61.

Paquet, Gilles, and J.-P. Wallot. "Crise agricole et tensions socio-ethniques dans le Bas-Canada, 1802-1821." *Revue d'histoire de L'Amérique française* 26 (September 1972): 185-237.

Séguin, M. "La Conquête et la vie économique des Canadiens." *Action nationale* 28 (1947): 308-326.

Séguin, M. *La Nation "canadienne" et l'agriculture (1760-1850)*. Trois Rivières: Boréal Express, 1970.

A Change in Climate: The Conquest and the *Marchands* of Montreal

JOSÉ IGARTUA

When the British government issued the Royal Proclamation of 1763, it assumed that the promised establishment of "British institutions" in the "Province of Quebec" would be sufficient to entice American settlers to move north and overwhelm the indigenous French-speaking and Papist population. These were naive hopes. Until the outbreak of the American Revolution, British newcomers merely trickled into Quebec, leading Governor Carleton to prophesy in 1767 that "barring a catastrophe shocking to think of, this Country must, to the end of Time, be peopled by the Canadian Race. . . . "[1] But the British newcomers, few though they were, had to be reckoned with. By 1765 they were powerful enough to have Governor Murray recalled and by 1777 they would be strong enough to command the majority of investments in the fur trade.[2] Did their success stem from superior abilities? Did the British take advantage of the situation of submission and dependence into which the Canadians had been driven by the Conquest? Did the newcomers gain their predominance from previous experience with the sort of political and economic conditions created in post-Conquest Quebec?

273

Historians of Quebec have chosen various ways to answer these questions. Francis Parkman was fond of exhibiting the superiority of the Anglo-Saxon race over the "French Celt."[3] More recently the studies of W.S. Wallace, E.E. Rich, and D.G. Creighton took similar, if less overt, positions.[4] One of the best students of the North West fur trade, Wayne E. Stevens, concluded: "The British merchants . . . were men of great enterprise and ability and they began gradually to crowd out the French traders who had been their predecessors in the field."[5]

The French-Canadian historian, Fernand Ouellet, attributed the rise of the British merchants to the weaknesses of the Canadian trading bourgeoisie: "Son attachement à la petite entreprise individuelle, sa réponse à la concentration, son goût du luxe de même que son attrait irrésistible pour les placements assurés étaient des principaux handicaps." No evidence is given for this characterization and the author hastens to concede that before 1775 "le problème de la concentration ne se pose pas avec acuité," but for him it is clear that the economic displacement of the Canadians resulted from their conservative, "ancien Régime" frame of mind, bred into them by the clergy and the nobility.[6] Ouellet painted

From *Historical Papers* (1974):115–34. Reprinted with the permission of the Canadian Historical Association.

British merchants in a more flattering light as the agents of economic progress.[7]

Michel Brunet has depicted the commercial competition between the British newcomers and the Canadian merchants as an uneven contest between two national groups, one of which had been deprived of the nourishing blood of its metropolis while the other was being assiduously nurtured. For Brunet the normal and natural outcome of that inequality was the domination of the conqueror, a situation which he sees as prevailing to the present day.[8]

Dale B. Miquelon's study of one merchant family, the Babys, shed new light on the question of British penetration of Canadian trade. It outlined the growth of British investments in the fur trade and the increasing concentration of British capital. The author concluded:

> The French Canadians dominated the Canadian fur trade until the upheaval of the American Revolution. At that time they were overwhelmed by an influx of capital and trading personnel. English investment in the top ranks of investors jumped by 679% and was never significantly to decline. Even without explanations involving the difference between the French and English commercial mentalities, it is difficult to believe that any body of merchants could recover from an inundation of such size and swiftness.[9]

This conclusion had the obvious merit of staying out of the murky waters of psychological interpretations. But Miquelon's own evidence suggests that the "flood theory" is not sufficient to account for the Canadians' effacement; even before the inundation of 1775-1783, British investment in the fur trade was growing more rapidly than Canadian. By 1772, to quote Miquelon, the "English [had] made more impressive increases in the size of their investments than [had] the French, and for the first time [had] larger average investments in all categories."[10]

It is difficult not to note the ascendancy of the British in the fur trade of Canada even before the American Revolution. The success of the British merchants, therefore, was rooted in something more than mere numbers. It was not simply the outcome of an ethnic struggle between two nationalities of a similar nature; it was not only the natural consequence of the Canadians' conservative frame of mind. It arose out of a more complex series of causes, some of them a product of the animosities between Canadians and British, others inherent to the differences in the socioeconomic structures of the French and British Empires; together, they amounted to a radical transformation of the societal climate of the colony.

The aim of this paper is to gauge the impact of the Conquest upon a well-defined segment of that elusive group called the "bourgeoisie" of New France. It focuses on Montreal and its Canadian merchants. Montreal was the centre of the fur trade and its merchants managed it. Historians of New France have traditionally seen the fur trade as the most dynamic sector of the colony's economy; by implication it is

274

generally believed that the fur trade provided the likeliest opportunities for getting rich quickly and maintaining a "bourgeois" standard of living.[11] It is not yet possible to evaluate the validity of this notion with any precision, for too little is known about other sectors of the economy which, in the eighteenth century at least, may have generated as much or more profit. Research on the merchants of Quebec should provide new information on the wealth to be made from the fisheries, from wholesale merchandising, and from trade with Louisbourg and the West Indies. But if one is concerned with the fate of Canadian merchants after the Conquest, one should examine the fate of men involved in the sector of the economy of Quebec which was the most dynamic *after* the Conquest, the fur trade. The paper examines the impact of the arrival of (relatively) large numbers of merchants on the Montreal mercantile community, the attitude of British officials towards the Canadians, and the changing political climate of the colony. It is suggested that it was the simultaneous conjunction of these changes to the "world" of the Montreal merchants, rather than the effect of any one of them, which doomed the Canadian merchants of Montreal.[12]

275

The Montreal Merchants at the End of the French Regime

In 1752 a French Royal engineer passing through Montreal remarked that "la plupart des habitants y sont adonnés au commerce principalement à celui connu sous le nom des pays d'en haut."[13] It was only a slight exaggeration. By the last year of the French regime one could count over one hundred *négociants*, merchants, outfitters, traders, and shopkeepers in Montreal. The overwhelming majority of them had been in business for some years and would remain in business after the Conquest. Over half were outfitters for the fur trade at some time or other between 1750 and 1775; these men comprised the body of the merchant community of Montreal. Above them in wealth and stature stood a handful of import merchants who did a comfortable business of importing merchandise from France and selling it in Montreal to other merchants or directly to customers in their retail stores. Below the outfitters a motley group of independent fur traders, shopkeepers, and artisans managed to subsist without leaving more than a trace of their existence for posterity.[14]

The fur trade, as it was conducted by the merchants of Montreal before 1760, had little to do with the glamorous picture it sometimes calls to mind. For the outfitter who remained in Montreal, it was not physically a risky occupation; its management was fairly simple and the profits which it produced quite meager. For the last years of the French regime the fur trade followed a three-tier system. Fort Frontenac (present-day Kingston) and Fort Niagara were King's posts; they were not lucrative and had to be subsidized to meet English competition. The trade of Detroit and Michilimackinac, as well as that of the posts to the South West, was open to licencees whose numbers were limited. Some *coureurs de bois* (traders without a licence) also roamed in the area. The richest posts, Green Bay and the posts to the northwest past Sault Sainte-Marie, were monopolies leased by the Crown to merchants or military officers.[15] The export of beaver was undertaken by the French *Compagnie des Indes*, which had the monopoly of beaver sales on the home market. Other furs were on the open market.

The system worked tolerably well in peace time: there was a stable supply of furs, prices paid to the Indians had been set by custom, the prices paid by the *Compagnie des Indes* were regulated by the Crown, and the prices of trade goods imported from France were fairly steady. There was competition from the Americans at Albany and from the English on the Hudson Bay, to be sure, but it appeared to be a competition heavily influenced by military considerations and compliance with Indian customs.[16]

The system faltered in war time. Beaver shipments to France and the importation of trade goods became risky because of British naval power. Shipping and insurance costs raised the Canadian traders' overhead, but the Indians refused to have the increase passed on to them. This was the most obvious effect of war, but it also produced general economic and administrative dislocations which led H.A. Innis to conclude that it " . . . seriously weakened the position of the French in the fur trade and contributed to the downfall of the French *régime* in Canada."[17]

Nevertheless, outside of war-time crises, the fur trade of New France was conducted with a fair dose of traditionalism. This traditionalism resulted from two concurrent impulses: Indian attitudes towards trade, which were untouched by the mechanism of supply and demand and by distinctions between commercial, military, political, or religious activities; and the mercantilist policies of France, which tried to control the supply of furs by limiting the number of traders and regulating beaver prices on the French market. While the fur trade structure of New France had an inherent tendency towards geographic expansion, as Innis argued, it also had to be oligopolistic in nature, if investments in Indian alliances, explorations, and military support were to be maximized. Open competition could not be allowed because it would lead to the collapse of the structure.[18]

It is not surprising, therefore, that most outfitters dabbled in the fur trade only occasionally. On the average, between 1750 and 1775, the Canadian merchants of Montreal invested in the trade only four times and signed up about eleven *engagés* each time, not quite enough to man two canoes. Few merchants outfitted fur trade ventures with any regularity and only six men hired an average of twelve or more *engagés*,

276

more than twice before 1761 (See Table 1). Three of these were unquestionably wealthy: Louis Saint-Ange Charly, an import merchant
who, unlike his colleagues, had a large stake in the fur trade, realized
100 000 livres on his land holdings alone when he left the colony for
France in 1764; Thomas-Ignace Trotier Desauniers "Dufy," who in a
will drawn up in 1760 bequeathed 28 000 livres to the Sulpicians; the
illiterate Dominique Godet, who in a similar document of 1768 mentioned
5000 livres in cash in hand, land in three parishes in the vicinity of
Montreal, "Batiment & Bateaux qui en dependent," around 5000 livres
in active debts, and two black slaves.[19] Two other large outfitters left
relatively few belongings at the time of their death: Alexis Lemoine Monière left less than 1000 livres, all of it in household goods, and François L'Huillier Chevalier just slightly more.[20] Little is known about the
sixth man, Jean Léchelle.

If the fur trade made few wealthy men among those who invested
heavily in it, it would be hard to argue that less considerable investors
were more successful. It is not unreasonable to conclude that the fur
trade was not very profitable for the overwhelming majority of outfitters
and that it only sustained a very limited number of them each year.
Yet the French had reduced costly competition to a minimum and had
few worries about price fluctuations. How would Canadian outfitters
fare under a different system?

277

The Advent of the British Merchants

With the arrival in Montreal of British traders, the workings of the fur
trade were disrupted. At first, the licensing system was maintained and
some areas were left to the exclusive trade of particular traders.[21] But
from the very beginning the trade was said to be open to all who wanted

TABLE 1   Largest Canadian Fur Trade Outfitters in Montreal, 1750–1760

Name	Total No. of Years	Total No. of Hirings	Yearly Average
Charly, Louis Saint-Ange	6	85	14.1
Godet, Dominique	5	85	17.0
Léchelle, Jean	4	130	32.5
Lemoine Monière, Alexis	7	300	42.8
L'Huillier Chevalier, François	7	90	12.6
Trotier Desauniers, Thomas-Ignace "Dufy"	5	129	25.8

Source: "Répertoire des engagements pour l'ouest conservés dans les Archives judiciaires de Montréal,"
Rapport de l'Archiviste de la province de Québec (1930–31):353–453; (1931–32):242–365;
(1932–33):245–304.

to secure a licence, and the result could only be price competition. With individual traders going into the fur trade, the organization of the trade regressed. The previous division of labour between the *Compagnie des Indes*, the import merchants and outfitters, the traders, the voyageurs, and the *engagés* was abandoned and during the first years of British rule the individual trader filled all of the functions previously spread among many "specialists."

The story of Alexander Henry, one of the first British merchants to venture into the upper country, illustrates the new pattern of trade. A young man from New Jersey, Alexander Henry came to Canada in 1760 with General Amherst's troops.[22] With the fall of Montreal Henry saw the opening of a "new market" and became acquainted with the prospects of the fur trade. The following year, he set out for Michilimackinac with a Montreal outfitter, Étienne Campion, whom he called his "assistant," and who took charge of the routine aspects of the trip.[23] Henry wintered at Michilimackinac. There he was urged by the local inhabitants to go back to Detroit as soon as possible for they claimed to fear for his safety. Their fears were not without foundation, but Henry stayed on. His partner Campion reassured him: " . . . the Canadian inhabitants of the fort were more hostile than the Indians, as being jealous of British traders, who . . . were penetrating into the country."[24] At least some of the Canadians resented the British traders from the outset and a few tried to use the Indians to frighten them away.[25]

Henry proceeded to Sault Sainte-Marie the following year. In the spring of 1763, he returned to Michilimackinac and witnessed the massacre of the British garrison during Pontiac's revolt.[26] He was eventually captured by the Indians and adopted into an Indian family with whom he lived, in the Indian style, until late June 1764. Undaunted, Henry set out for the fur trade again, exploring the Lake Superior area. He was on the Saskatchewan River in 1776, tapping fur resources which the French had seldom reached.[27] Finally he settled down in Montreal in 1781 and while he did join the North West Company after its formation, he seldom returned to the upper country himself.[28]

Henry was not the first British merchant to reach the upper country. Henry Bostwick had obtained a licence from General Gage before him in 1761,[29] and the traders Goddard and Solomons had followed Henry into Michilimackinac in 1761. By early 1763 there were at least two more British merchants in the area.[30] In Montreal alone there were close to fifty new merchants by 1765. Governor Murray's list of the Protestants in the district of Montreal gives the names, the origins, and the "former callings" of forty-five.[31] Over half of them came from England and Scotland and 20 percent were from Ireland. Only 13 percent came from the American colonies and an equal number came from various countries (Switzerland, Germany, France, Guernsey). In the proportion of more than three to one, the newcomers had been merchants in their "former calling." The others had been soldiers and clerks. Many of the newcomers were men of experience and enterprise. Among them were Isaac Todd, Thomas Walker, Lawrence Ermatinger, Richard Dobie, Edward Chinn, John Porteous, William Grant, Benjamin Frobisher, James Finlay, Alexander Paterson, Forrest Oakes, and the Jewish merchants Ezekiel and Levy Solomons, all of whom became substantial traders.[32]

The arrival of so many merchants could only mean one thing: strenuous competition in the fur trade. Competition ruthlessly drove out those with less secure financial resources or with no taste for sharp practices. Among the British as among the French, few resisted the pressures. The story of the trader Hamback is not untypical. Out on the Miami River in 1766 and 1767, he found that competition left him with few returns to make to his creditor William Edgar of Detroit. "I live the life of a downright exile," he complained, "no company but a Barrel of drunken infamous fugitives, and no other Comfort of Life."[33]

The Canadian merchants of Montreal had competition not only from British merchants in their town, but also from American merchants moving into Detroit and Michilimackinac. William Edgar, a New York merchant, was at Niagara in late 1761.[34] In 1763 he was established at Detroit, where he conducted a brisk trade supplying individual traders at Michilimackinac and in the South West District.[35] From Schenectady, the partnership of Phyn and Ellice also carried on a profitable supply trade for the fur traders of the interior.[36]

Competition also came from the French on the Mississippi, who were trading in the Illinois country and the Lake Superior region. These French traders could all too easily link up with French-speaking traders from Canada, whose help, it was feared, they could enlist in subverting the Indians against British rule.[37] This always troubled Sir William Johnson, the Superintendent for Indian Affairs, who refused to abandon his suspicions of the French-speaking traders from Canada.

This many-sided competition produced a climate to which the Canadian merchants were not accustomed. The increased numbers of fur traders led to frictions with the Indians, smaller returns for some of the traders, and unsavory trade practices.[38] Even the retail trade was affected. Merchants from England flooded the market at Quebec "with their manufactures, so much so that they are daily sold here at Vendue Twenty per Cent. below prime Cost."[39] In 1760 alone, the first year of British occupation, £60 000 worth of trade goods had been brought into Canada.[40] From 1765 to 1768 the pages of the *Quebec Gazette* were filled with notices of auctions by merchants returning to England and disposing of their wares after unsuccessful attempts to establish themselves in the trade of the colony.[41]

By 1768 some thought the Canadians still had the advantage in the fur trade, even though there was "Competition" and a "strong jealousy" between Canadian and English. The Canadians' "long Connections with those Indians," wrote General Gage, "and their better Knowledge of their Language and Customs, must naturaly for a long time give the Canadians an Advantage over the English. . . . "[42] Sir William Johnson had expressed a similar opinion the previous year and had deplored the British merchants' tactics: "The English were compelled to make use of Low, Selfish Agents, French, or English as Factors, who at the Expence of honesty and sound policy, took care of themselves whatever became of their employers."[43]

Another observer, the Hudson's Bay Company trader at Moose Factory, complained of "Interlopers who will be more Destructive to our trade than the French was." The French had conducted a less aggressive trade: they "were in a manner Settled, their Trade fixed, their Standards moderate and Themselves under particular regulations and restrictions, which I doubt is not the Case now."[44] Competition was forcing the British merchants in Montreal into ruthless tactics, a development which upset the Hudson's Bay Company man and which would unsettle the Canadians.

The pattern of British domination of the fur trade began to emerge as early as 1767. Trading ventures out of Michilimackinac into the North West were conducted by Canadians, but British merchants supplied the financial backing. The North West expeditions demanded the lengthiest periods of capital outlay, lasting two or three years. British merchants, it seems, had better resources. Of the fifteen outfitters at Michilimackinac who sent canoes to the North West in 1767, nine were British and six were Canadian; the total value of canoes outfitted by the British came to £10 812.17 while the Canadian's canoes were worth only £3061.10. The British outfitters — most notably Alexander Henry, Isaac Todd, James McGill, Benjamin Frobisher, Forrest Oakes — invested on the average £1351.12 and the Canadians only £510.5. The average value of goods invested in each canoe stood at £415.17 for the British and £278.6 for the Canadians.[45] The Canadians' investment per canoe was only two-thirds that of the British and the Canadians were already outnumbered as outfitters in what would become the most important region of the fur trade.[46]

Open competition was not conducive to the expansion of the fur trade and an oligopolistic structure reminiscent of the French system soon reappeared as the only solution.[47] This led to the formation of the North West Company in the 1780's but already in 1775, those Montreal merchants who had extended their operations as far as the Saskatchewan felt the need for collaboration rather than competition. Again developments in the more remote frontiers of the fur trade foretold of events to occur later in the whole of the trade: the traders on the Saskatchewan were almost all of British origin.[48] The fur trade was returning to the structures developed by the French, but during the period of competition which followed the Conquest the Canadians were gradually crowded out. There was some irony in that. Why had the Canadians fared so badly?

The Attitude of Government Officials

Much has been made of the natural sympathies of Murray and Carleton towards the Canadians and their antipathies towards the traders of their own nation. Yet for all their ideological inclinations there is no evidence that the governors turned their sentiments into policies of benevolence for Canadians in trade matters. Rather, it is easier to discover, among the lesser officials and some of the more important ones as well, an understandable patronizing of British rather than Canadian merchants. Colonial administrators may not have set a deliberate pattern of preference in favor of British merchants. But the Canadian merchants of Montreal, who put great store by official patronage, cared not whether the policy was deliberate or accidental; the result was the same.

Official preferences played against the Canadian traders in many ways. First, the lucrative trade of supplying the military posts was given to British and American merchants as a matter of course, and this occasion for profit was lost to the Canadians. Under the French regime some of the Montreal merchants, notably the Monières and the Gamelins, had profited from that trade.[49] Now it fell out of Canadian hands. This advantage did not shift to the sole favor of the British merchants of Quebec. New York and Pennsylvania traders were also awarded their share of the trade. The firms of Phyn, Ellice of Schenectady and Baynton, Wharton, and Morgan of Philadelphia received the lion's share of that business while the upper country was under the jurisdiction of Sir William Johnson.[50] But this was of little comfort to the Canadians.

Less tangible by-products of the British occupation of the former fur trading areas of New France are more difficult to assess than the loss of the supply trade; they were, however, quite real. One was the British military's attitude towards Canadians. The military were wary of French-speaking traders in Illinois and on the Mississippi. Although the French from Canada had been vanquished, French traders in the interior could still deal with France through New Orleans. No regulations, no boundaries could restrain French traders operating out of Louisiana from dealing with the Indians, and the Canadians who were confined to the posts protested against the advantage held by the French traders.[51] But who were these French traders? Did they not include Canadian *coureurs de bois* and wintering merchants? How could one really tell a French-speaking trader from Canada from a French-speaking trader out of New Orleans? Were not all of them suspect of exciting the Indians against the British, promising and perhaps hoping for France's return to America?[52] As late as 1768, when Indian discontent in the West threatened another uprising, General Gage failed to see any difference between French-speaking Canadians and the French from New Orleans:

281

> There is the greatest reason to suspect that the French are Endeavoring to engross the Trade, and that the Indians have acted thro' their Instigation, in the Murders they have committed, and the Resolutions we are told they have taken, to suffer

no Englishman to trade with them. And in this they have rather been Assisted by the English Traders, who having no Consideration but that of a present gain, have thro' fear of exposing their own Persons, or hopes of obtaining greater influence with the Indians, continually employed French Commissarys or Agents, whom they have trusted with Goods for them to Sell at an Advanced price in the Indian Villages.[53]

Gage's suspicions of the French traders were nurtured by Sir William Johnson, who had to keep the Indians on peaceful terms with one another and with the British. It was part of Johnson's function, of course, to worry about possible uprisings and about subversive individuals. His job would be made easier if he could confine all traders to military posts where they could be kept under surveillance. But the traders had little concern for Sir William's preoccupations. If British traders were irresponsible in their desires of "present gain," the Canadian traders' vices were compounded by the uncertainty of their allegiance to the British Crown:

282

Since the Reduction of that Country [Canada], we have seen so many Instances of their [the Canadian traders'] Perfidy false Stories & Cª. Interested Views in Trade that prudence forbids us to suffer them or any others to range at Will without being under the Inspection of the proper Officers agreeable to His Majesty's Appointment. . . . [54]

Johnson's attitude spread to the officers under him, even though Carleton had found nothing reprehensible in the Canadians' behavior.[55] Johnson's deputy, George Croghan, believed there was collusion between the French from Canada and the French from Louisiana.[56] In 1763 the commandant at Michilimackinac, Major Etherington, had displayed a similar mistrust of the Canadians.[57] Major Robert Rogers, a later commandant at Michilimackinac, checked the Canadians by trading on his own account.[58]

The British military's mistrust of the French traders from Canada was understandable. Before 1760, one of the major reasons for the American colonials' antagonism towards New France had been the French ability to press the Indians into their service to terrorize the western fringes of American settlement. Thus there was a historical as well as a tactical basis for the military's attitude towards the Canadians. But British officers failed to recognize that not all Canadian traders were potential troublemakers and that there was indeed very little tangible evidence, as Carleton had reminded Johnson, of any mischief on their part. The military's attitude was directed as much by ethnic prejudice as by military necessity.

The Canadian traders could not fail to perceive this prejudice, and it dampened their spirits. Perhaps the military's attitude, as much as competition, forced the Canadians into partnerships with British merchants. (The express purpose of the bonds required for the fur trade was to ensure loyal conduct; what better token of loyalty could there be for a Canadian trader than a bond taken out in his name by a British partner?) The military's mistrust of the Canadian traders did not lessen with time. The advantage which this prejudice gave British traders would continue for some twenty years after the Conquest, as the American Revolution rekindled the military's fears of treasonable conduct by the Canadians.

Other patronage relationships between British military officials and British traders also deprived the Canadians of an equal chance in the competition for furs. It is hard to evaluate precisely the effect of such patronage; only glimpses of it may be caught. Late in 1763 a Philadelphia merchant who had lost heavily because of Pontiac's uprising wrote to William Edgar in Detroit that Croghan was in England where he was to "represent the Case of the Traders to his Majesty" and that General Amherst had "given us his faithful promise that he will do everything in his power in our behalf."[59] In 1765 Alexander Henry was granted the exclusive trade of Lake Superior by Major Howard, the military commandant at Michilimackinac. Nine years later Henry received the support of such patrons as the Duke of Gloucester, the consul of the Empress of Russia in England, and of Sir William Johnson in an ill-fated attempt to mine the iron ore of the Lake Superior area.[60]

These were obvious examples of patronage; other forms of cooperation were less visible. Another correspondent of William Edgar, Thomas Shipboy, asked Edgar to represent him in settling the affairs of a correspondent at Detroit and at Michilimackinac where, he added, "if you find any Difficulty in procuring his effects I dare say the Commanding officer will be of Service to you if you inform him in [sic] whose behalf you are acting. . . ."[61] Benjamin Frobisher also asked Edgar to "use your Interest with Capt. Robinson" to put a shipment of corn aboard the government vessel which sailed from Detroit to Michilimackinac.[62] Such shipping space was scarce and was only available through the courtesy of military officers or the ships' captains. Here again British traders put their social connections to good use. A last resort was sheer military force. Out on the Miami River, the trader Hamback saw "little hope of getting any thing from [Fort]St. Joseph at all, if I don't get protected, by the Commanding Officer, who might easily get those [Canadian] rascals fetch'd down to Detroit if He would. . . ."[63]

None of this patronage appears to have been available to Canadians. It is impossible to ascertain the degree to which military suspicions and patronage lessened the Canadians' chances in the fur trade. But more important, perhaps, than the actual loss of opportunities was the psychological handicap imposed upon the Canadians. What heart could they put in the game when the dice were so obviously loaded?

283

The Merchants' Political Activities

The enmity between British merchants and the military, the merchants' growing agitation in favour of "British liberties," and their sentiments of political self-importance have been ably told by others and need not be retold here.[64] What needs to be underlined is that political agitation was unfamiliar to the Canadians. They had had no experience in these matters under French rule. Only on rare occasions during the pre-Conquest years had the Canadian merchants engaged in collective political representations; such representations were elicited by the governor or the intendant to obtain the merchants' advice on specific issues.[65] As French subjects, the Canadian merchants of Montreal had lacked the power to foster their economic interests through collective political action.

After 1760, the Canadian merchants would gradually lose their political innocence under the influence of the British merchants. During the thirty years which followed the Conquest they would make "l'apprentissage des libertés anglaises" and in 1792 they would take their place in the newly created legislative assembly more cognizant of the workings of the British constitution than the British had expected.[66] But that is beyond the concern here. In the years preceding the American Revolution the Montreal merchants were still looking for bearings. They showed their growing political awareness by following in the *Quebec Gazette* the political and constitutional debates which were rocking the British Empire. The merchants also began to voice their concerns in petitions and memorials to the authorities in the colony and in London.

The *Quebec Gazette* was the province's official gazette and its only newspaper before 1778. The paper published public notices for the Montreal district and occasional advertisements sent in by Montrealers as well as matters of concern to Quebec residents. It also made an effort to publish Canadian news of a general character. It closely followed the debates raging across the Atlantic over the Stamp Act and the general issues of colonial taxation. It reported on changes in the Imperial government and on contemporary political issues in England, notably the Wilkes affair.[67]

The pages of the *Gazette* also served on occasion as a forum for political discussion. In September 1765 a "Civis Canadiensis" declared his puzzlement at all the talk of "British liberties" and asked for enlightenment. The following year, a Quebec resident wrote a series of letters arguing that the colony should not be taxed.[68] In 1767, a debate arose on the British laws relating to bankruptcy and their applicability in Quebec.[69] Because of the pressures of Governor Carleton the *Gazette* stifled its reporting of controversial issues after 1770 and thereafter had little to print about American affairs.[70] In 1775 the *Gazette*'s political outpourings were directed against the American rebels and towards seuring the loyalty of those Canadians who might be seduced by revolutionary propaganda.[71] The paper had become more conservative in its selection of the news but those Canadians who read the *Gazette* had been made familiar with the concepts of personal liberty, of "no taxation without representation," of the limited powers of the sovereign, and of the rights of the people. The *Gazette*'s readers most probably included the leading merchants of Montreal.

The *Gazette* was not the only instrument for the learning of British liberties. Anxious to give the appearance of a unanimous disposition among all merchants in Montreal, the British merchants often called on their Canadian confreres to add their names to various memorials and petitions dealing with the political and the economic state of the colony. The Canadian merchants who signed these petitions and memorials represented the top layer of the Canadian mercantile group in Montreal. Those who signed most often were the import merchants and the busy outfitters.

These Canadian merchants followed the political leadership of the British merchants. From 1763 to 1772 their petitions were either literal translations or paraphrased equivalents of petitions drafted by British merchants. It was only in December 1773 that they asserted views different from those of their British counterparts.[72] They petitioned the King that their "ancient laws, privileges, and customs" be restored, that the province be extended to its "former boundaries," that some Canadians be taken into the King's service, and that "the rights and privileges of citizens of England" be granted to all.[73]

The Canadians were becoming aware of their own position and were seeking to consolidate it against the attacks of the British element. The demand for the maintenance of the "ancient laws" was designed to counter British demands for British laws and representative institutions. The Canadians opposed the latter since, in their view, the colony was "not as yet in a condition to defray the expences of its own civil government, and consequently not in a condition to admit of a general assembly."[74] The demand for "a share of the civil and military employments under his majesty's government" came naturally to those who had lived under the French system of patronage. The Canadians had been accustomed to seek official patronage as the main avenue of upward mobility. The prospect of being denied such patronage was "frightful" to them, since they had little familiarity with alternate patterns of social promotion.[75]

In style as well as in content the Canadian merchants' petitions and memorials revealed differences in attitudes between Canadians and British. British memorials and petitions were rarely prefaced by more than the customary "Humbly showeth" and went directly to the point. In their own memorials and petitions, the Canadians first took "the liberty to prostrate themselves at the foot" of the royal throne and surrendered themselves to the "paternal care" of their sovereign. They often appealed to the wisdom, justice, and magnanimity of the King.[76] Their formal posture of meekness contrasted sharply with the self-assertion of the British. The Canadians' "Habits of Respect and Submission," as one British official put it,[77] may well have endeared them to Murray and Carleton, but those habits constituted a psychological obstacle against their making full use of their new-found "British liberties" to foster their own economic interest.

Conclusion

With the fall of Montreal to British arms in September 1760 something was irrevocably lost to the Canadian merchants of that city. More than the evil effects of the war or the post-war commercial readjustments, the most unsettling consequence of the Conquest was the disappearance of a familiar business climate. As New France passed into the British Empire, the Montreal outfitters were thrown into a new system of business competition, brought about by the very numbers of newly arrived merchants, unloading goods in the conquered French colony and going after its enticing fur trade. In opening up the trade of the colony to competition, the British presence transformed Canadian commercial practices. The change negated the Canadian merchants' initial advantage of experience in the fur trade and created a novel business climate around them.

Competition in trade, the new political regime, the Canadian merchants' inability to obtain the favors of the military, all these created a mood of uncertainty and pessimism among the Montreal merchants. The merchants could only conclude from what was happening around them that the new business climate of the post-Conquest period favored British traders at their expense. They can be understood if they were not eager to adapt their ways to the new situation.

It may be argued, of course, that the changes which produced the new situation are subsumed under the notion of "Conquest" and that the previous pages only make more explicit the "decapitation" interpretation advanced by the historians of the "Montreal school."[78] It is true enough that the new business climate described here may not have been created after the Seven Years' War had Canada remained a French possession. But there is no guarantee that other changes would not have affected the Montreal merchants. During the last years of the French regime they had reaped few profits from the fur trade. After the Conquest they continued in the fur trade much on the same scale as before. The Montreal merchants were not "decapitated" by the Conquest; rather, they were faced in very short succession with a series of transformations in the socioeconomic structure of the colony to which they might have been able to adapt had these transformations been spread over a longer period of time.

This paper has attempted to show that the fate of the Canadian merchants of Montreal after the Conquest followed from the nature of trade before the Conquest and from the rate at which new circumstances required the merchants to alter their business behavior. But it should be remembered that the decapitation hypothesis still remains to be tested in the area of the colony's economy which was most heavily dependent upon the control of the metropolis, the import-export trade of the Quebec merchants. Only a detailed examination of the role and the activities of the Quebec merchants, both before and after the Conquest, will fully put the decapitation hypothesis to the test.

NOTES

[1] Public Archives of Canada [hereafter PAC], C.O.42, vol. 27, f. 66, Carleton to Shelburne, Quebec, 25 November 1767; quoted in A.L. Burt, *The Old Province of Quebec*, 2 vols. (Toronto, 1968), 1:142.

[2] See Burt, *Old Province*, vol. 1, ch. 6; Dale B. Miquelon, "The Baby Family in the Trade of Canada, 1750-1820" (Unpublished Master's thesis, Carleton University, 1966), 145-46.

[3] Francis Parkman, *The Old Regime in Canada* (27th ed., Boston, 1892), ch. 21, especially 397-98.

[4] W. Stewart Wallace, ed., *Documents Relating to the North West Company* (Toronto, 1934); Wallace, *The Pedlars from Quebec and Other Papers on the Nor'Westers* (Toronto, 1954); E.E. Rich, *The Fur Trade and the Northwest to 1857* (Toronto, 1967); Rich, *The History of the Hudson's Bay Company*, vol. 2 (London, 1959); D.G. Creighton, *The Empire of the St. Lawrence* (Toronto, 1956).

[5] Wayne E. Stevens, *The Northwest Fur Trade, 1763-1800* (Urbana, Ill., 1928), 25.

[6] Fernand Ouellet, *Histoire économique et sociale du Québec, 1760-1850* (Montreal, 1966), 77.

[7] Ouellet, *Histoire économique*, 104-106.

[8] Michel Brunet, *Les Canadiens après la Conquête, 1759-1775* (Montreal, 1969), 173-74, 177-80.

[9] Miquelon, "The Baby Family," 158.

[10] Miquelon, "The Baby Family," 142.

[11] The implication is unwarranted. A given economic sector can be dynamic and even produce the largest share of marketable commodities and still provide individual entrepreneurs with meager profits. The macro-economic level of analysis should not be confused with the micro-economic level. Jean Hamelin showed that only around 28 percent of the profits from the beaver trade remained in Canada. Since the Canadians had an assured market for beaver, one can wonder how much more profitable it was for them to deal in other peltries. See Hamelin, *Economie et Société en Nouvelle-France* (Quebec, 1960), 54-56.

[12] The obvious economic explanation for the downfall of the Canadian merchants after the Conquest has to be dismissed. The liquidation of Canadian paper money by France hurt most of all those British merchants who bought it from Canadians for speculation. Canadian merchants had already compensated in part for the anticipated liquidation by raising prices during the last years of the Seven Years' War. Those Montreal merchants who had the greatest quantity of French paper were not driven out of business; on the contrary the most prominent merchants were able to open accounts with British suppliers soon after the Conquest without too much difficulty. See José E. Igartua, "The Merchants and *Négociants* of Montreal, 1750-1775: A Study in Socio-Economic History" (Unpublished Ph.D. thesis, Michigan State University, 1974), ch. 6.

[13] Franquet, *Voyages et mémoires sur le Canada en 1752-1753* (Toronto, 1968), 56.

[14] For a more elaborate description of the size and the socioeconomic characteristics of the Montreal merchant community at this time, see Igartua, "The Merchants and *Négociants* of Montreal," ch. 2.

[15] See H.A. Innis, *The Fur Trade in Canada* (Rev. ed., Toronto, 1956), 107-113.

[16] See Abraham Rotstein, "Fur Trade and Empire: An Institutional Analysis" (Unpublished Ph.D. thesis, University of Toronto, 1967), 72.

[17] Innis, *Fur Trade*, 117. For his discussion of the impact of war on the fur trade and on New France, see 114-18.

[18] In theory, the French licensing system set up to restrict the trade remained in operation from its re-establishment in 1728 to the end of the French regime; only twenty-five *congés* were to be sold each year. In practice, military officers in the upper country could also acquire for a modest fee

exclusive trade privileges for their particular area. With some care, concluded one author, they could make an easy fortune. See Emile Salone, *La Colonisation de la Nouvelle-France* (Trois-Rivières, 1970), 390, 392-93. No clear official description of the licensing system was found for the period from 1750 to 1760, but the precise way in which the fur trade was restricted matters less than the fact of restriction.

19 On Charly see PAC, RG 4 B58, vol. 15, 19 September 1764, pass by Governor Murray to "Monsr. Louis Saint-Ange Charly [and his family] to London, in their way to France agreeable to the Treaty of Peace . . . "; Archives Nationales du Québec à Montréal [formerly Archives judiciaires de Montréal; hereafter ANQ-M], Greffe de Pierre Panet, 16 août 1764, no. 2190. Trotier Desauniers "Dufy"'s will is in ANQ-M, 29 juillet 1760, no. 1168, and Godet's will is in ANQ-M, 28 décembre 1768, no. 3140.

20 The inventory of Monière's estate is in ANQ-M, 28 décembre 1768, no. 3141; that of L'Huillier Chevalier's in ANQ-M, 15 [?] juin 1772, no. 3867.

21 See Alexander Henry, *Travels and Adventures in Canada* (Ann Arbor, University Microfilms, 1966), 191-92.

22 W.S. Wallace, *Documents Relating to the North West Company*, Appendix A ("A Biographical Dictionary of the Nor'Westers"), 456.

23 See Henry, *Travels*, 1-11, 34.

24 Henry, *Travels*, 39.

25 Henry, *Travels*, 50. Cf. the rosier picture by Creighton, *The Empire of the St. Lawrence*, 33.

26 Henry, *Travels*, 77-84. The Indians killed the British soldiers but ransomed the British traders, giving to each according to his profession.

27 Henry, *Travels*, 264-92.

28 See Wallace, *Documents*, 456; Milo M. Quaife, ed, *Alexander Henry's Travels and Adventures in the Years 1760-1776* (Chicago, 1921), xvi-xvii.

29 Henry, *Travels*, 11; Quaife, *Henry's Travels*, 12 n. 6.

30 Rich, *History of the Hudson's Bay Company*, 2: 9.

31 See PAC, C.O.42, vol. 5, ff. 30-31, Murray's "List of Protestants in the District of Montreal," dated Quebec, 7 November 1765.

32 See Miquelon, "The Baby Family," 181-87.

33 PAC, MG 19 A1, 1, William Edgar Papers, 1: 97, F. Hamback to W. Edgar, 2 November 1766. See also 1: 95, Hamback to D. Edgar, 29 October 1766, and 1: 104-106, same to Edgar, 23 March 1767.

34 William Edgar Papers, 1: 12.

35 See William Edgar Papers, vols. 1 and 2.

36 R.H. Fleming, "Phyn, Ellice and Company of Schenectady," *Contributions to Canadian Economics* 4 (1932): 7-41.

37 See Marjorie G. Jackson, "The Beginnings of British Trade at Michilimackinac," *Minnesota History* 11 (September 1930): 252; C.W. Alvord and C.E. Carter, eds., *The New Regime, 1765-1767* (Collections of the Illinois State Historical Library, vol. 11), 300-301; Alvord and Carter, eds., *Trade and Politics, 1767-1769* (Collections of the Illinois State Historical Library, vol. 16), 382-453.

38 See "Extract of a Letter from Michilimackinac, to a Gentleman in this City, dated 30th June," in *Quebec Gazette*, 18 August 1768; see also Rich, *History of the Hudson's Bay Company* 2: 26: "The suspicions between the Pedlars [from Quebec], and their encouragements of the Indians to trick and defraud their trade rivals, especially by defaulting on payments of debt, were widespread and continuous."

39 *Quebec Gazette*, 7 January 1768.

40 Burt, *Old Province*, 1: 92.

41 The flooding of the Quebec market by British merchants was part of a larger invasion of the colonial trade in North America. See Mark Egnal and Joseph A. Ernst, "An Economic Interpretation of the American Revolution," *William and Mary Quarterly*, 3rd series, 29 (1972): 3-32.

42 Quoted in Alvord and Carter, eds., *Trade and Politics*, 288.

43 Alvord and Carter, eds., *Trade and Politics*, 38.

44 Quoted in E.E. Rich, *Montreal and the Fur Trade* (Montreal, 1966), 44.

45 These figures are somewhat distorted by the inclusion of a single large British investor, Alexander Henry, who outfitted seven canoes worth £3400 in all. See Charles E. Lart, ed., "Fur-Trade Returns, 1767," *Canadian Historical Review* 3 (December 1922): 351-58. The definition of the North West as including Lake Huron, Lake Superior, and "the northwest by way of Lake Superior" given in Rich, *Montreal and the Fur Trade*, 36-37, was used in making these compilations. The French traders were "Deriviere," "Chenville," St. Clair, Laselle, "Guillaid [Guillet]," and "Outlass [Houtelas]."

46 See Rich, *Montreal and the Fur Trade*, 36-37.

47 Jackson, *Minnesota History*, 11: 268-69.

48 Rich, *History of the Hudson's Bay Company* 2: 68.

49 On the Monières, see Igartua, "The Merchants and *Négociants* of Montreal," ch. 2. On the Gamelins, see Antoine Champagne, *Les La Vérendrye et les postes de l'ouest* (Quebec, 1968), passim.

50 See R.H. Fleming, *Contributions to Canadians Economics* 4: 13; on Baynton, Wharton and Morgan, see *The Papers of Sir William Johnson* [hereafter *Johnson Papers*], 14 vols. (Albany, 1921-1965), vols. 5, 6, 12, *passim*.

[51] PAC, C.O.42, vol. 2, ff. 277-80, petition of the "Merchants and Traders of Montreal" to Murray and the Council, Montreal, 20 February 1765; *Johnson Papers* 5: 807-15, memorial and petition of Detroit traders to Johnson, 22 November 1767; 12: 409-414, 1768 trade regulations with the merchants' objections.

[52] See Alvord and Carter, eds., *The New Regime*, 118-19, and *Trade and Politics*, 39, 287; see also Stevens, *The Northwest Fur Trade*, 44.

[53] Johnson Papers, 12: 517, Thomas Gage to Guy Johnson, New York, 29 May 1768.

[54] *Johnson Papers* 5: 481. See also Alvord and Carter, eds., *The New Regime*, 118-19; *Johnson Papers* 5: 362; Alvord and Carter, eds., *Trade and Politics*, 39; *Johnson Papers* 5: 762-64; 12: 486-87; Stevens, *The Northwest Fur Trade*, 28.

[55] PAC, C.O.42, vol. 27, ff. 81-85, Carleton to Johnson, Quebec, 27 March 1767.

[56] *Johnson Papers* 12: 372-75, Croghan to Johnson, 18 October 1767.

[57] Henry, *Travels*, 71-72.

[58] See PAC, C.O.42, vol. 26, f. 13, Court of St. James, Conway [Secretary of State] to the Commandants of Detroit and Michilimackinac, 27 March 1766. See also Alvord and Carter, eds., *Trade and Politics*, 207-208, Gage to Shelburne, 12 March 1768; 239, Johnson to Gage, 8 April 1768; 375, Gage to Johnson, 14 August 1768; 378, Gage to Hillsborough, 17 August 1768; 384, Johnson to Gage, 24 August 1768; 599, Gage to Hillsborough, 9 September 1769. More than trading on his own account, Rogers was suspected of setting up an independent Illinois territory. He was eventually cleared. See "Robert Rogers," *Dictionary of American Biography*, vol. 16 (New York, 1935), 108-109, and *Johnson Papers*, vols. 5, 6, 12, 13, *passim*.

[59] PAC, William Edgar Papers, 1: 43-44, Callender to Edgar n.p., 31 December 1763.

[60] Henry, *Travels*, 191-92, 235.

[61] PAC, William Edgar Papers, 1: 90, Thos. Shipboy to Rankin and Edgar, Albany, 21 August 1766.

[62] William Edgar Papers, 1: 201, Benjamin Frobisher to Rankin and Edgar, Michilimackinac, 23 June 1769.

[63] William Edgar Papers, 1: 104-106, F. Hamback to Edgar, 23 March 1767.

[64] The most detailed account is given in Burt, *Old Province*, vol. 1, ch. 6 and 7. See also Creighton, *Empire of the St. Lawrence*, 40-48.

[65] See for instance E.-Z. Massicotte, "La Bourse de Montréal sous le régime français," *The Canadian Antiquarian and Numismatic Journal*, 3rd series, 12 (1915): 26-32.

[66] See Pierre Tousignant, "La Genèse et l'avènement de la Constitution de 1791" (Unpublished Ph.D. thesis, Université de Montréal, 1971).

[67] See *Quebec Gazette*, 15 September 1766 and the issues from June to September 1768.

[68] See *Quebec Gazette*, 26 September 1765. Tousignant, "La Genèse," pp. 21-39, points out the political significance of this letter.

[69] See texts by "A MERCHANT" in the 10 and 17 December 1767 issues, and rebuttals in the 24 and 31 December 1767 and 7 and 21 January 1768 issues.

[70] Tousignant, "La Genèse," 39.

[71] See issues of 13 and 27 July, and 5 October 1775.

[72] Canadian notables of Quebec broke with the "Old Subjects" earlier: a petition, thought to date from 1770 and signed by leading Canadians of that city, asked for the restoration of Canadian institutions. See Adam Shortt and Arthur G. Doughty, *Documents Relating to the Constitutional History of Canada* (2nd. ed., Ottawa, 1918) [hereafter *Docs. Const. Can.*], 1: 419-21.

[73] The petition and the memorial are reproduced in *Docs. Const. Hist. Can.* 1:504-506, 508-510.

[74] *Docs. Const. Hist. Can.* 1: 511. The British merchants of Montreal signed a counter-petition in January 1774, requesting the introduction of an assembly and of the laws of England. See 1: 501-502.

[75] Recent historians have highlighted the influence of the military and civil administrations as sources of economic and social betterment in New France. See Guy Frégault, *Le XVIIIe siècle canadien* (Montreal, 1968), 382-84; W.J. Eccles, "The Social, Economic, and Political Significance of the Military Establishment in New France," *Canadian Historical Review* 52 (March 1971): 17-19; and Cameron Nish, *Les Bourgeois-Gentilshommes de la Nouvelle-France* (Montreal, 1968), *passim*.

[76] See PAC, C.O.42, vol. 24. ff. 72-73v.; ff. 95-95v; vol. 3, f. 262; *Docs. Const. Hist. Can.* 1: 504-508.

[77] See *Docs. Const. Hist. Can.* 1: 504.

[78] Maurice Séguin, of the History Department of the Université de Montréal, was the first to present a systematic interpretation of the Conquest as societal decapitation. His book, *L'Idée d'indépendance au Québec: genèse et historique* (Trois-Rivières, 1968), which contains a summary of his thought, was published twenty years after its author first sketched out his thesis. Guy Frégault's *Histoire de la Nouvelle-France*, vol. 9, *La guerre de la Conquête, 1754-1760* (Montreal, 1955) is a masterful rendition of that conflict, cast as the *affrontement* of two civilizations. Michel Brunet, the most voluble of the "Montreal school" historians, has assumed the task of popularizing Séguin's thought. See Brunet, "La Conquête anglaise et la déchéance de la bourgeoisie canadienne (1760-1793)," in his *La Présence anglaise et les Canadiens* (Montreal, 1964), 48-112. Brunet developed the point further in *Les Canadiens après la Conquête*, vol. 1, *1759-1775* (Montreal, 1969). An abridged version of Brunet's position is provided in his *French Canada and the Early Decades of British Rule, 1760-1791* (Ottawa, 1963). For a review of French-Canadian historiography on the Conquest up to 1966, see Ramsay Cook, "Some French-Canadian Interpretations of the British Conquest: une quatrième dominante de la pensée canadienne-française," Canadian Historical Association, *Historical Papers* (1966): 70-83.

The Road between York and Kingston, Upper Canada, 1830, *a watercolour by James Pattison Cockburn.*

"Despite the Simcoe plan of trunk roads and the setting aside of road allowances as part of the land survey, much of the basic network before 1825 grew from Indian paths through the forest."

R. Louis Gentilcore and David Wood, "A Military Colony in a Wilderness: The Upper Canada Frontier"

The Society of Upper Canada

The social history of settlement in British North America in the late eighteenth and early nineteenth centuries is really a collection of separate regional stories. Two French-speaking populations existed — the French Canadians in the St. Lawrence Valley and the Acadians in New Brunswick. English-speaking communities had been established in the Maritime colonies and in Newfoundland, in the St. Lawrence Valley, and in Upper Canada. The readings in this section review Upper Canadian developments.

With the Constitutional Act of 1791, Upper Canada emerged as a new British colony, composed largely of Loyalists escaping from the newly independent thirteen colonies. How did this colony differ from the other English-speaking British North American colonies, and why? What role did women play in the formative years of Upper Canada?

Historical geographers Louis Gentilcore and David Wood discuss Upper Canada's beginnings in "A Military Colony in a Wilderness: The Upper Canada Frontier." Using newspaper sources, historian Jane Errington sketches out a portrait of women in Upper Canada in her "'Woman . . . Is a Very Interesting Creature': Some Women's Experiences in Early Upper Canada."

Although a growing literature now exists on Upper Canada, the best introductory text is still Gerald M. Craig's *Upper Canada: The Formative Years, 1784–1841* (Toronto: McClelland and Stewart, 1963). Important sources on the Loyalists who settled in the new colony include Bruce Wilson, *As She Began: An Illustrated Introduction to Loyalist Ontario* (Toronto: Dundurn Press, 1981); James J. Talman, ed., *Loyalist Narratives from Upper Canada* (Toronto: Champlain Society, 1946); and Janice Potter-MacKinnon, *While the Women Only Wept: Loyalist Refugee Women in Eastern Ontario* (Montreal and Kingston: McGill-Queen's University Press, 1993). Mrs. Simcoe's diary is an invaluable primary text for the early social history of the province; John Ross Robertson's fully annotated edition of the diary appeared under the title *The Diary of Mrs. John Graves Simcoe, Wife of the First Lieutenant-Governor of the Province of Upper Canada, 1792–6* (Toronto, 1911; reprint Toronto: Coles Publishing, 1973). Mary Quayle Innis edited an abridged version, entitled *Mrs. Simcoe's Diary* (Toronto: Macmillan, 1965).

Currently, a great deal is being published on the economic and political history of Upper Canada. Economic issues are introduced in Chapter 6 ("Upper Canada") of Kenneth Norrie and Douglas Owram's *A History of the Canadian Economy* (Toronto: Harcourt Brace Jovanovich, 1991), 160–74, and, in greater depth, in Douglas McCalla's "The 'Loyalist' Economy of Upper Canada," *Histoire Sociale/Social History* 16, 32 (November 1983): 279–304, as well as in his *Planting the Province: The Economic History of Upper Canada, 1784–1870* (Toronto: University of Toronto Press for the Ontario Historical Society Series, 1993). For the early history of Upper Canadian politics, see Jane Errington, *The Lion, the Eagle and Upper Canada: A Developing Colonial Ideology* (Kingston and Montreal: McGill-Queen's University Press, 1987), and David Mills, *The Idea of Loyalty in Upper Canada, 1784–1850* (Montreal and Kingston: McGill-Queen's University Press, 1988).

For background on the Amerindian history of Upper Canada, consult Charles M. Johnston, ed., *The Valley of the Six Nations: A Collection of Documents on the Indian Lands of the Grand River* (Toronto: Champlain Society, 1964); Peter Schmaltz, *The Ojibwa of Southern Ontario* (Toronto: University of Toronto Press, 1991); and Donald B. Smith, *Sacred Feathers: The Reverend Peter Jones (Kahkewaquonaby) and the Mississauga Indians* (Toronto: University of Toronto Press, 1987). Daniel G. Hill's *The Freedom-Seekers: Blacks in Early Canada* (Agincourt, Ont.: Book Society of Canada, 1981) is a popular summary of the history of blacks in Upper Canada and in British North America in general. An important study of a British immigrant group is Marianne McLean's *The People of Glengarry: Highlanders in Transition, 1745–1820* (Montreal and Kingston: McGill-Queen's University Press, 1991).

Pierre Berton has written two popular accounts of the War of 1812: *The Invasion of Canada, 1812–1813* (Toronto: McClelland and Stewart, 1980), and *Flames across the Border, 1813–1814* (Toronto: McClelland and Stewart, 1981). A more recent study is Wesley B. Turner's *The War of 1812: The War That Both Sides Won* (Toronto: Dundurn Press, 1990). George F.G. Stanley's *The War of 1812: Land Operations* (Toronto: Macmillan, 1983) provides the best review of the war's military history. George Sheppard examines the Upper Canadian militiamen's accomplishments in "'Deeds Speak': Militiamen, Medals, and the Invented Traditions of 1812," *Ontario History* 83, 3 (September 1990): 207–32.

For biographical sketches of leading Upper Canadians in the late eighteenth and early nineteenth centuries, consult the multivolume *Dictionary of Canadian Biography* (Toronto: University of Toronto Press, 1966–   ), particularly volumes 4 to 8.

Three of the most perceptive contemporary witnesses of early Upper Canada are women: Catharine Parr Traill, Susanna Moodie, and Anna Jameson. Catharine Parr Traill's *The Backwoods of Canada* (1836) and

The Canadian Settler's Guide (1854), Susanna Moodie's *Roughing It in the Bush* (1852), and Anna Jameson's *Winter Studies and Summer Rambles in Canada* (1838) are available, in abridged editions, in McClelland and Stewart's New Canadian Library Series. Marian Fowler's *The Embroidered Tent: Five Gentlewomen in Early Canada* (Toronto: House of Anansi, 1982) contains sketches of these women's lives. Alison Prentice et al., *Canadian Women: A History* (Toronto: Harcourt Brace Jovanovich, 1988) examines changes in the lives of British North American women in the late eighteenth and early nineteenth centuries.

A Military Colony in a Wilderness: The Upper Canada Frontier

R. LOUIS GENTILCORE and DAVID WOOD

293

The settlement geography of British North America was set on a new course by the revolt of the American Colonies. In the wake of the conflict, British territory had to provide a haven for American Loyalist refugees. Three areas were available. Nova Scotia (which included New Brunswick until 1784) was the most accessible and had the longest experience with British settlement; it received by far the majority of the Loyalists. Only a token number went to what was to become Lower Canada (in 1791), but they constituted the first immigration of an English-speaking group to the former French colony. West of Montreal, in what was to become Upper Canada, practically no white settlement had taken place. That territory awaited only alienation from Indian claims to expedite two British quests: land for the Loyalists, and a military base flanking the United States on the northwest. Ultimately Nova Scotia and New Brunswick received about 30,000 Loyalists, and Lower Canada about 7,000. If one can rely on the figure for land granted to Loyalists (nearly three million acres) in Durham's 1839 report, then it seems likely that Upper Canada received roughly 9,000 such refugees by the end of the 1780s, not counting the loyal Six Nations Indians.[1]

Settlement by Design

Early settlement in Ontario was directed by military authorities. The first occupied places were military posts from which the taking up of land was organized, as the Crown sought to build a viable, defensible

From *Perspectives on Landscape and Settlement in Nineteenth-Century Ontario*, ed. David Wood (Toronto: Macmillan, 1978). Reprinted with the permission of the authors.

community. The British design was given concrete expression by its first Lieutenant Governor, John Graves Simcoe. The observant La Rochefoucault-Liancourt said of him, in 1795,

> He is acquainted with the military history of all countries; no hillock catches his eye without exciting in his mind the idea of a fort, which might be constructed on the spot. . . . ,[2]

and Simcoe, explaining something of his intentions in 1793, said

> . . . for every purpose of Civilization, command of the Indians, and general De-fence . . . on the Confluence of the main Branches of the Thames the Capital of Upper Canada, as soon as possible, ought to be Situated. But . . . it is not my intention at present to establish myself upon the Forks of the River Thames. . . . I shall content myself with rendering the Road between Burlington Bay and the River Thames . . . sufficiently commodious as a military Commu-nication . . .
>
> . . . as . . . the safety of this Province should not depend upon so feeble a Barrier as (comparatively) the contemptible Fortress of Niagara, it is with great pleasure that I offer to you some Observations upon the Military Strength and naval Conveniency of Toronto (now York) which I propose immediately to occupy.[3]

The first component in Simcoe's plan was military movement. Two primary roads were planned. Dundas Street would run from Lake On-tario to the site of the future provincial capital at the head of navigation on the Thames River, a place safe from attack yet affording ready access to Lake Erie and border points to the south. The road would facilitate movement into the interior and help consolidate control over this part of the province. Yonge Street, north from Lake Ontario, was conceived as a military route to provide rapid communication with the upper lakes. A second component of the plan was a set of nucleated settlements, to be planted at intervals along the roads, at road and water junctions.

The Simcoe plan is incorporated in one of the earliest printed maps of Ontario. The map, accurately depicting provincial districts, counties, townships, main villages, towns, and Indian settlements, also includes roads and towns proposed by Simcoe but not in existence in 1800. For example, at this time there was no London, or Oxford (later Woodstock), nor a Dundas Street extending to them (although it had been surveyed). But many places which later become important urban centres were con-ceived as part of the plan. Toronto, the provincial capital, was the out-standing example. The plan also provided the impetus for places like Newmarket, Barrie, Penetanguishene, Woodstock, London, and Cha-tham. One of its achievements was that it helped to direct population inland at a time when most of it still clung tenaciously to navigable waterways.

An operational analysis of the plan by Kirk, shortly after World War II, provided military terminology fitting to Simcoe's intentions. Kirk, extrapolating from Simcoe's correspondence, outlined the tactical advantages of the various nodal points in the resulting network and identified "bridgeheads" at the extremities of the military roads adjacent to the United States border (summarized in Map 1).[4]

Setting and Settlement

Combining with the Crown's efforts to direct settlement was a physical geography that both hindered and aided occupation and development. Most dominant was the forest, sensed, feared, and appreciated in varying degrees as settlement advanced; so overpowering that new settlers had to be given detailed instructions on what to do for survival when lost in the woods. Not the least oppressive element in the partially cleared

295

MAP 1 Kirk's 1949 Summary of Simcoe's Plan, Southwestern Upper Canada

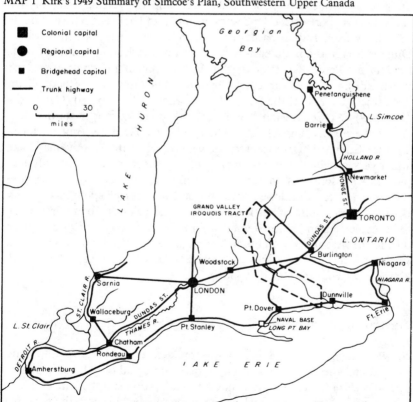

Donald W. Kirk, "Southwestern Ontario/The Areal Pattern of Urban Settlements in 1850," unpublished doctoral thesis, Northwestern University, 1949.

countryside was the multitude of insects which afflicted both man and his beasts. W.H. Smith, in a wry aside in his *Gazetteer*, says

> . . . mosquitoes are apt to form an early and sometimes rather *too intimate* acquaintance with the newly arrived emigrant.[5]

The forest was both enemy and friend, an obstacle to be removed but also an asset, a source of food, building material, and forage. It was in the woods that agriculture began. Land was cleared most commonly by cutting and burning, which might require from a settler one month or more of hard labour per acre. Even then stumps were left standing, a reminder that the toil of clearing was not yet complete.[6] Fortunately, the task was not without early benefit. Clearing produced the settlers' first "cash crop." Ashes from the burned trees were preserved and sold to potash manufacturers. In some cases, especially where the settler had partially processed the ash himself, the "crop" might yield enough to pay the costs of clearing and fencing the land.[7]

296

The woods also contained the beginnings of Ontario's road network. Despite the Simcoe plan of trunk roads and the setting aside of road allowances as part of the land survey, much of the basic network before 1825 grew from Indian paths through the forest. For example, rivalling Dundas Street as a main east–west route was the Iroquois Trail, crossing the Niagara Peninsula at the foot of the escarpment and continuing westward. Adrian Marlet, surveying north of "The Governor's Road" (Dundas Street) just east of the Grand River valley in 1816, noted (Concession II, lot 19) "At Concession X old Mohawk Road," a north–south route.[8] Along the north shore of Lake Ontario, the Lakeshore Trail vied with Dundas Street. The importance of water-side routes is obvious. Lakes and rivers provided the best means of transport; roads were only supplements. As long as settlement was thinly strung out along water routes, the road pattern developed little beyond a series of spontaneous links between the clusters of settlers, ignoring the gridiron road allowances.[9] (The extension and improvement of roads as a communication system during the first generation of settlement are dealt with by McIlwraith . . . [in his article in *Perspectives on Landscape and Settlement in Nineteenth-Century Ontario*, ed. David Wood].)

Agricultural Beginnings

Slowly, the high roof of leaves was broken. But given the abundance of land and the small population, agriculture could only be an extensive operation. Implements were crude and cultivation simple. The emphasis was on grains, particularly wheat. In some places, however, the first food was Indian corn, which was easier to grow and produced more food, more reliably on new land. But, in less than a decade, wheat was the leading crop in all the settlements.[10] In the same period, wheat also became a cash crop. As early as 1795, the fort at Kingston was collecting wheat, together with peas and salt pork, for export. If pioneering is to be equated with subsistence agriculture, its presence in early Ontario is very short-lived. From the impetus provided by the fort settlements, commercial agriculture, based on wheat production, expanded into the nineteenth century (cf. Osborne on Kingston . . . [in *Perspectives on Landscape and Settlement*]). Indeed, wheat growing quickly dominated or replaced what one might expect to be persistent traditional crops, such as potatoes among Irish and oats among Scots. The wooded landscape was replaced by open stretches of cultivated fields, though commonly, in the opinion of a priggish visitor, "ill-ploughed, . . . disfiguring the face of the country" where "Corn succeeds corn, until the land is nearly exhausted."[11] Increasing familiarity with the conditions leading to farming success resulted in demand for better lands and particularly those adjacent to the roads to main markets. It is reported that although La Rochefoucault-Liancourt in 1795 had thought Toronto to be a small swampy break in the woods (containing a fort and twelve log huts), by the mid-1840s "the three great thoroughfares — the western, the northern, and the Kingston roads — are each planked or macadamised for about twenty miles [out from Toronto]; and for the same distance nearly every lot fronting on the roads is taken up, settled, and under cultivation."[12]

297

The clearing of the woods also provided another major commodity for trade. The value of timber exports exceeded that of all agricultural products shipped from the province in the second quarter of the nineteenth century. The trade had been promoted by British policy dating back to the Napoleonic Wars.[13] Timber ships returning empty to North America offered the cheap link to complete the emigration chain. This symbiotic relationship sometimes was continued into Upper Canada through the demand of the timber camps for provisions and winter labourers. The most vigorous timber exploitation developed on the Ottawa River early in the nineteenth century, tapping many areas better suited to lumbering than to agriculture. Further southwest, the Trent River, on the edge of the Shield, also moved sizeable quantities of timber. Elsewhere, smaller scale exploitations were associated with numerous minor rivers and creeks throughout the province. (See Head's paper on forest exploitation in . . . [*Perspectives on Landscape and Settlement*].)

The Port and Administration Functions

The increasing importance of exports fortified the early and persistent relationship between populated places and water, illustrated on the map of "populated places" in 1825 (Map 2). The map also emphasizes the role of ports as entry points. Only three places, all ports, had populations of at least 1,000: Kingston, the leading port; York, later Toronto, the capital; and Niagara, the original capital. Each occupied a key site in Simcoe's settlement plan; each was nurtured by a major fort from which settlement was deployed to nearby hinterlands and to which produce and equipment moved for handling and shipment. Between 1825 and 1851, the province's population increased from 158,000 to 952,000 (which surpassed that of the former Lower Canada). In 1806, it had been 71,000, compared to Lower Canada's 250,000. Populated places advanced in a wave across parts of the formerly uninhabited interior. But the attachment to water survived, tied to the increased trade in timber, flour, and wheat. There were now eighteen places with a population exceeding 2,000; thirteen were ports (Map 3).

298

Another function contributed to growth. From the inception of settlement, centres awarded administrative responsibilities possessed unique advantages. The division of the province into districts led to the management of local affairs by the district court from 1788 to 1841. The appointed Justices of the Peace, meeting as the Court of Quarter Sessions in the district centre, not only tried court cases, but also supervised road and bridge construction contracts and issued various licences, including those for taverns.[14] Their duties were administrative as well as judicial. Consequently, the places chosen for their meetings took on the role of district capitals. Once created, they became the leading central places for the areas around them. Initially, the choice of district centres was governed by military considerations and accessibility by water. As settlements grew, new districts had to be formed and new places chosen as their "capitals," a process accompanied by considerable political manoeuvring (Ennals's paper . . . [in *Perspectives on Landscape and Settlement*] on Cobourg and Port Hope documents a comparable competition). Throughout, a close relationship was maintained between district centres and concentrations of population.

The Dominant Urban Nuclei

The dominant places in 1851 were those that had been able to combine port and administrative functions. The largest of these was Toronto. Offering the advantages of defensibility and a good harbour, the site had been selected for a key settlement in the Simcoe plan (Map 4). A naval arsenal and the provisional government headquarters were established there. By 1796, the original town lots were granted, Yonge Street was opened to the north, and the first farms were emerging along it. Simcoe's view that the location was a logical one for the advancement of settlement into the interior would be borne out. But at the time, the community gave little indication of its future prominence. Even the Yonge Street

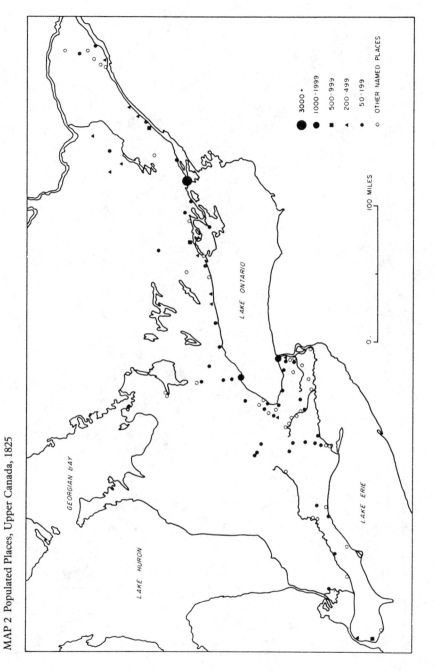

MAP 2 Populated Places, Upper Canada, 1825

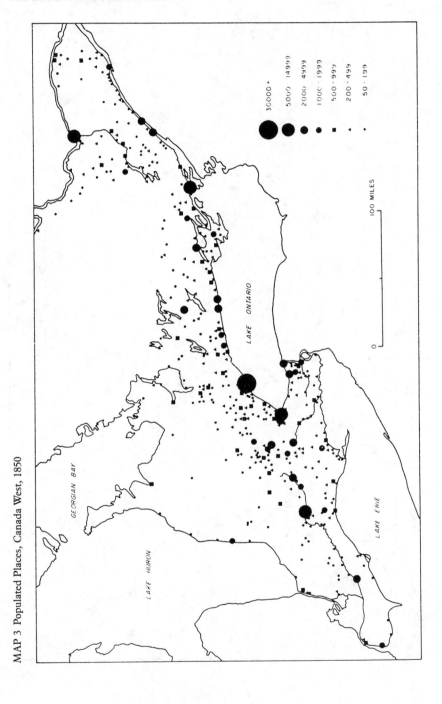

MAP 3 Populated Places, Canada West, 1850

artery was maintained irregularly and without conviction. York possessed only twelve cabins and a hinterland practically devoid of white population. There was no church, school, or inn and only one store. In 1810, its population had risen to a modest 600, but the physical framework for growth had been established. The planted settlement continued to grow. By 1825, the population had more than doubled, to 1,677; at city incorporation, in 1834, it was 9,252; in 1851, it stood at 30,775.[15] The city had held on to its function as the provincial capital, its port was a busy one, and its hinterland was no longer wilderness but productive and prosperous farmland, contributing wheat for export and drawing immigrants to its unsettled margins. Despite its prominence, Toronto differed little in appearance from other urban places in the province. It still struck visitors as a backwoods settlement. There were no paved streets; houses were small; the buildings were of wood, one storey high, except for a few three-storey brick buildings in the main business area. The buildings sprawled along the blocks, including rows of sheds and huts, housing workers and the poor, in places betraying the outlines of incipient ghettoes.[16] There also were many examples of gaping vacant lots being held for speculation. But appearance masked the reality. By mid-century, Toronto dominated the urban geography of Ontario. It was the province's main wholesaling and distributing centre; banks and businesses, workshops, and stores vied for space. In the early 1840s, building ground in the business area sold at the "incredible" rates of £10 to £20 a foot. The loss of its capital function for a few years in the 1840s and disastrous fires in 1847 and 1849 were only minor setbacks to Toronto's growth. The fires cleared away old buildings to make way for the new, a process that would become increasingly characteristic of the city as the rate of growth accelerated.

301

Second in size to Toronto in 1851, with about one-half its population (14,112) was the young city of Hamilton (Map 3), which is not even on the map of 1825. Like Toronto, Hamilton had begun as an administrative centre in the wilderness. Despite the claims of a number of thriving centres around it, the Hamilton townsite was chosen in 1816 as the centre for the new district of Gore. Later, in 1830, a port function was added with the cutting of a channel through the bar that separated the town's potential harbour from Lake Ontario. By 1840, most of the grain produced in the farmlands west of Lake Ontario was moving to Hamilton. The city also vied with Toronto as a main entry point for immigration. New roads were built and old ones improved, including one to Port Dover on Lake Erie for the transport of iron mined and smelted on Long Point Bay. Other transportation improvements helped the settlement. The completion of the Welland Canal by 1830 provided a replacement for the Niagara portage as the main route from Lake Erie to Lake Ontario, and incidentally fulfilled a longstanding desire of colonial administrators to move the passage away from the United States

MAP 4 Plan of York Harbour, 1793

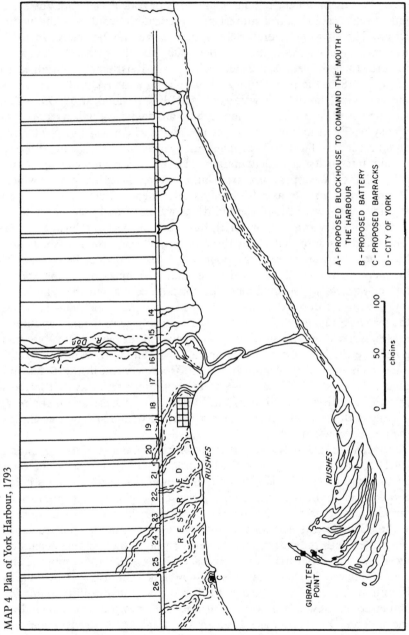

A - PROPOSED BLOCKHOUSE TO COMMAND THE MOUTH OF
    THE HARBOUR

B - PROPOSED BATTERY

C - PROPOSED BARRACKS

D - CITY OF YORK

By A. Aitken, by order of Lt. Gov. Simcoe, 1793. Original in Public Record Office, London, Ont.

boundary. Simcoe, in his correspondence (vol. 1, p. 90), misguidedly expressed the hope that a water route via the Upper Thames would "annihilate the political consequence of Niagara & Lake Erie." Hamilton used the canal, ironically, to import coal from Lake Erie ports in the United States, installing steam power facilities that would serve as a base for the expansion of industry. The ascendancy of Hamilton over other places in the area was typical of new urban growth in the province. Older settlements that were dependent upon intermittent water supplies for power and that had limited shipping facilities were declining in importance. Replacing them were urban centres on good harbours with easy access to new sources of power. In the Niagara Peninsula, a new alignment of centres had been brought about by the construction of the Welland Canal (compare Maps 2 and 3). Settlements on the Niagara River, including Niagara, the former capital, were now eclipsed by those on the canal, particularly St. Catharines, the terminus on Lake Ontario.

Ontario's third city in 1851 had been its leading one before 1825. *303* Kingston grew up around the major fort built to guard entry into eastern Ontario and to organize its settlement. From the fort, a number of townships were surveyed for occupancy by refugee loyalists from the United States in the early 1780s. The townsite was laid out in 1788. By 1800, there were half a dozen quays in operation. Their number and extent increased as Kingston took advantage of its harbour and its location at the junction of lake and river navigation. The town grew rapidly; in 1825, its population was 3,000. Although maintaining its administrative and port functions, it steadily lost ground to Toronto and Hamilton as trade was diverted from the Lake Ontario–St. Lawrence route to the United States via the Erie Canal. In 1851, it had a population of 11,697. (Osborne's essay, later in . . . [*Perspectives on Landscape and Settlement*], traces Kingston's rise and fall). Port cities above and below Kingston also were marked for decline (and even Montreal's "tradeshed" was truncated). But they were prominent in the urban geography of the province in 1825 and even in 1850, when they were still able to tap productive hinterlands.

Another settlement whose fortunes were tied to water was Bytown, Ontario's fourth largest in 1851. The Bytown location had developed as a centre for the lumber trade, beginning with the floating of squared white pine logs down the Ottawa River to Quebec; in the late 1830s and through the 1840s, the watershed was the largest producer of timber in North America. A second and more immediate impetus to growth was selection of the site as terminus and headquarters for the building of the Rideau Canal between the Ottawa River and Kingston. The town's population had reached 7,760 by 1851. Bytown was eventually made a district centre and later, rechristened "Ottawa," it began a new life on the strength of an administrative impetus *par excellence*.

The only sizeable inland city in 1851 was London, whose population of 7,035 made it the fifth largest in Ontario. Although the site had been chosen by Simcoe as the future provincial capital, there was no town or village there in 1825. But the crown had retained the proposed townsite and made it a district centre in 1826. Drawing sustenance from a well-settled hinterland and assisted by business generated from its administrative operations, London grew steadily, the pace quickening in the 1840s in response to increasing agricultural production.

Growth was not assured everywhere in the province even by the vital functions of port and administration. For example, Goderich on Lake Huron was planned as the administrative centre for the colonizing activities of the Canada Company in western Ontario. The settlement had a good harbour, served as the terminus of two main roads and was also a district centre. But the port was never active and no sizeable population emerged. Goderich could not overcome the disadvantages of a peripheral situation. The area around it was sparsely populated and the main settled parts of the province were too far away. Similar difficulties confronted other western settlements, including those along the Detroit River. Amherstburg was a military settlement, at the junction of the Detroit River and Lake Erie, which also failed to grow. By 1850, it was being overshadowed by the more favourably situated Windsor-Sandwich area, which would draw strength from its location across from the city of Detroit and its role as a district centre.

Hindrances to growth in Upper Canada were not merely "situational." Nor are they encompassed within a broader category including land quality, which would largely explain the failure of settlement on the Laurentian Shield a generation later. As identified by the impatient Robert Gourlay (1817ff.) and recognized by the famous report by Lord Durham (1839), there were considerable social hindrances. Gourlay was concerned about privilege, which embraced the alienation of scattered lots of potential farmland granted to friends of government and to Crown and Clergy. The quantity of such land is astonishing. Durham's report calculates that, *omitting* Crown but including Clergy reserves, these grants amounted to nearly half the 17,000,000 surveyed acres in the province! W.H. Smith's *Gazetteer* (1846) shows the various kinds of grants in a table in which the sums tend to be a little higher than Durham's. Smith's table has an air of authenticity, but no source is given and it is difficult to compare with the exhaustively mined data presented by Lillian Gates in her 1968 publication.[17] The wildness of much of the reserved land irritated and inconvenienced bona fide settlers all across the province. There are numerous examples of speculators who held thousands of acres widespread throughout the province before the middle of the century. "Privilege" also embraced a patronizing and aloof style of governing, which dominated Upper Canada through the 1830s, and which was blatantly at odds with the equality of opportunity underlying the influential American Doctrine of Success.[18]

Conclusion

The pattern of urban development in mid-nineteenth century Ontario cannot be divorced from the countryside in which it was imbedded. The growth of market and service centres accompanied increasing wheat and timber production, particularly after 1825. But those places in which growth was quickened possessed certain advantages over their neighbours. Principal among these were administrative and port functions, spawned in some cases by a plan of development proposed for the province when settlement was in its infancy. By 1850, the major urban places had emerged. They retained the traditional association with well-established transportation routes. But more important was the increasing concentration in a cluster around Toronto and Hamilton, at the western end of Lake Ontario, the forerunner of today's "Golden Horseshoe." In the decades that followed, the province would move from a simple resource exploitation economy, focussed on agriculture, toward a more industrial and commercial one, ushered in by the coming of railways in the 1850s. But these developments would not change the urban pattern. They would work within it, concentrating growing populations in a limited number of places whose propensity for growth had been indicated before 1850. This was the most momentous of the legacies of John Graves Simcoe to Ontario.

305

NOTES

This paper is based, in part, on R.L. Gentilcore, "Ontario Emerges from the Trees," *Geographical Magazine* 45, 5 (February 1973): 383–91 (by courtesy of *The Geographical Magazine*, London).

[1] Cf. Gerald M. Craig, *Upper Canada/The Formative Years/1784–1841* (Toronto: McClelland and Stewart, 1963), chap. 1.

[2] *La Rochefoucault-Liancourt's Travels in Canada, 1795 . . .* , edited with notes by William R. Riddell, published as *Thirteenth Report of the Bureau of Archives for the Province of Ontario . . . (1916)* (Toronto, 1917), 38–39.

[3] *The Correspondence of Lieut. Governor John Graves Simcoe, with Allied Documents Relating to His Administration of the Government of Upper Canada*, collected and edited by E.A. Cruikshank (Toronto: Ontario Historical Society, 1923), 1: 338, 339 (31st May, 1793).

[4] Donald W. Kirk, "Southwestern Ontario/The Areal Pattern of Urban Settlements in 1850," unpublished doctoral thesis, Northwestern University, 1949, especially Figure 12, p. 56.

[5] W.H. Smith, *Smith's Canadian Gazetteer . . .* (Toronto: H. & W. Rowsell, 1846; reprinted in Coles Canadiana Collection), 241.

[6] Kenneth Kelly, "Wheat Farming in Simcoe County in the Mid-Nineteenth Century," *Canadian Geographer* 15 (1971): 95–112, gives an extended description of the common stages of clearing. See also Kelly's essay in [*Perspectives on Landscape and Settlement in Nineteenth-Century Ontario*, ed. David Wood (Toronto: Macmillan, 1978)].

[7] William Cattermole, *Emigration: The Advantages of Emigration to Canada . . .* (London: Simpkin and Marshall, 1831; reprinted in Coles Canadiana Collection), 85–86.

[8] Marlet's survey notebook of Dumfries township is on file at the Survey Records Office, Ontario Department of Natural Resources. The prime source on the survey books is R.L. Gentilcore and K. Donkin, *Land Surveys of Southern Ontario/An Introduction and Index to the Field Notebooks of the Ontario Land Surveyors/1784–1859*, Cartographica monograph no. 8, York University, B.V. Gutsell, 1973.

[9] Andrew Burghardt, "The Origin and Development of the Road Network of the Niagara Peninsula, Ontario, 1770–1851," *Annals*, Association of American Geographers, 59 (1969): 417–40.

10 R.L. Gentilcore, "The Beginnings of Settlement in the Niagara Peninsula (1782-1792)," *Canadian Geographer* 7 (1963): 72–82, and K. Kelly, "Wheat Farming in Simcoe County . . . ," *Canadian Geographer* 15 (1971): 95–112.

11 John Howison, *Sketches of Upper Canada, Domestic, Local, and Characteristic* . . . (Edinburgh: Oliver and Boyd, 1821; reprinted in Coles Canadiana Collection), 193, 146.

12 W.H. Smith, *Smith's Canadian Gazetteer* . . . , 1846, p. 244.

13 A.R.M. Lower provides the classical analysis in "The Trade in Square Timber" (1933), reprinted in W.T. Easterbrook and M.H. Watkins, eds., *Approaches to Canadian Economic History*, Carleton Library no. 31 (1967), 28–48.

14 Frederick H. Armstrong, *Handbook of Upper Canadian Chronology and Territorial Legislation* (London, Ont.: University of Western Ontario, 1967), 137, 149 *passim*.

15 Peter G. Goheen, *Victorian Toronto, 1850 to 1900: Pattern and Process of Growth*, University of Chicago, Department of Geography, Research Paper no. 127 (1970), 49. A standard source is Donald Kerr and Jacob Spelt, *The Changing Face of Toronto — A Study in Urban Geography*, Memoir 11, Geographical Branch, Canada Dept. of Mines and Technical Surveys, Ottawa, 1965.

16 F.H. Armstrong, "The Toronto Directories and the Negro Community in the Late 1840s," *Ontario History* 61 (1969): 111–19.

17 John George Lambton, Lord Durham, *The Report of the Earl of Durham* . . . , new ed. (London: Methuen, 1902), 155, 158; W.H. Smith, *Smith's Canadian Gazetteer* (Toronto, 1846), 242; Lillian F. Gates, *Land Policies of Upper Canada*, Canadian Studies in History and Government no. 9 (Toronto: University of Toronto Press, 1968), 139, 140.

18 Fred Landon, *Western Ontario and the American Frontier* [1941], Carleton Library no. 34 (Toronto: McClelland and Stewart, 1967), Foreword, *passim*.

"Woman . . . Is a Very Interesting Creature": Some Women's Experiences in Early Upper Canada

JANE ERRINGTON

In 1802, the *Niagara Herald* reprinted a short article on "Traits of Women — from Sacred History." "Woman, with all her weaknesses, is a very interesting creature," it began. "Without her we should sometimes have fewer troubles; but should have no joys." The author, "Philo Billos," then proceeded to explain that woman was created by God to be a "help mate" for man. "Bone of [his] bone, flesh of [his] flesh," Eve initiated Adam into the "sacred rites of marriage." She gave him love and support and made his life whole. Truly, woman was "the last, best gift of heaven."[1]

Although it is almost invisible in written history, there is no question that at the turn of the nineteenth century, many Upper Canadians recognized the important contribution that their women were making to the development of colonial society. Certainly, the natural increase in the colonial population depended on the ability and willingness of women to bear children. Just as important, Upper Canadian women — the colony's daughters, wives, mothers, school mistresses, and scullery maids — were dedicating their labour, their thoughts, and all their energy to establishing and maintaining a strong, stable society on the North Amer-

From *Historic Kingston* 38 (1990): 16–35. Reprinted with the permission of the author.

ican frontier. Not only were women necessary, as "Philo Billos" concluded, for man's "happiness,"[2] but their presence and efforts were also essential for the survival of the colony.

Unfortunately, our knowledge of the lives of women in early Upper Canada is still woefully incomplete.[3] Few early Upper Canadian women left explicit records of their thoughts and experiences. Those who did, like their male counterparts, tended to inhabit the upper levels of the social and economic order. These records are invaluable, yet they tell only part of the story. The experiences of most women, the servant girls and tavern keepers, farm wives and land girls, have to be carefully and painstakingly re-created from fragments of the archival records — petitions, land and probate records, immigrant records and accounts, and surviving manuscripts, travel accounts, and colonial records. One of the richest sources for a study of women in the early period is the colonial press. The dozens of Upper Canadian newspapers published in the first two generations of provincial development provide the basis of this paper. *307*

Throughout much of the early period, Upper Canadian newspapers were the public voice of the political, social, and economic elite in the colony.[4] The views expressed in the press most often reflected the values that various provincial leaders were attempting to promote and inculcate as social and political norms. At the same time, local newspapers also provided residents with information essential for making the day-to-day decisions. Almost half the newspaper was given to advertisements and legal, military, and social notices which had little to do with the social and political ideals of the paper's patrons. Thus, the four pages (and later the larger editions) of the weekly paper unconsciously reflected the complexity of early colonial society. They provide the historian with a unique window into the life of the colony in its formative years, a brief picture of the rhetoric of what the colony was supposed to be, and the reality of some of everyday life. Women were an integral part of both worlds.

Even the most cursory examination of the colonial press, from its inception in 1793 (two years after the colony was officially created) to 1830, suggests that many leading Upper Canadians were preoccupied with the role women should assume in the community. Hundreds of articles and short stories appeared in the local newspapers extolling the virtues of the good woman, who eagerly filled her "natural," divinely appointed role as a wife and mother. On the frontier, where the wilderness posed a constant threat to social and political stability, she was expected to provide the primary defence of social order. The "good" woman, in fact, became a symbol for the type of society influential colonists hoped to create.

Ironically, the same newspapers that so assiduously portrayed the "good" woman, with happy children on her knee and a contented husband at her side, also provide the historian with momentary and often contradictory glimpses of another side of life for many, if not most, women in Upper Canada. Advertisements tell of single women landowners, shopkeepers, artisans, and merchants who acted alone, and many rather successfully, in the marketplace. Minutes of court proceedings document sexual, physical, and emotional abuse against women. Brief news items report instances of drunkenness, theft, robbery, assault, murder, and suicide committed by and against women. And perhaps most significantly, hundreds of desertion notices tell of a world of family strife and violence and apparently frequent marriage breakdown.

Undoubtedly a number of women in early Upper Canada willingly accepted the dictates of what American historian Barbara Welter has termed "the cult of true womanhood."[5] Like those women who trekked to the American West between 1840 and 1860, for some Upper Canadian women, particularly those of affluent and influential families, the frontier experience only "served to reinforce many conventional familial and cultural ideals"[6] of their former lives. There appear to have been a great many women in the colony, however, who would not or could not accept such personal definitions or social roles. This is not surprising. Frontier society demanded not social niceties but the physical participation of all residents, female and male, just to ensure survival. Indeed, this preliminary probe into the life of women in early Upper Canada suggests a dynamism and intricacy of relationships which mirrored that of society as a whole. Clearly, the rhetoric articulated by colonial leaders in the newspapers of women's place in society was often at odds with what many women were actually doing and saying — very much, it may be argued, as the political rhetoric of the time and activities of the majority of the population at large were often at variance.

I

To colonial leaders, there was no question that women were fundamentally different from men. It was not, many Upper Canadians explained, that women were "in any respect inferior to men, except in a few particulars connected with their Physical texture."[7] Each sex, however, inhabited "a separate department" in society and had correspondingly different "duties to perform."[8] The exterior world of the market and business "which was [admittedly] the most extensive" was the domain of men, who were naturally aggressive, keen of mind, and able to cope with the thrust and parry of business and politics. The "true" woman, with her "soft heart"[9] and "purity of mind"[10] rightfully belonged in the interior, personal world of the home. "Women," it was noted, "are not formed for great care themselves, but to soften ours."[11] As the vine which has long twisted its grateful foliage around the oak and been lifted by it into the sunshine," so too was woman "the mere depend and ornament of man in his happier hours." Yet, "it is [also] beautifully ordered by Providence that woman" was man's "stay and solace when smitten by sudden calamity." Like the vine, she wound "herself into the rugged recesses of his nature, tenderly supporting the drooping head and binding up the broken heart."[12] The one institution which enabled women to fulfill their natural, God-given vocation was marriage. Moreover, when women "stray beyond this, they are out of their proper sphere, and consequently without grace."[13]

In Upper Canada in the early nineteenth century, as in much of the western world, marriage was considered both the natural state of mankind and the basis of all personal happiness. Without a wife, a man was "a roving restless being, driven by pleasure, by romantic speculation . . . the sad victim of untamed passions";[14] an unmarried woman was denied real love and security and consequently became a bereft tragic figure.[15] Yet, to many prominent Upper Canadians in the early years of development, the institution of marriage was far more important than just a vehicle to promote individual happiness. In a frontier community, which lacked many of the social and political institutions which ensured internal stability and respect for authority, enduring marriages and strong families were the only secure foundation of a just, well-ordered, and stable society. Marriage was therefore a duty, articles and short stories in the Upper Canadian press explicitly and implicitly asserted, that both men and women owed not only to themselves but also to society. And it was the duty primarily of the wife, all asserted, to ensure that the marriage remained happy, productive, and secure.

309

> Happy is he, sincerely bless'd
> The man who by propitious fate
> Is of a virtuous wife possessed
> A careful, kind and loving mate;
> No cares nor fears his quiet can destroy
> Nor shake the solid basis of his day.[16]

First and foremost, to be a good wife, a woman had to be a good woman. Only "a virtuous and discreet wife,"[17] it was constantly asserted, could ensure that her home was "a temple pure and uncontaminated,"[18] a haven from the tumults and immorality of the world. In short stories, poetry, and specifically prescriptive articles (often purported to be by a mother or father to a daughter) printed in local newspapers, young Upper Canadian women were warned to guard their virtue and nurture those qualities which graced their sex alone.[19] Short stories graphically illustrated that young girls without innocence were brought to despondency and despair. A "ruined" daughter could never expect to marry and certainly did not make a good wife. An indiscreet, ill-mannered, bad-tempered, and faithless wife was a disgrace to herself and her family — violating the sanctity not only of her marriage but of society at large. The influence of a good wife, however, was incalculable.

"In the fate of a woman," a letter from "a Lady to her Daughter" in the York *Weekly Register* in 1825 commented, "marriage is the most important crisis. It fixes her in a state of all others the most happy or the most wretched."[20] And a woman's happiness or unhappiness in marriage was largely of her own making. A woman's first duty was to her husband — to love, honour, and obey him, to look after his temporal and physical needs and to be a lifelong support and companion. "It is the innate office of the softer sex," matrimonial maxims to married ladies maintained, "to soothe the tumults of others."[21] At all times, it was asserted, a woman was to be "never out of temper"[22] with her husband. "Sweetness of temper, affection to husband, and attention to his interests constitute the duties of a wife,"[23] one woman reminded her daughter. A father counselled his daughter, "a difference with your husband ought to be considered the greatest calamity" and one that had "to be assiduously guarded against."[24] This was despite the fact that men were acknowledged to be "prone to sudden passions and irrational acts." "Even the best men," a Mrs. Bennington noted in the *Upper Canadian Gazette* in 1807, "are sometimes so inconsistent with themselves" and have "some oddities of behaviour, some peculiarities of temper" so as to be subject to "accidental ill humour or whimsical complaints."[25] Do not, she and others warned women, upbraid or berate him. Rather, "study your husband's temper" and "deny yourself the trifling satisfaction of having your will or gaining the better of an argument."[26] A good wife can make a good husband, young wives were told. With tenderness, "a man's manners will soften" and his soul "will be animated by the most tender and lively sensation."[27] A woman's power, as well as her happiness, ultimately rested in her husband's esteem and love. It was in her interest, therefore, to preserve and increase it.

Women were not, however, to be completely submissive. Within her own world, a woman had to take an active and knowledgeable interest in her husband's concerns.[28] A well-bred woman was "well informed in every species of general knowledge,"[29] continuously cultivated "rational ideas about religion and general world affairs,"[30] and was able "to converse well."[31] Moreover, "the office of a good wife," one lady told her daughter, "includes the exertions of a friend; a good one must strengthen and support that which a bad one would endeavour to overcome. There are situations," she continued, "where it is not enough to love, cherish, and obey; she must teach her husband to be at peace with himself, to be reconciled to the world, to resist misfortune, to conquer adversity."[32] And although at least until 1830 the colonial press paid little attention to the specific and undoubtedly often tedious everyday responsibilities of running a household, it was generally noted that "domestic order and regularity"[33] in the home were essential. Women were warned to "let your expenses and desires be ever within the reach"[34] of their husbands' circumstances. If they did not, misery and dissension would inevitably ensue.

It was sometimes acknowledged that men did have some responsibilities in establishing and maintaining a happy marriage. A man and his wife were "equally yoked," John Strachan reminded residents of Kingston[35] and "the idea of power on either side [had to] be totally banished from the system." Yet, though the reverend gentleman declared that both should "yield one to another,"[36] in the case of dispute, the male head of the household had the final authority and had a right and a God-given duty to chastise his wife when she failed to perform her appointed tasks adequately.[37] It was ultimately the wife's responsibility to ensure that the marriage was a happy, satisfying, and productive union. "It is a fact incontestable," one leading Upper Canadian roundly asserted, "that he who finds his home a paradise will seldom stroll into the wilderness of the world." On the other hand, "the scolding wife and hot house have driven away many a wretched husband to a tavern or tipling shop, where cards, women and wine have sealed his own fate and the destruction of the family."[38]

II

Though the colonial press gave most attention to the duties a wife owed her husband, it was recognized that a home was not complete until the union had been blessed by children. Articles and stories in early nineteenth century newspapers almost never discussed sexuality within the marriage or explicitly considered the hardships of pregnancy and childbirth. They did, however, discuss at some length the responsibilities of motherhood. Certainly, there was no picture "more charming than that of an intelligent, virtuous mother assiduously instructing her infant offspring and using her daily endeavours to both inform their minds and fashion their hearts aright."[39] A mother should be "her children's best friend and possess their earliest love."[40] Parents, and particularly a mother, had to ensure that their children were well mannered, obedient, healthy, and pure of heart. This responsibility was considered especially important in the case of daughters. It seems to have been presumed that sons would be sent off to school or an office to learn a trade. Most girls, however, remained under the parental roof until marriage, and their mothers had a particular duty to ensure that their daughters were fitted to assume, in their own time, the onerous and important tasks demanded of a wife and mother.

"Girls . . . require much more care and attention in bringing up than parents generally suppose,"[41] a fictitious character in one of the many articles on the subject observed. Colonial mothers were reminded that "daughters are to be the mothers of the generation," and "a race of heroes and statesmen, men of vigorous minds and strong constitutions" could not be produced "from a pale, weakly, soft mother."[42] From their earliest years, mothers had to ensure that their daughters were healthy, prudent, virtuous, wise, and well trained in all the arts of wife and motherhood. The advantages of such training were many. It ensured a girl's later happiness when she was herself a wife; it taught a girl the advantages of hard work and discipline; and as one matron noted, it prevented the nation's daughters "from forming improper attachments" as youths.[43]

In addition to lessons in "the domestic arts,"[44] sewing and the gentle art of conversation, mothers also had to teach their daughters to prefer "substance to shadow; to admire solid rather than showy acquirements."[45] In dress and demeanour, girls had to learn to ignore "the tinsel arts"[46] and to appreciate restraint in words, actions, and relationships. Upper Canadians seemed particularly concerned with the apparently growing tendency of young girls to become fashion plates. "When I see others bringing up their daughters to look gay and dress fine, without instilling into their minds the principles of virtue," "Poor Robert" commented in the *Kingston Gazette*, "when I see more pains taken to furnish the outside of the head with laces and combs than the inside with ideas, I cannot help thinking that some doting lover will find to their sorrow . . . that 'he has got nothing but a squash.'"[47] "Modesty and purity of manners" were "the true ornament of women,"[48] it was asserted.

As the colony matured, and disposable income increased, a number of community leaders began to advocate that young girls receive instruction beyond that available in the home. "Nothing short of the refinements of education," mothers were told, "can give dignity and elevation to the female character; nothing can so well qualify them for participating to advantage in all the pleasures desirable for a mutual intercourse with the polished circles of life."[49] Not all Upper Canadians, however, accepted that women should — or, indeed, could — be educated. There were also some men who apparently distrusted educated women. Contributors to the colonial press frequently felt obliged to defend, sometimes quite vehemently, the need for formal education for women. "A woman's senses are generally as quick as ours," it was maintained. Those men who found educated women threatening were reassured "that where there is most learning, sense and knowledge, there is observed to be the greatest modesty and rectitude of manners."[50] Educated women were not to be shunned or feared; rather they were an asset to a discerning man, to his home, and to the future of their community. "She whose mind has been expanded and feeling so elevated," one concerned individual wrote in 1829 to the *Farmer's Journal*, "will have neatness, economy, and regularity in all her domestic advocations; she will never debase herself by associating with the vulgar and the mean; she will cheerfully discern that her dwelling is the centre of her companion's happiness."[51]

Although it is likely that not all residents were convinced by such assertions, after 1815 articles in the colonial press increasingly encouraged parents to send their daughters to schools. Between 1815 and 1830, at least a dozen schools for young girls were opened in Upper Canada, and by the end of the period, each centre in the colony had at least one "ladies' academy" that catered to those who could afford to pay fees.[52] Teachers, themselves women of the highest character and respectability, taught the standard subjects — English grammar, writing, spelling, reading, arithmetic, and geography. In addition, young ladies were "instructed in all that is necessary for a person of their sex." This included "all that concerns housekeeping," plain and fancy needlework, and lessons that "could be useful in the world."[53] Some also received tutoring in French, penmanship, and music, dancing, and painting. Moreover, and perhaps most important to parents, all the schools stressed that particular attention would be paid "to the manners and morals"[54] of the students. Soon-to-be wives and mothers could be safely left in the care of the school mistresses and masters, it was asserted; and it was implied that Upper Canadians were well advised to take advantage of such opportunities.

The appearance and apparent viability of so many academies for young ladies was, in part, an indication of the growing maturity and sophistication of Upper Canadian society. In the pre–War of 1812 years, few residents could afford to send their daughters to schools. After 1815, colonial society was becoming increasingly differentiated economically and socially. Now, not only did the most affluent and influential families accept and promote a special role for their women, but a growing "middling" economic group of colonists, the merchants and shopkeepers, well-to-do artisans, and landholders, also could afford and were apparently eager to take advantage of such a service. This group undoubtedly aspired to the social position of their "betters." And if they themselves could not attain it, their children, with the proper preparation, could.

313

On a broader scale, the growing numbers of ladies' academies were perhaps also an indication of Upper Canadians' increasing acceptance of the cult of true womanhood and an attempt by the patrons of such schools to institutionalize it. In part, many colonists were undoubtedly influenced by those social practices current in the United States and Great Britain.[55] In addition, though Upper Canada was still a pre-industrial society, the gradual social and economic diversification of colonial life was making the division between a man's and a woman's sphere of activity more distinct.[56] There seemed to be growing consciousness of place and position in society, which brought with it quite distinct and defined roles for men and women. Yet the press's advocacy of education for women and the growing number of formal schools for girls also suggests that many influential Upper Canadians remained concerned that their women were not adequately filling their appointed duties.

The rhetoric of domesticity and the image of the true woman were articulated and directed at the upper and middle levels of society — the wives and daughters of professional men, businessmen, government officials, and relatively affluent, well-established residents. And though obituary notices were but part of the rhetoric — often formulated in-cantations of social norms — they were a reflection of social expectations, and perhaps of some women's willingness to conform. After their deaths, the wives of leading merchants and other influential residents were ex-tolled as "possessing those virtues that adorn humanity and rendered them a pattern of their sex."[57] In life, many women, like Mrs. McGill, wife of the Solicitor General of Lower Canada, apparently "apprised themselves a tender wife, and an affectionate parent and a steady and sincere friend."[58] In life, they apparently had "possessed united with every elegant female accomplishment, a sweetness of disposition and an affability of manners which conciliated the warmest affection of all."[59] And in death, they invariably exhibited "the most exemplary patience and Christian resignation."[60]

Not all women in Upper Canada in the formative period were such paragons of virtue. There were a few, like an anonymous Mrs. Laughlan, who died, as a notice in the *Upper Canada Gazette* announced, as a result of having fallen into a fire while drunk.[61] And as the colonial press in-advertently indicates, there were many women who proudly worked out-side the home or who, finding that marriage did not provide the happiness or security so glibly offered in short stories and articles, left their hus-bands and homes to strike out on their own. Indeed, it is likely that for the vast majority of women in Upper Canada between 1793 and 1830, the rhetoric of true womanhood had little to do with the reality of their lives.

III

What is immediately evident from the advertisements, legal notices, court reports, and a few letters to the editor or short, apparently autobiograph-ical reports which appeared in the Upper Canadian press between 1793 and 1830 was that many women in the colony were and remained alone. Some chose not to marry; many were widowed, often quite young, and chose not to remarry. A number undoubtedly remained permanently sep-arated from their husbands. For many of these women, it seems that living all or a large part of their lives in such an "unnatural state" — either without benefit of a husband or working outside the home — was not the personal tragedy that the rhetoric of true womanhood sug-gested. Undoubtedly, the pioneering nature of Upper Canadian society encouraged women to assert their own independence.[62] Certainly, eve-ryone implicitly accepted that some women would become involved in some aspects of trade and commerce and in other traditionally male pursuits.

There were a number of occupational opportunities open to women in early Upper Canada which were not only quietly condoned but were

314

also essential for the well-being of the colonial elite. Upper Canada seemed to have a chronic lack of domestic servants. Until abolition, this problem was partly alleviated by the presence of slaves.[63] Before the War of 1812, notices frequently appeared in the colonial press from interested patrons who wanted to either buy or sell a slave, or who were attempting to retrieve a runaway.[64] For the most part, however, and particularly after slavery was abolished in 1804, most well-to-do Upper Canadians were dependent on mobile and apparently all too often poorly trained servants to meet their needs. Both women and men of "good character" and "sober and steady habits" who were willing to work for good wages were at a premium.[65] The hundreds of advertisements in local newspapers indicate that single women were in particular demand as maids, house-keepers, cooks, laundresses, companions, and governesses. Youth did not seem to be a criterion for employment. Frequently, genteel Upper Canadians looked for an "elderly single woman" with experience, to take on a responsible position "superintending arrangements of the whole family."[66] After 1815, advertisements from prospective employers began to be matched by notices of hopeful employees, most of whom seemed to be recently arrived immigrants looking for their first position. As a service to both employers and employees, a number of local printers after 1820 established "intelligence offices"[67] for domestic servants and la-bourers. Prospective candidates and particularly immigrants were encouraged to register at the local newspaper office, so that their credentials could be made known to interested employers.

Upper Canadians readily accepted single women entering domestic service. At its most basic level, this fulfilled what at the time were ongoing requirements of any upper class household. In addition, domestic service kept women in the home. It provided single women with the opportunity to develop and use skills considered to be most suited to their sex, and enabled those who needed it to earn a living wage within an apparently secure and natural environment. There were a few other occupations open to women which also utilized the special nurturing, homemaking propensities of women. Between 1793 and 1830, there was considerable call for wet nurses. In addition, a few women practised midwifery, though by the end of the period, professional male doctors were beginning to usurp this traditional female occupation.[69] The largest field open to women after domestic service, however, was in education, and the numbers of school mistresses and female assistants steadily increased over the decades.[69] Particularly after 1815, a number of young women, newly arrived from Britain, offered their services to affluent colonial families as governesses. Others came determined to establish or teach in the growing number of girls' academies. These educated and often highly trained ladies clearly took pride in their professional and commercial abilities and they received the approval and in some cases the patronage of the best of Upper Canadian society.[70]

In all of these endeavours, whether working in a household for wages or training the colony's daughters, these working women continued to conform to society's expectations and preoccupations. Even though usually unmarried, they nonetheless were engaged in occupations which demanded those nurturing, homemaking, supportive qualities considered peculiarly characteristic of their sex. Yet, it is clear that particularly in the early years of colonial development, other single or widowed women pursued careers in what was traditionally considered the "man's" world of the marketplace.

Advertisements in the colonial press confirm that a new widow sometimes continued to run her husband's business, as had been and continued to be the case in the United States.[71] Catherine Chesney, for example, informed the good people of York in 1812 that she intended to carry on her husband's saddlery business as usual.[72] Jane Marian "returned her sincere thanks to the public for past favours" and requested the continuance of the patronage her husband, Paul, had received in the "baking business and keeping a house of entertainment."[73] Notices in the press indicate that women also ran a number of inns, taverns, and boarding houses in the colony.[74] In addition, a few actively managed their own land.[75]

One of the most visible groups of public women were the "she" merchants, who established their own clothes and hat shops. The first notice from such a businesswoman appeared in 1808, when Marie de Dieman announced to the ladies of York that she was commencing "mantuamaking in all its branches" and respectfully requested their patronage.[76] Within fifteen years, she was joined by over a dozen women in Kingston, Niagara, and York who had all established "millinery, mantua making and hat shops," a number of which clearly became prosperous and expanding businesses.[77] Some women proprietors, like Frances Murray, began to take on apprentices[78] and by the end of the period, others had acquired specialized machinery for the making and cleaning of women's clothes.[79] In addition to the permanent shops, there were a few apparently well-respected itinerant saleswomen who regularly visited the colony. One of the first to arrive was a Miss Leigh, from Montreal, who brought "a fashionable assortment of frocks"[80] to the women of Niagara. In the 1820s, a Mrs. Metzner, also from Montreal, began annual visits to all the principal towns of Upper Canada, selling "an extensive and elegant assortment of millinery and fancy goods."[81] There was obviously a demand for such services, for by the end of the decade, some women were touring the colony twice a year.

Though women tavern owners and shopkeepers did not seem to conform to the behavioural norms established by society for those of their sex, their presence (and for some, at least, success) suggests that their activities were required and generally accepted. It must be stressed, however, that the notices and advertisements in the newspapers indicate that

316

acceptable opportunities for women's employment outside the home were quite restricted. The vast majority of advertisements placed by women merchants all concerned businesses which catered to a largely female clientele. There was no mention of women proprietors of a general merchandising or transhipment establishment, or of a transportation business. It seems that for the most part, women could be employed either in women's work, or to serve other women's needs. Thus, even in a frontier situation, where all were needed to contribute their labour to the development of the community and social expectations necessarily declined, women's activities were still restricted.

IV

Despite the presence of she merchants, landowners, and tavern keepers, most women in the colony were wives, mothers, or young girls preparing to take their appointed place in a man's home and apparently his heart. And yet for a great number of these women, marriage did not bring the emotional fulfilment or even physical security that stories in the Upper Canadian press so glibly guaranteed. Indeed, in the early years of the colony, relations between the sexes and even marriage itself seemed for many to be a perilous pursuit. In this young frontier society, where order and stability were often lacking and violence was quite common, women were always in a particularly vulnerable position.

317

Numerous reports from the courts and a few apparently autobiographical accounts in the press tell of a world where women were readily taken advantage of and abused. "In this small community," one matron in York wrote at the turn of the century, "unmarried women make up the majority; and it must awaken pity in every mind, not rendered callous by vice," she noted, "to witness the dissipation which reigns."[82] All too often, she observed, young girls were abused or raped by older men. Theft and violence against women were rife and illegitimate birth was a common occurrence. In almost all cases, the unfortunate girl, not the offending man, had to bear all the consequences. An unmarried, pregnant young woman was "invariably avoided by the wise and the good; we see them unpossessed of rank and respect,"[83] the matron noted. Certainly, the options open to such an unfortunate girl and her family were limited at best.

One, Mary Bowen, a single girl who was apparently pregnant, did attempt to stop her former lover, Thomas Harris, from marrying another woman. He was guilty, she stated in the *Kingston Chronicle*, of the breach of promise of marriage, "and by his false insinuations" had "caused me to go astray from the path of my duty to myself and my God and by that means has involved me in trouble and shame and caused the displeasure of my parent and my God to fall on me by depriving me of my home and communion which I formerly held with my brother and my God."[84] Subsequent issues of the *Kingston Chronicle* are silent as to Mary's success. One father, Mr. Fuller, did successfully take a Mr. Secord to court to recover damages for "the loss of reputation and services of his daughter."[85] It was the exceptional woman or family, however, who was willing to pursue the matter publicly in court or in the press. Most were forced to cope with the situation privately as best they could. The colonial papers sometimes reported instances of young girls who in desperation had killed their newborn infants in an attempt to hide their transgression or had chosen to kill themselves.[86] Yet it may be that illegitimacy, or at least pregnancy before marriage, was quite acceptable amongst some groups of Upper Canadians. In a number of cases, the young girl probably moved, or had her child and continued with her life as best she could.

318 For many women, their vulnerable situation did not seem to be improved within the bonds of marriage. Wife-beating was apparently considered by many men necessary to ensure the obedience of their spouse. Many women had to be tamed, like Kate in *The Taming of the Shrew*,[87] one anonymous Upper Canadian wrote. It was only when such acts "put her life in jeopardy"[88] that a wife was justified in defending herself, or in taking the ultimate response, leaving her husband. It was only in those instances which resulted in death that society became involved. Violence in marriage was undoubtedly exacerbated by the prevalence of alcohol in Upper Canada. Certainly, a common complaint of both wives and husbands was that their spouses were drunk,[89] a state which often led to verbal and physical abuse and sometimes led to death. Remedies for this were scarce. Women were told first to forebear and be forgiving, and change the situation by quiet example. Only if the situation became chronic should they take action, though the options society and the law made available to them were very limited. It is likely that physical abuse was one of the leading contributory factors which caused marriage breakdown in early Upper Canada.

In almost all cases of marriage breakdown, men considered themselves the aggrieved parties, and the law and society unquestioningly accepted this interpretation. The standard separation notices which appeared in the colonial gazettes were always signed by the husband, and placed the onus for the dissolution of the marriage on the wife, who had "left" or "absconded" or "eloped" from the home, usually "without any cause or just provocation."[90] A number of notices went beyond this standard formula and listed specific grievances. In some cases, husbands charged that their wives had left them "to improperly reside" with another man. A frequent complaint was that wives had "behaved in an unbecoming manner." This seemed to include everything from refusing to return, failure to perform her duty, neglecting her work, running her husband into debt, deserting her children, or physically abusing her husband, to the most serious instance of establishing a house of ill repute. In some cases, the husband was undoubtedly the injured party. Some women undoubtedly did abuse their husbands, verbally and physically. A number of women, like their male companions, did drink to excess; children were abandoned. Yet it was always women who in law were in the most vulnerable position. It was women who were most often the victims, and not the perpetrators, of emotional or physical violence. But the very fact that a wife had left her husband, whether by choice or by force, was enough to establish her guilt and "rendered her unworthy of being [a] wife."

Some men did seem willing to resolve marital differences. Often a separation notice would conclude with a plea from the husband that if his wife returned "she shall be cheerfully received and kindly treated."[91] And even when reconciliation was not possible, a number of couples were able to resolve their differences apparently quite amicably, as attested to by a few separation notices printed in the local press. John and Jane Milton of Kingston, for example, informed the public that they had "mutually agreed to part." The notice then detailed the subsequent division of property, which implicitly recognized Jane's ability and willingness to run the farm: she received a portion of the livestock and farm implements and the right to remain in the marital home. In addition, the two agreed "not to molest each other."[92] Such notices were, however, rare.

What was more prevalent was that for many men there was obviously no urgency in informing the public of the breakdown of their marriage. It was sometimes months and even years after the separation that a notice appeared. In some cases, this may have been the result of the husband's hope that his wife would return. Often, it seems that the wife had originally left the district and it was only on her return that a man felt compelled to absolve himself legally of all responsibility for the situation.[93] In a number of instances, men may have been embarrassed about their inability to control their wives. Regardless of the cause cited for the marriage breakdown or the apparent agreement or disagreement of the two parties to separate, it must be remembered that it was the husband who legally controlled the relationship and whose actions were socially sanctioned. Very few women could or would publicly challenge this right. What are therefore perhaps rather surprising and provide interesting insights into both marital affairs in Upper Canada and some women's sense of independence are those few instances when women expressly and publicly replied to their husband's charges, or even went so far as to take independent action.

Though in law, married women lost all rights to their property and a separate income, unless protected by a pre-nuptial contract, it seems clear that a few women did retain some financial independence and control of their property after their marriage. Magdeline Utter, in 1799,

319

for example, replied to her husband's standard separation notice that he would "not be responsible for her debts" by stating that the economic situation in their household was quite at variance with the "norm." "As the poor man had never paid any occasion or even any expense on my account, on the contrary, as he has expended considerable of my property for his debts and [I] am still dunned on his account, this is to give the public notices that I shall pay no debts of his contracting after this date."[94] Twenty-six years later, Mary Buckley of Kingston was prompted to insert a similar caution to the public against her husband Barnard.[95]

Some wives attempted to assert their legal rights to maintenance in other ways. Anticipating her husband's separation notice, Charlotte Reid of Kingston cautioned the townspeople in 1819 not to purchase any property from her husband, Dr. Reid, as she refused to relinquish her dower right.[96] Elizabeth Dieurran, also of Kingston, cautioned the public in 1814 from buying any property from her husband John, who had left her, "for there is no property which he can produce but that formerly belonged to me before marriage."[97] It is not known if any of these and the other claims which were aired in the local newspapers were successful. It is nonetheless clear that though most women were undoubtedly forced to accept a submissive and subordinate role in law, a few were not. This suggests an assertiveness on the part of at least some women completely at variance with society's and indeed the law's normal practices — an assertiveness that may have resulted from the frontier nature of early colonial society.

Most women who felt compelled to respond publicly to their husband's charges against them did not attempt legal remedy. They acknowledged their husband's "right by law" to forbid anyone "trusting" them.[98] What these women objected to were the causes their husbands cited for the marriage breakdown. Nancy Durham replied to her husband's accusation in 1799 that she *"prefers other men"* by stating emphatically that "in the sense you mean, the assertion is *false* and *scandalous.*" She continued, "in another sense it is true," however, "because there are but few men who less deserve any affection and none excepting yourself." Her husband, John, she charged, had tricked her into marriage and then left her for three years, during which time he had become a fugitive from justice. "I have never refused to do my duty," she asserted, "and share the disgrace you have incurred." And rather pathetically she concluded, "it is my fate to be tied in marriage to the basest of men."[99] Nancy Durham was obviously not alone in her plight.

In a very long reply to her husband in 1824, Elizabeth Sheltenburgh told the story of how her husband, John, had refused to make a home for her and to provide support, and was most often away altogether. "It is plain from your conduct," she wrote to the *Niagara Gleaner*, "that your sole object with me is to gratify a brutal passion without any trouble or cost to yourself." John, she charged, continued to come to her bed, despite his public renunciation. "You forbid the world to trust me," she declared, "and yet, wretched man, you can trust yourself asleep and unprotected in my very arms. Oh duplicity! Thou art personified and thy name is John Sheltenburgh."[100] In January 1820, Hannah Snider considered it a duty, not only to herself but also to her children, to set the record straight concerning her marriage. She had not left her husband. Rather, he "himself withdrew from me and his children," she stated, leaving them "without the means of support or bedding at that inclement season of the year." Moreover, she considered "it necessary to state that his conduct has been for many years past, marked with the utmost severity and a total want of feeling either to myself or his children."[101]

One of the most telling marital disputes erupted in 1819 between Catherine and William Woodward of Kingston. In a reply to the standard notice to the public, Catherine stated that it was not she but her husband who had "turned me off without provocation." To make matters worse, he had "traded upon her money" and had made a fortune, and had then abandoned her for another woman.[102] In the next issue of the *Kingston Chronicle*, William told his side of the story. During the nine years of the marriage, he wrote, he had "by industry and perseverance" improved and added to his property and the marriage had presumably been satisfactory. It was when his daughter, by a previous marriage, had arrived from the United States that tension and acrimony had developed. His wife, he charged, had used his daughter "in a shameful and unnatural manner." The subsequent two and a half years of constant abuse had forced him to propose a separation, to which Catherine had agreed. It was only after, he carefully explained, at his daughter's prompting, that he had begun to help and support his sister's daughter, whose husband had left her. He had provided his niece with "asylum in his house for the winter" and, in return, his daughter was receiving help in the management of the household affairs. It was "from this circumstance," he concluded, that his wife "thought fit to publish her ridiculous statement, and to endeavour to injure me in the opinion of my friends and traduce the character of an innocent woman. I therefore consider it a duty I owe to myself to caution any person from trusting the said Catherine."[103]

The rights and wrongs of any of these and other disputes are beyond the ability of the historian to determine. What is clear, however, is that in early Upper Canada marriage and the position of women in the home were often not what community leaders attempted to depict. Many marriages were fraught with tension, dissatisfaction, anger, and violence. Over 250 desertion notices as well as a number of brief reports and comments in the colonial press indicate that many relationships were not permanent or long term. Second and perhaps third marriages may have

321

occurred frequently, and marriage breakdown was certainly common, perhaps with the exception of those in the upper economic and social levels of the community.

The implications of this for most women in Upper Canada were profound. In a pioneering society, women had to take an active part, both in and outside the home, to ensure their and their children's survival. The constant demands of food, shelter, and family and the fluidity and mobility of pioneer life did not encourage or even permit the existence of purely separate spheres for men and women. Moreover, the pressure and constant toil imposed by the wilderness both contributed and exacerbated tension within a marriage. The apparently high incidence of marriage breakdown and of physical abuse reported in the courts indicate that many women in Upper Canada were never really secure economically or emotionally. By law and custom, they were expected to be subordinate to the male head of the household, whether husband or father. Yet, even within these restraints, a number of women in Upper Canada of all income levels took an active part in shaping their lives. Though many undoubtedly accepted the private world of the home as their own separate and unique sphere, when circumstances demanded it, a number were compelled or willing to abandon this and make a life for themselves in the public world of men.

322

These problems did not seem to have confronted that minority of well-to-do women in Upper Canada. Certainly, marital breakdown in the upper levels was not publicized in the press. The few specific references to the ladies who lived in the big houses show them as employers, not employed. Fulfilling their roles as nurturing, supportive wives, mothers, and members of society, they gave to the poor while secure in their own world. It was these women who were willing — and, it would seem, economically able — to embrace the cult of true womanhood and, at least in public, to present the image of "the kindred wife, an affectionate parent and the steady and sincere friend."[104]

V

In a pioneering society like Upper Canada, such divisions in life style between the rich and the poor, the well-established secure women and the many who were actively involved in the economy and working in the home, were inevitable. As the colony matured economically and socially, it is likely that the gap did begin to narrow. Yet, there would always be different economic levels, which perpetuated distinctive life styles, expectations, and activities. At no time would or could the rhetoric of domesticity, so important to community leaders, be accepted by all. The reality of women's lives and experiences varied too greatly and too many women were unwilling or unable to conform.

The result of this schism and its implications in the life of the colony as a whole need far more exploration. It is likely that it tended to exacerbate the already existing tensions between the colonial elite and the majority of residents. It may also have formed an integral part of the impetus to social reform which took hold in the colony after 1820. Before we can fully appreciate and assess the impact of varying roles and expectations of women in Upper Canada, however, there are a host of other questions which must be considered. What were the well-to-do women doing and thinking throughout the early period? What were their relations with their servants, with the poor, and with others of their sex? Was there a women's world quite different from that of men, with its own integrity and sense of unity based on gender rather than class? Did Upper Canadian law, particularly in the early years, meet the demands of a pioneering society in such a way as to alter fundamentally the British common law equity tradition? Did the bonds of true womanhood tighten and, if so, how was it entrenched?

323

The foregoing has made no attempt to address any of these questions. Rather, it is intended only as a preliminary probe into the lives, experiences, and expectations of women in early Upper Canada. Clearly, there is much more work to be done before we have any real understanding of the dynamics and undercurrents of a community which was the precursor of our own.

NOTES

[1] *Niagara Herald*, Aug. 14, 1802.

[2] Ibid.

[3] Women in early Upper Canada have received almost no attention from historians. In addition to Marian Fowler's collected biography, *The Embroidered Tent* (Toronto, 1982), there are Beth Light and Alison Prentice's *Gentlewomen in British North America* (Toronto, 1980) and a few articles and Ph.D. dissertations.

[4] Errington, *The Lion, the Eagle and Upper Canada* (Montreal, 1987).

[5] Barbara Welter, "The Cult of True Womanhood," *American Quarterly* 18 (1968): 151–74. See also Barbara Cott, *The Bonds of Womanhood* (New Haven, 1977).

[6] Julie Jeffrey, *Frontier Women: The Trans Mississippi West, 1840–1860* (New York, 1979), 106.

[7] *Kingston Gazette*, May 12, 1812.

[8] *Kingston Gazette*, Aug. 11, 1812. See also *Kingston Chronicle*, July 19, 1828; *Farmer's Journal*, Dec. 16, 1829.

[9] *Upper Canada Gazette*, Jan. 2, 1817; Jan. 1, 1825. See also *Canadian Freeman*, July 24, 1826; *Farmer's Journal*, Feb. 15, 1826; *Brockville Gazette*, Nov. 6, 1829; *Kingston Gazette*, Apr. 2, 1812; *Kingston Chronicle*, July 30, 1819.

[10] *Niagara Herald*, Sept. 12, 1801.

[11] *Farmer's Journal*, June 17, 1829.

[12] *Farmer's Journal*, Feb. 6, 1828. See also *Upper Canada Gazette*, Jan. 1, 1828; *Farmer's Journal*, Feb. 15, 1826; July 16, 1826; *Niagara Herald*, Aug. 14, 1802. The flower metaphor was used extensively by Upper Canadians when describing women. For example, see *Upper Canadian Gazette*, Aug. 26, 1796; Oct. 26, 1796; Jan. 20, 1825; *Farmer's Journal*, Apr. 9, 1826; *Kingston Gazette*, Apr. 7, 1812.

[13] *Farmer's Journal*, June 17, 1829.

[14] Ibid., Sept. 5, 1827. See also Aug. 2, 1826; *Kingston Chronicle*, Feb. 4, 1820.

[15] There were numerous satirical and didactic references in the press to the plight of the "old maid" during this period. A few examples include *Kingston Gazette*, Apr. 9, 1811; *Farmer's Journal*, May 21, 1828; *Upper Canada Gazette*, May 11, 1821.

[16] *Upper Canada Herald*, Aug. 23, 1825. A good deal of the poetry printed in the local newspapers extolled the virtues of a good marriage and a good wife.

17 *Farmer's Journal*, Dec. 16, 1827. See also *Kingston Gazette*, Sept. 16, 1827; *Colonial Advocate*, Dec.10, 1829; Mar. 3, 1826; *Niagara Gleaner*, Apr. 7, 1828.

18 *Upper Canada Gazette*, Aug. 30, 1800. See also *Kingston Chronicle*, July 19, 1829; *Farmer's Journal*, Dec. 16, 1829; *Colonial Advocate*, Nov. 8, 1828; *Upper Canada Herald*, Aug. 23, 1825.

19 *Kingston Gazette*, Dec. 10, 1811. See also *Niagara Herald*, Aug. 15, 1802.

20 *Weekly Register*, Mar. 24, 1825.

21 *Farmer's Journal*, Apr. 2, 1828.

22 Ibid. See also *United Empire Loyalist*, July 7, 1827; *Farmer's Journal*, July 11, 1827; *Upper Canada Gazette*, Sept. 16, 1824.

23 *Upper Canada Gazette*, Mar. 24, 1825. See also Sept. 16, 1824; *Kingston Gazette*, May 21, 1811; *Farmer's Journal*, May 30, 1827.

24 *Colonial Advocate*, Nov. 12, 1829. See also *Kingston Chronicle*, May 7, 1818; *Kingston Gazette*, Aug. 11, 1812; *Farmer's Journal*, Aug. 30, 1826; May 30, 1827.

25 *Upper Canada Gazette*, May 23, 1807. See also Mar. 24, 1825.

26 *Upper Canada Gazette*, Sept. 16, 1824; *Farmer's Journal*, July 11, 1827. Perhaps one of the worst faults of any woman was the tendency to nag and scold, and scolding women were frequently put to ridicule. See, for example, *Upper Canada Gazette*, Sept. 21, 1799; Feb. 14, 1801; Nov. 17, 1804; Mar. 24, 1825; *Colonial Advocate*, Nov. 12, 1829; *Niagara Herald*, Aug. 8, 1801; *Farmer's Journal*, Aug. 30, 1826.

27 *Kingston Gazette*, Apr. 16, 1811. See also *Farmer's Journal*, May 30, 1827.

28 Idle or malicious curiosity was never condoned, however, and there were several references in the press to the downfall of curious women. See, among others, *Kingston Gazette*, Dec. 17, 1811; *Upper Canada Gazette*, Oct. 19, 1805; Aug. 15, 1815; Sept. 16, 1824; *Kingston Chronicle*, Sept. 26, 1829; *Farmer's Journal*, May 30, 1827.

29 *Upper Canada Gazette*, Sept. 16, 1824.

30 *Colonial Advocate*, Dec. 3, 1829.

31 *Upper Canada Gazette*, Sept. 16, 1824.

32 *Upper Canada Gazette*, Mar. 24, 1825. See also Aug. 30, 1800; Aug. 23, 1825; *Kingston Gazette*, Sept. 16, 1817; *Colonial Advocate*, Dec. 10, 1829.

33 *Upper Canada Gazette*, Sept. 16, 1824. See also Nov. 12, 1803; *Farmer's Journal*, Feb. 14, 1826; July 11, 1827; *Kingston Gazette*, July 2, 1811; *Colonial Advocate*, Dec. 30, 1828.

34 *Farmer's Journal*, July 11, 1829. See also *Colonial Advocate*, Nov. 12, 1829.

35 *Kingston Gazette*, Aug. 11, 1811.

36 Ibid. See also Apr. 16, 1811; June 11, 1811; Aug. 11, 1812; *Kingston Chronicle*, May 7, 1819; *United Empire Loyalist*, July 7, 1827; *Farmer's Journal*, July 11, 1827; Aug. 30, 1826.

37 The right of a husband to punish his wife, physically if need be, was rarely discussed in specific terms in the many articles and short stories of instructions. Yet, in many, that was certainly implied (*Colonial Advocate*, Apr. 12, 1827) and as noted in subsequent discussion, many women were beaten by their husbands.

38 *Farmer's Journal*, Aug. 30, 1826. This was the conclusion that appeared in almost all articles of advice to married women. See previous references.

39 Ibid. See also Aug. 5, 1826; Oct. 6, 1827; Mar. 1, 1828; *Niagara Gleaner*, June 4, 1825; *Farmer's Journal*, Oct. 16, 1829.

40 Ibid.

41 *Kingston Gazette*, Dec. 3, 1811. See also Aug. 18, 1812; *Farmer's Journal*, Sept. 26, 1827; *Upper Canada Gazette*, Aug. 3, 1805.

42 *Kingston Gazette*, Aug. 18, 1812.

43 *Kingston Gazette*, Dec. 3, 1811. See also *Upper Canada Gazette*, Oct. 19, 1805.

44 *Kingston Gazette*, Dec. 3, 1811. See also Aug. 18, 1812; *Farmer's Journal*, Sept. 26, 1827; *Upper Canada Gazette*, Aug. 3, 1805.

45 *Kingston Gazette*, Dec. 3, 1811.

46 *Upper Canada Gazette*, Aug. 3, 1805.

47 *Kingston Gazette*, Aug. 11, 1812. See also Jan. 18, 1818; Dec. 12, 1811; *Farmer's Journal*, Sept. 26, 1827.

48 *Upper Canada Gazette*, Aug. 3, 1805.

49 *Farmer's Journal*, Apr. 9, 1828. See also *Kingston Gazette*, Aug. 18, 1812.

50 *Upper Canada Gazette*, Nov. 25, 1797.

51 *Farmer's Journal*, Dec. 16, 1827. See also *Upper Canada Gazette*, Aug. 3, 1805.

52 Advertisements and references to girls' schools which appeared in the colonial press are too numerous to list. Most schools charged tuition, and took girls from the age of 7. One school which does not fit those discussed here was a "nocturnal" school, established in York in 1810 for young servant girls who could not attend during the day. *Upper Canada Gazette*, Sept. 19, 1810.

53 *Upper Canada Gazette*, June 19, 1817.

54 Ibid., Nov. 27, 1817.

55 I argue in *The Lion, the Eagle, and Upper Canada* that members of the colonial elite consciously looked to the United States and Great Britain for political ideas and practices. It is likely that the same was true of social norms and beliefs. This cross-cultural interaction needs far more exploration, however.

[56] Ryan, in *Cradle of the Middle Class*, argues that the "frontier was, by definition, temporary" (p. 20), lasting at most only two generations. After settlement was secure and social and political institutions firmly established, the distinctions between the public and the private world solidified. See also Jeffrey, *Frontier Women*, and Ryan, *Womanhood in America* (New York, 1978). This has yet to be tested in the Upper Canadian context, however.

[57] *Upper Canada Gazette*, Dec. 14, 1798, noting the death of Mrs. Hamilton.

[58] *Upper Canada Gazette*, Nov. 25, 1819. See also June 17, 1824, Mrs. Consitt; Feb. 24, 1827, Mrs. Claus; *Brockville Gazette*, Oct. 23, 1829, Mrs. Racheal Wilter; *Kingston Gazette*, Dec. 24, 1824, Mrs. Grant.

[59] *Upper Canada Gazette*, Mar. 17, 1804.

[60] Ibid., Aug. 11, 1825.

[61] Ibid., Nov. 11, 1824.

[62] See Ryan, *Cradle of the Middle Class*, Chap. 1; Jeffrey, *Frontier Women*.

[63] See, among other references, *Upper Canada Gazette*, July 4, 1793; Aug. 19, 1795; Jan. 25, 1797; Oct. 4, 1797; Sept. 17, 1803; Dec. 22, 1800; Nov. 28, 1801; Feb. 22, 1806; *Niagara Herald*, Jan. 9, 1802; Nov. 7, 1801.

[64] The whole question of slavery, indentured servants, and apprenticeship needs to be fully explored in the Upper Canadian context. There are surprisingly few references to indentured servitude. See *Niagara Herald*, Sept. 21, 1801.

[65] There are far too many notices for servants to even begin to list them. Almost each issue contained at least one, and the number steadily increased throughout the century.

[66] See, for example, *Kingston Gazette*, Nov. 20, 1811; *Upper Canada Gazette*, Dec. 13, 1828; Aug. 27, 1818.

[67] *Upper Canada Gazette*, Dec. 11, 1823; March 29, 1828; *Niagara Gleaner*, July 30, 1825.

[68] See *Upper Canada Gazette*, Aug. 13, 1821; Sept. 13, 1828; *Colonial Advocate*, May 1, 1828; Oct. 10, 1829; Oct. 24, 1829. See also Wendy Mitchinson's work on the medical profession, including her article in Burt, Code, and Lindsay, eds., *Changing Patterns* (Toronto, 1988).

[69] Alison Prentice, "The Feminization of Teaching," *The Neglected Majority*.

[70] There are numerous references to this. See, among others, *Upper Canada Gazette*, June 3, 1826; Aug. 11, 1827; Oct. 20, 1827; *Colonial Advocate*, Jan. 20, 1825. Note that Mrs. Goodison's school in York was under the patronage of Mrs. Maitland, the wife of the lieutenant governor. *Upper Canada Gazette*, Dec. 24, 1822.

[71] See Ryan, *Womanhood in America*, Part 2; Mary Beth Norton, *Liberty's Daughters* (Boston, 1980); Linda Kerber, *Women of the Republic* (Chapel Hill, 1980).

[72] *Upper Canada Gazette*, Mar. 25, 1812.

[73] Ibid., May 7, 1805. See also May 8, 1808, and Oct. 1, 1821 for other examples of widows continuing their husbands' businesses.

[74] *Niagara Spectator*, Mar. 2, 1820; Apr. 4, 1825; *Colonial Advocate*, July 11, 1827; Aug. 2, 1828; *Upper Canada Gazette*, Feb. 9, 1828; Jan. 15, 1810; Aug. 21, 1817.

[75] *Upper Canada Gazette*, July 2, 1808; July 29, 1815; Sept. 3, 1818; *Niagara Spectator*, Feb. 14, 1817; May 29, 1819; *Niagara Gleaner*, June 11, 1825; *Farmer's Journal*, Aug. 16, 1826.

[76] *Upper Canada Gazette*, Dec. 21, 1808.

[77] Ibid., Dec. 19, 1810; Oct. 9, 1810; Sept. 11, 1817; Feb. 10, 1820; *Niagara Spectator*, Apr. 9, 1818.

[78] *Upper Canada Gazette*, Jan. 28, 1811.

[79] *Niagara Gleaner*, May 26, 1828; Apr. 26, 1826.

[80] *Niagara Herald*, Feb. 7, 1817.

[81] *Upper Canada Herald*, June 14, 1825; *Upper Canada Gazette*, July 7, 1825; Aug. 30, 1828; Jan. 21, 1828.

[82] *Upper Canada Gazette*, Feb. 14, 1801. See also *Farmer's Journal*, Oct. 11, 1826; Nov. 25, 1829.

[83] *Upper Canada Gazette*, Feb. 14, 1801.

[84] *Kingston Chronicle*, Oct. 6, 1820.

[85] *Colonial Advocate*, Aug. 19, 1824.

[86] See reports in the *Upper Canada Gazette*, July 27, 1805; Aug. 21, 1823; *Farmer's Journal*, Feb. 16, 1829; *Brockville Gazette*, Oct. 16, 1829; *Colonial Advocate*, Oct. 29, 1829.

[87] *Colonial Advocate*, Apr. 12, 1827.

[88] Ibid., Apr. 6, 1827; *Brockville Gazette*, July 24, 1829.

[89] See, for example, *Upper Canada Gazette*, Sept. 21, 1799; *Colonial Advocate*, Apr. 6, 1826.

[90] The following discussion is based on an examination of over 250 separation notices which appeared in the colonial newspapers between 1793 and 1830. Most were a single, standard "notice" or "caution" to the public.

[91] *Farmer's Journal*, Aug. 27, 1828; *Canada Constellation*, Sept. 6, 1799; *Niagara Gleaner*, May 19, 1827; *Colonial Advocate*, Aug. 5, 1830.

[92] *Kingston Gazette*, Sept. 23, 1817. See also *Upper Canada Gazette*, May 5, 1811; Apr. 22, 1812; Dec. 26, 1810; *Canada Constellation*, Sept. 6, 1799; *Niagara Gleaner*, May 19, 1827; *Colonial Advocate*, Aug. 5, 1830.

[93] See, for example, *Canada Constellation*, Dec. 28, 1799; *Upper Canada Gazette*, Nov. 23, 1805; July 2, 1808; July 29, 1815; *Farmer's Journal*, May 23, 1827.

[94] *Canada Constellation*, Oct. 2, 1799.
[95] *Kingston Chronicle*, July 21, 1826.
[96] *Kingston Gazette*, July 30, 1811.
[97] Ibid., May 18, 1814.
[98] *Canada Constellation*, Dec. 14, 1799.
[99] Ibid.
[100] *Niagara Gleaner*, Dec. 11, 1824.
[101] *Upper Canada Gazette*, Jan. 20, 1820.
[102] *Kingston Chronicle*, Dec. 10, 1819. The husband's original notice appeared Dec. 3, 1819.
[103] Ibid., Dec. 17, 1819.
[104] *Brockville Gazette*, Oct. 23, 1829, for Mrs. Wiltse.

Patriote insurgents at Beauharnois, Lower Canada, during the Rebellion of 1838. Watercolour over pencil by F. Ellice.

The inescapable fact is that the Patriot movement was a fundamentally masculine phenomenon, in its style as well as its philosophical orientation.

Allan Greer, "Josephte and Jean-Baptiste: Gender in the Lower Canadian Rebellion of 1837"

Topic Nine

The Rebellions of 1837–1838 in Lower Canada

The rebellions in Lower Canada followed a long period of constitutional strife. The appointed Executive and Legislative councils were predominantly English-speaking, while the Assembly was almost entirely French-speaking. In 1837, Louis-Joseph Papineau, an articulate bilingual lawyer, led a number of the Lower Canadian reformers into open revolt against the entrenched conservative elite who retained control of the provincial revenue.

Were the causes of the uprisings of 1837–38, however, purely political? Did the Patriotes, in rebellion, present a united front against British rule? What would women have gained from a Patriote victory? Why were the British able to suppress the insurrections of 1837–38 so quickly? In his short contribution "The Insurrections," from *Canada: Unity in Diversity*, Fernand Ouellet introduces the economic as well as the political factors that contributed to the Rebellions of 1837–38. Allan Greer looks at the revolutionaries' attitudes toward women in his "Josephte and Jean-Baptiste: Gender in the Lower Canadian Rebellion of 1837." Valuable information on Louis-Joseph Papineau also appears in Topic Ten, in the reading by Cole Harris (see "Of Poverty and Helplessness in Petite-Nation"). Elinor Kyte Senior adds the military dimension to the discussion of the revolutionaries' defeat in "Suppressing Rebellion in Lower Canada: British Military Policy and Practice, 1837–38."

Fernand Ouellet's *Lower Canada, 1791–1840* (Toronto: McClelland and Stewart, 1980) is essential for any understanding of the Lower Canadian rebellion. Helen Taft Manning's *The Revolt of French Canada, 1800–1835* (Toronto: Macmillan, 1962), an older study, covers the constitutional struggle. A popular account is Joseph Schull's *Rebellion* (Toronto: Macmillan, 1971). Ramsay Cook has edited a valuable collection of essays on the background to the rebellion, entitled *Constitutionalism and Nationalism in Lower Canada* (Toronto: University of Toronto Press, 1969). For the agricultural situation in the 1830s, see R.M. McInnis, "A Reconsideration of the State of Agriculture in Lower Canada in the First Half of the Nineteenth Century," in *Canadian Papers in Rural History*, ed. Donald H. Akenson, vol. 3 (1982), 9–49, and Allan Greer's important study *Peasant, Lord and Merchant: Rural Society in Three Quebec Parishes, 1740–1840* (Toronto: University of Toronto Press, 1985). In *Les Rebellions de Canada 1837–1838* (Montréal: Éditions du Boréal Express, 1983), historian Jean-Paul Bernard includes a summary of the various interpretations of the Lower Canadian uprisings. Elinor Kyte Senior reviews the military history of the rebellions in *Redcoats and Patriotes: The Rebellions in Lower Canada, 1837–38* (Stittsville, Ont.: Canada's Wings, 1985). Parallel developments in Upper Canada are reviewed by Colin Read in *The Rebellion of 1837 in Upper Canada*, Canadian Historical Association, Historical Booklet no. 46 (Ottawa: CHA, 1988).

For the impact of the rebellions see Jacques Monet, *The Last Cannon Shot: A Study of French-Canadian Nationalism, 1837–1850* (Toronto: University of Toronto Press, 1969), and Maurice Séguin, *L'idée d'indépendance au Québec: Génèse et historique* (Trois-Rivières: Le Boréal Express Limitée, 1968). Chester New's *Lord Durham's Mission to Canada* (Toronto: McClelland and Stewart, 1963; first published in 1929) continues to be useful. For an overview of subsequent developments in the 1840s, see J.M.S. Careless, *The Union of the Canadas: The Growth of Canadian Institutions, 1841–1857* (Toronto: McClelland and Stewart, 1967). Micheline Dumont et al., *Quebec Women: A History*, trans. R. Gannon and R. Gill (Toronto: Women's Press, 1987) reviews the history of women in the St. Lawrence Valley in the early and mid-nineteenth century.

The Insurrections

FERNAND OUELLET

The Origins of the Rebellions

To understand fully the nature and real repercussions of the rebellions of 1837–1838, it is not sufficient simply to cite the reactions to Russell's Resolutions, any more than it is to emphasize the preceding political conflicts. It is just as important to take into consideration the economic, social, demographic, and psychological aspects of this revolutionary attempt, since it is impossible to believe that the rural population with its low level of education and its traditions could have been aware of the constitutional principles involved in the debate. They were not trying to promote a democratic society by their action. The reaction of the habitant sprang from sources more intimately connected with his everyday existence and his mental outlook.

Nor is it correct to assume that the insurrection was in the hands of isolated individuals, drawn at random from all social strata. Rather,

From *Canada: Unity in Diversity*, ed. Paul Cornell, Jean Hamelin, Fernand Ouellet, and Marcel Trudel (Toronto: Holt, Rinehart and Winston, 1967). Reprinted with the permission of the author.

it was the activating of certain social groups and the reacting of others against them. This indicates that a certain amount of cooperation was taking place among individuals working to transform society to conform to their common ideals. A knowledge of this social background is indispensable to the understanding of the events that ushered in the establishment of a new order.

THE ECONOMIC INSTABILITY

The economic trends taking form at the turn of the century were thrown into sharper relief after 1815. As the decline of the fur trade gathered momentum, the agricultural situation of Lower Canada was becoming more critical. The lower prices which had prevailed for so long accentuated the problems facing the inhabitants of Lower Canada. This economic crisis was not, however, universal. The development of the lumbering industry and the expansion of agriculture in Upper Canada, in spite of violent fluctuations, did a great deal to alleviate the existing problems. Nevertheless, the economic situation remained, on the whole, unfavourable.

331

The decline in wheat production, in spite of occasional increases, continued without interruption after the War of 1812. Surpluses for export became progressively smaller, until after 1832 the deficits became chronic. At this stage the consumer in Lower Canada was obliged to import a large part of the grain necessary for subsistence either from Upper Canada or from the United States. The decline could not be attributed to a lesser demand from foreign markets, for as time went on these demands increased. Nor was its main cause the epidemic of wheat rust, since this did not occur in full force until 1835. It was owing, rather, to the continuance of outmoded techniques which inevitably caused an exhaustion of the land; however, it has a much greater significance for it was an expression of the deep agricultural crisis existent in Lower Canada during these times.

This decisive turn of events resulted in the restriction of agricultural production until it was aimed at mere subsistence. The habitant, in order to feed himself, was obliged to increase the number of his cattle and swine and resort to replacement crops, such as the potato, that had no foreign outlets. Furthermore, the impoverished farmer found it more difficult to obtain textiles and wools imported from Great Britain, and therefore was forced to devote more attention to the raising of sheep and the production of linen. In concentrating his efforts in this direction the habitant, instead of participating in the internal markets, was rather obeying a defence mechanism which led him to assert his agricultural independence. This reaction explains why Lower Canada remained a heavy importer of dairy products and butchered meats during this period. Technical progress did not keep pace with the increase in the quantities produced. Thus, after 1832, when the crisis forced the agricultural producer to substitute commodities, he was inevitably forced to watch a reduction in animal husbandry.

The extent of the crisis became more apparent as 1837 approached; it plunged the peasantry into debt, imperilled patrimonies, and engendered rancour and discontent. Instead of looking for a remedy to his problems through technical improvements, the French-Canadian farmer was led to look outward for the responsibility for his misfortunes. The political elite, although occasionally rather patronizing toward the agricultural groups, did help the farmers to find scapegoats in the capitalist, the immigrant, the local government, and, before long, in the British Government as well — in a word, the *English*.

THE DECLINE IN PRICES

After 1815, the habitant was faced with further difficulties — a universal fall in prices. This fall was consistent in spite of several vacillations and had a profound effect on the regional economics. It accented the seriousness of a problem already critical. The peasants' revenue tended to fluctuate in direct proportion to the general price vacillations, as did the salaries of city workers and agricultural labourers. The pressure affected even the seigneurs who reacted to it by demanding more from their tenants. Neither the business classes, nor the liberal professions escaped it. Profits were directly threatened by the economic situation, and this forced the merchants to look for solutions to the problems.

THE NEW IMAGE OF THE SEIGNEURIAL SYSTEM

During these years the seigneurial system acquired an image that was considerably less benevolent than before. The idea of profit had by this time penetrated deep into this stratum of society and became more and more a motivating force. The seigneurs, whether they were businessmen, descendants of the older families, lawyers, or ecclesiastics, were sensitive to the implications of the new definition of property. Property was becoming more mobile and took on a more personalized and intrinsic character. The new outlook and behaviour of the seigneurs is partly explained by the economic situation.

The new practices were most pronounced in the seigneuries owned by merchants where disposable land was more abundant. With a view to increasing the value of landed property and seigneurial rights, the holders of seigneuries restrained the rate of land concession. Not having the right to sell unsettled or uncleared land, the seigneurs did it indirectly. They demanded a gratuity (*pot-de-fin*) from those inhabitants desirous of obtaining a concession; or even transferred parcels of land to friends, retrieved them for non-clearance, and then sold them afterward. If, in the older seigneuries, whose rates had been fixed at a time of rising prices, the proprietors confined themselves to exercising their rights, other seigneurs did not hesitate to raise the rates of *cens et rentes*. They also redoubled their own privileged rights in contracts and restored privileges that had fallen out of use, even going so far as to establish new rights. In addition, the surge in the lumbering business led all seigneurs, whatever their initial origin, to reserve the wood on their lands for themselves.

The seigneurial regime, which the merchants, even those who owned seigneuries, wished to abolish, became an increasingly heavy burden for the habitants. But the political upper castes were watchful. Fearing that the peasants would turn their aggressiveness upon this institution, which they considered as being of ultimate national value, the French-Canadian political leaders tried to divert the rural discontent against the English merchants, the habitant's main creditors. In this manner they hoped to preserve French Civil Law.

333

LUMBERING

The preferential tariffs promoted considerable expansion in the exploitation of the forests during this period by supporting two sectors of the economy: naval construction, with its centre in Quebec, and the export of lumber which spread most of its benefits in the same area. At such a difficult time, lumbering had a profound significance. Not only did it sustain an important section of the middle classes, but it provided a wage to a large portion of the population, both urban and rural. This business tended, therefore, to temper the shock produced by the agricultural crisis and the drop in prices and to lessen the effect of the seigneurs' reaction to these events. It is of note that the political and social conflicts did not degenerate into a general crisis until the time when lumbering began to follow the other industries down the road of decline. These recessions, especially in the lumbering industry, never lasted more than a year or two. It might also be said that, in the circumstances, the British regime had been saved by the lumbering industry.

DEMOGRAPHIC PRESSURE

Astonishing as it may seem, the rate of increase of the French-Canadian population remained the same during this entire period. It is evident (taking into account the economy at this period) that the population as a whole tended to become poorer year by year. The land not only produced less, but it became scarcer throughout the entire seigneurial region. By about 1820 the majority of the seigneuries were overpopulated or nearly so. The habitant was no longer able to settle his sons around him and felt that he was witnessing the dissolution of the family.

It was at this stage that the migrations began. Some of the emigrants were content to leave the seigneurie and move to the townships where they might settle near their former parishes. Others left their original localities and went further afield in search of land. A final group began to emigrate to the United States, a trend that continued and expanded during the nineteenth century.

The habitant had become, naturally enough, extremely sensitive to the problem of land. He felt limited in his natural expansion by the borders of the townships; and since he was frequently in debt, he feared he would lose the small portion of soil that was his basis of security. He held the government responsible for the scarcity of seigneurial land and reproached it for not converting the townships into seigneuries, and so giving him access to all the land in Lower Canada. He reproached the capitalists for their desire to possess land which he regarded as his right.

334

This hostility toward the capitalists and the State expressed itself most forcibly in the attitude toward the English immigrant. Immigration after 1815, instead of being a modest flow as before, became an actual tidal wave; and in the eyes of the rural French Canadian the immigrant was a competitor for land and employment; therefore, he represented a vital danger both to the rural population and to the inhabitants of the towns. The pressure of overpopulation, then, as it was experienced by the rural groups, promoted the racial conflicts to the same degree as the agricultural crisis.

SOCIAL ILLS

The social misunderstandings were not solely the product of economic conditions, but were caused as well by purely social factors that in themselves implied conflicts of ideals and interest. The economic situation merely threw into bold relief the ambitions of the different groups composing the society.

Obviously the economic problem preoccupied the merchant classes most. The decline in the cultivation of wheat in Lower Canada affected the business groups, who tried to revive its traffic by encouraging the clearance of new lands. The merchants, therefore, attached considerable importance to the development of Upper Canada. Having lost all hope of a renewal of agriculture in the lower province, these merchants looked to the immigrants as the only future hope for economic improvement. But the drop in prices and the distances between the centres of production necessitated a lowering in transportation costs; especially at a time when the Erie Canal, finished in 1825, had strengthened American competition to the point where it was seriously threatening the leadership of Montreal.

The building of a road network the length of Lower Canada and the system of canals on the Saint Lawrence constituted the two essential measures needed to revive the economy of the two Canadas. These improvements were impossible to attain without government support and the cooperation of the French-Canadian members in the legislative assembly; for they implied a new concept in public finance and a reassessment of tax responsibility. In addition, the support of Upper Canada was of the essence in this mutually beneficial project.

It was not enough to agree to these reforms and organize credit. Since foreign competition was so strong, it was essential to firmly unite the efforts of the two provinces against the English free-trade movement that was battling with increasing success against the tariffs protecting Canadian wood and lumber on the English market. Finally, for economic and social reasons, the mercantile middle class demanded the dissolution of the institutions that were the basis of the old social regime, namely the *Coutume de Paris* and the seigneurial system. They were, however, content with an extensive revision of these structures. The proposed program encountered the determined resistance of the liberal professions and a large part of the French-Canadian rural population. In their discouragement, the merchant interests became more and more aggressive, and finally demanded, both in Canada and in London, the union of the two Canadas.

335

THE LIBERAL PROFESSIONS

The influence of the liberal professions, especially the French-Canadian elements, deteriorated during this period, partly as a result of economic difficulties. However, the excessive multiplication of professional practitioners as a result of the growth of the classical colleges was another aspect of the problem. The professional men were living for the most part in hardship and, therefore, tended to place a high value on the security of former times and to share the fears of the rural population.

The professional men came, more and more, to identify their own future with that of the French Canadians. Their mistrust of the merchant classes and the objectives they advocated became more extreme. They felt that the French-Canadian nation was disappearing as a result of the prevailing circumstances and the aims of the Anglo-Saxon group. The lumbering industry and the fur trade seemed opposed to their interests for they supported their political and social adversary. Their reaction was the same toward the banks and the preferential tariffs which the professional men saw as a gross attack upon individual liberty. The efforts of the merchants to modify the *Coutume de Paris* and to abolish the seigneurial system were regarded as aimed at depriving the French-Canadian nation of the institutions essential to the support of the social structure and its upper classes. The proposals to revamp the transportation system were regarded as the logical concomitants of this general program to undermine French-Canadian institutions. They believed that its only possible objective was to flood Lower Canada with English im-migrants in order to achieve union of the two Canadas, and thereby to drown the French Canadians in an Anglo-Saxon sea. The aggressive attitude of the more militant-minded British simply seemed to confirm them in their convictions. Above all, they feared the domination of large capitalists, Anglo-Saxon for the most part, upon whom a mass of salaried workers would be forced to depend.

Goaded by these fears and by their class ambitions, the professional men intensified their efforts to attain a greater control of the political structure, since it was at this level they believed that they might succeed in solving their own problems and those of the nation. Of course there were many who refused to look at the situation in such a tragic light, and believed in policies founded on moderation and a spirit of compromise.

But the most influential factions moved deliberately toward intran-sigence and radicalism. An unstable rural population exerted an addi-tional pressure on the decisions of the professionals.

THE CLERGY

The clergy did not remain unaffected by the trends that became evident after the turn of the nineteenth century. They were temporarily discon-certed by the rapidity of the changes, and did not hesitate in their reac-tion. The actions of the Anglican bishop, the State intervention in ed-ucation, and the attraction of the new liberal ideas upon the upper-class laity contributed to the rise of new problems. Under Mgr. Plessis, the reaction of the clergy went no further than an opposition to new in-novations. In addition, the clergy was deeply divided over the proposed establishing of a new episcopate at Montreal. But the founding of new classical colleges and schools, supervised by the curates, demonstrates that the episcopate had become aware of the need for positive action.

It was under Mgr. Lartigue that the counter-offensive of the clergy really began. Mgr. Lartigue, the first bishop of Montreal, a cousin of Papineau and a former lawyer, did not have the same prejudices as his predecessors toward nationalism. What he deplored most about this new ideology was its association with liberalism, that flower of the French Revolution. But once the idea of brotherhood had been excised, nation-alism might well serve to build up a society respectful of tradition and, perhaps, even theocratic in nature. Mgr. Lartigue had been educated under the influence of the French theocratic school of De Maistre, De Bonald, and Lammenais, a school directly opposed to the Gallican school of which Mgr. Plessis was an advocate. Thus his hostility toward the French Revolution and to liberal and democratic ideas was even more pronounced.

Mgr. Lartigue was not content to confine his efforts to waging a fierce and desperate war against revolutionary ideas and their advocates, but worked diligently to restore the moral and temporal influence of the Church and to make the clergy the accepted dominant class. In struggling against the Royal Institution and the legislative assembly's scheme for public schools he hoped to restore the exclusive jurisdiction of the Church over education. He felt that education on all levels (primary, secondary, and university) was solely the responsibility of the Church. Mgr. Lartigue, in addition to planning a religious revival in the population, worked to extend the social radius of the Church. The counter-offensive begun in these years carried on during the course of the nineteenth century.

Thus, relations between the liberal professions, especially those elements of it engaged in the political struggle, and the clergy had become increasingly strained. The attitude of Mgr. Lartigue during the rebellions of 1837–1838 stemmed from these social and ideological controversies. *337* Moreover the clerical influence had not been strong enough to prevent the *patriote* movement from exerting a large measure of influence over the rural population.

The Principal Actors

The critical economic situation, the pressures of overpopulation, and a society in which racial delineations tended to coincide with class boundaries, together formed the stage upon which the political drama was to unfold. The aims and policies of the emergent political parties remained consistent with the circumstances of the particular sectors of society from which they arose. It would be wrong, however, to underestimate the influence of the individual personalities in the foreground; for instance, the personalities and attitudes of the governors influenced public affairs according to their support of one group or another. Historians have frequently been misled by contemporary caricatures of the governors engaged in the conflicts of that time. "Francophile" or "Anglophile" were the most common descriptions, and these often obscured the real issues and occasionally led to errors in diagnosing causes.

Among the outstanding personalities, none stands out more clearly than Louis-Joseph Papineau, who was born in 1786 and was educated at the Quebec Seminary. His father was a notary who had been politically active since the establishment of parliamentary institutions. After leaving the Seminary the young Papineau decided to become a notary; dissatisfied by his studies there, he shortly thereafter chose law, which he also disliked. In 1818, he bought the seigneurie of Petite-Nation from his father. He would have liked very much to live there but his wife objected, and although he was attracted by the charm and solitude of country life, he was too much in need of an audience to enjoy himself fully in the country. In 1809, he entered politics which seemed to bring him the outlet he needed.

In reality, Papineau did not especially like politics. He constantly complained that he was engaged in a combat he was not suited for; and moreover, attributed his continuing this way of life to a sense of patriotic duty and an ardent desire to rescue his countrymen from the ills that threatened them. However he rationalized it, it is true that Papineau was not cut out for political life; he was a visionary and intransigent, and was disposed to take upon himself the perils threatening the French-Canadian group and to assume the ambitions and interests of the liberal professions.

At the outset of his career, he did not belong to the extremist wing of the *Parti Canadien*, but among the moderates; and when the question of a successor for Pierre Bédard and Antoine Panet arose, Papineau was the only deputy to finally poll the majority of his party's votes. It was only after 1818 that he adopted his extreme attitudes. He gradually became the natural leader of the French Canadians whose hopes he claimed to represent. A reformer until 1830, he subsequently came to desire independence and to wish for the establishment of a French-Canadian republic, with himself as president. His ineptitude in practical action, which drove him to specialize in verbal action, was the source of his setbacks. Despite his deficiencies, Papineau was nonetheless the most outstanding personality of the period upon which he left his mark.

338

The Political Conflicts

All these factors were transposed to the political level, where the fluctuations followed those of the economy and the society. Two political parties, representing different social and ethnic groups were locked in combat. The *Parti Canadien* drew its support mainly from the rural sector of the population and was led by an elite drawn from the liberal professions; the merchants' party was supported by the capitalists and landed interests, and rallied the British and the affluent. Until 1830, the clergy and the old seigneurial families supported or disapproved, more or less openly, the one or the other of the two parties, depending on the circumstances.

On the political scene there were as many irreconcilable views and opposing political ideas as there were in the social sphere. Each group wished to control the political structure in order to promote its own exclusive views on economic and social matters. Under these conditions, the constitutional issues were not, in themselves, very significant. If the legislature demanded "ministerial responsibility" and the control of finances, it was simply because they saw in these innovations a way to allow the liberal professions to assume not only political leadership, but also the social leadership, which would permit them to promote their concept of the future of the French-Canadian people. Until 1830, the French-Canadian political leaders were convinced that the mother country was not ill-disposed toward them; but the moment they believed that the latter did not favour the abolition of what they called the "reign of the oligarchy," they took the road toward political independence and the inauguration of a republican regime modelled upon the American political design. The *Parti Canadien*, which had become the *Patriote* party in 1826, was not truly democratic; but was dominated by a nationalistic ideology, and thought it could attain its reactionary objectives by means of democratic institutions. On the other hand the Bureaucratic party, formerly the merchants' party, in spite of its urge for innovation in economic and social affairs, took the opposite course, putting its faith in a reactionary defensive policy executed with a measure of realism.

After 1830, the political atmosphere deteriorated more and more until *339* the conflict between the legislative assembly and the councils, and between the lower house and the governors became so sharp that any compromise became extremely difficult, if not impossible. Elections were not only stormy, but they frequently gave rise to organized violence. During this period, associations were formed which merely aggravated the feeling of anarchy that reigned everywhere. The cholera epidemics and the acuteness of the economic crisis complicated the situation, and with the Ninety-Two Resolutions passed in 1834, the turbulence reached a peak. The extremists of both camps spoke of taking up arms, with the result that the slightest incident threatened to unleash an insurrection. The stage for revolution was set in the spring of 1837, when Lord John Russell presented to the Parliament in London a series of resolutions which constituted a total rejection of the demands of the *Patriotes*.

Russell's Resolutions rejected the *Patriotes'* demands for an elective legislative council and granted power to dispose of government funds without permission from the legislative assembly. The adoption of these Resolutions took place at the most inopportune moment. The agricultural crisis reached a new low; for the general crop failure, after several years of deficits that were more or less universal in the colony, had accentuated the discontent among the farmers. The recession in the lumbering industry and in naval construction, and the effects of a contemporary English financial crisis reached country and town at the same time. This critical situation added to the social instability and to the privations already suffered by the most underprivileged groups in society. On the political level, the atmosphere was even more strained as a result. The explosive nature of the Resolutions is understandable in this light.

A challenge had been presented to the *Patriotes*, which left them no alternative but to surrender or to take up arms. The first alternative was impossible in such troubled times; they could only turn to insurrection. It could not, however, be a spontaneous uprising, for practical preparations had to be made and some supplementary agitation undertaken to rouse the populace. Although the extremists in the *Patriote* party had wanted an armed confrontation ever since 1830, they had taken no practical steps in this direction.

The Pre-Revolutionary Period: April 1837 to November 1837

It is difficult to ascertain with any degree of certainty the *Patriotes'* decisions following the divulgence of the contents of Russell's Resolutions, since they took care to destroy any documents likely to appear compromising. It is, however, obvious that they followed a precise program, whose general outlines can be traced both in their actions and through various sources of information.

340

The *Patriotes* were not unanimous in their aims. Some believed that the English Government would never stop at the stand taken by Russell, and that the only realistic solution was to organize the revolutionary forces as soon as possible and throw them into action. Others, nursing their illusions, continued to believe that systematic agitation would be sufficient to force England to revise her policy, and that recourse to armed rebellion would be unnecessary. Finally the two groups, the former one led by Dr. W. Nelson and the latter by Papineau, seemed to have agreed on a single plan.

The plan included two distinct phases. The first was constitutional agitation which was either to lead to the backing down of England, or to pave the way for revolutionary action should the English authorities refuse to yield to pressure. The armed uprising was projected for the beginning of December. The so-called constitutional agitation occurred on three levels. Firstly, a series of large public meetings were held to stir up the populace in both the urban and rural areas. A boycott of regular imports and the use of smuggling was also prescribed with a view to combating the merchant classes. Thirdly, a show of force was to be prepared either by enlisting volunteers or some other means.

During the summer of 1837, the campaign waged by the *Patriotes* throughout the province produced the desired results. From one assembly to the next the fever mounted, especially in the rural areas. Although the leaders tried, by and large, to remain within the legal limits, they did not always succeed, and were occasionally carried away by the atmosphere they created. After July, others, particularly the extremists, did not hesitate to incite the populace to revolt, and numerous incidents occurred throughout the countryside. The founding of the revolutionary *association des Fils de la liberté* ("Association of the Sons of Liberty") increased the unrest in the city of Montreal. It had its counterpart in the *Doric Club*, a society equally counter-revolutionary.

Tension reached the breaking point when the *Patriotes* organized the "Assembly of the Six Counties." The speeches were extremely violent, and the nature of the meetings indicated that the climax was fast approaching. A declaration of human rights was issued at the meeting, and measures that were plainly revolutionary were adopted. It was decided that officers of the militia and justices of the peace, previously named by the government, were to be replaced by officials elected by the populace. The new organization set itself up to a certain extent as independent. From this point on the actual revolutionary phase had begun.

The Revolt

The increasing tension, which spread in the rural areas and the city of Montreal, was expressed with new vigour after the formation of the Assembly of the Six Counties. The British minority became alarmed and demanded that the government intervene, but the latter continued to interpret the movement asa blackmailing operation until the beginning of November 1837. Monseigneur Lartigue, Bishop of Montreal, was the first to feel it necessary to intervene; and on October 24, at the time the *Patriotes* published the manifesto of the Assembly at St. Charles, he sent out a letter unequivocally condemning the actions of the French-Canadian leaders. He condemned their revolutionary intentions and the liberal ideas that bore them, and implicitly formulated the penalties the Church attached to actions intended to overthrow the established order. In spite of this clerical influence the revolutionary movement swept on.

It was November before the government finally decided to act and ordered the arrest of the principal *Patriote* leaders. Some of them hid in the parishes, one small group headed toward St. Eustache and St. Benoit, and others went to St. Charles or St. Denis. Camps were established in these places as rallying points for the peasant forces. After the incident at Longueuil between the police and the *Patriotes*, the government sent an expedition against St. Denis which was repulsed on November 23, 1837; but two days later the government forces captured St. Charles, at which point the resistance of the *Patriotes* collapsed. Colborne afterward succeeded in pacifying the parishes to the north of Montreal, and St. Eustache fell to him in spite of strong resistance from a small group of *Patriotes* commanded by Jean-Olivier Chénier.

The rapid collapse of the *Patriote* movement was not the result of a lack of planning of the revolt, but of weakness in the leadership. The *Patriote* chiefs, as far as the practical side of their venture was concerned, showed themselves to be very poor organizers; in combat, they were lamentable. Only Dr. Nelson, Charles-Ovide Perrault, and Chénier were equal to the task. Papineau, the commander-in-chief, left St. Denis just before the battle; moreover, his conduct during the entire revolutionary

341

period was most inconsistent. His continual hesitation, his fear of responsibility, and his physical cowardice explain his flight in disguise, and account for a large part of the climate of anarchy that existed. It is true that the government forces mobilized much more swiftly than the *Patriotes* expected, but this is hardly a sufficient explanation. The French-Canadian leaders undoubtedly put too much faith in the ability of the farmer to act alone. Without well-established leadership, the habitants were a disorganized and ineffective fighting force.

The Mission of Lord Durham in Lower Canada

The revolt in Lower Canada and the troubles in Upper Canada profoundly shocked public opinion in England. The problems could not be regarded lightly. English political leaders now became preoccupied with finding the source of the problems and the nature of the conflicts, and with formulating satisfactory solutions. Lord Durham's mission was the result of this desire to rectify these ills.

Durham arrived in Quebec in May 1838 with two types of responsibilities. He was to decide the future of the political prisoners and set up committees of inquiry to study the causes of the uprising. All this was not easy. The atmosphere was extremely strained and each group seemed bent on securing official validation and forwarding its own version of events. Therefore, the commissioner had to avoid compromising himself in the eyes of all the different elements of the population. In such circumstances, impartiality would not be easy.

The most pressing task was to decide the fate of the political prisoners. Many different solutions were possible, of course, but Durham was quick to realize that trial by jury was unthinkable. With emotions running high, justice could not have been dispensed fairly whatever the jury chosen. On the other hand, a trial without a jury would have resulted in a long series of particularly severe condemnations. The great volume of proof accumulated against the *Patriote* leaders guaranteed this. Wishing to avoid another popular uprising, Durham preferred another solution. He freed those prisoners who had played only a subordinate role in the insurrection, but showed more severity toward the principal instigators of the movement, exiling them to Bermuda. Those who had escaped to the United States he forbade to return under threat of punishment.

During this time, the committees formed by Durham were accumulating a large body of material dealing with all aspects of life in Lower Canada and in the other colonies. With the help of this material and his own personal observations, Durham was soon in a position to diagnose the problems of Lower Canada. Influenced by the European climate of ideas, "Radical Jack" had thought he would find a genuine liberal conflict in Canada. He did discover traces of it, especially in Upper

Canada, but to him it seemed that the conflict in Lower Canada had an entirely different character. The intensity of the racial conflict, which the liberal element masked but did not hide, seemed to him the most striking feature in the colony. "I found two nations warring in the bosom of a single State. . . . "

According to Durham, these two nations not only possessed different characteristics of language, race, and religion, but they differed in their degree of evolution as well. The French-Canadian society, he assumed, was essentially static and destined, as a result of its outlook, to remain so. The British, on the other hand, were sensitive to currents of progress in all their forms. Influenced by the atmosphere that existed in the society at the time of his stay, Durham finally concluded that the French sector was forever entrenched in inferiority and obstruction. He even saw in this element some organic and immutable tendency to be so. Hence the extreme nature of some of his recommendations.

Therefore, because he had observed the struggle at its greatest intensity, Durham saw no other solution to the ethnic problem except the assimilation of French Canadians into the English culture. For this reason he recommended the union of the Canadas and the undertaking of a policy aimed at absorbing the French group into the Anglo-Saxon. His *raciste* attitude was based on a distorted view of relations between the ethnic groups. Apart from the establishment of the union, necessary for other reasons, his solution was illusory. The future progress of Canada did not depend on the destruction of French culture, but on a change in attitude on the part of the French-Canadian population toward progress. In this sense, the French Canadians themselves held the key. By reversing their stand, they might prove Durham's conclusion unfounded. Instead of promoting assimilation, the union of the Canadas would prove to be no more than a means of achieving a number of economic and institutional reforms.

In his *Report*, which was published in the spring of 1839, Durham perceived another reform as indispensable as the union — the establishment of responsible government. His recommendation is not, of itself, startling. The commissioner had long been one of the main proponents of the English liberal movement, and even bore the reputation of being a radical. His background, together with a desire to find a solution to certain Canadian problems, explains Durham's proposal for ministerial responsibility. His recommendation seemed to him to be in tune with the natural evolution of the British Empire toward a thorough remoulding of its colonial structures. Ministerial responsibility, for Durham, was to be the political expression of this development, implying an increased autonomy of the colonies. It is from this point of view that the Durham Report marked a step toward the complete reform realized in 1848.

Fortunately, the enormous amount of work accomplished by his committees allowed Durham time to accumulate the information necessary to draw up his report, because his mission ended abruptly in 1838. He

343

learned that the government in London had just overruled the decision he had made regarding the political prisoners. There was no other alternative under the circumstances but to tender his resignation.

The Second Outbreak: November 1838

A few days after Durham's departure another insurrection broke out in Lower Canada which was not, however, linked to the events surrounding his mission. It was, rather, a movement organized at long range by the Canadian refugees in the United States. After the setback of 1837, the *Patriotes* had never ceased to dream of avenging themselves; but deeply divided, they needed more than six months to recover and to agree on a new plan.

However, after July 1838, the *Patriote* leaders, having more or less rejected Papineau, succeeded in achieving a certain unanimity among themselves, and in establishing the *Société des Frères-Chasseurs*, a secret revolutionary organization drawing its adherents from the parishes of Lower Canada. The leaders counted on American aid in their insurrection planned for November 3. They hoped to capture St.-Jean, Chambly, and Laprairie quickly, before marching on Montreal. Once Montreal was in their hands, they proposed to move on Quebec.

Events, however, did not occur as planned. On November 3, the *Frères-Chasseurs* agitated in all the parishes south of Montreal, and several thousand of them gathered at Napierville, where independence for the country was once again proclaimed by two of their leaders, Robert Nelson and Côté. Anarchy prevailed everywhere. Once again the leaders were found incapable of commanding the movement and guiding it toward the desired objectives. A large mass of people gathered at Napierville but the majority dispersed before seeing any action, and government forces encountered no serious opposition.

This resounding failure, followed by severe repressive measures, was to have a profound influence upon the future course of the French Canadians. In 1840, the *Patriote* experiment had completely collapsed, and men with different objectives assumed the leadership of the French-Canadian group.

Josephte and Jean-Baptiste: Gender in the Lower Canadian Rebellion of 1837

ALLAN GREER

> Do you want to know men? Study women. This maxim is general, and up to this point everybody will agree with me. But if I add that there are no good morals [manners] for women outside of a withdrawn and domestic life; if I say that the peaceful care of the family and the home are their lot, that the dignity of their sex consists in modesty, that shame and chasteness are inseparable from decency for them, that when they seek for men's looks they are already letting themselves be corrupted by them, and that any women who shows herself off disgraces herself; I will be immediately attacked by this philosophy of a day which is born and dies in the corner of a big city and wishes to smother the cry of nature and the unanimous voice of humankind.
>
> Jean-Jacques Rousseau[1]

345

> Women's role is not to be found in public life, the life of action and agitation, but truly in the internal life, that of sentiment and of the tranquility of the domestic hearth . . .
>
> Pierre-Joseph Proudhon[2]

> I see that this harmful philosophy is infecting everybody and that Rousseau's *Social Contract* makes you forget St. Paul's Gospel: "Wives, be subject to your husbands."
>
> Louis-Joseph Papineau to his wife, 1830[3]

Queen Victoria ascended the throne of England in August 1837, just as the tensions that would soon lead to armed insurrection in Lower Canada were coming to a boil. There is no indication that the seventeen-year-old monarch gave much thought to the political squabbles wracking her North American possessions, but the celebrations surrounding her coronation provided Canadians with an occasion to express their strongly held views for or against the British connection. It was the Te Deum ordered for the middle of August by the bishop of Montreal, as was usual on such occasions, that aroused the greatest controversy. At St Polycarpe, where the curé dared to say a few words in praise of the new monarch, local Patriots managed to stop the ceremony.

> No sooner did the *Te Deum* commence, than the people quitted the church bodily, leaving the women and *marquilliers* (churchwardens) to keep his Reverence company. The deputy beadle was beginning to ring the bell when the people got out, but the parishioners stopped him, telling him that the bell belonged to them, and not the Queen of England, and that it should not be rung . . .[4]

Note the language used by *The Vindicator* to describe this incident — the counterposing of "the *people*" and "the *women*." Half the population

This article, originally written in English, appeared in a French translation by Suzanne Mineau, in Revue d'histoire de l'Amérique française 44, 4 (Spring 1991): 507–28. Reprinted with permission. The English text of the article is included in Allan Greer, The Patriots and the People: The Rebellion of 1837 in Rural Lower Canada (Toronto: University of Toronto Press, 1994).

of the province might well have viewed these words as ominous signals, emanating as they did from the presses of a journal dedicated to the principle of popular sovereignty!

That this was no accidental slip is underlined by the sexual references in protests against the coronation Te Deum. In the parish of Contrecoeur a radical merchant led an exodus from the church shouting, "It is painful to have to sing the Te Deum for the damn queen, whore with her legs in the air." A Patriot orator addressing the people of Nicolet from the church porch was reported to have said, "As for the king, he is nothing but a big zero to whom Canadians pay a pension . . . The proof that kings are nothing but zeros is that we are now governed by a young queen seventeen years of age." Later, at the time of the battles of November and December, an American Patriot sympathizer got into trouble at St Athanase by throwing "ridicule on the person of the sovereign by saying the loyalists were governed by a little girl, that they were governed by petticoats."[5] Such language would certainly have shocked English radicals; they were well disposed towards the young queen, who seemed to them a much more sympathetic figure than her notorious uncle, William IV.[6] At the same time, it alerts us to the importance of gender in understanding the Patriot movement and the Rebellion of 1837-38.

The fact that the Patriots objected to monarchy, to British rule over Lower Canada, and, therefore, to the queen should come as no surprise. But why did they have to make an issue — and in such a cruel and personal way — of Victoria's sex? Well, certainly their sensitivity to gender was not unique in the international republican community of the period. Recent scholarship has demonstrated that considerations of sexual difference were of central concern to political writers and revolutionaries of the late eighteenth–early nineteenth century period. To the degree that they challenged existing hierarchies on egalitarian grounds and insisted that "the people" ought to rule, philosophes, Jacobins, and American Patriots had to grapple with the question of what "the people" was. It certainly was not all human beings resident in a given territory; that is to say, not everyone was to participate equally and in the same way in sovereign authority. Women in particular tended to be excluded from direct political participation in the republican city. Pronouncements may have been cryptic and susceptible to multiple interpretations, with much assumed and little expressed; the effect was nonetheless for gender to become increasingly the primary dividing line between rulers and ruled in the age of the great bourgeois revolutions. Partly this was by default, as older conceptions of political privilege based on birth, sacerdotal status, and so on came under attack, but also it derived from a profoundly gendered republican conception of citizenship.

Inspired by a particular reading of the history of ancient Greece and Rome, modern republicans such as Jean-Jacques Rousseau believed that men were uniquely qualified for the responsibilities of citizenship.[7]

They were better suited for military combat and, it was felt, all good citizens had to be prepared to defend their country on the battlefield. More fundamentally, Rousseau thought that males were by nature more apt to subordinate selfish and sectional interests for the good of the whole community. Women, by contrast, were necessarily associated with child-birth and nurturing; consequently, their orientation was to the family, a particularistic allegiance which they could not fully transcend without denying their nature. Thanks to their looser attachment to specific loved ones, men had the potential to develop the civic virtue — that is, the dedication to the common good — required in any healthy republic. It is important to note, however, that Rousseau did not consider women inferior to men. On the contrary, he attached great value to the loving and nurturing domestic sphere where women found their true calling. His effusions over motherhood and conjugal bliss underline the fact that, for Rousseau, women's familial role was the essential complement of active male citizenship. Domestic life and public life, he implied, were equally important elements of civilized existence. In order to discharge her duty, the republican woman needed to exercise a special sort of virtue: not public-spirited courage, but "sexual innocence and chastity" were her distinguishing characteristics and, as an outward guarantee of monogamous behaviour, she had to confine herself to the private realm.[8]

Rousseau was in no simple sense a male-supremacist; indeed, his contemporary defenders insist that he accorded a great deal of legitimate power to women, though it was covert power, exercised through their sexual influence over particular men.[9] Moreover, with his emphasis on liberty and on the cultivation of the individual personality, he can plausibly be seen as the intellectual ancestor of modern women's liberation. One need only extend to females the reasoning that the philosopher applies to "Man" and unsettling conclusions soon follow. (Indeed, the quotation at the head of this article shows that at least one Lower Canadian noticed these possibilities in Rousseau!) The fact remains that Rousseau himself did not present a feminist reading of Jean-Jacques. Everywhere one turns in his writings, the needs of men take precedence and women appear in a positive light to the degree that they are helpful.

I have dwelt on Rousseau, not because his works provided an instruction manual for Lower Canadian Patriots, but because he was one of the few writers of the period who gave sustained and explicit attention to the gender dimension of politics. Without denying the originality of his genius, I think it is fair to suggest that many of the essential features of Rousseau's thought in this area were characteristic of the international republican movement. Certainly echoes can be detected in the Patriot press of the notion that men and women possessed complimentary but fundamentally different moral natures. An article published in *La Minerve* under the title "Les deux républiques" makes this point quite explicitly.

> The moral world is a mixture composed of men and women and it owes to this combination the greatest part of its customs, usages, and ceremonies; if there were no more women in the human race, men would be unrecognizable. It is only in seeking to please the opposite sex that they manage to refine themselves . . . Women, for their part, owe everything to that other half of the human race, to which they find themselves joined . . . It is to the desire to please him [man] that they owe that gracious air, those eyes which say so many things, that modest blush which embellishes their complexion, that voice so soft and touching. This reciprocal desire is indeed a precious instinct in both sexes, one which tends towards the perfection of each of them. Thus a man with no interest in women will ordinarily become a savage; by the same token, a woman, intended by nature to get along with and to appear with man, can scarcely hate or despise him without becoming a ferocious and unbearable creature.[10]

Such sentiments were by no means limited to republican circles. Indeed, the basic notion that women belonged in a (valorized) domestic setting while men should run the state and the community became widely prevalent everywhere the bourgeoisie gained the ascendancy through the eighteenth century and well into the nineteenth. During the French Revolution, for example, there was some initial encouragement for the politicization of women, but it was soon followed by a policy of rigid exclusion from public life on the grounds that both the polity and the family suffered when women strayed into the male realm of active citizenship. Such treatment at the hands of the Jacobins led the feminist/royalist Olympe de Gouges to protest that "Women are now respected and excluded, under the old régime they were despised and powerful."[11] Earlier, American women had been treated similarly during "their" revolutionary war.[12]

But women were not always "respected" under the new order: witness the Patriots' misogynist and obscene verbal assault on Queen Victoria. In this respect, too, Lower Canadian behaviour seems to reflect widespread attitudes of the period, attitudes that are particularly characteristic of republicanism. While what one might call the "vulgar Rousseauian" outlook venerated the virtuous woman who kept to the domestic sphere, it was profoundly suspicious of any woman who ventured into the political realm. Quite apart from the fact that women were not by nature equipped to cope with public affairs, their attempts to take part in politics posed a direct danger to the hallowed conjugal family. This is because public life was conceived of in republican discourse as entailing a literally *public* performance open to the gaze of the community. And, whereas for men publicity was the guarantee of virtue, the opposite case applied for women. Self-display was repugnant to good women because it signified sexual immorality, just as surely as female confinement to private pursuits indicated chastity. As Rousseau put it, "A woman's audacity is the sure sign of her shame." Thus were the two meanings of the phrase "public woman" — that is, politically prominent individual and prostitute — elided in the republican mind of our period.[13]

Sexual disorder on the part of women, as evidenced by political self-assertion, was of course considered deplorable for all sorts of reasons, but it is important to note that it posed specifically *political* dangers from the republican point of view. When women forsook the family hearth, they could not support their husbands or raise their sons as good future citizens. More fundamentally, they acted against their chaste and modest nature; the result, since women are so important and men so highly dependent on them, was to denature men, to make them effeminate and therefore susceptible to tyranny. Thus it was that republicans tended to associate political corruption among males — and this of course was the primary threat to liberty — with sexual corruption among females.[14] It is when we recognize this linkage among public roles for women, sexual disorder, and political corruption and tyranny that we begin to understand why the Patriots could even conceive of accusing Victoria Regina — innocent, young, but undeniably a prominent public figure — of being a "whore."

A reader might well protest at this point that neither Rousseau nor the Patriots invented patriarchy. The notion that "a woman's place is in the home" and under the authority of her husband was of course quite ancient, as Papineau made clear when he quoted Scripture to chastise his wife's independence." What was new in the early nineteenth century was the peculiarly insistent emphasis on the "cult of female domesticity," and the concomitant male monopoly over public affairs. Under an earlier tradition (what one might call, in a very loose sense, the "ancien régime"), matters were less clear-cut, particularly where politics were concerned, and there was no justification for asserting that men should partake of the sovereign power of the state simply because they were men. Most people were regarded as *subjects* and, to that degree, men and women were politically on a par. Conversely, some women — from Madame de Pompadour in France to Madame Péan in Canada — did exercise great influence over affairs of state.[15]

The mass of the population was not supposed to have a political voice, according to the ideologues of absolutism, but of course they could make their views felt through the threat of demonstration, riot, and insurrection; and women often played a prominent part in these activities. In eighteenth-century French Canada, women were at the forefront in several community battles with Church authorities over parish boundaries, and protests over food shortages and rationing during the Seven Years' War were almost entirely the work of women.[16] Later, when rural insurrection broke out during the American occupation of Canada in 1775, women once again played an important role in many localities. At Pointe-aux-Trembles, two women went from door to door blackening the faces of all their neighbours who had cooperated with the British militia call-up. Elsewhere, it was reported:

> The widow Gabourie, nicknamed the "Queen of Hungary," has done more damage in this parish than anyone else. She often held meetings at her home at

349

which she presided and which tended to excite people against the government and in favour of the rebels.[17]

For many years, Lower Canadian women even enjoyed the suffrage, at least to some extent.[18] The legislation establishing the colonial government in 1791 had accorded the vote in Legislative Assembly elections on the basis of a property qualification, with no mention of sex. Accordingly, women possessed of the requisite property (normally this meant widows) often cast their votes. Female suffrage was not universally accepted, however. Evidence from surviving poll books indicates that, depending on the election and on the constitutency, substantial numbers of women might vote or none at all.[19] Certainly there were returning officers who turned women away from the hustings "in consequence of their sex." In one case, this provoked objections from men whose candidate stood to benefit from a sex-blind franchise. "Property and not persons," they insisted, "is the basis of representation in the English government," pursuing an argument for female suffrage that, in the context, can only be called "conservative."[20] (We might note in passing a fact that has escaped the attention of nationalist/feminist historians: this partial and contested feminine franchise was not unique to Lower Canada. It was not unheard of for women's votes to be accepted in Britain and her colonies in the eighteenth century and there were French women who helped elect representatives to the Estates-General of 1789.)

The spectacle of women voting appeared increasingly anomalous to Lower Canadian parliamentarians and in 1834 they passed a bill formally disenfranchising women. It is worth noting that this was not a controversial measure, nor did it even seem very important to its supporters. The clause in the law regulating elections which disenfranchised women in fact received less attention than such matters as the appointment of returning officers and the administration of oaths. It was originally proposed by John Neilson, a moderate from Quebec City who had earlier broken with Papineau and the more radical Patriots. Nonetheless, Papineau threw his full support behind the measure, in spite of his bitter feud with Neilson. Indeed, I have been unable to find a trace of any sort of objection to the exclusion of women from the electoral process. Lower Canadian newspapers of every political stripe (needless to say, they were all written by men and for men) either ignored the measure or treated it as a straightforward housekeeping matter.[21] Even in the turbulent and fiercely partisan 1830s, then, there were subjects on which the parties could agree!

Louis-Joseph Papineau was in fact the only member of the Assembly to articulate a justification for an exclusion the necessity of which seemed entirely self-evident to his colleagues. Significantly, in framing his argument against feminine voting, he did not allude to any sort of defect in judgement or political understanding that ought to disqualify women. What concerned Papineau was rather the danger posed to the domestic sexual order by women participating in the public exercise of the suffrage (recall that this was long before the introduction of the secret ballot). "It is ridiculous," he declared, "it is odious to see women dragged up to the hustings by their husbands, girls by their fathers, often against their will. The public interest, decency, and the modesty of the fair sex require that these scandals cease."[22] Never mind the fact that all this anxiety about fathers and husbands is quite irrelevant in a situation where almost all the female voters were widows. We might even pass over the irony of this gentleman casting himself in the role of gallant protector of frail femininity as he substantially narrows the political rights of women. What seems to me impossible to ignore — and characteristically republican — about Papineau's speech is the way it associates three things: (1) "the public interest," (2) feminine chastity and "modesty," and (3) the withdrawal of women from the public arena. Such a linkage is of course right in line with Rousseau's convictions. It seems entirely fitting, then, that, while male politicians of every persuasion were in basic agreement on gender-political issues, it should be a radical who took the strongest stand.

351

And yet there were countercurrents, possibilities — however limited — for an alternative construction of the republican discourse on gender and political rights. In Lower Canada, as in Europe and the United States, the rhetoric of equality, and even the language of "separate spheres," could be appropriated to serve proto-feminist purposes. On the eve of the Rebellion, one lonely contributor to *La Minerve* appealed to the nationalism of the Patriots, calling on them to recognize sexual equality as a distinguishing feature of the French-Canadian nation.[23] "Adelaide" (it was customary to use pseudonyms in letters to the editor) began by observing an insidious English practice that was creeping into the old Canadian custom of celebrating the pre-nuptial signing of a marriage contract. When called upon to witness the contract, some married women in Montreal were apparently signing with their own christian names coupled with their husband's surnames. This abandonment of the established practice whereby women signed with the "maiden names" was disturbing to Adelaide for it suggested more fundamental shifts in conceptions of marriage. The use of the pre-marital family name was associated with a legal and moral system that allowed a married woman to preserve her property and her identity. Adelaide draws a sharp contrast, in this regard, between Lower Canada and England, where, she believes, wives could not own property and were completely subordinate to their husbands. Among French Canadians, the management of family property and the raising of children is by *"collaboration mutuelle,"* (the phrase is underlined in the original). "Our laws, in harmony with our customs [moeurs], make the woman the partner of the man as well as his wife."

"Adelaide's" propositions on marital law and custom do not exactly represent a bald description of reality. They should instead be read as a programmatic and normative statement, one which puts the accent on French-Canadian tendencies in the direction of sexual equality while conveniently ignoring contrary tendencies. For example, she neglects to mention that, while husbands and wives were accorded equal shares of family property under the Custom of Paris, the law clearly stated that "the husband is master of the conjugal community."[24] It is true that the civil law of Canada protected the property rights of widows and of inheriting offspring of both sexes to a much greater extent than did English law. Accordingly, a French-Canadian *pater familias* did not dispose of the economic leverage or the threat of disinheritance to bully his "dependents," as could the domestic tyrants that populate so many English novels of the eighteenth century. However, this does not mean that French Canada was not a patriarchal society, it just means that male power was based on different mechanisms of control. For example (and this is only one element in a patriarchal complex with too many ramifications to be adequately discussed here), under the French régime, disobedience on the part of wives and children could be a punishable criminal offence.[25]

It is nevertheless true that the institution of the conjugal community and the inheritance provisions of the Custom of Paris requiring equal division among sons and daughters did constitute important safeguards for girls and women, subject though the latter were to a male ascendancy in other realms of life. And yet, in the pre-Rebellion decades, these safeguards were eroding. Most contemporaries were probably unaware of it, so gradual was the change, but more and more habitants were finding ways to bequeath all or most of their property to their sons, leaving their daughters to be beholden to future husbands for whatever wealth they might acquire.[26] Behind this partial abandonment of the rules of French-Canadian civil law lay a number of factors, such as the growing scarcity of land for new settlement. The influence of English legal traditions may also have played a role in encouraging the belief that a man should be able to dispose of "his" property as he saw fit (with emphasis on the unspoken, but crucial, assumption that family property ought to be vested in the father/husband). Perhaps that is why the writer of the "Adelaide" letter was so worried about the adoption of English practices in the comparatively insignificant matter of signing marriage contracts.

At any rate, it is clear that Adelaide was presenting what amounted to a plea for greater sexual equality. And she made her case in the only terms that could be expected to appeal to readers of *La Minerve*: those of nationalist republicanism. Like other early feminists, including Wollstonecraft, she was unable to mount a fundamental challenge to the prevalent conception of female domesticity. Instead, she insisted on the virtues of harmony, mutuality, and equality within the private conjugal sphere. Obviously, this was not an argument for feminine "independence" as the late twentieth century would understand the term but, in the real world that "Adelaide" inhabited, much would have had to change if all couples were to live together with genuine cooperation and mutual respect.

And was her appeal to the men of the Patriot party successful? Not if one judges by the absence of any response to her letter in subsequent editions of *La Minerve*. Nor did the behaviour of the radicals during the Rebellion suggest a deep attachment to Adelaide's conception of French-Canadian marital equality. When the conjugal community régime came up as an issue in 1837–38, it did so because Patriots were demanding its abolition as an infringement on a man's right to control "his" property freely![27] In addition, the sources connected with the insurrection tell of one case of vicious wife-battering on the part of an active rebel. Jean-Baptiste Lague of St Mathias mercilessly beat his pregnant wife, Marie-Desange Brunette, on more than one occasion in late 1838. Accusing her of being a pro-government "bureaucrat," he threatened to kill her or to have her arrested by the Patriots. And indeed Marie, aided by a neighbour woman, did go to the authorities and denounced Lague's secret revolutionary activities.[28] In a case of this sort, one can hardly separate the personal and the political dimensions of Madame Lague's decision to turn in her husband; indeed, her political stance (if indeed she was a convinced Constitutionalist, as Jean-Baptiste said) and her attitude towards her mate were no doubt inextricably connected. The violence of Lague may well have been exceptional (though who can know how common wife-battering was at that time?), but his political disagreement with his wife does seem symptomatic of a general tendency for French-Canadian men and women to diverge politically at the time of the Rebellion.

This said, it is important to note that the crisis of the summer of 1837 began with a rather awkward attempt on the part of the Patriots to attract the active support of women. It was in the context of the campaign to boycott British imports that radical men turned to their wives and mothers for support. In both the boycott itself and in the consequent mobilization of women, the Patriots were following the pre-Revolutionary American experience, as Papineau and his associates were well aware.[29] Women were thought to have a critical role to play, in the first instance as consumers. Since textiles accounted for a large part of British exports to Canada, the Patriot press felt called upon to lecture the ladies of the country on the need to forgo foreign finery in favour of plain homespun.

> Women of Canada! Little as ye think it, it is in your power partly to avert the awful storm now threatening us with such terrific fury . . . There is a demon rapidly destroying your country's prosperity, the virtue of your children, and the happiness of your own hearts. You feel it not; you know it not; yet it is a thousand times more terrible in its influence than the all-devouring serpent in days of yore . . . The demon that I speak of, that hath taken possession of, and sullied, the purity of your minds, *is an inordinate love of dress* . . .

353

Leaving aside the question of how anyone with that kind of writing style could presume to champion the cause of chaste simplicity, we might note the typically republican linkage of national salvation with feminine modesty. The article concludes with a ringing call to the women of Lower Canada: "Throng not your city's streets clothed in foreign apparel. Let the leading ones among you assume the dress of humble *toile*, and, believe me, by so doing, they will have tended more to the preservation of their country's *rights* and *trade*, than the numberless resolutions of the greybeards and councillors."[30]

Who was to spin the yarn and weave it into patriotic *toile*? Certainly not the greybeards and councillors! The non-importation campaign entailed the mobilization of women above all in the role of domestic producers. In some parts of the province — particularly the Richelieu valley — women did take up the challenge. At St Charles, a man later recalled, "Even the women shared the general enthusiasm . . . And they competed with one another to produce the finest cloth."[31] Previously ignored in Patriot discourse, women began to appear repeatedly in the radical press, though usually in anonymous and stereotyped terms. At a banquet at Contrecoeur, for example, 56 men raised their glasses to toast "Josephte, the wife of Jean-Baptiste, as patriotic as she is beautiful, no less virtuous than she is pleasant, she will make a powerful contribution to the happiness of the country by her industry and by her efforts to encourage domestic manufactures."[32]

First they take away Josephte's vote, then they ask her to toil at the hand-loom in order to free the country! The temptation is great to treat the Patriot appeal to women with complete cynicism. Yet there was some complexity to the position of the radical men and some hints of movement in the direction of fuller citizenship for women as the crisis of 1837 deepened. A newspaper reprinted extracts from Harriet Martineau's work on "The Political Non-existence of Women."[33] It also gave favourable reports of the formation of patriotic women's associations in several rural parishes. Little is known about these organizations themselves but, by September 1837, they seem to have extended their attention to other matters in addition to the boycott.

HONOR TO OUR PATRIOTIC LADIES

A party of two hundred and fifty ladies, belonging to the parish of St. Antoine, celebrated, on Thursday, the 10th inst. their love of country and their patriotism, by a public dinner, from which every *imported* article was rigidly excluded. Various patriotic toasts, appropriate to the spirit of the times, were proposed. A guard of honor, composed of forty men belonging to the parish, was in attendance with their muskets, and occasionally complimented the fair party by firing a *feu de joie*. So far from being frightened by the smell of powder, or the roar of musketry, many of the ladies, to prove that they can act in case of need, took the muskets and discharged them with the most admirable tact and courage. When the *women* of Canada are displaying such patriotism, it is not very probable the *men* will be backward when the day of trial comes.[34]

354

Of course no one really expected women to shoulder arms in the coming struggle. Still, behind the condescending treatment of the "patriotic ladies," lies a recognition of the importance of women's contribution to the national mobilization. Like other middle-class radicals in other countries, the Patriots found themselves impelled by the revolutionary situation itself to modify their views somewhat in order to bring women into the movement. Their more democratic approach to poor men was analogous. But, where women were concerned, there was perhaps a more deeply felt ambivalence about this widening process, because the relationships involved were more intimate than those of class. Thus, while it tried to stimulate and encourage women's politicization, the radical press constantly betrayed, by repeated reference to the ladies' weakness and beauty, its anxiety about the dangers of subverting the sexual hierarchy. With some misgivings, Patriot men stretched and extended the malleable concept of female domesticity in ways that allowed women to become more directly involved in the national struggle; they emphatically did not abandon the ideology of separate spheres, however.

355

The inescapable fact is that the Patriot movement was a fundamentally masculine phenomenon, in its style as well as in its philosophical orientation. Orators at the protest meetings held in the summer of 1837 emphasized themes of independence, honour, and manly valour in appeals clearly addressed to men. Women were certainly a presence at these meetings; in fact, Constitutionalist newspapers liked to declare that the crowds attending anti-coercion rallies were mostly composed of women and children. The response of the Patriot press was revealing: rather than challenging the assumption that a female presence detracted from the seriousness of the proceedings, *The Vindicator* would instead insist that "the handsome and patriotic ladies" had confined their participation to waving handkerchiefs from the windows of nearby houses.[35]

None of this was calculated to further the Patriots' attempts to appeal to women and neither, presumably, was the movement's pronounced anti-clericalism. In Lower Canada at this time, as in other parts of the Catholic world, religion was becoming a peculiarly female affair within the family.[36] One finds evidence of this trend in statistics on membership in various devotional sodalities. Whereas men formed an overall majority in the seventeenth century, women became more numerous in the first half of the eighteenth century and their numerical predominance only increased over the years.[37] Though the official Church remained subject to a strictly masculine hierarchy, women of all classes were tending to develop a special relationship with the clergy. For all its authoritarianism, the Church did have a place for women in a way that the republican movement did not.

It is hardly surprising then that women did not, on the whole, embrace the Patriot cause with great enthusiasm. To say this is not to deny or to belittle the very real suffering of the hundreds of women who found themselves with their possessions stolen, their homes in ashes, and their husbands in prison in the wake of the battles of 1837 and 1838. We know, moreover, that, in addition to their efforts on behalf of the non-importation campaign, women sewed banners, sheltered fugitives, and otherwise aided the insurgents; one woman even acquired a reputation in the parish of St Benoit by composing satirical songs directed against the local priest, a loyalist "*chouayen*."[38] Yet, aside from these auxiliary contributions, evidence of active female commitment to the Patriot cause is almost non-existent. Among the 1356 names on the official lists of political prisoners for the Rebellion period, not one can be identified as a woman.[39] The thousands of depositions and other narrative sources convey a similar impression: nowhere did women play a prominent or even a very active role, either as fighters or as spies, agitators, or journalists.[40] Now it is true that women have generally been slighted in the records favoured by historians, but it would be a serious mistake to attribute the resounding silence on this score merely to documentary bias.

Women do appear in the sources, but they do so principally in a stance of opposition to the Patriots and their insurrection. The testimony of dozens of witnesses and prisoners mentions wives urging their husbands to stay home rather than report to a rebel camp. Of course contemporaries explained this as nothing more than the weakness of the weaker sex, but one wonders whether the women concerned might not have displayed greater firmness had they found the cause more inspiring. Certainly there is no reason to think that the women of French Canada held back from full support of the Rebellion out of any ingrained timidity or "conservatism." Their record of anti-government activism in the eighteenth century is sufficient refutation of that hypothesis. Obviously something had changed between 1775, when the "Queen of Hungary" had led the peasants of the Île d'Orléans, and 1837, when the anti-government forces could boast no heroines. One new factor on the scene was of course the Patriot movement, which, in spite of half-hearted attempts to sponsor women's organizations, clearly stood for a masculine — indeed, a masculinizing — politics in which women were not really welcome. And, no doubt, many women had no desire to be involved in political struggle, for or against the British colonial régime in Lower Canada. After all, the evolving ideology of female domesticity was not the exclusive property of Patriots, nor was it limited to men alone. As it gained hegemonic status throughout the Euro-Atlantic world,[41] women themselves tended increasingly to subscribe to the notion that national affairs should be left to men.

Not every woman was prepared to accept the assigned role, however. Indeed, the tense pre-Rebellion period saw two heroines in the Madeleine de Verchères mould gain province-wide notoriety thanks to their willingness to engage in dangerous armed confrontations. Hortense Globensky, the wife of Guillaume Prévost, a Ste Scholastique notary, was a staunch Constitutionalist who earned the hatred of local Patriots during the July troubles in Two Mountains county. Taking up a rifle at the approach of a hostile crowd which she truly thought was about to ransack her home, she organized the household defences so effectively that the "mob" went away without pressing the attack. Even in the fall of 1837, she was not afraid to plunge into Patriot meetings denouncing sedition. However, her habit of brandishing a loaded pistol on such occasions did get her into some trouble; Ste Scholastique's Patriots had her charged with illegal possession of a firearm. Tory Montreal, on the other hand, made a great fuss over her, for she had proved that "even a woman" could put the cowardly mob to flight. Urban Constitutionalists expressed their appreciation in the form of a silver tea urn, which they presented to Madame Prévost, as the English inscription read, " . . . in memory of her heroism, greater than that expected of a woman . . . "[42]

An even more formidable champion of Constitutionalism was Rosalie Cherrier ("Madame St Jacques") of St Denis.[43] Like Hortense Globensky, she was a courageous and outspoken opponent of radicalism right in the heart of Patriot country, but no one ever offered Madame St Jacques an engraved teapot; so defiantly unconventional was she in her personal life as well as her politics that heroine status with the respectable Tory press was out of the question. Cherrier's loyalist convictions certainly did not come from her family, for she was the sister of a Patriot politician and cousin to Louis-Joseph Papineau. As a matter of fact, Rosalie Cherrier seems to have been completely alienated from her family. Some time before the Rebellion, she had separated from her schoolteacher-husband and this may have been at the origin of the breach with her relations. Living in St Denis with her two teen-aged daughters, as well as a young American man who lodged with her as a semi-permanent guest, Madame St Jacques was a prime target for sexual slander in a small town. There she was known as "la Poule," the kept woman of Sabrevois de Bleury, one-time Patriot lately gone over to the government, who herself kept a young man around the house to satisfy her depraved appetites. To make matters worse, the radical press reported after she had fallen afoul of local Patriots, she was known to walk the streets of St Denis at night, dressed in the habit of a soeur de la Congrégation, arm in arm with her lover. A deviant in her domestic arrangements as well as in her political allegiance, Rosalie Cherrier was a woman doubly at odds with her family and her community.

Obviously a very strong-willed person, Rosalie seems to have had no fear of confrontations. She made no secret of the fact that she wrote reports on regional affairs for the Constitutionalist paper, *Le Populaire*. When St Denis's Patriots staged a demonstration in September 1837 that featured the hanging in effigy of Governor Gosford and several of his Lower Canadian supporters, Cherrier marched out and tore down the signs attached to the effigies, while treating the shocked bystanders to her own views on the issues of the day. That evening a noisy crowd surrounded her house in the urban village, singing obscene songs and demanding that she leave the parish. Instead of fleeing, however, she went out and purchased a gun the next day and melted down her spoons for ammunition. An even larger group assembled to resume the charivari the following night, but Madame St Jacques was prepared for them. The crowd grew ever louder and more menacing until suddenly a shot rang out from a window of the house. It was never determined whether Rosalie herself or some other member of the household under her command actually fired the shot. What is clear, though, is that, after the dust had settled, two men who had come to enjoy the charivari lay seriously wounded (one almost died). Cherrier and her household escaped, and her home was reduced to a pile of rubble by the furious crowd.[44]

In the aftermath, journalists argued about whether this had been a political charivari or a traditional charivari, one aimed at a marital non-conformist, a partisan opponent, or a woman who had dared to intrude into the public sphere of political debate. Yet surely it was all these things. Feminine chastity and domesticity were the necessary counterparts of masculine civic virtue in the republican discourse of the period, and so, for the villagers of St Denis, as well as for the bourgeois Patriots of Montreal, Rosalie Cherrier's "immodest" political outbursts and her alleged sexual depravity were all of a piece. Her allegiance to the colonial régime simply confirmed both her and its basic corruption.

The defeat of the Rebellion and the crushing of the Patriots did not of course lead to any sort of liberation of Lower Canada's women. Indeed, the state structure and political order instituted after 1838 were, if anything, more thoroughly masculine than the incipient Patriot régime had been.[45] Meanwhile, women were taught more than ever before to concentrate on private, domestic, and familial matters. (Of course, in actual practice, the ideology of domesticity did not prevent women from playing important roles outside the household, particularly in the realms of charity, education, and moral and religious reform; in Lower Canada, the Church and the religious life offered significant outlets for ambitious girls.[46]) All in all, the emergence of the Victorian régime of "separate spheres" (to use a rather inadequate shorthand phrase) continued apace.[47]

Important changes were in train during the 1830s and 1840s, changes implying a fundamental restructuring of political relations between the sexes. The state gained unprecedented powers, the content of formal politics narrowed, and women were increasingly alienated from affairs of state. All this was an international phenomenon observable in one form or another throughout the Euro-Atlantic world.[48] Closely associated with the rise of the bourgeoisie, it was hardly the exclusive work of any particular partisan faction; nor did it correspond to any simple political event or revolution. One can nevertheless see the Patriot party as the Lower Canadian spearhead of this wider shift in the politico-sexual order. Quite apart from their occasional misogynist outbursts in 1837, it was they who had enunciated the democratic conception of a "public sphere" open to every citizen without privilege or distinction. Since their definition of citizenship excluded women, their discourse of liberation was as much about sex as it was about politics. By the same token, one would be justified in regarding the Rebellion of 1837-38 as constituting, among other things, a significant moment in the process of gender formation in French Canada.

NOTES

I would like to thank Mariana Valverde, Bruce Curtis, Ed Hundert, and Micheline Dumont for their comments on an earlier version of this paper. Thanks also to the Social Sciences and Humanities Research Council for supporting my research and to my research assistant, Irshad Manji.

[1] Jean-Jacques Rousseau, *Politics and the Arts: Letter to M. d'Alembert on the Theatre*, trans. Allan Bloom (Glencoe, Ill.: Free Press, 1960), 82-83.

[2] Quoted in Jane Rendall, *The Origins of Modern Feminism: Women in Britain, France and the United States, 1780-1860* (London: Macmillan, 1985), 235.

[3] Quoted in Micheline Dumont et al., *Quebec Women: A History*, trans. Roger Gannon and Rosalind Gill (Toronto: Women's Press, 1987), 122. Papineau appears to have made this observation in jest, playfully inverting his wife's and his habitual roles as pious Christian and Enlightenment sceptic. Nevertheless, this is one of those jokes that reveals much about basic attitudes.

[4] *The Vindicator*, 1 September 1837.

[5] Archives nationales du Québec, collection événements de 1837-1838 (hereafter ANQ, 1837), no. 324, déposition du Baron Augustin de Diemar, 21 December 1837 (author's translation); ibid., no. 242, déposition de Joseph-Louis Pinard, 1 February 1838; ibid., deposition of Thomas Casson, 31 December 1838 (cf. ibid., no. 1483, Lacombe to Walcott, 23 August 1837). The loyalists, for their part, struck a chivalrous posture, vowing to "make any sacrifice in maintaining the legitimate authority of our young and beauteous Queen." Speech by Hon. Mr. McGill, Montreal, 23 October 1837, in Jean-Paul Bernard, ed., *Assemblées publiques, résolutions et déclarations de 1837-1838* (Montreal: VLB éditeur, 1988), 239.

[6] Dorothy Thompson, personal communication.

[7] This point is made in several studies, but I found particularly useful Joel Schwartz, *The Sexual Politics of Jean-Jacques Rousseau* (Chicago: University of Chicago Press, 1984). The basic texts are the *Discourse on the Origins of Inequality*, the *Social Contract*, *Letter to M. d'Alembert*, and *Emile*.

[8] Joan B. Landes, *Women and the Public Sphere in the Age of the French Revolution* (Ithaca: Cornell University Press, 1988).

[9] Schwartz, *Sexual Politics*.

[10] *La Minerve*, 28 July 1836 (author's translation).

[11] Darline Gay Levy, Harriet Branson Applewhite, and Mary Durham Johnson, eds., *Women in Revolutionary Paris, 1789-1795* (Urbana: University of Illinois Press, 1979); Sîan Reynolds, "Marianne's Citizens? Women, the Republic and Universal Suffrage in France," in *Women, State and Revolution: Essays on Power and Gender in Europe since 1789* (Amherst: University of Massachusetts Press, 1987), 101-22; Landes, *Women and the Public Sphere*. The de Gouges quotation is from Dorinda Outram, "Le langage mâle de la vertu: Women and the Discourse of the French Revolution," in *The Social History of Language*, ed. Peter Burke and Roy Porter (Cambridge: Cambridge University Press, 1987), 126.

[12] Linda Kerber, *Women of the Republic: Intellect and Ideology in Revolutionary America* (Chapel Hill: University of North Carolina Press, 1980).

[13] Landes, *Women and the Public Sphere*. The quotation from Rousseau is from p. 75 of this work.

[14] Outram, "Le langage mâle." A wonderful illustration of this outlook can be found in the work of Rousseau's English contemporary and fellow-republican Edward Gibbon. Gibbon devotes several long and salacious pages in Chapter 20 of *The Decline and Fall of the Roman Empire* to the misdeeds of the sixth-century empress Theodora, whose fond husband, Justinian, committed the fundamental error of making his wife not a consort, but a co-ruler. Long before she managed to seduce Justinian, Gibbon explains, Theodora was renowned in Constantinople and beyond for her beautiful face and figure.

But this form was degraded by the facility with which it was exposed to the public eye, and prostituted to licentious desire. Her venal charms were abandoned to a promiscuous crowd of citizens and strangers, of every rank and of every profession: the fortunate lover who had been promised a night of enjoyment was often driven from her bed by a stronger or more wealthy favourite . . .

And so on.

[15] "This social system," writes Colin Coates, referring to New France and to the tribulations of Madeleine de Verchères, seigneuresse and military heroine, "though patriarchal, allowed certain women to wield a great deal of power." He might have added the qualification "overtly" to better distinguish the eighteenth century from the nineteenth, when men still expected elite women to wield power, but quietly and privately. Colin Coates, "Authority and Illegitimacy in New France: The Burial of Bishop Saint-Vallier and Madeleine de Verchères vs. the Priest of Batiscan," *Histoire sociale/Social History* 22 (May 1989): 65-90.

[16] Louise Dechêne, *Habitants et marchands de Montréal au XVIIe siècle* (Paris and Montreal: Plon, 1974), 464; Terence Crowley, " 'Thunder Gusts': Popular Disturbances in Early French Canada," Canadian Historical Association, *Historical Papers* (1979) 19-22.

[17] "Journal . . . pour l'examen des personnes qui ont assisté ou aider les rebels . . . 1776," *Rapport de l'Archiviste de la Province de Québec (RAPQ)* (1927-28), 480 (author's translation). See also pp. 447, 450, 470, 496.

[18] W.R. Riddell, "Woman Franchise in Quebec, a Century Ago," Royal Society of Canada, *Proceedings and Transactions* 22 (1928), section 2, pp. 85-99; Fernand Ouellet, *Le Bas-Canada, 1791-1840: changements structuraux et crise* (Ottawa: Éditions de l'Université d'Ottawa, 1976), 42-43, 350; David De Brou, "Mass Political Behaviour in Upper-Town Quebec, 1792-1836," Ph.D. thesis, University of Ottawa, 1989, 94-98.

[19] In addition to the works noted above, see Archives nationales du Canada (hereafter ANC), Lower Canada Election Records, vol. 21, poll books for Quebec county, 1804 (no women voted); Charlesbourg county, 1817 (no women voted); borough of William Henry, 1827 (three women attempted to vote; one was rejected). In the Montreal West election of 1832, on the other hand, Ouellet found 199 women among the 1533 voters.

[20] Petition of divers electors, Upper Town, Quebec, 1828, in *Documents relating to the Constitutional History of Canada, 1819-1828*, ed. A.G. Doughty and N. Story (Ottawa: King's Printer, 1935), 520.

[21] *L'Ami du Peuple*, 27 January 1834; *Montreal Gazette*, 1 February 1834; *La Minerve*, 3 February 1834. *Le Canadien* and *L'Echo du Pays* took no notice of the disenfranchisement of women. It should be noted that the electoral bill of 1834, after sailing through the House of Assembly, was held up at subsequent stages of the legislative process and, for reasons quite unconnected with the clause relating to female voters, it never seems to have been enacted into law. Nevertheless, women do not seem to have been admitted to the hustings after 1834. Just to be sure, the Parliament of the province of Canada prohibited women from voting in 1849.

[22] *La Minerve*, 3 February 1834 (author's translation). See also *Montreal Gazette*, 1 February 1834.

[23] Ibid., 2 February 1837.

[24] François-Joseph Cugnet, *An Abstract of Those Parts of the Custom of the Viscounty and Provostship of Paris, which Were Received and Practised in the Province of Quebec, in the Time of the French Government* (London, 1772), 56; Allan Greer, *Peasant, Lord and Merchant: Rural Society in Three Quebec Parishes, 1740-1840* (Toronto: University of Toronto Press, 1985), 53-56.

[25] John F. Bosher, "The Family in New France," in Barry Gough, ed., *In Search of the Visible Past* (Waterloo: Wilfrid Laurier University Press), 9.

[26] Greer, *Peasant, Lord and Merchant*, 80-81, 223.

[27] See *La Minerve*, 14 August 1837.

[28] ANQ, 1837, no. 1666, déposition de Marie Desanges Brunette, 2 December 1838. Cf. ibid., no. 1665, déposition d'Agathe Vient, 30 December 1838.

[29] See Papineau's speech as reported in *The Vindicator*, 6 June 1837. Cf. Kerber, *Women of the Republic*.

[30] *The Vindicator*, 27 June 1837. Though presented here specifically in relation to the anti-British boycott, the moral danger posed more generally by women's weakness for fancy clothes was a favourite theme for nineteenth-century bourgeois commentators. See Mariana Valverde, "The Love of Finery: Fashion and the Fallen Woman in Nineteenth-Century Social Discourse," *Victorian Studies* 32 (Winter 1989): 169-88.

[31] ANC, MG24, B82, "Quelques notes historiques sur les événements politiques de 1837 en Canada," 9.

[32] *La Minerve*, 17 August 1837 (author's translation).

[33] *The Vindicator*, 4 July 1837.

[34] Ibid., 22 September 1837.

[35] See, for example, the accounts of the meetings at Ste Scholastique and Napierville in *The Vindicator*, 6 June 1837 and 25 July 1837.

[36] Jean-Pierre Wallot, *Un Québec qui bougeait: trame socio-politique au tournant du XIXe siècle* (Sillery: Boréal, 1973), 203.

[37] Marie-Aimée Cliche, *Les pratiques de dévotion en Nouvelle-France: comportements populaires en encadrement ecclésial dans le gouvernement de Québec* (Québec: Les Presses de l'Université Laval, 1988), 181-83, 208, 232.

[38] Marcelle Reeves-Morache, "La canadienne pendant les troubles de 1837-1838," *Revue d'histoire de l'Amérique française* 5 (June 1951): 99–117; Dumont et al., *L'Histoire des femmes au Québec*, 146.

[39] Irish University Press Series, *British Parliamentary Papers* 14: 405–25. Of course a man was more likely to be arrested than a woman, even if they committed the same political offences. Nevertheless, in spite of the obvious bias in arrest figures, the complete and absolute absence of women political prisoners is remarkable.

[40] Some have attempted (see works by Reeves-Morache and Dumont et al. cited above) to maek Emilie Boileau of Chambly into a nineteenth-century Madeleine de Verchères, but their case is quite unconvincing. It seems to rest on a passage in the memoirs of R.S.M. Bouchette in which Bouchette describes a gathering of Patriots at the home of Emilie and her husband, Timothée Kimber, during the crisis of 1837. Bouchette was impressed by the fact that Madame Kimber was holding a pistol. However, there is no indication that she ever fired this weapon, or that she brandished it in any encounter with anti-Patriot forces; in fact, there is no reason to believe that she ever carried it outside her own house!

[41] Among other studies suggesting a parallel tendency in various countries for women to retreat in the nineteenth century from political activism that seemed normal in the eighteenth century, see Janet L. Polasky, "Women in Revolutionary Belgium: From Stone Throwers to Hearth Tenders," *History Workshop* 21 (Spring 1986): 87–104.

[42] *Dictionnaire biographique du Canada* (Québec: Les Presses de l'Université Laval, 1972), vol. 10; *Le Populaire*, 12 July 1837; *Montreal Gazette*, 26 October 1837.

[43] J.-B. Richard, *Les Événements de 1837 à Saint-Denis-sur-Richelieu* (St Hyacinthe: Société d'histoire régionale de Saint-Hyacinthe, 1938), 21–27; *Montreal Gazette*, 30 September 1837; *La Minerve*, 12 October 1837; *The Vindicator*, 29 September 1837; *Le Populaire*, 29 September 1837, 2 October 1837, 9 October 1837, 16 October 1837; ANC, MG11, Q238-1:190, Gosford to Glenelg, 12 October 1837; Toronto Public Library, George Nelson journal, p. 6.

[44] Rosalie Cherrier was captured the following day and taken to Montreal, where she stood trial for attempted murder; apparently she was acquitted. Unfortunately, the relevant judicial records for this period are not open to researchers.

[45] See Lykke de la Cour, Cecilia Morgan, and Mariana Valverde, "Gender and State Formation in Nineteenth-Century Canada," in Allan Greer and Ian Radforth, eds., *Colonial Leviathan: State Formation in Nineteenth-Century Canada* (forthcoming).

[46] See Marta Danylewycz, *Taking the Veil: An Alternative to Marriage, Motherhood, and Spinsterhood in Quebec, 1840-1920* (Toronto: McClelland and Stewart, 1987).

[47] Distinctions between public and private, political and social, masculine and feminine were, as ever, contested, changing, and ambiguous. Thus, we can hardly speak of any simple process by which men seized control of all that was "public," while women were relegated to a strictly "private" sphere. For a critique of the excessively static and mechanical conception of "separate spheres," see Linda K. Kerber, "Separate Spheres, Female Worlds, Woman's Place: The Rhetoric of Women's History," *Journal of American History* 75 (June 1988): 9–39.

[48] On the United States, see Paula Baker's suggestive essay, "The Domestication of Politics: Women and American Political Society, 1780-1920," *American Historial Review* 89 (June 1984): 620–47.

Suppressing Rebellion in Lower Canada: British Military Policy and Practice, 1837–1838

ELINOR KYTE SENIOR

In the event of insurrection — whether in Ireland, in Jamaica, or in Canada — the usual British military practice in the early 1800s was to seize the papers of rebel chiefs, burn their homes, and imprison leaders when caught. Rank and file insurgents were less likely to have their homes burnt unless those buildings had been used by insurgents to fire upon Crown forces. "Free quartering" of troops was often imposed on a disaffected populace as part of the punitive measures, but exile or hanging

From *Canadian Defence Quarterly* 17, 4 (Spring 1988): 50–55. Reprinted with permission.

of rebel leaders were measures of last resort. Imposition of martial law meant the suspension of civil government, a step contemplated with as much anxiety by loyal citizens as by disaffected elements. Government and military authorities clearly believed that rebels had to be punished, and that such punishment should be evident, not only to the loyal part of the population but to the neutral and wavering elements as well.

Most British officers and soldiers of this period who served abroad were familiar with coping with disturbed areas. It was then usual military practice to send regiments to Ireland prior to a posting overseas, as the Irish station was considered an excellent training ground both for use of troops in aid of civil power and for training in ceremonial procedures. Colonel George Cathcart of the 1st King's Dragoon Guards, for instance, had served in Ireland and then in Jamaica during the slave revolt there in the 1830s. When faced with insurrection in Lower Canada, he made use of his experience, particularly with regard to combined police-military operations. His expertise in these matters enabled him to exercise great influence in the reorganization of the Montreal police both during and after the rebellions.[1] Similarly, Colonel Charles Grey of the 71st Highland Light Infantry urged civil authorities to make use of the Irish Insurrection Act of 1798 to compel each Montreal householder to post on the front door a list of all residents and order them to be within the house by a certain hour each night.[2]

362

Outbreak of the First Rebellion

Even before the first actual battle of the 1837 rebellion occurred in Lower Canada, the British military command had formulated a policy of home burning as a punitive measure. This policy was instituted as a reaction to the rescue of arrested *Patriote* chiefs by a body of armed *Patriotes* under Bonaventure Viger. These insurgent leaders had been arrested in Saint Jean on 16 November 1837 by Montreal bailiffs, who were escorted by troopers of the Royal Mounted Cavalry under the command of Lieutenant Charles Oakes Ermatinger, an Ojibway chief. Lieutenant Ermatinger was hit by the first shot of the first rebellion, a shot fired by the insurgent son of a half-pay Scottish officer, Patrick Murray.[3] In the ensuing melée, the men of the Royal Montreal Cavalry were scattered, their prisoners freed, and authorities faced the first open defiance of government and military forces. The Commander of the British forces in Canada, Sir John Colborne, immediately sent a strong contingent of regulars back to the spot where the cavalry had been attacked, with orders to arrest the men who had fired on the troopers. "Should they resist the civil power or fire on the troops, you will fire on the rebels, also destroy any house from which they may fire."[4] On returning to Saint Jean, however, the troops found the houses deserted, the women and children hiding in the woods. The men had gone to Boucherville to reinforce insurgent ranks there under Bonaventure Viger. Some prisoners were taken, but no homes put to the torch.

Battles of Saint Denis and Saint Charles

This rescue of the Saint Jean *Patriote* chiefs was, however, the incident that triggered Sir John Colborne to move against the radical centres of Saint Denis and Saint Charles, on the Richelieu River, with some 800 troops, ostensibly as "an aid to civil power." The troops were to accompany magistrates with warrants to arrest the *Patriote* leaders Louis-Joseph Papineau, Doctor Wolfred Nelson, Thomas Storrow Brown, and others, who were then forming armed camps on the Richelieu.

Colborne's military policy was to move swiftly against the armed camps. In a two-pronged pincer movement, one brigade was to move south from Sorel toward Saint Denis, and a second would march from Chambly against the armed camp at Saint Charles. It was expected that the brigade headed to Saint Denis would pass through that small village with little opposition. When put into practice, however, this plan proved only partly successful. Bad weather and bad tactics on the part of Colonel Gore allowed rebel reinforcements to get to Saint Denis during the battle. The regular troops were exhausted after an all-night march in the frightful November weather, and victory ultimately went to the insurgents, who fought vigorously from a strong defensive position.

By contrast, two days later, good weather and effective military leadership enabled the Chambly brigade to move decisively against Saint Charles in a triumphant two-hour battle. Following this battle the first of the punitive military measures began — the burning of houses and barns from which rebels had fired on Crown forces. The armed camp at Saint Charles was destroyed, except for the manor house of Pierre-Dominique Debartzch, which the insurgents had used as their main headquarters.[5] Some twenty buildings were put to the torch immediately. Prisoners were rounded up and lodged in the parish church until sent to jail in Montreal, where they joined those *Patriote* chiefs from Montreal who had already been arrested since 16 November.

With the suppression of the rebel camp at Saint Charles, a brigade of some 500 regulars, with field artillery and a cornet's detachment of the Royal Montreal Cavalry, returned to Saint Denis on 1 December. They entered the village unopposed, and there was no sign of Doctor Wolfred Nelson, Papineau, or other rebel leaders. The officer commanding the regulars, Colonel Gore lost no time in putting the torch to the fortified stone building which a week earlier the rebel forces had defended so effectively that regular soldiers had been unable to storm it.

363

Adapted from Elinor Kyte Senior, *Redcoats and Patriotes: The Rebellions in Lower Canada, 1837–38* (Stittsville, Ont.: Canada's Wings, 1985).

Home-Burning: A Policy of Punishment and Repression

In his first report to Colborne on 1 December 1837, Gore stated, "The fortified house has been burned and several others from which we were fired on." He added, "Wolfred Nelson's property will be destroyed tomorrow."[6] The destruction of Nelson's property and of other buildings was thus carried out as a punitive and as a repressive measure — to punish rebels and to prevent future uprisings. The British succeeded in the first, but failed in the second.

During and immediately after the first military engagements in Lower Canada, some 184 homes were burned. About 30 of these were disciplined military acts. The rest represented plunder and vengeance. After the battle of Saint Eustache, for instance, troops were ordered to "free quarters." This was a euphemism for plunder, as officers and soldiers fully understood. One regular officer described the pillaging at Saint Eustache as "equalling or surpassing that which followed the sack of Badajoz in Spain."[7] Only two homes were ordered burned in Saint Eustache — those of the local *Patriote* leaders, the merchant William Henry Scott and Doctor Jean Chenier.[8]

When "unofficial" fires broke out after the battle, troops were ordered out to protect property, but without much effect, and some 60 houses were gutted.[9] There was probably a certain element of calculation on the part of the military authorities with regard to these unofficial burnings. Colborne had warned the men of nearby Saint Benoit that their village would be put to fire and the sword if a single shot was fired as the Crown forces approached the village. Not a shot was fired, but the village was gutted nonetheless. Colborne had ordered three homes burnt in Saint Benoit, those of the three principal *Patriote* leaders — Notary Jean-Joseph Girouard, Doctor Luc Masson, and J.B. Dumouchel. The rest were put to the torch by local volunteers and residents. The church at Saint Benoit was set on fire three times; twice troops put out the flames, but the third time the church burned to the ground. Regular troops then marched through the disaffected area of the Lake of Two Mountains for three days. On orders, they burned two homes, took up surrendered arms and received the oath of allegiance from rural inhabitants. Their final duty was to escort to Montreal some of the 361 political prisoners that crowded the jails over that Winter.[10]

Terror and Persecution

Arrested rebels were expected to give depositions before magistrates about their part in the uprisings. Floggings and half-hangings, so much a part of the Irish rebellion scene in 1798, did not, however, form part of the repressive measures in Lower Canada in 1837. Rather, an atmosphere of terror was temporarily created by widespread police interrogation carried out under Pierre-Edouard Leclère, head of the newly raised police. No one could know to what extent a neighbour's testimony might implicate one in treason, and there was thus a continual flight over the American border of rebels and their sympathizers. They were undoubtedly frightened, but they were not so terrorized that they refrained from engaging in border raids from their safe haven in the United States.

The military reaction to these first border raids was to order the Glengarry Highlanders to move from Upper Canada in the Spring of 1838 to police areas south of the Saint Lawrence, and regular officers were brought over from England on "particular duty," that is, to act as intelligence officers. They were scattered in a number of small towns south of the Saint Lawrence, with the task of reporting to Colborne any suspicious behaviour of the *habitants* and those suspected of disaffection. It was no wonder that *Patriote* chiefs over the border spoke uneasily of "spies being sent throughout the agricultural districts."[11]

By May of 1838 additional troops from Great Britain were pouring into Lower Canada. The Grenadier Guards and the Coldstream Guards, along with two cavalry regiments, arrived under the command of Sir James Macdonell. In addition, three other regiments were brought in from the Maritime colonies. This brought Colborne's regular force up to a strength of 5,000 and, with his local volunteer troops numbering about 4,000, this combined military force exceeded the peacetime strength of the army of the United States.

In spite of the increasing size of the regular garrison, the *Patriotes* over the American line began preparations for a second uprising, this time through the agency of a secret society — *Les Frères Chasseurs*. Border raids were called off temporarily. With this lessening of border tension, Colborne released 200 of the lesser rebels from jail, a move that provoked considerable resentment on the part of the well-affected populace. Colborne went even farther. He agreed to a policy of general amnesty, expecting that such leniency would remove from the border the more turbulent spirits thought to be plotting another insurrection. Thus, six months after the first rebellion, all political prisoners had been released except for eight leaders who were sent into exile in Bermuda. Disaffected elements had accurately predicted this release of prisoners, and openly boasted that government dared not bring any of them to trial. Exile there was, then, for eight *Patriote* chiefs, but no executions. In fact, the only execution during the first rebellion in Lower Canada was that of a loyalist French-Canadian volunteer, executed by rebel forces who accused him of being a government spy.[12] This was in sharp contrast to what had happened in the upper province, where civil authorities promptly hanged two captured rebel leaders.

The Second Rebellion: The Scottish Suppression

When the second insurrection broke out in Lower Canada in November of 1838, if faced a well-prepared government which suppressed it within a week. The rebellion, and its suppression, had something of a Scottish tone about it. The leader of the *Chasseur* conspiracy in Montreal was

John de Bélestre Macdonell, son of a half-pay Scottish officer who had settled in Glengarry County and married into the prominent de Bélestre family. It was out of Macdonell's law office in Montreal that the head lodge of the *Chasseurs* operated and funnelled money to Doctor Robert Nelson, leader of the insurgent forces south of the American line.

On the other side of the coin, the officer in charge of the harsh repressive measures after the second insurrection was Major-General Sir James Macdonell, brother of the late Highland Chieftain from Glengarry. It was thus not surprising that Colborne had no hesitation in ordering Glengarry Regiments from Upper Canada to cross the provincial line and surround insurgent forces in the Beauharnois area. Numerous Macdonells and other volunteers from Glengarry were delighted to join forces with their kinsman as he moved west from Quebec City with a brigade of Guards, doubly indignant that a man by the name of Macdonell was numbered among the rebel leaders.

The insurgents' fear of the Scots was clearly stated by one of them — himself half-Scot. Pierre Reid claimed that the reason the insurgents tried to disarm the Caughnawaga Indians just prior to the second uprising was because they feared "the Indians were coming with the Scotch to massacre us."[13] Reid's fear contained some element of reality: Captain Edmund Thomas Campbell of the 7th Hussars was in charge of suppressing the insurgents at Chateauguay; Colonel George Cathcart of the 1st King's Dragoon Guards scoured the area around La Prairie; and still another Campbell, Major John Campbell, commanded the Huntingdon Volunteers as they moved down the Chateauguay River against a rebel encampment at Baker's Farm. It is no wonder then that the pipers of the Stormont Highlanders gaily played "The Campbells are Coming" as they marched into the Huntingdon camp, accompanied by 60 warriors from the Indian village of Saint Regis, just opposite Cornwall. The combination of the Scottish bagpipes and the Indian warcries proved to be too much for the insurgents a short distance away: they silently slipped away overnight.

On their march from Beauharnois towards the major rebel encampment at Napierville, the Glengarries boasted that they left a trail six miles wide as they came along "burning and pillaging."[14] The Scottish wife of Edward Ellice, *seigneur* of Beauharnois, described them as a "wild set of men — very like what one imagines the old Highlanders in Scotland and equally difficult to manage." She concluded that the rural *habitants* were less afraid of the Indians than of the Glengarries, and with reason. The Highlander who rowed her and her husband to safety at Lachine after they were rescued from the insurgents laconically told them "the houses they had spared in coming down the country, they would surely burn going back."[15]

A border raid on the windmill at Prescott sent the Highlanders scurrying back to defend their own province. Having come as infantry, most

367

of them returned as cavalrymen, mounting, as they claimed, "stray French ponies they found on the wayside."[16] The horses were on the loose because the *habitants* had freed their animals, fearing that their properties would be burned as part of the repressive military measures. The use of the Glengarries and the Indians was part of a military policy of instilling terror amongst the rebel forces, a policy that succeeded, for fighting took place only briefly at Lacolle and Odelltown, on the frontier, and at Baker's Farm and Beauharnois. In none of the areas that rose during the previous Autumn was a shot fired, evidence of the efficacy of the repressive measures by the military in those areas.

A Harsher Policy: Fear of a Third Rebellion

This second revolt, coming so swiftly on the heels of the first, faced a harsher military policy. Colonel Charles Grey, son of a former British Prime Minister, expressed the common military attitude. "You certainly cannot allow people to give you all this trouble and to act as they have towards the loyal part of the population, and then go to their homes without any punishment."[17] Once the second insurrection was suppressed, a policy of "dragooning" was adopted, designed to check any possible attempt at a third uprising. The spectre of a third rebellion was indeed raised by Curé François-Xavier Bellamin Ricard of Île Perrot. Identified as one "well acquainted with all the secret plans and designs of the late revolt," Curé Ricard visited Beauharnois in the wake of the troops on Sunday, 11 November 1838. He was horrified by what he saw, just as Jane Ellice was as she "stood watching the village in flames — an awful sight."[18]

As soon as Curé Ricard returned to his own parish from Beauharnois, he predicted that "they would revolt again next year and would be unsuccessful, but that in the year 1840, they would rise again in rebellion and be revenged for their injuries." Strangely, Ricard said this before a house full of people, among them two loyalist volunteer officers who immediately informed military headquarters of the priest's speech. "The prediction is the groundwork of a future insurrection."[19]

Military authorities did not need evidence of continuing disaffection in order to initiate a harsher policy. Having, as they believed, treated disaffection with great leniency the previous year — no executions, and all but eight of the prisoners freed — they concluded that their former policy had been interpreted as weakness. Many of the loyalists repeatedly insisted that a lenient policy would lead to fresh outbreaks of rebellion. Henceforth, troops were quartered south of the Saint Lawrence, some 3,000 regulars and 1,000 volunteers. Homes were searched for rebels and arms, arrests made, and oaths of allegiance exacted. Houses of suspected insurgent leaders and of those thought to be still consorting with sympathizers across the American border were burnt.

Home-Burning Intensified

At Napierville, a village of about 80 houses, military authorities at first intended to burn all rebel homes. Non-commissioned officers from regular regiments were selected for the task, and had actually begun when the order was countermanded by Sir John Colborne. Colonel Charles Grey claimed that the countermand order arrived too late "to prevent several homes being burnt, among them Dr. Côté's which we saw in full blaze after we left the place."[20] Grey was heading towards Saint Edouard, accompanied by Captain Sydney Bellingham of the Royal Montreal Cavalry; their objective was to "burn the houses of the leaders of the insurgents." Bellingham described how the policy of burning had been adopted. It was largely the work of Attorney-General Charles Richard Ogden. "He (Ogden) discovered the authors of the outrages to which the loyal inhabitants had been exposed, and as the principal actors took refuge beyond the frontier, and secretly returned to excite the population, Mr. Ogden came to the conclusion that the best method of punishing them was to burn their homesteads. The officers in command of troops merely obeyed orders."[21]

369

A Montreal newspaper dolefully reported that not a single rebel home was left standing south of the Saint Lawrence. This was far from the case. At least 1,500 men took up arms in the second insurrection and there were as many as 7,500 among the disaffected, yet the number of homes burnt in the second uprising, even counting those burned at Beauharnois and Chateauguay immediately after military engagements, were probably under 100.[22]

Not all burnings were, however, authorized by the military.

At Beauharnois, for example, a village of about 45 homes, some 23 houses were burned by loyalists, who reasoned that it was the only punishment the rebels would receive.[23] The Lachine Volunteers were responsible for at least ten homes out of the 20 that were burned at Chateauguay. These were unauthorized burnings, and the Lachine Volunteers involved were put under military arrest.

In early 1839 the military burnings had ceased. But by then disaffected elements over the border had renewed raids and had started to burn properties themselves. In most cases, the border burnings were confined to barns, but in two cases homes of loyalist volunteers were set on fire. With regard to "free quarters," or pillaging, regulars and volunteers engaged in both with equal gusto, sometimes legitimately, as in the case of the church funds of Napierville, where insurgents had confiscated them from the local priest. In their haste to clear out of Napierville as regular troops neared, the rebels left the cart containing the funds behind. They took time out only to set fire to the house they used as their arms depot. Soldiers of the 71st Highland Light Infantry pulled the cart out of the way and, as they did so, it upset. The chest containing the "sacred silver" broke open, whereupon the delighted soldiers helped themselves. Colonel Grey regarded this as legitimate plunder, but he had harsh words for other incidents of pillage. "The sort of plunderers that the Guards, the Artillery and the 7th Hussars are, I think I never saw. There was this excuse for killing animals to eat, that no rations were issued to the men . . . but the slaughter of poultry of all sorts by the Guards and the Hussars in particular I never saw equalled."[24] His own regiment was not totally innocent, and pillaging ceased only after five men had been sentenced to twelve months imprisonment for plundering.

Effect of Persecution and Harsh Measures

The effect of this persecution, together with the courtsmartial of some 111 prisoners and the hanging of twelve insurgents in Montreal, drove at least 3,775 *Patriote* sympathizers over the border by 1839.[25] Some of these political refugees continued to think in terms of limited border raids, hoping to provoke war between Great Britain and the United States. But this new round of border outrages caused such negative reactions in the United States that *Chasseur* leaders as far away as Baltimore wrote to insurgent leaders on the border deploring the raids. "Tell our friends to cease these martial excursions," one wrote. "They do only harm to our cause."[26] Moreover, the firm stand against the raiders now being taken by the American Generals John Wool and Winfield Scott convinced military leaders in Montreal that the American government was anxious to avoid war.

370

By 1840 only a few desultory border raids were made. But the refugee communities were quick to denounce them as "individual private acts, not being pushed by the chiefs."[27] Many over the border were longing for home. Others had found work and established their families over the line, and were now anxious to raise the image of French Canadians in the eyes of their fellow American citizens.

By creating an atmosphere of terror, dragooning had done its job. Those disaffected elements who had sought safety across the American border soon learned that there was no chance of American military aid. And without such aid, they recognized the folly of continued resistance, for all hopes of a successful insurrection were predicated on an uprising *en masse* of the *habitants*, coupled with American aid. Thus, directly or indirectly, military policy and practice stamped out insurrection in Lower Canada.

NOTES

[1] Elinor Kyte Senior, *British Regulars in Montreal: An Imperial Garrison, 1832-1854* (Montreal, 1981), 28-30.
[2] Lt. Col. Charles Grey to his father, 5 November 1838, in William Ormsby, *Crisis in the Canadas, 1838-39* (Toronto, 1964), 155.

[3] Elinor Kyte Senior, *Redcoats and Patriotes: The Rebellions in Lower Canada, 1837-38* (Stittsville, 1985), 54–55.

[4] Deputy Quarter Master General Sir Charles Gore to Lt.-Col. George Wetherall, 17 November 1837, PAC: MG11/Q239/2: 10.

[5] Wetherall to Gore, 28 November 1837, PAC: RG4/S390/A1/2: 147; Pierre Meunier, *L'Insurrection à Saint-Charles et le Seigneur Debartzch* (Quebec, 1986), 216.

[6] Gore to Major Goldie, 2 December 1837, PAC: Colborne Papers, MF24/A40/8043.

[7] Statement of Captain Joseph Swinburne in PAC: Wily Memoirs, PAC: MG29/E1/94.

[8] *Gazette*, Montreal, 16 December 1837.

[9] Lord Charles Beauclerk, *Lithographic Views of the Military Operations in Canada* (London, 1840), 12.

[10] *Transcript*, Montreal, 18 December 1837; Maitland to Gore, 16 December 1837, PAC: Q239/346-7; Colborne to Somerset, 22 December 1837, PAC: RG8/C1272/57.

[11] E.B. O'Callaghan to Thomas Falconer, 24 June 1838, PAC: Chapman Papers, MG24/B31/1: 37–44.

[12] For details see Senior, *Redcoats and Patriotes*, 101.

[13] Pierre Reid's testimony, in *Report of the State Trials* (Montreal, 1839), 1: 42–44.

[14] Grey to his father, 13 November 1838, in PAC: Grey Papers, MG24/A10/2: 127.

[15] Ellice diary, PAC: MG24/A2/50, see entry 14 November 1838.

[16] John Fraser, *Canadian Pen and Ink Sketches* (Montreal, 1890), 105.

[17] Grey to father, 11 November 1838, PAC: Grey Papers, MG24/A10/2: 124.

[18] Major J.A. Mathison's deposition, 12 November 1838, in Archives nationales de Québec: Documents relatifs aux événements de 1837-38, #2953; Ellice diary, PAC: MG24/A2/50, entry dated 10 November 1838.

[19] Captain Edward Jones' deposition, 23 November 1838, ANQ: Documents relatifs aux événements de 1837-38, #2951.

[20] Ormsby, *Crisis in the Canadas*, 147.

[21] Bellingham Memoirs, PAC: MG24/B25/2: 126.

[22] This figure is estimated from *First Report of Commissioners to enquire into losses occasioned by the troubles during the years 1837-38, Appendix to the Journal*, 1846, no. 2, app. X, see claims for over £100; see also Robert Sellar, *History of Huntingdon* (Huntingdon, 1888), 604; Fraser, *Pen and Ink Sketches*, 91; F.X. Prieur, *Notes of a Convict, 1838* (Australia, 1949), 49–55.

[23] Ormsby, *Crisis in the Canadas*, 150.

[24] Grey to father, 11 November 1838, PAC: Grey Papers, MG24/A10/2: 124.

[25] For figures, see Elinor Kyte Senior, "The Presence of French Canadians in American Towns Bordering Lower Canada 1837-1840: Disaffection, Terror or Economic Pulls," in *Journal of the Northern New York American-Canadian Genealogical Society* (Plattsburgh, N.Y.) 4, 2 (Fall 1987): 17–30.

[26] Dr. Henri Gauvin to Louis Perrault, 5 April 1839, PAC: Duvernay Papers, MG24/C3/3: 1351.

[27] Assemblie de comité de l'association des Refugiés Canadiens d'état de Vermont, 29 août, 1840, PAC: Duvernay Papers, MG24/C3/3: 1860.

The Habitant Farm *(1856), oil on canvas, by Cornelius Krieghoff.*

... French-Canadian society in most of the older parishes and seigneuries of the St. Laurence lowland had sealed itself from outsiders; not only were there few if any non–French Canadians in many parishes, but as time went on there were fewer French Canadians who had not been born in the immediate vicinity. . . . Petite-Nation, in contrast, was being settled and it attracted different people.

Cole Harris, "Of Poverty and Helplessness in Petite-Nation"

The Society of the Canadas

On the eve of the Act of Union of 1841, the United Canadas had a population of roughly 1 100 000. Canada East (Lower Canada) had 650 000 inhabitants; Canada West (Upper Canada) had 450 000. Two groups, the Americans and the British, predominated in Canada West. The Americans arrived in two waves — the United Empire Loyalists in the 1780s, who settled mainly in the Niagara Peninsula and along the St. Lawrence River, and the later settlers, many with no Loyalist background, who arrived between 1791 and 1812. The British migrants came in great numbers between 1830 and 1860. Naturally, such rapid population growth created a society in transition. In contrast, the population of Canada East remained predominantly French Canadian.

The selections included here examine various aspects of the society of the Canadas from the 1830s to the 1860s. L.F.S. Upton's article, "The Origins of Canadian Indian Policy," looks at the evolution of a uniform policy toward the Amerindians in the mid-nineteenth century. The evolving system of confinement and control of Canadian Amerindians in some ways parallels developments in the areas of mental health and the penal system. Daniel Francis and C. James Taylor review these topics in "Institutions of Confinement: The Origins of Canadian Mental Hospitals and Penitentiaries." In another sense, poverty also "imprisoned" Canadians. In "Of Poverty and Helplessness in Petite-Nation," Cole Harris provides an in-depth study of extreme poverty in a seigneury in Canada East.

The best overview of the Canadas remains J.M.S. Careless's *The Union of the Canadas: The Growth of Canadian Institutions, 1841–1857* (Toronto: McClelland and Stewart, 1967). R. Cole Harris provides a survey of Quebec and Ontario in *Canada before Confederation: A Study in Historical Geography* (Toronto: Oxford University Press, 1974), 65–109 and 110–68, respectively. On Canada West, J.K. Johnson's *Historical Essays on Upper Canada* (Toronto: McClelland and Stewart, 1975) and his second collection of articles under the same title, edited with Bruce G. Wilson, (vol. 2; Ottawa: Carleton University Press, 1989), as well as Roger Hall, William Westfall, and Laurel Sefton MacDowell, eds., *Patterns of the Past: Interpreting Ontario's History* (Toronto: Dundurn Press, 1988), are very useful.

For a full review of the Iroquois residents of Canada West and their society in the early nineteenth century, consult *The Valley of the Six*

Nations: A Collection of Documents on the Indian Lands of the Grand River, ed. Charles M. Johnston (Toronto: Champlain Society, 1964). Donald B. Smith tells the story of the Mississauga Indians in *Sacred Feathers: The Reverend Peter Jones (Kahkewaquonaby) and the Mississauga Indians* (Toronto: University of Toronto Press, 1987). A general review of the changes in Indian society is provided by Elizabeth Graham in *Medicine Man to Missionary: Missionaries as Agents of Change among the Indians of Southern Ontario, 1784–1867* (Toronto: Peter Martin Associates, 1975). For developments in Canada East, see Daniel Francis, *A History of the Native Peoples of Quebec, 1760–1867* (Ottawa: Indian Affairs and Northern Development, 1983), and Hélène Bédard, *Les Montagnais et la réserve de Betsiamites, 1850–1900* (Quebec: Institut québécois de recherche sur la culture, 1988). Several chapters in Robin W. Winks's *The Blacks in Canada* (Montreal: McGill-Queen's University Press, 1971) deal with the arrival and the lives of blacks in the Canadas. Allen P. Stouffer looks at the antislavery movement in Canada West in *The Light of Nature and the Law of God* (Montreal and Kingston: McGill-Queen's University Press, 1992). Richard Menkis examines attitudes toward Jews in his "Antisemitism and Anti-Judaism in Pre-Confederation Canada," in *Antisemitism in Canada: History and Interpretation,* ed. Alan Davies (Waterloo: Wilfrid Laurier University Press, 1992), 11–38.

A number of valuable social histories of the Canadas in the mid-nineteenth century now exist. They include David Gagan, *Hopeful Travellers: Families, Land and Social Change in Mid-Victorian Peel County, Canada West* (Toronto: University of Toronto Press for the Ontario Historical Studies Series, 1981); Michael Katz, *The People of Hamilton, Canada West: Family and Class in a Mid-Nineteenth Century City* (Cambridge, Mass.: Harvard University Press, 1975); and Jack Little, *Crofters and Habitants: Settler Society, Economy, and Culture in a Quebec Township, 1848–1881* (Kingston and Montreal: McGill-Queen's University Press, 1991). For a survey of life in rural Canada East, consult Serge Courville and Normand Séguin, *Rural Life in Nineteenth-Century Quebec,* Canadian Historical Association, Historical Booklet no. 47 (Ottawa: CHA, 1989).

Alison Prentice et al., *Canadian Women: A History* (Toronto: Harcourt Brace Jovanovich, 1988) provides a review of Canadian women's lives in the mid-nineteenth century. Micheline Dumont et al., *Quebec Women: A History,* trans. R. Gannon and R. Gill (Toronto: Women's Press, 1987) summarizes developments in Canada East alone during the same period.

Two of the best Canadian biographical studies are about the two leading political antagonists of the 1850s: D.G. Creighton's *John A. Macdonald,* vol. 1, *The Young Politician* (Toronto: Macmillan, 1952) and J.M.S. Careless's *Brown of the Globe,* vol. 1, *The Voice of Upper Canada, 1818–1859* (Toronto: Macmillan, 1959). These volumes also contain many glimpses into the social history of the Canadas, as do the portraits of the mid-nineteenth century Canadians included in the relevant volumes of the *Dictionary of Canadian Biography* (Toronto: University of Toronto Press, 1966–   ).

374

The Origins of Canadian Indian Policy

L.F.S. UPTON

By 1830 the British Empire no longer needed the Indians of the two Canadas. These Indians had been key allies in the struggle for continental power as late as 1814, but except in the memory of a few veterans of the Indian Department, this military potential was of no further use. They had once been vital to the fur trade, but the trade had departed westward. There was no need to employ Indians as cheap labour on white plantations, for the family farm was the unit of settlement. Nor were there enough Indians to provide a worthwhile market for British manufacturers. The only economic interest that the Empire had in the Indians was to arrange for the peaceful transfer of the land to which their possessory title had been acknowledged by the Proclamation of 1763. This process was going ahead to the complete destruction of the Indians' economic, social, and cultural life. And to ease this process the British Colonial Office adopted a new policy after 1830: to assimilate the Indians into white society. It was a policy that was later generalized across the Dominion after 1867 and has guided the official conduct of Indian affairs down to the present day.

375

The policy of assimilation was the result of a concurrence of sentiment and interest: the sentiment that a superior race (the British) had definite responsibilities towards an inferior (the Indians) coincided with the self-interest of the British government in cutting the costs of colonial administration. The British never for a moment questioned their own superiority. They could see it in every example of European contact with native peoples, who were inferior in terms of political organization, military equipment, religious beliefs, business skills, and attitudes to work. The 1830s, with their immense advances in the technology of steam, further emphasized the gulf between superior and inferior. At a time when the excessive expense of Empire was a matter of frequent debate, no one questioned the desirability of lessening the burden on the British taxpayer.

When it came to forming opinions on the Indian "problem" the Colonial Office did not rely simply on the reports of its officials on the spot. Men such as Lord Glenelg and James Stephen had behind them a body of literature which included the works of scientists, social scientists, travellers, humanitarians, and missionaries. After all, the Amerindian had long been the best-known outsider of the European world. For two centuries the noble savage had been a stereotype for writers anxious to show up the foibles and pomposities of western civilization.[1]

From *Journal of Canadian Studies/Revue d'études canadiennes* 8, 4 (November 1973): 51–61. Reprinted with permission.

The Indian was noble in word, deed, and physique. As Benjamin West exclaimed on first seeing the Apollo Belvedere, "My God, a Mohawk!"[2] Although this type of sentimentality was discounted in the nineteenth century, few whites who travelled among the Indians could avoid at least a twinge of envy. Sir Francis Head, who had earlier admired the life of the Indians of the Argentine pampas, was impressed all over again when he went to Upper Canada fresh from building poorhouses in East Kent: The Indian

> breathes pure air, beholds splendid scenery, traverses unsullied water, and subsists on food which, generally speaking, forms not only his sustenance but the manly amusement, as well as occupation of his life.[3]

Indians always contrasted favourably with those languid natives of the tropics, who had only to reach out an arm to pluck food provided by an overabundant nature.

376   The romantic image of the Indian had been challenged by the more analytical approach of the social scientist. William Robertson's *History of America*, published in 1777, asked why the Indian had failed to progress as had the white living on the same continent. The answer lay in the isolation of the Indian and the harsh conditioning of the hunting life he led. This environment dictated his virtues, freedom, independence, eloquence, bravery; and also his vices — notably, improvidence.[4]

By the beginning of the nineteenth century, anthropology was struggling into existence as a science, cataloguing the various members of the human race, establishing their characteristics, both physical and moral. From the first, the science assumed white superiority as a fact, sometimes on little more evidence than that white was familiar to the writer. Where else, asked Charles White in 1799, could one find

> that nobly arched head, containing such a quantity of brain . . . ? Where that variety of features, and fulness of expression; those long, flowing, graceful ringlets; that majestic beard, those rosy cheeks and coral lips? Where that . . . noble gait? In what other quarter of the globe shall we find the blush that overspreads the soft features of the beautiful women of Europe, that emblem of modesty, of delicate feelings . . . ? Where, except on the bosom of the European woman, two such plump and snowy white hemispheres, tipt with vermillion?[5]

A second constricting feature of early anthropological studies was the need to work within the time limits laid down in the Bible. There was precise dating for the Creation, 4004 B.C., and for the Flood, 2350 B.C., which had destroyed practically all life. How could the great differences between men be explained if they had developed in so short a time? One answer, which defied explicit scriptural authority, was that there had been several independent creations, and that men were not all of the same species. If whites chose, as they did, to see themselves as the superior species, polygenesis had great implications for their treatment of others: for if there were several species of men it was easy to place blacks, Indians, Mongolians, orangutans, on the same, declining scale in the animal world. By the 1820s this idea had been successfully rebutted in England, although it lingered long in the United States as a justification for slavery.[6]

One prominent supporter of monogenesis was William Lawrence, whose influential *Lectures on Physiology, Zoology, and the Natural History of Man* (London, 1822) explained the differences among men as the result of the varying size of human crania, a study of which showed the superiority of the whites.

> The retreating forehead and the depressed vertex of the dark varieties of man make me strongly doubt whether they are susceptible of . . . high destinies; — whether they are capable of fathoming the depths of science; of understanding and appreciating the doctrines and mysteries of our religion.[7]

Lawrence expected that such obstacles doomed most men to an inferior, subordinate lot, although inferiority did not mean a total absence of virtue. The savage tribes of North America had

> lofty sentiments of independence, ardent courage, and devoted friendship, which would sustain a comparison with the most splendid similar examples in more highly gifted races.[8]

377

But there was obviously a very low ceiling to the Indians' development.

Lawrence's reputation was second only to that of J.C. Prichard, whose writings dominated British anthropological thought until Darwin. Prichard was much more optimistic about the dark races, for he felt that the common origin of all men meant that they had the same basic mental faculties. But no one looking at the plates in his book would mistake the Apollo Belvedere for a Mohawk. There was no doubt that the darker races were inferior, but only through the absurd notion of polygenesis could anyone argue that they must always be so. The Indians, Prichard argued, had a definite advantage over other races, for their monotheistic religion meant that they were well suited to civilization and Christianity. Whole tribes had already become Christian and agricultural, and, given the short time in which the human race had developed its differences across the world, improvement could come with great rapidity.[9]

Another item in the intellectual baggage of the day was the travelogue. Travellers had a ready audience for their accounts of distant parts, and occasionally moved from description to judgement. John Howison published *European Colonies in Various Parts of the World Viewed in their Social, Moral and Physical Conditions* in 1834. His Indians were much addicted to liquor, for only its stimulation could overcome "the languor of a contemplative state of existence," which lacked domestic amusements, or any taste for music or poetry. The Indians were so improvident that the loss of their hunting grounds did not bother them at all. Christianity and civilization had no effect on them, for unlike other savage peoples, "they refuse to admit our superiority," and would not conform to white ways.[10] Howison may have had in mind the Indian he had once met in the Upper Canadian twilight: "His half-unsheathed scalping knife gleamed in the ruddy light of the flames. He grasped his rifle with one hand, while the other rested upon a tomahawk." But, as the alarmed traveller quickly noted, the Indian was only skinning a deer. The two men fell into conversation, for the Indian spoke excellent English. "To my astonishment he made enquiries about the Reform meetings then very common throughout Britain, and seemed anxious to learn the cause of them, and their object." For all his polite interest, the Indian hunter made it quite clear that such antics of the whites were beneath his contempt.[11]

The most conscientious moulders of opinion were the humanitarians and missionaries. Their basic concern at this period was with the evils of black slavery and the frequent killings of Bushmen, Xhosa, and the aborigines of Australia. The Canadian Indian was generally peripheral to their concern. A survey of the condition of the native peoples in the British Empire would show that the Indians were the most fortunate of them all. Professor Herman Merivale of Oxford University attributed this situation to the fact that the Indians were

378

> possessed of higher moral elevation than any other uncivilized race of mankind, with less natural readiness and ingenuity than some, but greater depth and force of character, more native generosity of spirit and manliness of disposition, more of the religious element.[12]

And yet these virtues created their own difficulties, because, as Howison had noted, they made the Indian that much more difficult to include in any pattern of white civilization.

One of the essential attributes of the humanitarian was guilt. The evils that the whites inflicted on native peoples all over the globe were endlessly paraded in ritual self-examinations.

> We hand over to the care of the missionary and magistrate not the savage with his natural tendencies and capacities, and his ancestral habits, but a degraded, craving, timid and artful creature familiarised with the powers and the vices of the whites.[13]

Guilt prefaced almost every account of the Indian in this period: guilt for destroying his independence, his manliness, for killing him through war and disease, and demoralizing him with liquor. Frequently the London-based humanitarian put the blame squarely on the riff-raff white settlers on the frontier. Guilt shows through the voluminous Parliamentary enquiries of 1835/36 into the aborigines of the Empire. As the committee chairman, Thomas Buxton, wrote a friend in South Africa:

> Oh! we Englishmen are, by our own account, fine fellows at home. Who among us doubts that we surpass the world in religion, justice, knowledge, refinement and practical honesty? but such a set of miscreants and wolves as we prove when we escape from the range of the laws, the earth does not contain.[14]

Guilt never led to any thought that the whites might leave others alone to go their own way. There was never any thought of stopping the flow of emigration, which could only increase as the century progressed. Guilt had to be atoned for by accepting responsibility for the protection and civilization of inferior and perverse people, for if the natives were debauched by white contact it was partly their own fault. Hence they must be made over into white men.

For the Canadian Indian the path led to assimilation. First of all it would be necessary to overcome his preference for his own way of life, which was doomed to vanish in the face of white settlement. To do this it would be necessary to Christianize him, and the missionaries would be the executive arm of assimilationist policy. Unless sanctioned by religion, "civilized life is too tame, too insipid, to charm the roving barbarian," explained one witness before the Parliamentary enquiries.[15] Chief Kahkewaquonaby (the Reverend Peter Jones) described in a letter how "all the tribes that have embraced the Gospel" immediately "applied to the Governor and missionaries to enable them to settle down in villages." He cited the Credit River mission, whose Indians had comfortable

379

> houses, furniture, window curtains, boxes and trunks for their wearing apparel, small shelves fastened against the wall for their books, closets for their cooking utensils, cupboards for their plates, cups, saucers, knives and forks; some had clocks and watches.

Previously they had been content without owning any of these things. Christianity had given them the material desires of white men, and for that reason the Indian now had to work like a white man. He could no longer be drunken, indolent, improvident.[16] He had been inducted into civilization, on his way to assimilation — the end which, as Merivale rather gracelessly put it, was "the only possible euthanasia of savage communities."[17]

It was Merivale who gave the best summation of the conventional wisdom of Empire (as it stood) at the end of the 1830s. The lectures he gave on "Colonization and the Colonies" marked him as the successor of James Stephen at the Colonial Office. His synthesis of a decade of intensive soul-searching by Britons can be assumed to be the definitive one. Three alternatives, said Merivale, faced all natives in the presence of white settlement: their extermination, their civilization in communities isolated from the whites, or their amalgamation with the colonists. Merivale favoured the last alternative. Other races were not inferior to the whites for any immutable physical cause; their inferiority was cultural and could be remedied by training in civilized ways. Britain therefore had two duties to perform: first, to protect, second, to civilize the native peoples of the Empire.[18]

* * *

How well had the twin responsibilities of protecting and civilizing the native peoples been carried out in the Canadas?[19] The traditional policy towards the Indians had been simple: keep them content, so that when war broke out with the Americans, they would fight on the British side, or at least not on the American. The Indian Department was a branch of the military establishment and as such directly under the Governor General. The Indian agent was a mediator in peace, a leader in war. His duties were described by Sir James Kempt in 1829:

> It is essential that he should conciliate the good will of the several Indian tribes, and possess their confidence; attend to their endless representations, remedy their grievances, or report them to the commander of the forces, adjust their differences, and arbitrate in their bargains, advise them in their difficulties, collect their rents, and distribute in detail their presents and occasional rations, &c &c. In war they also command the Indians in the field.[20]

The Department's main routine responsibilities were the annual distribution of presents, and the guardianship of Indian lands. In theory the Indians of both Canadas were administered as a unit, but in practice the Lieutenant Governor of Upper Canada was always consulted about the natives of his province. The precaution was a wise one, for the situation in the two colonies was very different. There were some 3,000 Indians in Lower Canada, and they had been long in contact with whites. Many were, at least to English eyes, "nearly, if not quite on a par with the lower class of their Canadian neighbours."[21] The Roman Catholic church was an old and strong influence, jealously on guard against interference from Protestant missionaries or Protestant government.[22] The only outsiders were 300 or so Indians who wandered in from New Brunswick for their annual presents. The Indians of Upper Canada had not been in contact with the whites for very long, and then usually in connection with war. These Indians numbered some 6,500 and in addition some 3,000–4,000 more, residents of the United States, arrived every year to receive their presents.[23] Comparatively few of the western Indians were settled or within the reach of missionaries, and so preserved their accustomed way of life to a much greater extent than the Indians of Lower Canada.

What did the Indian have that needed protection? His life, both physical and cultural, and his lands. His life was reasonably safe in Canada. He was not being hunted down (as in Newfoundland or Tasmania) nor was he being militarily destroyed. All the same, his numbers were decreasing, and the birth rate was too low to maintain the population at the existing level.[24] His way of life was under continuing threat due to the advance of white settlement, but to an extent the appurtenances of life, at least as they had become known in the previous 150 years, were maintained by the annual distribution of presents, featuring the traditional trade goods of bygone years: blankets, tobacco, gunpowder, shot, cloth. Their effect was to assist the Indian in the nomadic hunting life and maintain his accustomed style of dress. In fact the presents were increasingly criticized by whites during the 1830s simply because they did protect the Indian from new influences. By contrast, the Indians clung tenaciously to their presents and resisted every effort at abolition with frequent reminders of the debt of honour owed them by the British. As 94-year-old Saro Oriwagati explained: never, in three bloody wars that he had fought on the side of the British, had he ever had occasion to doubt the good faith of the Great Father, and his promise, "Presents so long as we should remain a Tribe."[25] The suggestion that the presents be commuted for cash was strongly resisted by Indian and Indian agent alike on the grounds that ready money would be instantly squandered on liquor and contribute nothing to the Indians' welfare.[26] To a considerable extent, then, the distribution of presents in goods could be regarded as one aspect of protection.

When it came to lands, the argument that the Indian enjoyed some kind of protection from government is not so strong. True, individuals could not buy lands from the Indians, nor is there any indication of large-scale overt theft of their lands; but even the official documents indicate that the white squatter on Indian lands could usually get away with it, if he improved his acquisition into a useful family farm.[27] Moreover, the Indian Department oversaw massive transfers of Indian lands to settlers in its capacity as administrator of moneys arising from land sales. The Department arranged for Indian land both on and off reserves to be sold outright to the Crown or conveyed to the Crown for sale piecemeal to settlers. The moneys realized went to the Commissioner of Crown Lands and were credited to the account of the Indians. Land surrenders took place on a large scale. Nine tribes gave up 11,277,480 acres outright for annuities between 1818 and 1838. They received annual payments totalling £6,653, all but £1,400 of which was to be in goods. In addition to this were 201,926 acres deeded over to Crown agents for sale.[28] An example of what happened to one tribe can be seen by following the surrenders of the Mohawks of the Bay of Quinté. They had been allotted reserves of 92,700 acres in 1793. They surrendered 33,280 acres in 1820 for £450 a year. The Commissioner of Crown Lands thereupon deducted 14,773 acres as Crown and Clergy reserves. In 1835 the band deeded 27,850 acres of their land in trust to be sold for their benefit, leaving them with 16,500 acres. Seven years later, their last surrender had yielded only £1,500 in sales, and £1,000 of that was earmarked for a stone church.[29]

The way in which the Indian Department handled the moneys entrusted to it showed less than a scrupulous regard for the protection of Indian interests. The investments made for the Six Nations in the disastrous Grand River Navigation Company is the most glaring example of abuse. The Indians were supposed to determine among themselves how their money was to be spent, but £38,000 had gone without consultation.[30] But at least the Six Nations had a record of their land sales; all other tribes were lumped together in the Department's records so that who had sold what for how much was almost impossible to determine. There was no checking or auditing of the warrants of payment made

381

on behalf of the Indians, and no statements of expenditure were submitted to the governor. The rough and ready system of accounting that did exist frequently showed income from Indian lands as less than the costs of administration charged to them.[31] The Department's discharge of its duties in connection with Indian lands can be characterized in one word: fraudulent.

* * *

The implementation of the idea that the British had a duty to civilize the Indian came into official policy through the back door of self-interest. The Colonial Secretary, Lord Goderich, started it, almost predictably, in one of the British government's periodic drives for economy. He wrote Lord Dalhousie in 1828 questioning the need for an Indian department in the Canadas and urged that it be scaled down with a view to its eventual abolition.[32] Dalhousie ordered the Superintendent of the Indian Department, Major General Darling, to draw a survey of the state of the Indians and make recommendations for their future. Threatened with the loss of his department, Darling turned in a report that advanced a new function for it: to promote civilization by settling the Indian on farms, making him educated and Christian. This report, dated July 24, 1828, is the founding document of the whole "civilizing" programme.[33] It was accepted at the Colonial Office and expanded in detail by Sir James Kempt, Dalhousie's successor. Indians should be collected into villages with only enough land for their agricultural support. The government should provide for their religious instruction, elementary education, and training in agriculture. It should encourage them to build houses and acquire tools and seed. But it would be expensive: £14.3.4 to settle a family of five on cleared land and £100 on forest land. Therefore the Indians should pay the cost of their own assimilation by using the moneys from land sales to buy the necessary equipment. Further changes in the Indians' way of life could be encouraged by varying the nature of the presents, substituting, for example, ready-made trousers and shirts for blankets.[34]

The Colonial Secretary, Sir George Murray, agreed that Britain had the duty of reclaiming the Indians "from a state of barbarism and of introducing amongst them the industrious and peaceful habits of civilized life." However, costs must be held down, and so the Indian Department was transferred from military to civil control and its budget was brought under the annual scrutiny of the British parliament.[35] Throughout the 1830s the Colonial Office kept prompting governors to dismiss as many officials as possible. Artisans and schoolteachers disappeared from the payroll. In 1835 a House of Commons Select Committee renewed the demand that the Department be abolished. Out went interpreters and even superintendents. The Department knew that if "civilization" ever succeeded, they would be the first victims of its success.[36]

The Department's officials were trapped. London wanted to hear of the success of the policy of "civilization," so they had to provide evidence that they were still performing a useful function. One showcase was the Credit River settlement referred to above. Another was Coldwater. Captain Anderson, the superintendent there, wrote in 1835:

> I trust . . . I shall not be considered impertinent in expressing my Opinion that the Indians are not a degraded Race; all the higher Attributes are possessed by them; their Minds are strong; their imaginative Powers highly fertile, their Morals in their natural State are pure.

But the Indians, the "original proprietors of the soil" had been demoralized by the whites, and so had "claims on our Humanity." Coldwater showed this humanity in action. Farming had been introduced, drunkenness overcome; the sabbath was observed, hunting had dropped off; log houses had been built and the Indians wanted to own furniture. "If concentrated and civilized," Anderson explained, all the Indians would become "useful and loyal Subjects during Peace, and an important Support to the Government."[37] Sir John Colborne waxed very enthusiastic about the success of the assimilation policy in one of his last official letters:

383

> . . . all the Indian Tribes in Canada are collected in Villages . . . Schools are instituted for their benefit . . . they are placed under the Care of Persons interested in their Welfare . . . few cases of Intoxication now occur, except among the visiting Indians chiefly resident in the United States.[38]

Colborne's letter to the Colonial Secretary crossed one from Glenelg to the new Canadian Governors, Lord Gosford and Sir Francis Bond Head. Glenelg wanted a progress report on Indian relations and recommendations for future policy.[39] Gosford, wise in the ways of administration, struck a Council committee to prepare his answer for him. Head devised his own policy on the spot and put it into effect right away with a massive assault on the whole concept of assimilation.

Head based his policy, as he eventually informed the Colonial Secretary, on his personal observations and his previous knowledge of the aborigines of the Argentine. The whites had systematically plundered and destroyed the Indians over the years, and Christian missionaries were still killing them by herding them into villages, where they died of consumption. The process was irreversible: the Indian was doomed to extinction. Agriculture was a complete failure. Head had visited practically all the Indian villages in Upper Canada, entering "every Shanty or Cottage" to see how civilization was progressing. It was not. Consequently he proposed to remove all the Canadian Indians to the 23,000 islands of the Manitoulin area, where their last years could be spent happily, free of the whites. These islands, Head maintained, provided good enough soil, and an abundance of game and berries and fish, and would never be attractive to white settlers.[40] At the ceremony of issuing the presents at Amherstburg in 1836 he had the Hurons surrender two thirds of their lands along the River Thames, and the Moravian Indians a further six miles square in the same area. While distributing the presents at Manitoulin, Head also arranged for the Ottawa and Chippewa to give up the islands of the region and got one and a half million acres from the Saugeen.[41]

Lord Glenelg was overwhelmed when he received news of these vast surrenders. He was impressed, he wrote, with Head's "vigilant Humanity" and his incomparably superior resources for judging the plight of the Indian. The King had been pleased to approve all the arrangements and wanted "no Measure . . . unattempted which may afford a reasonable prospect of rescuing this Remnant of the Aboriginal Race from the calamitous Fate" of contact with the whites. But having said this much, Glenelg then asked for any further suggestions Sir Francis might have to enable the Indians "to share in the Blessings of Christian Knowledge and social Improvement . . . "[42]

Head's policy created outrage among the missionaries in Canada. The 1836 annual address of the Wesleyan Methodist Conference in Upper Canada to the British Conference spoke of the most "trying and afflictive year yet" due to "Circumstances as strange as they were unexpected." In 1837 the Conference reported great unrest in Upper Canada among the Indians. Every settlement of Indians now felt itself in danger, and the whole drive towards Christianity, civilization, and progress was slowed by the threat that their lands would be taken from them and that they themselves would be removed to the Manitoulin Islands. Only secure land titles, the missionaries argued, would now persuade the Indians to continue improving themselves.[43] The Aborigines Protection Society joined in the denunciation of Head's policy of removal, which had seen the exchange of three million acres of rich land for 23,000 barren islands. His argument that the fate of the Indians was already sealed had been used time and again to justify European aggression the world over: it must not be allowed to succeed any more. The Secretary of the Wesleyan Methodist Society, R. Alder, appealed to Glenelg as a Christian statesman to undo Head's work. It was an appeal Glenelg had no wish to resist.[44]

While controversy raged around Head's policy, the Council of Lower Canada submitted its report on Indian policy prepared by a committee under the chairmanship of William Smith. It was a safe document, the work of men familiar with the latest in humanitarian precepts, and it also reflected the different state of the Indians in Lower Canada. The committee could not believe that any race of men was doomed to extinction, as Sir Francis maintained contrary to "Reason and Experience." The experiment in farming had not failed, because many Indians had in fact been farmers for generations. Rather than remove them, the committee would prefer to see more land given to Lower Canadian Indians.

Presents should still be issued to resident Indians, but European clothing and farm tools should replace trinkets to encourage settlement. Schools should be maintained to provide basic education in literacy, the French and English languages, agriculture, and handicrafts. School attendance could be encouraged by making the issue of presents to parents dependent upon it. All Indians should be collected in compact groups "not very remote from existing settlements." The report was pure balm to nerve sorely frayed by events in Upper Canada.[45]

In vain did Sir Francis try to defend his policy of removal. The missionaries, he charged, wanted to get the Indians title deeds to make themselves trustees of their lands. Peter Jones was the organizer of a "Radical Meeting of all the Indians in the province at the Credit Village," which was prevented only at the last moment.[46] But Lord Glenelg was no longer listening. Anxious to exculpate himself from his earlier approval of Sir Francis' actions, he stressed that he had always believed the Indians could profit from "the Doctrines of Christianity [and] . . . the Habits of civilized Life." His faith had been strengthened by re-reading the relevant documents. Accordingly, he suspended the operation of the Indian treaties Head had negotiated.

In August, 1838, the Colonial Office issued its statement of official policy for the Canadian Indian. The document was a comprehensive statement of the duty to civilize the natives. Wandering Indians had to be settled down; those who were more or less settled had to be made farmers. They had to be given a sense of permanency on their lands, "attached to the soil," with title to their locations under the Great Seal of the province. Still, their lands would be protected from creditors and be inalienable without the threefold consent of governor, principal chief, and resident missionary. Education was basic to assimilation. The government gave its blessing to the missionaries by instructing the Indian Department agents to co-operate cheerfully with them. The sum total of British policy, Glenelg concluded, was "to protect and cherish this helpless Race . . . [and] raise them in the Scale of Humanity."[47]

To those who formulated Canadian Indian policy in the 1830s, protection and civilization were part and parcel of the same process. The protection of the Indians' accustomed way of life was never contemplated, for that would have meant imposing severe restrictions on the expansion of white settlement. The Indian could not be protected unless he were assimilated. But the government had no intention of putting public money into the venture: rather, the Indian was to pay his own way and so indirectly relieve the Treasury of the expense of a special department to minister to his peculiarities. And the missionary, who financed himself, came to be seen as an increasingly important agent of assimilation.

To those who now live with the legacies of white imperialism, the policy fits into place in a world picture. Nineteenth-century racism has been explained as a rationalization for the exploitation of non-whites by

Europeans who "fostered the elaboration of a complex ideology of paternalism and racism, with its familiar themes of grownup childishness, civilizing mission, atavistic savagery, and arrested evolution."[48] Philip Mason, examining patterns of racial dominance, proposes four groups of relationships: dominant, paternalist, competitive, and racially fluid. The events related in this paper conform to the model in which a dominant migrant group, attracted by sparsely populated land in a temperate zone, drives back the natives and sets up small family farms that need no outside labour. Since they are not needed, the surviving natives are put on reserves. This total dominance would lead either to the extinction of the native, or, if he were to survive, to the creation of plural cultures within the state. But the situation in Canada was not simply one of unchecked dominance by the white settlers. The second category, paternalism, had a visible part to play. In this model, native affairs are controlled by a mother country through officials who have no intention of settling permanently in the colony. Priding itself on its impartiality, metropolitan policy aims at integrating the weaker into the dominant group.[49] In Canada there was a hybrid situation, because the creation of policy lay with the mother country but its execution was in the hands of men who had an economic stake in the colony. Hence the contrast between the high-sounding notions of "civilization" and the actual practice of administering Indian lands. In its pattern of race relations, Canada at this time fell somewhere between dominance and paternalism.

But let one of the actors of the day have the last line. As Glenelg wrote Lord Durham, the Indians had once been

> under the special care of the Jesuit Missionaries, a Class of Men of whom it must be admitted that whatever their Delinquencies in the Old World, they have in the New, been known chiefly as the Protectors and Civilizers of a Race forsaken or trampled upon by all beside. It is Time for us to emulate their Example, and to supply, however tardily, the Place of the Instructors of whom our Conquests have deprived the original Possessors of the Soil.[50]

386

NOTES

This paper is based on one read at the Great Northern Plains History Conference in Winnipeg, October, 1972. The author would like to acknowledge the valuable advice given to him in the shaping of this paper by Robert Kubicek, Peter Moogk, Allan Smith, and Christina Boom of the Department of History, University of British Columbia, and his appreciation of the comments made on this paper by Jean Usher of the Museum of Man, Ottawa.

ABBREVIATIONS IN NOTES

J.L.A.C. 1844-5, *J.L.A.C.* 1847: "Report on the Affairs of the Indians in Canada." Sections 1 and 2 are in the *Journals*, Legislative Assembly of Canada, 1844–1845, Appendix EEE. Section 3 is in the *Journals*, 1847, Appendix T. There is no pagination for this report.

PP 1834: "Reports from Governors of British Possessions in North America, on the present state of the Aboriginal Tribes," House of Commons, *Sessional Papers*, 1834, sec. 44.

PP 1837: "Report from Select Committee on Aborigines (British Settlements)," House of Commons, *Sessional Papers*, 1837, sec. 7.

PP 1839: "Copies or Extracts of Correspondence since 1st April, 1835, of Correspondence between the Secretary of State for the Colonies and the Governors of the British North American Provinces Respecting the Indians in those Provinces," House of Commons, *Sessional Papers*, 1839, sec. 34.

[1] Hoxie N. Fairchild, *The Noble Savage: A Study in Romantic Naturalism* (New York, 1961), 22.

[2] Roy H. Pearce, *The Savages of America: A Study of the Indian and the Idea of Civilization* (Baltimore, 1953).

[3] Sir Francis B. Head, *The Emigrant* (New York, 1847), 88; *Journeys across the Pampas and among the Andes* (Carbondale, 1967), ch. 8, "The Pampas Indians."

[4] Pearce, *Savages*, 86–88.

[5] Charles White, *Account of the Regular Gradation in Man* (London, 1799), 135.

[6] William Stanton, *The Leopard's Spots: Scientific Attitudes towards Race in America, 1815-1859* (Chicago, 1960), 30, *passim*.

[7] Lawrence, *Lectures*, 433.

[8] Ibid., 417.

[9] James C. Prichard, *The Natural History of Man*, 3rd ed. (London, 1848), 5–6, 131–32, 497.

[10] Howison, *European Colonies*, 417–18, 426–28.

[11] John Howison, *Sketches of Upper Canada* (Edinburgh, 1825), 177–78.

[12] Herman Merivale, *Lectures on Colonization and Colonies* (London, 1928), 493.

[13] Ibid., 489.

[14] Charles Buxton, ed., *Memoirs of Sir Thomas Fowell Buxton, Baronet* (London, 1848), 367.

[15] "Report of the Committee on Aborigines," *PP* 1836, sec. 7, 533.

[16] Ibid., 47–48.

[17] Merivale, *Colonization*, 511.

[18] Ibid., 492.

[19] There are accounts of Canadian Indian policy in the 1830s by Duncan C. Scott, "Indian Affairs, 1840 [*sic*] — 1867," in *Canada and Its Provinces* 5: 331–64, and by George R. Mellor, *British Imperial Trusteeship, 1783-1850* (London, 1951), 368–405. R.J. Surtees takes a sanguine view of one aspect of this decade in "The Development of an Indian Reserve Policy in Canada," *Ontario History* (June 1969): 87–98. The complexities of administration within the Indian Department are described in J.E. Hodgetts, *Pioneer Public Service* (Toronto, 1955), 213–19.

[20] Sir James Kempt to Sir George Murray, May 16, 1829, "Papers Relative to the Aboriginal Tribes in British Possessions," *PP* 1834, 375–79.

[21] *J.L.A.C.* 1847, n.p.

[22] Witness the successive failures of Protestant Indian schools in Lower Canada. For example, Rev. Joseph Marcoux at Caughnawaga was reported to have threatened withholding the sacraments from families of those who attended a school set up by the Montreal branch of the Society for Promoting Education and Industry in Canada. "Report of . . . Mr. Justice Pyke," January 10, 1837, "Correspondence Respecting the Indians in the British North American Colonies," *PP* 1839, 275–76.

[23] For details of the Indian population figures, see *J.L.A.C.* 1845.

[24] The 1837 report of the Lower Canadian Council stated that there were on average five children (including half-breeds) for each four Indian married couples. By contrast, there were four children for each white married couple. *PP* 1839, 246.

[25] Enclosure 7 in Earl of Gosford to Lord Glenelg, July 13, 1837, *PP* 1839, 259–60.

[26] For example, Grand Chief Tekanasontle, enclosure 10, *PP* 1839, 263–64.

[27] *J.L.A.C.* 1847, n.p.

[28] For details, see *J.L.A.C.* 1847, Appendices 66 and 67, and Part 3, Section 3.

[29] Ibid., n.p.

[30] This investment absorbed the Six Nations' income from land sales and put them a further £10,000 in debt to meet instalments. What construction took place resulted in the flooding of prime land on the reserve. Incidentally, the Chief Superintendent of Indian Affairs, Upper Canada, in 1843–44 was a director of the Grand River Navigation Company and also received £150 a year from Six Nation funds to manage their finances. Ibid.

[31] The Assembly committee was highly critical of land management practices. Ibid.

[32] Lord Goderich to Earl of Dalhousie, July 14, 1827, *PP* 1834, 343.

[33] Lord Dalhousie to Sir George Murray, October 27, 1828, enclosing the report. Ibid., 360–73.

[34] Sir George Murray to Sir James Kempt, December 3, 1828; Sir James Kempt to Sir George Murray, May 16, 1829, ibid., 374, 375–91.

[35] Sir George Murray to Sir James Kempt, January 25, 1830, ibid., 425–27.

[36] For details on staff reductions, see figures for 1829 and 1837, *PP* 1834, 372–73; *PP* 1839, 238, 373–74.

[37] Report of Captain T.G. Anderson, September 24, 1835, in Sir J. Colborne to Lord Glenelg, January 22, 1836, *PP* 1839, 336–40.

[38] Ibid., 336.

[39] Lord Glenelg to Earl of Gosford (and Sir Francis B. Head), January 14, 1836, ibid., 219–22.

[40] Sir Francis B. Head to Lord Glenelg, November 20, 1836, *PP* 1839, 342–50.

387

[41] Same to same, August 20, 1836, Ibid., 340–42.
[42] Lord Glenelg to Sir Francis B. Head, October 5, 1836, ibid., 290.
[43] Enclosures 1 and 2 in Lord Glenelg to Sir George Arthur, August 22, 1838, ibid., 308–17.
[44] Enclosure 4 in ibid., 319–20.
[45] Report of June 13, 1837, in Earl of Gosford to Lord Glenelg, June 13, 1837, ibid., 245–87.
[46] Sir Francis B. Head to Lord Glenelg, August 15, October 18, 1837, ibid., 367–70, 375–78.
[47] Lord Glenelg to Sir George Arthur, August 22, 1838, ibid., 304–308.
[48] Pierre L. van den Berghe, *Race and Racism: A Comparative Perspective* (New York, 1967), 15–17.
[49] Philip Mason, *Patterns of Dominance* (Oxford, 1971), 107, 126, 129, 159.
[50] Lord Glenelg to the Earl of Durham, August 22, 1838, *PP* 1839, 223–27.

Institutions of Confinement: The Origins of Canadian Mental Hospitals and Penitentiaries

DANIEL FRANCIS and C. JAMES TAYLOR

388

Introduction

Societies have dealt in a variety of ways over time with individuals who cannot or will not conform to accepted standards of behaviour. Early in the nineteenth century, theorists and social reformers began to argue — first in Europe, then in North America — that criminals and the mentally disturbed could be successfully "treated" and rehabilitated. Assuming that insanity and criminal behaviour resulted from an undesirable social and/or personal environment, they maintained that deviant behaviour could be corrected in an improved environment which emphasized discipline and proper standards of conduct. This approach underlay the design of new institutions for the confinement of criminals and the insane — the penitentiary and the asylum. These institutions have remained central to the rehabilitation of deviants down to the present day.

Asylums, as early mental hospitals were called, and penitentiaries may appear to have different purposes, but both were created at about the same time to put into practice similar theories on dealing with deviance. Both were intended to be therapeutic, as opposed to simply custodial, institutions. Both served as "laboratories" for new techniques of behavioural management. Both attempted to use architecture as a force for moral development. Both were created in a burst of reformist optimism, and both deteriorated, partly through mismanagement, into examples of man's inhumanity to man. For all these reasons the penitentiary and the asylum are like non-identical twins; despite their apparent differences, they were simultaneously conceived under the same circumstances.

From *Canada's Visual History* 1, 76 (1986): 1–5. Reprinted with the permission of the Canadian Museum of Civilization.

The Emergence of the Age of Confinement

At the beginning of the nineteenth century, jails in British North America functioned mainly as holding tanks for offenders between stages in the judicial process; suspects were held in jail until they were tried, then confined until punishment was meted out. For serious crimes, such as treason, murder, and even robbery, hanging was the usual punishment. Criminals convicted of lesser offences might be branded or placed in stocks. Between these two extremes lay an uncertain area of flexible sentences. Although the law defined many crimes against property as capital offences punishable by death, many magistrates became increasingly reluctant to send criminals to the gallows for crimes other than murder. Since stocks and branding did not seem severe enough for serious crimes, other punishments, such as exile, were implemented. In the Canadian colonies at the beginning of the nineteenth century, short-term jail sentences and exile were the most common modes of punishment. Because jails were seldom used for prolonged incarceration, they did not have the importance they would gain later in the century.

Virtually no institutional framework existed for handling the mentally ill during the early 1800s. If they could support themselves, and broke no laws, the deranged were often at large in the community. Those with sufficient means or wealthy relatives resided in private "madhouses," while others were cared for by their families or religious groups. It was only when mentally disturbed people became criminals or paupers that they were sent to either a workhouse or a jail.

In the 1820s and 1830s a few reform-minded laymen and doctors in British North America began to complain about the inadequacy of the care given to the mentally ill. Inspired by examples in Europe and the United States, they petitioned the various colonial governments to provide publicly funded and properly managed treatment centres for the insane. Their concern was fuelled in part by new ideas regarding the nature of insanity. Previously, mental illness had been considered a spiritual condition rather than a disease. Robbed of their reason, lunatics were thought to have lost the essence of their humanity. On the assumption that they could not feel pain, loneliness, or sorrow in the same way as healthy human beings, they were treated as dumb beasts or worse. Proponents of the newer theories believed lunacy was a disease rooted in environmental factors such as poor health, poverty, and damaging family relationships. They believed that by taking the "diseased organ" away "from the cares of his ordinary life, from his bad habits, from that circle . . . in which he finds permanent danger of relapse," one could cure a person suffering from mental illness in healthy, sympathetic surroundings. This approach to madness required a new method of handling the insane, one which provided therapy and not simply confinement.

At the same time, there emerged a growing body of opinion, in both Europe and North America, in favour of improving the penal system. Depending on what motivated them the most, these would-be reformers fell into three categories: those who complained of the barbarity of the prevailing modes of punishment; those who believed it possible to alter rather than just punish criminal behaviour; and those who wanted a more rational system of punishment to better deter crime. The champion for all three of these groups was Englishman John Howard, who in 1777 published a two-volume study entitled *Prisons and Lazarettos*. In this work a number of British and some European prisons were described. Howard criticized British prisons for being squalid schools for crime where young offenders languished in the company of hardened criminals. He claimed that in Europe there were institutions where criminals were led by the very nature of their prison experience to improve their behaviour and that this behavioural change was not brought about simply through punishment but also through penitence and moral reform. In one of the European prisons that Howard visited, inmates were kept in separate cells arranged around a central altar. By reflecting on their crimes and expressing their guilt and sorrow to God, criminals atoned for their sins. Believing that crime, like lunacy, was connected with general social ills such as poverty, ignorance, drunkenness, and other vices, Howard argued that prisoners must be subjected to rigid discipline involving hard work and reflection if they were to be morally reformed. He was thus responsible for developing and popularizing the concept of the penitentiary, which during the nineteenth century became the principal mode of treating serious criminal offenders.

It was not until the second quarter of the nineteenth century that these new institutions of confinement were imported into Canada. Before then the old-fashioned jail system handled most deviants; moreover, the population was so small and scattered that large institutions of any kind were unnecessary and impractical. Following the Napoleonic Wars, however, a flood of immigrants to Canada created widespread concern about what was thought to be a general increase in criminality, mental disease, and deviance.

Recognizing that the existing jails and madhouses could not cope with the need to confine greater numbers of people, Canadians looked to Europe and the United States for alternative models. Americans were concerned about the effects of massive immigration, modernization, and new democratic attitudes on the stability of society. There, too, reform groups were influenced by a belief that society could be perfected through social engineering. In the 1820s the Boston Prison Discipline Society became a leading exponent of new penitentiary theories and helped popularize these new theories in Canada.

By the end of the eighteenth century, mental institutions had been created in England and France that utilized a technique known as moral treatment. Also called the "humane method" or the "soothing system," this approach quickly gained the endorsement of asylum promoters in North America. Not really a treatment in the medical sense, the moral method relied on compassion and gentle discipline. The modern asylum provided a strictly regulated environment in which the deranged mind could find order to calm itself. Patients were no longer roughly handled. Rather than being locked away to brood over their morbid delusions, they were now to engage in activities that would distract them from their former preoccupations. Ample exercise, plenty of hard work, cheerful amusements, and a healthy diet were the elements of moral treatment that constituted this new daily regime.

As the term moral treatment implies, such therapy was concerned with reasserting the prevailing moral standards. The stress on morality derived from the belief that sin or immorality was an important cause of madness. Accordingly, any kind of anti-social behaviour, including drunkenness, gambling, overeating, adultery, and masturbation, was thought to jeopardize one's sanity. The asylum was therefore rigidly organized to reinforce self-control and to promote socially acceptable standards of conduct. Productive labour, religious observances, regular habits, and cleanliness were of such paramount importance that they overshadowed any medical procedure. The asylum was a system. Everything from the location of its buildings to the inmates' table manners was designed to transform behaviour through the internalization of correct moral standards.

The construction of penitentiaries based on these new theories generally lagged behind that of asylums. Medical men — Dr. George Peters in New Brunswick, Dr. Charles Duncombe in Upper Canada, Dr. Henry Hunt in Newfoundland, Dr. James Douglas in Lower Canada — agitated for the construction of mental asylums in British North America. In the course of their work, they had been touched by the lunatic's plight. Confident that they knew how to remedy mental illness, these reformers led the campaign for public support. Insanity, stated Charles Duncombe, was as easily cured "as the ordinary diseases of the climate." Treatment in the early stages was seen as crucial. If the afflicted person was removed from his home to an asylum within the first three months, a cure was virtually assured. Whereas the family had once been the primary agent of care, medical opinion and eventually the conventional wisdom became that "no insane man recovers at home." Insanity required moral treatment and moral treatment required the asylum.

Initially, however, the reformers' zeal outpaced the public's willingness or ability to provide separate hospitals for the insane. The early institutions were consequently makeshift and inadequate. The first mental hospital in British North America was located in the basement of a converted cholera hospital in Saint John, New Brunswick. It opened its doors in 1836. In Toronto the small, wood-frame Home District Gaol was emptied of prisoners in 1841 to be turned into a temporary asylum for "insane persons." On the outskirts of Quebec City an old stone manorhouse at the seigneury of Beauport was fitted out as an asylum and received its first patients in the fall of 1845. In Newfoundland a farm was pressed into service; in British Columbia, a former smallpox hospital. In every case, the inmates probably enjoyed better care than they would have had before, but hand-me-down facilities could not bring about the revolution in mental health care that activists desired.

By the middle of the century the process of replacing these earliest mental institutions with large permanent hospitals providing the modern "moral" treatment was under way. Once again New Brunswick was in the forefront: a new asylum, overlooking the Reversing Falls, was opened in Saint John in 1848. The Provincial Lunatic Asylum began operations in Toronto in 1850, to be followed by institutions in Newfoundland (1854) and Nova Scotia (1859). In Western Canada, where smaller populations made the need less acute, asylums were not built until the last quarter of the century.

All of the institutions mentioned above were publicly owned except the ones in Quebec, where the government chose to adopt a "farming out" system. The asylum at Beauport, and subsequent mental hospitals in that province, were privately owned and operated. The Quebec government gave proprietors an annual per capita grant for the maintenance of patients unable to pay for their own care.

Up until Confederation, the only serious effort to implement modern theories of criminal treatment and reform via the establishment of a new penal institution was in Upper Canada. Early in the 1830s, a committee of the Legislative Assembly visited several institutions in Britain and the United States and recommended the construction of a penitentiary along the lines suggested by Howard. "The aim of a penitentiary," the report stated, was "not only to protect society and punish offenders, but by inducing a penitent attitude in prisoners to effect a reformation of their characters." The government approved the report and in 1832 work began at a site near Kingston. Although the building proceeded in stages, the design not being fully realized until the 1850s, it became one of the most up-to-date institutions of its day.

The Kingston Penitentiary featured several of the latest innovations in penal architecture, including a central rotunda and radiating wings containing cell blocks. It "treated" inmates with a systematic form of prison discipline. This method, based on theories of John Howard, involved a strict routine of hard work in communal silence by day, and separate confinement in individual cells by night. "To rescue the child of ignorance and vice from almost certain destruction to which he hastens; to guard from contamination the venial offender . . . ; to implant religious and moral principles and industrious habits on the inmates of the Penitentiary; and to strengthen and encourage him in his struggles with the world when he is discharged from confinement" the penitentiary suppressed prisoners' individual identity and subjected them to a routine of rigid conformity.

The Kingston institution remained the only full-fledged Canadian penitentiary until after Confederation. With the union of Upper and Lower Canada in 1841, convicts from Quebec were sent there. Elsewhere, some county jails, such as those in Halifax and Toronto, incorporated features of the penitentiary system, and by Confederation most provincial jails had facilities for the separate confinement of prisoners.

After 1867 the responsibility of rehabilitating criminals was divided between the provincial and federal governments. Offenders convicted of lesser crimes entailing fines or sentences of under two years came under the jurisdiction of the provincial government, while those subject to the death penalty or long prison sentences became the responsibility of the federal government. Although the provinces did establish penitentiaries for the incarceration of prisoners serving short sentences, the duration of their term was not considered sufficient for prison discipline to have any real effect. Provincial institutions therefore tended to be less rigorous in their enforcement of the system of silent labour, although the buildings were constructed according to the design of the day, which included cell blocks and catwalks.

During the 1870s a building program was initiated to establish federal penitentiaries in each region of the Dominion. A former boys' reformatory was enlarged into a penitentiary at St. Vincent de Paul, near Montreal, in 1873. Identical buildings were constructed in Manitoba and British Columbia in 1876 and 1878, and the following year a penitentiary was completed near Moncton at Dorchester, New Brunswick. During most of the nineteenth century, these institutions were all run according to the Kingston model and the philosophy upon which it was based: that prisons were "schools where the ignorant are enlightened and the repentant strengthened — in which expiation for crime is not lost sight of, but the permanent moral reform of the convict is the chief aim."

The End of Optimism

The new institutions of confinement were established in a spirit of great optimism. The confidence that deviant behaviour could be corrected under the right circumstances was widespread. Mental illness, for instance, was everywhere believed to be in retreat before the combined forces of moral treatment and the asylum.

Unfortunately, it was not long before the new institutions disappointed their founders. In the case of mental hospitals, effective moral treatment required a strict system of classification, a manageable number of patients, and a sympathetic staff. Instead, asylums overflowed with an inmate population that included epileptics, retardates, and the senile. Once the practice of institutionalizing the mentally ill was aggressively adopted, hospitals could not handle the large number of patients being thrust upon them. Toronto's Provincial Lunatic Asylum, built to accommodate two hundred and fifty inmates, was crowded with close to four hundred in the 1860s. As lack of space made classification difficult, the mildly depressed often lingered with the wildly frantic. Staff was ill-trained and poorly paid. At one time it was even claimed that in Prince Edward Island "an ordinary labourer" was in charge of the asylum. Given these circumstances it may have been inevitable that physical restraints were again used to control inmates. A British asylum reformer, Daniel Hack Tuke, visited the Quebec asylums in 1884 and discovered many patients bound in restraining devices. The inmates he saw inhabited tiny, windowless cells. They communicated with their warders through a wicket in the door. Many were shackled in handcuffs and passed their days wandering the gloomy corridors. Others were strapped to their beds. These conditions were duplicated in other provinces. In Nova Scotia's Mount Hope Asylum, for example, there were documented cases of inmates freezing to death in their cells. Some inmates were placed in a kind of solitary confinement called a "dark room," where they were deliberately starved to weaken them and make them submissive. In British Columbia mental patients were routinely beaten and ducked in water.

Penitentiaries continuously faced the problem of keeping on the right side of the fine line between discipline and brutality. Periodic investigations into the Kingston Penitentiary found evidence of cruel treatment of prisoners, although faith in the perfectibility of the system was maintained. Critics often pointed to the low qualifications of the prison staff, yet much of the harsh treatment was inherent in the system itself. Inmates were confined for much of each day in stone cells large enough only for a bed, a stool, and a bucket. Cells were cold, damp, smelly, and dark. Talking between prisoners was forbidden and work was intended to be hard and boring. Visitors were not allowed. When regulations were broken, inmates were punished severely.

As the statistics on repeat offenders showed, the penitentiary system failed to correct criminal behaviour. Instead of rehabilitating prisoners, it turned out hardened criminals. Administrators tinkered with the system in an attempt to achieve better results. They tried lenience; they tried harsh discipline; they tried longer sentences; they tried indeterminate sentences. Nothing had an appreciable effect; the number of inmates continued to grow.

Attempts to arrest the deterioration of mental hospitals also failed. Asylums became a provincial responsibility following Confederation and various governments conducted formal investigations into charges of patient abuse. Since overcrowding was thought to be the main problem, several new hospitals were opened in the last quarter of the nineteenth century. By 1900 Quebec had four institutions and Ontario seven. Some of the new facilities were intended solely to care for chronic cases whose prognosis was poor or whose illness was due to congenital defect, disease, or senility. In Nova Scotia, for example, there were fifteen county asylums housing inmates who were never expected to recover and go home.

Other changes recommended by those investigating mental hospitals were improved training for asylum personnel, better classification of inmates, and the banning of sightseers. While some of these changes may have improved life in the asylums, they did not succeed in either giving moral treatment a second chance or introducing new therapeutic methods.

By the end of the century the optimism that earlier characterized the treatment of the mentally ill had been replaced by resignation and a very limited sense of what could be done. It was taken for granted that a small percentage of patients would never be cured. "Out of four hundred and forty-two patients," admitted the superintendent of the New Brunswick asylum in 1881, "only sixteen were expected to be restored to mental health." Like the penitentiary, the mental institution had come full circle. Once again it was perceived as a place of confinement in which the mentally ill languished without therapy and with almost no expectation that they would ever recover.

Conclusion

Until quite recently, historians typically characterized the creation of asylums and penitentiaries during the nineteenth century as examples of the moral progress of mankind. Invoking images of the lunatic in chains or the criminal bound in stocks, these traditional reform historians believed that asylums and penitentiaries represented an improvement over the "barbaric" practices that had preceded them. Not only were the institutions more humane, they argued, they were also more enlightened, because they substituted therapy and rehabilitation for simple confinement.

In the last two decades, historians have increasingly questioned the proposition that incarcerating large numbers of people in asylums and penitentiaries during the last half of the nineteenth century constituted an improvement on former practices. Some say that the institutions of confinement represented not reform but a new form of repression; that they merely substituted psychological coercion for physical coercion; and that corporal punishment lost favour not because it was inhuman but because it was inefficient. Others regard the new asylums and penitentiaries as agents of social control, isolating deviants and maintaining order at a time when rapid industrialization was disrupting society. Some claim the institutions were part of a defensive strategy by which the middle class, made nervous by social change, imposed their own values on the rest of society.

What all these explanations have in common is a disdain for the reform model and its claims to moral superiority. Revisionist historians look beyond the rhetoric of asylum and penitentiary promoters to the social conditions in which crime, insanity, and institutional confinement flourished. They believe that the new institutions were created not because they were morally advanced but because they served specific purposes in a society challenged by industrialization and urban growth.

Today, about one hundred and fifty years after they were created, penitentiaries and mental hospitals are still familiar forms on the social landscape. Increasingly, however, it is being argued that incarceration is not the only, or the best, way of dealing with deviant behaviour. Modern reformers insist that institutions have become too large and impersonal and that they tend to exacerbate the behaviour they were created to correct. These reformers now argue for de-institutionalizing some criminals and mental patients. Obligatory community service rather than imprisonment, for example, is beginning to be seen as appropriate punishment for certain types of crime. Criminals are already being sent to half-way houses, and there is renewed interest in treating mental patients in the home. While these approaches are being debated, mental asylums and penitentiaries remain with us.

Of Poverty and Helplessness in Petite-Nation

COLE HARRIS

During the three hundred and fifty years of white settlement along the lower St. Lawrence River there have been three major migrations of French-speaking people: the first bringing some 10,000 Frenchmen across the Atlantic before 1760; the second, beginning shortly before 1820, taking French Canadians to the Eastern Townships, to New England, or to the Canadian Shield; and the third, following closely on the second, gradually urbanizing French Canadian society. Each of these migrations was predominantly a movement of poor people, and each characteristically involved individuals or nuclear families rather than groups or communities. Their results, however, have been vastly different. The first created a modestly prosperous base of agricultural settlement along the lower St. Lawrence. The third has brought French Canadians into

From *Canadian Historical Review* 52 (1971): 23–50. Reprinted with the permission of University of Toronto Press Incorporated.

the technological orbit of the modern world. But the second, especially
when it turned north to the Canadian Shield, led to poverty as acute
as that of any Negro sharecropper in the American South, and then,
often within a generation or two, to land abandonment and migration
to the cities. The magnitude of the third migration was partly a product
of the failure of the second, and this failure still echoes through contemporary Quebec.

This paper deals with the French-Canadian migration to and settlement in the seigneurie of Petite-Nation, a small segment of the Quebec
rim of the Canadian Shield some forty miles east of Ottawa. It describes
the coming of French Canadians to Petite-Nation and their way of life
there before approximately 1860, then considers the reasons for the extreme poverty and the institutional weakness which were, perhaps, the
dominant characteristics of French-Canadian life in the seigneurie. Although in most general respects the habitant economy and society of
Petite-Nation were reproduced throughout the Shield fringe of southern   *397*
Quebec, there is some justification for a close look at this particular place.
It belonged to Louis-Joseph Papineau, the leading French-Canadian nationalist of his day and a man who believed, at least in his later years,
that the seigneurial system and a rural life were central to the cultural
survival of French Canada; and it can be studied in detail in the voluminous Papineau Papers in the Quebec Provincial Archives. This paper
considers the ordinary French-Canadian inhabitants of Petite-Nation,
and a subsequent paper will consider its elite.

The Occupation of Petite-Nation

Although the penetration of the Shield for agricultural purposes had
begun as early as the 1730s,[1] it gained little momentum until well into
the nineteenth century. By 1820 a great many *rotures* in the older seigneuries had been subdivided until they produced a minimum subsistence
living. French-Canadian agriculture, inflexible, uncompetitive, and
largely subsistent, was incapable of supporting a growing population.
Some of the young French Canadians whom the land could no longer
support moved to the local village, finding there a way point, a time
and a place of transition between the closely knit society of kin and *côte*
and a new life among strangers. Others moved directly from the parental
roture to a destination outside the St. Lawrence lowland. Whether from
farm or village, French Canadians left the parish of their birth as individuals or in nuclear families, those going into the Shield travelling
a relatively short distance from the adjacent lowland. Habitants settling
in Petite-Nation before 1820 had come from the Island of Montreal,
Île Jésus, and the surrounding mainland seigneuries. Most later settlers
came from a scattering of parishes in the lower Ottawa Valley (see Map

MAP 1 Place of Birth of Adults in the Parish of Ste-André Avellin, Petite-Nation, 1861

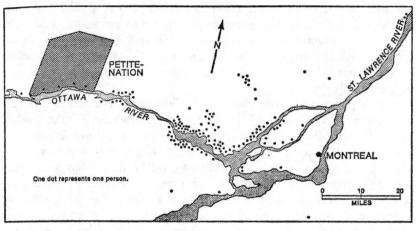

One dot represents one person.

Nominal census of 1851.

1).[2] A few of the earliest settlers had been brought to Petite-Nation by the seigneur,[3] a few others had scouted out the land and brought some capital to their destination,[4] but the great majority came unassisted and penniless. They had heard that there were jobs and land up the Ottawa Valley, they had set out with no specific place in mind, had perhaps worked here and there, and arrived, almost by chance, in Petite-Nation.[5]

Petite-Nation was a tract of land approximately fifteen miles a side and bounded on the south by the Ottawa River. Barely a tenth of the seigneurie lay in the Ottawa River plain; the rest, in the hilly southern fringe of the Canadian Shield.[6] Only approximately a third of the land was at all suited to agriculture, the rest being too rough, too swampy, or its soils too thin and acidic. The best soils, although they were hardly good even by the standard of those in Quebec, had developed on the marine clays of the lowland or on alluvial material in the north-south valleys in the Shield that once had been glacial spillways. The forest cover of this abrupt, knobby land was a typical segment of the mixed Laurentian forest:[7] white, red, and jack pine, fir, and white spruce predominated in rocky, excessively drained areas; black spruce, cedar, and larch dominated the bogs; and a beech–maple–birch association that included white ash, red oak, poplar, and a few coniferous species was common on more moderate sites. The climate was considerably more severe than at Montreal. Along the Ottawa River the average frost-free period was 125 days; it was less than 115 days along the northern border of the seigneurie. The climatic limit of wheat cultivation crossed Petite-Nation along the boundary between the Shield and the lowland.

The white settlement of this tract of land began in 1807 or 1808, when Joseph Papineau, then seigneur of Petite-Nation, contracted to cut a small quantity of squared timber,[8] and brought some twenty French-

Canadian woodcutters to the seigneurie.[9] Early in 1809 he sold two-fifths of his seigneurie for £7220 to a Boston timber merchant, Robert Fletcher,[10] who in March of that year arrived in Petite-Nation with 160 well-provisioned New Englanders.[11] Within a year Fletcher defaulted on payments, committed suicide,[12] and his portion of the seigneurie reverted to Joseph Papineau. In 1817, when Joseph Papineau sold the entire seigneurie — mills, domain, back *cens et rentes*, and unconceded land — to Louis-Joseph Papineau,[13] his eldest surviving son, there were perhaps three hundred people there, a third of them the remnants of Fletcher's New Englanders, and almost all the rest French Canadians. One of the latter was Denis-Benjamin Papineau, younger brother of Louis-Joseph, a resident of Petite-Nation since 1808 and seigneurial agent for his brother until the late 1840s. For some twenty years after Louis-Joseph purchased the seigneurie, only a few settlers trickled into Petite-Nation each year: in 1828 there were 517 people,[14] in 1842 only 1368.[15] In the 1840s the rate of immigration increased sharply as population pressure in the older settlements dislodged a steadily larger number of French Canadians, and declined again in the 1850s when almost all the cultivable land in Petite-Nation had been taken up. Over 3000 people lived in the seigneurie in 1851, and some 4000 a decade later.[16] By this date five-sixths of the population was French Canadian.

399

Settlers in Petite-Nation, as in all other Canadian seigneuries, acquired a *roture* (a farm lot or, legally, the final form of land concession within the seigneurial system), which they held from the seigneur. Joseph Papineau had made forty such concessions before 1817,[17] and by the mid-1850s the rotures shown in Map 2 had been conceded, most of them by Denis-Benjamin Papineau. The Papineaus adopted without modification the cadastral system of the St. Lawrence lowland, conceding land in long lots laid out, as far as the interrupted terrain of Petite-Nation permitted, in côtes (or *rangs*) along the Ottawa River and its tributaries.[18] They charged surveying to the *censitaires*, which meant that it was usually inadequately done,[19] and they expected the censitaires to build their own roads.[20]

There is no evidence that the Papineaus withheld rotures from prospective censitaires while Petite-Nation was still a sparsely settled seigneurie. They were well aware, however, that some rotures were better than others and that it was advantageous to establish responsible settlers in new areas. From time to time Louis-Joseph wrote from Montreal to his brother in the seigneurie with instructions about the settlement of specific rotures.[21] By the late 1840s rotures were becoming scarce — almost invariably there were several applications for each new lot available[23] — and Louis-Joseph, who had returned from exile in France and spent much of his time in the seigneurie, granted land more cautiously. His prejudices ran strongly against English-speaking applicants — finding "foreign squatters . . . infinitely less satisfactory than our Canadians"[23] — partly because they were wont to cut his timber. In 1848 he

400

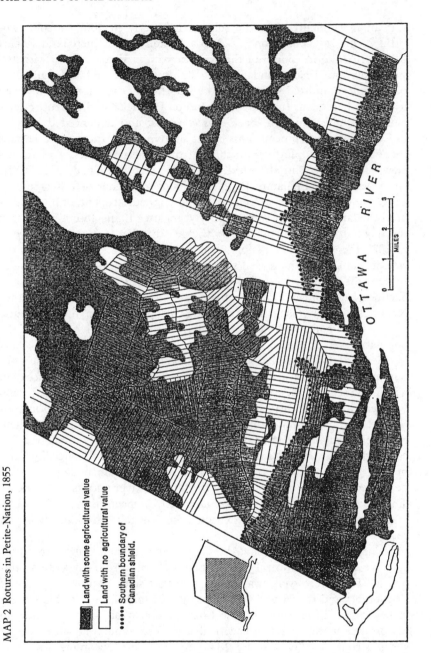

MAP 2 Rotures in Petite-Nation, 1855

began withholding formal title to any new roture until the settler had cleared six arpents (1 arpent equals approximately five-sixths of an acre). Each applicant was informed that until that time he was a tenant, not a censitaire,[24] a procedure that was unheard of during the French regime, when seigneurs were required to grant unconceded rotures to any applicant for them.[25] One habitant, wrote Louis-Joseph, "had the insolence to tell me that I was obliged to grant him land."[26] He also required anyone taking an abandoned roture to pay all the back cens et rentes.[27] As the back dues frequently equalled the value of the land, this was, in effect, a sale.

In Petite-Nation, as in most other seigneuries in the nineteenth century, roture contracts were standardized, printed forms with blanks left for the addition in longhand of information about the particular censitaire and roture. Joseph Papineau had prepared the original contract, and when these forms ran out Louis-Joseph ordered a second and almost identical printing.[28] Apart from their printed form and much greater consistency, these contracts differed in two principal respects from any drawn up during the French regime: they increased the seigneur's access to timber, and they stipulated a higher cens et rente. To achieve the former purpose, roture contracts in Petite-Nation permitted the seigneur to cut oak and pine for profit on the roture and forbade the censitaire to do so. They allowed the seigneur to confiscate up to six arpents for the construction of a mill, and prevented the censitaire from building either a sawmill or a grist mill without the seigneur's written consent. Before 1760 many seigneurs had the right to cut timber on their censitaires' rotures for the construction of the banal mill or the seigneurial manor, but they never had the right to cut oak and pine there commercially.[29] Some contracts had given the seigneur power to confiscate an arpent or two, but not more, for a mill. Although the seigneur always had first claim to the grist mill banality, roture contracts had never forbidden the censitaires to build grist mills.[30] Sawmilling had not been a banal right, and during the French regime any censitaire had been allowed to build a sawmill provided that, in so doing, he did not interfere with the operation of the seigneur's grist mill. In Petite-Nation all of this had been changed, with the result that rights to all important forests on conceded as well as on unconceded land, and to the milling of timber, rested entirely with the seigneur.

The rotures granted by Joseph Papineau before 1817 and by his son thereafter paid an annual cens et rente of one *minot* of wheat (1 minot equals 1.07 bushels) and two *livres tournois* for each thirty arpents, a rate which was a third higher than the highest rate consistently charged during the French regime.[21] For a roture in Petite-Nation the annual charge was six and two-thirds minots of wheat plus thirteen livres, six sols, eight deniers (approximately $2.50 Halifax).[32] The Papineaus charged in wheat rather than in capons because the price of wheat was more tuned to inflation.[33] In Montreal in the first half of the nineteeth

401

century, the average price of wheat was between five and six livres a minot, twice the average price a century earlier.[34] In 1813 wheat sold in Petite-Nation at fourteen livres ($2.58) a minot, and the cens et rentes for that year were calculated on this basis. These prices could almost quadruple a cens et rente: at two and one-half livres a minot a roture of 200 arpents paid thirty livres ($5.50) a year, at six livres a minot it paid just over fifty-three livres ($9.70), and at fourteen livres a minot it paid more than 106 livres ($19.40). Because wheat rarely ripened on Shield lots in Petite-Nation, and was a subsistence crop on lowland farms, cens et rentes were usually paid in the cash equivalent of the minots of wheat owed.[35]

After acquiring land on these terms, a settler usually built a tiny log cabin and cleared a little land. Most of the first cabins were shanties of perhaps ten to twelve feet long, with a one-slope roof, a dirt floor, and a chimney usually made of short green rounds heavily chinked with clay. In a few years a settler might build another, larger cabin, some fourteen to eighteen feet long, with gable ends, a stone chimney, and a plank floor. Most of these buildings were of *pièce-sur-pièce* construction (squared logs laid horizontally and pegged to vertical timbers at the corners and at intervals along the walls), but some were made of round logs cross-notched at the corners,[36] and a few were frame. By the 1840s a cabin was typically in a clearing of some ten arpents.[37]

The Habitant Economy

The occupations of working men and boys in Petite-Nation in 1851 are given in Table 1. At this date more than 90 per cent of the working French-Canadian men in Petite-Nation gave their occupation to the census enumerator as farmer, labourer, or river man. Most of the remainder described themselves as artisans or tradesmen, and only sixteen, some of them members of the Papineau family, as merchants, clerks, or professionals. Of those describing themselves as farmers, the great majority were heads of households, married men with several offspring. The labourers and river men were largely youths, some of them only twelve or thirteen years of age, who still lived on the parental roture, and many of the tradesmen listed in the first column were boys working with their fathers. Some men gave two occupations — *cultivateur et menuisier, négociant et cultivateur* — and many of those describing themselves only as farmers must also have worked intermittently in the logging camps.

Although the nominal census indicates that farming was the dominant occupation in Petite-Nation in 1851, agriculture had developed slowly in a rocky seigneurie that had first been settled for its timber. In the first years both Joseph Papineau and Louis-Joseph had sent biscuit and pork from Montreal,[38] and Denis-Benjamin, who doubted that agriculture was climatically possible in Petite-Nation, had imported wheat.[39]

TABLE 1 Occupations of Working Males in Petite-Nation, 1851

Occupation	All Male Residents[a]		All Heads of Households[b]	
	Fr. Can.	Others	Fr. Can.	Others
farmer	384	67	344	52
labourer[c]	287	30	46	1
river man[d]	40	7	2	
carpenter or joiner	22	2	14	2
blacksmith	12	4	6	1
woodcutter	1			
fisherman	2		2	
baker	1	1	1	
mason	4		3	
sawyer		1		1
tanner	4		1	
cooper	6	1	4	1
tinsmith	1		1	
painter	1		1	
carter	1		1	
saddler	2	1	1	
miller	2		1	
shake maker	3		2	
sextant	2		2	
bourgeois		1		1
innkeeper		2		1
merchant	7	8	7	6
doctor	1	1		1
clerk	5	6	4	1
priest or minister		2[e]		1
bailiff		1		1
clerk of the JP		1		1
clerk of the court	1		1	
notary	1		1	
surveyor	1		1	

Source: Based on the nominal census of Petite-Nation, Nominal Census, 1851, reels C-1131 and C-1132.
[a]This column includes all male residents of Petite-Nation under seventy years of age for whom an occupation is listed in the census.
[b]This column includes all married men and widowers under seventy years of age for whom an occupation is listed in the census.
[c]Including *journaliers* and *engagés*.
[d]In French, *voyageur*. Some of this group may have been hired on the river boats, but most must have had some connection with the timber drives.
[e]Comprising a Belgian priest as well as a Methodist minister.

403

Only by the 1820s were the logging camps supplied locally and most settlers self-sufficient in basic foods. Even in 1842, when the first agricultural census was taken in Petite-Nation, virtually all habitant farms were subsistence operations on a few arpents of cleared land. The habitants were not selling produce to the lumber camps, which were supplied almost entirely by a handful of large farms. Table 2 gives examples of both subsistence and commercial farm types. In 1842 there were six large commercial farms in Petite-Nation. One of them (Farm 3 in Table 2) belonged to Denis-Benjamin Papineau, the other five to English-speaking settlers, among them Alanson Cooke, the sawmill operator, and Stephen Tucker, the timber merchant. Between the commercial and subsistence farm types illustrated in Table 2 there were a few semi-commercial operations, and of these three belonged to French Canadians.

By 1861 there were twenty-five commercial farms in Petite-Nation, a quarter of them held by French Canadians. Farms 1 and 2 in Table 2 still describe characteristic habitant farms, except that by 1861 there were likely to be fifteen to twenty cleared arpents and corresponding increases in crop acreage and livestock. Without manuring or adequate crop rotation, seed-yield ratios on the thin soils of Petite-Nation were extremely low, probably not higher than 1:6 for wheat or 1:12 for oats.[40] Livestock were scrub animals that browsed or grazed in the bush for most of the year. Such a farm rarely produced a marketable surplus. With clearing proceeding at an average rate per farm of well under one arpent per year, and with women and children doing much of the farm work, it required no more than a man's part-time attention.

The farmers and farmers' sons who sought off-the-farm employment usually worked in the sawmills or logging camps, thereby providing most of the labour for the Papineaus or the English-speaking timber merchants who controlled the forests. Joseph Papineau and his son Denis-Benjamin had managed the earliest sawmills, but when Louis-Joseph acquired the seigneurie he leased the mill rights in the western half of it to Thomas Mears, a timber merchant from Hawkesbury.[41] Peter McGill, nephew

404

TABLE 2   Farm Types in Petite-Nation, 1842

	Arpents										Number of			
	held	cleared	in wheat	barley	rye	oats	peas	potatoes	meadow & pasture	other	cattle	horses	sheep	pigs
Subsistence farms														
Farm 1	100	7	2	1		2		1		1	1		1	3
Farm 2	120	7	1	¼	1	2½	1	1			2			2
Commercial farms														
Farm 3	1229	320	1			10	3	1	300	5	36	7	57	12
Farm 4	90	40	1					2	37		36	2	18	5

Source: Derived from examples in the nominal census of Petite-Nation, 1842, Nominal Census, 1842, reel C-729.

and heir of the director of the Bank of Montreal, took over the lease
in 1834, but the mills were managed by Alanson Cooke, son of one of
the early settlers from New England.[42] In 1854 Louis-Joseph sold the
mills and timber rights for ten years in the western half of the seigneurie
to Gilmour and Company, a firm of Scottish origin then based in Liverpool, and with British North American operations on the St. John
and Mirimichi rivers as well as the Ottawa. Besides these mills, Asa Cooke,
father of Alanson, operated a small mill in the first range;[43] and in the
eastern part of the seigneurie another New Englander, Stephen Tucker,
held a concession to cut and square timber.[44] A few habitants cut firewood
for the steamers on the Ottawa River,[45] and others made potash. There
were fourteen asheries in Petite-Nation in 1842, eight of them belonging
to French Canadians. In 1851 there were thirty-nine asheries, two-thirds
of them in the hands of habitants. These were part-time, family operations, each producing three to five barrels of ash a year.[46]

The number and the aggregate income of the men employed in the
forests and mills of Petite-Nation cannot be determined exactly.[47] Although most of the labourers and some of the farmers listed in Table
1 worked intermittently in forest industries, the census enumerator noted
that only thirty to forty men were employed in Alanson Cooke's mill
and another ten at his father's in 1851, and did not list the number of
men cutting or squaring timber.[48] In 1861 Gilmour and Company employed 147 men in Petite-Nation, and Stephen Tucker employed sixty.[49]
Certainly, during the 1850s there were sawmill jobs for perhaps half the
year for not more than fifty to sixty men, jobs in the lumber camps
for four or five winter months for not more than another 150 to 200,
and jobs in the spring timber drives for perhaps fifty.[50] Seeking these
jobs were the great majority of able-bodied French Canadians in Petite-
Nation. At any given time most of them were unemployed or were engaged in work around the farm that brought almost no cash return. In
these conditions wages were extremely low. Mill hands earned $12 to
$14 a month in 1861, and wages had been even lower.[51] While some
French Canadians earned as much as $100 a year in the forest industries,
a great many more earned far less. In the 1850s sawmill and forest jobs
could not have brought more than $20,000 in cash or credit into the
seigneurie each year.[52]

Among the approximately 1300 people in Petite-Nation in 1842 there
were only twelve artisans and tradesmen, nine of them French Canadians.[53] The two merchants then in the seigneurie were English-speaking.
In the next decade the population almost trebled, and the number of
artisans and tradesmen increased to the point shown in Table 1. As along
the lower St. Lawrence at the same time, the number of tradesmen was
essentially a reflection of poverty. With not enough work available in
the forests, and little good farm land, several men would turn to carpentry,
for example, when there was the opportunity. Of the handful of French-

405

Canadian merchants and professionals in Petite-Nation in 1851, the doctor was a Papineau; the notary, Francis Samuel MacKay, was the son of an immigrant Scot and a French Canadian; the clerk of the lower court was another Papineau; and the eight French-Canadian merchants were small shopkeepers.

Essentially, then, the habitants in Petite-Nation were farmers, loggers, or sawmill hands. Farming was a subsistence activity that attracted few young men, who instead competed for scarce jobs in the forests or mills. When the family depended entirely on farming, as was frequently the case, its annual cash income can rarely have exceeded $25, and often must have been virtually nothing. When the father worked on his roture and one or two unmarried sons had some work in the lumber camps, the family income would likely have been between $50 and $150 a year. In a few cases, as when the father was employed in the sawmill or had a trade, and two or three unmarried sons worked through the winter in the forests, the family income would have exceeded $200. Almost certainly, however, the gross annual income of most habitant families in Petite-Nation was between $50 and $150 a year.

Arriving without capital in Petite-Nation, taking out a roture that only slowly became a subsistence farm, finding intermittent and poorly paid work in the sawmills or logging camps, and facing payments for basic supplies and for land, almost all habitants in Petite-Nation quickly found themselves in debt. By 1822 the holders of forty-eight rotures in Petite-Nation owed Louis-Joseph over 11,000 livres ($2017).[54] In 1832 only ten lots, several of them belonging to the Papineaus, were free of debt; fifty-one lots each owed more than 500 livres ($92), and five owed over 1000 livres.[55] Indebtedness had become a chronic condition, most of the habitants owing their seigneur a sum that was approximately equivalent to the value of a man's labour for six months in the sawmill. Many habitants had tried to reduce their debt by subdividing their rotures — as early as 1822 a third of the sixty-six rotures along the river had been broken up[56] — but after a few years even these fractions were likely to owe several hundred livres. Others attempted to escape from debt by selling their rotures, but the seigneur could exercise his *droit de retrait* in these sales, taking over the roture by paying his former censitaire the difference, if any, between the sale price and the debt.[57]

In the twelve years from 1825 to 1836 Denis-Benjamin Papineau collected just over 19,000 livres ($3480) from the censitaires in Petite-Nation.[58] As the cens et rentes accumulating during this period amounted to 55,000 livres ($10,080), and the *lods et ventes* to some 20,000 livres ($3670), he collected each year about a quarter of the annual dues. At least 20,000 livres were also owing for the years before 1825. Louis-Joseph had made several short visits to the seigneurie partly with the hope of collecting more of his debts, but found his censitaires no more able to pay him than his brother. He could sue his debtors but, although he blustered and threatened, in these years he rarely did so. Restraining him was the high cost and inconvenience of court action,[59] the advice of his brother Denis-Benjamin,[60] and undoubtedly, also, Papineau's recognition of the plight of his censitaires.[61]

When Louis-Joseph returned to Canada in 1845 after eight years in exile, he began to manage his seigneurie much more rigorously. He was no longer as involved in politics and had more time for his own affairs; he was more cantankerous, more concerned about his own rights; and he was planning to build an expensive manor house, a project that depended entirely on the collection of debts.[62] In letter after letter Louis-Joseph railed against his brother for allowing "ces animaux" (the censitaires) to fall so heavily into debt,[63] against the high cost of justice, against the sheriff ("maudite invention anglais comme tant d'autres") for pocketing a commission on the sale of rotures. He could also write: "We will threaten court action and we will sue a few people, but in such a new area there is really so much poverty that I feel more repugnance in suing than they do in paying. Lack of foresight, ignorance, the tendency to become indebted to the merchants are the common failings of all the habitants without exception, but a few have acted out of ill will . . . which it is certainly necessary to rectify."[64] When a censitaire lost his roture after court action, it was sold by public auction, usually to the seigneur. As Louis-Joseph pointed out to his brother, "the certainty that the creditor is owed as much as the land is worth and that the debtor has not and never will have other means to pay means that the creditor is in reality the proprietor."[65]

Most habitants in Petite-Nation were also indebted to at least one merchant. At first Denis-Benjamin had acted as merchant, but he was neither particularly astute nor demanding, which may explain why, around 1830, the New Englander Stephen Tucker became the principal, and for a time the only, merchant in Petite-Nation. Tucker was a Baptist, a man, according to Denis-Benjamin, "so filled with the missionary spirit that he has promised up to $40.00 to any of our poor Canadians who will agree to join his sect."[66] Some years later he was still described as the most fanatical Protestant in Petite-Nation; nevertheless the Papineaus and a great many habitants bought from him. Of 145 *obligations* (statements of indebtedness) drawn up between 1837 and 1845 in Petite-Nation by the notary André-Benjamin Papineau, ninety-one recorded debts to the seigneur, and forty-nine debts to Stephen Tucker.[67] By the mid-1850s Tucker owned forty-four rotures,[68] almost all of them confiscated from his debtors.

Stephen Tucker and Louis-Joseph Papineau disliked each other intensely, and in the late forties and fifties, when Louis-Joseph lived in the seigneurie, disputes between them were frequent. On one occasion, when the value of many rotures would not cover the debts owed to the two creditors and Tucker complained bitterly about prospective losses, Louis-Joseph — who, as seigneur, had prior claim — replied icily: "You forget the high credit prices of goods; the interest charges on back accounts, and what you have received from many when I had the right of being paid before you. If you advanced too much with too many, it was your choice."[69] From the habitants' point of view both men were creditors to whom their farms were vulnerable, but Tucker, who combined economic and religious coercion and was usually the more insistent, must have been the more feared.

The Habitant Society

By the 1820s French-Canadian society in most of the older parishes and seigneuries of the St. Lawrence lowland had sealed itself from outsiders; not only were there few if any non–French Canadians in many parishes, but as time went on there were fewer French Canadians who had not been born in the immediate vicinity. These areas exported many of their young while, with almost no immigration, the people who remained formed an increasingly consanguinous population. Petite-Nation, in contrast, was being settled and it attracted different people: French Canadians from many parishes and seigneuries, New Englanders, Englishmen, Irishmen, and some English-speaking people of Canadian birth. In several cases Catholic Irishmen and French-Canadian girls married in Petite-Nation, and the progeny of these matches were quickly assimilated into French-Canadian society.[70] At least three Protestants in Petite-Nation had also married French Canadians.[71] For the most part, however, the two groups kept to themselves socially. In 1842 forty-seven of the fifty-three English-speaking families in Petite-Nation had another such family in an adjacent lot, while 205 of 208 French-Canadian families lived next to a French-Canadian household.[72] In 1861 the interior parish in Petite-Nation was overwhelmingly French Canadian (with only four Irish by birth and 1489 Catholics against forty-five Protestants), whereas most English-speaking people lived on the Ottawa Valley plain towards the western corner of the seigneurie (in the parish of Ste-Angélique, with 1007 French Canadians against 545 others). By this date there were three tiny villages in the seigneurie, and in only one of them, Papineauville in the parish of Ste-Angélique, were French- and English-speaking people in Petite-Nation likely to live close together. The habitants encountered the English-speaking settlers as employers, as merchants, as creditors, and occasionally as co-workers, but rarely in the ordinary social round of their lives.

The social importance of nuclear family, nearest neighbour, and côte in habitant life in Petite-Nation was not different, as far as can be ascertained, from that in the older settlements of the St. Lawrence lowland.

However, migration into the Shield had weakened drastically the importance of kin group and parish. Not only had settlers in Petite-Nation come as individuals but they had come recently and in relatively large numbers. At mid-century most adults were still immigrants and, because of the speed of settlement, many of their sons had not found land close to the parental roture. Table 3, which compares the kin affiliations in Petite-Nation with those in Lotbinière, a long-settled seigneurie on the south shore of the St. Lawrence some forty miles east of Quebec City, illustrates the effect of migration on the kin groups. The French Canadians who straggled up the Ottawa Valley had left a web of blood ties which they could not quickly recreate. Habitants in Petite-Nation were far less likely to have a relative as nearest neighbour, or even a relative in the same côte, than were habitants in the older seigneuries. Where kin groups existed in Petite-Nation, they rarely extended beyond sibling and parent–child relationships.

In many ways the parish in Petite-Nation resembled the parishes *409* along the lower St. Lawrence in the late seventeenth and early eighteenth centuries.[73] For many years the seigneurie was visited briefly twice a year by a missionary priest, who arrived in January on snowshoes and in June by canoe.[74] The first resident priest, an Irishman, was appointed in 1828 and stayed three years; his successor stayed for two years, and in 1833 the parish reverted to the missionary system.[75] In 1835 the Bishop appointed another priest, who, in turn, soon begged to be relieved. When in 1838 the Bishop acquiesced, Petite-Nation was left without a resident priest for another four years. In this interval missionaries continued to visit the parish twice a year, but these were short visits, their essential purposes to baptise babies and to say mass for the dead. For the most part, Catholics in Petite-Nation were left alone, and exposed, as one missionary priest put it, "to fatal communications with methodists and baptists."[76] In 1841 the Bishop established yet another priest, and this man stayed until 1849, when, amidst bitter factional quarrels over the school tax and the location of a new church, he left for a newly constructed

TABLE 3   Surnames in the Seigneuries of Petite-Nation and Lotbinière, 1842

	Petite-Nation	Lotbinière
No. of families	267	458
No. of different surnames	143	126
Per cent of families with the most common surname	3	12
Per cent of families with one of the ten most common surnames	9	43
Per cent of families with unique surname	33	14

Source: Nominal Censuses of Petite-Nation and Lotbinière, 1842, reels C-729 and C-730.

chapel and presbytery in the interior of the seigneurie.[77] The Bishop attempted to placate the feuding parties by dividing Petite-Nation into three parishes,[78] but for several more years the two parishes along the river were visited irregularly by their former curé or by the curé from l'Orignal, a seigneurie twenty miles away.

Priests did not stay in Petite-Nation because their financial support was inadequate. They could not have lived on the tithe (in Canada one twenty-sixth of the grain harvest) had it been paid regularly, and agreed to come only after the habitants had subscribed a sum for their maintenance. Yet, whatever the financial arrangements, priests in Petite-Nation were rarely paid. The first complained that he was reduced to "scratching among the stumps"[79] for a living, another that he paid out twice what he received from the habitants and was indebted to the merchant.[80] On one occasion the habitants agreed to tithe in potatoes,[81] but when the new priest arrived in a buggy pulled by two horses, the habitants decided that he was rich and refused to pay either tithe or subscription. The priest explained to his bishop that the buggy was old and had cost only a few dollars. "The mistake," he wrote, "is that I had it varnished, and that gives an appearance of luxury."[82] One priest noted bitterly that the habitants could support several taverns,[83] and in 1833 the bishop informed Denis-Benjamin that "experience has proved that the habitants could not *or would not* pay even half of what they owed without being forced by law."[84] The priests had attempted to curtail the heavy drinking[85] and some adulterous behaviour in Petite-Nation, and this may have led to a reaction against them; but in the light of many meetings to petition for a priest, the number of times that funds were subscribed for his support, and the bitter rows over the location of a church, it is clear that most habitants wanted to have a resident priest but that he was a luxury they could hardly afford.

After 1840 a number of civil functions, notably the assessment and collection of taxes and the maintenance of roads and schools, were organized within the parish.[86] These civil functions were open to all parish residents, whatever their religious affiliations (the parish corresponding in this sense to the township in Ontario), and in Petite-Nation most responsible parish positions were held either by members of the Papineau family or by New Englanders. Illiteracy alone disqualified almost all the habitants. New Englanders had established a school in Petite-Nation in 1820, but only two French Canadians (one of them Denis-Benjamin) sent their children to it. The habitants saw no need for formal education, and most of the effort to create schools had to come from outside the seigneurie.[87] The first major initiative in this direction came with the Common School Act of 1841,[88] which provided for the election of five school commissioners in each parish, for the division of parishes into school districts, for an assessment of £50 ($200) on the inhabitants of each district for the building of a school, and for a monthly fee of one

410

shilling and three pence for each child at school. These were heavy charges on a poverty-stricken people who attached no value to formal schooling.[89] Then, when three of the first five school commissioners were English-speaking (elected because the New Englanders had attended the organizational meeting in greater number), the priest began preaching that the three English-speaking school commissioners were agents of religious and cultural assimilation.[90] In these circumstances schools were built slowly and then were often closed for want of pupils. The School Act was modified in 1846 to provide more operating revenue from property taxes whether or not parents sent their children to school.[91] Even so, Denis-Benjamin estimated in 1851 that not one French Canadian in thirty in Petite-Nation was literate.[92] The habitants usually became viewers of ditches and fences, the New Englanders the tax assessors and collectors.[93]

Although the seigneur or his agent was a powerful presence in Petite-Nation, the seigneurie itself was not a social unit. All censitaires had acquired land from the Papineaus; all paid, or were supposed to pay, annual charges for their land; almost all were in debt to the seigneur. This, coupled with Louis-Joseph's fame, his sense of himself as a leader, his excellent education and meticulous knowledge of Canadian civil law, and, after 1849, his mansion at Montebello, which was by far the finest residence that most habitants in Petite-Nation had ever seen, made him an awe-inspiring figure in the seigneurie. Louis-Joseph liked to think of himself as the leader of a flock,[94] but the habitants undoubtedly viewed him with fear. He was a force in rural life as seigneurs had not been during the French regime, but not the focus of a rural society. As during the French regime, seigneurial boundaries were irrelevant to social patterns.

Until Louis-Joseph settled at Montebello, Denis-Benjamin Papineau, Stephen Tucker, and the two Cookes had been the most powerful men in the seigneurie. At one time or another each was a justice of the peace. In 1840 Denis-Benjamin was elected unanimously to represent Petite-Nation in the newly formed District Council; four years later he was succeeded by Alanson Cooke. In 1842 Denis-Benjamin was elected to the Legislative Assembly. His son was parish clerk and, at times, surveyor of roads in Petite-Nation, and for several years Stephen Tucker was the tax collector. Several prosperous farmers and merchants, all of them English-speaking, were fringe members of the elite.[95] The position of all this group rested, finally, on economic power. Denis-Benjamin's authority depended on his position as seigneurial agent, Tucker's on his role as employer and creditor, the Cookes' on the many jobs they controlled in the sawmills. The habitants elected these men to the District Council, to the Legislative Assembly, or to a local parish office because their livelihood, however meagre, was controlled by them. Moreover, the elite were the only men in the seigneurie who met the property qualification of £300 ($1200) for such public offices as district councillor or justice of the peace.

411

Petite-Nation in 1860

By 1860 parts of Petite-Nation had been settled for more than fifty years. The Ottawa Valley plain was cleared, long lots were conceded across it, and much of the land was farmed. Farm houses stretched in côtes along the river, and two small villages, Montebello and Papineauville, had taken shape towards opposite ends of this line. In the Shield, the patterns of clearing and settlement were much more irregular, but most of the fertile pockets in the valleys were farmed. In the largest of these valleys, the village of St-André Avellin contained a church, a number of stores, and even a few streets laid out, but still largely unoccupied, at right angles to the main road. North and west from St-André Avellin, where côtes had been settled in the previous two decades, there were still many shanties in tiny clearings amid the bush that was the aftermath of logging. Still farther north, pine and spruce were being cut and floated down the Petite-Nation River to Gilmour and Company's sawmill. In all, some 4000 people lived in Petite-Nation. Rough as in many respects it was, with stumps in many fields and the slash of recent logging almost everywhere, a settled place had emerged where just over fifty years before there had been only forest.

412

In this place there were three principal groups of people, and three landscapes associated with their different lives. In the manor he had built in 1848 and 1849 at Montebello lived Louis-Joseph Papineau and as many of his immediate family as he could entice away from Montreal.[96] His was one of the finest country houses in Lower Canada, its main unit forty by sixty feet and twenty-four feet high,[97] and its architectural inspiration an amalgam of ideas that Louis-Joseph had brought back from France. The house was sheltered by a row of towering pines, and overlooked a spacious garden to the river. In the village of Montebello just outside the gate to his domain, Louis-Joseph had considerably widened the through road from Montreal to Hull, and had lined the streets with trees, naming each street after its particular tree: rue des cèdres, rue des érables, rue des pins, rue des ormes, rue des sapins.[98] Several miles to the west, in the village of Papineauville and its surrounding farms, lived Denis-Benjamin Papineau and a group of prosperous New Englanders. Most of their houses were white clapboard in the New England style, or the brick or frame buildings with italianate trim that were becoming common in Ontario. Their large, well-managed farms produced oats, potatoes, hay, oxen, and meat for the logging camps, and their stores in Papineauville supplied settlers in much of the seigneurie. Throughout most of the rest of the coastal plain and in the cultivable valleys of the Shield were the tiny log houses, the barns, the fields, and the côtes of the French-Canadian habitant. However imperfectly, three traditions had emerged in the human landscape of Petite-Nation: that of the aristocrat,[99] that of the Yankee trader, and that of the habitant community of the lower St. Lawrence.

Underlying and shaping the habitant landscape in Petite-Nation were the two essential characteristics of French-Canadian life in Petite-Nation, its poverty and its weak institutions. The habitants faced the world individually or in nuclear families supported by nearest neighbour or côte. The seigneur was a creditor, not a leader, the parish priest was more often absent than not, the kin group was barely forming, and the local government was dominated by those who controlled the habitants' livelihood. Paradoxically, the New Englanders, who valued self-reliance, created more institutional support in Petite-Nation for their way of life than did the habitants, who tended to value community. To conclude this paper it is necessary to consider why this was so.

An explanation for the character of French-Canadian settlement in the Shield lies only partly in nineteenth-century Quebec, and even less in the physical character of the Canadian Shield or the commercial ascendancy of the English. The same soils on which French Canadians scratched out a living also supported large and prosperous farms. The forests in which the habitants worked for a pittance made the fortunes of others. English-speaking timber merchants exploited the habitants. So did Louis-Joseph Papineau. The Papineau manor at Montebello, Stephen Tucker's forty-four rotures confiscated from debtors, and the profits of the Mears, the McGills, and the Gilmours who built and operated the sawmills in Petite-Nation all rested on a poor habitant population. Seigneur and lumberman profited from the situation in Petite-Nation, but neither had created it. Rather, to understand the habitant landscape and society in Petite-Nation is to understand the evolving character of French-Canadian rural society over the previous century and a half.

413

What apparently had happened was this.[100] The few emigrants who crossed the Atlantic to the lower St. Lawrence in the seventeenth and early eighteenth centuries were, for the most part, poor and dispossessed people who had only a toehold in French society before they crossed the Atlantic. Among them were approximately 1000 girls from Paris poorhouses; 2000 petty criminals (mostly salt smugglers); over 3000 ordinary soldiers, most of whom had been pressed into service; and perhaps 4000 engagés, who came largely from the same group of landless labourers and unemployed as the soldiers. Many of the engagés were young, merely boys, according to the intendants, and not very robust. These people came as individuals or within the type of temporary social structure — that of a poorhouse, a prison, or an army — in which they had never intended to spend their lives, and which was irrelevant to the settlement of Canada. Along the lower St. Lawrence they found an abundance of land that, when cleared, yielded a higher standard of living than that of most French peasants. They found an opportunity to settle along the river, away from official eyes, and in a setting where their lives could not be controlled. And they found in the untrammelled life of the fur trade contact with largely nomadic Algonkian Indians whose rhetoric, courage, and apparent lack of regime they admired and emulated.

Out of this emerged a habitant population characterized by bravado, insouciance, and a considerable disdain for authority. The habitants lived boisterously, spending their income, enjoying the independence and modest prosperity of their lives in the côtes, and, perhaps too, the Indian girls along the upper Ottawa; it was a style of life that grew partly out of their French background but probably more out of the opportunities of a new land. They had brought few institutions with them, and needed few in Canada. The Canadian seigneurie was neither a social nor an economic unit, while the parish was emerging only slowly as a social unit at the end of the French regime. The village was almost absent; collective open-field agriculture never appeared. The côte did become a loose rural neighbourhood, as time went on neighbours were frequently kin, and, after perhaps the earliest years, the nuclear family was always important. In the background was the colonial government, eager to promote the settlement of the colony, paternalistic, tending to side with the habitants in disputes with the seigneurs. The government could not impose itself on the habitants, but it could offer certain services — inexpensive regional courts, for example, or the right of free appeal to the intendant. In operating hospitals, orphanages, and poorhouses, the religious orders did the same. Such support only increased the independence of the habitants, who were not forced to compensate for an oppressive officialdom by a tighter social organization at the local level.

414

In the century after the Conquest, this way of life had slowly changed. Habitant mobility was constrained by the declining relative importance of the fur trade and, after 1821, by its loss to Hudson's Bay; by English-speaking settlement in Upper Canada; and by growing population pressure along the St. Lawrence lowland. Farm land was becoming scarce as the seigneurial lands filled up; the value of land rose, and that of labour gradually fell. Seigneurs found their revenues rising, and close seigneurial management a paying proposition. They kept accounts regularly, insisted on payment of debts, and began to build sizeable manors throughout the lower St. Lawrence. Without an intendant to interfere, they often increased their cens et rentes[101] (indeed, they interpreted the seigneurial system to the English), and as alternative land became scarcer, the habitants had no alternative but to accept these charges. A situation which once had favoured the censitaire had turned to favour the seigneur.

At the same time French Canadians were losing control of commerce to more single-minded and better-connected Englishmen, Scots, and New Englanders. A government which had never controlled but had often supported the habitants during the French regime was taken over by an alien people with a different language, religion, and values. This was no longer a government to turn to as the habitants had turned to the courts and the intendant during the French regime. For a time the Conquest connected French Canada to a larger market for its agricultural products, but not to the larger world of social and intellectual change. It shielded

French Canadians from the full impact of the French Revolution, for which most of them were thankful, and it filtered the late eighteenth- and nineteenth-century world through the eyes of the English-speaking merchant, the colonial administrator, or, especially in the nineteenth century, the parish priest. The fragment of France which had crossed the Atlantic to settle the côtes of the lower St. Lawrence and become the largely illiterate habitant population of the French regime had been poorly connected before 1760 to contending French values and ideologies, and the long-term effect of the Conquest had been to prolong its isolation.

In this situation, French-Canadian life had become increasingly rural. Before 1760, 20 to 25 per cent of the people along the lower St. Lawrence were townsmen, but by 1815 only 5 per cent of the French Canadians were. The central business districts and the upper class residential areas of Montreal and Quebec were overwhelmingly English-speaking. French-Canadian seigneurs who once had lived in the towns now lived in their seigneuries. In this rural introversion there were two deep ironies. French Canadians were turning to a rural life at a time when, for the ordinary habitant on the ordinary roture, such a life meant subsistence farming, poverty, debt, and, eventually, the departure of most of his children. Then, too, many of them gloried in an image of the French regime, of a rural way of life before the coming of the English built around seigneurie, parish, and Coutume de Paris,[102] without understanding that in the vastly different conditions of the French regime these institutions had been extremely weak. Economically and institutionally, the rural core around which French Canada had folded was hollow.

All that could be done was to make the most of what they had. The parish, which had been slowly gaining strength after the decision taken in 1722 to establish resident priests, gradually became more vital after the Conquest, and would have developed more rapidly had there not been a serious shortage of priests.[103] The extended family or kin group enlarged and probably strengthened and, with less rural mobility within its seigneurial lowlands, the côte and nuclear family may have strengthened as well. The Coutume de Paris, with its emphasis on family rather than on individual rights, and its protective view of landholding that became more relevant to the lower St. Lawrence as the population increased, became an essential prop, in many nationalist minds, of French-Canadian life. The seigneurial system, although neither a social nor an economic unit of habitant life, had become profitable for the seigneurs, most of whom insisted that the survival of French Canada depended on the survival of the system. These institutions, particularly the kin group and the côte, provided a measure of stability, but they did not provide an institutional framework for change, especially as parish priest and seigneur usually defended the status quo. French-Canadian society had achieved some strength in rural isolation, in closely knit, interrelated communities, and in a retrospective outlook, but had not the ability to

415

cope with change, least of all with the internal problem of population pressure.

When young French Canadians were pushed out of the St. Lawrence lowland, they left in much the condition in which their forebears, a century and a half before, had crossed the Atlantic. They were young, illiterate, often destitute, and, in the sense that they were not part of groups bound by ties of blood and tradition, alone. Immigrants in the late seventeenth century had found an abundance of agricultural land and a heady outlet in the fur trade. The many more French Canadians who settled in the Shield found a far more meagre agricultural land and lumber camps and sawmills operated by another people. In this setting, they had no defence against what they became, subsistence farmers and underpaid labourers. When their children or grandchildren left for the cities, they too left as their predecessors had come to the Shield. The years in the Shield had availed French Canadians nothing but poverty and some lag in the adjustment to changed conditions.

Finally, the tragedy of French-Canadian settlement in Petite-Nation lay perhaps less in poverty than in the habitants' inability to maintain a distinctive way of life. The values of the closely knit rural communities of the lower St. Lawrence were neither those of an aristocrat such as Louis-Joseph Papineau, nor those of liberals such as Stephen Tucker or Alanson Cooke. The habitants' outlook was more collective than that of the New Englanders, more egalitarian than that of Louis-Joseph Papineau. But communities such as those along the lower St. Lawrence in the nineteenth century depend on isolation and internal stability. When either is removed they are likely to be undermined, as they were for the habitants in Petite-Nation, who stood almost alone to face a changing world.

416

NOTES

This paper has been written with the support of a Fellowship from the J.S. Guggenheim Foundation and a Grant-in-Aid-of-Research from the University of Toronto. The author acknowledges with gratitude the research assistance of Mr. John Punter and Mr. Ian Walker.

[1] In St-Féréol, behind the present settlement of Ste-Anne de Beaupré, after the Séminaire de Québec had conceded all the land along the Côte de Beaupré.

[2] See Michel Chamberland, *Histoire de Montebello, 1815–1928* (Montréal, 1929), chap. 7, for a description of early immigration to Petite-Nation. The data in Map 1 are derived from the nominal census of 1851. The place of birth of approximately one-half the heads of households in St-André Avellin is given in the census.

[3] Ibid., 58–59.

[4] See, for example, J. Papineau à son fils Benjamin, Île Jésus, mai 1824, *Rapport de l'Archiviste de la province de Québec* [*RAPQ*] (1951–52, 194–96; and a letter of 9 Feb. 1826, ibid., 231.

[5] This process is described here and there in the Denis-Benjamin Papineau correspondence. See, for example, Denis-Benjamin Papineau à Louis-Joseph Papineau, fév. 1836, Archives de la province de Québec [APQ], Archives Personnelles [AP], P, 5, 29.

[6] The physical geography of Petite-Nation is well surveyed in Paul G. Lajoie, *Étude pédologique des comtés de Hull, Labelle, et Papineau* (Ottawa, 1968), 14–31.

[7] A detailed description of the forest in Petite-Nation before very much of the seigneurie had been cleared is in Joseph Bouchette's Field Book of the Line between the Seigniory of La Petite-Nation and the Augmentation of Grenville, beginning 1 Oct. 1826, APQ, AP, P, 5, 48.

8 Joseph Papineau à son fils Benjamin, Montréal, 22 juil. 1809, *RAPQ* (1951-52), 173. Joseph Papineau does not give the date of the contract in this letter, but apparently it was made in the previous year or two.

9 Chamberland, *Histoire de Montebello*, 58-59.

10 Vente de partie de la Seigneurie de Petite-Nation par J. Papineau, Ecr. à Robert Fletcher, Ecr., 17 jan. 1809, APQ, AP, P, 5.

11 *La Gazette de Québec*, 9 mars 1809, no 2289.

12 This account of Fletcher's death is given by Judge Augustin C. Papineau in a short history of Petite-Nation written in 1912. Copy of original manuscript by J.T. Beaudry, Oct. 1819, APQ, QP, P, 5.

13 Vente par Joseph Papineau à Louis-Joseph Papineau, 2 mai 1817, APQ, AP, P, 5, 46. In this case the sale was for £5000.

14 Lettre de D.-B. Papineau à Mgr Lartigue, Petite-Nation, 25 fév. 1828, APQ, PQ, P, 5, 29; Chamberland, *Histoire de Montebello*, 79-81, gives 512 people in 1825.

15 Public Archives of Canada [PAC], Nominal Census of Petite-Nation, 1842, reel C-729.

16 Ibid., 1851, reels C-1131 and 1132; 1861, reel C-1304.

17 Tableau de la Censive de la Petite-Nation, 1818, APQ, AP, P, 5, 48.

18 J.-B.N. Papineau, son of Denis-Benjamin, pointed out in 1852 that rotures in Petite-Nation had been laid out "along the course of the Ottawa River or the Petite-Nation River and its tributaries so that the rivers can be used for roads until such time as the censitaires are able to build them." Nominal census of Petite-Nation, 1851, remarks of enumerator on back of page 131, 6 March 1852, reel C-1132. See also, Instructions de Denis-Benjamin Papineau sur l'arpentage, 1839, APQ, AP, 5, 46.

19 With inadequate surveying there was always a good deal of confusion about property lines, particularly in the irregular pockets of cultivable land in the Shield, for which the cadastral system of long lot and côte was quite ill suited.

20 During the French regime seigneurs had been expected to build and the censitaires to maintain the roads. The title to Petite-Nation, however, did not specify the seigneur's responsibility to build roads, and there is no indication that the Papineaus built any roads in Petite-Nation other than a few short roads to mills.

21 Louis-Joseph Papineau à Benjamin Papineau, Montréal, 22 nov. 1829, APQ, AP, P, 5, 5 (folder 153a); and also Joseph Papineau à son fils Benjamin, Île Jésus, mai 1824, *RAPQ* (1951-52), 194-96.

22 Louis-Joseph Papineau à Alanson Cooke, Petite-Nation, 22 oct. 1850, APQ, AP, P, 5, 48 (bundle Alanson Cooke).

23 Louis-Joseph Papineau à Benjamin Papineau, 23 oct. 1848, APQ, AP, P, 5, 5 (folder 185).

24 Louis-Joseph Papineau à Benjamin Papineau, 11 oct. 1848, ibid. (folder 184).

25 The legal position in this regard of the seigneur during the French regime is discussed in R.C. Harris, *The Seigneurial System in Early Canada: A Geographical Study* (Madison, 1966), 106-108.

26 Louis-Joseph Papineau à Benjamin Papineau, Petite-Nation, 22 oct. 1850, APQ, AP, P, 5, 5 (folder 203). The title deed to the seigneurie of Petite-Nation, unlike most others, did not specify that the seigneur was required to sub-grant land, but it is doubtful that an intendant during the French regime would have permitted Louis-Joseph to grant land as he did.

27 Louis-Joseph Papineau à Benjamin Papineau, 11 oct. 1848, ibid. (folder 184).

28 For an example of a roture contract in Petite-Nation see: Concession de roture no 2, côte du Moulin . . . à Alanson Cooke, 20 oct. 1846, APQ, AP, P, 5, 51.

29 In many seigneurial titles, even the seigneur had been forbidden to cut oak anywhere on the seigneurie.

30 Indeed, by an Arrêt du Conseil d'État of 4 June 1686, seigneurs during the French regime could lose their banal right if they did not put up a grist mill within a year.

31 Harris, *The Seigneurial System*, 63-69, 78.

32 All dollar values are given in Halifax dollars, such a dollar being worth five English shillings, and approximately one and one-half livres tournois. Thus one livre tournois was worth approximately eighteen cents Halifax currency.

33 Louis-Joseph was fully aware that seigneurs who fixed their charges in money payments were not likely to prosper in the long run from their holdings. He discusses this matter at some length in Tableau statistique des Seigneuries, circa 1851, APQ, AP, P, 5, 55.

34 A graph of wheat prices during the French regime is in J. Hamelin, *Économie et société en Nouvelle France* (Québec, 1960), 61, and a similar graph for the later period is in Fernand Ouellet, *Histoire économique et sociale du Québec, 1760-1850* (Montréal, 1966), 603.

35 In the seigneurial account books the charge for each year was always listed in livres rather than in minots, and depended on the price of wheat in that year. It was not possible for a censitaire to accumulate several years of debt and then, when the price of wheat was low, pay back his seigneur in kind.

36 Pièce-sur-pièce was the most common form of log construction during the French regime, and was still widespread in the nineteenth century. Round log construction probably had entered Quebec from New England in the late eighteenth century and was widely adopted in the Shield by both French Canadians and Irish. French-Canadian and Irish houses in the Shield were often almost indistinguishable, both being essentially simple versions in wood of a Norman house, one brought from the St. Lawrence lowland, the other from southeastern Ireland. The heavily flared eaves, the porches,

417

and the elevated ground storey, all characteristics of the vernacular French-Canadian house of the nineteenth century, often did not penetrate the Shield, presumably because of the additional work and cost associated with them.

[37] In 1842 the median amount of cleared land per roture was ten arpents, and by 1861 it was 19 arpents (Nominal Census of Petite-Nation, 1842, reel C-729).

[38] See, for example, lettre de Joseph Papineau à son fils Louis-Joseph, Montréal, 28 fév. 1818, *RAPQ* (1951–52), 182.

[39] Lettre de Denis-Benjamin Papineau à son oncle Frs. Papineau, Petite-Nation, 29 fév. 1812, APQ, AP, P, 5, 29.

[40] These figures are calculated from data on yields in the Nominal Census of 1861. They assume that French Canadians sowed one and a half minots of grain per arpent. A good deal of land in 1861 was still within a few years of first cultivation. Later, without a change in agricultural technology, yields would have been substantially lower.

[41] This lease was arranged sometime before 1822. There is a receipt, dated 1822, for £75 ($300) for lease of the mill in the Papineau Papers (APQ, AP, P, 5, 48).

[42] Lease from 1 Nov. 1833 . . . between the Hon. L.-J. Papineau and the Hon. P. McGill, 20 Sept. 1834, ibid. (bundle Alanson Cooke).

[43] Nominal Census of Petite-Nation, 1851, reel C-1132.

[44] This was a long-standing arrangement, its terms varying over the years. See, for example, D-B. Papineau à Stephen Tucker, 10 fév. 1844, APQ, AP, P, 5, 30.

[45] Joseph Papineau à son fils Louis-Joseph, Montréal, 25 mars 1840, *RAPQ* (1951–52), 299.

[46] Nominal Census of Petite-Nation, 1851, reels C-1131 and C-1132.

[47] An exact statement would be possible only if the records of all timber concerns operating in Petite-Nation had survived. As it is, there are, apparently, no such records.

[48] Nominal Census of Petite-Nation, 1851. Some of the information given here is listed on the back of folio sheets and is not photographed on microfilm.

[49] Ibid., 1861, reel C-1304. At this date Gilmour and Co. and Stephen Tucker were the only major employers in Petite-Nation, and it can be taken that only just over 200 men worked in forest industries in the seigneurie in 1861.

[50] These figures are my estimates, which probably err on the side of more rather than fewer jobs. In much of the Ottawa Valley the same men were hired to cut and square timber and then to raft it to Quebec. Stephen Tucker may well have hired in this way; if so, the fifty to sixty raftsmen given in these estimates were the same men as fifty to sixty of those estimated to have worked in the logging camps.

[51] The 1861 wages are given in the census (Nominal Census of Petite-Nation, 1861, reel C-1304). Wages at Hull, forty miles away, were $10 a month in 1820 and $12 a month in 1840, and there is no reason for those in Petite-Nation to have been different. See C.H. Craigie, "The Influence of the Timber Trade and Philemon Wright on the Social and Economic Development of Hull Township, 1800–1850" (M.A. thesis, Carleton University, 1969), 94.

[52] My estimate, and probably too generous, based on the wage scale and inventory of jobs given above.

[53] Nominal Census of Petite-Nation, 1842, reel C-729.

[54] Tableau d'arrérages, 1822, APQ, AP, P, 5, 48. In 1825 46 rotures owed over 20,000 livres (ibid., 1825, APQ, AQP, P, 48).

[55] État des dettes au 11 nov. 1832, APQ, AP, P, 5, 48. By this date the 73 rotures along the Ottawa River owed approximately 40,000 livres.

[56] Tableau d'arrérages, 1822, ibid.

[57] There are numerous indications in the documents that the Papineaus exercised this droit de retrait. See, for example, J. Papineau à son fils Benjamin, Montréal, 7 jan. 1825, *RAPQ* (1951–52), 198–99.

[58] Comptes entre D-B. Papineau et L-J. Papineau, 1825–37, APQ, AP, P, 5, 48.

[59] At this date there was no court in the Ottawa Valley, and, as a result, minor disputes rarely reached a court. See D-B. Papineau to Philemon Wright, 14 May 1833, PAC, Wright Papers, MG24, D8, vol. 19, p. 8179.

[60] Denis-Benjamin was always an easy-going seigneurial agent, often too much so for his brother's liking. Once, for example, when Louis-Joseph was determined to sue, Denis-Benjamin would go only so far as to tell the censitaires in question that they would be taken to court if their debts were not paid in three years. "Je ne scais si cela conviendra à [Louis-Joseph] Papineau," he told his father, "mais je ne pense qu'a moins de déposseder les habitants l'on puisse exiger d'avantage" (J. Papineau à son fils Louis-Joseph, St. Hyacinthe, 27 sept. 1838, *RAPQ* [1951–52], 291–92).

[61] Although he rarely sued, Papineau did expect to be paid, and he pushed his censitaires as hard as he could short of actual eviction. During one brief visit to the seigneurie he wrote to his wife, "je vois que je n'en retirerai rien, il est trop tard, leur grains sont mangés" (Louis-Joseph Papineau à sa femme, Petite-Nation, 9 avril 1828, *RAPQ* [1953–54], 247–49).

[62] "Oh il faudrait vivre ici pour reussir à une petite partie des améliorations que je rêve et pour forcer la rentrée des arrérages qui me permettraient de les tenter" (L-J. Papineau à Benjamin Papineau, 23 oct. 1848, APQ, AP, P, 5, 5 [folder 185]).

[63] Louis-Joseph Papineau à Benjamin Papineau, Montréal, 6 mai 1848, ibid. (folder 175).

[64] Louis-Joseph Papineau à son fils Amédée, 28 avril 1852, APQ, AP, P, 5, 7 (folder 327).

[65] Louis-Joseph Papineau à Benjamin Papineau, 12 mars 1848, APQ, AP, P, 5, 5 (folder 173). In French

law the debts against land were not revealed at the time of its sale, and in this circumstance, bidders were unwilling to pay more than a pittance for rotures sold for the non-payment of dues. The seigneur could acquire them for next to nothing.

66 Chamberland, *Histoire de Montebello*, 165. Denis-Benjamin did not here mention Tucker by name, but other reports about him and the fact he was the only Baptist merchant in Petite-Nation leave no doubt who was being described. There is some indication that his offer was not always rejected. In the nominal census of 1851 Aureole Gravelle and his wife, both French Canadians by birth, are listed as Baptists.

67 Liste alphabétique des actes reçues par Andre-Benjamin Papineau, notaire à St-Martin . . . transactions en la Seigneurie de La Petite-Nation de 1837 à 1845 inclusivement, APQ, AP, P, 5.

68 Stephen Tucker to Louis-Joseph Papineau, Papineauville, 25 May 1855, APQ, QP, P, 5, 48; and also, Reciprocal Discharge and acquittance from and to the Honourable Louis-Joseph Papineau and Stephen Tucker, 14 July 1858, APQ, AP, P, 5, 48. Tucker had not been paying the back dues on these rotures and in 1858 he owed approximately £900 on them.

69 L-J. Papineau to Stephen Tucker, Montebello, 27 May 1858, ibid.

70 One priest, however, reported that there was "beaucoup d'animosité" between French Canadians and Irish in Petite-Nation (Lettre de M. Bourassa à Mgr Lartigue, 23 mars 1839, cited in Chamberland, *Histoire de Montebello*, 174). And, of course, there were many accounts in the Ottawa Valley of strife between rival gangs of French-Canadian and Irish workers.

71 One of these Protestants was a Lutheran, another, brother of the first, a Universalist, and the third, an Anabaptist.

72 This information is calculated from the nominal census of 1842.

73 Resident priests were not established in rural parishes until the 1720s, and before that time parishes were visited intermittently, as in Petite-Nation, by missionary priests.

419

74 Copies of all the correspondence between Joseph Raupe, the first missionary priest to visit Petite-Nation, and Joseph Papineau are preserved in the Papineau Papers (APQ, AP, P, 5, 49). Together these letters give a vivid picture of the Ottawa Valley mission in its earliest years.

75 This intricate history is treated more fully in Chamberland, *Histoire de Montebello*, chaps. 9–11.

76 Lettre de M. Brady, missionaire ambulante à l'évêque, Petite-Nation, 4 nov. 1838; cited in Chamberland, *Histoire de Montebello*, 171–73.

77 Ibid., p. 188.

78 Correspondence entre D-B. Papineau et Mgr de Guigues, Evêque de Bytown, 1850–51, APQ, AP, P, 5; see also L-J. Papineau à son fils Amédée, 21 jan. 1851, APQ, AP, P, 5, 7 (folder 299).

79 Chamberland, *Histoire de Montebello*, 135.

80 M. Brunet à Mgr Lartigue, 1838, cited in ibid., 167.

81 Procès verbal d'une assemblée des habitants de la Paroisse de Notre Dame de Bonsecours, 14 juil. 1844, APQ, AP, P, 5, 46. "Cette assemblée est d'opinion qu'en payant les dîmes de patates en sus des dîmes de tout grain, tel que pourvu par la loi, la subsistence du Curé de cette paroisse serait assurée . . . "

82 Lettre de M. Mignault à Mgr Guigues, 18 oct. 1854, cited in Chamberland, *Histoire de Montebello*, 218–19.

83 Ibid., 155.

84 Mgr Lartigue à D-B. Papineau, Montréal, 15 juil. 1833, APQ, AP, P, 5, 28 (folder 1).

85 There are many references to drunkenness. "Il faut dire," wrote one missionary, "que l'ivrognerie regne en maitresse . . . " (M. Bourassa à Mgr de Telenesse, 10 avril 1839, cited in Chamberland, *Histoire de Montebello*, 174).

86 An ordinance to prescribe and regulate the Election and Appointment of certain officers in the several Parishes and Townships in this Province . . . , 29 Dec 1840; 4 Vic., c. 3; *Ordinances Passed by the Governor and Special Council of Lower Canada*, 1840 and 1841, pp. 9–16. See also 4 Vic., c. 4.

87 In 1833 D-B. Papineau and the priest did attempt to raise money for a school. Although they obtained over £40 in subscriptions, the project apparently collapsed (D-B. Papineau à Louis-Joseph Papineau, Petite-Nation, 17 mai 1833, APQ, AP, P, 5, 29).

88 *Ordinances Passed by the Governor and Special Council of Lower Canada*, 4–5 Vic., c. 18, 1841.

89 "Le goût de l'Education . . . n'existe pas dans la classe qui en a le plus besoin . . . plusieurs fois des parents ont été assez deraisonnables pour retirer leurs enfants de l'Ecole sans aucune juste raison de plainte contre le maître; quelquefois par animosité à cause de quelque châtiment merité infligé aux enfants; quelquefois par pique personnelle contre quelque commissaire ou Syndic; d'autres fois par un motif ignoble de vengeance, qui les portait à faire tout en leur pouvoir pour faire manquer l'Ecole" (D-B. Papineau au Gouverneur Général, Petite-Nation, 22 mai 1843, APQ, AP, P, 5, 29. "You, nor no one else not being amidst our rural population could ever conceive the extravagant notions which they entertain respecting that Great Bug Bear 'The Tax' [the school tax] and designing Scoundrels are prowling about the Country raising still more the heated minds of the Habitants . . . " (D.M. Armstrong to D-B. Papineau, 8 avr. 1845, APQ, AP, P, 5, 28 [folder A]).

90 L-J. Papineau à D-B. Papineau, 26 sept. 1846, Chamberland, *Histoire de Montebello*, 193–94. See also letters from Denis-Benjamin to Mgr de Guigues, Evêque de Bytown, 18 Dec. 1850, and 1851 (more specific date not given), APQ, AP, P, 5.

91 9 Vic., c. 27, 1846.

92 D-B. Papineau à Mgr de Guigues, Evêque de Bytown, 1851, APQ, AP, P, 5.

[93] In 1843, for example, the following men were parish officials in Petite-Nation: parish clerks: J.B.N. Papineau; assessors: Thomas Schryer, Charles Cummings, and Asa Cooke; collector: Stephen Tucker; inspector of roads and bridges: Ebenezer Winters; inspector of the poor: Asa Cooke; commissioners of schools: Mr Sterkendries (priest), Asa Cooke, Stephen Tucker, Bazile Charlebois, Charles Beautron; road viewers: Jean Lavoie, Henry Baldwin, Antoine Gauthier, François Gravelle, Elezear Frappier, Augustin Belile; fence and ditch viewers: Louis Chalifoux, Edward Thomas, Paul Sabourin, Daniel Baldwin, Antoine Couillard, Louis Beautron (Book of Proceedings of the Civil Corporation of the Seigneurie of Petite-Nation persuant of the Ordinance of the Special Council of the 4th Victoria, c. 3, APQ, AP, P, 5, 46).

[94] "Et moi aussi je suis chef de colonie" (lettre de L-J. Papineau à Eugène Guillemot, ex-ministre de France au Brésil, 10 jan. 1855; printed in F. Ouellet, ed., *Papineau*, Cahiers de l'Institut d'Histoire, Université Laval, p. 99).

[95] The periods of office of all the elite can best be worked out from the Book of the Civil Corporation of . . . Petite-Nation, APQ, AP, P, 5, 46.

[96] Louis-Joseph's wife was especially uneasy about leaving Montreal and competent medical attention. In his later years Louis-Joseph often took to task this or that member of the family for not spending more time in the seigneurie, where he most loved to be.

[97] L-J. Papineau à son fils Amédée, 26 juin 1848, APQ, AP, P, 5, 6 (folder 281).

[98] L-J. Papineau à Mgr Guigues, 29 mars 1856; printed in Chamberland, *Histoire de Montebello*, 221–22. All these names have since been changed to saints' names.

[99] This characterization of Louis-Joseph hardly does justice to the complex, many-sided character of the man, although in his later years it is probably the single word which fits him best. Louis-Joseph's relationship with Petite-Nation will be looked at much more closely in another paper.

[100] The tentative sketch of the social evolution of habitant Quebec that concludes this paper is based largely on work I have undertaken since the publication of *The Seigneurial System in Early Canada*. It will be given fuller treatment in subsequent essays.

[101] Changes in the rate of the cens et rentes after 1760 cannot be described simply. In many seigneuries they did not change, and in many others changes were spasmodic. As yet there is insufficient evidence to support the claim that English or French seigneurs, as a group, adjusted these changes in a certain way.

[102] The Coutume de Paris had provided a base of civil law throughout most of the French regime, but it was a French law, evolved in conditions far different from those in early Canada, and some of its tenets were irrelevant to Canadian life for many years.

[103] By the 1820s and 1830s, perhaps even earlier, the parish was undoubtedly a strong institution in rural French-Canadian life, and this image of it, as of many aspects of French-Canadian life in the early nineteenth century, has been projected back to the French regime.

Toronto Rolling Mills, Mill Street, 1864. Pastel drawing by William Armstrong.

Toronto's development is therefore explained not only by the growth of its own hinterland but also by a start to its commercial penetration of other regions. In the process it began its escape from the control of Montreal.

John McCallum, *Unequal Beginnings: Agriculture and Economic Development in Quebec and Ontario until 1870*

Topic Eleven

Urban and Commercial Development in the Canadas in the Mid-Nineteenth Century

The colony of the United Canadas in the mid-nineteenth century was still predominantly rural and agricultural. Out of a population of roughly two million, only 135 000 — approximately 8 percent — lived in the three major urban centres of Montreal (60 000), Quebec (45 000), and Toronto (roughly 30 000). Yet already these urban centres were emerging as focal points for the commercial and social life of the Canadas. John McCallum explains why this was so in "Urban and Commercial Development until 1850," a chapter from his *Unequal Beginnings: Agriculture and Economic Development in Quebec and Ontario until 1870*.

The British decision to abolish the old imperial preferences for Canadian flour and grain in the late 1840s forced British North Americans to look within North America for their trade and livelihood. This shift in emphasis necessitated in turn an extensive railway system that could link the urban centres of British North America with one another and with the prosperous American cities. The railways had decided advantages over the existing canal system for trade and communications: they were faster, more flexible in terms of location, and operational year round. Together, the railways and the St. Lawrence canals held the potential to make the colony of the United Canadas one of the major centres of North American trade.

The 1850s became the great age of railway building in British North America. At the beginning of the decade, only 106 km of primitive track existed, but by the end, more than 3000 km of new track had been laid. The construction of the Grand Trunk, which extended from Sarnia to Quebec City, developed into the most ambitious of all the projects. With 1800 km of track, it was, at the time, the longest railway system in the world.

One of the immediate effects of the railway industry was the rapid rise of towns and cities along the rail lines. Toronto in particular became an important trading centre, with rail links to the northern part of the colony (the Georgian Bay area); the American midwest; New York, via Buffalo; and Montreal and Quebec City. Railways also brought the industrial revolution to the Canadas: iron foundries, locomotive shops, and rolling mills were established in Toronto, Montreal, and other important Canadian towns. In "Transportation Changes in the St. Lawrence–Great Lakes Region, 1828–1860," Gerald Tulchinsky reviews the impact of the development of canals, and later railways.

H.V. Nelles's introduction to T.C. Keefer's *Philosophy of Railroads* in the Social History Series edition (Toronto: University of Toronto Press, 1972) provides a valuable introduction to the topic of railways in the Canadas. For a general history of railway development, consult the first volume of G.P. de T. Glazebrook's *A History of Transportation in Canada* (Toronto: McClelland and Stewart, 1964). Peter Baskerville offers a useful summary of developments in present-day Ontario in "Americans in Britain's Back Yard: The Railway Era in Upper Canada, 1850–1880," *Business History Review* 55 (1981): 314–36. For a short review of the effect that the railway had on small towns, see J.J. Talman, "The Impact of the Railway on a Pioneer Community," Canadian Historical Association, *Report* (1955), 1–12. Jacob Spelt's *Urban Development in South-Central Ontario* (Toronto: McClelland and Stewart, 1972) reviews urbanization of the north shore of Lake Ontario.

424

The best short review of the growth of cities in the Canadas is J.M.S. Careless's *The Rise of Cities in Canada before 1914*, Canadian Historical Association, Historical Booklet no. 32 (Ottawa: CHA, 1978). *The Canadian City: Essays in Urban and Social History*, ed. G.A. Stelter and A.F.J. Artibise (Don Mills, Ontario: Oxford, 1984) contains articles on the early urban history of the Canadas. Three important studies of Canadian city life in the nineteenth century are David T. Ruddel's *Quebec City 1765–1832: The Evolution of a Colonial Town* (Ottawa: National Museums of Canada, 1987), J.M.S. Careless's *Toronto to 1918: An Illustrated History* (Toronto: Lorimer, 1984), and John C. Weaver's *Hamilton: An Illustrated History* (Toronto: Lorimer, 1982). For an overview of economic developments in British North America in the mid-nineteenth century, see the chapters entitled "Wood, Banks, and Wholesalers: New Specialties, 1800–1849" and "The Steam Revolution" in Michael Bliss's *Northern Enterprise: Five Centuries of Canadian Business* (Toronto: McClelland and Stewart, 1987), 129–92. John A. Dickinson and Brian Young examine the economic history of mid-nineteenth century Canada East in their *A Short History of Quebec*, 2nd ed. (Toronto: Copp Clark Pitman, 1993), while Douglas McCalla does the same for Canada West in *Planting the Province: The Economic History of Upper Canada, 1784–1870* (Toronto: University of Toronto Press for the Ontario Historical Studies Series, 1993). Allan Greer and Ian Radforth look at the expansion of the government of the Canadas in their edited work, *Colonial Leviathan: State Formation in Mid-Nineteenth Century Canada* (Toronto: University of Toronto Press, 1992).

Urban and Commercial Development until 1850

JOHN McCALLUM

Urban development in Quebec and Ontario is a study in contrasts. Between 1850 and 1870 the two largest cities of Quebec made up about three-quarters of the urban population of that province, while the equivalent figure for Ontario was between one-quarter and one-third. To arrive at the share of Quebec's urban population held by Montreal and Quebec City, one would have to include the fifteen largest towns of Ontario in 1850 and the thirty largest towns in 1870. Looking at the matter in a different way, dozens of urban centres filled the Ontario countryside, but outside Montreal and Quebec City the population of Quebec was overwhelmingly rural.

425

It is clear from Table 1 that these differences in urban structure had been firmly established by 1850 and that the differences merely intensified in the following two decades. Between 1850 and 1870 the number of towns increased faster in Ontario than in Quebec, and, while the share of Ontario's two largest cities in the urban population actually fell from one-third in 1850 to one-quarter in 1870, Montreal and Quebec City accounted for close to three-quarters of Quebec's urban population throughout the period. The causes of the basic differences in urban structure are therefore to be found in the years before 1850, and this chapter focuses on those years. Urban growth after 1850 cannot be separated from industrial and transportation developments.

Ontario

Regional patterns of wheat production and urban and industrial development may be seen at a glance in Maps 1 to 4. In mid-nineteenth century Ontario there was a striking concentration of activity in the triangle bounded roughly by York County, the Niagara River, and London. The region varies somewhat, sometimes extending further east along Lake Ontario and sometimes stopping short of London on the west; but as a snapshot of a rapidly changing scene the general outline is remarkably

From *Unequal Beginnings: Agriculture and Economic Development in Quebec and Ontario until 1870*, by John McCallum (Toronto: University of Toronto Press, 1980). Reprinted with the permission of University of Toronto Press Incorporated.

TABLE 1 Population in Quebec and Ontario, 1850–70

1. Number of towns:

Town size:	Quebec			Ontario		
	1850	1860	1870	1850	1860	1870
25,000+	2	2	2	1	1	2
5000–25,000	0	1	3	4	8	10
1000–5000	14	18	22	33	50	69
Total	16	21	27	38	59	81

2. Urban and rural population (thousands):

Town size:	Quebec			Ontario		
	1850	1860	1870	1850	1860	1870
25,000+	100	141	167	31	45	83
5000–25,000	0	6	20	41	83	95
1000–5000	31	39	42	67	108	149
Total urban	131	187	229	139	236	328
Total rural	759	925	962	813	1160	1293
Total population	890	1112	1192	952	1396	1621
Urban as percentage of total	14.7	16.8	19.2	14.6	16.9	20.2

Source: Census of Canada

clear: the areas of highest wheat production tended also to be the areas of greatest urban and industrial development. This was so despite the very recent settlement of the western regions, which, at mid-century, were in the midst of their period of most rapid growth. This pattern suggests that wheat was at the root of urban development, a supposition that will be confirmed by an analysis of the growth of Ontario towns.

TORONTO

It was only by virtue of its position as provincial capital that the town of York, with its "very trifling"[1] trade and its undeveloped hinterland, had reached the grand total of 1700 inhabitants by 1824. Starting in the mid-1820s, settlers poured into the Home district, and the district population of 17,000 in 1824 increased at an annual rate of 8.6 per cent to reach 168,000 in 1851. York (or Toronto, as it became in 1834) grew with its agricultural hinterland, attaining a population of 9252 in 1834 and 30,800 in 1851.[2]

The driving force behind the growth of Toronto was the demand for goods and services from the immigrant and farm population. Financed initially by the savings of British immigrants, this demand was maintained by the farmers' cash income from wheat. In the earlier years of settlement, the demand from new arrivals was the major element. In the second half of the 1820s, according to T.W. Acheson, "the provision

MAP 1

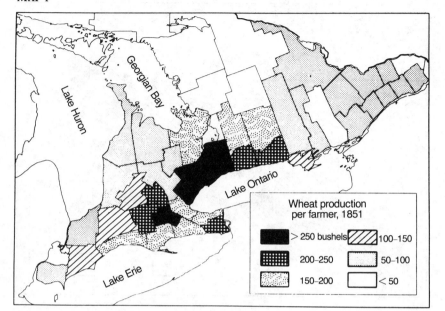

Wheat production per farmer, 1851

> 250 bushels   100–150

200–250   50–100

150–200   < 50

MAP 2

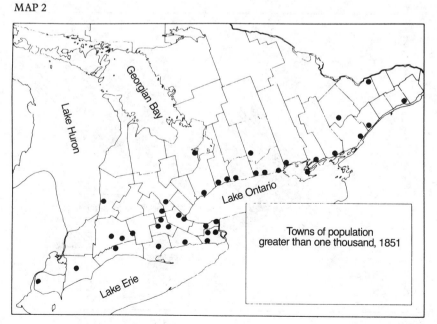

Towns of population greater than one thousand, 1851

Source: Census of Canada.

MAP 3

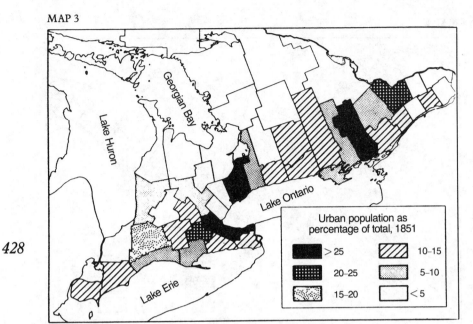

428

MAP 4

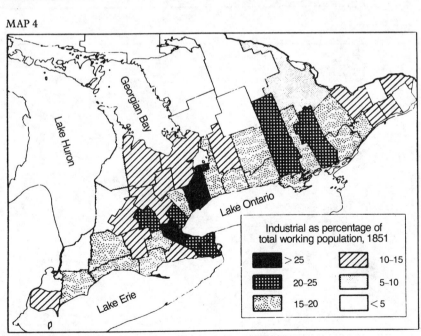

Source: Census of Canada.

of housing, food, clothing, and tools for several hundred new family units each year created a demand which provided the economy with a dynamism otherwise inconceivable."[3] At the time of the peak immigration of 1831–32, immigrants deposited not less than £300,000 in the Bank of Upper Canada.[4] As exports of wheat and flour accelerated during the 1840s, the demand for goods and services from established farmers was felt with ever-increasing intensity. Throughout the period wheat and flour dominated the export trade of Toronto, accounting for more than three-quarters of exports at mid-century.[5]

As population and trade increased, the importance of the city's position as provincial capital declined correspondingly. Thus, in 1845 W.H. Smith, author of the *Canadian Gazetteer*, wrote: " . . . the seat of government was moved to Kingston in 1841. . . . Had this event taken place ten years sooner, it might have had a serious effect upon the prosperity of the town, but in 1841 Toronto had become a place of too great a commercial importance to feel much ill effect from the removal of the government offices, and the loss of the expenditure of a few thousand pounds per annum."[6]

429

Under these circumstances the primary functions of Toronto were to export flour and to import goods for sale to established and prospective farmers. Acheson described the operations of the retailers around 1830. About 90 per cent of the market of Toronto's retailers was in rural areas, and consequently the pattern of sales was determined by the farming seasons. Peak sales occurred in October following the harvest, and business remained fairly strong throughout most of the winter when the farmers transported their wheat and flour to the town. Demand fell off during the spring thaw, and it picked up again in July, when there was a steady demand for tools and implements. The "struggling" patrons purchased cotton cloth and thread, glass, nails, scythes, and hardware supplies, while the more prosperous customers bought luxury articles such as Madeira, snuff, and silk. These prosperous customers, presumably mainly attached to government activities, were small in number, and it was the agricultural population which determined both the seasonal fluctuations and the principal commodity composition of retail sales.

Behind the retailers were the wholesalers. These were larger commercial enterprises which not only sold goods to the retailers but also purchased and exported flour. Manufacturing made modest progress in the years to 1850, and the goods supplied by the wholesalers were mainly imported. In the early years most imports were British goods purchased through Montreal, but after the opening of the Erie Canal in 1825 the wholesalers began to import more American goods. In the prosperous years of the late 1820s and early 1830s, larger and more specialized wholesalers established themselves, and to stay in business it became necessary to import goods directly from Britain.[7] In 1832 York had eight wholesalers; by 1850 this number had increased to twenty, fifteen of which had jettisoned retail activities altogether.[8]

Indeed, by mid-century a rising commercial group led by the wholesalers was challenging the position held by the old Toronto families. This group had arrived in the 1830s, and included such men as William McMaster (wholesaler and later banker) and F.C. Capreol (commercial salesroom operator and later railway promoter). Many of the old members of the Family Compact were still important in the economic life of the city, but by 1850 they were losing power to the newer group led by the wholesalers.[9]

While this commercial development based on settlement and wheat exports applied on a smaller scale to most other Ontario towns, a number of special factors favoured Toronto over other places. Between 1824 and 1829 York had the only bank in the province, but in the latter year the Bank of Montreal established a branch in York, and banks were established in Hamilton and Kingston in the first half of the 1830s. While the Bank of Upper Canada was sometimes credited with York's growing prosperity, it was remarked in 1831 that "the fine back Country does infinitely more for the advancement of York than the Bank can do."[10] To the advantages of an early lead in banking and an exceptionally large and fertile back country were added a good harbour, an early road, and the town's position as provincial capital, which made it a focal point for new arrivals to the province. It was only natural, then, that Toronto should be the main beneficiary of any trends in the direction of increased geographical concentration of economic activity.

In the years to 1850, such forces of concentration were limited. Toronto's export trade was not markedly higher than that of other lake ports, and according to Jacob Spelt its presence did not have any influence on the size or number of manufacturing establishments in York County. The one important sector of the economy in which forces of concentration had begun to assert themselves by mid-century was wholesale trade. In 1851 the value of direct imports to Toronto was $2.6 million, as compared with $2.2 million for Hamilton and $1 million for Kingston. The next largest importer was Chippewa at $318,000. By 1850 Toronto had established itself as the major distributing point for such ports as Oakville, Port Credit, and Whitby. There were economies to be gained in limiting the number of contacts with British and American suppliers, and "it was only natural that this trade should concentrate on the capital, the largest city and market with the biggest banks and one of the best ports."[11]

Furthermore, Toronto had started to invade the territory formerly held by Montreal. The city's direct imports (as opposed to goods imported through Montreal wholesalers) rose dramatically in the 1840s and imports from the United States more than doubled in the two years between 1849 and 1851. It has been seen that Toronto wholesalers began to import goods directly from the early 1830s, and in the same period they started to replace Montrealers as suppliers to merchants in smaller

Ontario towns. Also, from the late 1840s a rising proportion of wheat and flour was shipped through the United States instead of through Montreal.

Toronto's development is therefore explained not only by the growth of its own hinterland but also by a start to its commercial penetration of other regions. In the process it began its escape from the control of Montreal. On the whole, however, the city's growth up to 1850 depended mainly on growth within its own territory, for, with the partial exception of wholesale trade, dispersion rather than concentration remained the hallmark of economic activity.

Finally, associated with all this was the accumulation of capital. Funds were derived first from the savings of immigrants and from the disposal of land held by the government and its associates, and then increasingly from the activities of the rising merchant class and its agricultural hinterland. Local governments, deriving their revenue directly from the wealth of the towns and countryside, were also important contributors. The point to be emphasized at present is that all these sources may be traced to the twin processes of settlement and wheat exports.

431

HAMILTON

Hamilton owed its early growth to its position at the head of Lake Ontario. According to W.H. Smith, "Hamilton is admirably suited for carrying on a large wholesale trade with the West, — being at the head of navigation of Lake Ontario, and in the heart of the best settled portion of the Province, it possesses peculiar advantages for receiving goods, and distributing them through the interior, while its central position makes it the depot of a large extent of grain and other produce."[12] The town's population reflected the course of settlement and the wheat trade. The Burlington Bay Canal, which connected Hamilton with Lake Ontario, was completed in 1825, and in 1831 it was said that "since the Burlington Canal started, Hamilton has increased from 3 to 18 stores. Its former trifling trade and its houses have doubled." Population rose from 1400 in 1833 to 3600 in 1837, 4300 in 1842, and 14,000 in 1851.[13]

As in the case of Toronto, this growth resulted from the rapid settlement of the city's back country and the acceleration of wheat exports during the 1840s. The population of the Gore district was 150,000 in 1851, or more than six times as high as in 1831. Exports of wheat and flour more than tripled between 1838 and 1844, and they had tripled again by 1850. By mid-century, Hamilton exported more wheat and flour than any Ontario town except Port Dalhousie, located at the mouth of the Welland Canal.

As Smith indicated, Hamilton was the major wholesale centre for points west of Lake Ontario. Douglas McCalla has produced a map that reveals, for the year 1857, the deep penetration into western Ontario by Hamilton's largest wholesaler, Buchanan, Harris and Company. Eighty centres from Niagara to Amherstburg and from Lake Erie to points north of Goderich contained one or more customers of this firm, and the most concentrated group of customers was located between London and Hamilton.[14]

Hamilton, then, was a commercial town. In his exhaustive study of the town in 1851 Michael B. Katz wrote that " . . . men in commerce, about a quarter of the workforce, controlled nearly 59% of the wealth, a figure which underscores the clear commercial basis of the city." As in Toronto, the industrial sector, operating overwhelmingly in local markets, played a passive role in the years up to 1850. The settlement and development of Hamilton's rich and rapidly growing agricultural hinterland was the basis not only of the town's growth but also of the wealth and capital accumulation of the commercial class. The export of wheat and flour, the importation and distribution of manufactured goods, land speculation, and personal profit derived from municipal funds[15] were all based directly or indirectly on the settlers' supply of wheat and demand for land and other goods and services. This capital accumulation and general prosperity may be seen in a number of developments: the replacement of wooden structures with brick buildings and the "vast improvement" in the character of the city's buildings in the last few years of the 1840s, the location of two bank headquarters and four branches in Hamilton, improvements such as the introduction of gas lighting in 1851, and the ambitious but misguided decision of the city to subscribe £100,000 for the construction of the Great Western Railway.[16]

This is not to paint a picture of general affluence and social harmony. As Katz demonstrated minutely, inequalities were enormous and individual business failures were commonplace. The large-scale Irish immigration brought problems of disease, riots, and violence. Nevertheless, during the last decade of the pre-railway age, Hamilton underwent a total transformation in its population, trade, social infrastructure, and wealth. It is impossible to attribute this transformation to anything other than agricultural settlement and the growth of wheat and flour exports.

OTHER ONTARIO TOWNS

Maps 1 to 4 indicate that the three westernmost counties of Ontario were not large-scale wheat producers and that they were relatively underdeveloped in terms of both urban and industrial growth. The only two towns of a thousand or more were Amherstburg (1880) and Chatham (2070). The former was a frontier post and naval depot during the War of 1812, and it continued to be a garrison town until after 1850. In 1850 and 1851 almost all enumerated exports consisted of wheat, but the quantities involved were not large. By Ontario standards Amherstburg was stagnant. Joseph Bouchette in 1831 gave the population as over 1200 and mentioned "the wealth and respectability of its inhabitants."[17] In the twenty years to 1851 population rose by only 50 per cent. The difficulties of wheat growing in the region and the correspondingly low production levels would seem to have limited the growth of the town. Chatham, on the other hand, was a product of the wheat boom. Its population rose from 812 in 1841 to 2070 in 1851, and, according to Smith, "Being situated in the midst of a fine agricultural country, it is a place of considerable business." Or in the words of F.C. Hamil, "The principal source of prosperity for the town was the prolific country about it, settled by industrious, intelligent, and thrifty farmers."[18] During the 1840s property values rose rapidly, bank branches were established, and brick houses began to replace less solid structures. In 1850 the town had two steam grist mills, two steam sawmills, two foundries and machine shops, a brewery, two tanneries, a woollen factory, and four distilleries.[19] Nevertheless, taken as a whole, the three counties of the Western District grew relatively little wheat, and difficulties in this area had led to an effort to expand tobacco production and in general to adopt a more diversified agriculture. Tobacco and other products were not good substitutes for large quantities of wheat, and the overall development of the district was meagre.

433

Moving eastwards, London, St. Thomas, and Ingersoll were within about thirty miles of each other in Middlesex, Oxford, and Elgin counties. The maps indicate that in 1850 this area was more developed than the counties to the west and somewhat less developed than the counties along the shores of Lake Ontario. This was a newer region which at mid-century was in the middle of its period of most rapid growth: the population of the London District tripled during the 1840s, while the town of London grew from 1100 in 1834 to 2600 in 1842 and 7000 in 1851.[20] London became the district town in 1826, and in 1838 an imperial garrison was stationed in the town. These factors were the major non-agricultural influences on London's development, and, while they may explain the town's ascendancy over St. Thomas, they were relatively unimportant in the urban development of the region as a whole. Some town in the region had to be the district centre, and, while the coming of the garrison in 1837 was a shot in the arm for the town's economy, its departure in 1853 was "almost unnoticed."[21]

After London was given the right to hold a public market in 1835, it quickly became the trade focus of a rich but very partially settled agricultural area. It was during the 1840s that London's economy became firmly based on wheat. In the words of Orlo Miller: "By the late 1840's, London's economy had become tied to a more stable commodity than either litigation or logistics [that is, district centre or garrison town]. That commodity was wheat. . . . By the middle of the nineteenth century Western Ontario had become one vast granary and London one of its principal market towns and shipping centres."[22]

As London grew, it attracted men with capital to invest and enriched those who were already there. Some of the town's leading citizens arrived with the settlers in the 1820s and early 1830s. This group included George Goodhue, merchant and land speculator, and Ellis Hyman and Simeon Morrill, both tanners. Men such as Elijah Leonard, iron founder and steam engine maker; John Birrell, dry goods wholesaler; and Thomas Carling, brewer, arrived soon after the Rebellion of 1837. John K. Labatt, brewer; Charles Hunt, miller; and the McClary brothers, warehousing, arrived in the late 1840s and early 1850s. These manufacturers and wholesalers served an area that "stretched west to Chatham, Windsor, and Sarnia, north to Goderich, St. Mary's, and Stratford, east to Ingersoll and Woodstock, and south to St. Thomas and Port Stanley." Strong commercial ties with Hamilton were developed from an early date. By 1850 London had four bank branches, two building societies, several insurance companies, three "extensive" foundries, one grist and sawmill, three breweries, two distilleries, two tanneries, and three newspapers. While provincial funds were spent generously on London roads because the position of public works commissioner was held by a London citizen, it was the local capital of such families as the Labatts and Carlings which paid for the road to the Huron Tract in 1849 and for the London–Port Stanley railroad in the 1840s.[23]

434

Ingersoll, Woodstock, and St. Thomas were rivals of London in the 1820s and 1830s, but by 1850 they were clearly of secondary importance. To some extent they suffered from London's success, as in the case of Elijah Leonard's departure from St. Thomas to London in 1838 on the conviction that London was "sooner or later to become the hub of Western Canada."[24] Nevertheless, the populations of Ingersoll and Woodstock grew extremely rapidly in the late 1840s, and it was not until the railway age that these towns suffered severely from the forces of concentration. At mid-century they were market centres surrounded by a booming agriculture, and each had its five to ten mills and manufactories. The same was true on a lesser scale for the fifteen to twenty smaller villages which dotted the countryside within a twenty-mile radius of London.

Goderich served as district town headquarters of the Canada Company and port for the surrounding country. Population rose from 300 in 1831[25] to about 1300 in 1851, and in the latter year the town had the usual assortment of mills, newspapers, and bank and insurance company agents. Exports were still very low, and the most important function in 1850 was to supply settlers bound for the northern sections of the Huron Tract.

In Norfolk County only the district town of Simcoe had as many as one thousand people. Lumber was more important in this county than elsewhere, and in 1850 Ports Dover, Ryerse, and Rowan exported mainly wood, although in the first of these, which was much the largest, wheat and flour made up close to half the total value of exports. None of these ports contained as many as a thousand residents. Simcoe, which had the usual quota of mills and other establishments, derived its existence from a combination of wood, wheat, and administrative functions.

We come now to the largest cluster of towns, those within about forty miles of Hamilton in Brant and Wentworth counties and in the Niagara Peninsula. A glance at Map 1 shows that this region was second only to the neighbourhood of Toronto in its wheat production. In Brant County wheat production per farmer was the highest in the province in 1851 (370 bushels), and this county contained Paris and Brantford, with a combined population of 5800 or 23 per cent of total county population. Brantford, the largest of these towns, increased its population rapidly in the few years before 1850. It had the advantage of being located on the Grand River and on the Hamilton–London road. In 1850, 350,000 bushels of wheat and flour (just under three-quarters of the total value of shipments) were shipped from Brantford along the Grand River, and in addition "large quantities of flour, whisky and ashes are teamed down to Hamilton and shipped there." The manufacturing establishments seem to have been larger than average, for Smith lists "four grist mills, one of which is a large brick building; two foundries, doing a large business; a stone-ware manufactory, the only one yet in operation in the west of Canada . . . two tanneries, two breweries, four distilleries, a planing machine and a sash factory, &c. &c."[26]

The other towns on the Grand River had similar, if somewhat lesser manufacturing activities, and they too profited from their position on the river in the midst of highly productive wheat farming. Galt and Guelph had originated as supply centres for the Canada Company, but by mid-century most of the lands in the region had been settled. Dunnville was located at the mouth of the Grand River and was a point of trans-shipment of imports as well as an export point. In 1850 wheat and flour made up about three-quarters of the town's exports.

In Niagara District the largest town, St. Catharines, benefited from its position on the Welland Canal and had six grist mills. Thorold was also on the Welland Canal, and it had grown rapidly in the few years prior to 1850, taking advantage of the hydraulic powers of the canal to establish a number of large grist mills and other enterprises. Niagara and Chippewa had declined somewhat with the opening of the Welland Canal: in 1851 they had a combined population of about 4500.

The Lake Ontario wheat ports east of Hamilton and west of Belleville were so similar that they may be described as a group. According to figures contained in Smith, for six of the eight ports in this region wheat and flour accounted for at least 80 per cent of total exports. The two exceptions were Port Hope and Cobourg, but these were also the only two towns (except Toronto) for which figures on exports to places other than the United States were not available. Most of the towns had wheat and flour exports between 175,000 and 300,000 bushels and total exports

435

of $160,000 to $320,000, while the value of imports varied more widely. The ports competed for their respective back countries, and leading citizens were active in promoting and financing roads, and later railroads, to tap their agricultural hinterlands. Financial services and small-scale manufacturing of the type already described had developed in all of these towns by 1850.

This survey of towns in the wheat-producing areas of Ontario ends with Barrie and Peterborough, which were inland towns north of Lake Ontario. Barrie, with a population of 1007 in 1851, was the main supply centre for the settlers and farmers of Simcoe County, as well as the county town. Its growth had been moderate, and it contained a tannery, brewery, newspaper, and bank agency in 1850. Peterborough was more substantial, with a population of 2191 in 1851. Immigration and the settlement of the surrounding districts remained the town's most important function until about 1840, after which the export of wheat, flour, and lumber increased in importance. In 1850 wheat and flour exports were of about the same importance as exports of lumber and square timber.[27]

We come now to the towns in the part of the province which did not produce wheat as a staple product. From Hastings County eastwards there were in 1851 nine towns with population exceeding one thousand, of which the largest were Kingston (11,600), Bytown (7800), Belleville (4600), and Brockville (2200). For the region as a whole, the urban population made up 15.1 per cent of the total. This was a lower proportion than in the former districts of Niagara (19.1 per cent), Home (21 per cent), and Gore (18 per cent), but it was higher than in most counties west of Brant. Considering that this eastern section had been settled earliest, its urban development up to 1850 was not impressive.

In 1830 Kingston had a larger population than York and about four times as many people as Hamilton; by 1851 it had been surpassed by Hamilton and had less than 40 per cent of the population of Toronto. The economy of Kingston had traditionally been based on its position as entrepôt, together with civilian and military government establishments, the lumber trade through the Rideau Canal, and shipbuilding. The town's unproductive back country was said to have restrained its growth, and it suffered setbacks with the movement of the capital to Montreal in 1844 and the decline of its role as entrepôt. Smith wrote that "the Government establishments, naval and military, with the shipping interest, are the principal support of the City."[28]

Bytown (later Ottawa) was clearly a lumber town, and Belleville exported mainly wood in 1850, although wheat and flour were significant (28 per cent of exports). To a large extent, Prescott and Brockville were dependent on St. Lawrence shipping, while Perth was originally the supply centre for local settlers and in later years had been connected to the Rideau Canal by private company. Cornwall lost population between 1845 and 1850, and the small towns of Napanee and Picton were market centres. Of the nine towns, only Belleville, Kingston, and Bytown had significant exports in 1850. Taken as a whole, the region from Belleville eastwards experienced slightly more than a doubling of its urban population between 1835 and 1850. West of Belleville, urban population rose by a factor of five over the same period.[29]

This analysis has covered the years up to 1850. In the next twenty years the number of towns increased from 38 to 81. Three-quarters of the newly established towns were located west of Trenton, and most of these were in the more recently settled inland counties which accounted for a rising proportion of wheat production as the older lands became exhausted. Dispersion remained the keynote of urban structure, as the share of the five largest cities in the urban population actually fell from 51 per cent in 1850 to 40 per cent in 1870.

Three sets of conclusions flow from this analysis. First, wheat was the driving force behind at least twenty-six of the twenty-nine towns west of Belleville (Amherstburg, Simcoe, and Peterborough were partial exceptions). All of these towns were either export ports or inland transportation terminals for Ontario wheat, all were market centres for the agricultural population, most had been supply centres for settlers, and many were import ports or wholesale centres. Wood and garrisons had been of secondary or passing importance. In addition to the centres of over a thousand people, there were literally hundreds of lesser centres, concentrated in the most productive wheat-producing areas, which performed similar functions on a smaller scale. By producing the region's only major export and by providing the market for its imports, agriculture was the foundation of commercial activity. Also, it was this wheat-generated activity that attracted men of capital to the region's commercial and nascent industrial sectors, that provided the basis for further capital accumulation, and that provided the tax base and savings that financed the roads and other projects of the time.

437

Furthermore, by the standards of the day the wheat economy of 1850 was an economic success story. In the words of I.D. Andrews, the compiler of the most comprehensive statistics on the trade of the province, "The population of Toronto has doubled in the last 10 years, and is now 30,000. Hamilton, now containing 14,000, has been equally progressive. The imports show their commercial program to have been equally rapid; and there can be little doubt that in Upper Canada the export of produce, and the import and consumption of all the substantial and necessary products of civilization, are as high, per head, as in the best agricultural districts of the United States."[30]

The second conclusion is that wood had much weaker effects on urban growth than wheat. The eastern part of the province had been settled earlier, and the Ottawa Valley was the major contributor to Canada's very large exports of forest products. Yet urban growth in this region had been meagre. The reasons for this are discussed in a later chapter.

The final conclusion concerns the pattern of urban growth. Why was this growth so dispersed instead of highly concentrated in a single city, as in the case of Winnipeg in the prairie wheat economy? Why, indeed, was the commercial activity located in Ontario at all, when, for example, most of the commercial activity associated with southern cotton and much of that flowing from prairie wheat took place outside the staple-producing region? To these questions, so vital to the prospects of any staple-producing region, there are two basic answers. The technology of the mid-nineteenth century favoured dispersion. We have already mentioned the case of the tiny port of Oakville which transported the wheat to its warehouses, constructed the steam engines and flour mill machinery that converted the wheat to flour, and built and manned the ships that carried the finished commodity to Montreal.[31] In 1847 a small Peterborough foundry manufactured most of the threshing mills used in the district, as well as a wide variety of the agricultural implements.[32] Such examples could be multiplied, but, in general, technology in the areas of transportation and manufacturing favoured the very local retention of a very high proportion of the linkages flowing from the wheat staple.

This technological bias in favour of the local level naturally promoted the retention of commercial activity within the province. However, even in 1850 technology favoured a higher degree of concentration of imports and wholesalers, and in subsequent years technological changes promoted centralization of other activities. The question was whether these centralized activities would take place in Ontario or Quebec, and it was the availability of direct American imports and the American trade route that tipped the balance in favour of Ontario. By contrast, fifty years later the prairie wheat economy had no such escape from eastern control, for the high Canadian tariffs and the monopolistic American freight rates made it difficult to import goods or export wheat through the United States.[33] In the case of Ontario, the effective challenge to Montreal's monopoly position had permitted a growing independence on the part of Toronto wholesalers from the 1830s, and the story was to be repeated in banking, transportation, and industry. Nevertheless, this was a gradual and partial process, for it will be seen in the next section that Montreal derived much benefit from the Ontario wheat economy.

Quebec

MONTREAL

Much, if not most, of the literature on this period has concerned itself with the commercial empire of the St. Lawrence, and there is no need to repeat the story of the Montreal merchants here.[34] Suffice it to say that a series of shocks in the 1840s destroyed both the old colonial system and Montreal's aspirations for the trade of the American west. Abandoned by Britain and excluded from American produce and markets, the Montreal merchants were driven to the Annexation Manifesto of 1849, in which they declared that the only solution to their problems lay in "going to prosperity, since prosperity will not come to us."[35]

Excluding for the moment its role as supplier of cheap labour, Quebec agriculture had little to do with the development of Montreal. The local farmers had made no significant contribution to exports since the early years of the century, their demand for imports was limited by their low and fluctuating incomes, and their role in capital formation was minimal. They supplied a portion of the city's livestock requirements, little of its wheat, and most of its limited requirements for other vegetable products.

On the other hand, Ontario agriculture was a major factor in the economy of Montreal. While Montreal never became the great emporium of the American mid-west, such shipments as it did receive came increasingly from Ontario rather than from the United States. Thus, wheat and flour shipments via the St. Lawrence rose from 2.9 million bushels in 1840 to a peak of 5.8 million bushels in 1847, and by 1851 shipments were 4.3 million bushels. Ontario produce was less than half the total in 1840 and virtually all of it in 1850. In the latter year, wheat and flour made up 78 per cent of the total tonnage passing down the St. Lawrence canals. This excludes lumber products, which accounted for 10 per cent of the tolls collected.[36] Thus, by 1850 Ontario wheat and flour were of dominant importance in the shipments received at Montreal via the St. Lawrence canals. The total tonnage, while not as great as had been anticipated, would have been almost negligible without the wheat and flour of the upper province.[37]

439

Montreal's imports were closely tied to conditions in Ontario. According to Fernand Ouellet, even by 1820 the incomes of Montreal importers were "directement fonction de l'agriculture haut-canadienne."[38] As indicated by the following figures, the volume of merchandise passing up the Lachine Canal to Ontario rose dramatically:[39]

1826	1,500 tons
1830	8,300 tons
1835	15,800 tons
1844	27,500 tons
1850	70,000 tons

In 1851 *direct* imports to Ontario towns via Montreal amounted to $3.0 million, as compared with $9.2 million entered as imports at Montreal.[40] A significant but unknown percentage of the latter figure would have been re-exported to Ontario.

Thus Ontario provided the great majority of Montreal's exports and absorbed perhaps one-half of the imports which reached the city. For

Montreal, the upper province was the one bright spot in an otherwise gloomy decade. This is all the more remarkable in the light of Ontario's shift to the American route for both its imports and exports: the province's growth was so rapid that Montreal's declining share of the trade did not prevent the city's absolute level from growing at impressive rates.

There was little progress in manufacturing during the 1840s, and this, together with the commercial disappointments of the decade, led to the emigration of large numbers of workers. Referring to "Montreal and Quebec workmen" as the first class of emigrants, a Select Committee of the Legislative Assembly in 1849[41] described the causes of this emigration in the following terms:

— unsettled trade and industry for several years past
— want of manufactories for those previously in lumbering
— increase in U.S. wages and fall here
— lack of public works

440

It was not until the industrial growth of the 1850s and 1860s that Montreal began to call on the surplus labour of rural Quebec.

OTHER QUEBEC TOWNS

The timber trade and shipbuilding dominated the economic life of Quebec City. Local agriculture was of minor importance. Neither did Ontario agriculture exert much influence on Quebec, for while the city was a major exporter of wheat this trade was much less important than the trade in timber and ships.

In the rest of the province the major activity was agriculture, and Quebec agriculture was a miserable base for urban growth. Worse than this, the crisis in Quebec agriculture destroyed the economic base of established merchants and artisans, and rural artisans who were "réduits à la misère par l'effondrement du revenu de leurs clients" were forced to emigrate. The Select Committee of 1849 ascribed the emigration of "workmen who had settled in the villages and county parts" to the fact that the farmers "do themselves almost everything they might require from a tradesman," with the result that "the workmen . . . have little employment and lose courage." Also, the inability of the inhabitants to repay debt to "the fearful number of those who carry on trade in our country parts on a small scale" brought financial ruin to debtor and creditor alike.[42]

Outside Montreal and Quebec City the urban population made up 4 per cent of the total population in 1850 and 6 per cent in 1870. Even these figures understate the differential impact of agriculture in the two provinces. While the great majority of Ontario towns owed their existence to the wheat economy, most Quebec towns depended in large measure on activities other than agriculture. This has already been demonstrated for Montreal and Quebec City, and it was also the case for most of the remaining fourteen towns of mid-nineteenth-century Quebec.

The growth of Lachine was obviously not dependent on agricultural conditions, while Aylmer was an Ottawa Valley lumbering town. The economy of St Jean was based on its role as entrepôt for trade between Canada and the United States. Trois-Rivières was in the midst of a region of very poor soil and an agricultural back country which had little to buy or sell. Growth was based on the town's position as a half-way point between Quebec and Montreal, a minor administrative centre, and, from 1840, the exporter of wood from the country along the St Maurice. Laprairie was a commercial centre at the head of communication from Montreal to St Jean and the Richelieu, while Ste Thérèse was a lumbering centre.[43]

In Quebec the railway age began slightly before 1850. The Longueuil–St Hyacinthe section of the St. Lawrence and Atlantic Railway was completed in 1847, and these towns had become distribution points based on the railway.[44] Sherbrooke, which had 350 people in 1830, had 2998 in 1851, thanks in large part to the local railroad construction going on at the time of the census. Without the railroad, Sherbrooke "n'aurait jamais dépassé la taille d'un Lennoxville ou d'un Richmond."[45] Joliette, or Industrie, as it was called before 1864, originated as a sawmill site in 1823. Under the energetic direction of its founder, the site acquired a flour mill in 1824, a wool factory and nail factory in 1825, a distillery in 1840, and an foundry in 1844. In 1850 a railway was constructed at a cost of $55,000, and at that time population doubled to about 2500. The towns of L'Assomption and Berthier were the two terminal points of this railway.[46]

441

Sorel and Berthier had been important centres of the wheat trade in earlier years, and the timber trade and shipbuilding were also important in the former. Population of both towns slightly more than doubled in the twenty years to 1850.[47] Finally, Montmagny, which with the exception of Quebec was the only town east of Trois-Rivières with as many as a thousand people, was dependent on local agriculture. Small manufacturing enterprises were encouraged by water power, local raw materials, river transport, and "l'emploi de l'abondante main-d'oeuvre d'origine agricole."[48] Thus, Quebec towns were only partly based on agriculture. The wood industry and entrepôt and administrative functions were also important, and in some cases railways provided stimuli unrelated to local agriculture.

Consequently, the agricultural sector of mid-nineteenth-century Quebec sustained less than 20,000 town-dwellers. By contrast, the great majority of Ontario's 130,000 urban residents owed their livelihood to economic activity spawned by the wheat staple, and even Montreal, after its grander designs had been shattered during the 1840s, saw its fortunes tied increasingly to the Ontario wheat economy. On the other hand, the forestry sector, supporting a few small towns in both provinces as well as Bytown and Quebec City, had proven to be a much less potent generator of urban growth.

NOTES

[1] This was the phrase of John Howison, *Sketches of Upper Canada* (1821; Toronto, 1965), 55.

[2] Population figures for Toronto are from Edith G. Firth, ed., *The Town of York, 1815-1834* (Toronto, 1966), xxvi; and Census of Canada, 1870, iv, 83, 131, 178. Unless otherwise stated, figures on town population are from the census.

[3] Acheson, "The Nature and Structure of York Commerce in the 1820's" (1969), in J.K. Johnson, ed., *Historical Essays on Upper Canada* (Carleton Library no. 82, 1975), 171.

[4] Jacob Spelt, *Urban Development in South-Central Ontario* (Carleton Library no. 57, 1972), 79.

[5] Unless otherwise stated, information on export and import values is from I.D. Andrews, *Report on the Trade, Commerce, and Resources of the British North American Colonies . . .* 31st Congress, 2nd Session, ex. doc. no. 23 (Washington, 1851), and Andrews, *Report on the Trade and Commerce of the British North American Colonies and upon the Trade of the Great Lakes and Rivers*, 32nd Congress, 1st Session, ex. doc. no. 136 (Washington, 1853).

[6] Smith cited in Spelt, *Urban Development*, 94.

[7] Firth, *Town of York*, xxvi-xxviii.

[8] Barry D. Dyster, "Toronto, 1840-1860: Making It in a British Protestant Town," unpublished Ph.D. thesis, University of Toronto, 1970; and Firth, *Town of York*, 75-76.

[9] Donald C. Masters, *The Rise of Toronto, 1850-1890* (Toronto, 1947), 21-26; and Dyster, *"Toronto, 1840-1860,"* 293.

[10] John Macauly, agent of the bank at Kingston, cited in Firth, *Town of York*, xxxi.

[11] Spelt, *Urban Development*, 75-76, 79.

[12] Smith, *Canada: Past, Present and Future*, 2 vols. (Toronto, 1851), 1: 223.

[13] *Western Mercury*, cited in Marjorie Freeman Campbell, *A Mountain and a City: The Story of Hamilton* (Toronto, 1966), 65; population statistics, 62.

[14] McCalla, "The Decline of Hamilton as a Wholesale Center," *Ontario History* 65 (1973): 253.

[15] Katz, "The People of a Canadian City: 1851-2," *Canadian Historical Review*, 53 (1972): 411. Katz, in *The People of Hamilton, Canada West* (Cambridge, Mass., 1975), provides evidence that these were the primary sources of income of the "entrepreneurial" class.

[16] Smith, *Canada* 1: 220-28; Campbell, *A Mountain and a City*, 76.

[17] Bouchette, *The British Dominions in North America . . . and a Topographical Dictionary of Lower Canada*, 2 vols. (1831; New York, 1968), 1: 105-106.

[18] Smith, *Canada* 1: 16; Fred Coyne Hamil, *The Valley of the Lower Thames, 1640 to 1850* (Toronto, 1951), 263.

[19] Unless otherwise stated, information on the industrial and commercial establishments of each town in 1850 is from Smith, *Canada*.

[20] The population figure for 1834 is from Frederick H. Armstrong and Daniel J. Brock, "The Rise of London: A Study of Urban Evolution in Nineteenth-Century Southwestern Ontario," in Armstrong et al., eds., *Aspects of Nineteenth-Century Ontario* (Toronto, 1974), 89.

[21] Orlo Miller, "The Fat Years, and the Lean: London (Canada) in Boom and Depression," *Ontario History* 53 (1961): 76.

[22] Miller, "The Fat Years," 74.

[23] Armstrong and Brock, "Rise of London," 83-84, 91; Miller, "The Fat Years," 76.

[24] Cited in Armstrong and Brock, "Rise of London," 91.

[25] Bouchette, *British Dominions* 1: 118.

[26] Smith, *Canada* 1: 237-39.

[27] Thomas W. Poole, *A Sketch of the Early Settlement and Subsequent Progress of the Town of Peterborough* (Peterborough, 1867), 93-99. Estimate of price of square timber is from Smith, *Canada* 2: 229.

[28] Smith, *Canada* 2: 278. Direct imports by Kingston were 74 per cent of direct imports of all Ontario ports in 1842. This ratio declined to an average of 30 per cent in 1844-46 and 10 per cent in 1848-51. Andrews, *Report on the Trade, Commerce, and Resources*, 198-99; *Report on the Trade and Commerce*, 457-58.

[29] Estimates of urban population in 1835 are from Albert Faucher, *Québec en Amérique au XIXe siècle* (Montreal, 1973), 301.

[30] Andrews, *Report on the Trade and Commerce*, 430.

[31] Hazel C. Mathews, *Oakville and the Sixteen: The History of an Ontario Port* (Toronto, 1953), 204, 212.

[32] Poole, *Sketch of the Early Settlement*, 62.

[33] In comparison with mid-century Ontario, the prairies also faced more highly developed manufacturing and financial centres to the east, as well as a transportation network which denied to its nascent

industry the "natural protection" enjoyed by Ontario in its early years of industrial growth. The comparison with the prairies is analysed further in Chapter 8 [McCallum, *Unequal Beginnings*].

34 Works in this area include D.G. Creighton, *The Commercial Empire of the St. Lawrence, 1760–1850* (Toronto, 1937); Gilbert N. Tucker, *The Canadian Commercial Revolution, 1845–1851* (New Haven 1936); and R.T. Naylor, "The Rise and Fall of the Third Commercial Empire of the St Lawrence," in Gary Teeple, ed., *Capitalism and the National Question in Canada* (Toronto, 1972).

35 Cited in Tucker, *Canadian Commercial Revolution*, 186.

36 Andrews, *Report on the Trade, Commerce, and Resources*, 276–77.

37 As noted above, the exclusion of shipments to Lower Canada and the Maritimes gives a false impression of the relative importance of the American route. This misleading impression is compounded by considering only wheat, in which case, according to Easterbrook and Aitken, as cited in Jean Hamelin and Yves Roby, *Histoire économique du Québec, 1851–1896* (Montreal, 1971), 47–48, the volume of Upper Canadian wheat exported by the American route was more than fifteen times that exported via the St. Lawrence in 1850. The more meaningful figure, as given in Table S.2, includes flour shipments as well as shipments destined to Lower Canada and the Maritimes, and on this basis St. Lawrence shipments were one-third greater than those via the United States in 1850 and 88 per cent greater in 1851.

38 Ouellet, *Histoire économique et sociale du Québec, 1760–1850* (Montreal, 1971), 265.

39 1826: *Journals of the Legislative Assembly of Lower Canada* (*JLALC*), 1830, app. D; 1830: *JLALC*, 1831, app. L; 1835: *JLALC*, 1835–36, app. Q; 1844: *Journals of the Legislative Assembly of Canada* (*JLAC*), 1844–45, app. AA; 1850: Andrews, *Report on the Trade, Commerce, and Resources*, 282–83. All figures refer to the Lachine Canal except in the year 1850, which refers to the St. Lawrence canals. However, these would seem to be almost identical, since in 1844 shipments were 26,600 tons via the St. Lawrence canals and 27,500 tons via the Lachine Canal.

40 Andrews, *Report on the Trade and Commerce*, 454–55, 458.

41 *JLAC*, 1849, app. AAAAA, 3.

42 Ouellet, *Histoire économique et sociale*, 475; *JLAC*, 1849, app. AAAAA, 3, 11.

43 Raoul Blanchard, *Le centre du Canada français* (Montreal, 1947), 153–56, 159–62, 166–68; *L'ouest du Canada français* (Montreal, 1953), 139, 145.

44 Hamelin and Roby, *Histoire économique*, 122–23, 125.

45 Blanchard, *Le centre du Canada français*, 320.

46 Blanchard, *L'ouest du Canada français*, 144.

47 Bouchette, *British Dominions* 1: 210, 305–306.

48 Raoul Blanchard, *L'est du Canada français*, 2 vols. (Montreal, 1935), 1: 177.

Transportation Changes in the St. Lawrence–Great Lakes Region, 1828–1860

GERALD TULCHINSKY

Transportation has always been vital to Canadian economic life and was, in fact, the key to the movement of goods and people and to the expansion of various economic frontiers. The Canadian nation itself was realized when modern transportation systems joined scattered regions. In the short period from 1828 to 1860, creative and revolutionary transportation developments in the St. Lawrence–Great Lakes region laid the basis for the transportation system that eventually linked East and West. Steamboats came into general use; rivers were dredged; channels were marked; and major canals, docks, and lighthouses were built. There were early experiments in aerial transport by balloon, and the first railway networks were laid down.

From *Canada's Visual History* 1, 2 (1974): 1–5. Reprinted with the permission of the Canadian Museum of Civilization.

These new and dramatic transportation developments in Canada during the mid-nineteenth century were stimulated by the ancient and continuing pattern of exploiting the country's agricultural and forest resources, a process which H.A. Innis called "staple economy." Another economic historian, H.G.J. Aitken, sees in these transportation developments an example of another long-standing Canadian tradition, which he calls "defensive expansionism," or government-assisted growth of facilities which would prevent the United States from dominating British North America. Both themes are highly important in understanding the connections between improved transportation facilities and Canada's place as an underdeveloped economy in the international trading system. They explain, too, the strategy of continental expansion, in which government played a crucial role. Resource exploitation and "defensive expansionism" were carried out by the business class, which promoted transportation innovations and also profited from them. The relationship between these businessmen and the politicians, whose legislative measures largely shaped the climate of business enterprise, is interesting and complex. Transportation developments touched other sectors of the economy as well. Perhaps the most profound effects were felt by the Canadian people in the course of their daily lives.

444

Canals

One of the major problems which arose during the settlement of Upper Canada was the high cost of transportation for goods coming from Montreal, the principal port of entry on the St. Lawrence River. These difficulties were more than just financial; there were very long delays and serious hazards in the movement of commercial goods and vital military supplies. In the aftermath of the War of 1812–14, the British government feared that these problems would hamper troops guarding the posts along the Upper Canadian frontier. It was this combination of commercial and military concern which prompted the construction of the earliest major canals built along the St. Lawrence–Great Lakes system in the 1820's and 1830's. These were the Lachine Canal, the Welland Canal (the first stage of which was completed in 1829 to by-pass Niagara Falls), and the Rideau Canal between Bytown and Kingston. The latter two were major feats of engineering, labour mobilization, and capital investment. Certainly these projects could not have been completed without the direct involvement of government.

After a weak and inadequate start under the auspices of a private company, the legislature of Lower Canada, despite a reputation for being anti-commercial, undertook financial responsibility for the construction of the Lachine Canal around the dangerous Lachine rapids above Montreal. The British government accepted a similar responsibility for the extremely costly (almost one million pounds) Rideau Canal which, in their view, would serve both military and economic strategies. Indeed, the Rideau was built under the supervision of British army engineers, who employed local contractors to construct various portions of the work. Like the Lachine Canal, the Rideau was built mainly by Irish immigrants assisted by Scottish and French-Canadian artisans. A different engineering and financial influence can be seen in the earliest of the Welland canals, where New York State had supplied capital, technical experts, and even a substantial number of the same working men who had only recently finished the Erie Canal. Yet, even here, large sums of Upper Canadian and smaller amounts of Lower Canadian government funds were invested, and when the first Welland Canal proved to be flimsy and inadequate, it was quickly taken over as a public work. This was a very common pattern throughout North America; in the neighbouring United States most of the major canal systems, including the immensely successful Erie, were state or local projects. Although entrepreneurs were not lacking, local capital was scarce; and there was no easy mechanism in Canada until later in the nineteenth century for drawing upon foreign, chiefly British, capital.

445

The importance to Canada of these canals of the 1820's and early 1830's was incalculable. Even though the canals did not succeed in drawing the vast trade of the entire mid-continental interior, they were highly important parts of a more efficient Canadian transportation system. Together with the competing Erie Canal, they perhaps aided in the extension of Upper Canada's agricultural frontier by greatly lessening transportation costs for imports, exports, and passengers. At the same time they opened up regions like the Rideau Lakes area, which had been inaccessible. These projects provided brief employment for thousands of immigrants who often worked under hazardous conditions for low wages. Employers often used the truck system of payment, by which men were paid in commodities, such as liquor, rather than in money. Canal labourers who organized to fight this situation (for example, the Lachine Canal strike of 1843) were among the first labour union agitators in Canada. Canal construction brought huge sums of money into the country and generally stimulated economic activity even though the funds filtered unevenly through the various regions and segments of the population. The demands for labour, food, supplies, hardware, and horses created expansion throughout the primitive economy of Canada.

Following the dramatic and significant burst of canal activity during the 1820's and early 1830's, nearly ten years intervened before a new era of significant waterway improvement was undertaken in the Canadas. Exhaustion of financial resources (the British government was furious at the huge cost of the Rideau Canal), economic stagnation, and political conflict deterred further activity until the union of the Canadas in 1840 introduced a new era of stability and optimism.

A vast and comprehensive new program was begun as a Canadian government public works project with the assistance of the British government, who guaranteed the interest on the funds borrowed to build the canals. Planners aimed at improving the navigability of the St. Lawrence waterway between Montreal and Prescott, where rapids and shallows had always impeded shipping. Canals were cut at Beauharnois, Cornwall, and Williamsburg; and the Lachine and Welland canals were widened. When completed, at the huge expense of nearly two million pounds, which the Province of Canada had borrowed in London, these canals provided an integrated, through-waterway from Montreal to Lake Erie for large vessels.

Although the canals succeeded only moderately as an outlet for the produce from the Canadian and United States regions bordering the Great Lakes, they constituted another important addition to the Canadian transportation network. It was cheaper to ship goods to the interior from Montreal than from New York City, but New York long continued to hold its advantage over Montreal as an ocean port because it did not freeze in winter. Furthermore at least one of the canals provided an important source of power for industrial use; during the late 1840's the Lachine Canal in Montreal became the site of dozens of new factories, which manufactured flour, sugar, tools, lumber, clothing, steam engines, boats, and a substantial range of other goods. To encourage such industrialization, the government leased industrial sites at low rates. Consequently, manufacturers and speculators seized the opportunity to establish in Montreal and hence created a new aspect of economic life. Montreal had hitherto been principally a commercial city. By 1854, some twenty new factories employing approximately two thousand people had made Montreal the largest manufacturing centre in Canada.

Steamboats

The major canal building programs of the 1820's and 1830's as well as the several minor programs along the lower Ottawa, the Richelieu, and the St. Lawrence rivers were accompanied by a rapidly increased use of steamboats on Canadian waterways. While steamboats did not completely replace the bateaux, Durham boats, sloops, schooners, or rafts that were used to carry cargo and passengers, they were used increasingly for premium (high value) freight and passenger services. Starting in 1809, steamboats ran on the lower St. Lawrence River, and became common on the Great Lakes by the end of the following decade. During the next several years the "puffing billies," almost all of them built in Montreal shipyards, were to be found on inland waterways throughout the settled areas of British North America.

The building of steam engines for marine and stationary use developed into a major industry after the introduction of steamships. As early as 1818, a small foundry was set up by Americans in Montreal to build engines to meet the growing demand. This and similar factories established in Montreal and, later, in Kingston and Toronto formed the basis of the early Canadian engineering industry. A key link between the era of simple staple economy and the period known as the "age of steam and iron," they initiated Canada's transportation revolution. Both transportation and industrial activity were concentrated at the major commercial centres, and urban growth during these years was directly related to the growing connection between the two. This relationship became even clearer during the 1850's, when railways encouraged the rapid growth and expansion of iron foundries and other industries.

Railroads

The age of steam and iron, which was foreshadowed in Canada by the launching of John Molson's steamship *Accommodation* in 1809, was to become an established fact of economic, social, and political life during the 1850's. Successful experiments in the use of steam engines on railroads in England during the 1820's inspired a flurry of railway construction in Britain and the United States during the next two decades. The enthusiasm for railways was at an extremely high pitch during the 1840's and, quite naturally, Canadians interested in improved transportation and profits readily took up the idea. In his famous pamphlet, *The Philosophy of Railroads*, published in 1850, Thomas Keefer, a distinguished Canadian engineer, extolled the virtues of railways in the following grandiloquent terms:

447

> The civilizing tendency of the locomotive is one of the modern anomalies, which, however inexplicable it may appear to some, is yet so fortunately patent to all, that it is admitted as readily as the action of steam, though the substance be invisible and its secret ways unknown to man. Poverty, indifference, the bigotry or jealousy of religious denominations, local dissensions or political demagogism, may stifle or neutralize the best intended efforts of an educational system; but that invisible power which has waged successful war with the material elements, will assuredly overcome the prejudices and mental weaknesses or the design of mental tyrants . . . it waits for no convenient season, but with a restless rushing, roaring assiduity, it keeps up a constant and unavoidable spirit of enquiry or comparison; and while ministering to the material wants, and appealing to the covetousness of the multitude, it unconsciously, irresistibly, impels them to a more intimate union with their fellow men.

Since the 1830's there lay strong interest in the possibility of building railways. Railways were discussed in the newspapers and in the Legislative Assemblies which would supply financial assistance to these projects; and the country's first railway, a fourteen-mile portage line from Laprairie, near Montreal, to St. Jean, on the Richelieu River, was completed in 1836. By the mid-forties, with general prosperity and the example of successful railway projects in Britain and the United States, lines were being planned to run between many Canadian towns and cities and there were visionary schemes of extending railways east to the other British North American provinces and west to the Pacific. At this relatively early date, the "philosophy of railroads" included estimates of social and economic benefits, and conceived of railways as instruments of policy, as means of better communications between existing communities and distant frontiers, and as aids to the strategy of British North American defence. Toronto and Montreal became the two major centres of Canadian railway promotion. Montreal entrepreneurs planned lines to winter ports on the Atlantic coast, and Toronto businessmen projected rail routes into new hinterlands to the north and west of the city.

It soon became apparent, however, that without strong government assistance, only a few short portage-type railways could be built; and, in 1849, the Canadian Legislature passed the Guarantee Act by which the payment of interest (up to 6%) on bonds issued by railways over 75 miles long would be guaranteed by the government once the railway was at least half-completed. This legislation was designed for big railway projects such as the Northern, which was to connect Toronto and Georgian Bay; the St. Lawrence and Atlantic, between Montreal and Portland, Maine; and the Great Western, from Toronto to Windsor. Behind the protective skirts of this act, these projects went forward very rapidly and all were completed by 1854. There was a huge inflow of capital from Britain and the United States, but a considerable proportion was raised by private Canadian investors. More important, the granting of charters to these railways and many others (most of which were never built) reflected the rise of new groups of businessmen. There were the promoters of these lines, the speculators in railway stock issues or in land, the suppliers of building and operating equipment, the contractors, and a host of others. And there emerged, also, the entrepreneurs who often combined a number of these interests and who, by especially adroit manipulation, sometimes garnered huge profits. Although their actions are often extremely difficult to trace, those entrepreneurs who became wealthy through their railway interests often had close connections with politicians who sponsored and supported railway legislation. Sir Allan MacNab, leader of the Conservative party in Upper Canada, declared without hesitation, "my politics are railways." Few dissented and there are indications that huge numbers of politicians were obligated to the entrepreneur, Samuel Zimmerman, the key figure in the Great Western Railway.

The greatest railway project of this era was the Grand Trunk Railway, a Montreal to Toronto line begun in 1853, which was intended to be the Canadian section of an inter-colonial railway that would run through British North America from Halifax to Windsor. When Canadian railway promoters and politicians got through with this project, some had pocketed huge profits; and the public was saddled with a staggering debt

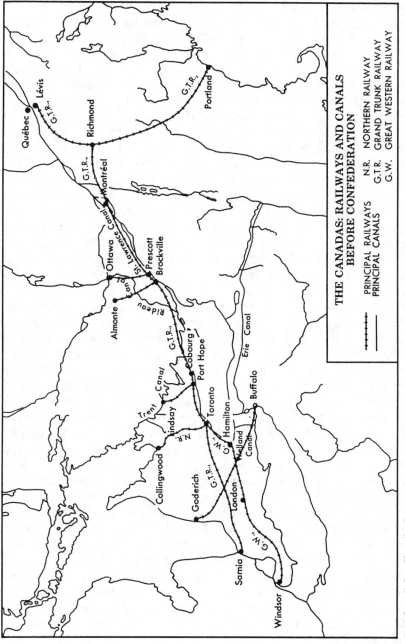

THE CANADAS: RAILWAYS AND CANALS
BEFORE CONFEDERATION

PRINCIPAL RAILWAYS   N.R. NORTHERN RAILWAY
PRINCIPAL CANALS   G.T.R. GRAND TRUNK RAILWAY
                           G.W. GREAT WESTERN RAILWAY

449

Paul Cornell, Jean Hamelin, Fernand Ouellet, and Marcel Trudel, eds. *Canada: Unity in Diversity* (Toronto: Holt, Rinehart and Winston, 1967), 239.

of $26 million. This debt absorbed a large portion of government revenue just to pay the interest on the loans (really outright gifts) that the government had extended to the company. The generous "legacy" the government allowed the Grand Trunk has been overshadowed by the even more generous grants of land, cash, railway lines, and other valuable benefits which were given to the Canadian Pacific Railway Company during the 1880's. Nevertheless, the Grand Trunk scheme was beset by waste, mismanagement, and some very dextrous sleight-of-hand. By 1853 the Grand Trunk company struggled under the ailing St. Lawrence and Atlantic Railway, the Quebec and Richmond line, a commitment to build the Victoria Bridge across the St. Lawrence River at Montreal, and the cost of constructing some two hundred additional and unnecessary miles of line from Toronto to Guelph and Sarnia, a region already served by the Great Western. Promoters A.T. Galt, Luther Holton, Casimir Gzowski, and David L. Macpherson were among the principal beneficiaries. British stock and bondholders and the Canadian people were left with an overly elaborate, expensive, debt-ridden, and unprofitable railway built on a gauge different from that of the western United States railways it was intended to join.

450

There were, however, some benefits to this extensive construction. The most substantial of them was probably the rapid acceleration of economic growth during the 1850's, when capital formation, much of it for railway construction, ran up to a staggering $100 million. With the exception of a brief but serious business depression in 1857, this was a decade of significant economic expansion. Yet, it would be unwise to attribute all or even most of that expansion to the spin-off of railway construction. The rapid rise in the price of wheat during the Crimean War (1853–1856), the expansion of the American market for sawn lumber and other commodities, and the continuing expansion of Upper Canada were, in fact, the crucial elements in this prosperity. It is arguable, also, that the railways did not alone create the high rate of immigration or the general widespread industrial expansion in this era. Certainly some of the basic framework for the latter was clearly laid by 1850, before the railway age began in earnest. Nor can it be proven that railways were almost indispensable to the movement of commodities and to the expansion of the agricultural and lumbering frontier. For these, the lake, river, and canal systems were increasingly effective and, along with improvements to the road network, probably could have been extended with less cost than the amounts expended on railways. What the railways did accomplish, however, was to open the country to year-round transportation.

This did not mean, however, that commerce went on evenly twelve months of the year. The bulky cargoes of wheat, lumber, and timber moved mainly by water, still a far cheaper form of transportation than rail, and, railways notwithstanding, these staple industries remained seasonal. Even though the completion of the Victoria Bridge in 1859 made it possible to run trains from Sarnia and Windsor to Portland, Maine (Montreal's winter port), a very small proportion of the staples went over that route. Indeed, very large quantities of Canadian exports were still carried to tide-water on American canals or railways. Still, it was the age of railways, and a healthy skepticism about the benefits commonly attributed to them should not blind one to the fact that practically everyone believed that railways were bound to bring prosperity in their wake.

Despite their questionable economic necessity, the railways became almost a sign of the times. Rail lines crossed the peaceful countryside and pushed into most of the major towns and cities; tracks were laid in the middle of streets; and locomotives spewed out smoke and noise, enraging concerned citizens. Railways considerably altered the areas in which they were built and deeply affected the lives of ordinary citizens by making relatively rapid transit available. Railway passage was cheap and fast. By reaching into the back townships where a less expensive *451* right of way could be purchased, rail transportation served a broader segment of the population than steamboats had readily done. Although initially problem-ridden by derailments and other accidents, the railways soon became a very popular form of travel. Those who could afford it enjoyed comfortable sleeping and dining accommodations; there were upholstered chairs in second class and simple wooden benches in third class.

Railways gave rise to a whole new segment of the Canadian working class within a relatively short period. The railways were built by large gangs of labourers, among them immigrants, who, not yet settled, were more mobile than earlier settlers. After the road beds were constructed, the tracks laid, and the bridges erected, the railroad still required regular maintenance. Often the road bed needed improvement, and large sections of most railways required a reduction in the grades. Men were needed to operate trains and repair equipment. The demand for locomotives and other railway stock created a broader market and stimulated expansion in the engine foundries and other metal working shops of Montreal. Railway-related factories arose in Kingston, Toronto, Hamilton, and London. The railway companies, in particular the Grand Trunk and the Great Western, erected what were, in those days, huge shops at their rail yards in Montreal and Hamilton. By 1860, Canadian railways employed a total of 6,600 men on their combined payrolls, and many more men worked in the factories that arose in several towns and cities to supply equipment.

Although one must concede that railways were just one part of the continuing transportation revolution, one should not underestimate their impact. The railways were a powerful engine of rapid change in the commercial and social fabric of the country. The railway was destined to expand. By 1860 the railway network in Ontario and Quebec extended along the more settled St. Lawrence–Great Lakes Valley, but promoters were now planning to build lines up the Ottawa Valley, east to Quebec, and on into the Maritimes. There was the recurrent idea of building an east–west line to span the continent. Elsewhere in British North America, notably in the Maritime colonies, where a highly ambitious, separate railway development program had been under way during the 1850's, there were several plans to connect cities and open new regions. Many of these schemes took decades to realize; yet with massive federal, provincial, and municipal government assistance, together with huge sums of foreign capital, many major railways were built. Indeed, one of the most important features of the railway era was the extent of government involvement in these schemes, many of them of questionable general utility. Growing sophistication in the ability to manipulate the financial structure of railway companies and to influence all levels of government created vast profits for an increasingly aggressive group of entrepreneurs.

452   Notwithstanding the St. Lawrence–Great Lakes region had entered the railway age, it must be emphasized that the region still depended heavily on its maritime strength, which, through canal developments, river improvements, and such important technological innovations as the screw propeller, grain loader, and iron hull, continued to grow during this period of rapid transition and diversification.

An engraving of the Saint John waterfront, circa 1879, from the Canadian Illustrated News.

Central to the business activity of all leading merchants was involvement in or ownership of one or more of the three vital elements in city commerce: the banking system, the wharves of the port, and the ships.

T.W. Acheson, "The Great Merchant and Economic Development in Saint John, 1820–1850"

Topic Twelve

The Economy and Society of the Maritime Colonies in the Mid-Nineteenth Century

There were very few ties between the Atlantic colonies and the Canadas in the mid-nineteenth century. Halifax and Saint John, the leading ports of Nova Scotia and New Brunswick, respectively, lay much closer to the great American ports of Boston and New York than to the Canadian harbours on the St. Lawrence; moreover, in winter, ice completely severed what links they did have with Canada. Thus, rather than westward to the interior, the Atlantic colonies, before the building of a rail link with the Canadas, looked eastward to Britain and southward to the American Atlantic seaboard and the West Indies.

Of the Maritime colonies, Nova Scotia was the most significant in the mid-nineteenth century. It had the greatest strategic importance, being located at the entrance to the Gulf of St. Lawrence and on the shipping lanes of the North Atlantic. It had the most balanced economy of the four, with excellent fisheries, good lowland farmland, and supplies of iron and coal. In 1861, Nova Scotia's population of 330 000 exceeded that of any of the other three Atlantic colonies.

Like Prince Edward Island, with its reliance on agriculture, New Brunswick depended on a single staple industry. The colony had some good farmland in the Saint John River Valley, but lumbering remained the mainstay of its economy.

The commercial ambitions of the merchants of the leading city in New Brunswick are examined by T.W. Acheson in "The Great Merchant and Economic Development in Saint John, 1820–1850." Graeme Wynn offers a broader view of mid-nineteenth century life and society in the Maritimes in "Ideology, Society, and State in the Maritime Colonies of British North America, 1840–1860."

For an understanding of the Maritime region in the mid-nineteenth century, consult W.S. MacNutt's *The Atlantic Provinces, 1712–1857* (Toronto: McClelland and Stewart, 1965). MacNutt has also written *New Brunswick, A History: 1784–1867* (Toronto: Macmillan, 1963). Also of importance is Graeme Wynn's *Timber Colony: A Historical Geography of Early Nineteenth Century New Brunswick* (Toronto: University of Toronto Press, 1981). For Prince Edward Island, consult *The Prince Edward Island Commission of 1860*, ed. Ian Ross Robertson (Fredericton: Acadiensis Press, 1988), and Douglas Baldwin's popular history of the Island, *Land of the Red Soil* (Charlottetown: Ragweed Press, 1990). William Menzie Whitelaw provides a general overview of all aspects of life in the Atlantic colonies in the mid-nineteenth century in "The Atlantic Provinces and Their Neighbors," a chapter in his book *The Maritimes and Canada before Confederation* (Toronto: Oxford University Press, 1966; first published in 1934), 9–37. Important essays on the Maritime colonies are contained in *Historical Essays on the Atlantic Provinces*, ed. G.A. Rawlyk (Toronto: McClelland and Stewart, 1967). Thomas H. Raddall's *Halifax, Warden of the North*, rev. ed. (Toronto: McClelland and Stewart, 1971) provides a readable account of that city's past. The metropolitan ambitions of the business community in Halifax are examined by David Sutherland in "Halifax Merchants and the Pursuit of Development, 1783–1850," *Canadian Historical Review*, 59, 1 (1978): 1–17. In "The Relief of the Unemployed Poor in Saint John, Halifax, and St. John's," *Acadiensis* 5, 1 (1975): 32–53, Judith Fingard reviews the early system of poor relief, a topic often ignored. Fingard's *Jack in Port: Sailortowns of Eastern Canada* (Toronto: University of Toronto Press, 1982) describes the life of merchant sailors in Saint John and Halifax. T.W. Acheson has provided a model study of Saint John in his *Saint John: The Making of a Colonial Urban Community* (Toronto: University of Toronto Press, 1985).

Students should consult the volumes of the journal *Acadiensis* (since 1970), which contain many important articles on Atlantic history. A collection of essays from back issues of *Acadiensis* is available under the title *The Atlantic Provinces before Confederation* (Fredericton: Acadiensis, 1985), ed. P.A. Buckner and David Frank.

The Great Merchant and Economic Development in Saint John, 1820–1850

T.W. ACHESON

One of the liveliest debates in recent Canadian business history has centred on the role of the nineteenth-century merchant in promoting or retarding the development of a locally controlled British North American industrial base. Supporters of the retardation theory usually argue

From *Acadiensis: Journal of the History of the Atlantic Region* 8, 2 (Spring 1979): 3–27. Reprinted with permission.

that the colonial merchant was nurtured in a system based upon the export of raw and semi-finished produce and the import of fully manufactured materials. Dominating the ports and the transportation systems of British North America, he became the principal defender of the economic *status quo*, viewing any substantial re-arrangement of economic relations as a threat to his world. Thus he remained the harbinger of a form of economic colonialism which bound the destiny of British North America and of the forming Dominion of Canada in a subservient relationship to more advanced national economies, particularly those of the United Kingdom and the United States. Opponents of this theory have accepted the primacy of the merchant in the colonial economies but have argued that the gulf separating the merchant from other dynamic elements in the business community was less wide than the retardationists would have us believe. They maintain that the dramatic shift from commercial to industrial emphases and from external to internal markets in the last half of the nineteenth century occurred with the consent and participation of this dominant commercial element.[1]

457

There are several difficulties within this general argument. One of the most basic concerns the definition of "merchant." The meanest cordwainer in the mid-nineteenth century offered his shoes for sale to the general public; conversely, many important shippers and wholesalers owned, in whole or in part, the means to process the basic staple commodities of their region. Even a restricted use of the term leaves a group of businessmen involved in a variety of commercial, financial, and transportation functions. In colonial Saint John, for example, "merchant" was a legal status conferred on certain men at the time of their admission to the freedom of the city. Within the hierarchy of occupations which were admissible as freemen, that of merchant was clearly the most important and this importance was reflected in the fees required of those admitted to the status. Although a merchant might also be a sawmill owner, a legal and social line was clearly drawn between merchants possessing a sawmill and sawmill owners by occupation, whose status was lower. Moreover, there were a number of commercial functions characteristically performed by merchants, including the importing and wholesaling of produce, the export of fish and wood products, the transport of other people's goods, the purchase of staples produce on other people's accounts, the sale and auction of other people's goods, private banking, and acting as agents or directors for chartered banks, fire, marine, and life insurance companies. In village business a single merchant might have exercised most of these functions; the most successful urban merchants were those who focussed their efforts on three or four. In time, the development of competing interests sharply limited the issues on which merchants were able to speak as a class or community. Indeed, on many issues, it is doubtful whether colonial boards of trade and chambers of commerce spoke for anything more than one of several elements within the business community.

Another important question raised by the retardation debate concerns the extent to which "normal" merchant behaviour was modified by the local environment. There can be little doubt but that all merchants in British North America responded to short-term opportunities and that only rarely were they willing to sacrifice these opportunities on the altar of national, colonial, or civic interest.[2] Yet, over time, a merchant became attached to the community in which he lived, his response to opportunity conditioned by the idiosyncracies of the local economy, the nature of the relationship between the local and metropolitan economies, and the impact of the economic cycle in reducing the short-term profitability of existing relationships. Any final assessment of the merchant's role in the economic development of British North America will therefore have to await the completion of a number of case studies of individual communities and firms.[3] The paper which follows is an attempt to explore the role of the merchant in the economic development of colonial Saint John. The city affords an interesting case study both because of its size — in 1840 it was the third largest urban centre in British North America — and because of the central role played by the trade in timber and deals in its economic life.

Traditionally the central problem in the study of the economy of Saint John has been to explain the failure of the city to make the necessary adjustments to compensate for the dislocations occasioned by the stagnation of the wood trade following Confederation. Recently, Peter McClelland has put the date of that stagnation back to mid-century, arguing that the shipbuilding industry, the most dynamic element in the provincial economy after 1850, added little to the well-being or growth of that economy.[4] McClelland has highlighted the role of New Brunswick businessmen in this problem by demonstrating the tenacity with which they stood behind the wooden shipbuilding industry, investing perhaps $8 million between 1870 and 1879 in a technology which was effectively obsolete.[5] These businessmen failed to make the transition to metal ships or to establish backward linkages from the shipbuilding industry — particularly those relating to the outfitting of ships and the manufacture of chains and anchors — which could develop in time into significant industries. McClelland has explained this failure in terms of "the absence of alternatives capable of giving to regional growth the sustaining force which timber was losing" after 1850.[6] But even if it is admitted that shipbuilding was unable to play this dynamic role — a thesis that is much more compelling in 1870 than in 1840 — McClelland offers scant evidence to prove that manufacturing and, to a lesser extent, fishing and agriculture, could not have contributed a dynamic element to the regional economy. To support his contention, he is forced to argue that they could not because they did not, an idea grounded in the assumption that by mid-century New Brunswick was backward relative to other colonial economies. To demonstrate this position McClelland offers an out-

458

put analysis of New Brunswick and Ontario agriculture at the end of the nineteenth century, and points to the inability of some New Brunswick consumer goods producers to compete with central Canadian producers on the central Canadian market in the post-Confederation period. Much of this can be demonstrated for 1890, but it all presumes that what was true at that time must have been true a half-century earlier, and that the absence of a particular resource, say coal, must preclude the development of any industry which employed that resource.

The doubts raised by the ahistorical nature of this analysis are heightened by the persistence with which the provincial business community pursued and supported the wood trade and the wooden ship, even in the face of a technological obsolescence which by 1870 was obvious to all observers. This persistence suggests a commitment to a declining economic base understandable in the small resource-based village economies of much of the province, but more difficult to comprehend in the context of the complex, differentiated economy which existed in Saint John. Indeed, the continuance of these forms of activity and the failure of other kinds of development to occur may have been more the result of human factors than the absence of any particular material resource. Certainly Saint John in the colonial period possessed considerable potential. In 1840 the city was one of the largest urban centres in British North America, with a population of about 27,000. Its merchants possessed a monopoly of the commerce of the Saint John River Valley and its tributaries, a market of nearly 100,000 people. They also dominated the commercial life of the Bay of Fundy counties of New Brunswick and Nova Scotia, containing another 90,000 people.[7] The population of the Saint John River Valley exceeded that of the Home District of Upper Canada, while the city's whole market area compared favourably with that of the Quebec City District of Lower Canada.[8] Shipbuilding had been an important feature of the city's economy for two full generations by 1840 and the Saint John industry was clearly the most significant in British North America.[9] In addition, a substantial and diversified manufacturing sector designed to service both the timber trade and the growing consumer market of the area had emerged over the previous two decades, a development reflected in the strong labour movement which had become an important feature of city life in the years following the War of 1812.[10] By 1840 Saint John was marked as a growth centre with a distinct advantage over any other community in the Atlantic region. And this is of special significance because nineteenth-century manufacturing growth tended to be cumulative: early leaders generally improved their advantage over other communities as James Gilmour has demonstrated in his study of the spatial evolution of manufacturing in Ontario.[11]

In many ways the 1840s was the most critical decade of the colonial period. It witnessed the collapse of the preferences for colonial timber on the British market, a disaster which Saint John businessmen were

459

able to overcome mainly by making the transition from the export of timber to the export of deals. Nonetheless, the trade in wood products reached its largest volume in that period and thereafter stagnated; the economy of the province grew increasingly dependent in the 1850s on the still further processing of wood into ships and their sale on the British market. The abrogation of the Old Colonial System was marked by several short-term economic downturns which severely mauled the wood trades and raised serious doubts about the viability of an economy based upon them. At this point in time any group which persisted in subordinating all other interests to the needs of an already failing industry, it could be argued, can be perceived as contributing to the retardation of the provincial economy at a critical juncture in its history. If, by virtue of their influence within the political framework of the colony and their control of the principal sources of capital, merchants were able to promote or to inhibit certain kinds of development, then their role in determining the economic destiny of the city and its hinterland was as important as the presence or absence of any specific resource.

460

The study which follows will test this hypothesis in the context of merchant behaviour in the city of Saint John between 1820 and 1850. It will do so by examining the extent and nature of merchant wealth and the role of leading merchants in promoting or opposing development strategies in the first half of the nineteenth century. A major problem is the sheer size of the city's merchant community. During the colonial period about 800 men held the legal status of merchant and a number of others illegally participated in merchant functions. There were large numbers of transients whose residency in the city was confined to a few years, and even larger numbers of minor businessmen whose sole claim to the status of merchant seems to have been their role as small-scale importers. Their impact on the commercial life of the city was marginal and any attempt to include them in a study of this nature — even if sufficient information were available — could seriously distort its purpose. At the other extreme, the council of the Chamber of Commerce provides a definite group of the influential merchants but these might represent only one faction of important merchants. To overcome both of these difficulties an effort was made to determine which merchants played important roles in the commercial and public life of the city and province over a number of years. The criteria used in the selection included ownership of significant shipping, wharfing and waterfront facilities, directorships of important financial agencies, public esteem and influence as manifested in the press and in public documents, public service, and personal wealth. Although the final decision of who to include is both arbitrary and subjective, for the purpose of this study forty leading commercial figures have been identified as "great" merchants. Members of this group comprehended a variety of commercial interests, but all participated in vital shipping and financial concerns of the port and all possessed substantial personal resources. Their influence stemmed not only from this control over most of the city's financial resources, but also from their ability to create a climate of public opinion which identified their interests with the welfare of the community at large,[12] and from their access to the political institutions of the colony.[13] The group included 19 men who held the legal status of merchant, 4 mariners, 2 grocers, 1 fisherman, 1 clerk, and 3 who were not freemen of the City.[14]

The great merchants were drawn from all elements within the broader community, but the most numerous were those of Loyalist or pre-Loyalist origins. Several, notably Ezekiel and Thomas Barlow, Noah Disbrow, Ralph Jarvis, John Ward, Stephen Wiggins, and John M. and R.D. Wilmot, were scions of important Loyalist merchant families. Several others, such as Nehemiah Merritt, and Thomas and William Leavitt, were children of frugal Loyalist fishermen. Still a third group was the Simonds connection, the principal landed interest in the province, which included the pre-Loyalist Charles Simonds and the two fortunate young Loyalists who married his sisters, Thomas Millidge and Henry Gilbert. Equally as important as the natives were the British immigrants. By far the most significant were the Scots, Lauchlan Donaldson, John Duncan, James Kirk, Hugh Johnston, John Robertson, and John Wishart, who greatly outnumbered the Protestant Irishmen, John Kinnear and William Parks.[15] All of these immigrants were the offspring of prosperous families and came to the colony as young men of substance, bringing with them at least some capital resources. From positions of comparative advantage in the early nineteenth century, these merchants rode the crest of the timber trade to wealth by the 1840s. Virtually all were involved, to some degree, in the timber trade itself. Frequently they shipped timber which their crews had harvested. More often they bought timber or deals from the producer or took them in trade. Sometimes they would ship them on consignment to the British market. Rarely was the timber merchandising a single activity. Usually it was part of a pattern of business endeavour which included the wholesaling and retailing of British and American imports, coastal shipping, and the purchase, use, and sale of sailing vessels.[16]

Central to the business activity of all leading merchants was involvement in or ownership of one or more of the three vital elements in city commerce: the banking system, the wharves of the port, and the ships. Most sat on the directorates of at least one of the three local public banks or the local advisory committee of the Bank of British North America.[17] Indeed, given the centrality of credit to the commercial system of the province, it was unthinkable that any substantial local firm would not have easy access to the financial stability which the banks offered, an access ultimately controlled by the bank directors, whose committees met twice weekly to approve all loans. Access to the city wharves and water lots on the east side of Saint John harbour, the most valuable

461

mercantile property in the colony, was also critical. The water lots had been leased in perpetuity by the city in return for the lessees' agreement to construct and maintain the wharves. In return for an annual rental of between £5 and £31, depending on location in the harbour, a merchant received the right to erect improvements on the wharf, to provide free wharfage for his ships and goods, and to charge the legal rates of wharfage to all ships choosing to load or unload at this landing.[18] Possession of this vital harbour resource provided the merchant with both the most geographically advantageous terminal for his sea and river commerce and a modest but continuous income.

The central feature of New Brunswick trade was its de-centralization. Most great merchants were not involved in the timber-harvest or the sawmilling industry. Similarly, although they bought, sold, and contracted for the construction of vessels, they rarely participated directly in the shipbuilding industry. The role of most merchants was that of entrepreneur closing the links between the harbours of Saint John and Liverpool. Their vehicle was the sailing vessel and by 1841 the port possessed nearly 90,000 tons of shipping, about equally divided between small coasting vessels and those designed for trans-Atlantic crossings.[19] There were great differences in patterns of ownership among the city's major mercantile firms. More than half of the port's tonnage was owned by its great merchants, several of whom possessed sizeable fleets. John Kirk owned 14 vessels, totalling over 7,000 tons; Stephen Wiggins, 10 vessels, of nearly 7,000 tons; and John Wishart, 9 vessels, of 4,500 tons. At the other extreme, a number of merchants actually owned very little shipping, apparently preferring to ship through others. The large firm of Crookshank and Walker, for example, had only a single vessel in 1841. The different ownership patterns reflected the kinds of mercantile specialization that had developed by 1840. The large shipowners were heavily committed to the timber trade, both as merchants and as carriers; Crookshank and Walker were West Indies merchants with strong ties to the coasting trade and played the role of commission merchant and auctioneer. But whatever the area of specialized activity an individual firm might tend to follow, the collective control by the great merchants of the financial structure, harbour facilities, and shipping industry of Saint John placed them in the position both to accumulate personal wealth and to play a significant role in determining the kind of economy which might emerge in the city and the colony.

Most great merchants built up sizeable fortunes at some point in their careers. And while time and fortune were not always kind to them, the great majority managed to avoid calamitous failures.[20] Any attempt to establish the extent of personal wealth of an individual over time is an exceedingly treacherous enterprise, but it is possible to get a glimpse of the collective resources of the merchant community and to establish with some accuracy the holdings of most merchants at one point in their lives. Something of the size of Saint John merchant capital can be glimpsed in the city's fleet. Assuming an average price of £5 a ton, a conservative estimate of the value of vessels registered in Saint John in 1841 would be £450,000, and the capital investment of firms such as those of James Kirk or Stephen Wiggins would have been in the order of £30–40,000.[21] All firms had a basic business investment in offices, stores, warehouses, and the harbour-area land or wharves on which they were located. While the size of this investment varied with the scope of the facilities, even a single store in the harbour area was worth £3,000 by mid-century and the larger facilities of many merchants plus the value of stock on hand could multiply that figure five or six times. Yet few merchants committed most of their assets to their mercantile activities. In 1826 the firm of Crookshank and Walker, one of the largest in the city, owned assets valued at more than £50,000 ($200,000). Of this total only 20 per cent was represented by vessels (the firm owned four) and less than 10 per cent by goods on hand.[22] The remainder consisted of investments in property and notes. Johnston withdrew from the firm in 1826 and received the sum of £25,000 from his partner. He also retained ownership of his own firm, H. Johnston & Co., and his total personal assets in that year amounted to over £40,000.[23] Similar stories of substantial capital investment outside the major mercantile operation can be constructed for other great merchants. Nehemiah Merritt died in 1843 possessed of an estate worth about £60,000 ($240,000) exclusive of ships and business stock.[24] In 1864 Stephen Wiggins left more than $700,000 to his heirs, about half of it composed of assets not connected with the firm.[25] And still later, in 1876, "The Lord of the North," John Robertson, passed on $454,000 for the benefit of his children.[26] By 1840 there may have been a dozen merchants with assets exceeding a quarter of a million American dollars each, and a large part of this capital was available for investment beyond the primary enterprises of their holders.

Not surprisingly the most important uses to which the great merchants of Saint John devoted their wealth were those designed to further the development strategies which the merchant community deemed essential to its economic well-being. While direction and emphasis of these strategies changed from time to time in response to external circumstances, the broad outline is clearly visible throughout the first half of the nineteenth century. Like their counterparts in most North American ports, Saint John merchants emphasized a combination of financial institutions, transportation links, resource exploitation, and urban development to enable them to facilitate trans-Atlantic trade and to dominate a hinterland extending for 200 miles around the city. By 1840 their dominance in shipping had turned the Bay of Fundy into a Saint John lake and their location had made the entire Saint John Valley a satrapy of the city. Their greatest concerns were the development of transportation facilities into the interior and to the north shore of the province and the exploitation of the natural resources found within this natural zone of control. To achieve the first, the merchants pressured for a canal system to open the Grand Lake, some 60 miles from the city. After 1835 they sought to extend the city's control to the North Shore by means of a combined ship–railroad system which would involve construction of short railway lines between Grand Lake and Richibucto and between Shediac and Moncton. To exploit the natural resources of the area, they proposed to develop the sources of water power at the mouth of the Saint John River and at the Grand Lake, to mine the coal resources of the Grand Lake area, and to promote the Bay of Fundy and southern whale fisheries.[27]

The most important institutions necessary to the maintenance of this commercial system were financial organizations, notably banks and insurance companies. Banks facilitated the transfer of funds in trans-Atlantic trade and control of the province's major credit agencies gave the leading merchants considerable leverage in their dealings with other parts of New Brunswick society. The Council of New Brunswick had co-operated with the merchant community to charter the first bank in British North America in 1820.[28] But the conservative policies and limited capital resources of the Bank of New Brunswick could not keep pace with the financial needs of merchants in a rapidly expanding colony and by 1836 they had secured royal charters for two more banking institutions, the Commercial and the City banks, over the opposition of the Executive Council of the province.[29] By 1845 the three banks possessed a paid up capital of £250,000 ($1,000,000), most of which was probably held within the city by the merchant community.[30] Through the period 1830–50 banking stock never yielded less than 8 per cent a year and was viewed not only as an excellent security but also a first-class opportunity for speculation. Similar emphasis was placed on the city's two marine insurance companies, and on its fire insurance company. The £50,000 capital of the N.B. Marine Company, the largest of these firms, yielded an annual dividend of 10% to 60% in the 1840s,[31] and more than 80% of the stock of that company was held by city merchants in 1841.[32] The stock of these companies not only yielded an excellent dividend income, but provided the basis for a flourishing speculative trade in stocks.

Nonetheless, the most important single investment made by Saint John merchants was in land. It is interesting to speculate on the reasons behind this phenomenon. Land was clearly acquired both incidentally, in payment for debts owed, and because of the high degree of security which it offered. As well, many merchants saw an opportunity to achieve a certain status in the possession of well-known farms and favoured city residences. The nature of the acquisitions reveals several motives on the part of the purchasers: a desire to emulate a landed gentry, to create the security of rental income, to speculate on rising land prices and, in the case of purchases outside New Brunswick, to escape the consequences of the provincial bankruptcy laws in the event of commercial disaster. All merchants maintained one and sometimes two city residences. A large land-holder such as Noah Disbrow owned 12 city lots and 5 houses,[33] while John Robertson paid city taxes on real estate assessed at £25,000 ($100,000) — which almost certainly greatly underestimated its true market value — and held long-term leases, through his brother, on more than 100 city lots.[34] At his death in 1876 Robertson owned city real estate valued at $250,000.[35] Virtually all merchants owned several city lots and most possessed long-term leases on substantial tracts of city land in the harbour area.

Perhaps the most obvious case of land speculation on the part of leading merchants was the development of the suburban lands lying along the Marsh Road area directly north and west of the city. As early as 1819 most of this land had been acquired from the Hazen estate by several merchants — notably Nehemiah Merritt, Stephen Wiggins, Henry Gilbert, Hugh Johnston, and Walker Tisdale — as building lots and farms.[36] By mid-century most of the land remained in the hands of the merchant-buyers, who were in the process of subdividing it into township building lots. The same assumptions concerning the development of the interior of the province marked the merchant's land acquisition in the Saint John River Valley. Instead of buying up timber land, most merchants deliberately set about to acquire land bordering on the river. Their holdings were marked by a high proportion of intervale land, working farms and tenants, and comprised some of the most valuable agricultural resources in the province. The estate of Hugh Johnston alone contained nearly 12,000 acres of Valley land in 25 separate holdings scattered through Queens, Sunbury, York, and Carleton counties in 1835.[37] A number of merchants also acquired extensive holdings in other areas, notably Nova Scotia, Maine, New York, and Upper Canada. Nehemiah Merritt, for example, owned three houses at Greenwich & Amos streets in New York City,[38] and he and Walker Tisdale each possessed more than 2,000 acres of land in Northumberland and Durham counties, Upper Canada.[39]

In addition to ownership of lands and financial institutions, the Saint John merchant sought security through the public sector of the economy. The debt of the city and the province and the financing of public utilities within the city offered ample opportunity for investment. The city, in particular, had no agency through which it could carry long-term debt contracted for the construction of essential public works and from 1819 onward the merchant came to play an important role as city creditor.[40] By 1842 the municipal funded debt totalled £112,000, of which 40 per cent was held directly by merchants and their families and another 20 per cent by Saint John banks and insurance companies.[41] The city's major public utilities were promoted and financed by its merchants. The water company was formed following the cholera epidemic of 1832 and by 1844 had expended £27,000 on the system.[42] The Gas Light Company and

465

Reversing Falls Bridge Company were founded in the 1840s under the inspiration of the same group.[43]

Of all the potential investments in New Brunswick, the one that found least favour with the merchant community was secondary industry. Most merchant investment in this sector was related to the processing of natural resources produced in the province. In the wake of the growing English demand for deals in the mid-1830s several merchants acquired or constructed sawmills in conjunction with their shipping activities. Within the city John Robertson erected a large steam sawmill powered by sawdust and offal,[44] while less impressive operations were conducted by Robert Rankin & Co., Stephen Wiggins, R.D. Wilmot, Thomas and Ezekiel Barlow, and Nehemiah Merritt.[45] Outside the city the Kinnear brothers operated the Wales Stream mill.[46] Several others lent their support to the Portland Mills and Tunnel Company which proposed to cut tunnels through the Reversing Falls gorge to provide water power for a sawmill complex in Portland.[47] The most important industrial undertaking of any merchant before 1850 was the establishment of the Phoenix Foundry by the Barlow brothers in the 1820s. During the first two decades of its existence the firm introduced a number of technical innovations into the city, including construction of the first steamship manufactured entirely in the colony.[48] However, these examples were the exceptions rather than the rule. Most leading merchants had no financial involvement with secondary industry before 1840; those who did, with exception of Robertson and the Barlows, had a very limited investment in the undertakings. There was little investment in the city's major secondary industry — shipbuilding — and most lumber, even in the Saint John area, was made in 49 sawmills owned by a different group of men.[49] Quite clearly, comprehensive industrial development stood low on the list of merchant priorities in the period.

In view of the rapid pace of industrial growth in the city between 1820 and 1840, the low level of merchant participation is surprising. In 1820, apart from a few shipyards, sawmills, and flour mills, Saint John's secondary industry consisted of a wide variety of traditional crafts practised in dozens of small workshops. Over the course of the next three decades, in response to the needs of a rapidly expanding provincial society, the city and its environs was transformed into an important manufacturing centre. This development occurred along a broad front. Most obvious and most significant was the growth of the shipbuilding and sawmilling industries. But there was also a host of industries producing for provincial consumers. Apart from the enterprises of the master tailors and shoemakers, these included 24 tanneries, 16 flour mills, 4 iron foundries, 2 brass foundries, 12 furniture and 4 soap manufacturers, 8 carriage makers, 2 breweries, a paper mill, and a number of minor industries.[50] The capacity and resources of these firms is perhaps best illustrated in the flour industry, which by 1840 represented a capital investment of over £50,000 in mills capable of annually producing more than 150,000 barrels of flour, enough to feed the entire population of the province.[51] The tanners — 4 of whom were capable of generating more than 60 horsepower from their steam engines — made a similar claim for their industry.[52] The Harris Foundry comprised a block of buildings in 1846 with a replacement value of more than £10,000.[53] Most of these firms were developed by local entrepreneurs using their own skills and either their own capital or that of their family or friends.

Before 1840 most merchants either held this development at arm's length or viewed it with outright hostility. Wood and fish processing and shipbuilding were regarded as important elements in the commercial system and some merchants were prepared to invest in these undertakings. When local grain and livestock production was expanding in the 1820s, several merchants indicated some support for the tanners in their efforts to exclude the cheap Canadian leather from the province, and even promoted the first steam flour mill to grind local wheat.[54] However, such support was rare. More common was a violent negative reaction. The special objects of the merchants' wrath were the millers and bakers. The latter had long protested because American flour entered the colony with 5 shilling-a-barrel duty while bread entered free.[55] The merchants' reply was to demand the removal of provincial tariffs on both.[56] A clearer indication of the merchants' view of early industrial development is seen in the issues on which they took no position. These included virtually every request for assistance, support, or tariff protection by every manufacturing industry and interest in the city between 1820 and 1840. Given the rapid growth of the manufacturing sector during this time, this lack of participation by the merchant community stood in sharp contrast to the support which the manufacturers were able to command in almost every other major segment of urban society.

The principal organization of the merchant community was the Chamber of Commerce and the world which the merchant sought to create and maintain before 1840 is clearly visible through its petitions to the municipal, provincial, and imperial governments. The central doctrine in these petitions was the reciprocity of mercantilism and imperial economic preference in return for colonial deference and loyalty in matters economic and political. The merchant identified the prosperity of the colony with his right to buy cheaply and sell dear. To do this he must not only be able to sell colonial produce in a protected imperial market, but to purchase that produce in as free a market as possible. The latter doctrine carried a special significance for colonial producers for the merchant was prepared to use American timber and foodstuffs to keep costs as low as possible in the timber trade. Indeed, on any issue deemed vital to the prosecution of the timber trade the ranks of the great merchants never broke in nearly half a century. Thus woods resources held by the crown and after 1836 by the province must be

467

leased at nominal fees;[57] severe penalties must be imposed on those stealing timber or making lumber, timber, fish, and flour of inferior quality;[58] debtors must continue to be imprisoned lest British creditors lose confidence in the colony's will to protect them and cheap justice must be provided to permit the collection of debts;[59] no provincial duties could be imposed on timber, lumber, flour, bread, pork, or manufactured tobacco; and provincial tariffs must stand at no more than 5 per cent so that the merchant might keep control of the commerce of the Annapolis Valley of Nova Scotia.[60] Until 1843 imperial regulations permitted the merchant to treat the entire eastern seaboard of the United States and New Brunswick as a single commercial entity for the purposes of the timber trade,[61] and New Brunswick timber makers found their prices set by American competition. Even more significant, in terms of its implications for the fortunes of farmers and millers, was the merchants' bitter and continued opposition to any attempts by either provincial or imperial parliaments to establish or maintain duties on flour or salted provisions, an opposition which finally led lieutenant-governor Sir John Harvey to express doubts as to what extent the Saint John Chamber of Commerce "represents the real commercial interests of the province."[62]

468

By 1840 there is some evidence to suggest that a minority of merchants were prepared to dissent from the Chamber on economic issues not directly related to the timber trade. The flour trade was a case in point. While most fleet owners strongly supported free trade in wheat and flour in order to assure the cheapest provisions for their crews, a number of other great merchants came to see the commercial possibilities of a high tariff on foreign wheat and flour which would enable them to ship wheat from England for processing in Saint John mills. And the rapidly expanding domestic market had persuaded a few that not only could greater returns be obtained by importing wheat, rather than flour, but that flour mills offered the best return of all.[63] Nonetheless, until the 1840s the vast majority of merchants still believed that low tariffs were essential.

After 1841 the assumptions upon which the merchants' system had been built were undermined by external factors. The first major jolt was the dramatic recession of 1841, occasioned by the collapse of the British timber market. As the ripples of this unusually severe crisis spread through the local economy, the layers of provincial society collapsed hierarchically, beginning with the ships labourers, passing into the minor shopkeepers and journeymen craftsmen, then into the ranks of the master craftsmen, shipbuilders, traders, contractors, small merchants, and lawyers,[64] finally claiming its victims among even the most stalwart, with the bankruptcies of leading merchants such as James Hanford, Alex Yeats, and J. & H. Kinnear in 1843.[65] Just as the economy was recovering from the recession in 1843, the British Government began its gradual dismantlement of the mercantilist structure with the regulations prohibiting the import of Maine-produced timber into the United Kingdom under the preferential tariff.[66] In the short run the regulations produced no significant impact on the timber trade other than to limit the merchants' choice of producers. The long-run effect of the tariff declension between 1843 and 1849 was a sharp decline in the quantity and value of timber shipped from Saint John, and a corresponding increase in the export of lumber and deals.[67]

The rapid change and threat of change in the early 1840s produced a crisis of confidence in the mercantile assumptions which had dominated the economy of New Brunswick since Napoleonic times. The producer, whether shoemaker, farmer, sawmill owner, or founder, had existed in a gray area of semi-protection since the creation of the colony. Although the combination of imperial protective tariffs and provincial revenue duties had been sufficient to keep most local produce competitive with that from the United States, British produce entered the colony burdened only by the small revenue tariff. Provincial duties on British manufactures, for example, were fixed at 2½ per cent while those levied on American were 10 per cent.[68] The proposed elimination of the imperial tariff threatened to visit further disaster on an already badly demoralized artisan community. Hundreds of Saint John artisans and mechanics had abandoned the city during the recession of 1841–42 and the exodus continued through 1842 and 1843 as economic prospects for the colony dimmed. By 1843 the city was divided by acrimonious debate between those prepared to follow the mother country into free trade, and those who argued that the wealth of the colony was being dissipated on imported produce to the detriment of the producing classes. These protectionist views were strengthened by the emergence of a significant mechanics' revolt against what was perceived as the tyranny of the merchants. Out of the thriving mechanics community which had developed in the 1830s was formed, late in 1843, the Provincial Association, which brought together representatives of every major group of producers in the province.[69] The Association advocated protection and promotion of the interests of farmers, fishers, mechanics, and manufacturers, through the use of duties, bounties, model farms, and mechanics fairs. Among other things it urged the imposition of a substantial tariff on cordage and canvas, coupled with the payment of a bounty to farmers to grow hemp and flax.[70]

By 1844 the debate between free traders and protectionists had been transferred from the meeting hall to the Legislative Assembly, where the protectionists succeeded in imposing a compromise on the merchant interests after six close divisions in the House. Provincial duties were raised to 25 per cent on clocks, 20 per cent on wooden ware and chairs, 15 per cent on furniture and agricultural implements, 10 per cent on castings, cut nails, and brick, and specific duties were imposed on cattle, oxen, horses, and apples. At the same time any product required for the building of ships or the provisioning of crews, including flour, was placed on the free list. The debate over the most hotly contested duties, those on footwear and clothing, ended in a tie when a 10 per cent duty was imposed on footwear (a 5 per cent proposal was narrowly defeated) and clothing was admitted under a 4 per cent tariff.[71]

The compromise was only a temporary truce. Led by the St. John Chamber of Commerce, the free traders counterattacked at the 1845 sitting of the Assembly. Winning the support of several farmers who had voted with the protectionists the previous year, the free traders succeeded in reducing the tariff schedule to its 1843 levels, cutting some duties by as much as 60 per cent.[72] In response, one outraged protectionist leader vented his spleen in the columns of *The Morning News* on the "Free Trade Chamber of Commerce" of Saint John, those "few selfish individuals" who were prepared to impose "this vicious system of one-sided free trade" on the "productive classes . . . the bone and sinew of the country."[73] However, this setback was temporary. Much to the chagrin of leading reformers like George Fenety, protection became a basic political issue during the 1840s and 1850s, one that cut across the constitutional issues so dear to the hearts of reformers.[74] The Revenue Bill of the province was prepared each year by a select committee of the Assembly which acted on resolutions passed at each sitting of the Legislature. In 1847 the House, by a 21–10 majority, accepted the principle that "in enacting a Revenue Bill, the principle of protection to home industry, irrespective of revenue, should be recognized by levying duties on those productions and manufactures of foreign countries which the people of this province are capable of producing and manufacturing themselves."[75] The thrust of this resolution was directed against American produce and the Revenue Bill of that year introduced differential duties on British and foreign manufacturers. After 1850, however, the protectionists on the select committee were able to develop a policy of modest protection for a number of local industries. This included a 15 per cent tariff on footwear, leather, furniture, machinery, iron castings (stoves, ranges, boilers, furnaces, grates), most agricultural implements, wagons and sleighs, veneers, cigars, hats, and pianos.

The merchant community of Saint John was ill-prepared to meet the threat posed by the rise of the Provincial Association. By 1843 it was still recovering from the blows dealt it by the collapse of 1841–42 and it perceived the major threat to its security among the British free traders rather than in a diverse group of local protectionists. While the Chamber of Commerce traditionally had been the principal vehicle of merchant views, by 1843 it had come to represent the great fleet owners in their struggle against the threats to the protected status of the colonial timber trade. The Chamber's initial reaction to the Provincial Association and its proposals to divert provincial resources from the timber trade into agriculture and manufacturing was negative. In strongly worded petitions to the provincial and imperial authorities it reiterated support for traditional mercantilist policies in the timber trade and for a maximum 5 per cent duty on all provincial imports.[76] Yet, while the majority apparently accepted the Chamber of Commerce position, a significant minority came out in support of the Provincial Association and its policies of economic diversification and protective tariffs.[77] Among the heretics were R.D. Wilmot, William Parks, the Jarvises, Henry Gilbert, John Walker, Noah Disbrow, Charles Ward, and Walker Tisdale.[78] The principal spokesman for the movement in Saint John in the mid-1840s was R.D. Wilmot. When the Provincial Association entered the political arena with its platform of the "new New Brunswick," Wilmot was returned to the House of Assembly where he replaced his cousin, Lemuel Allan Wilmot, as the province's leading protectionist. Meanwhile, in an effort to restore a semblance of unity to the divided merchant community, the Chamber of Commerce was re-organized in the spring of 1845 and the membership of its new directorate reflected the attempts made to provide representation from a wide range of merchant opinions and interests.[79] At the final crisis of mercantilism, in 1849, the Chamber played an important part in the organization of the New Brunswick Colonial Association which brought together the city's most distinguished citizens in an effort to define the province's role in the new economic order.[80] The early programme of the Association clearly represented an attempt to reconcile all viewpoints and included a proposal urging the encouragement of home industry.[81] These efforts muted but could not entirely conceal the tensions between merchant free traders and protectionists.

471

By 1850 the Colonial Association had dropped its proposal for the encouragement of home industry and offered reciprocity in trade and navigation with the United States as the sole panacea for the province's economic ills.[82] And in the House of Assembly the merchants and their supporters were able to impose a compromise on the protectionists the effect of which was to create two economic systems. The artisan and manufacturer were granted a moderate tariff on material not required in the prosecution of the wood trades, while virtually everything necessary to the lumber industry, the timber trade, the building of wooden ships, and the victualling of crews was admitted free to the New Brunswick market. The latter included mill engines, anchors, chain, canvas, cordage, tackle, felt, sails, spikes, cotton ways, and iron bolts, bars, plates, and sheating, as well as rigging, tin and copper plate, sheathing paper, grain, flour, meal, bread, meats, fruit, and vegetables.[83] In effect, every backward linkage that the rapidly growing shipbuilding and shipping industry might have provided to the provincial economy was discouraged by provincial policy. Ship builders were encouraged to import all materials required in the building process, other than wood. Merchants were rewarded both with the transportation costs of the building materials and with cheap vessels which they sold in the United Kingdom. It was a policy which permitted the application of a limited range of skills and the use of a small capital to produce a product which was competitive on the British market. Unfortunately such a policy conferred only limited benefits on the provincial economy and did not provide the flexibility or profit margins that gave the ship builder either the capital resources or the incentive to undertake any extensive technological innovation. More important it did not allow the development of substantial industries, dependent on these backward linkages, which might have promoted these changes.

Nonetheless, the activities of the Provincial Association remained an important theme in city politics into the 1850s. Of the 37 great merchants still living in Saint John after 1842, 16 lent their support to at least some significant part of the protectionist programme and 12 of these consistently supported its general objective.[84] Not surprisingly, the merchants split on the issue of protection in terms of the emphasis which their business activities gave to the timber trade. Those with the most significant trading concerns — like John Ward, John Wishart, and John Robertson — remained largely divorced from the concerns of other elements within the broader community. They were, as well, the major shipowners and their focus remained on the trans-Atlantic community. They did not, necessarily, oppose the protectionist impulse *per se*, but they did fear its emphasis on economic self-sufficiency, its inefficiencies, and, particularly, the stated goal of protectionists to transfer resources out of the timber industry and into manufacturing, agriculture, and fishing.[85] Yet, while leading merchants opposed protectionist policies where they threatened to make the New Brunswick shipping industry uncompetitive on international runs by imposing substantial tariffs on flour, bread, and pork, a number were prepared to accept the new order. Although it is difficult to generalize about them, they tended to include men whose principal activities had centred on the merchandising activities of the wholesaler and those whose interests were more concerned with New Brunswick than the trans-Atlantic community. While they were men of substance, none could match the personal fortunes amassed by the more substantial timber merchants, particularly those with heavy investments in ships. At his death in 1853, Noah Disbrow left over $80,000 (£20,800) to be divided among his 6 daughters and 2 sons,[86] and three years later Munson Jarvis' brother, William, a prominent dockside merchant, left $50,000.[87] The next year William Parks placed a value of £17,484 (about $70,000) on the assets of his firm.[88] By comparison, Stephen Wiggins' share of the firm of Stephen Wiggins & Son was valued at $389,000 in 1863, most of which would have been in shipping.[89] Over the course of the 1850s, however, a minority of the great merchants did play an increasingly important role in the industrial development of the city through promotion of enterprises as diverse as woollen mills and coal oil refineries. As their industrial interests grew, their involvement in the staples trade became less significant. Several had been or became agents for the transfer of resources from the staples to the manufacturing sector of the provincial economy in an attempt to create a more balanced economy. The Barlow brothers have been mentioned already in connection with the secondary iron industry. The hardware merchant, William Henry Scovil, established his cut nail factory in the early 1840s, while the wholesale grocer, William Parks, ended his career in the 1860s as proprietor of one of the first cotton mills in British North America.

Those who identified most closely with the community were generally most willing to commit capital to its internal development; those with strong British ties and alternatives were usually much less willing to make this commitment. The former characteristic is reflected in the relatively high proportion of merchants of Loyalist origins who supported the Provincial Association and its objectives. In essence, they viewed Saint John as the central element in a limited regional economy, in preference to its position in the larger metropolitan economy. It was merchants who had developed these more limited horizons and who saw their future in terms of local enterprise who came to the support of the manufacturers and artisans of the city, the group largely responsible for the not inconsiderable manufacturing development of the period from 1820 to 1850. The manufacturers and artisans were drawn from different origins, participated at different levels of civic society, and enjoyed a distinctly inferior status to their mercantile counterparts. Their special interests and ideas received serious consideration by the leaders of the community only during periods of economic crisis, such as the 1840s and 1870s. Even then the producers were able to achieve a position of influence only in alliance with a portion of the merchant community. When merchants closed ranks, they were able to establish the goals of the community at large and these goals were almost always designed to further the integration of the region into a larger trading complex in which the region was subordinated to the interests of a metropolitan community. So long as the imperial economic system was possible, the merchants used their capital and their great influence to maintain and further that system, largely ignoring the interests of farmers, manufacturers, and other producers in the province. Nowhere was this more evident than in the crucial area of credit. Not only did they use the financial institutions in the city to direct the available credit to their own commercial purposes, but they successfully thwarted every effort by producers to obtain their own banking facilities.

473

The great merchants certainly organized and financed the commercial and financial super-structure needed for the conduct of the timber trade in a major sea port and they played important roles in providing capital for the exploitation of the natural resources of the region and for the construction of public works and utilities within the city. A minority, distinguished by their wholesaling concerns and native origins, began to participate in some fashion in the development of a more diversified urban economy. But the majority of great merchants retained a commitment to an unmodified staples economy. In the early nineteenth century it was this group which produced the dominant economic class, the institutions, and myths — particularly that of commerce as the great creator of prosperity — which formed the community of Saint John. Throughout the period they were able to mould the economy to their essentially interregional export-oriented needs. In so doing, they exploited the province's natural resources of timber and stimulated the development of major sawmilling and shipbuilding industries, both of which produced significant short-term benefits for the economy. Ancillary benefits were derived from the provision of shipping, credit facilities, and insurance services.

The manufacturing sector of the New Brunswick economy did grow rapidly in the 1850s and 60s. Gordon Bertram has demonstrated that in 1871 the *per capita* output of the province's manufacturing industries rivalled that of Ontario and Quebec and was nearly twice that of Nova Scotia.[90] Nearly half of the industrial output of New Brunswick was produced in and around the city of Saint John.[91] McClelland suggests that there was an average annual growth of 1 per cent in New Brunswick's deal and lumber exports during the period.[92] Not surprisingly, the largest components of the province's industrial output were sawmill products and wooden ships (44% for the province and 38% for the city).[93] Apart from these traditional staples, however, virtually every industry which had received even a modest degree of protection in the previous generation flourished. Foundry products, footwear, and clothing all exceeded shipbuilding in value, while furniture and carriage making, boiler making, saw and file manufacture, and tin and sheet iron output and leather making all played significant roles in the local economy.[94] Some backward linkages from shipbuilding, which earlier tariff policies had done so little to encourage, were also able to develop by the later 1860s. The most obvious example was the small rope-making industry functioning in the city and there can be little doubt that at least some of the foundry activity was stimulated by the market created by the ship builders.[95]

Yet the outlines of the earlier emphases were still visible in the city's industrial structure. There was, apparently, no industry capable of producing the chain, anchors, and canvas used in the shipbuilding industry, nor to provide the machinery employed in the province's 565 sawmills.[96] Although steam engines had been constructed in Saint John in the 1840s, there was no engine-building firm in the province by 1870.[97] A similar situation existed in the basic food industries. The ancient flour industry had been virtually eliminated and only a minuscule meat-curing industry survived.[98] There were no distilleries and only four small breweries.[99] The debate over the virtues of the ordered pastoral life as opposed to the disordered and transient nature of the timber industry was a recurring theme in nineteenth-century New Brunswick. The debate came to be couched in such explicit moral terms that it is difficult to make any assessment from it of the economic viability of provincial agriculture in the period, or to determine the extent to which the agricultural development of the province was affected by the timber trade.[100] The rapidity of agricultural development between 1840 and 1870 would seem to indicate that there was some truth to the charges of the timber critics; at the very least, the combination of rewards which the trade could offer to the rural inhabitants, coupled with the refusal of the provincial legislature to provide any protection for the nascent colonial agriculture, severely retarded the development of a substantial agriculture in the early nineteenth century.[101]

The retardation was of vital importance to the health of the colonial economy. New Brunswick ran a perennial deficit in its current account and in most years the entire trade imbalance resulted from the substantial imports of foodstuffs for use within the province. The most prominent example of this phenomenon was American wheat and flour, but it was reflected, as well, in large imports of rye flour, Indian meal, pork, beef, lamb, butter, potatoes, vegetables, fruit, and even oats. The proportion of agricultural products ranged from just over 20% of the province's total imports in 1840 to just under 40% in 1855.[102] Wheat and flour imports alone exceeded the value of timber exports by 1852, and by 1855 the 170,000 barrels of flour and 110,000 bushels of wheat, worth £334,000 in all, rivalled the £380,000 in deals shipped from the province.[103] New Brunswick agricultural conditions were not particularly suited to the production of wheat, although the doubling of output following the National Policy of 1879 indicates that a much larger production than occurred up to Confederation was possible.[104] But it is more difficult to explain the import of most other foodstuffs which could be produced domestically. Given the fact that substantial quantities of these products were grown in the province in the 1840s, that the land for producing more was readily available, and that there was a substantial local demand for these foodstuffs which could not be met by local producers, it seems probable that the incentives offered by the timber trade, and the refusal of the province to afford even nominal protection to local producers were the major factors in inhibiting the growth of a more substantial agricultural sector before 1850.

In the final analysis there is no simple answer to the question of merchant responsibility for economic growth or retardation in Saint John and New Brunswick. While they agreed on the validity of the concept of economic growth, merchants rarely spoke with a single voice when the subject of a specific development strategy was raised. Most were prepared to permit, and some to support a strategy which included the development of certain kinds of secondary industry. These efforts were generally successful although this success was due more to the efforts

475

of the city's artisans than to its merchants. Merchant endeavours were particularly aimed at supporting and preserving the traditional timber staple and its milling, shipping, and shipbuilding ancillaries. The manufacture of producers' goods used in any of these activities, including mill engines and machinery, shipbuilding materials, and domestic foodstuffs needed for ship crews, woods workers, and mill labourers, were afforded no encouragement. In effect two economic systems based upon mutually exclusive values were the result of the synthesis which emerged from the conflict of the 1840s. The most obvious victim of that synthesis was the shipbuilding industry, potentially the most dynamic element in the provincial economy, which was locked into the more conservative timber-trade economy. Thus a city containing a number of secondary iron and steel firms, which for decades had possessed the capability of manufacturing complete steamships and engines, and a labour force skilled at working in both wood and iron was unable to manufacture metal ships or even to make any substantial adjustment in the face of technological changes which were gradually eroding this vital industry. In the course of the 1860s and 1870s the ship builders built and the timber merchants bought and sold ships in the traditional way simply because they could not perceive the industry apart from the timber trade or from the lumber which was basic to both building and trade. While the timber merchants were not alone able to shape the provincial economy to their perceptions, they provided an effective and powerful leadership to substantial interests in the province which identified with the traditional timber trade. By 1871 the economy was becoming increasingly diversified and self-sufficient and the dynamic elements in this development were to be found in secondary industry and in agriculture, but the influence of the great merchants delayed this development by two critical decades. In this sense they contributed to the retardation of a viable industrial base in the city.

NOTES

[1] The literature of this debate has been explored by L.R. MacDonald in "Merchants against Industry: An Idea and Its Origins," *Canadian Historical Review* 56 (1975): 263–81 [hereafter *CHR*].

[2] A point most recently made by Professor Gerald Tulchinsky in *The River Barons* (Toronto, 1977), 234.

[3] Nonetheless, a good beginning has been made with Tulchinsky's examination of the Montreal business community at mid-century, and in David Sutherland's study of the business strategies of Halifax merchants in the colonial period. Tulchinsky, *The River Barons*; David Sutherland, "Halifax Merchants and the Pursuit of Development, 1783–1850," *CHR* 59 (1978): 1–17.

[4] Peter D. McClelland, "The New Brunswick Economy in the Nineteenth Century," Ph.D. thesis, Harvard University, 1966, 3–4. McClelland argues that shipbuilding may have added no more than 2.6% to the gross regional product (p. 189) and that it had few significant backward or forward linkages.

[5] McClelland, "New Brunswick Economy," 229–30.

[6] McClelland, "New Brunswick Economy," 4.

[7] New Brunswick, *Journal of the House of Assembly*, 1841, xvii–xxx; Canada, *Census of 1871*, 4: 125.

[8] Canada, *Census of 1871*, 4: 128.

[9] The early development of this industry is discussed by Lewis R. Fischer in "From Barques to Barges: Shipping Industry of Saint John, N.B., 1820-1914," unpublished paper read to the Atlantic Canada Studies Conference, Fredericton, 1978.

[10] Eugene A. Forsey, *The Canadian Labour Movement, 1812-1902* (Ottawa: Canadian Historical Association, 1974), 3-4; J. Richard Rice, "A History of Organized Labour in Saint John, New Brunswick, 1813-1890," M.A. thesis, U.N.B., 1968), ch. 1.

[11] James M. Gilmour, *Spatial Evolution of Manufacturing: Southern Ontario, 1851-1891* (Toronto, 1972).

[12] For the extent to which they succeeded in this goal see the testimonials to the merchants delivered by George Fenety and Henry Chubb, the city's most respected and influential newspaper editors in the 1840s. See *The Commercial News and General Advertiser* (Saint John), 10 September 1839, and *The New Brunswick Courier* (Saint John), 10 February 1843.

[13] This thesis is argued by Stewart MacNutt in his "Politics of the Timber Trade in Colonial New Brunswick, 1825-40," *CHR* 30 (1949): 47-65.

[14] This group includes L.H. Deveber, Thomas Barlow, Ezekiel Barlow, Jr., Issac Bedell, Robert W. Crookshank, Noah Disbrow, Jr., Lauchlan Donaldson, John Duncan, Henry Gilbert, James T. Hanford, John Hammond, David Hatfield, James Hendricks, Ralph M. Jarvis, Hugh Johnston, Sr., Hon. Hugh Johnston, Jr., John H. Kinnear, James Kirk, Thomas Leavitt, William H. Leavitt, Nehemiah Merritt, Thomas Millidge, D.L. McLaughlin, Thomas E. Millidge, William Parks, John Pollok, Robert Rankin, E.D.W. Ratchford, Hon. John Robertson, W.H. Scovil, Hon. Charles Simonds, Walker Tisdale, John V. Thurgar, John Walker, John Ward, Jr., Charles Ward, Stephen Wiggins, John M. Wilmot, R.D. Wilmot, John Wishart.

[15] David Macmillan explores the early development of the Saint John Scottish community in "The New Men in Action: Scottish Mercantile and Shipping Operations in North American Colonies, 1760-1825," *Canadian Business History: Selected Studies, 1497-1971* (Toronto, 1972), 82-99.

[16] A good description of these activities is found in Graeme Wynn, "Industry, Entrepreneurship and Opportunity in the New Brunswick Timber Trade," in Lewis R. Fischer and Eric W Sager, eds., *The Enterprising Canadians: Entrepreneurs and Economic Development in Eastern Canada, 1820-1914* (St. John's: Memorial University of Newfoundland, 1979).

[17] Reports revealing the directors and the financial state of affairs of each bank were published annually in *Journal of the House of Assembly*.

[18] Schedule of Real Estate Belonging to Saint John, Wharf Leases in Perpetuity, Records of the Executive Council, REX/PA, Miscellaneous, Provincial Archives of New Brunswick [hereafter PANB].

[19] This description of the Saint John fleet, containing information on the date of acquisition, size, and ownership of each vessel, is found in "Customs House Account, Returns of Shipping, Port of Saint John, New Brunswick," *Journal of the House of Assembly*, 1842, cclvii-cclxvii.

[20] Two notable failures were the firms John M. Wilmot, in 1837, and James Hanford, Alex Yeats, and J. & H. Kinnear, in 1843. *The New Brunswick Courier*, 4 March, 18, 25 November 1843; A.R.M. Lower, *Great Britain's Woodyard* (Toronto, 1973), 151.

[21] Prices for New Brunswick-built vessels fluctuated between £5 and £12 a ton throughout the 1830s and 1840s.

[22] Account Book I, 5-10, Hugh Johnston Papers, New Brunswick Museum [hereafter NBM].

[23] Schedule of Real and Personal Effects, May 1826, Hugh Johnston Papers.

[24] Last will and testament of Nehemiah Merritt, Records of the Court of Probate, City and County of Saint John, Book G, 131 ff., PANB. The totals include estimates of property values.

[25] Stephen Wiggins, 1864, RG 7, RS 71, PANB.

[26] John Robertson, 1876, RG 7, RS 71, PANB.

[27] New Brunswick, Records of the Legislative Assembly [RLE], 1834, Petitions, vol. 2, no. 41; 1836, Petitions, vol. 5, nos. 70, 75, 81; 1834, Petitions, vol. 6, no. 130, PANB.

[28] James Hannay, *History of New Brunswick* (Saint John, 1909), 2: 428-29.

[29] NB, RLE, 1836, Petitions, vol. 5, no. 64, PANB; Hannay, *History of New Brunswick*, 430-32.

[30] These estimates are drawn from Bank of New Brunswick dividend payments, newspaper accounts of bank stock sales, and wills. There was no public statement disclosing the ownership of bank stock in colonial New Brunswick.

[31] The annual reports of the N.B. Marine Insurance Company between 1830 and 1850 may be found in the appendices of the journals of the New Brunswick House of Assembly.

[32] New Brunswick, *Journal of the House of Assembly*, 1842, Appendix — Returns of Incorporated Companies, The N.B. Marine Insurance Company.

[33] Records of the Court of Probate, City and County of St. John, Book H, 454 ff., PANB.

[34] John Robertson to Common Council, 10 October 1849, Saint John Common Council Supporting Papers, vol. 20, Saint John Manuscripts, PANB; Saint John Schedule (etc.), 1842, REX/PA, Miscellaneous, PANB.

[35] John Robertson, 1876, RG 7, RS 71, PANB.

[36] Extract of Cash Received for Land Sold 1814-1821, Hon. William F. Hazen Papers, Daybook and Journal 1814-34, NBM.

[37] Inventory of Estate of Hugh Johnston, 1 May 1835, Hugh Johnston Papers, Account Book I, NBM.

[38] Probate Records, Book G, 131, PANB.

[39] Probate Records, Book I, 267.

40 The city debt rose from £4413 in 1822 to £115,366 in 1845. Minutes of the Common Council, vol. 5, 5 April 1822; vol. 17, 10 September 1845, Common Clerk's Office, Saint John City Hall.

41 Common Council Supporting Papers, vol. 6, 7/8–12/13 September 1842, Saint John Manuscripts, PANB.

42 NB, RLE, 1844, Petitions, vol. 7, no. 181, PANB.

43 *The New Brunswick Courier*, 27 March 1843.

44 *The New Brunswick Courier*, 11 September 1852.

45 *The Morning News* (Saint John), 23 April 1841.

46 *The New Brunswick Courier*, 25 November 1843.

47 NB, RLE, 1834, Petitions, vol. 2, no. 41; 1836, Petitions, vol. 5, no. 75; 1839, Petitions, vol. 2, no. 43, PANB.

48 Common Council Minutes, vol. 15, 23 December 1840, 14 January 1841, Common Clerk's Office, Saint John City Hall.

49 The most important of these was probably George Bond, who held the lease for the tidal-powered Carleton mills, the most significant power source in the Saint John area.

50 NB, RLE, 1840, Petitions, vol. 4, no. 122; 1843, Petitions, vol. 6, no. 149; 1850, Petitions, vol. 17, no. 357; 1850, Petitions, no. 414; 1836, Petitions, vol. 5, no. 112, PANB; *The New Brunswick Courier*, 12 October 1850, 5 July 1851.

51 NB, RLE, 1840, Petitions, vol. 4, no. 122, PANB.

52 NB, RLE, 1845, Petitions, vol. 9, no. 298.

53 *The New Brunswick Courier*, 27 June 1846.

54 NB, RLE, 1834, Petitions, vol. 4, no. 91; 1828, Petitions, vol. 2, no. 43, PANB.

55 NB, RLE, 1835, Petitions, vol. 4, no. 124; 1842, Petitions, vol. 3, no. 54.

56 NB, RLE, 1833, Petitions, vol. 3, no. 102; 1840, Petitions, vol. 4, no. 121; 1842, Petitions, vol. 12, no. 237; 1851, Petitions, vol. 15, no. 457; *The New Brunswick Courier*, 4 February 1843.

57 W.S. MacNutt, "Politics of the Timber Trade in Colonial New Brunswick, 1825–40," 47–65; Graeme Wynn, "Administration in Adversity: The Deputy Surveyors and Control of the New Brunswick Crown Forests Before 1844," Acadiensis 7 (Autumn 1977): 49–65.

58 NB, RLE, 1839, Petitions, vol. 3, no. 80; 1824, D, Petitions, no. 6, PANB.

59 NB, RLE, 1831, F. Petitions, vol. 2, no. 10.

60 NB, RLE, 1850, Petitions, vol. 6, no. 138; *The New Brunswick Courier*, 24 February 1849.

61 *The New Brunswick Courier*, 20 January 1844.

62 Sir John Harvey to Lord Glenelg, 15 May 1838, CO 188/59, ff. 733–42, but also see Petition of Saint John Merchants, 17 February 1834, CO 188/49, ff. 169–71; Sir John Harvey to Lord John Russell, 4 September 1840, CO 188/69, ff. 152–53; Sir William Colebrooke to Stanley, 29 March 1842, CO 188/75, ff. 341–45. Both Harvey and Colebrooke feared the economic and social consequences of an over-specialized staples economy.

63 NB, RLE, 1840, Petitions, vol. 4, no. 122, PANB. Among the dissenters were N. Merritt, R. Rankin, John Walker, D. Wilmot, I. Bedell, Wm. Parks.

64 *The New Brunswick Courier*, 4 March, 3 June, 15 July, 7 October 1843.

65 *The New Brunswick Courier*, 4 March, 18, 25, November 1843.

66 NB, RLE, 1843, Petitions, vol. 9, no. 244, PANB.

67 Between 1840 and 1849 the value of timber exports from New Brunswick declined from £271,000 to £179,000; that of deals and boards increased from £180,000 to £266,000. New Brunswick, *Journal of the House of Assembly*, 1841, 1850, Customs House Returns.

68 *Journal of the House of Assembly*, 1842, Appendix, cclxxiv.

69 *The New Brunswick Courier*, 4 January 1844.

70 *The New Brunswick Courier*, 10 February 1844.

71 New Brunswick, *Journal of the House of Assembly*, 1844, 152–57.

72 *The Morning News*, 24 March 1845. The defectors included Barbarie from Restigouche, Earle from Queens, Hanington and Palmer from Westmorland. See New Brunswick, *Journal of the House of Assembly*, 1845, 219–21.

73 *The Morning News*, 19 March 1845.

74 Editor and publisher of *The Morning News* and later Queens Printer under the Liberals, Fenety was unsympathetic to the views of the protectionists. G.E. Fenety, *Political Notes and Observations* (Fredericton, 1867), vol. 1, chs. 5, 21. On the other hand both Lemual Allan Wilmot and Samuel Leonard Tilley supported the protectionist position.

75 New Brunswick, *Journal of the House of Assembly*, 1847, 190–91.

76 *The New Brunswick Courier*, 4 February 1844.

77 *The New Brunswick Courier*, 10 February 1844.

78 NB, RLE, 1843, Petitions, vol. 6, no. 143, PANB.

79 *The Morning News*, 2 April, 16 April, 6 May, 7 May 1845; 25 February 1846.

80 *The New Brunswick Courier*, 28 June, 4 August 1849.

81 *The New Brunswick Courier*, 15 September 1849.

82 *The New Brunswick Courier*, 8 June 1850.

83 The evolution of New Brunswick policy between 1837 and 1860 is illustrated through the following commodities:

478

	1837		1842		1844	1845	1848		1855	1859
	Brit.	For.	Brit.	For.			Brit.	For.		
Wagons	2.5%	10%	2.5%	10%	10%	4%	4%	30%	15%	15%
Footwear	2.5%	5%	2.5%	10%	10%	7.5%	4%	30%	15%	15%
Agricultural										
Implements	Free	Free	Free	Free	10%	4%	4%	15%	15%	15%
Stoves	2.5%	10%	2.5%	10%	10%	7.5%	4%	15%	15%	15%
Chain	2.5%	10%	2.5%	10%	Free	Free	Free	Free	1%	1%
Canvas	Free	Free	Free	Free	Free	Free	Free	Free	1%	1%
Cordage	Free	Free	Free	Free	Free	Free	Free	Free	1%	1%
Mill Engines	Free	10%	Free	10%	Free	Free	Free	Free	10%	12.5%
Meat	Free	Free	Free	Free	Free	Free	Free	Free	Free	Free
Bread										
Flour	Free	Free	Free	Free	Free	4%	4%	10%	Free	Free

Source: Statutes of New Brunswick, 7 William IV, c.1.; 5 Victoria, c.1.; 7 Victoria, c.1.; 8 Victoria, c.2.; 11 Victoria, c.1.; 18 Victoria, c.1.

[84] NB, RLE, 1850, Petitions, vol. 6, no. 416, PANB.

[85] NB, RLE, 10 February 1843, 23 February 1850.

[86] Noah Disbrow, 1853, RG 7, RS 71, PANB.

[87] William Jarvis, 1856, RG 7, RS 71, PANB.

[88] Partnership Agreements, William Parks Papers, F #3, NBM. This figure does not include Park's personal estate.

[89] Stephen Wiggins, 1853, RG 7, RS 71, PNB.

[90] Gordon W. Bertram, "Historical Statistics on Growth and Structure in Manufacturing in Canada, 1870-1957," in J. Henripin and A. Asimakopulas, eds., Canadian Political Science Association Conference on Statistics 1962 & 1963 (Toronto, 1964), 122. The figures for Ontario, Quebec, New Brunswick, and Nova Scotia were $69.60, $62.60, $59.80, $30.70.

[91] Saint John County output totalled $8,312,627; that of the province was $17,367,687. Canada, Census of 1871, vol. 3, Table 54.

[92] McClelland, "The New Brunswick Economy," 124.

[93] McClelland, "The New Brunswick Economy," Tables 22, 39.

[94] The shipbuilding industry produced vessels to a value of $538,042 and employed 647 men. Foundry output, including fittings, nails, and tacks, was $786,000 (507 employees); clothing $826,660 (1033 employees); footwear $539,230 (565 employees). Canada, Census of 1871, vol. 3, Tables 21, 22, 23, 24, 36, 39, 45, 51, 52, 53.

[95] Canada, Census of 1871, Table 50.

[96] The number of sawmills in the province had declined in the 1860s. There were 609 Water-powered and 80 steam-powered sawmills in 1861. Canada, Census of 1871, 4: 336-43.

[97] Canada, Census of 1871, vol. 3, Table 46.

[98] Canada, Census of 1871, Tables 21, 37.

[99] Canada, Census of 1871, Table 35.

[100] Soil maps would seem to indicate that the agricultural potential of the province is limited. However, since the arable area comprises several million acres of land, this source is only useful as an indicator of the upper limits of agricultural growth. In the short run the province possessed a considerable potential as the rapid growth of mid-century reveals.

[101] Acreage of cultivated land increased from 435,861 in 1840 to 1,171,157 in 1870 at a rate much more rapid than that of population growth. Consequently the number of cultivated acres per capita rose from 2.7 to 4.6. In the single decade of the 1860s the number of farmers in the province rose by nearly 30%; the population by 13%. Canada, Census of 1871, 3: 90-91; 4: 129, 336-43.

[102] New Brunswick, Journal of the House of Assembly, 1841, cclxxvi-cclxxvii; 1856, clxiii-clxvi.

[103] Flour and wheat to the value of £169,000 was imported in 1854. This compared with exports of 134,000 tons of timber valued at £165,000. Two years later the respective values of the two commodities were £286,000 and £160,000, and in 1855 imported flour and wheat totalled £377,000, a value rivalling that of the province's lumber output (£437,000). See New Brunswick, Journal of the House of Assembly, 1853, 1855, 1856, Customs House Returns.

[104] Canada, Census of 1881, 3: 42-43, 120-21, 158-59. New Brunswick wheat output rose from 204,911 bushels in 1871 to 521,956 in 1881.

Ideology, Society, and State in the Maritime Colonies of British North America, 1840–1860

GRAEME WYNN

By North American standards, the three colonies that came to be called the Canadian Maritime provinces are — and were — small. New Brunswick, approximately 73,000 square kilometres in area, is less extensive than Maine and South Carolina; Nova Scotia (55,000 square kilometres) does not match West Virginia in area and is barely double the size of Maryland; among all the states and provinces of North America, only Rhode Island is smaller than Prince Edward Island, which, at less than 6,000 square kilometres, is approximately the area of Delaware. Together, the three colonies are substantially smaller than the New England states, and in the mid-nineteenth century the area of the united Canadas was more than six times theirs. So, too, in population. In 1851, the three Maritime colonies had 534,000 inhabitants (Nova Scotia, 276,000; New Brunswick, 194,000; Prince Edward Island, 64,000), little more than half the total in Canada West, and some 50,000 fewer than in the neighbouring state of Maine. Ten years later, when the six states of New England had more than 3 million inhabitants, the population of the Maritimes was 682,000; Montreal, a city of 100,000, had 20,000 more residents than Prince Edward Island.[1]

Perceived from afar as a unit — in the early nineteenth century they were often described collectively as the Lower Provinces, and participants in the Confederation debates of the 1860s sometimes referred to them as the Maritime Provinces — these colonies were deeply divided in politics, economy, ethnicity, and religion. Separate jurisdictions, in 1840 and 1860, each had its own lieutenant-governor, council, and assembly. Commercially, they generally looked east and south, with strong links to Britain, the British West Indies, and the northern States. But within this matrix, economies cross-cut political boundaries. Most of New Brunswick's people lived in the Saint John–Fundy catchment and looked to Saint John as their commercial capital (as indeed did many settlements on the Nova Scotian side of the Bay of Fundy); on the northern (gulf) shore of New Brunswick, and in Prince Edward Island, however, Halifax held greater commercial sway than Saint John. Across the colonies, fish-

From *Colonial Leviathan: State Formation in Mid-Nineteenth Century Canada*, ed. Allan Greer and Ian Radforth (Toronto: University of Toronto Press, 1992), 284–328. Reprinted with the permission of University of Toronto Press Incorporated.

480

ing, shipbuilding, lumbering, and farming underpinned local life, but the first three were, largely, separate spheres that gave markedly different casts to landscapes, economies, and societies in those areas in which they dominated. Further, although perhaps eight of every nine inhabitants of the Maritimes in 1860 were native-born, most identified strongly with the ethnic, religious, and other traditions of their forebears, who in the process of settlement had made the colonies a patchwork quilt of different "allegiances" — Acadian, Loyalist, pre-Loyalist, Palatinate, Yankee, Scots, Irish, English — fragmented by adherence to one or another of a dozen different religions.[2]

Reflecting these patterns, diversity, complexity, fragmentation, and heterogeneity have become the *leitmotivs* of scholarly reflection upon the region. For all its modest size, it is commonly portrayed as a place without a "unifying configuration of physical features," a world of "islands, peninsulas, and river valleys" marked by particularism, small-scale competition, and cross-purposes. Within provincial bounds "local interests were thoroughly schooled to grudge ambitions to others"; considered as a whole, and compared to territories of similar or greater size elsewhere, this region appears "unusually divided against itself." Even the surrounding sea — which some have seen as a unifying influence, if only by implying that Maritimers are people who "smell of salt to the Prairie" — "provides a matrix rather than a focus."[3]

481

Faced with this mountain of regional complexity, it is surely wiser to contemplate it at some remove — to describe its peaks and vales, corries and couloirs as they diversify and give shape to its formidable bulk — than to attempt an assay of its every grain and crystal. From the vantage of distance, light and shadow, pattern and form can be picked out and interpreted against the backdrop of the whole; with skill and appropriate emphases, diversity and dissimilarity can be rendered intelligible, labyrinthine reality can be ordered and understood. By contrast, the assay-master stands to be overwhelmed by the sheer magnitude of his task. Yet in the end we cannot rest content — with Charles G.D. Roberts, looking again over the marshes of Tantramar — to "Muse and recall far off." The poet, fostering memories and the comforting vision of an unchanging landscape, might well stay his steps, "lest on too close sight" he "Spy at their task . . . the hands of chance and change." But if we would truly grapple with the multifaceted complexity of the Maritimes, we cannot afford "not [to] go down to the marshland," across the hillsides, along the roads, through the towns, and into the villages of the region, to observe the actions, chart the ideas, and explore something of the everyday lives of its people, and to assess the imprint of those ever-busy hands of chance and change upon its fabric.[4]

The pages that follow are intended to carry us on just such a journey. Comprising a series of discrete vignettes, drawn from many corners of the three provinces, they provide a varied parade of scenes from the rich tapestry of two decades of regional life.[5] Adits driven into the mountain of regional complexity, they seek to reveal more of the area's nooks, crannies, strata, and structure than it is possible to espy from the vantage of distance without burying comprehension beneath the endless detail of the everyday. Like most travel itineraries, these vignettes offer only glimpses of a wider picture, and they share — with the encounters and experiences of almost any adventurous exploration of new territory — a random or markedly kaleidoscopic quality that belies their interconnected, reflexive character.[6] Just as the cumulative impressions of alert travel provide the basis for heightened understanding of the country through which one has passed, however, these vignettes offer evidence for reflection upon the particular conjuncture of ideology, society, and state in the mid-nineteenth-century Maritime colonies. The final third of the paper is given to focusing these reflections, to teasing order and interpretation from the hues, shapes, interpenetration, and arrangement of the several kaleidoscopic fragments of the preceding pages.

482

Glimpses of a Troubled City

Encompassing three parishes in the mid-1850s, the city of Saint John was a bustling commercial and manufacturing centre with more than 30,000 residents.[7] The major city of its province, the hub of the Bay of Fundy, and the leading centre of the timber trade in southern New Brunswick, it was a place of compact neighbourhoods, many of them densely built up with three-storey tenements and two-storey duplexes on the narrow lots that were characteristic of the settlement. The fact that approximately three-quarters of Saint John's 4,200 family heads had been born in the British Isles reflected the rapid growth of the city in the nineteenth century and its position at the western end of an active transatlantic trading system. Native New Brunswickers, descendants of the city's Loyalist founders or migrants from the colonial countryside, made up most of the remaining population. Almost two-thirds of the inhabitants of this urban area lived in the peninsular parish of St. John; slightly more than 10,000 people occupied the neighbouring parishes of Carleton (across the harbour) and Portland (north and west of St. John parish). On the peninsula that formed the heart of the urban area almost three of every five households were headed by men (or women) of Irish birth, and well over a third of all residents in Saint John and Portland had been born in the Emerald Isle. A clear majority of these had lived in the city for a decade or more. Participants in the steady exodus from Ireland that brought tens of thousands of Irish men, women, and children to British North America before 1840, they were mainly artisans and tenant farmers from the northern counties, strongly Protestant in religion and generally sympathetic to the British monarchy. By 1850, a substantial number of them were employed in white-collar, artisanal, and semi-skilled jobs. If relatively few lived in the city's better neighbourhoods — near the business district and on the Courtenay Bay side of the peninsula — they were otherwise widely scattered through the town. In contrast, the significant minority of Saint John's Irish households headed by Catholics included a disproportionate number of unskilled workers. Recent arrivals, refugees from the Irish famines of the 1840s, they were crowded into substandard housing in two small areas of the city: York Point in the northwestern corner of the peninsula, and the wharf area of Portland, which lay in the shadow of Fort Howe, directly across the Mill Pond (and Portland Bridge) from York Point.

The decade that produced this distinctive, divided ethnic geography was a tumultuous one for the residents of Saint John. A quickening tide of immigration turned into a flood between 1845 and 1849, when more than 30,000 newcomers, almost all of them Irish, disembarked in the port. Heavily tied to the timber trade, the economy of the city was buffeted during the 1840s by recurrent crises of confidence, price instability, and fluctuating demand precipitated by the British government's decision to dismantle the system of preferential tariffs under which the colonial timber trade had grown up. Prophecies of economic collapse were common. With the abolition of old imperial trading policies culminating in the repeal of the Navigation Acts in 1849, barriers to trade with the United States fell; artisans and farmers who produced for local markets saw their livelihoods jeopardized. Between 1840 and 1842, the number of tailors in the city fell by 85 per cent, the number of shoemakers by almost the same proportion. In the middle of the decade the newly formed Provincial Association carried a monster petition (with 2,500 signatures) to the colonial legislature requesting protection for the farmers, fishermen, and manufacturers of New Brunswick. Tariffs of 10 and 20 per cent were levied on a range of manufactured goods, but did little to stave off depression at the end of the decade; hundreds of artisans and labourers were reported to have left Saint John, some of them for the distant — and doubtful — prospects of California gold.

At the same time the city was deeply divided by a series of increasingly violent confrontations among its citizens.[8] In both 1841 and 1842, Irish Catholics clashed with members of the Orange lodges (which had begun to proliferate in city and colony) in the streets of Saint John. The first was a minor skirmish precipitated by the erection of a commemorative arch by the Orange Order; the second degenerated into a riot on 12 July, when several hundred Catholics gathered to jeer outside a house flying an orange-beribboned Union Jack. A year later, to the day, Catholics and Protestants clashed again, although there was no official parade to mark King William's victory at the Boyne. In 1844, Squire Manks, a prominent local Orangeman, shot and killed a Catholic Irishman in York Point, and nine months later the year ended with a week

483

of disturbances in which Catholics and Orangemen picked fights with "certain . . . obnoxious individuals." On the following St. Patrick's Day, celebrating Catholics were fired upon by Orangemen, and general rioting ensued. Two years of "calm" hardly broke the pattern. Through the 1840s, poverty and privation spurred robberies and assaults that the city's magistrates and watchmen were powerless to control. Then, on 12 July 1847, Orangemen followed a band playing sectarian songs into York Point. They were met with sticks and stones and driven back across the bridge to Portland. Adding firearms to their numerical reinforcements, they marched again into the Catholic ghetto. Shots broke out and the ensuing general mêlée ceased only with the calling out of the military at midnight. Through the weeks that followed, vengeance assaults and murders occurred in Saint John. In July 1848 the city was quiet as Orangemen celebrated the anniversary of their 1847 victory in Fredericton; but in 1849 violence erupted again, when Saint John Orangemen invited their provincial brethren to the city for a massive procession. Early on 12 July, heavily armed Orangemen from the parishes of Portland and St. John gathered to meet Carleton lodge members disembarking from the harbour ferry. Together they marched through York Point to Indiantown, where they would greet brethren from the Saint John Valley. Outnumbered by a jeering Catholic crowd, they suffered the humiliation of dipping their banners beneath a pine-bough arch at the foot of Mill Street. After the arrival of the valley men, however, they returned 600 strong to York Point despite the entreaties of city officials. Five hundred Catholics lay in wait. In a hail of bullets and bricks, possibly a dozen or more people were killed and hundreds wounded before the Orangemen emerged from York Point to continue their march through the city while troops, stationed in Market Square earlier in the day, moved in to seal off the Catholic ghetto and prevent further skirmishes.

Back of these confrontations lay a complex, changing grid of sentiment, affiliation, and power in the rapidly expanding Irish population of Saint John. Earlier, secular organizations that sought to advance the interests of all those of Irish descent in the city (such as the St. Patrick's Society established in 1819) were challenged by new, more aggressive, and increasingly partisan representatives of sectoral interests. Early in the 1840s the Saint John Sons of Erin supported Daniel O'Connell's vision of a Catholic Irish state, and there was an active Repeal Association in the city; a decade before, the Sons had celebrated St. Patrick's Day before a "harp surrounded by shamrocks and orange lilies entwined to form the motto United We Stand: Divided We Fall."[9] At the same time, Saint John Catholicism became more self-conscious with the consecration of New Brunswick's first Catholic bishop and the growth of ultramontanism in the province. On the Protestant side, the Orange Order expanded in tandem. As late as 1840, prominent citizens filled leadership roles in both the Sons of Erin and the emerging Orange movement.

Two years later, the so-called Protestant Conservative Association claimed to have enrolled 600 men at a single meeting. By 1846 the city had ten active Orange lodges, some with more than 100 members. For those who refused to join the secret, quasi-military Orange organization or to take a pew in St. Malachi's Church, newspapers provided a ready source of partisan opinion. The *Mirror* favoured recourse to violence if that were necessary to repeal the Union of Great Britain and Ireland; the *Liberator* denounced those Catholics who questioned clerical authority; and the *Loyalist* defended and promoted the Orange cause with skill and vigour.

With lawlessness, violence, and confrontation seemingly endemic in the 1840s, the Common Council of Saint John sought ways to control the city. At the beginning of the decade an eleven- or twelve-man "watch" was charged with keeping the city's night-time peace. There was no equivalent in Portland. Employed by the Common Council, but underpaid, understaffed, and overwhelmingly Irish Protestant, the Saint John watch was described by the Grand Jury as "lamentably inefficient either for the preservation of good order or the prevention of crime."[10] Nor, some claimed, were the elected aldermen, who served as magistrates for their wards, and their constables, much more effective in policing the city and apprehending criminals. Lamenting the dangers of being abroad at night, the editor of a leading city newspaper suggested that citizens follow the lead of New Orleans' residents, and carry weapons if they ventured out in the dark.[11] By the end of 1841, 400 or so of the city's freeholders (or their sons) had joined the Saint John Mutual Protection Association to patrol the streets. Through the following years the question of how best to police the city was hotly debated. Few doubted the need for improvements, but tough decisions about the distribution of power and control had to be made. At least the watch might be increased in size without infringing upon traditional prerogatives. But this posed its own problems. As the mayor recognized, recruits would have to be drawn from "classes whose feelings, sympathies and prejudices all make them partisans on one side or the other, and so increase in place of putting down the agitation."[12] There were proposals to appoint stipendiary police magistrates and police forces responsible to the province's Executive Council — but these foundered on the reluctance of the Saint John Common Council to relinquish powers. Other possibilities were mooted and rejected. Crime and violence continued. Then in 1847 the lieutenant-governor moved to secure establishment of a permanent police force under a stipendiary magistrate in Portland. Soon thereafter the Saint John council doubled the size of the watch. By 1849 a stipendiary magistrate with administrative responsibility for the police force had been appointed in Saint John. Constables' salaries were raised, and their number increased. Uniformed, armed, and accorded new status as part of a professional bureaucracy, they succeeded in bringing order to

485

the city's streets in the 1850s, as the economy improved and the influx of immigrants waned.

A Colonial Parable

When he wrote to the printer of the *St. Andrews Standard* in March 1840, Patrick Medley described himself as a settler in southwestern New Brunswick whose aim was to depict life in his neighbourhood "way back near the Bailey Settlement."[13] His was a neatly conceived tale. "Dennis Snug" and "Slouch" were its protagonists. The former was a diligent farmer who worked hard on his land, took care of his stock, and lived in comfort. "Slouch" was also a farmer — of sorts. Not content with devoting his every effort to the productivity of his back-country acres, he spent his winters "trivin away at all kinds of lumberin." To feed his oxen engaged in the heavy work of getting out timber, the hay from Slouch's farm was taken to the woods, while the cattle at home starved. "Between hauling provisions and river drivin, and the likes of that," there was precious little time to attend to the farmer's winter chores. "Nothin [was] done about fences except maybe putin up the old rotten poles." When spring came, very little seed was put in the ground. Overworked in the woods, Slouch's oxen were too weak to plough, so Slouch had to "wait till Dennis Snug got his work all done before he could borrow his oxen to plough a place for to rase a few prataes on, and then there was little or no manuer, and to tell the truth how could there be! for the poor starvin critters of cattle got nothin to ate but a trifle mornin and evenin and then turned out of doors in the cauld." To make matters worse, when the surveyor came to measure Slouch's logs, he found one was small, another "shakey," the next rotten; together they amounted to very little. Provisions consumed in the woods also turned out to be more costly than anticipated. At the end of the day Slouch had to sell some of his land to pay his debts.

A Pamphlet on Agriculture

Anxious for guidance, many an "improving farmer" of the mid-nineteenth-century Maritime colonies turned to one or more of the several texts on agriculture that circulated in the region before Confederation. In the libraries of local agricultural or scientific societies, or on the shelves of like-minded friends, there was plenty of choice. Many classics from abroad circulated in the colonies, among them the works of the renowned agricultural chemist J.F.W. Johnston (who paid an extended visit to New Brunswick in 1849), Henry Stephens, William Youatt, and Arthur Young. From the United States came Jesse Buel's *Farmer's Companion* and

486

Farmer's Instructor, as well as several books by Johnston's student John P. Norton. For those who preferred homegrown instruction there were, of course, John Young's *Letters of Agricola* — published in Halifax in 1822, yet full, according to J.F.W. Johnston a quarter of a century later, of "sound knowledge," "honest common sense," and "warm but prudent zeal" — and James Dawson's *Contributions toward the Improvement of Agriculture in Nova Scotia*, which shared (with Agricola's letters and similar works) the derivative quality reflected in its subtitle: *Compiled from Youatt, Johnston, Young, Peters, Stephens &c.* Less voluminous, but in its way no less important, there was also James Ross's *Remarks and Suggestions on the Agriculture of Nova Scotia.*[14]

Published by James Bowes and Sons of Halifax in 1855, this pamphlet claimed distinction. Its author was a practical farmer, the occupant of Faddan Farm on the flanks of the Rawdon Hills, east of Windsor, some fifty kilometres from the provincial capital. His remarks and suggestions, he was at pains to point out, were "not the fanciful productions of fireside speculation, but the sober conclusions at which . . . [he] had arrived, during a moderately long life entirely spent in the laborious pursuits of Agriculture." Critical of the gentlemen farmers enthused by Agricola, who conducted their farms with "ruinously profuse" expenditures, as well as of "imported knowledge" advanced without local experience, Ross sought to redeem Nova Scotia's agricultural reputation and to provide useful guidance for ordinary settlers who depended upon their farms for their livings.

487

Not surprisingly, much of his booklet offered very specific advice. On new farms, "fields should never exceed . . . four acres each"; the beginning farmer should establish a seven-field rotation as soon as possible, and then extend it to nine to give him thirty-six acres under cultivation. Because manure would be scarce initially, it should be applied to the potatoes, turnips, and other green crops; later, as stock numbers were increased, fields should be fertilized in sequence, with carefully collected barnyard manure applied at the rate of fifty-five cartloads per acre. With similarly detailed discussions of drainage techniques, of the range and value of labour-saving implements available to Nova Scotian farmers, and of the variety and productivity of the different types of land in the colony, this was a manual to which farmers with a bent for improvement, settlers perplexed by the challenges before them, and colonists in need of basic information might turn for help.

Those who did so would quickly recognize that Ross's intentions were larger than the simple provision of facts. His booklet sought to set the earnest farmer on a distinct and demanding course. Ross was firmly against display. Show was not evidence of prosperity. Economy in farming was a great virtue. "He who acts judiciously," he wrote, "will prefer commodious barns and stables for his crops and cattle to a fine house." More than this, Ross was critical of those archetypal Nova Scotian jacks-of-all-trades who divided their attentions among several pursuits as whim or weather dictated. Recognizing that necessity obliged the settlers of young countries to turn their hands to "a great variety of labour," and that this both encouraged the "versatility which is naturally inherent in man" and called "many of his best energies into action," he nonetheless insisted that such multifaceted activity was a "misallocation of energy" in most parts of mid-nineteenth-century Nova Scotia. In his mind there was no question that the "skillful farmer will . . . allot his time" and complete the jobs assigned to a particular period on schedule. On Ross's favoured farm, years and days were divided into three. As the seasons turned there came times for sowing, for cultivating, and for harvesting. This everyone knew; but Ross would allocate specific numbers of days to these tasks: planting should be done by the tenth or twelfth of June; no more than three weeks should be given to making hay; two weeks were sufficient for the grain harvest. So, too, it was important to observe the divisions of the day with undeviating attention, never permitting "the labours of one part to interfere with those of another." The various small jobs that demanded attention on every farm should be taken care of before 8:00 a.m.; between 9:00 and 1:00 and 2:00 and 6:00 the plough or cart should be yoked, and an acre of land ploughed or a certain quantity of manure carried to the fields. The evenings were for care of the stock and "those numerous small pieces of labour of which every careful farmer will find abundance in a well-regulated establishment." Holding himself as a model, Ross concluded: "Unless on very extraordinary occasions I never permit any thing to interrupt the completion of work so arranged . . . Knowing that there is a reasonable time for every part of my work, I never say, if I can get this or that done, but having made my arrangements, I endeavour to put them in execution in their proper season, and the man unaccustomed to systematic effort can scarcely form an accurate conception of the amount of labour which can thus be done, even by an individual."

488

A Year at New Rhynie

> Snowing
> The End of 1853
> The end of the year 1853
> Three times I say this is the End of
> the year 1853

So wrote John Murray in the journal of New Rhynie farm in the late evening of Saturday, 31 December 1853, after a day spent cutting firewood and cobbling shoes.[15] Day by day, without fail through the year, he had recorded the business of life on his 112-acre farm fronting on Haliburton Stream a mile or so from the town of Pictou. Home to a substantial family of six children ranging in age from fifteen-year-old James to toddler William, New Rhynie was one of the better farms in its county. Valued at £700 in the census of 1851, it had approximately sixty acres under the plough, its stock included twenty-two cattle, twenty-five sheep, and a couple of horses, and its occupants lived in a large new house some twenty or thirty yards back from the road that led from Pictou to River John and on to New Brunswick.

A native of Aberdeenshire in his sixtieth year, John Murray was a man of some standing in his community. Departing Scotland in his early twenties, he had spent two years in Halifax before migrating again to "Dominica" in the West Indies. Fourteen years later he had returned to Nova Scotia to purchase the Pictou property that he named after the parish of his birth and on which, in 1853, he had lived for almost two decades. Two years after his arrival in the county he married Scottish-born Jane Irving of Mount Thom, who was twenty years his junior, and three years later the first of their five sons was born. John Murray quickly began to play a significant part in local affairs. One of the overseers responsible for the deployment of statute labour on county roads during the late 1830s, he was also, in 1837, a founding member of the Pictou Agricultural Society, and a member of its committee of management in 1839. Through the next several years he played an active role in the affairs of the society, judging its ploughing matches, purchasing small quantities of the new seed wheats imported by the society, and taking several premiums for stock at its annual exhibitions. Late in the 1840s, Murray began to participate more fully in the life of Pictou's First Presbyterian Church, where he and Jane had been married; less than two years after he thrice bade farewell to 1853, Murray was elected an elder of the congregation and would discharge the duties of that office "with exemplary fidelity and conscientious devotedness" until his death in 1873. A neighbour of long-serving county sheriff John Harris, and an associate in church and agricultural society of many of Pictou's leading citizens, including merchants J.D.B. Fraser, William Matheson, John Yorston, and James Fogo, sometime provincial superintendent of education James W. Dawson, and others such as Israel Stiles, James Purvis, Henry Lowden, and E.M. McDonald, Murray was by wealth and connection among the loosely defined élite of the mid-nineteenth-century Pictou countryside.

489

With a productive farm and easy access to Pictou, John Murray made frequent trips to town, to sell his produce, to purchase the services of a blacksmith, or to acquire necessities and luxuries for his household. Trips to local mills and to neighbouring farms also provided opportunities for sales of small quantities of eggs, butter, potatoes, and so on. On average through the year such off-farm journeys occurred better than twice a week (although their incidence was highly variable and clearly seasonal). Not every such trip brought a sale or purchase. On occasions

Murray went to town to assess the state of the market (before deciding, for example, to slaughter one of his animals); on others he returned home with the goods he had hoped to sell. In the meticulous accounts of "Articals Bought" and "Articals Sold" that Murray kept in addition to his journal in 1853, however, sales are recorded on almost 100 days of the year; purchases of goods were just as frequent. In total, farm sales for the year amounted to almost £70, two-thirds of which was accounted for by butter (300 lbs.), meat (three carcasses of beef, eleven of pork, and twelve and a half of lamb), hides, skins, and flour. Total recorded expenditures, which amounted to less than £46, included the "Parsons Stypends," a stud fee for "Jets mare," school fees and supplies for the older children, taxes of £1.1.4, wages for servants Christy Ann (who left for Canada in May), "Ellonar Jane Carmicle," and May "Mattall" (each of whom stayed approximately a month in the late summer and early fall), and various sums for spinning, weaving, and the use of a threshing machine.

490

Omitted from the accounts, but just as central to the operation of New Rhynie farm, were the reciprocal exchanges that enmeshed John Murray and his family in a web of mutual interdependence and more or less formal obligations. Some of these were straightforward enough — simple payments in kind to neighbours in return for certain goods or assistance with a specific task. Thus on 6 June, Murray gave two bushels of oats to John Curry for his help in killing a pig. Some were acts of neighbourly charity, as for example when Murray took oats and wheat to the mill "for Alexander McKay that got his house burnt fully." Communal responsibilities — the three days of statute labour on the roads required of John Murray in June, or the less formal "breaking of roads" after major snowstorms — formed a third category of obligations. Others ensued from complex, continuing relationships, built perhaps on proximity and friendship, whose rich nuances it is now impossible to uncover. Favours were done, favours were returned; in a loose way there may have been some informal reckoning of the balance of obligation; but in the end it was the mutual identification of a general equilibrium of give and take (and perhaps in the case of youthful labour simply the chance of change and company) rather than the strict tally of shillings and pence that defined these associations. So "Elicksonder" Young helped the Murrays with their hay harvest on at least two late July days; two and a half months later, Murray's sons James and Mercer (aged thirteen) were across the line fence that marked the western boundary of New Rhynie "with the Ponie assisting J.W. Harres Shurref at Threshing."

Far more intricate, because it was close and continuing, was the Murrays' relationship with the mason, James Dawson. Dawson was a relatively frequent visitor to New Rhynie. On several occasions he came to borrow the Murrays' pony; in February he was on hand to help with the slaughtering of an ox; and in April he put his special skills to use in building a chimney on the east end of the Murrays' house. A few days after the chimney was finished, Murray got four loads of manure from Dawson, and took him one and a half bushels of potatoes. In June and September there was more manure from Dawson's stable for New Rhynie's fields. In rough return, Murray hauled several loads of sand for the mason, and in October delivered a load of cabbages to him. None of this figured in John Murray's accounts. But several years later his son John D. would marry James Dawson's daughter Jane.

For Jane (Irving) Murray, life on New Rhynie farm followed a rhythm very different from that of her husband during 1853. Because the New Rhynie journal is generally silent about the activities of the sabbath, we might assume that she and her children joined John in the family pew of the Prince Street church on most Sundays of the year. We might also assume that she accompanied her husband on a few of his numerous trips into Pictou and that she probably attended the funerals of Christopher Underwood and Jane Curry at his side. But in the journal record of market visits, trips to the mill, and the incessant round of work in the fields and barns, the only three references to Jane Murray note her absence from New Rhynie: in March, when she went to Cariboo; in mid-September, when she, James, and Mercer visited New Glasgow; and later that month, when she and John and six-year-old Charles visited her family in Mount Thom. By implication her place was in the home.

Although she had more help around the house than most of her rural counterparts, and was thus relieved of the chores of spinning and weaving, thirty-nine-year-old Jane Murray's days were full. With four children under the age of eight, the family had added a female servant to their household since the census of 1851, but on the departure of Christy Ann they were unable, for whatever reason, to retain regular help. Jane's mother came from Mount Thom for extended stays, through most of May and most of July. There were nevertheless innumerable chores to which Jane must have turned her daily attention, from cooking and washing to churning butter, tending the hens, ducks, and turkeys, caring for the garden, and putting up provisions. In the fall there were the additional demands of the harvest, with its long days, large appetites, and extra mouths to feed. Occasional visits from Mount Thom relatives broke the routine and brought news, as, presumably, did the enforced overnight stay of five travellers on their way to New Brunswick who were marooned by a heavy mid-April snowstorm. Still, Jane's was likely a life of closely circumscribed horizons, an existence structured (as was John Murray's) by a demanding routine of work, but lived within much narrower spatial limits and devoid (by contrast) of opportunities for casual social intercourse.

Mounts of Hope

Rambling among the Bluenoses in the summer of 1862, Andrew Lear-mont Spedon of Chateauguay County, Canada East, remarked upon the progress of Saint John, a "once dirty, insignificant hamlet" now "swallowed up by the magnificent city, whose wealthy and elegant edifices, designed by the lights of science and projected by the hand of industry . . . [stood] as the unmistakable evidence of . . . wealth and prosperity."[16] Especially worth remark were the 600-foot-long suspension bridge spanning the river just below the falls and, beyond it, in the parish of Lancaster on the West bank of the Saint John, the Provincial Lunatic Asylum — "a splendid building, having a front 300 feet in length with two wings projecting from the main body, each 160 feet long . . . " set amid forty acres of well-cultivated ground. Completed fourteen years earlier, on a site that was "a mere waste," it possessed, observed Spedon, "a commanding position, and a fine view of the city and surrounding country."

492

Six years before, Halifax's natal day had fallen into American humourist Frederic S. Cozzens' *Month with the Blue Noses*.[17] Special because it included a ceremony to mark the return of the 62nd and 63rd regiments to Halifax from the Crimea, this day of celebration in 1856 also saw a great procession with a particular and unusual purpose. As Cozzens described the "luckless pilgrimage," upon which "the jolly old rain poured down": "There were the 'Virgins' of Masonic Lodge No. - , the Army Masons, in scarlet; the African Masons, in ivory and black; the Scotch-piper Mason, with his legs in enormous plaid trowsers . . . the Clerical Mason in shovel hat, the municipal artillery; the Sons of Temperance, and the band. Away they marched, with drum and banner, key and compasses, BIBLE and sword, to Dartmouth, in a great feather, for the eyes of Halifax were upon them." Their purpose was to lay "the corner stone of a Lunatic Asylum," a feat accomplished by Lieutenant-Governor LeMarchant with the assistance of Alexander Keith, provincial grand master of Freemasons in Nova Scotia, New Brunswick, Prince Edward Island, and Newfoundland (who had participated in a similar ceremony in Lancaster, New Brunswick, in 1847) and framed by artillery salutes. Built on an eighty-five-acre site, the asylum, like the New Brunswick institution and the asylum and house of industry erected at Brighton on the York River a mile and a quarter from Charlottetown in the late 1840s, had a picturesque situation a short remove from the province's major city.[18] The building, occupied in 1857, though not completed for some years, was just as impressive as its Lancaster counterpart. Built of brick in the Georgian style, its central four-storey structure was flanked by wings of two and three storeys. Called Mount Hope, it stood on rising ground with noble views of village, farm, wood, and harbour. Its grounds, surrounded by a hawthorn hedge, included lawns, grain fields, a garden, and a nursery of trees and shrubs. Altogether it offered "very decided proof of provincial advance" and was a "credit to the country."

The similarities of site, situation, and structure among the lunatic asylums of the three colonies were not accidental. Although construction of these institutions spanned a decade and more, each was intended to provide a carefully designed and closely controlled environment in which the minds of the afflicted could be coaxed back to sanity. Advocates of new facilities for the accommodation of the insane in the colonies after 1835 borrowed heavily from the doctrines of American reformers, which depended, in turn, upon the pioneering works and writings of William Tuke in England and Philippe Pinel in France. By these lights, the location of hospitals for the insane "should not be near a large city, nor within half a mile of any street which is, or will likely become, a populous part of the town." The site "should be so elevated as to command a full view of the surrounding country." The asylum should be situated "where the scenery is varied and delightful." At best it should command views of "a navigable river bearing on its basin a variety of water craft, public roads thronged with the evidences of life and business, but not so near as to be exciting, [and] a populated and cultivated country." And its buildings, surrounded by ornamented grounds, "should be in parallel lines and as nearly in a right line as they can be."

According to current wisdom, both the external appearance and the internal economy of the asylum exerted an important corrective influence on its occupants. Work, play, and worship were the cornerstones of life in the institutions, but of these work was the most vital. It occupied the mind and stayed the patients' morbid, melancholy inclinations. It taught industry and fostered useful skills. And it drained the excess energy that produced frenzied behaviour. Field and dairy, threshing floor and woodpile, workshop and sewing room were "as indispensable as the strong rooms have been for the refractory in times past." But work was most useful if closely integrated into a highly organized routine. Authorities held little hope of improvement for the insane outside the asylum; "without system there . . . [would not] be success," reported the Nova Scotia commissioners appointed to consider construction of an asylum in 1846. But it was confidently anticipated that appropriately designed, located, and managed institutions offering "the most humane and enlightened treatment" would reduce "the numbers of Insane in proportion to the population."

493

Of Acadians and "People of Colour"

Two pictures open Frederic Cozzens' *Month with the Blue Noses*. These, asserts the author, are "the first, the only real likenesses of the real Evangelines of Acadia."[19] Travelling with the lines of Longfellow's poetry firmly in mind, and seeking to write an "Evangeliad," Cozzens was disappointed by his first glimpse of Chezzetcook, the largest Acadian settlement in the vicinity of mid-nineteenth-century Halifax. Its cottages were "not the Acadian houses of the poem, 'with thatched roofs and dormer windows projecting'" but comfortable homely looking buildings of modern shapes, shingled and unweathercocked. There were "no cattle visible, no ploughs, nor horses," but the boat builders and coopers who worked on the shore — very poor people with no milk, ale, or brandy for thirsty travellers — were "simple, honest, and good tempered enough."

At daybreak, a few women from Chezzetcook might be seen, fleetingly, in Halifax — the two who provided the frontispieces for Cozzens' book were among them, though, he took great pains to explain, it was no easy task to capture them on daguerrotypes, for "as soon as the sun is up [they] vanish like the dew." "A basket of fresh eggs, a brace or two of worsted socks, a bottle of fir-balsam" — these things comprised "their simple commerce." To sell them, they walked the twenty-two miles from Chezzetcook, and then returned on foot. This journey was "no trifle," agreed Cozzens, "but Gabriel and Evangeline perform it cheerfully, and when the knitting-needle and the poultry shall have replenished their slender stock; off again they will start on their midnight pilgrimage, that they may reach the great city of Halifax before daybreak."

Expressing surprise that a "mere handful" of Acadians should live so near the colonial capital, yet remain so isolated that their "village of a few hundred should retain its customs and language, intact, for generation after generation," Cozzens was quickly given an explanation for what he considered unaccountable. The reason was "because they stick to their own settlement; never see anything of the world except Halifax early in the morning; never marry out of their own set; never read — I do not believe [said his informant, that] one of them can read or write — and are in fact *so slow*, so destitute of enterprise, so much behind the age . . . "

"I went into the jury court," wrote J.F.W. Johnston in Halifax at the beginning of his North American tour in 1850, "where the author of *Sam Slick* was the presiding judge, and I was both surprised and pleased to see a perfectly black man sitting there in the box as a juror."[20] For Johnston this was evidence enough that in British North America "people of colour" enjoyed "the same political privileges as are possessed by other classes of her Majesty's subjects." Some of them — descendants of eighteenth-century immigrants to Nova Scotia, reported Johnston — were industrious owners of small farms. Yet most of those the traveller saw in the streets of Halifax were "acting as porters and in other humble employments." Generally they were spoken of "as indolent, as hanging about the towns and as suffering much from the severity of the winter."

494

Had Johnston done as other commentators of the period did and crossed the harbour to travel north and east along the Nova Scotian coast, he might have added detail to these fleeting impressions. "We saw," recorded one who passed this way in 1856,

> a log house perched on a bare bone of granite that stood out on a ragged hillside, and presently another cabin of the same kind came in view. Then other scare crow edifices wheeled in sight as we drove along; all forlorn all patched with mud, all perched on barren knolls or gigantic bars of granite, high up like rugged redoubts of poverty, armed at every window with a formidable artillery of old hats, rolls of rags, quilts, carpets and indescribable bundles, or barricaded with boards to keep out the air and sunshine.[21]

This was "a Negro settlement," inhabited, explained the traveller's guide, by "a miserable set of devils" who would not work. During most of the year, he continued, "they are in a state of abject want, and then they are very humble. But in strawberry season they make a little money and while it lasts are fat and saucy enough. We can't do anything with them; they won't work. There they are in their cabins, just as you see them, a poor woe-begone set of vagabonds; a burden upon the community; of no use to themselves, nor to anybody else."

495

Taking a Census

When on 9 April 1860, the legislature of New Brunswick passed "An Act to provide for taking a Census" (23 Vic. cap. 49), it followed a relatively well-worn path. Decennial censuses had been taken (by rather different methods) in the United States since 1790, and in England and Wales since 1801; increasingly detailed enumerations of New Brunswick had been conducted in 1824, 1834, 1840, and 1851; and there was growing conviction, in the middle of the statistical nineteenth century, that such exercises were valuable: census returns, readers of the Saint John *Morning Freeman* were informed, "afford much useful information, dispel many erroneous ideas, and form the basis of most important legislation."[22] Yet in April 1860 the precise nature of this "useful information" remained to be decided. According to the enabling act, the taking of the census meant "the taking an account of the Population and such other inquiries relative thereto, or relative to the Agricultural, Mechanical, Lumbering or other resources, or such other Statistics as the Governor in Council shall prescribe." Much remained to be done in deciding upon the categories of enumeration and in establishing the means by which data were to be collected. At minimum, appropriate geographical divisions had to be established, enumerators chosen and appointed, and rules and regulations and schedules drawn up, before the enumeration could be conducted and the results tabulated. Recognizing as much, the legislature provided that 23 Vic. cap. 49 should come into effect on 1 January 1861.

Still, it was March 1862, almost two full years after passage of the census act, before the results of that vaguely defined initiative were presented to the Assembly.

By the end of February 1861, the "schedule of enquiries" had been finalized. The census was to elicit information in six broad categories: population, buildings, agriculture, manufactures, minerals, and fisheries. The first and second schedules each included sixteen questions, the last a mere five; manufacturers were listed, according to their product, in a dozen subcategories and, as with minerals (of which six and a catch-all "other" were identified in the schedule), the name of the producer and the number of hands employed were to be recorded. Agriculture was by far the most complex category: because both the yields and acreages of crops were sought, a nominal thirty-five questions might entail, at maximum, forty-eight entries per farmer. Taken as a whole, this was a concerted effort to identify salient characteristics of the developing colony, far more ambitious than its 1851 predecessor. Still, the emphasis of this enumeration was economic. Schedule I sought information about religious adherence and "race," and listed the numbers of "sick and infirm," "deaf and dumb," "blind," and "lunatic and idiotic," as well as the births, marriages, and deaths of the preceding year. Schoolhouses and places of worship were counted in Schedule II, but in essence this census documented production.

In July, the provincial secretary began to appoint his census enumerators, one for each of the 160 census districts into which the province was divided. Paid at the rate of ten shillings per day, these were desirable appointments; unsolicited applications for the position of census-taker began to reach the governor in council in September 1860, almost a year before the census would be taken, and a further three dozen were received in the next ten months. But the great majority of appointments were by recommendation; hard on the heels of the New Brunswick election in June, the provincial secretary asked members of the Assembly for nominations from their districts. Hardly surprisingly, relatives, friends, and supporters were prominent among those whose names were forwarded. So, for example, Samuel Freeze and S. Nelson Freeze were appointed census-takers in Norton and Sussex parishes on the recommendation of George Ryan, MLA for Kings, who had married Miriam Freeze three decades earlier, and John Farris, MLA for neighbouring Queens, left no room for ambiguity in suggesting his brother-in-law, among others, to the provincial secretary: "I wish to inform you the men that I want appointed to take the census of the county . . . these are the men that I want appointed and please appoint the same."

According to the instructions given to the enumerators, the census was to be taken "with the least possible delay" and should "represent the state of the country as it existed on the 15th August." Yet there were delays and complications from the start. The enumerator for Upper

Queensbury, twenty-five kilometres upriver from Fredericton, was not appointed until 3 September; in at least one instance, an enumerator's blank schedules were sent to the wrong post office, where they lay for weeks; other census-takers found themselves without blanks of one or more schedules well into September; and at least three enumerators failed to realize that Schedule VI was on the back of Schedule V. Even when appointments were made and schedules provided on time, the enumeration was sometimes slowed by the difficulties of travel, illness, and the absence of people from their homes. One enumerator did not begin work until 20 November. Although slightly more than half the returns reached Fredericton by the end of October, eight remained outstanding at the beginning of the new year, and the last was not received until 23 January 1862. Generally, enumerators spent between twenty and forty working days at their task, but it required a full two and a half months for W.L. Prince to enumerate the inhabitants of Moncton. Such a protracted process clearly jeopardized the accuracy of the census: how many could recall, accurately, the state of their farms on 15 August, two or three months after that date? How many simply assumed the date of this enumeration to be the point of reference in reporting the number of births or deaths in the preceding year?

497

There were also problems in the formulation of census categories. Schedule III required a return of "Pork, slaughtered, pounds," but enumerators were not informed whether they should enter "the quantity to be slaughtered [in] the fall of 1861 or what . . . [they found to] have been slaughtered on the 15th of August . . . or what . . . [had] been slaughtered in the fall of 1860." Similarly, there was ambiguity in the "Hands Employed" column of the agricultural schedule: did it mean "Hired Laborer or all belonging to the Family able to work"? Those enumerators who sought clarification were instructed to enter their own estimates of "the number of males and females that could do the work if steadily/continuously employed." When the returns were finally compiled, many essentially arbitrary decisions had to be made. The numerous farmer-lumbermen and fishermen-farmers of the "Rank or occupation" columns had to be shoe-horned into one of the compilers' broad occupational categories: Professional, Trade and Commerce, Agricultural, Mechanics and Handicraft, Mariners and Fishermen, Miners, Labourers, and Miscellaneous. So inconsistent were the returns on "race" that this categorization was omitted from the printed tabulation. And the picture was little clearer in respect to religious affiliation. "Owing to misconception on the part of a large number of Enumerators," explained compilers Charles Everett and James Beek, "it became necessary in the abstract to include the Baptists and Free Christian Baptists in one body and the adherents of the Church of Scotland, Free Presbyterian Church and Presbyterian Church of New Brunswick in another body." By chance (or more confusion), Samuel Freeze of Kings County appeared on two enumerators' returns, his own and A.B. Smith's. The returns were completed a month apart, Freeze's at the end of December, Smith's in January. Both, of course, should have referred to the state of Freeze's household and farm on 15 August. By Freeze's own account he was an Episcopalian tavern-keeper with 30 improved acres on a 200-acre farm valued at $2,000, whose household included a servant, Matilda Hoggins, and two labourers, Richard Bigelow and John Golding. According to Smith, Freeze was an innkeeper and farmer and a member of the Free Baptist Congregation; 40 of his 200 acres were improved and his farm was worth $2,400; his servant was Emily Driscoll, he had only one labourer, Bigelow, and one of his sons, aged three by Freeze's count, was now four. Well might Everett and Beek have reflected at the end of their task on the fact that it was "without doubt, extremely difficult to devise such forms of schedule as will tend to procure accurate accounts of the several matters which it may be considered advisable to embrace in the Census Returns."

498

Greeting a Prince

On the morning of 30 July 1860, the weather in Halifax was "anything but agreeable"; "drizzling showers" fell from a grey sky. Yet almost all Haligonians were out of doors. In buoyant spirits they crowded the waterfront and lifted their voices in "thrilling and vociferous cheers which rang loud and long" as the Royal Squadron bearing His Royal Highness, Albert Edward, Prince of Wales, anchored in front of the city. Once ashore, the prince was mounted upon a "fine high-mettled charger" to take his place in a procession that included the Union Engine and Axe fire companies; the North British and Highland societies; the Charitable Irish Society; the St. George's Society; the Carpenter's Charitable Society; the African Society; the Sons of Temperance; the Volunteer Artillery and Rifle companies; and representatives of Her Majesty's forces. Through streets lined with soldiers and volunteers, thronged by thousands, and decorated with at least seventeen arches, as well as "transparencies," flags, banners, and evergreens, the parade followed the firemen, who bore "a trophy fifty feet high, surmounted by a colossal figure holding a hose-pipe," as "thirty five hundred school children, dressed in white and blue . . . sang the National Anthem." In the next three days, His Royal Highness reviewed troops, witnessed Indian Games (where he laughed "heartily at the ludicrous scene" presented by a war dance), mingled with zest at a grand ball attended by 3,000, watched displays of fireworks, and (it was said) "sat on his horse nobly and never flinched" when drenched by a sudden shower.[23]

Through early August, the Prince's grand progress continued, to Saint John, to Fredericton, and then to Charlottetown, before he took ship from the Island on the eleventh, bound for Quebec. In detail, the royal itinerary differed from day to day, but the general pattern of community responses to the Prince's visit was as constant as the weather was miserable. There were levees, balls, and formal presentations of addresses; "National and Trade Societies and Volunteers" — of which there were "great number" and whose members were invariably pronounced "a fine-looking body of men" — paraded; streets were decked with bunting and whole cities beautifully illuminated; bonfires were built, bells rung, and guns fired; "people cheered and cannon roared"; enthusiasm and joy knew no bounds, even when planned fireworks displays "were completely destroyed by the immense deluge of rain."

Testaments to colonial loyalty were everywhere. At the grand ball in the Provincial Building in Charlottetown, one of the "many beautiful devices" that graced the scene carried the message:

> Thy grandsire's name distinguishes this isle;
> We love thy mother's sway and court her smile.

499

In Saint John, 5,000 "fancifully dressed" and flower-bedecked school children added three verses to their rousing rendition of "God Save the Queen," ending:

> Hail, Prince of Brunswick's line,
> New Brunswick shall be thine:
> Firm has she been
> Still loyal, true, and brave
> Here England's flag shall wave
> And Britons pray to save
> A nation's heir.

And on 7 August, when His Highness returned to the mouth of the Saint John River en route to Windsor, Pictou, and Charlottetown, "a party of stalwart though gentle firemen" unharnessed the horse from his carriage and pulled " 'their dear little prince' as they delighted to call him," across the Suspension Bridge to the wharf.

Even Bishop Medley (who excused his decision to preach a stentorian sermon on the text of Romans 14, verse 12 — "So, then everyone of us shall give an account of himself to God" — to those who crowded into Fredericton's Christchurch Cathedral with the Prince on 5 August by claiming that he had "a higher mission to discharge" than simply to voice the "language of congratulation") could not entirely avoid the spirit of loyal adulation that gripped his fellow colonials. "When we look round among the nations of the earth and consider the past and present conditions of countries favoured with a fruitful soil and a more genial climate than our own," intoned the Bishop in the middle of a sermon full of eloquent warnings of the awful power of God's judgment,

> how inestimable is the price of our manly, rational, and constitutional freedom,
> how deeply should we cherish, how diligently should we guard and preserve,

the integrity of our limited monarchy, the nice balance of our respective estates and realms, the just and merciful administration of our laws and the various expressions of freedom and safe-guards against license with which a gracious Providence has endowed us. Our monarchy, our language, our religion are rich in all the associations of the past . . . Our sufferings and our joys are the common property of the empire. One year our bosoms throb with fear and sorrow at the massacre of Cawnpore, in another we hail the coming of a Prince, not, like his great ancestor reaping his youthful harvest of renown and blood inflicted upon a foreign land, but sent forth by the love of the Mother of our country, to consolidate the affection of a distant empire and to bring nearer in loyalty, love, and friendship the claims which science and commercial action have already united.

Little wonder that the young prince claimed to leave the lower provinces with "an endearing regard and sympathy" for their inhabitants, in whom he found "the love of freedom . . . combined with a deep-rooted attachment to the mother country, and the institutions in which we have all been nurtured."

500

Reflections

Good geographers, it has been said, have stout boots. By this simple maxim, those who lack these essential pieces of research equipment are, at best, pretenders to the proud title "geographer," "armchair" scholars bound to the comforts and limited horizons of their studies; at worst they are traitors to the traditions of their discipline, men and women of blinkered vision whose understanding is sorely compromised by their failure to range over reality in all its complex, interconnected variety. Now there is much to be said for field-work; no map, document, or census table can adequately convey the look of the land, and neither computer tapes nor dusty library stacks can illuminate the patterns and processes that shape places in quite the way that the physical exploration of a territory may do. But good boots do nothing to ensure good thoughts. Just as the traveller who embarks without information and curiosity is likely to arrive broadened in the beam rather than the mind, so the geographer who goes into the field without careful preparation — and thus unable to formulate well-grounded, if still tentative, explanatory hypotheses to account for what is seen — is likely to reap little intellectual reward from the effort. Whether cosseted tourist, wild rover, or well-shod field-geographer, in short, the strict empiricist is destined to return far richer in observations than understanding.[24]

By the same token, we cannot come to grips with the past simply by retrieving fragments of it. The facts do not speak very eloquently for themselves. Many and various as they are, the vignettes that comprise the bulk of this paper provide a terribly incomplete rendering of the diversity of land and life, economy and society in the mid-nineteenth-century Maritime colonies. Taken on their own they form a rather incongruent assortment of snapshots — so many grains of sand, as it were, arrayed on the page. True, their number could be multiplied, almost endlessly. But in the end such proliferation would only exacerbate the sense of discord, and bring us closer to the assay-master's dilemma. Still, none of this justifies retreat from our engagement with the variety, nuances, and textures of life as it was lived, for it is just such intricate, multifaceted reality that we must seek to grasp if we would justify and sustain the vitality of our inquiries. The challenge, for those who would make sense of places — be they travellers, geographers, or historians — is surely to confront complexity in ways that can heighten understanding instead of simply adding to our store of factual knowledge.[25]

In the broadest and most ambitious of terms this means approaching the places and people in whom we are interested with a curiosity honed on the whetstones of contextual understanding, pertinent comparison, and theoretical insight, in an effort to locate them on those "grand maps of history" that promise to illuminate and explain how the world came to be as it is.[26] In a more concrete, mundane, and certainly more circumspect vein, it means approaching the vignettes that comprise the body of this paper not as so many unconnected word pictures of a hopelessly disparate realm, but as a series of ethnographic jottings, each and all of which capture something of the assumptions, aspirations, and attitudes, the classifications and regulations, the constructions and constraints that gave shape and meaning to life in the settings that they encapsulate. Perceived thus, woven back into the rich contextual fabric of provincial existence from which they are drawn as so many threads, and considered against recent discussions of the sources of social power, the processes of state formation, and the development of modernity, these vignettes reveal much about ideology, society, and state in the mid-nineteenth-century Maritimes.[27]

501

In reviewing them in this light we recognize first the pervasiveness of what Max Weber called the ethos of modern Western capitalism — calculating, rational, "sober bourgeois capitalism" — in the rhetoric of the colonies.[28] In its emphases on time discipline and the division and specialization of labour, James Ross's pamphlet on agriculture embodies the confidence of the Victorian age in the benefits of system and the possibilities of improvement. In rural Nova Scotia, the doctrines of Adam Smith and the practices of English factory owners would redeem both the productivity and reputation of the colony's most important industry. With farmers committed to unwavering, persevering, and above all systematic effort, with their energies no longer dissipated by want of calculation and design, individual profits and colonial prosperity were regarded as certain. Doubters need only consider the plight of Nova Scotia's negro settlers, a plight produced, according to prevailing views, by the failure of these "vagabonds" to work as industriously as they ought. Nor was it incidental that work and system were touted as cures for insanity. That the judicious application of labour and capital to the myriad activities of the farm required careful assessment of inputs, outputs, expenditures, and returns escaped mention in Ross's pamphlet, but was well understood by other leading agricultural improvers of the period. Through books, newspapers, and county agricultural societies the importance of system and science, and with it the importance of detailed record keeping of the sort practised by John Murray of New Rhynie, was driven home to those colonial farmers who would listen.

Patrick Medley's parable of "Snug" and "Slouch" spoke in different tones to much the same project. At base its message was simple: those who "cleared land, developed their farms and lived on them were the real producers." Farming was a stable, enduring occupation; the well-managed farm was a "permanent enterprise oriented to constantly renewed profit." Lumbering was a precarious, adventitious speculation, a lottery attractive for its promise of "spectacular ad hoc killings." As "O'Leary," a stereotypical Irish ex-lumberman who appeared in a series of letters from Paul Jones to the *New Brunswick Courier*, had it, the lumber industry was "a game of haphazard."[29] Those who engaged in it might prosper temporarily, but in the end they would find "their farms mortgaged [and] their houses . . . tumbling down wid hardly a light of glass in them but stuffed wid ould rags hats and straw." By contrast, the settler who invested in "the bank of earth" would dwell in a "neat and smart" house, and his "ould wife" would always have "'siller' in her pouch."

By the middle decades of the nineteenth century these were well-established themes in the formal discourse of colonial life. Given full and self-conscious expression in Thomas McCulloch's "Letters of Mephibosheth Stepsure" early in the 1820s, they were reiterated time and again in vice-regal pronouncements, in the columns of the provincial press, in the apological observations of travellers, and in the reports and injunctions of the provincial and local agricultural societies, whose formation and continued activity rested upon the fiscal support of the three colonial governments.

Closely associated with these rhetorical and administrative attempts to influence the construction of aspirations and to entrench the ethos of rational capitalism in the colonies was a moral agenda. Here farmers and lumberers again found themselves the metaphorical centrepieces of a wider tableau. They were "as unlike each other *professionally* as . . . the black Ethiopian and the White European *personally*." Lumberers lived a "toilsome and semi-savage life"; they were men of "spendthrift habits and villainous and vagabond principles," strangers "to every rational enjoyment"; their work was demoralizing and debilitating; they "spent their winters in the woods and their summers lounging about the towns." "Happy" farmers, by contrast, followed "a pursuit of in-

502

nocence and peace," derived their pedigree from the patriarchs, and stooped to no man; their characteristically neat cottages surrounded by rich and cultivated land betokened their elect status. Farmers were snug by virtue of their sober and industrious characters; profane, sabbath-breaking, gambling lumberers were poor, indifferent, lazy, idle, loutish, and slovenly fellows — slouches indeed.

That these were thoroughly derivative arguments drawn from the ancients and the agricultural literature of Renaissance Europe mattered not a whit. Nor was it of much moment to those who used them that they caricatured — rather than characterized — the colonial scene. Their purpose was to cajole, not to describe. They sought to define a moral universe, to encourage particular forms of behaviour by portraying them as normal, appropriate, and acceptable, and to discourage others by representing them as inept and repugnant. Nor were they the only vehicles for the promotion of a sober, industrious, bourgeois mentality. The temperance movement, which flourished in the region during the 1840s and 1850s, was directed to similar ends.[30] Teas, picnics, processions, and excursions brought the sons, daughters, and cadets of temperance together, developed a sense of camaraderie among them, and heightened the visibility of their cause. In 1852, 9,000 people petitioned the New Brunswick Assembly for a ban on the import of alcoholic beverages; passed into law, their resolution imposed official prohibition on the colony through 1853, but quickly proved unworkable. "Conceived in tyranny," as Attorney-General Lemuel Allen Wilmot recognized, it soon led to "fanaticism and violence," and was rescinded in 1854.[31] Still, the temperance movement had revealed its political power and its moral authority in "urg[ing] upon other men, as good, such lines of conduct as are good for them, whether good or evil to the other people."[32]

Nowhere were the contours of the emerging social order more clearly revealed than in mid-nineteenth-century Saint John. Here the endemic disorder and ethnic rioting — and the responses of city officials to both — reflected and helped to frame prevailing convictions about the nature of colonial society. Orangemen in New Brunswick shared with their brothers on both sides of the Atlantic an unswerving loyalty to the Crown and a fervent belief in the superiority of Protestantism. Irish famine immigration was resisted because it was seen as one part of a massive campaign to establish the authority of the Vatican around the globe: "A great . . . conflict is at hand," warned the Saint John *Church Witness* in September 1853, "between Protestant Truth and Popery leagued with Infidelity."[33] And "Popery," it was alleged, had formidable troops on its side: "no one can deny," claimed the *Loyalist and Conservative Advocate*, "that the lower orders of the Roman Catholic Irish are a quarrelsome, headstrong, turbulent, fierce, vindictive people." One might as well attempt to "wash the Ethiope White" as to "tame and civilize" the native of Connaught and Munster. Time and again, editorials in the "Orange" press played on these themes. Almost every contemporary newspaper carried anecdotes and "Irish jokes" that mocked the Celtic newcomers as barbaric or ignorant or both. When economic arguments were added to these ethnic (or racial) slurs — for the destitute immigrants formed a large pool of cheap labour in direct competition with unemployed native labourers during the "hungry forties" — they formed a powerful goad to Protestant nativism. Fully half of New Brunswick's mid-nineteenth-century Orangemen were born in the colony; their membership in the Ulster-based organization was a measure of its attraction as a defender of Protestantism and British hegemony.

When Orange fervour spilled over into vigilante action and the provocation of conflict by ceremonial invasions of Catholic areas of the city, the processes of colonial justice generally ensured more lenient treatment of Protestant than Catholic participants. When the worshipful master of the Wellington Orange Lodge shot a Catholic Irishman in 1844, he was placed in protective custody rather than arrested and was quickly exonerated of any crime — on the claim of self-defence — by city magistrates. After riots in 1842, an all-Protestant force of special constables arrested several Irish Catholics who were subsequently convicted of rioting. Three years later, both Orangemen and Irish Catholics were arrested after fierce fighting in the streets, but the all-Protestant Grand Jury refused to bring their co-religionists to trial. And in 1849, when the clash of Orange and Green forces was widely anticipated, and the route of the Orangemen's approach to York Point was clear well in advance, garrison troops were deployed not to ward off conflict by barring entrance to the Catholic district, but to seal off the riot once the Orange parade had moved through the area, and thus to allow the procession to continue, unmolested, through the core of the city. Here the sentiments and convictions of Saint John's powerful majority were made clear: Irish Catholics were rejected for their cultural and religious differences; disparaged in the vigorous rhetoric of the day, they became legitimate targets of attack as the authorities turned myopic eyes on the provocative actions of vehement nativist Protestants.

Elsewhere, anti-Catholic ideology also ran strongly during the 1840s and 1850s. In Prince Edward Island, "Romanism" became an issue in the elections of the late 1850s, campaigns that turned on "a serious and most unaccountable misunderstanding" over the place of the Bible in the educational system and that produced an all-Protestant administration in a colony whose population was almost half Roman Catholic.[34] In Nova Scotia, "Popery" was seen as a threat to established values, denounced for undermining colonial attachments to Britain, and criticized as an obstacle to colonial improvement.[35] "The Popery of the [D]ark [A]ges . . . [was] the Popery of the present generation." Catholic countries published fewer books and had fewer miles of railway than Protestant ones; thus "Protestant areas nourished 'progress' while Catholic lands promoted ignorance and lethargy." As Scottish-born Free Church minister the Reverend A. King told a Halifax audience, and readers of his pamphlet *The Papacy: A Conspiracy against Civil and Religious Liberty* (1859), Catholic priests nipped "in the bud in the first appearance of . . . that assertion of liberty to think and act for himself, which belongs to man as a moral and accountable being." Little wonder, in this view, that the Acadians of Chezzetcook were "*so slow*, so destitute of enterprise, so much behind the age."

Beyond all this lay various, more or less explicit, "official" initiatives and strategies that worked to shape and confirm social and political identities in the three Maritime colonies. When colonial governments embarked on the construction of asylums for the insane, their actions implied more than the simple provision of facilities for the unfortunate. The new institutions were trophies in the landscape, placed there with appropriate fanfare to symbolize the progressiveness of their creators. They reflected the growing embrace of the asylum for treatment and correction, and were but single — if important — pieces in a larger mosaic of corrective institutions. By 1860, Halifax had a handful of penitentiaries, homes for juvenile delinquents, and rescue homes for prostitutes, as well as a poor's asylum and Mount Hope.[36] Saint John likewise, in the dozen years or so before the opening of its institution for the insane, built a cholera hospital, a county gaol/house of correction, an almshouse–workhouse–infirmary, and an emigrant orphan asylum. Nor did these developments lack significance as colonial initiatives. In 1845 the erection of a combined asylum for the three provinces was mooted but came to naught in the face of perceived "difficulties" and the conviction that "separate establishments for each of the provinces would be more desirable."

By the mid-nineteenth century, there was a growing consciousness, among their élites, of Nova Scotia, New Brunswick, and Prince Edward Island as separate communities. Peter Fisher published the first *History of New Brunswick* as early as 1825, and (according to D.C. Harvey, at least) Nova Scotians *as such* had begun to emerge between 1812 and 1835, when the record of literary achievement shows them "rubbing the sleep out of their eyes and facing their own problems, in various ways, but with discernment and energy."[37] Certainly there is no gainsaying the importance of T.C. Haliburton's writings, with their portrayal of the Nova Scotian as half-Yankee, half-English, the best product of his race.[38] And of Prince Edward Islanders, it was proclaimed in 1853: "removed as they are from all intercourse with the world, these narrow-minded Provincials really fancy themselves *par excellence* THE people of British North America."[39]

To a degree such identifications were fostered by the legislatures, sessions, courts, and grand juries that formed the essential infrastructure of these mid-nineteenth-century colonial "states."[40] Communities returned representatives to provincial assemblies and by and large were administered through courts of session composed of justices of the peace (appointed by the governor and council), who served, on paper, to extend the influence of central government into local affairs. Although the Common Council of Saint John, established in 1785, held legislative, executive, and judicial powers, and a few other towns and cities in the region gained autonomy through incorporation after 1840 — viz Halifax (1841), Fredericton (1848), and Moncton, Charlottetown, and Sydney (1855) — local government by sessions was the norm in both Nova Scotia and New Brunswick until the late 1870s. Moreover, many local officials — such as the supervisors of New Brunswick's great roads and the fire-wardens of Fredericton — were appointed by the lieutenant-governor in council.

That these officials and institutions were tentacles of the "state" is indubitable, but their strength in that capacity should not be over-estimated. Technically subject to central control, most justices enjoyed a great deal of freedom in their conduct of local business; many indeed fell sorely short of the demands of their offices. Furthermore, proposals for municipal incorporation in the 1840s were rejected as "en-croach[ments] upon the liberties of the people." Colonial politics re-volved, for the most part, around the local distribution of government largesse rather than the development of a coherent political ideology at the centre and its implementation on the periphery. For all the social importance of politics and its undoubted role in shaping the channels of power in individual communities, in the 1860s as in the 1830s it was essentially about local patriotism. As Joseph Howe noted in the 1840s, the central administrative duty of the government lay in "dispensing the patronage of the County"; the fact that assemblymen were consulted about the appointment of justices of the peace was "a substantial concession from the Crown to the People."[41] New Brunswick lawyer and assemblyman George S. Hill voiced similar conclusions more colourfully in arguing that "the Russians under Peter the Great thought the privilege of wearing long beards the essence of liberty — our people judge it to consist in the right of sending members to the Fredericton legislature to get their by-road and school money — all beyond is a *terra incognita*, which they have no curiosity to explore."[42]

The role of the colonial "state" in staking out a cognitive territory with which its citizens could identify and the severe limits to its effective authority were clearly revealed by New Brunswick's attempt to count its people in 1861. By mounting a census of the colony, the legislature instantiated conceptions of New Brunswick as a distinct and, in some sense, unitary territory; by establishing — whether *de jure* or *de facto* — the categories of that enumeration, it defined, however implicitly, those things that it held to be important; and, inadvertently or no, it served to blur distinctions (between Baptists and Free Christian Baptists, for example) that others held dear. Yet the fumbling, bumbling manner in which the census was conducted was a stark testament to the limits of central power. Without a professional bureaucracy to conduct the work, New Brunswick's authorities fell back upon traditional channels of patronage in selecting their census-takers; among the motley crew of enumerators that this produced, few, apparently, were cowed by instructions to complete their work with "the least possible delay." In its many confusions and inaccuracies the census of 1861 stands as a measure of the very real constraints limiting the totalizing power of the "state" in the mid-nineteenth-century Maritime colonies.

This is not to suggest that progress towards the development of more powerful and effective instruments of government was absent during the early nineteenth century. In both Nova Scotia and New Brunswick, the widespread disregard of statutes intended to control access to both land and timber was gradually restricted by refinement of both the relevant regulations and the means of their enforcement. So "squatters" and "trespassers" — official descriptions of those who claimed natural or moral rights of access to the abundant resources of the colonies — were evicted and fined, and provincials were increasingly forced to acknowledge the property rights legitimized by the state and to conform to the terms of lease and sale that it established for them.[43] So, too, the development of a uniformed, bureaucratic police force in mid-century Saint John marked a significant extension of the effective range of control by centralized authority. But always there remained, through the mid-century decades, large segments of colonial life that lay, to all intents and purposes, beyond the effective everyday sway of the colonial "state."

To throw these patterns into bolder relief, it is useful to consider the mid-nineteenth-century Maritime colonies against the framework of societal types outlined in the writings of Anthony Giddens.[44] Primarily concerned to provide a perspective on the novel world of the late twentieth century, Giddens identifies several salient contrasts between traditional (so-called class-divided) and modern states. Foremost among them are those related to the range over and intensity with which economic and political power can be exercised. In traditional states, Giddens avers, "the administrative reach of the political centre is low"; in modern ones it is extensive. So, traditional states have frontiers, modern ones borders. In the former, most people live lives shaped by the rhythms of the seasons, structured by personal contact, and bounded by the limits of domestic production; they occupy relatively closed pockets of local order that combine to make of any more extensive territory a cellular, segmented space within which ruling groups — concentrated in the cities — are generally unable to influence the day-to-day lives of their subjects, although they utilize their control of "authoritative resources" (generally military power) to pacify and extract surplus production from the people. In the latter, new technological and organizational means of overcoming

507

the barriers of time and space allow for interaction and the co-ordination of activities without face-to-face contact; here control over "allocative" (economic) resources is critical; there is a high level of internal order; government is polyarchic, in the sense that it is responsive to the preferences of the people; codes of conduct tend to be spatially extensive, patterns of production are highly integrated, and administrators characteristically have an enormous capacity to shape even the most intimate features of their subjects' daily activities. Fundamental to this transformation has been the growing power to bridge distances: by the development of writing and, later, other forms of information storage (which opened out the possibilities of social interaction beyond those provided by the evanescent spoken word and heightened the prospects of central surveillance); by the acceptance of money (which enlarged the radius of exchange beyond that possible in a barter economy and led eventually to the commodification of everyday life); and by improvements in the transportation / communication system that produced time–space convergence (or a reduction in the friction of distance — measured in terms of time or cost — between places) and thus facilitated system integration.

508

At base, this conceptualization rests upon an essential distinction between "the state" as an instrument of government or power and "the state" as "the overall social system subject to that government or power," or, in other words, between the state as an administrative apparatus and the wider "civil society" of which it is a part. Recognizing as much, we can associate the contrasts between traditional and modern societies sketched above with a decisive shift in the ability of the state, as instrument, to penetrate the civil realm. In traditional societies, substantial spheres of life "retain their independent character in spite of the rise of the state apparatus." Thus the classic contrast between city and countryside — markedly distinct places despite their interdependence. With the rise of the modern (nation-)state (as an administrative organ), however, the distinction blurs and then disappears; few areas or spheres of life survive beyond the administrative reach of the state, and those that do "cannot be understood as institutions which remain unabsorbed by . . . [it]."

Against this backdrop — barely and inadequately sketched as it is here — the contours of Maritime distinctiveness begin to stand out. On the face of it, the mid-nineteenth-century colonies embodied elements of both "traditional" and "modern" archetypes. There were close and finite limits to the administrative state's ability to penetrate and organize the colonial countryside; the provinces were a patchwork of social, ethnic, and religious fragments; relationships built on barter and reciprocity integrated people into local worlds; many colonists remained remote from central authority, unaware of many of its dictates, and prepared in many cases to transgress against others with scant fear of detection. Colonial administrators, on the other hand, sought to shape and circumscribe the lives of colonial residents by defining property rights, requiring road work, and administering justice. They took account of the colonists and their production. And they brought some of them under even more continuous surveillance in the asylums, prisons, and rescue homes that were built during these years. These colonies were, moreover, territories with clearly identified boundaries, capitalist societies without limitations on the alienability of property, and places in which steam trains and steam-ships had begun to revolutionize transport by 1840.

Yet it would be a mistake simply to classify the colonies, on this evidence, as "transitional." Rather than standing at some intermediate point in this conjectural framework, they form a special variant of the models identified by Giddens. Outliers of empire, they were neither modern states nor traditional "class-divided" societies. Shaped by the encounter of post-Enlightenment Europe with a remote and essentially undeveloped wilderness, they were peculiar hybrids. They exhibited many of the forms of the modern administrative state, but lacked final sovereignty and were poorly integrated, by virtue of their colonial status and the difficulties of communication and time–space co-ordination across their territories. Janus-like, they present different appearances to our gaze. Viewed from their political centres — Halifax, Fredericton, and Charlottetown — these small, and recent, colonial societies reveal many characteristics of the modern state and its substantial administrative apparatus. Courts and assembly chambers provided forums for the defence and advancement of civil and political rights; restrictions on the (male) individual's freedom to join organizations, express opinions, hold public office, and vote were few; newspapers offered several alternative sources of opinion, provided readers with a steady flow of "decontextualized" information, and broadened the sense of membership in a political community; political leaders competed for support; and elections determined the composition of governments. Statutes applied colony-wide; surveyors of land and timber were appointed far and near to administer regulations framed in the capitals; institutions were created to adjust "deviants" — criminal or insane — to the norms of "acceptable behaviour"; public accounts were subject to scrutiny; and colonial census statistics began to provide the basis of that "reflexive self-regulation" so essential to the administrative power of the state. Official documents, reports, and correspondence reveal much about these aspects of colonial administration. Their real effects upon the rank and file of colonists are considerably harder to assess, however.

It is clear, nonetheless, that to view these societies from their peripheries — from the fields, camps, dories, and kitchens of their predominantly rural populations — it is to see them in a very different guise. Through most of the region, the sanctions of religion and the local community were more important than formal policing in maintaining "order";[45] among people dispersed upon their farms, working

509

in the woods in small, informal groups, or fishing in crews of one or two, there could be little surveillance over production. Although the colonies were defined and bounded spaces, they were hardly "conceptual communities"; their people spoke different languages (the Gaelic language, reported mid-nineteenth-century visitors to Cape Breton, was more common there than in Scotland; French was the language of Acadian areas; Lunenburgers clung to their German; and so on); and they worshipped in different churches; in these relatively new-settled places there was little shared history (or, yet, symbolic historicity of the sort that would be provided by celebrations of the Loyalist centenary in the 1880s).[46] Even colonial government — the central structure of the administrative state — failed to override the profoundly fragmented and local character of colonial life; late in the 1850s, Lieutenant-Governor Sir Edmund Head of New Brunswick lamented the absence of "public" (communal rather than individual, colonial rather than parochial) interest among the assemblymen of his province.[47] However impressive in the colonial capitals, many tentacles of the administrative state reached but weakly into the provincial hinterlands. Distance — the formidable time and cost of movement in this new world — was a significant barrier to integration of the corners of colonial life with the centre.[48] Elaborated and refined through the first half of the century, the administrative apparatuses of these colonial states (which owed much to the model of the developing English nation-state) cast longer, more solid shadows in 1860 than in 1800 or 1830, but their penumbras were wide, and they clearly failed to blanket several facets of colonial life.

510

All of this leaves us, finally, with an important and infinitely elusive question: how was the world made sense of by inhabitants of these three colonies? If there is an easy yet broadly accurate answer it is, simply, differently. Consider, for example, the black juror in a Halifax courtroom noted by J.F.W. Johnston. To Johnston, and no doubt to many leading citizens of the province, his presence suggested the equality of political privileges in British North America. But the reality of circumstances in those nearby "redoubts of poverty" — described by other travellers — that were home to many of the colony's black residents surely conveyed a different message to those who lived in them. In the end we can do no more than allude to the range of this diversity and recognize its complex manifestations. Yet in doing so we demonstrate, again, the magnificent, messy complexity of this "naughty world," which can be illuminated but neither entirely boxed in nor completely explained by our theories of it.[49]

Consider first John and Jane Murray. In a very real sense, John Murray lived in several worlds. He was a colonial Briton, a resident of Nova Scotia subject to its statutes (which were themselves subject to disallowance in London), and entitled to participate in the election of a representative from his county to the House of Assembly in Halifax.

But quite how strongly he felt his provincial identity, and whether it was as important to him as his identification with Pictou, Hardwood Hill, the small cluster of people who lived between Haliburton Stream and the harbour, or the larger congregation of First Presbyterian Church, we will never know. Certain it is, though, that as a prosperous, improving farmer, John Murray was a participant in the agricultural enlightenment, rational, observant, and calculating in the operation of his farm. A devout Presbyterian, he gave a significant part of his time to the affairs of his church. A Scot in Pictou, he found his religious identity reinforced by his ethnic allegiance. Sometime overseer of district roads, prizewinner, judge, and committee member in the local agricultural society, he was both recipient and (indirectly) dispenser of small sums of provincial-government largesse. Connected firmly to the market, he was also enmeshed in a web of local exchange and mutual interdependence. For Murray these, surely, were not separable spheres. Life involved a complex set of obligations, involvements, decisions, and actions. It was centred *511* on New Rhynie and essentially local, despite the wider economic, political, and intellectual horizons to which many of Murray's contacts ultimately led. And how much more decisively was this true of Jane Murray. If the state impinged little on the everyday existence of her husband, its presence was almost entirely absent from hers. She was not, of course, entirely removed from its orbit. In denying her a vote because she was a woman, the statutes of Nova Scotia limited her participation in political life and circumscribed her ability to influence the exercise of political power in her society. In ascertaining how much butter and homespun she made in the course of a year, provincial authority "invaded" her home — but it did so in the person of a neighbour, and then only once a decade. So far as we can judge, and on balance, in short, "state activities, forms, routines and rituals" neither greatly affected the conduct of life nor played much part in the constitution of Jane Murray's identity (or that of countless other mid-century Maritime colonists).

Recognizing as much, we are drawn to conclude that religion was a far more powerful influence upon everyday life in these mid-century colonies than was the influence of the provincial "state." Consider, in support of this contention, Bishop Medley (who, on 5 August 1860, at least, was inclined to give credit to "gracious Providence" for the constitutional freedom enjoyed by New Brunswickers). Or contemplate those who marched behind Orange banners through the streets of Saint John in the 1840s. Remember those Catholic Irish who resisted Protestant incursions into their districts of the city. Recall those Presbyterians who objected to the failure of provincial census-takers to record accurately the nuances of their sectarian subdivisions. And bring to mind those Acadians of Chezzetcook whose houses clustered around their chapel. Generally closely associated with the tragic myths on which each of the ethnic/immigrant groups of the region built cohesion out of their pasts, religion was in some important sense the substance of the region's several mid-nineteenth-century cultures, the means of social integration through which collective memories were organized and constructed to form a far more effective basis for definitions of "us" and "other" than was provided by the still relatively feeble fabric of the colonial state.[50] Colonial politics in the mid-nineteenth-century Maritimes were what W.L. Morton described twenty years ago as "limited politics": for most people they were secondary to the more compelling preoccupations of religion, ethnicity, business, and survival.[51]

None of this is to deny the existence of what might broadly be called a "political culture" in the Maritimes. But as Greg Marquis has argued recently, this was a culture with its roots firmly planted across the Atlantic.[52] Editorial and other contributions to the provincial press and speeches made in councils and assemblies leave no doubt that "the plain language of [Maritime colonial] politics . . . came from English history." In relatively recently settled colonies, whose people were deeply divided by religion, ethnicity, and experience; whose economies were equally fragmented into distinct sectors (with different needs and interests); and which lacked the communications infrastructure to integrate scattered peoples into a single community, reference to an English past (and all that heritage stood for in terms of industrial ascendancy, imperial achievement, and political tradition) provided a ready symbolic touchstone for the majority of the region's peoples. They were — as they never tired of reiterating in protest at the reduction of British preferential tariffs or tenancy in Prince Edward Island — British *subjects*, their rights, implicitly, those secured by the Glorious Revolution of 1688, rather than the "rights of man" due "citizens."[53] Guard and cherish and preserve the integrity of "our limited monarchy," the "nice balance" of "our respective estates and realms," urged Bishop Medley. "Our sufferings and our joys are the common property of the empire."

Time and again, colonials looked to developments in seventeenth-century England to give meaning to their circumstances. For Orangemen the references were specific and the images vivid. Ritual, songs, and parades celebrated the Protestant Succession, revered William III, and commemorated the Battle of the Boyne. In lodge after lodge, members of the order learned a particular version of the past that made much of loyalty to the Crown and the need for eternal vigilance against popish intrigue. For others, the lessons of history were framed in less explicit and extreme terms, but they were nonetheless important. If the tenants of Prince Edward Island were downtrodden, they could find hope in "acquaintance with English history," which revealed "the historic tendency of the race to throw off oppression." When, in 1868, Canadian initiatives were seen to threaten Nova Scotian liberties, they were compared to the rule of the Stuarts. And seventeenth-century "Country Party" rhetoric, suspicious of centralized government, opposed to taxation, and attached to local custom, echoed through the pre-Confederation Maritimes.[54]

Of all this there was no better symbol than the monarchy, and there is no better indication of its significance in the Maritimes than the events surrounding the visit of the Prince of Wales to the region in 1860. Although Halifax publisher William Annand made available a collection of Joseph Howe's letters and speeches in 1858 — and in the next decade or so the "discontinuity" of (impending) Confederation spurred publication of documents pertaining to the early-eighteenth-century history of Nova Scotia, a new, political history of New Brunswick, and other reflections of a developing awareness of provincial distinctiveness — through the mid-century decades, "loyal, true, and brave" Maritimers courted Victoria's smile.[55] To the degree that they did so, the "colonial state" remained in some important sense a limited state.

And so, in the end, there is perhaps no better way of making sense of this kaleidoscopic picture than with a simile. Recognizing with historical sociologist Michael Mann that social life is built upon the overlapping skeletons of state, culture, and economy, but that these are very rarely congruent, we might conceptualize the frameworks that gave pattern to life in the mid-nineteenth-century Maritimes as the parts of a wheel.[56] In this view, London appears as the ideological and emotional hub of the "political culture" of the Maritimes; the colonial state becomes the rim, linking people together and exercising certain authority over them, but generally in a weak and provisional way — peripherally; and religion, ethnicity, and locality, coupled with those quintessentially Victorian doctrines of system, sobriety, thrift, and toil (especially on the land), assume the position of spokes, giving shape and form and structure to the everyday lives and identities of most colonists.

513

NOTES

This paper represents a first effort to bring to bear on the Maritimes some of the literature and ideas that have been the focus of discussion among human geographers at the University of British Columbia for some time now. I am indebted to that group — especially Trevor Barnes, Derek Gregory, Cole Harris, Dan Hiebert, David Ley, and Gerry Pratt — for the lively, challenging, but always pleasant and thought-provoking exchanges we have shared. Although I gladly give credit for the stimulus I have derived from these fine colleagues, I also absolve them of responsibility for the particular interpretive paths I have chosen. My debt to the Killam Program of the Canada Council is substantial. Their award of a 1988-90 Research Fellowship provided the vital freedom to read and think that lies behind this essentially experimental paper. I also thank Marlene Shore and Ramsay Cook for their comments; and I am grateful to Greg Marquis for providing me with a copy of his unpublished paper "In Defence of Liberty."

[1] For more extended comment on the development of the region, see G. Wynn, *Timber Colony: A Historical Geography of Early Nineteenth Century New Brunswick* (Toronto: University of Toronto Press, 1981); W.S. MacNutt, *The Atlantic Provinces: The Emergence of Colonial Society, 1712-1857* (Toronto: McClelland and Stewart, 1965), 213-70; and W.M. Whitelaw, *The Maritimes and Canada before Confederation* (Toronto: Oxford University Press, 1934), 7-37. J. Gwyn, "'A Little Province Like This': The Economy of Nova Scotia under Stress, 1812-1853," *Canadian Papers in Rural History* 6 (1988), 192-225, is the most important recent work.

[2] Some of these cleavages were explored, for example, in A.H. Clark, "Old World Origins and Religious Adherence in Nova Scotia," *Geographical Review* 50 (1960), 54–72; A.H. Clark, *Three Centuries and the Island* (Toronto: University of Toronto Press, 1959). For a general review of the ethnic-diversity theme, see G. Wynn, "Ethnic Migrations and Atlantic Canada: Geographical Perspectives," *Canadian Ethnic Studies/Études Ethniques au Canada* 18 (1986), 1–15.

[3] The point is evident in almost all general surveys of the region's history and/or geography. In addition to the works noted above, see G. Wynn, "The Maritimes: The Geography of Fragmentation and Underdevelopment," in L.D. McCann, ed., *Heartland and Hinterland: A Geography of Canada* (Scarborough, Ont.: Prentice-Hall, 1987), 174–246; J.G. Reid, *Six Crucial Decades: Times of Change in the History of the Maritimes* (Halifax: Nimbus Publishing, 1987). For quotations in this paragraph, see A.G. Bailey, "Creative Moments in the Culture of the Maritime Provinces," in his *Culture and Nationality: Essays by A.G. Bailey* (Toronto: McClelland and Stewart, 1972), 49; R.C. Harris and J. Warkentin, *Canada before Confederation* (Toronto: Oxford University Press, 1974), 169; MacNutt, *Atlantic Provinces*, 268; C. Bruce, "Words Are Never Enough," in R. Cockburn and R. Gibbs, eds, *Ninety Seasons: Modern Poems from the Maritimes* (Toronto: McClelland and Stewart, 1974), 62. See also on this theme G.A. Rawlyk, ed., *Historical Essays on the Atlantic Provinces* (Toronto: McClelland and Stewart, 1967), 1; D.C. Harvey, "The Heritage of the Maritimes," *Dalhousie Review* 14 (1934), 29; J.M. Beck, "The Maritimes: A Region or Three Provinces?" *Transactions*, Royal Society of Canada, Series 4, 15 (1977), 301–13.

[4] C.G.D. Roberts, "Tantramar Revisited," in D. Pacey, ed., *The Collected Poems of Sir Charles G.D. Roberts* (Wolfville, N.S.: Wombat Press, 1987), 78–79.

[5] That the focus of what follows is more heavily upon New Brunswick and Nova Scotia than Prince Edward Island reflects my own disproportionate knowledge of the mid-nineteenth-century Maritime colonies as much as the relative thinness of good work on the Island (which the researches of Ian Ross Robertson, in particular, are at long last beginning to overcome). Throughout, I have kept footnoting to the major works upon which particular sections of my discussion depend; fuller details of the sources of quotations are generally available in these works.

[6] Rather than proclaim a renowned model or deep philosophical roots in justification of the rather idiosyncratic organization of this paper, I trust that the point of this structure, and the travel/exploration metaphor — neither of which is entirely irrelevant to the wider purposes of this essay — will become evident in its conclusion. If any single piece of writing shaped my initial experimentation with this form it was perhaps my recollection of K.S. Inglis, "Ceremonies in a Capital Landscape: Scenes in the Making of Canberra," *Daedalus* (Winter 1985), 85–126, although a second reading of it, after I had embarked on my own piece, left me disappointed that it fell short in the task of interpretation.

[7] T.W. Acheson, *Saint John: The Making of a Colonial Urban Community, 1815–1860* (Toronto: University of Toronto Press, 1985) offers a full and careful treatment of most of the material summarized here; as elsewhere in this essay, emphases and arguments are not necessarily those of the works from which information is drawn.

[8] Acheson, *Saint John*, 92–114, is complemented here by S.W. See, "The Orange Order and Social Violence in Mid-Nineteenth-Century Saint John," *Acadiensis* 13 (1983), 68–92.

[9] Acheson, *Saint John*, 100.

[10] Ibid., 219.

[11] *New Brunswick Courier* (Saint John), 9 Jan. 1841.

[12] Acheson, *Saint John*, 224.

[13] This tale can be found in the *St. Andrews Standard*, 14 and 21 Mar. 1840, in the form of two letters from Patrick Medley to the Printer.

[14] J. Ross, *Remarks and Suggestions on the Agriculture of Nova Scotia* (Halifax, 1855); further discussion of this literature and its place in the agricultural improvement movement can be found in my "Exciting a Spirit of Emulation among the 'Plodholes': Agricultural Reform in Pre-Confederation Nova Scotia," *Acadiensis* 20:1 (1990), 5–51.

[15] J. Murray, "New Rhynie" Farm Diary and Accounts, 1853. Public Archives of Nova Scotia, MG100, vol. 194, no. 16.

[16] A.L. Spedon, *Rambles among the Bluenoses; Or, Reminiscences of a Tour through New Brunswick and Nova Scotia* (Montreal: J. Lovell, 1863), 59–65.

[17] F.S. Cozzens, *Acadia: Or a Month with the Blue Noses* (New York: Derby and Jackson, 1859), 33.

[18] The fullest treatment of the development of these asylums is in H.M. Hurd, ed., *The Institutional Care of the Insane in the United States and Canada*, 4 vols. (Baltimore: Johns Hopkins University Press, 1916–17), 1:427–97; 4:37–119, 203–18. D. Francis has summarized much of this material in his "The Development of the Lunatic Asylum in the Maritime Provinces," *Acadiensis* 6 (1977), 23–38.

[19] Cozzens, *Acadia*, iv.

[20] J.F.W. Johnston, *Notes on North America, Agricultural, Economical and Social*, 2 vols. (Edinburgh: Blackwood, 1851), 1:7.

[21] Cozzens, *Acadia*, 40–41.

[22] This discussion derives in large part from A.A. Brookes, " 'Doing the Best I Can': The Taking of the 1861 New Brunswick Census," *Histoire Sociale/Social History* 9 (May 1976), 70–91.

[23] Details of the royal progress can be found in the appropriate provincial newspapers, but there is a full and effective summary in *The Tour of H.R.H. The Prince of Wales through British America*

and the United States, by a British Canadian (Montreal: J. Lovell, 1860), 25-51, from which most of this discussion is derived.

24 I think back here to one of the distant roots of my discipline, to the work of Grove Karl Gilbert, geologist and explorer of the American West, who argued over a century ago (in "The Inculcation of Scientific Method by Example," *American Journal of Science*, 3rd ser., 31 [1886], 286-87) that "The great investigator is primarily and pre-eminently a man who is rich in hypotheses"; that "A phenomenon having been observed, or a group of phenomena established by empiric classification, the investigator invents an hypothesis in explanation"; and that "In the testing of hypotheses lies the prime difference between the investigator and the theorist. The one seeks diligently for the facts that may overthrow his tentative theory, the other closes his eyes to these and searches only for those which will sustain it." For more on Gilbert, see R.J. Chorley, A.J. Dunn, and R.P. Beckinsale, *The History of the Study of Landforms; Or the Development of Geomorphology*, vol. 1 (New York: J. Wiley and Sons, 1964), 546-72.

25 The arguments of this paragraph have, of course, been well made several times; for examples old and new, see M. Bloch, *The Historian's Craft* (New York: Vintage Books, 1953), and B. Bailyn, "The Challenge of Modern Historiography," *American Historical Review* 87 (1982), 1-24.

26 I borrow the "grand maps" phrase from D. Gregory, who has used it in his forthcoming "'Grand Maps of History': Structuration Theory and Social Change." As Gregory points out, it was used originally by Theda Skocpol to refer to the recovery of sociology's historical imagination.

27 The essential books in the rapidly growing literature against which the vignettes are considered in the pages that follow are M. Mann, *The Sources of Social Power*, vol. 1, *A History of Power from the Beginning to A.D. 1760* (Cambridge: Cambridge University Press, 1986); P. Corrigan and D. Sayer, *The Great Arch: English State Formation as Cultural Revolution* (Oxford: Blackwell, 1985); A. Giddens, *The Constitution of Society: Outline of the Theory of Structuration* (Cambridge: Polity Press, 1984); A. Giddens, *A Contemporary Critique of Historical Materialism*, 2 vols.: vol. 1, *Power, Property and the State* (London: Macmillan, 1981); vol. 2, *The Nation State and Violence* (Berkeley: University of California Press, 1987). Here, I trust, some of the reasons for the travel metaphor around which this paper is built begin to come into focus. In a sense this essay is intentionally double-edged. Its first purpose is to look at the Maritimes through the lenses provided by the above-mentioned literature; this, so to speak, involves a certain "rummaging in the hold of history" in an effort to rearrange some of the cargo borne by Clio's large Maritime fleet. Its second is to respond to the challenge of "evolving an appropriate style, a mode of discourse" capable of wedding evidence and theory, of transcending the dualism between "analytic" and "narrative" history, and of dealing coherently with space, time, agency, and structure; on this challenge, see P. Abrams, "History, Sociology, Historical Sociology," *Past and Present* 87 (1980), 3-16. It may well be that I hit neither target squarely here, but it does seem important that the effort to ground Giddens' ideas (in particular) be made, because in much of his writing "particular contexts are used more as passive illustrations than as active explanations," N. Thrift, "Bear and Mouse or Bear and Tree? Anthony Giddens's Reconstitution of Social Theory," *Sociology* 19 (1985), 621.

28 M. Weber, *Economy and Society* (Berkeley: University of California Press, 1978), 1:100-105; Corrigan and Sayer, *Great Arch*, "Afterthoughts," 182-85; Giddens, *Nation State and Violence*, 123-33. Through this first section of the conclusion, I attempt to realize, in a way, Giddens' claim that theoretical concepts (such as those of structuration theory) are "sensitizing devices," and that being theoretically informed does not mean "always operating with a welter of abstract concepts." Thus such "theorizing" as there is here is deliberately unobtrusive; given the focus of the workshop for which this paper was written, it draws most explicitly from Corrigan and Sayer, *Great Arch*.

29 Paul Jones to the Editors, *New Brunswick Courier*, 5, 12, and 26 Jan., 2, 9, and 16 Feb., 2 Mar. 1850. This item and several of those discussed below are considered at greater length in my "'Deplorably Dark and Demoralized Lumberers': Rhetoric and Reality in Early Nineteenth Century New Brunswick," *Journal of Forest History* 24 (1980), 168-87.

30 The temperance movement is treated in J.K. Chapman, "The Mid-Nineteenth-Century Temperance Movement in New Brunswick and Maine," *Canadian Historical Review* 35 (1954), 43-60, and in E.J. Dick, "From Temperance to Prohibition in 19th Century Nova Scotia," *Dalhousie Review* 61 (1981), 530-52.

31 W.S. MacNutt, *New Brunswick, a History: 1784-1867* (Toronto: Macmillan, 1963), 351. Further thought on this general theme is provoked by J. Fingard, "The Relief of the Unemployed Poor in Saint John, Halifax, and St. John's, 1815-1860," *Acadiensis* 5 (1975), 32-53.

32 J.S. Mill, cited in Corrigan and Sayer, *Great Arch*, 129.

33 See "Orange Order," 79-80.

34 I.R. Robertson, "The Bible Question in Prince Edward Island from 1856 to 1860," *Acadiensis* 5 (1976), 3-25; see also his "Party Politics and Religious Controversialism in Prince Edward Island from 1860 to 1863," *Acadiensis* 7 (1978), 29-59.

35 A.J.B. Johnston, "Popery and Progress: Anti-Catholicism in Mid-Nineteenth Century Nova Scotia," *Dalhousie Review* 64 (1984), 146-53.

36 J. Fingard, "Jailbirds in Victorian Halifax," in P.B. Waite, S. Oxner, and T.G. Barnes, eds, *Law in a Colonial Society: The Nova Scotia Experience* (Toronto: Carswell, 1984), 89-102.

37 D.C. Harvey, "The Intellectual Awakening of Nova Scotia," *Dalhousie Review* 13 (1933), 1-22.

38 T.C. Haliburton, *The Clockmaker; Or the Sayings and Doings of Samuel Slick of Slickville*, 1st-3rd

515

Ser. (London: R. Bentley, 1839–40); nor indeed should the role of Joseph Howe be overlooked: see J.M. Beck, *Joseph Howe* (Kingston: McGill-Queen's University Press, 1982), vol. 1, *Conservative Reformer, 1804–48*, and vol. 2, *The Briton Becomes Canadian, 1848–73*.

[39] Robertson, "Bible Question," 3.

[40] S. Oxner, "The Evolution of the Lower Court of Nova Scotia," in Waite et al., eds., *Law in a Colonial Society*, 59–80; J.M. Beck, *The Evolution of Municipal Government in Nova Scotia, 1749–1973* (Halifax, 1973); H. Whalen, *The Development of Local Government in New Brunswick* (Fredericton, 1973), 11–39.

[41] J. Howe, *Lord Falkland's Government* (Halifax, 1842), 2–7.

[42] Cited in G. Marquis, "In Defence of Liberty: 17th-Century England and 19th-Century Maritime Political Culture," paper delivered at the Atlantic Canada Studies Conference, Edinburgh, 1988, 9.

[43] For examples see G. Wynn, "Administration in Adversity: The Deputy Surveyors and Control of the New Brunswick Crown Forest before 1844," *Acadiensis* 7 (1977), 49–65; S.J. Hornsby, "An Historical Geography of Cape Breton Island in the Nineteenth Century" (Ph.D. diss., University of British Columbia, 1986), 82–91.

[44] Sorely limited though it is, this discussion attempts to edge towards an exploration of the "fundamental *reciprocity* between theoretical constructs and empirical materials," an approach that some have found wanting in Giddens' writing; see, for example, N. Gregson, "Structuration Theory: Some Thoughts on the Possibilities for Empirical Research," *Environment and Planning* D 5 (1987), 73–91; for the reciprocity quote, see D. Gregory, "Thoughts on Theory," *Environment and Planning* D 3 (1985), 387. The most relevant of Giddens' writings to the discussion that follows is *Nation State and Violence*, but see also *Power, Property and the State* and *Constitution of Society*. The extensive literature commenting on Giddens' project is also useful in explicating its evolving pattern; in a mountain of material, see, for example, A. Callinicos, "Anthony Giddens: A Contemporary Critique," *Theory and Society* 14 (1985), 133–66; H.F. Dickie-Clark, "Anthony Giddens's Theory of Structuration," *Canadian Journal of Political and Social Theory* 8 (1984), 92–110; D. Gregory, "Space, Time and Politics in Social Theory: An Interview with Anthony Giddens," *Environment and Planning* D 2 (1984), 123–32; *Theory, Culture and Society* 1 (1982), 63–113, a "symposium" on Giddens; and D. Held and J.B. Thompson, eds., *Social Theory of Modern Societies: Anthony Giddens and His Critics* (Cambridge: Cambridge University Press, [1989]).

[45] For another variant, see J. Fingard, "Masters and Friends, Crimps and Abstainers: Agents of Control in 19th Century Sailortown," *Acadiensis* 8 (1978), 22–46.

[46] M. Barkley, "The Loyalist Tradition in New Brunswick: The Growth and Evolution of an Historical Myth," *Acadiensis* 4 (1975), 3–45.

[47] A.R. Stewart, "Sir Edmund Head's Memorandum of 1857 on Maritime Union: A Lost Confederation Document," *Canadian Historical Review* 26 (1945), 406–19.

[48] For some discussion of the geography of movement in the region during these years, see J.S. Martell, "Intercolonial Communications, 1840–1867," Canadian Historical Association, *Report* (1938), 41–61, and G. Wynn, "Moving Goods and People in Mid-Nineteenth Century New Brunswick," *Canadian Papers in Rural History* 6 (1988), 226–39.

[49] The allusions here are to M. Mann's observation that "societies are much messier than our theories of them," in *Sources of Social Power*, 4, and B. Kennedy's critique of rigid explanatory frameworks, especially those derived from physics, in "A Naughty World," *Transactions of the Institute of British Geographers* NS4 (1979), 550–58.

[50] For further comment on this idea, see S.F. Wise, "God's Peculiar Peoples," in W.L. Morton, ed., *The Shield of Achilles: Aspects of Canada in the Victorian Age* (Toronto: McClelland and Stewart, 1968), 36–61.

[51] W.L. Morton, "Victorian Canada," in *Shield of Achilles*, 311.

[52] Marquis, "In Defence of Liberty."

[53] Or, to provide another, earlier, example on the same lines, Joseph Howe's trial in 1835 is seen to have convinced him that "his countrymen would not secure the rights of Englishmen . . . through newspaper writing alone." J.M. Beck, "'A Fool for a Client': The Trial of Joseph Howe," *Acadiensis* 3 (1974), 27–44.

[54] Marquis, "In Defence of Liberty," has more on these matters; any serious sampling of the contemporary press throws up examples.

[55] W. Annand, *The Speeches and Public Letters of the Honorable Joseph Howe*, 2 vols. (Boston, 1858); T.B. Akins, *Selections from the Public Documents of Nova Scotia* (Halifax, 1869).

[56] Mann, *Sources of Social Power*, ch. 1.

516

Trader McPherson and his family: country-born, or English-speaking mixed-bloods. Photograph by the International Boundary Commission, 1873.

Were the English-speaking mixed-bloods and French-speaking métis of what is now western Canada separate and mutually hostile groups? Or were they friendly and closely linked with each other?

Irene M. Spry, "The Métis and Mixed-Bloods of Rupert's Land before 1870"

Topic Thirteen

Rupert's Land

By the mid-nineteenth century, a new and distinct society was evolving in Rupert's Land, the vast area of the North American continent controlled by the Hudson's Bay Company. In particular, a distinct and active society had taken shape at the junction of the Red and Assiniboine rivers, known as the Red River colony. By 1850, the colony had a population of more than 5000 mixed-bloods and several hundred white settlers. Of the mixed-blood population, roughly half were English-speaking Métis, or "Country-born," the descendants of the British fur traders and their Native wives. The other half were French-speaking Métis, the descendants of the early French fur traders and their Native wives.

Did these two groups of mixed-bloods create a cohesive society, or did they co-exist in a state of friction? Frits Pannekoek provides one answer in "The Flock Divided: Factions and Feuds at Red River." He argues that religion split the colony into two hostile factions. Fellow historian Irene Spry reaches the opposite conclusion in "The Métis and Mixed-Bloods of Rupert's Land before 1870." She argues that the two groups of mixed-bloods were united by their common aboriginal heritage. Any division that existed was class-based, relating to the occupational differences between the farmers and the hunters or plains traders.

Gerald Friesen's early chapters in *The Canadian Prairies: A History* (Toronto: University of Toronto Press, 1984) offer a good overview. D.N. Sprague looks at the Red River colony in the mid-nineteenth century in his introduction to *The Genealogy of the First Métis Nation: The Development and Dispersal of the Red River Settlement, 1820–1900* (Winnipeg: Pemmican Publishers, 1983), compiled by D.N. Sprague and R.P. Frye. Frits Pannekoek provides a full study of Red River society in *A Snug Little Flock: The Social Origins of the Riel Resistance, 1869–70* (Winnipeg: Watson and Dwyer, 1991). J.R. Miller reviews the secondary literature on the Red River colony in "From Riel to the Métis," *Canadian Historical Review* 69 (1988): 1–20. This study complements Frits Pannekoek's "The Historiography of the Red River Settlement, 1830–1868," *Prairie Forum* 6 (1981): 75–85. Important essays on the Métis appear in Jennifer S. Brown and Jacqueline Peterson, eds., *The New Peoples: Being and Becoming Métis in North America* (Winnipeg: University of Manitoba Press, 1985). Gerhard Ens provides an interesting insight into Red River society in his "Dispossession or Adaptation? Migration and Persistence of the Red River Métis, 1835-1890," Canadian Historical Association, *Historical Papers* (1988), 120-44. Other references are listed in the bibliographical section of Topic Two, "The Nature and Impact of the Fur Trade." Excellent maps of the Red River and all of Rupert's Land appear in Richard Ruggles, *A Country So Interesting: The Hudson's Bay Company and Two Centuries of Mapping, 1670-1870* (Montreal and Kingston: McGill-Queen's University Press, 1991).

Dale R. Russell provides a detailed review of the location of First Nations' groups on the territory that is now the Prairie provinces in *Eighteenth-Century Western Cree and Their Neighbours* (Hull, Que.: Canadian Museum of Civilization, 1991). This monograph can be supplemented by James G.E. Smith's "The Western Woods Cree: Anthropological Myth and Historical Reality," *American Ethnologist* 14 (1987): 434-48. Interesting excerpts from early travellers' accounts of what is now Western Canada appear in Germaine Warkentin's edited work *Canadian Exploration Literature: An Anthology* (Toronto: Oxford University Press, 1993). Hugh A. Dempsey's two biographies, *Crowfoot* (Edmonton: Hurtig, 1972) and *Big Bear* (Vancouver: Douglas and McIntyre, 1984), introduce the Plains Indians in the mid-nineteenth century. A recent study of Big Bear's tribe is John S. Milloy's *The Plains Cree: Trade, Diplomacy and War, 1790 to 1870* (Winnipeg: University of Manitoba Press, 1989). The Blackfoot experience is reviewed by John Ewers in *The Blackfeet: Raiders in the Northwestern Plains* (Norman, Okla.: University of Oklahoma Press, 1958).

A comparative description of two nineteenth-century families, one from the Red River colony and one from Prince Edward Island, is provided by J.M. Bumsted and Wendy Owen in "The Victorian Family in Canada in Historical Perspective: The Ross Family of Red River and the Jarvis Family of Prince Edward Island," *Manitoba History* 13 (1987): 12-18.

The Flock Divided: Factions and Feuds at Red River

FRITS PANNEKOEK

The settlement of Red River changed in the late 1850s and early 1860s. From a relatively quiet backwater, it became the confluence of the northward frontier of the American Republic and the western frontier of the

From *A Snug Little Flock: The Social Origins of the Riel Resistance, 1869-70*, by Frits Pannekoek (Winnipeg: Watson and Dwyer, 1991). Reprinted with permission.

Canadian colonies. In 1858 there were only a few buildings outside Upper Fort Garry at the forks of the Red and Assiniboine; but within ten years there was a drugstore, grist mill, gun shop, harness shop, bookstore, butcher shop, tinsmith, photography studio, carriage shop, two saloons, and a newspaper office. Steamboats, the *Anson Northup* (1859) and the *International* (1862), even attempted, although without great success, to navigate between Moorhead in Dakota and Red River.

Much of this change was due to a major influx of Canadian and American immigrants. Even before the immigration, however, Red River was changing of its own accord. During the six years before 1849, 1,232 new people were added to the colony. This growth was internal, rather than the result of immigration, since only twenty-eight families arrived in Red River between 1849 and 1856. This increase placed a substantial burden on the means of livelihood: the river lot and the hunt. Because the family lands could no longer be divided indefinitely among the numerous sons, as had been the tradition, many moved to the plains along the Assiniboine River. Others moved to the United States or into the western interior along the Saskatchewan River at places such as Victoria in what is now Alberta and Prince Albert in present-day Saskatchewan.

521

There were four major groups in the Red River settlement. The most significant were those of mixed-blood heritage. In 1871 the total population was 11,400. Of these 5,740 were Métis or Catholic French/Cree-speaking mixed bloods. These lived in the parishes south and immediately west of the junctions of the Red and Assiniboine rivers. The 4,080 Protestant and English-speaking mixed bloods lived in the parishes largely north of the junction of the two rivers and after 1854 around Portage la Prairie. It has been argued by some that the Indian blood tied these two groups together as one family. While that would seem common sense, in fact there was little unity between the two groups during the Riel Resistance. Indeed, the English-speaking Protestant mixed bloods, who proudly called themselves Halfbreeds, were at odds with Riel. Why? It would seem that the two groups should be of single mind. When the events in the decade preceding the resistance are examined closely, the influence of the Reverend Griffiths Owen Corbett in creating a split between the Halfbreeds and Métis is evident. This bizarre clergyman with his petty politics and religious bigotry managed to effectively divide the mixed-blood community into its Protestant and Catholic halves. Coincidentally he reinforced the Halfbreeds' anti–Hudson's Bay Company and pro-Imperial sentiments. When Riel attempted to appeal to the mixed bloods for unity in 1869 he would fail. Corbett had been too effective. The Canadians, with their anti-Catholicism and Imperial bombast, would find supporters in the Halfbreed parishes of Red River.

In the 1850s, at the same time that there were significant demographic and social changes in Red River, both Canada and Great Britain began to show a peculiar interest in the future of Rupert's Land. Red

Glenbow Archives, Calgary/Cat. no. 6383.2.

Upper Fort Garry from the south, from a watercolour by William Napier, mid-nineteenth century.

River, of course, chased every rumour of change and there were as many factions as there were alternatives. In the early 1860s Crown Colony status seemed most likely. The Duke of Newcastle, colonial secretary from 1859 to 1864, favoured the creation of a Crown Colony in Rupert's Land as a connecting link between Canada and British Columbia, all of which would eventually comprise a British North American federation. He was supported in his stand by substantial Canadian and British railroad and financial interests. But Red River was only vaguely aware of what was happening in the Colonial Office and at Hudson's Bay House, London. As rumour increased of Imperial support for the Crown Colony status after 1859, it seemed apparent to Red River that change of some sort was inevitable. The settlement hoped that it would be immediate. No firm plan was offered, however, by either the Canadian government, the Imperial government, or the Company. Confusion remained the only political certainty.

The agitation for change in Red River's political status started in 1856-57 in Canada and filtered through to Red River via the *Globe*, the Toronto newspaper read by many of the informed and literate. James Ross, Halfbreed son of Alexander Ross, historian and former sheriff, expressed the prevailing sentiments:

> We ought to have a flood of immigration to infuse new life, new ideas, and destroy all our old associations with the past, *i.e.*, in so far as it hinders our progress for the future — regular transformation will sharpen our intellects, fill our minds with new projects and give life and vigour to all our thoughts, words and actions.

The first petition for change came in June of 1856 from the Protestant clergy. Their demands were moderate, including only restrictions on the importing of alcohol and the introduction of the elective principle in the Council of Assiniboia. They did not wish the removal of the Councillors, only that vacancies be filled by election, and that the settlement be divided for that purpose into districts.

No serious pro-Canadian agitation developed until a few months later. On 26 February, William Dawson of the Dawson-Hind expedition, sent by the Canadian government to assess the fertility of the Assiniboine-Saskatchewan country, gave a lecture, "Canada Past and Present." Interest was high and the governor, the clergy, and some of the Company's active and retired gentlemen attended. There was, however, no open political movement at the parish level. Interest turned into open agitation only when William Kennedy returned to Red River on 7 February 1857 after a number of years of anti-Company agitation in Upper Canada. Like his relative Alexander Kennedy Isbister, who had been instrumental in the presentation of the 1847 petition to the Imperial Parliament, he was an embittered ex–Hudson's Bay Company employee.

From March to May, a number of meetings organized by Kennedy were held in the Kildonan school house and in the neighbouring Halfbreed parishes. An elder of the Presbyterian Church, Kennedy ingratiated himself with the Kildonan settlers, especially Donald Gunn, one of its leading members, and Rev. John Black, who had strong Canadian sympathies. The Company was severely criticized and annexation to Canada advocated. When Governor F.G. Johnson, who had succeeded Adam Thom as Recorder, attended one of the first March meetings, he was requested to leave. As a result of the meetings the younger settlers displayed their open sympathy with Kennedy and signed his petition for union with Canada. The older settlers, still believing that a certain deference was due the Company, hesitated to make a decision.

In May, Kennedy convinced some in Red River — the exact parishes cannot now be known, but probably they were those between the Upper and Lower Forts — to elect five members, including himself and Isbister, to serve in the provincial legislature of Canada. Kennedy for his part had allowed reports to spread that he was a representative of Canada. While he publicly denied these reports, he left the vague impression that he had to do so because he was a secret agent. The five members were actually sent off, but Kennedy had second thoughts about the legality of the proceedings. He chose to recall the delegates when he heard that Captain John Palliser was arriving at the head of the British expedition to the North-West and that he might have some concrete instructions for Red River's future.

This spelled the effective end of Kennedy's agitation. By the winter of 1858–59, the semblance of unity that momentarily had existed in Red River disintegrated under the force of new pressures. Rev. G.O. Corbett, arriving in the spring of 1858, was the cause.

Corbett, of the Church of England, was a contentious and difficult individual, spending much of his life quarreling with his bishops, the Hudson's Bay Company, his fellow clergymen, and the Colonial and Continental Church Society, which sponsored him. While not a charismatic leader, he was something of a gadfly with strong convictions about the rights of Englishmen, and even stronger convictions that these rights were being denied to the Halfbreeds by the tyranny of the Hudson's Bay Company and the Church of Rome. A popular and effective speaker, his views fell on the fertile ground of the political and social unrest in the late 1850s and early 1860s. Corbett aroused the Halfbreeds and directed their energies against both the Company and the Catholics, convincing them that their future lay within a Protestant Crown Colony firmly affixed to the British Empire. Crown Colony status seemed to guarantee an extension of the full rights and privileges of the British constitution and offered a fellowship of English-speaking people, under the loose British nationalism with which the Empire had always anointed its subjects.

524

When in 1862 Corbett found himself the centre of an unsavoury scandal and defended himself by identifying it as a Company plot to discredit him and his movement for Crown Colony status, feelings grew so intense that Red River split into two factions. The pro-Company group, who believed Corbett guilty, included strangely enough the Métis, who disliked his anti-Catholicism. The anti-Company group, who were the most fervent Crown Colony advocates, believed him innocent, and were composed principally of the Protestant English-speaking Halfbreeds. In the end the two groups verged on open war.

Rev. G.O. Corbett despised the Catholics, considered them barbarians, and used the newspaper to propagandize his sentiments. In a community torn by dissent and rife with status tensions, Corbett's anti-Catholicism was absorbed as eagerly as his anti-Company rhetoric. He taught the Halfbreeds that because they were Protestant they were superior to the Catholic Métis of Red River.

Corbett felt that the British liberties of Red River, a Protestant colony of a Protestant queen, were succumbing to the tyranny of the Church of Rome. Corbett, seeing, as he imagined, too many examples of the growing power of the Papal "anti-Christ," felt it his duty to warn of the dangerous consequences. His greatest concern was William Mactavish, the Governor of Assiniboia. Mactavish had married a Catholic daughter of Andrew McDermot in Saint-Boniface Cathedral, and in the following years baptized his children into the Catholic faith. All of Protestant Red River had considered the marriage an insult to Bishop Anderson of the Church of England, who had apparently expected to conduct the ceremony. Corbett was convinced that, with the governor a virtual Catholic, and with seven Catholics against seven Protestants on the Council of Assiniboia, "the balance of power [was] with the Pope of Rome."

When an official report of the legislative proceedings of the Council of Assiniboia referred to the Catholic Bishop as "Lord Bishop," Corbett had what he considered proof. Legally only Bishop Anderson, who wanted no part in the controversy and who unsuccessfully cautioned Corbett to moderate his stand, was entitled to the title. Only Anderson had been appointed by "Her Most Gracious Sovereign the Queen." Corbett considered use of the title for Bishop Taché both "insidious" and "unconstitutional." When the Council of Assiniboia continued its folly by passing a law forbidding all government activity on Catholic holidays, there was no longer any doubt in Corbett's mind — Red River had fallen to the Pope.

These religious tensions that had split the society asunder tended to centre on the settlement along the Assiniboine River, but their impact was felt throughout the whole of Red River. The *Nor'Wester* newspaper was particularly effective in ensuring that the controversies of the 1860s would continue to exacerbate social, religious, and racial divisions. Every imagined slight was well publicized and exaggerated. In 1860, for example, a heated battle waged between Henry Cook, a Halfbreed Anglican schoolmaster, and François Bruneau, one of the principal Métis, over the quality of Protestant and Catholic education. So virulent did Protestant sentiment become that James Ross, rather moderate in his anti-Catholicism and at times a restraining influence on Corbett, fearing a loss of Protestant business, refused on first request to publish an obituary and eulogy for Sister Valade, one of the first and most venerated sisters at Saint-Boniface. When in August 1861 Ross dared to publish an article suggesting that the Halfbreeds were superior to the Métis, the elder Riel visited Ross and "*il lui a chanté une chanson, la chanson du juge Thom.*" In other words Riel threatened Ross's life, just as he had done years earlier to Adam Thom, the first Recorder of Rupert's Land, who had voiced similar bigotries.

525

An understanding of these religious divisions is critical to the understanding of the crises which faced Red River as Corbett commenced his agitation for Crown Colony status in 1858. In December of 1858 Corbett and his cohort, Reverend John Chapman of St. Andrew's parish, the Company's chaplain, circulated their first petition advocating Crown Colony status. Corbett believed that annexation to Canada would place Red River "altogether in the hands of a subordinate power." He felt that if Red River were a Crown Colony, it would become the civil and commercial hub of the West, with its own elected Assembly — a feature that was central to all of Corbett's arguments. He believed that "whatever advantages Canada enjoys, apart from her natural position, she derives these from her connection with England as Crown Colony." He damned the Company for its alleged inability to maintain law and order and its obstruction of material progress. Both would be remedied, he believed, when Rupert's Land assumed its rightful place in the Empire as a Crown Colony.

Provincial Archives of Manitoba/N4793.

James Ross: Opting for Canada.

Donald Gunn, William Kennedy, and James Ross, the leaders of the Canadian party, vigorously opposed Corbett and circulated a counter-petition advocating annexation to Canada. At this point, William Kennedy and James Ross, both Halfbreeds with strong British Canadian connections, still felt Canada offered the best future — and Crown Colony status would offer continued domination by the Company. Both petitions were sent to the House of Lords, where they were ignored.

Corbett's agitation for political change assumed an even wider and more popular basis in the early 1860s. On 30 October 1862 the Council of Assiniboia petitioned the British government for troops in the face of a rumoured Sioux attack, a feared American invasion, and the growing local disaffection. The Council's petition made the rounds of Kildonan, Headingley, and St. Paul's parishes, gathering some 1,183 signatures. As the petition was circulating, Rev. G.O. Corbett, Rev. John Chapman, the former Company chaplain, and James Ross, who joined Corbett's party when it became apparent that Canada was no longer interested in annexation, circulated a counter-petition condemning the Council of Assiniboia and the Company, and requesting Crown Colony status. Ross also refused to publish the Council's petition in his newspaper, the *Nor'Wester*. The counter-petitioners claimed that troops were not so much needed as a more efficient government. There was considerable confusion as to who supported which petition, since many attempted to delete their signatures from the Council's petition in order to support the counter-petition. The Company, as a disciplinary action, deprived Ross of his public offices of sheriff, governor of the gaol, and postmaster. Both petitions were ultimately sent to the Colonial office, where they too were ignored.

The Council's petition was seen by the aroused Halfbreeds as a plot to crush their efforts to throw off the yoke of the Hudson's Bay Company. Consequently, when the lurid details of Corbett's presumed attempts to induce the miscarriage of his illegitimate child by Maria Thomas struck like a thunderbolt from nowhere, his protested innocence and his accusations of a Company conspiracy appeared completely credible to the Halfbreeds. After all, earlier that winter Maria had been persuaded in front of a magistrate to deny the rumours of an affair. The denial had been acceptable but when Corbett was jailed on the abortion charges and refused bail, in spite of precedent for granting such a request, the Halfbreeds were certain that the Company had resurrected a charge which had no substance and which had already been dismissed. Many were convinced that Maria Thomas's father, having pressed the charges, and Thomas Sinclair, the magistrate, were in the Company's pay. In effect, the question became not one of Corbett's guilt or innocence, but rather one of support for, or opposition to, the Company's supposed tyranny.

527

Corbett was charged with violation of 24 and 25 Victoria ch. 100, passed in 1861. It states that:

> Whosoever, with intent to procure the miscarriage of any woman, whether she be, or not be with child, shall unlawfully administer to her or cause to be taken by her, any poison or noxious thing, or shall unlawfully use an instrument or other means whatsoever with the like intent, shall be guilty of felony, and, being convicted thereof, shall be liable at the discretion of the Court to be kept in penal servitude for life, or for any term not less than three years, or to be imprisoned for any term not exceeding two years, with or without hard labour, and with or without solitary confinement.

In his charge to the jury on the ninth day of the Corbett trial, which was published on 12 May 1863 in the *Nor'Wester*, Recorder Black felt that he ought to elaborate on the law:

> I may state that the law regarding this crime has within the last 35 years, undergone various changes. At one time the law made a distinction between acts in which the attempt was made on a woman quick with child and one not quick with child. Previous to the passing of the statute under which the prisoner is indicted that which regulates this offence made it material whether or not the woman was pregnant. By a subsequent statute 7 Wm. IV, and Vic. ch. 85, that distinction was done away with, and there were some slight differences and alterations, which were embodied in the statute under which the prisoner is indicted.

The outcome of the case was not the result of this new "mass" concern with abortion that swept America and Great Britain in the 1850s through to the 1880s. Prior to the 1850s and 1860s life was construed to begin with "quickening" or "stirring in the womb," and abortion before "quickening" was not a felony. Corbett attempted to abort Maria Thomas's and his alleged child after the fourth month. The scurrilous *Nor'Wester* indicated that Corbett, whom they supported, had been unjustly accused of "murder." Nevertheless the abortion was not successful, and despite Maria Thomas's explicit testimony, Corbett was jailed for six months, an extremely light sentence given the damning evidence.

The trial commenced on Thursday, 19 February 1863, continued for nine days, and heard sixty-one witnesses. Rev. John Chapman described the shocking trial to the secretaries of the Church Missionary Society:

> What a spectacle . . . Mr. Corbett in one box & Maria Thomas a young girl of 16 years in the witness box, with her babe in her arms which she declares is Mr. Corbett's and whose embryo life he is charged with attempting to destroy by means of medicine, instruments &c.

528

The Bishop appointed Archdeacon James Hunter to conduct an independent church investigation and before the court made its own decision, he pronounced Corbett guilty as charged. The court then followed suit. Corbett refused to recognize the jurisdiction of the Court of Assiniboia, or to accept its decision, and continued his accusations of a conspiracy on the part of the Company and the Church of England. For the rest of his life, he insisted upon his innocence and he was supported in his view by many in Red River. Some indeed were prepared to resort to arms.

The first incident occurred at nine o'clock on the morning of Saturday, 6 December 1862. In response to the denial of bail for Corbett, one hundred and fifty to two hundred persons, principally from Headingley but with groups from St. James, St. John's, St. Paul's, and St. Andrew's, arrived at Fort Garry. Governor Alexander Grant Dallas, Simpson's unpopular successor from the Pacific coast, favoured a hard line, but when riot was threatened he allowed Corbett to address the crowd. Corbett, for his part, encouraged all to continue their fight for justice. Finally James Ross and ten to twelve of the more respected members of the crowd persuaded Dallas that he would have to allow bail or suffer the consequences.

The second instance of mob rule occurred during the third month of Corbett's six-month sentence. On 14 April the Halfbreeds submitted a petition signed by 552 of their number, requesting a pardon for Corbett. Six days later, after Dallas had refused to consider their pleas, Corbett was freed by force. The Governor responded by arresting James Stewart, the mixed-blood schoolmaster of St. James parish school and a ringleader in the agitation.

Governor Dallas, suspecting a plot to free Stewart, called upon twenty-five Métis and twenty-five Halfbreeds to defend the prison. Only five of the Halfbreeds would serve; the Métis, who had no use for "Corps Bête" as they called the anti-Catholic Corbett, appeared in full force. At ten o'clock on the morning of 22 April twenty-seven protestors, headed by William Hallett and James Ross, demanded an interview with Dallas. When Dallas refused to meet the insurgents, Ross sent a petition demanding the liberation of Stewart, the cessation of all discussion over the Corbett affair, and the removal of Sheriff McKenney, a supporter of the Company, who had replaced Ross. Dallas again refused, and Ross rode into the prison compound and liberated Stewart. It is evident that had Dallas not forbidden a violent confrontation, the Métis would have used force to stop Ross, which in turn would have triggered *une guerre civile* between Protestant and Catholic Red River. Fortunately, most of the twenty-five Métis were from Saint-Boniface and under the control of the moderate François Bruneau. Had *les hivernants*, the Métis boatmen and tripmen living at Cheval Blanc and Saint-Norbert, been involved, as had been initially intended, blood would most certainly have been shed. The "winterers" were hardly as charitable as their brethren at Saint-Boniface and after a long season of winter confinement would have been ready to flex their muscles in a Red River spring in order to teach the insolent Protestants a lesson. Consequently nothing was done to recapture Stewart.

529

The situation had deteriorated to such an extent that late in May, one month after the Corbett escape, John Bourke, who had been involved in all three acts of defiance, and James Stewart went so far as to attempt the organization of a "Provisional Government." It is probable that Corbett himself was involved. Stewart suggested that Headingley, St. James, and Portage la Prairie should secede from Red River and form an independent colony subordinate only to the Crown. Ultimately the proposal failed to gain sufficient support, and the conspirators, who lacked apparent organizational ability, gave up the plan.

Within the colony generally the jail breaks were followed by an increased questioning of Red River's traditional leaders. Even after suspension by both the Bishop and the Colonial and Continental Church Society, Corbett returned to Headingley, where he assumed his clerical duties. The Bishop sent replacements, including William Henry Taylor from the neighbouring parish, but the congregation locked the church doors and refused admittance to any clergyman save Corbett. In a ludicrous climax to the issue, John Chapman, formerly Corbett's ally, finally forced the door and preached to an empty church. The Bishop then ordered Corbett to leave Rupert's Land by 1 September 1863, but even in this he was defied and Corbett remained in the settlement until the following June.

In the neighbouring parish of St. James the persecution of the pro-Corbett group was equally vigorous if somewhat less successful. While James Stewart was allowed to teach for two months following his escape,

530

H.L. Hime/Provincial Archives of Manitoba/N12543.

"Bishop's Court — the residence of the Bishop of Rupert's Land, on the banks of the Red River," 1858.

Rev. William Henry Taylor, on poor terms with Stewart because of an earlier dispute over the location of the school, hired a replacement with the Bishop's approval. Stewart then opened a private school where the great majority sent their children, forcing Taylor to close his. Taylor never regained his popularity.

The parishes along the Red River were also affected by the upheaval. Not only did many refuse to attend church services, but Archdeacon James Hunter was attacked for his investigations into the Corbett case. John Tait, a carpenter and miller from St. Andrew's parish, circulated a number of vicious rumours against Hunter to prove that any untruth could find support in Red River. Consequently, he reasoned, Corbett was probably just as easily innocent as guilty. Bishop Anderson urged Hunter to sue but a court case was avoided when Tait signed an apology that was read from St. Andrew's pulpit, and paid Hunter £100. Hunter announced that he would distribute the sum among Tait's daughters and when he failed to do so, Tait sued but lost.

As a result of the gossip and ill-feeling generated by the Corbett and related affairs, both Bishop Anderson and Archdeacon Hunter, his presumed successor, resigned their positions. Hunter commented that "the storm is pitiless, *a systematic blackening of the characters of all*. No one can live in this land with this adversary, and my prophecy is that in two years there will not be four clergymen on the two rivers."

His prediction possessed a degree of truth and by 1867 all of the most prominent clergymen had left Red River: Anderson in 1864, Hunter in 1865, and Chapman and Taylor in 1867. Their numbers were further reduced by William Cockran's death in 1864.

By 1865, then, the Halfbreeds had achieved a degree of confidence about their own identity, largely through Corbett's influence. They were to liberate Red River from the two tyrannies of the Hudson's Bay Company and the Roman Church. With Red River a Crown Colony, they would then follow Corbett, a thoroughly Protestant Englishman. They would have the balance of power. In the first decades of the history of the settlement, identity had been based on race, and rank in the Company. With Corbett's agitation acting as a catalyst, racial ties were weakened. They did not see themselves as English-speaking Protestant versions of the Métis. They did not identify with the Métis Nation. They were not petty settlers in a squalid little Company settlement in the isolated and frigid heart of British North America. They were not poverty-stricken coloured parishioners of the white-missionary–dominated Church of England. They were Protestant subjects of Her Most Britannic Majesty's Empire, an Empire upon which the sun never set.

531

The Métis and Mixed-Bloods of Rupert's Land before 1870

IRENE M. SPRY

Were the English-speaking mixed-bloods and French-speaking métis of what is now western Canada separate and mutually hostile groups? Or were they friendly and closely linked with each other? Frits Pannekoek contends that the *country-born* (as he terms the English-speaking mixed-bloods)[1] and the métis of Red River Settlement "were at odds years before the [Riel] resistance, and the origins of that hatred lay in the nature of Red River society." He concludes: "In fact, upon closer examination of the origins of Métis–Country-born hatred, it becomes apparent that the first Riel resistance was in part caused and certainly exacerbated not by racial and religious antagonisms introduced by the

From *The New Peoples: Being and Becoming Métis in North America*, ed. Jacqueline Peterson and Jennifer S.H. Brown (Winnipeg: University of Manitoba Press, 1985). Reprinted with permission.

Canadians, but rather by a sectarian and racial conflict with roots deep in Red River's past."[2]

This view of the divisions within Red River Settlement is directly contrary to what a métis, Louis Goulet, remembered. Writing of 1867, when his family returned to Red River from the far western plains, he recollected:

> Something was missing in the Red River Colony: There wasn't the same feeling of unity and friendship that had always been felt among those people of different races and religions. And he [his father] wasn't the only one unhappy with the way things were going.
>
> The old-timers seemed to feel a strange mood in the air. Newcomers, especially the ones from Ontario, were eagerly sowing racial and religious conflict, banding together to fan the flames of discord between different groups in the Red River Settlement. These émigrés from Ontario, all of them Orangemen, looked as if their one dream in life was to make war on the Hudson's Bay Company, the Catholic Church and anyone who spoke French. . . . The latest arrivals were looking to be masters of everything, everywhere.[3]

532

Continuing tradition among twentieth-century English-speaking descendants of the Selkirk settlers supports Louis Goulet. As Miss Janet Bannerman of Old Kildonan recalled, "The relations between the French-speaking families and the rest of us in Red River were always of friendliness and goodwill. In the very earliest and hardest days of the settlement that friendship was established upon a lasting foundation by the French-Canadians and the métis who showed warmhearted kindness to the poor Scottish people when the lack of food at the Forks compelled them to go down to the buffalo hunters' headquarters at the mouth of the Pembina river in the winter time."[4] This, in turn, is consistent with Miss Anne Henderson's memories of walks, when she was a child early in this century, with her grandfather, who introduced her to all the friends he met, many of whom were French-speaking.[5] Similarly, George Sanderson, Jr., writing of his boyhood in Portage la Prairie, mentioned among his chums the "Pochas" [Poitras] and "Demers" [Desmarais] boys.[6]

Very little evidence of conflict, let alone "hatred," has come to light except in the clerical sources on which Pannekoek's conclusion seems in large measure to be based. Such sources, it is submitted, must be used with great reserve. Independent evidence is needed to test the testimony of writers who were concerned to convert the adherents of rival dogmas and to protect their own flocks from counter-conversion. Hostility between Catholic and Protestant divines was a byword in Rupert's Land.[7] Such antagonism as there may have been between French- and English-speaking communities was, indeed, largely sectarian, but it does not seem to have been racial in origin.

A preliminary survey of such non-clerical evidence as is available concerning the nature of the relationships of the natives of the country of Indian and French and Indian and other white descent[8] suggests that, far from being mutually hostile, métis and mixed-bloods were, as

W.L. Morton put it, linked by "ties of blood and of long association on hunt and trip.[9]

Alexander Ross's celebrated statement may, perhaps, be taken with a pinch or two of salt, but it must at least be considered:

> We have now seen all the different classes of which this infant colony was composed brought together. The better to advance each other's interest, as well as for mutual support, all sects and creeds associated together indiscriminately, and were united like members of the same family, in peace, charity, and good fellowship. This state of things lasted till the Churchmen began to feel uneasy, and the Catholics grew jealous; so that projects were set on foot to separate the tares from the wheat. . . .
>
> Party spirit and political strife has been gaining ground ever since. The Canadians became jealous of the Scotch, the half-breeds of both; and their separate interests as agriculturalists, voyageurs, or hunters, had little tendency to unite them. At length, indeed, the Canadians and half-breeds came to a good understanding with each other; leaving then but two parties, the Scotch and the French. Between these, although there is, and always has been, a fair show of mutual good feeling, anything like cordiality in a common sentiment seemed impossible; and they remain, till this day, politically divided.[10]

533

Significantly, Ross said nothing about the mixed-bloods as a separate group, except as he described where each community lived; on the contrary, in his book *The Red River Settlement*, he noted a number of apparent affinities among and cooperation between métis and mixed-bloods. Thus, in his account of talk among Rupert's Landers, Ross mentioned their "narrations." These were "made up of an almost unintelligible jargon of the English, French and Indian languages."[11] This suggests at least some mingling of the English- and French-speaking elements in the population of mixed descent, an impression borne out by a traveller's observation concerning a cart train south of Red River Settlement: "In the 'polyglot jabber'" of the métis drivers "he heard 'fine broad Scotch,' a scattering of Gaelic and Irish brogue, and a plentiful mixture of 'rapidly uttered French *patois*.'"[12] Another traveller in the Red River Valley in 1864 joined a cart train under the command of Antoine Gingras, who "knew English" as well as French, though his drivers spoke only Indian and French.[13] J.G. Kohl in the 1850s recorded a bilingual statement by a métis: "Ou je reste? Je ne peux pas te le dire. Je suis Voyageur — je suis Chicot, monsieur. Je reste partout. Mon grand-père était Voyageur: il est mort en voyage. Mon père était Voyageur: il est mort en voyage. Je mourrai aussi en voyage, et un autre Chicot prendra ma place. Such is our course of life."[14]

Louis Goulet, in describing the Frog Lake massacre, mentioned that he and his friends, André Nault and Dolphis Nolin, conversed in English mixed with a little French when they were held by the Cree.[15] He noted, too, that a French-speaking métis of Scottish descent, Johnny Pritchard, was interpreter to Tom Quinn. Presumably this meant that he could speak English.[16] A granddaughter of Norbert Welsh (an Irish-French métis), in enumerating the languages that her grandfather had at his command, ended the list with "and, of course, English."[17]

Similarly, some mixed-bloods spoke French — people such as Charles Thomas, who was in charge of the Hudson's Bay Company post at Reindeer Lake when Father Taché visited it in 1847.[18] "Big Jim" McKay, later to become the Honourable James McKay of Deer Lodge, whose father came from Sutherlandshire, spoke French,[19] as did members of another family of McKays, the "Little Bearskin" McKays, William McKay, his brother John ("Jerry") McNab Ballenden McKay, and his son Thomas.[20] Joseph Finlayson, one of the Roderick Finlayson family, also wrote and spoke French fluently.[21] It would appear, therefore, that many métis and mixed-bloods, at least among the elite, spoke both French and English, as well as one or more of the Indian languages, in which tongues those who did not speak both French and English could and did communicate. The English-speaking pioneer settlers of Portage la Prairie, for instance, were fluent in Cree, which "enabled them to associate freely with the French Half-breeds" of White Horse Plain, among whom most of them could claim cousins.[22]

No doubt the métis and mixed-bloods of Rupert's Land spoke this diversity of languages at least in part because they were the descendants of a rich diversity of ancestors. Their maternal forebears included Cree, Ojibwa, and Chipewyan, as well as French Canadians and Scots; their paternal ancestry included not only French and English, but also Orcadian, Scots, Irish, Shetland, and other European strains, notably the Danish ancestry of the numerous progeny of Peter Erasmus, Sr.[23] Baptiste Bruce, for instance, the guide with Dr. John Rae's Arctic expedition of 1848–49, claimed Highland and French as well as Indian descent.[24] Alick Fisher's mother was a métis.[25] Baptiste Robillard, a former guide with the Cumberland boat brigade, was accompanied out on the plains by a son-in-law, John Simpson, said to be the natural son of Thomas Simpson, the ill-fated Arctic explorer.[26] A long roster of names like Baptiste Kennedy attests to the complex mixture of origins among the métis. Among the mixed-bloods, similarly, there were many with French ancestry. "Big Jim" McKay had French antecedents through his mother, who was a Gladu(e).[27] Joe McKay, a "Little Bearskin," married one of the Poitras girls.[28] George Sanderson had two French grandmothers and a niece named Desmarais.[29]

It would be interesting to have a count of all mixed marriages, both *à la façon du pays* (according to the custom of the country) and those solemnized by the clergy. The fragmentary nature of the documentary record makes this impossible, but, even without such comprehensive information, it is evident that many marriages spanned the alleged gulf between the mixed-blood and métis groups. Among the marriages recorded in the Protestant parishes of Red River Settlement, a number involved couples with French and non-French names. It cannot, of course, be assumed that having a Scottish name meant that an individual was a mixed-blood, nor that all métis had French names. Some whose fathers came from Scotland or the Orkneys grew up speaking French and were assimilated to the culture of a French-speaking, Catholic métis mother, as in the case of the Bruce and Dease families.[30] In other cases, seemingly non-French marriages had in them a strong French element, as in the case of James McKay's marriage to Margaret Rowand[31] and Jeanette [Janet] Tate's marriage to Alex Birston.[32] Moreover, dominance in a family of French, Catholic culture did not necessarily exclude non-French influences any more than a dominant non-French culture excluded French or Catholic influences.

A further complication in an attempt to analyze marriages listed in the parish registers is that not all the apparently French–non-French marriages were between métis and mixed-bloods of whatever descent. At least a dozen Swiss–Swiss and a half-dozen French–French (or, more likley, Canadien–Canadienne) unions have been identified. Further, an apparently métis–mixed-blood marriage may turn out to be a Canadian–Scottish marriage. This adds uncertainty to the relevance of seeming cross-marriages to the question of métis–mixed-blood relationships. Norman Kittson, for example, who came from Quebec, married a daughter of Narcisse Marion, also from Quebec.[33]

535

Unfortunately, it has not been possible to analyze marriages in the Indian settlement, although some of the settlers there, such as Joseph Cook and his children,[34] were of mixed origin. Nor has it been possible to include data from the French-Catholic parishes. The fire that destroyed St. Boniface cathedral in 1860 destroyed most of the early formal records. There is, however, a list in the Provincial Archives of British Columbia of men married by the Catholic missionaries from the time of their arrival in 1818 to February 15, 1831.[35] Among the almost three hundred names listed, nearly twenty are non-French: mostly McDonnells, McLeods, and the like. Undoubtedly, some of their descendants had been assimilated to the culture of métis mothers, though the wives' names are not given.

Other scattered records that survive show that non-French names were, in some instances, changed to a spelling better suited to French pronunciation than the original spelling was. For example, "Sayer" became "Serre"[36] and "McKay" became "Macaille."[37] Similarly, French spelling was sometimes anglicized. Thus, the descendants of Michel Reine (Rayne and other variants), from Strasbourg, became "Wren."[38]

Despite all these gaps and ambiguities, the records in the Hudson's Bay Company and church registers of what appear to be cross-marriages between métis and mixed-bloods in the Protestant parishes of Red River Settlement from 1820 to 1841[39] are of considerable interest (see Table 1).

TABLE 1 Apparent Marriages between Métis and Mixed-Bloods

Entry Number	Cross-Marriage, with Date and Reference Number
13	Michael Lambere to Peggy (January 25, 1821 SJM[a] 1820–1835)
18	George Saunderson to Lisset Lajimoniere (March 30, 1821 SJM 1820–1835)
23	William Dickson to Justine Pacquette (June 9, 1821 SJM 1820–1835)
36	John Warring to Lydia Fournier (November 11, 1821 SJM 1820–1835)
37	Martin Norte to Catherine Treathey (November 11, 1821 SJM 1820–1835)
58	Joshua Halero to Francoise Laurain (November 18, 1823 SJM 1820–1835)
82	Henry Hallet, Jr., to Catherine Parenteau (October 18, 1824 SJM 1820–1835)
83	David Sandison to Louisa Giboche (October 19, 1824 SJM 1820–1835)
111	John Anderson to Mary (Murray?) [Desmarais] (January 31, 1826 SJM 1820–1835)
122	William Mackay to Julia Chalifoux (August 13, 1826 SJM 1820–1835)
124	James Swain to Margaret Racette (October 3, 1826 SJM 1820–1835)
125	William Birston to Hazelique Marchand (December 8, 1826 SJM 1820–1835)
129	William Bruce to Frances Andre (1827 SJM 1820–1835)
134	Andrew Spence to Susette L'Eunay (October 30, 1827 SJM 1820–1835)
167	George Kipling to Isabella Landrie (November 19, 1828 SJM 1820–1835)
176	Peter Pruden to Josette (Susette) Gothvier (May 7, 1829 SJM 1820–1835)
177	James Monkman to Nancy Shaboyee (May 12, 1829 SJM 1820–1835)
194	Pierre St. Pierre to Susannah Short (February 8, 1830 SJM 1820–1835)
202	Francis Desmarais to Harriet Spence (date and reference number missing)
212	John Batish Shurdan to Mary Lewis (January 6, 1831 SJM 1820–1835)
215	Aimable Hogue to Margarette Taylor (March 24, 1831 SJM 1820–1835)
221	Hugh Cameron to Mary Jordan (October 26, 1831 SJM 1820–1835)
236	John Aimable McKay to Lizette La Vallee (March 12, 1832 SJM 1820–1835)

Entry Number	Cross-Marriage, with Date and Reference Number
	TABLE 1 *(continued)*
253	Charles Desmarais to Harriet Favel (February 7, 1833 SJM 1820–1835)
272	William Spence to Loraine Truche (March 6, 1834 SJM 1820–1835)
287	James Swain to Josette Couteau (January 7, 1835 SJM 1820–1835)
289	William Sutherland to Suzette Truche (December 26, 1834 SJM 1835–1854)
308	James McNab to Sarah Michael (January 21, 1836 SJM 1835–1854)
331	John Swain to Mary Alerie (January 18, 1837 SJM 1835–1854)
332	Baptiste De Champ to Margaret Johnston (January 19, 1837 SAM[b] 1835–1860)
376	Baptist DeMarais to Sophia Erasmus (December 28, 1837 SJM 1835–1860)
390	Andrew Dennet to Mary Martinois (September 25, 1838 SAM 1835–1860)
434	Peter Warren Dease to Elizabeth Chouinard (August 3, 1840 SAM 1835–1860)

537

Source: Provincial Archives of Manitoba; HBCA, E.4/1b; parish registers for St. John's and St. Andrew's (Church of England Index to Parish Registers, 1820–1900).
[a]*SJM* — St. John's Marriages
[b]*SAM* — St. Andrew's Marriages

The spelling of names in these records varies from one to another and even from index to entry. It is, moreover, phonetic in character, and in many cases difficult to make out. Some marriage entries in the parish registers differ from those in the company registers and some either do not appear in the latter or are illegible. The usage adopted by the Provincial Archives of Manitoba in its index has therefore been followed.

Some of the men whose names appear in this list may have come from Europe. Certainly men from the Orkneys, Scotland, England, and elsewhere married women of mixed Indian–French ancestry, such as Hugh Gibson from the Orkneys, who married Angélique Chalifoux; Francis Heron and Henry Hallet, Sr., from England, who married Isabella Chalifoux and Catherine Dansee, respectively; meanwhile, Louis Gagnon from France married Jane McKay. John Wasuloski, probably a de Meuron, married Justine Fournier. George Saunderson (Sr.), from Scotland, married Lisset Lagimonère (Lagimodière), both of whose parents came from Quebec. There are other uncertainties in the list, but, imperfect as it is, it suggests that some thirty marriages among a total of 450, probably 5 percent or more, were marriages of men and women with French names to men and women with non-French names. This surely indicates that the métis and mixed-blood communities cannot have been rigidly isolated from each other. Indeed, the Reverend William Cockran bears witness to a French element in the mixture of origins among his parishioners at St. Andrews: In ninety-two families there were thirty-nine European males and one female. The rest were "Orkney, English, Scotch, French, Welsh, Norwegian, Negro, and Jewish half-breeds."[40]

The Company's register of marriages for 1841 to 1851[41] shows proportionately fewer apparent cross-marriages, only some nine or ten out of a total of more than four hundred, but even this must have meant that there was a certain amount of going and coming between the métis and mixed-blood groups.

Further, marriages recorded in the parish registers were only those formally solemnized by the clergy. Unregistered marriages, *à la façon du pays*, may well have involved a greater proportion of cross-marriages, since the clergy were not, in general, sympathetic to members of their own congregation marrying into a rival sect. Fragmentary evidence of marriages which do not appear to be listed in the official registers has come to light. A paper on James McKay mentions two such cross-marriages: John Rowand to Julie Demarais; Angus McKay to Virginia Boulette.[42] John Moar married Matilda Morrisseau at Lac Seul in 1859.[43] Angus Harper married Peggy La Pierre at Oxford House in 1830,[44] and Joseph Everette married Nancy McKay in 1846.[45] The financial records for Red River Settlement mention one Louise McLeod, widow of Baptiste Larocque.[46] Nancy McKenzie, the discarded country wife of Chief Factor J.G. McTavish, married Pierre Leblanc.[47] One of the Carrière sisters of St. Boniface married Roger Marion (son of Narcisse Marion), while the other became Mrs. Henry Donald Macdonald.[48]

That Protestant Anglophones and Catholic Francophones did, indeed, associate with each other is made still more clear by reminiscences recorded in W.J. Healy's *Women of Red River*. Father Louis-François Laflèche used to visit the Sinclair house to play the piano there and to exchange music with the Sinclair girls. Everybody in the Settlement seems to have gone to St. Boniface cathedral to hear Sister Lagrave play the organ built by Dr. Duncan, medical officer of the Sixth Regiment of Foot[49] and "Christmas midnight mass at St. Boniface cathedral was always attended by many parties from across the river."[50]

On the St. Boniface side of the river, the Narcisse Marion home was a centre of hospitality that included English-speaking Protestants. Mrs. Henry Donald Macdonald (née Angélique Carrière) related that it was a "great house for dances. . . . Many of the Kildonan people and the other people across the river used to come to our parties, and we went to theirs. We knew them all."[51] Indeed, it was Narcisse Marion who hospitably received the Reverend John Black when he arrived to become the first Presbyterian minister in the Colony, and arranged for

538

him to be taken across the river to the home of the leading Presbyterian, Sheriff Alexander Ross.[52]

Not only did colonists from the different parishes go to each other's parties, but also their children mixed with each other at school. Miss Janet Bannerman recalled that there were several children from well-to-do French-speaking families at her first school, St. John's parochial school. Among them she remembered Joseph and Marguerite Leclair, Emile Bouvette, Ambroise Fisher, Henri Laronde, and Baptiste Beauchemin.[53] By the same token, some Anglophone children went to school in St. Boniface, notably James McKay's three children.[54]

Mrs. W.R. Black, granddaughter of Kate and Alexander Sutherland of Kildonan, rounded off her recollections in this way: "I have said so much about the Riels and the Lagimodières because they and the other French-speaking families who were our neighbours are associated with my earliest memories almost as much as the English-speaking families of Red River." Her father, John Sutherland, built a new house across the river after the flood of 1852 swept away the original Sutherland house at Point Douglas. The whole family spoke French as well as English and John Sutherland became a confidant of his French-speaking neighbours and a link between them and the Kildonan settlers.[55]

Business transactions also linked the French- and English-speaking communities: grain from the Carrières' farm at St. Boniface was taken to Robert Tait's mill to be ground;[56] Moise Goulet, a noted plains trader, when illness forced him to retire, sold his whole outfit to A.G.B. Bannatyne;[57] Norbert Welsh, another prominent trader of Irish and Quebec descent, after a disillusioning transaction with "Bobbie" (Robert) Tait, took charge of Bannatyne's cart trains en route to St. Paul and, when he set up in business for himself, dealt with Bannatyne.[58] On January 1, 1846, Peter Garrioch went to see his friend Pascal Berlan[d], about getting some buffalo for him, in company with Peter Pruden and two others.[59] Frederick Bird was apprenticed to a Catholic blacksmith named Bovette.[60]

Although the evidence is scanty, it would appear that métis and mixed-bloods joined together in the great Red River buffalo hunt. Alexander Ross records that in 1840 the captain of the hunt was one Jean-Baptiste Wilkie, "an English half-breed brought up among the French," while one of Wilkie's captains was a member of the Hallett family.[61] Ross himself travelled with the hunt that year; the late Miss Sybil Inkster once spoke to me of her relatives going to the buffalo hunt; and Henry Erasmus "accompanied the buffalo hunters on trips to the prairies after meat," of which he got a full share, even though he did not actually take part in the hunt itself.[62] The Reverend John Smithurst wrote in June 1840 that most of his parishioners (all Anglicans) had gone either on the buffalo hunt or with the boat brigades.[63] In June 1845, Peter Garrioch was with the buffalo hunt, which certainly numbered métis families among those in the one hundred tents. Of these, Garrioch mentioned Francis Lauze [Lauzon] and Morin.[64] George Sa[u]nderson, Jr., gives a lively description of the way in which Francophone boys were trained to hunt buffalo. He appears to have watched these proceedings. He states explicitly that the "Pochas" [Poitras] family were on one hunt in which his family took part.[65]

Besides the buffalo hunt, the major occupation of the mixed-bloods and métis was freighting, in boat brigades to York Factory and up the Saskatchewan; in the Red River cart trains to the south, to St. Peter's and St. Paul, and west by the Carlton Trail and other traditional overland routes; and in winter with dog trains carrying the winter packet or other urgent freight.

Scattered data about the personnel of boat brigades suggests a mixture of racial origins. In the Hudson's Bay Company's account books the names of some of the tripmen who received advances are listed, especially in the case of advances made at York Factory. The record of advances at York in the summers of 1826 and 1830, for example, gives a mingle-mangle of French and non-French names: In 1826, ten men with French names and four with non-French names received advances. Five others with French names and one uncertain did not have accounts.[66] In 1830, ten French names appear, with four names that originated in the United Kingdom, two mixed names (François Whitford and François Bruce), and one Indian name.[67] It is possible, though not documented, that the crew of each boat was separated on the basis of French or non-French origin.

Information about the personnel of the cart brigades is also limited, but suggests a similar mixture. The *Daily Minnesotan* for July 22, 1854, stated that "Messrs. Kittson, Rolette, Caviller, Grant and others had arrived at Traverse des Sioux with nearly two hundred carts." The same journal published a letter on September 13, 1858, stating that the Sioux had killed two men on the plains, "Busquer" [Louis Bosquet], in charge of Henry Fisher's carts, and John Beads.[68] *The St. Paul Daily Pioneer* reported on July 12, 1870, that the *St. Cloud Times* had recorded seventy arrivals of Red River carts since July 9. They belonged to Gingras and Bannatyne.[69] The voyageurs' signatures to a Hudson's Bay Company contract to make the journey from Fort Garry to St. Peter's in 1850 included nine French names and seven Orcadian and other non-French names.[70]

Only one document has been found containing information about mixed personnel travelling in winter with dog trains. The party left from Île-à-la-Crosse, not from Red River, but it may be significant: Samuel McKenzie, writing on January 15, 1867, noted that "Peter Linklater and Michel Bouvier go with the North Packet to Carlton accompanied by Baptiste Payette and James Wilson."[71] A party was sent from Red River Settlement in 1832 to bring back a herd of sheep from the United States. It too was mixed, having had in it, besides Scots, a French Canadian, and an Irishman, two French half-breeds and two young English half-breeds.[72]

Some information is available about the voyageurs and hunters who accompanied the increasingly numerous expeditions engaged in exploration, surveying, and other official missions in the nineteenth century, to say nothing of pleasure parties travelling on the western plains in "search of adventure and heavy game."[73] John Rae's Arctic searching expedition of 1848–49, for example, included, besides Canadians and Shetlanders, Baptiste Bruce, the guide already mentioned, Baptiste Emelin [Hamelin], Baptiste Fredrique, Xavier Laplante [Antoine Plante], William Sabiston, and Edmund Stevenson, all natives of the country, and so, presumably, of mixed-blood or métis origin. The natives in his team in 1850–51 were John Fidler, John Hébert dit Fabien (not from Red River), Charles Kennedy, Alexandre Laliberté dit Lachouette, Peter Linklater, Baptiste Marcellais, Baptiste Peltier, and Samuel Sinclair, who was probably a native of the country. However, none of the Rupert's Landers with Rae's 1853–54 expedition had a French name. They were Jacob Beads; John Beads, Jr.; Henry Fidler; and James Johnstone.[74]

541

Palliser's expedition set out from Red River in 1856 with the following men, besides James Beads, the expedition's servant: John Ferguson, first guide; Henry Hallet[t], second guide; Pierre Beauchamp; Samuel Ballenden[dine]; George Daniel; Baptiste Degrace; Perre Falcon; Amable Hogue; Donald Matheson; [Antoine] Morin; John Foulds; George Morrison; Charles Racette; John Ross; John Simpson; Thomas Sinclair; Robert Sutherland; George Taylor; Joseph Vermette; and Pascal.[75] At least some of Palliser's "Red River contingent" in 1858 were of French origin: among the Red River men who stayed with him at Fort Edmonton during the winter of 1858–59 were Pierre Beauchamp and Baptiste La Graisse, while Chief Factor W.J. Christie, who, on behalf of Palliser, paid off those who returned to Red River, called out "*assez*" to each man when he had taken all the trade goods to which his wage entitled him. Others, such as Todd and Ballenden, were of at least partly non-French origin.[76] In the fall of 1858, James Beads returned from Edmonton to Red River, on hearing that his brother had been killed by the Sioux. When Beads came back in the spring of 1859 he brought with him the redoubtable hunter Jean-Baptiste Vital[le].[77]

When Henry Youle Hind set off in 1858 for the western plains, his party included "six Cree half-breeds, a native of Red River of Scotch descent [John Ferguson?], one Blackfoot half-breed, one Ojibway half-breed, and one French Canadian." It is noticeable that, with one exception, he did not consider the European derivation of the "half-breeds" of sufficient importance to be mentioned.[78]

The Boundary Survey of 1872–76 recruited a troop of native scouts styled "the 49th Rangers," under the command of William Hallett. The deputy commander's name was McDonald, and the names of the three sub-leaders were Gosselin, Lafournais, and Gaddy. The rank and file, too, included men of both French and Scottish or other descent.[79]

Records of sportsmen travelling in the West for pleasure do not always give the names of their voyageurs and hunters, but Hudson's Bay Company accounts show that the Comte de la Guiche had in his employment John Ferguson, Alexis Goulait, and Goulait's son,[80] in June 1851, when he left Red River on a trip to the Rocky Mountains. Lord Dunmore's party set out on August 22, 1862, with Jim McKay (spelled Mackay by Dunmore) as hunter-in-chief, Baptiste Valet as hunter, James Whitford, Pierre (?) and (?) De Charme as buffalo hunters and drivers, and Joe Macdonald as hunter, cook, and driver.[81]

None of this suggests any sharp segregation between Red River mixed-bloods and métis. Indeed, Palliser, describing the expedition's great buffalo hunt in 1858 in the neighbourhood of modern Irricana, Alberta, commented: "The run was magnificent, and there was considerable emulation between my Saskatchewan and my Red River men,"[82] a comment that indicates some solidarity of the group from Red River, regardless of descent, vis-à-vis the group from Lac Ste. Anne; elsewhere, however, Palliser commented on what seemed to him a remarkable difference in energy and progressiveness between the Canadian and French and the Scottish "half-breeds."[83]

Other mixed ventures include the party of emigrants from Red River to the Columbia River, which in 1841 made the extraordinary journey across the plains and through the mountains under James Sinclair's leadership. Its members numbered among them an almost equal balance of men with names suggesting French and non-French origin, all of them speaking either French or English. Table 2 shows the list of men in the original agreement between the emigrants and the Company. Cash advances were made to all but three of these men and to two not listed in the agreement: David Flett and Pierre Larocque, Jr.[84] John Flett is

---

TABLE 2   Emigrants from Red River Settlement to the Columbia River, in the James Sinclair Party, 1841

François Jacques	James Birston
Julien Bernier	John Cunningham
Baptiste Oreille or Rhelle	Alexander Birston
Pierre Larocque	Archibald Spence
Louis Larocque	François Gagnon
Pierre St. Germain	Joseph Klyne
John Spence	James Flett
Henry Buxton	John Tate
Gonzaque Zastre	Horatio Nelson Calder
William Flett	Toussaint Joyal
Charles McKay	[David Flett]

Sources: HBCA, B.235/d/82, p. 56; A.12/7, fo. 392d (agreement between emigrants to the Columbia River and Hudson's Bay Company, dated 31 May 1841); William J. Betts, "From Red River to the Columbia," *The Beaver* (Spring 1971), 50–55.

not in either list, but other evidence makes it clear that he was with the party.[85]

In contrast, none (or, at most, one)[86] of the second group of Red River emigrants to the Columbia, who, again under James Sinclair's leadership, went in 1854 to Walla Walla (Washington), seems to have had a French name, at least according to the list given by John V. Campbell, Sinclair's brother-in-law, who, as a lad, was a member of the party.[87]

Of greater importance than evidence of mixed parties freighting, travelling, and emigrating from Red River Settlement is the story of the joint mixed-blood–métis struggle against the claim of the Hudson's Bay Company to the exclusive right to trade in furs in Rupert's Land and, until the License to Trade lapsed in 1859, in the Indian territories beyond. W.L. Morton tells this story admirably in his introduction to *Eden Colvile's Letters, 1849-52*.[88] With a brief lull, while the Sixth Regiment of Foot were stationed at Red River from 1846 to 1848, the mixed-blood–métis population of Red River Settlement agitated throughout the 1840s for recognition of their "rights," as natives of the country, to take part in the fur trade and for redress of other grievances. The Sayer trial in 1849 established that, in practice, the joyful shout of the métis, "Le commerce est libre," was justified, but the natives of Rupert's Land still wanted a voice in the government of the colony.

543

Evidence in Peter Garrioch's diary of métis–mixed-blood friendship and fraternization has already been cited. Garrioch also makes it clear that the men who banded together in 1845 to resist the imposition by the Council of Assiniboia of an import duty on goods brought in from American territory were of diverse origins: Canadian, Irish, métis, and mixed-blood. Besides Peter Garrioch, they were Peter Hayden, Alexis Goulet, St. Germain (which Garrioch spelled Chagerma), Dominique Ducharme, Henry Cook, and Charles Laroque.[89]

On August 29, 1845, a larger group of mixed-blood and métis traders submitted a list of questions to Governor and Chief Factor Alexander Christie concerning their rights (see Table 3).[90] In another version of this list of signatures, given by Alexander Begg in his *History of the North-West*, four of these names are omitted: Pierre Laverdure, Edward Harmon [or Harman], James Monkman, and Edward [Antoine] Desjarlais, Sr.[91] Two others were added: Adal Trottier and Charles Hole [possible Houle]. Again, this is a not uneven mixture of métis and mixed-bloods.

In 1846, two parallel petitions, one in French and one in English, were drafted at a meeting held on February 26 in Andrew McDermot's house. The petitions contained demands for free trade and representative government. James Sinclair carried both of them to England, where Alexander K. Isbister submitted them to the Imperial Government.[92] As W.L. Morton noted: "The settlement was an Anglo-French colony, a European-Indian community, and the métis, excluded from public office like the English half-breeds, were only demanding that the institutions of the Colony should reflect its ethnic composition. In so doing they spoke for

TABLE 3 Signatories to the Letter to Governor C.F. Alexander Christie, dated 29 August 1845

James Sinclair	Peter Garrioch
Baptiste Laroque	Jack Spence
Thomas Logan	Alexis Goulait [Goulet]
Pierre Laverdure	Antoine Morin
Joseph Monkman	William McMillan
Baptiste Wilkie	Louis Letendre [dit Batoche]
Baptiste Farman (Famian)	Robert Montour
Edward Harman	Jack Anderson
John Dease	James Monkman
Henry Cook	Antoine Desjarlais, Snr.
William Bird	Thomas McDermot
John Vincent	

Source: HBCA, D.5/15, fos. 139a–139b; PAM MGZ 135, "Red River Correspondence"; Alexander Begg, *History of the North-West*, 3 vols. (Toronto: Hunter, Rose and Co., 1894–95), 1: 261–62. Begg omits Montour but adds Adel Trottier and Charles Hole.

the English half-breeds as well as for themselves, as they were to do again in 1869."[93] As well, "English half-breeds" such as James Sinclair spoke for their métis associates — as, for instance, in the Sayer trial, at which Sinclair represented the four métis defendants and their armed colleagues who had surrounded the court house.[94]

The younger generation of mixed-bloods and métis was frustrated and restless. The demand for representation on the council and for a free trade in furs was a demand for an outlet for ambition, energy, and enterprise.[95]

The métis organized a "council of the nation" and pressed upon Sir George Simpson still another petition when he arrived in the Settlement in June, 1849. Sent with a covering letter from Sinclair, dated June 14, 1849, this petition was signed by William McMalen [McMillan], Louis Rielle [Riel Sr.], Pascal Berland, Baptiste Fairjeu, Baptiste Laroque, Antoine Morein, Louis Letendre, Solomon Amelin, and Urbain Delorme.[96] A letter presented to Simpson when he was again in Red River Settlement in the summer of 1850 was signed by William McMillan, Solomon Amelin, Louis Riel, and eighteen others. They demanded that Recorder Thom should go and that they should have representation on the Council "chosen from our nation by ourselves."[97]

Yet another petition in 1851 reached the Company via the Aborigines' Protection Society and the Colonial Office asking "that Red River be granted British liberty, a Governor appointed by the Crown, a judge similarly appointed and able to speak English and French, power in the Governor to appoint Councillors in an emergency, the dismissal of Councillors who had forfeited public confidence or been subservient to the Company, and the removal of Thom to some other British colony." The 540 signatures were attested by five leading métis.[98]

These data, fragmentary and incomplete as they are, cannot be conclusive, but, as far as they go, they do suggest an intermingling of mixed-bloods and métis, fellow feeling and cooperation between the two groups, not separation or hostility. This impression is strengthened by yet another petition sent in 1857 to the Legislature of Canada "from Donald McBeath and others[,] inhabitants and Natives of the Settlement situated on the Red River, in the Assiniboine Country. . . . "[99]

This petition was promulgated by a mixed-blood, "Captain" William Kennedy of Arctic fame, who visited Red River in 1857 as an emissary of Canadian commercial interests. It bore the signatures of 119 men with French names or known to be French-speaking, as well as fourteen more who may have been of French origin, and two with mixed names, out of a total of 511, including a number with Indian or probably Indian names. Though not all the apparently French signatures were those of métis — that of Narcisse Marion, for example — the Francophone roster is considerable. This is surprising, since, according to Alvin C. Gluek, Jr., the Catholic clergy had discouraged their parishioners from signing the petition.[100]

As late as 1869–70, a contemporary observer, Walter Traill, commented: "The natives [of Red River Settlement], both English and French, though not resenting the newcomers from the newly formed Dominion, wonder why it is that they . . . should be slighted by Canadians who are coming to rule them." And again: "If the Canadian Government . . . had recognized the natives, both English and French, both would have given their loyal support."[101]

"Hostility" reported by rival clerics, if it existed, may well have reflected deference to the missionaries' wishes and pressures. However, at least one missionary, that turbulent priest Father G.-A. Belcourt, cooperated closely with Sinclair and Isbister. Besides Sinclair, Thomas McDermot, John Anderson, and Peter Garrioch attended the meeting on February 26, 1846, at which Belcourt presided, speaking in French. It appears that they were the only English-speaking people at this meeting.[102]

An observation made by Eugene Bourgeau, botanical collector with the Palliser expedition, is further evidence of mutual métis–mixed-blood friendship. A compatriot, Ernest St. C. Cosson, the eminent French botanist, said of Bourgeau: "Par l'influence que lui donnait sa double qualité de Français et de catholique, il se concilia l'amitié de ces peuplades [the natives of the West], qui ont gardé le souvenir de notre domination, comprennent notre langue, et sont restées fidèles aux principaux dogmes de notre religion."[103] This was the man whose account of the Sunday services held by Palliser (a staunch Protestant) led Charles Gay to write in *Le Tour du Monde*: "Touchant accord que celui de ces croyances si diverses, ailleurs si fécondes en antagonismes et en rivalités, se confondant, au pied des montagnes rocheuses, dans une même bonne foi et dans une commune simplicité!"[104]

545

Palliser, too, noted this harmony. The métis Catholics from Lac Ste. Anne asked leave "to attend Divine worship," despite the fact that the prayers read for the Red River men, who "belonged to the Church of England," were from that Church's service. Palliser, therefore, through an interpreter, "conducted the lessons and half the prayers in Cree." He mentioned "this circumstance to show the respectful tendency and absence of bigotry of these men, in their appreciation of Divine service."[105]

If, then, even religious differences did not go very deep, were there important cleavages in Red River society? The answer must surely be yes. There were two fundamental divisions,[106] but these were not divisions between métis and mixed-blood.

The first was a division between the well educated and well-to-do gentry, the officers and retired officers of the Hudson's Bay Company and those of their progeny who had achieved respectability, the clergy, and the prosperous merchants, in contrast to the mass of unlettered, un-propertied natives of the country — the "engagés" of the Hudson's Bay Company and of the Nor'Westers before them and their descendants. James Sinclair, for example, was recognized as a "gentleman"; he was a close friend of his British-born son-in-law, Dr. William Cowan, an officer of the Hudson's Bay Company, as well as of his brother, Chief Factor William Sinclair II, and even of Sir George Simpson, despite his battles with the Company.[107] This set him apart from the ordinary tripmen, whom he employed on his freighting ventures. The gap was one occasioned by ambition, affluence, education, and social status as against poverty and the inferior status of employees or, at best, of hunters, petty traders, or small farmers.

The second was the division between the professional farmer and the hunter and plains trader, between the sedentary population and those to whom the freedom of a wandering life out on the plains was more important than economic security and material comfort. This was the irreconcilable cleavage, so convincingly analyzed in George F.G. Stanley's classic, *The Birth of Western Canada*,[108] and described in Goulet's, Welsh's, and Sanderson's reminiscences.

As Jennifer Brown concludes in *Strangers in Blood*, the "half-breed" descendants of the men of both the North West and Hudson's Bay Companies "combined to define and defend common interests and finally to take military action in the Rebellions of 1869 and 1885."[109] Western Canada, as we know it today, was indeed born of conflict, conflict not between métis and mixed-blood, but between a wandering, free life and settlement; a conflict between agriculturalists, especially the flood of new-comers in search of landed property and wealth, and the old way of life that both métis and mixed-bloods had had in common with their Indian cousins, a way of life based on adjustment to the natural environment and the shared use of the free gifts of nature. That way of life was doomed

546

with the coming of surveyors, fences, police, organized government, settlers, and private rights of property in real estate and natural resources.[110] With it went the prosperity and independence of all but a small elite of métis and mixed-bloods alike.

NOTES

[1] Here the term *mixed-blood* is used (in spite of its biological ineptitude) instead of Pannekoek's term *country-born* to denote Anglophone Rupert's Landers of hybrid Indian and white ancestry. After all, the children of Jean-Baptiste and Julie Lagimodière and those of Kate and Alexander Sutherland and other Selkirk settlers were country-born even though they had no Indian ancestry. A possible alternative might be to use *métis* with a qualifying adjective, as Alexander Morris did: "The *Metis* who were present at the [North West] Angle [of the Lake of the Woods] and who, with one accord, whether of French or English origin. . . . " (*The Treaties of Canada with the Indians of Manitoba and the North-West Territories* [Toronto: Belfords, Clarke and Co., 1880], 51). Similarly, Isaac Cowie wrote of one man being an Irish and another a French Métis in his book, *The Company of Adventurers: A Narrative of Seven Years in the Service of the Hudson's Bay Company* (Toronto: William Briggs, 1913), 191, and George F.G. Stanley of "English Métis" in "Indian Raid at Lac la Biche," *Alberta History* 24 (Summer 1976) 3:25. It seems simpler, however, to use *mixed-blood* for the Anglophones of mixed ancestry as a reasonably close equivalent of *métis* for the Francophones of mixed descent.

[2] Frits Pannekoek, "The Rev. Griffiths Owen Corbett and the Red River Civil War of 1869-70," *Canadian Historical Review* 57 (June 1976) 2:134.

[3] Guillaume Charette, *Vanishing Spaces: Memoirs of Louis Goulet* (Winnipeg: Éditions Bois-Brulés, 1980; translated by Ray Ellenwood, from the original French edition, *L'Espace de Louis Goulet*, 1976), 59.

[4] W.J. Healy, *Women of Red River* (Winnipeg: Russell, Lang and Co. Ltd., 1923), 88.

[5] Personal conversation, Winnipeg, May 22, 1973.

[6] George William Sanderson, "'Through Memories [*sic*] Windows' as Told to Mary Sophia Desmarais, by her Uncle, George William Sanderson (1846-1936)," 2, Provincial Archives of Manitoba (hereinafter cited as PAM) MGI/A107.

[7] John Palliser wrote from Edmonton of "the black looks of the hostile divines. I understand that sometimes hostilities have proceeded further than mere looks. . . . " (HBCA, D.5/49, 1859 [2], fos. 245-46). I am grateful to the Hudson's Bay Company for kind permission to use material in its archives. The Rev. John Smithurst wrote in his journal: "We see the eagle of Rome watching to seize as its prey these precious souls. . . . " (PAC, MG19, E6, vol. 2, June 12, 1841). Father A.G. Morice, in his *Histoire de l'Église catholique dans l'Ouest canadien* (St. Boniface and Montreal: Granger Frères, 1915), 1:216, commented on the arrival of the Methodist missionaries that they "allaient se mesurer plutôt avec les enseignements de la Robe Noire et les pratiques religieuses que ses néophytes tenaient d'elles, qu'avec les ténèbres épaisses et l'immoralité révoltante dans lesquelles croupissaient encore plusieurs des nations barbares du Canada central" (i.e., western Canada). There are many similar passages throughout the work.

[8] Since the European origins of mixed-bloods included Highland and Lowland Scottish, Orcadian, Shetland, Swiss, Danish, and other strains, as well as French, the commonly used description, *English*, scarcely seems appropriate.

[9] W.L. Morton, ed., *Alexander Begg's Red River Journal and Other Papers Relative to the Red River Resistance of 1869-1870* (Toronto: Champlain Society, 1956), 12.

[10] Alexander Ross, *The Red River Settlement* (London: Smith, Elder and Co., 1856; reprinted Edmonton: Hurtig, 1972), 80-81. References are to the Hurtig reprint.

[11] Ibid., 79.

[12] Cited in Rhoda R. Gilman, Carolyn Gilman, and Deborah M. Stultz, *The Red River Trails: Oxcart Routes between St. Paul and the Selkirk Settlement, 1820-1870* (St. Paul: Minnesota Historical Society, 1979), 14. This "polyglot jabber" was, no doubt, Bungay, which the late Mrs. J.L. Doupe told me was widely used when she was a child in Winnipeg.

[13] J.A. Gilfillan, "A Trip through the Red River VAlley in 1864," *North Dakota Historical Quarterly* 1 (October 1926 to July 1927) 4:37-40.

[14] J.G. Kohl, *Kitchi-Gami: Wanderings round Lake Superior*, trans. Lascelles Wraxall (London: Chapman and Hall, 1860; reprinted Minneapolis: Ross and Haines, 1956), 260. I am indebted to Jacqueline Peterson for this reference.

[15] Charette, *Vanishing Spaces*, 119.

[16] Ibid., 116.

[17] Television broadcast, Ontario T.V., 1981. "The Last Buffalo Hunter," featuring Norbert Welsh.

[18] Barbara Benoit, "The Mission at Île-à-la-Crosse," *The Beaver* (Winter 1980):46.

547

[19] Inkster papers, typescript account of the career of "The Honourable James McKay — Deer Lodge," 1 and 5, PAM. See also Allan Turner, "James McKay," *Dictionary of Canadian Biography*, ed. Francess G. Halpenny and Jean Hamlin, 11 vols. (Toronto: University of Toronto Press, 1972) 10:473–75; N. Jaye Goossen, "A Wearer of Moccasins: The Honourable James McKay of Deer Lodge," annotated typescript published in substance in *The Beaver* (Autumn 1978):44–53; and Mary McCarthy Ferguson, *The Honourable James McKay of Deer Lodge* (Winnipeg: published by the author, 1972).

[20] Cowie, *Company of Adventurers*, 191–92.

[21] Ibid., 192.

[22] A.C. Garrioch, *The Correction Line* (Winnipeg: Stovel Co. Ltd., 1933), 200–201. I am indebted to Mr. Brian Gallagher for this reference.

[23] Irene M. Spry, "A Note of Peter Erasmus's Family Background" and "Family Tree," in Peter Erasmus, *Buffalo Days and Nights* (Calgary: Glenbow-Alberta Institute, 1976), 303–305, 324–28, and end papers.

[24] E.E. Rich, ed., *John Rae's Correspondence with the Hudson's Bay Company on Arctic Exploration, 1844–1855* (London: Hudson's Bay Record Society [HBRS], 1953), 353–54.

[25] Cowie, *Company of Adventurers*, 220.

[26] Ibid., 348. It is possible that Cowie was mistaken; Sir George Simpson also had a son called John.

[27] Inkster Papers, "James McKay," 1, PAM.

[28] Mary Weekes, *The Last Buffalo Hunter, As Told by Norbert Welsh* (New York: Thomas Nelson and Sons, 1939; Toronto: Macmillan of Canada, 1945), 23.

[29] Sanderson, "Memories," title and p. 8, and list of marriages, Table 1, p. 101, PAM, MGI/A107.

[30] Lionel Dorge, "The Métis and Canadian Councillors of Assiniboia," *The Beaver* (Summer, Autumn, and Winter 1974), especially Part 3, 56–57. Douglas N. Sprague, in his research on Sir John A. Macdonald and the métis, has analyzed cross-marriages on the basis of the 1870 census, from which he has been able to trace all marriages back for three generations.

[31] Goossen, "James McKay," 47.

[32] Charles A. Throssell wrote the following note on January 20, 1966: "John Tate — Who's [*sic*] only daughter, Jeanette, married Alex Burston about 1830. . . . They were both of French Canadian descent." This note was sent by Alex Burston's daughter, Mrs. Mary Burston Throssell, to Mr. William J. Betts of Bremerton, Washington. He very kindly sent me a copy on November 14, 1971. An entry in St. John's parish register states that Alex Burston [Birston] married Janet Tate on June 28, 1832, No. 237, St. John's Marriage Register, 1820–1835.

[33] W.L. Morton, Introduction in E.E. Rich, ed., *London Correspondence inward from Eden Colvile, 1849–1852* (London: HBRS, 1956), xiv, lxxx, 246.

[34] HBCA, E.4/1b, also recorded in PAM, Parish records. Some cross-marriages are recorded in the Indian church register of marriages, such as that of Sally Erasmus to Antoine Kennedy, December 23, 1847 (no. 57d), HBCA E.4/2.

[35] Provincial Archives of British Columbia (hereinafter cited as PABC), Add Mss 345, File 135.

[36] Les Archives de la Société historique de St. Boniface has the record of the marriage of "Guillaume Serre," alias William Sayer. I am indebted to Lionel Dorge for a copy of this record.

[37] Dorge, "Métis and Canadian Councillors," Part 3, 57.

[38] PABC, Wren Family papers; Spry, "Note on Family Background," in Erasmus, *Buffalo Days and Nights*.

[39] HBCA, E.4/1b and 2, and PAM microfilm of parish registers. There are some discrepancies between these two sets of records. Marriages of Barbara Gibson and Isabella Spence to James Louis have been omitted because James Louis was the son of a mulatto from New England, not, as might be supposed, of French extraction. A record of the marriage of Margaret Louis [or Lewis] is omitted for the same reason (HBCA, E.4/1b, fo. 221, and A.38/8, fo. 36). I am indebted to the keeper of the Hudson's Bay Company Archives for this information. Nancy Budd's marriage to Michel Reine is also omitted because he was from Strasbourg.

[40] John E. Foster, "Missionaries, Mixed-bloods and the Fur Trade: Four Letters of the Rev. William Cockran, Red River Settlement, 1830–1833," *Western Canadian Journal of Anthropology* 3 (1972) 1: 110 and 112.

[41.] HBCA, E.4/2.

[42] Goossen, "James McKay," 48.

[43] The marriage contract is reproduced in Sylvia Van Kirk, *"Many Tender Ties": Women in Fur-Trade Society, 1670–1870* (Winnipeg: Watson and Dwyer Publishing Ltd., 1980), 118.

[44] Ibid., 117–19.

[45] HBCA, B.239/Z/39, fo. 22.

[46] HBCA, B.235/c/l, fo. 248d.

[47] Van Kirk, *"Many Tender Ties,"* 188.

[48] Healy, *Women of Red River*, 119.

[49] Ibid., 34–35.

[50] Ibid., 208.

[51] Ibid., 119.

[52] Ibid., 68.

[53] Ibid., 87.

[54] Ferguson, *James McKay*, 60.

[55] Healy, *Women of Red River*, 59 and 61.

[56] Ibid., 119.
[57] Charette, *Vanishing Spaces*, 70.
[58] Weekes, *Last Buffalo Hunter*, 35–45, 57, 60–72, and 201–202.
[59] Garrioch Journal, January 1, 1846, PAM.
[60] Sanderson, "Memories," 12, PAM, MGI/A107.
[61] Ross, *Red River Settlement*, 248 and 271.
[62] Erasmus, *Buffalo Days and Nights*, 6.
[63] PAC, MG19 E6, vol. 2, journal entry for June 21, 1840.
[64] Garrioch Journal, June 10 and 16, October 1 and 2, 1845, PAM.
[65] Sanderson, "Memories," 3, PAM, MG9/A107.
[66] HBCA, B.235/d/26, fo. 2d, 1826.

John Ashburn	Louis Lapierre dit Brilliant
J. Bts [*sic*] Boisvert (no account)	François Laframboise (no account)
Alexis Bonamis dit Lesperence	William Malcolm
Rennes Cardinal (no account)	Simon Martin (no account)
Antoine Deschamps (no account)	Pierre Papin
Antoine Dagenais	Medard Poitras
Leon Dupuis	David Scott
Toussaint Joyal	Jacques St. Denis
Louis La Rive	David Sandison
Jacques Le'Tang (no account)	Louis Thyfault [*sic*]

[67] HBCA, B.235/d/44, 1830.

549

François Savoyard	Henry House [Howse?]
Carriole Lagrasse	Joseph Savoyard
Pierre Savoyard	Richd Favel
James Birston	Bte Boyer
Antoine Lambert	George Kipling
Alex Carrier	Charles Larocque
François Whitford	Amable Lafort
François Bruce	Joseph Delorme
Matouche	

Cowie wrote that Baptiste Kennedy was a guide in a brigade with steersmen from Red River Settlement named Cameron, Spence, Cunningham, and William Prince, an Indian (*Company of Adventurers*, 117).
[68] Minnesota Historical Society, St. Paul.
[69] St. Paul Public Library, Minnesota.
[70] PABC, Add Mss 345, vol. 2, file 70.
[71] HBCA, B.27/c/1, fo. 20.
[72] Robert Campbell, "A Journey to Kentucky for Sheep: From the Journal of Robert Campbell, 1832–1833," *North Dakota Historical Quarterly* 1 (October 1926 to July 1927) 1:36.
[73] A phrase used by Palliser of the two friends who joined him on his expedition. Captain Arthur Brisco and William Roland Mitchell (Irene M. Spry, ed., *The Papers of the Palliser Expedition* [Toronto: Champlain Society, 1968], 338–39).
[74] Rich, ed., *John Rae's Correspondence*, 350–78.
[75] Spry, ed., *Palliser Papers*, 37 n.1.
[76] Ibid., 340–41.
[77] Ibid., 403.
[78] *North-West Territory: Report on the Assiniboine and Saskatchewan Exploring Expedition* (Toronto: John Lovell, 1859), 39.
[79] John E. Parsons, *West on the 49th Parallel* (New York: William Morrow and Co., 1963), 53.
[80] HBCA, B.235/a/15, Upper Fort Garry Journal, June 16, 1851.
[81] "Log of the Wanderers on the Prairies in Search of Buffalo Bear Deer &c in 1862," ms. in the possession of Lord Dunmore.
[82] Spry, ed., *Palliser Papers*, 258.
[83] Ibid., 169.
[84] HBCA, A.12/7, fo. 392d. Agreement between emigrants to the Columbia River and Hudson's Bay Company, dated May 31, 1841, and HBCA, B.235/d/82, fo. 30. 56. cash paid to emigrants. Whether there were two Pierre Larocques is not clear. The accounts list Pierre Larocque Jr., the agreement simply Pierre Larocque.
[85] William J. Betts, "From Red River to the Columbia," *The Beaver* (Spring 1971):50–55, reproduces John Flett's own account of the journey.
[86] Toussaint Joyal may have been with the second group of emigrants.
[87] John V. Campbell, "The Sinclair Party — An Emigration Overland along the Old Hudson's Bay Company Route from Manitoba to the Spokane Country in 1854," *Washington Historical Quarterly* 8 (July 1916):187–201.

88 See also Irene M. Spry, "Free Men and Free Trade," unpublished paper submitted to the Canadian Historical Association meeting held in Saskatoon in 1979, and "The 'Private Adventurers' of Rupert's Land," in John E. Foster, ed., *The Developing West: Essays on Canadian History in Honor of Lewis H. Thomas* (Edmonton: University of Alberta Press, 1983), 49–70.

89 Garrioch Journal, March 1 and 9, 1845, PAM. See also E.H. Oliver, *The Canadian North-West: Its Early Development and Legislative Records*, vol. 1 (Ottawa: Government Printing Bureau, 1914), 315, which lists Charles Laurance, Dominique Ducharme, Peter Garriock, Henry Cook, Peter Hayden, and Alexis Goulait as petitioners to the Council. It does not include St. Germain.

90 Christie to Simpson, September 5, 1845, enclosing the letter from Sinclair et al. dated August 29, 1845, HBCA, D.5/15, fos. 139a, 139b. Sinclair's letter is reproduced in Lewis G. Thomas, ed., *The Prairie West to 1905* (Toronto: Oxford University Press, 1975), 56–57, with Christie's reply, 58–59. No source is given and the spelling of some of the names is different from that in the copy enclosed by Christie. Another copy of the letter is in PAM, RRS/RRC, 1845–47.

91 Alexander Begg, *History of the North-West*, 3 vols. (Toronto: Hunter, Rose, 1894–95), 261–62.

92 Correspondence Relating to the Red River Settlement and The Hudson's Bay Company, *British Parliamentary Papers*, vol. 18, 1849, Colonies, Canada (Shannon: Irish Universities Press, 1969).

93 Morton, Introduction in Rich, ed., *Eden Colvile's Letters*, lxxxix.

94 A good account of the trial and of the role of Sinclair and Garrioch is given in Morton, Introduction in Rich, ed., *Eden Colvile's Letters*, lxxxii–lxxxvi, and another in Roy St. George Stubbs, *Four Recorders of Rupert's Land* (Winnipeg: Peguis Publishers, 1967), 26–29.

95 Morton, Introduction in Rich, ed., *Eden Colvile's Letters*, lxxxix.

96 Ibid., citing HBCA, D.5/25, June 2, 1849, enclosed in Sinclair to Simpson, June 14, 1849.

97 Ibid., p.c., citing HBCA, D.5/28, June 1, 1850; HBCA, A.13/4, fos. 519–20; and A.12/5, Simpson, July 5, 1850.

98 Ibid., pp. cvii–cviii, citing HBCA, A.13/5, enclosure in a letter from F. Peel, C.O., to Pelly, dated December 30, 1851. Attempts to find the signatures in HBCA, the Public Record Office, London, England, and the Archives of the Aborigines' Protection Society, Rhodes House, Oxford, England, have failed, so it has not been possible to discover the origins of the signatories.

99 The original petition with all the signatures is in PAC, RG 14-C-I, vol. 64, petition no. 1176, received and filed May 22, 1857. Oddly, the signature of Roderick Kennedy is not among the 511 signatures attached to the petition, though he presented it to the Legislature, and his name is the only one given in the Select Committee version. It was printed in *The Toronto Globe* for June 12, 1857, and as Appendix 15 of the *Report of the Select Committee of the House of Commons on the Hudson's Bay Company, 1857*.

100 Alvin C. Gluek, Jr., *Minnesota and the Manifest Destiny of the Canadian Northwest* (Toronto: University of Toronto Press, 1965), 123–25.

101 Mae Atwood, ed., *In Rupert's Land: Memoirs of the Walter Traill* (Toronto: McClelland and Stewart, 1970), 204 and 208. Sanderson wrote of the Rising when he was captured by Riel's men, when he was with the Portage party: "I was not afraid of the French half-breeds . . . I knew Riel and many of his adherents, in fact I was related to some of his leaders" (PAM, MG9/A107, Part 2, 1).

102 Garrioch Journal, February 26, 1846, PAM.

103 *Bulletin de la Société botanique de France* vol. 13, 1866, liv, cited in Spry, ed., *Palliser Papers*, xxviii n. 5. The number of the volume is given incorrectly in this citation.

104 "Le Capitaine Palliser et l'Exploration des Montagnes Rocheuses, 1857–1859," *Le Tour du Monde: Nouveau Journal des Voyages* (Paris: 1861), 287, cited in Spry, ed., *Palliser Papers*, xxviii.

105 Spry, ed., *Palliser Papers*, 238 n.5.

106 A third cleavage might be identified, namely, the generation gap between the children and grandchildren of the well-established Principal Settlers of the colony and their aging precursors. See Morton, Introduction in Rich, ed., *Eden Colvile's Letters*, lxxxix.

107 This impression is derived from a wide range of material by and concerning both James Sinclair and William Sinclair II, including Journal of Dr. William Cowan, PAC, MG19 E8.

108 George F.G. Stanley, *The Birth of Western Canada* (Toronto: University of Toronto Press, 1960; 1963; reprinted from the original edition, Longmans, Green and Co. Ltd., 1936).

109 Jennifer S.H. Brown, *Strangers in Blood: Fur Trade Company Families in Indian Country* (Vancouver and London: University of British Columbia Press, 1980), 173.

110 Irene M. Spry, "The Tragedy of the Loss of the Commons in Western Canada," in *As Long as the Sun Shines and Water Flows: A Reader in Canadian Native Studies*, ed. Ian A.L. Getty and Antoine S. Lussier (Vancouver: University of British Columbia Press, 1983), 203–28.

Fort Victoria, Vancouver Island, in the mid-nineteenth century.

Well into the 1880s, and perhaps even to the nineties, the patterns of Victorian commercial society set between 1858 and 1864 continued as a basis; even while American or continental European elements within it decreased or were assimilated, and British and Canadian elements were enlarged.

J.M.S. Careless, "The Business Community in the Early Development of Victoria, British Columbia"

Topic Fourteen

The Pacific Coast

In the early nineteenth century, North West Company traders, operating out of Montreal, reached the Fraser and Columbia river-basins. Subsequently, the Hudson's Bay Company, after its union with the North West Company in 1821, extended fur-trading operations all along the North Pacific Coast. With the extension of the boundary between present-day Canada and the United States along the 49th parallel to the Pacific Coast in 1846, however, the Hudson's Bay Company was required to leave the Oregon Territory. It established its new commercial headquarters at Victoria, on Vancouver Island. The economic history of Victoria is outlined in J.M.S. Careless's "The Business Community in the Early Development of Victoria, British Columbia."

In 1858, the discovery of gold on the Fraser River opened up the mainland. Britain organized the separate colony of British Columbia that same year, to offset the domination of American prospectors. James Douglas, the governor of Vancouver Island, became governor of the new mainland colony as well, planting British institutions there, and making New Westminster the new capital. In 1866, the two colonies were joined under the title of British Columbia. Barry Gough offers an interpretative sketch of British Columbia in his "The Character of the British Columbia Frontier."

Barry Gough's *The Northwest Coast: British Navigation, Trade, and Discoveries to 1812* (Vancouver: University of British Columbia Press, 1992) discusses the maritime history of the Pacific Coast. W. Kaye Lamb has edited the journals of George Vancouver's expedition, 1791–95, in four volumes, *The Voyage of George Vancouver, 1791–1795* (London: Hakluyt Society, 1984). For the later period, see Barry Gough, *The Royal Navy and the Northwest Coast of North America, 1810–1914: A Study of British Maritime Ascendancy* (Vancouver: University of British Columbia Press, 1971), and his *Gunboat Frontier: British Maritime Authority and Northwest Coast Indians, 1846–90* (Vancouver: University of British Columbia Press, 1984). The maritime fur trade is reviewed in Robin Fisher's *Contact and Conflict: Indian–European Relations in British Columbia, 1774–1890*, 2nd ed. (Vancouver: University of British Columbia Press, 1992), and James R. Gibson's *Otter Skins, Boston Ships, and China Goods: The Maritime Fur Trade of the Northwest Coast, 1785–1841* (Montreal and Kingston: McGill-Queen's University Press, 1992).

Margaret A. Ormsby has written a valuable introduction to *Fort Victoria Letters, 1846–51* (Winnipeg: Hudson's Bay Record Society, 1979), edited by Hartwell Bowsfield. In "The Colonization of Vancouver Island, 1849–1858," *B.C. Studies* 96 (Winter 1992–93), 3–40, Richard Mackie reviews the colony's early years. On the history of coal mining in the early settlement period, see Lynne Bowen's *Three Dollar Dreams* (Lantzville, B.C.: Oolichan Books, 1987), and John Douglas Belshaw's "Mining Technique and Social Division on Vancouver Island, 1848–1900," *British Journal of Canadian Studies* 1 (1986): 45–65.

For an overview of developments on the mainland, see R. Cole Harris's "British Columbia," in *Canada before Confederation*, ed. R. Cole Harris and John Warkentin (Toronto: Oxford, 1974), 289–311. The standard, but now rather dated, history of the area is Margaret Ormsby's *British Columbia: A History* (Toronto: Macmillan, 1958). It should be supplemented by Jean Barman's *The West beyond the West: A History of British Columbia* (Toronto: University of Toronto Press, 1991). *British Columbia: Historical Readings*, ed. W. Peter Ward and Robert A.J. McDonald (Vancouver: Douglas and McIntyre, 1981), contains several valuable essays on early British Columbia history.

The Business Community in the Early Development of Victoria, British Columbia

J.M.S. CARELESS

The rise of Victoria from the Hudson's Bay fort of the 1850's to the substantial commercial city of the later nineteenth century may be readily associated with striking events like the Fraser and Cariboo gold rushes, the political course of able Governor Douglas and the somewhat colourful officialdom about him — or the still more colourful doings of Amor de Cosmos, a kind of dedicated opportunist in politics, working toward the crucial decision of federal union with Canada. Far less likely is Victoria's growth to be associated with the more prosaic, lower-keyed activities of the city's businessmen. None the less, their quieter, continuing operations played an essential part in making the Vancouver Island community the chief entrepot of young British Columbia. Nor was the process lacking in colour or in noteworthy figures of its own. To trace that process, the development of the business community in conjunction with Victoria itself, is thus the object of the present study.[1]

From *Canadian Business History: Selected Studies, 1497–1971*, ed. David S. Macmillan (Toronto: McClelland and Stewart, 1972). Reprinted with the permission of the author.

Before 1858, and the onset of the gold rush to the Fraser on the neighbouring mainland, Victoria was a tranquil little hamlet of some three hundred inhabitants clustered about a fur trade depot. For Victoria, founded in 1843, did have the distinction, of course, of being the Hudson's Bay headquarters on the coast, as well as seat of government for the colony of Vancouver Island that had been erected in 1849, still in the keeping of the fur trade company. As a part of a great British commercial and imperial enterprise, and on the open Pacific within the world reach of British seapower, Victoria was by no means wholly isolated or unchanging. Parties of colonists had arrived from the United Kingdom to settle among the Company's officers and employees. The mild climate and fertile soil of the adjacent districts produced good crops. The Company had opened valuable coal mines up the coast at Nanaimo in the early fifties, and the timber wealth of the Island's heavy forests was initially being tapped. Finally, there was an increasing trade southward in coal, lumber, and sometimes fish or potatoes to San Francisco, the bustling Californian gold metropolis, from where most of the colony's necessary imports were derived.

555

Nevertheless, Victoria had remained an outpost community of small endeavours and limited opportunities. It was not one to invite much business enterprise when the fur company dominated the major economic activities — not to mention political — and when markets were either local and scanty or far off and uncertain. True, the Hudson's Bay interests had worked at developing farms, mines, or sawmills, and had diversified their trading operations on the coast well beyond the traffic in furs. Yet problems of access to market and to sufficient shipping plagued them too, while the established, hierarchical ways of the old fur monopoly inevitably made new adjustments harder. Outside of the quasi-bureaucratic world of the Bay Company, moreover, there scarcely was a business community, other than well-to-do tavern-keepers like James Yates (a former Company employee), some artisans, and a few independent settlers engaged in trade.

John Muir, formerly a Company coal-miner, sent spars, piles, and lumber to Victoria from his small mill at Sooke, for shipment to the California market. Captain William Brotchie had pioneered in opening the spar trade, but found it hard to get adequate transport, and subsequently became Victoria's Harbourmaster. And Captain James Cooper, who had commanded Hudson's Bay supply vessels, had set up as an independent trader, bringing the little iron schooner *Alice* out from England in sections, then shipping cargoes like coal, cranberries, and spars to San Francisco and the Hawaiian Islands. The role of sea captains in early business development on Vancouver Island was notable, in fact. But shipmasters then had long been roving businessmen, used to trading where they could, seeking cargoes, and commissions in their own or others' service. They were particularly prominent in early lumbering on the Island. Of fourteen subscribers to the Vancouver Steam Saw Mill Company five were ship captains, the rest Hudson's Bay officials or associates.[2] The Company itself introduced the first steam saw mill machinery to Victoria in 1853, but the venture failed from lack of sufficient capital, and the mill did little before it was destroyed by fire in 1859.

This, then, was the restrictive climate for business enterprise in early Victoria: lack of funds outside the Company for any but the smallest scale of operations, and lack of stimulating demands generally. The San Francisco market itself was far from satisfactory, when the products of Washington or Oregon were competitive and closer, and also did not face duties there. During the California boom that reached a peak in 1853, demands had been high enough to make the Vancouver Island lumber trade important; and of the nineteen lumber ships that left Victoria that year eighteen were bound for San Francisco.[3] When the boom faded, however, so did much of the Island's wood trade. Coal did better, earning a place in the California market as good steamer fuel; but again it could suffer from price fluctuations and the competition of coal from Britain, Australia, or the eastern United States. In short, down to 1858, Victoria had not yet found a trade pattern that could encourage much business growth. Then came gold, to change the picture almost overnight.

In the spring of 1858, news of gold strikes in British territory along the lower Thompson and Fraser valleys reached San Francisco. The mass hysteria that makes gold rushes surged within the city, and thousands prepared to leave for a new El Dorado. Some might make their way to Puget Sound or by rough overland trails up through the mountainous interior, but most chose the quickest, surest route by sea, the four-day passage to Victoria. For here was a port of entry to the British far western domains, the one place of settlement in all that wilderness. It offered a base of supply and a point of transhipment for the river journey up the treacherous Fraser, unnavigable by large ocean-going vessels. The importance of already existing patterns of transport in focussing this flow of traffic is fully evident here. The mass of shipping that was now swept into highly profitable runs to Victoria was simply following a recognized lane to an established harbour that lay beside the entrance to the Gulf of Georgia, from where the fur trade had long maintained contact with the mainland posts of the interior by way of the Fraser route.

For Victoria, however, the flow of ships brought golden inundation by waves of eager miners, who needed food and shelter, transport to the interior, supplies beyond what they had carried with them, and had money to spend for it all. The first four hundred and fifty arrived in April on the American steamer *Commodore*. They came in ever-mounting numbers through the summer, until, it was estimated, the town's population had climbed to seven thousand.[4] Most of the newcomers soon had to be housed under canvas; Victoria became a veritable tent city. But construction proceeded rapidly, brick as well as wooden buildings

556

going up, while land values soared — rising for choice lots from an initial fifty dollars to three thousand dollars and more.[5] For with the miners had come entrepreneurs with capital, store and hotel keepers, commission merchants, and real estate buyers, who were ready to invest in the business which they envisaged would acrue to Victoria from its services to the gold fields.

Some, of course, were essentially speculators, planning to grab a quick return and move on. Others were agents of established San Francisco firms, seeking profitable new branches, and still others were more vaguely attracted by the thought of commercial opportunities in another California-like boom. Many would leave, especially after the initial enthusiasm of the rush ran out in disillusionment by the winter, and contraction and depression followed. But enough of the new commercial element remained, along with miners in the hinterland, to bring an enduring change to Victoria. And when the next year sufficient finds further up the Fraser kept the mining frontier going, then its main outlet continued to grow also as a town. Though Victoria's population had fallen back under three thousand by 1860,[6] it had indeed become an urban centre with a trading pattern of its own, supplying a considerable market on the mainland and exporting quantities of gold to San Francisco.

The pattern was strengthened in 1860, when Governor Douglas declared the town a free port. New Westminster, established near the mouth of the Fraser in 1858 as capital of the new mainland province of British Columbia, faced the burden of customs duties as well as the problems of Fraser navigation. It became little more than a river-steamboat halt, while Victoria remained the terminus for ocean shipping. The Vancouver Island town, indeed, had the best of both worlds: free external contact with an international, maritime traffic system, customs and licenses on the mainland to check encroachments on its inland trade from over the American border. Accordingly, although Victoria's business life, like its population, ebbed and flowed with the fortunes of gold mining, it nevertheless acquired substance and solidity as an entrepot, building a merchant group alongside the older Hudson's Bay and official elements that would steadily gain in stature.

Its business community grew particularly with the new rush to the Cariboo goldfields in 1862. Over the next two years, as Barkerville and other mining towns grew up far in the interior, as the Cariboo Road was opened to serve the fields, and as their deeper-driven mines increasingly needed capital and a greater volume of supplies, Victoria once more grew apace. But this time its business operations were necessarily on a bigger scale, in provisioning, transporting, and financing for the larger enterprises of the Cariboo — where, moreover, farming and ranching were soon widening the bases of hinterland activities. It was good evidence of growth when Victoria was incorporated as a city in 1862, and its Chamber of Commerce was organized in 1863. That year, indeed,

557

The British Columbian and Victoria Guide and Directory could say of the new city, "Her true position as the center and headquarters of commerce north of the Columbia has been placed beyond a doubt."[7]

In these early years of growth, Victoria's business community of several hundreds had acquired some significant characteristics, as well as many individuals worthy of note. One frequently remarked feature was the high proportion of Americans in the rising merchant group; another, its strongly marked cosmopolitan flavour as well. The former was to be expected from the commercial ties that made Victoria an outpost of San Francisco. The latter reflected the multi-national nature of gold rush society, whether among miners or those who would mine the miners, and whether in California or the British possessions to the north. But if Victoria had become "in effect, San Francisco in miniature,"[8] it none the less had features of its own. There were the continuing elements of the older settler society and the Hudson's Bay–official elite. Some of their members did quite well by the Victoria boom, in hotels, stores, and real estate; James Yates, for instance, piling up sufficient fortune to retire. Besides, other businessmen of British or British North American background arrived to share in the town's expansion, and later more generally stayed on, when Americans tended to withdraw. Finally, some of the "American" business migrants were better included in the multi-national category, since a number of them had earlier been immigrants to the United States; and, having moved on temporarily to San Francisco, had now moved on again.

In this regard, it has been noted that of the first 450 newcomers who arrived in 1858 aboard the *Commodore* from San Francisco, only about 120 were either British or Americans (about equally divided), the rest being mainly German, French, or Italian.[9] There was also a notable Jewish admixture in the cosmopolitan influx of the gold-rush era, not to mention a significant contingent of American Negroes, and additional numbers of Slavs, Hawaiians, and Chinese. The commercial community that took shape in Victoria was more Anglo-American in its upper ranks, more varied on the level of small shopkeepers or skilled tradesmen. Yet French, German, and Jewish names figured prominently on the higher levels, while two Negroes, Mifflin Gibbs and Peter Lester, set up the first large general store to compete effectively with that of the Hudson's Bay Company.[10]

Adolph Sutro, a cultivated German Jew, arrived in 1858 to extend the wholesale and retail tobacco business he and his brothers had established in San Francisco. The Sutro warehouse in Victoria continued under brothers Gustav and Emil, though Adolph shortly afterward returned to San Francisco, to make a fortune in the Comstock Lode and became one of the Californian city's most lavish benefactors.[11] In similar fashion David and Isaac Oppenheimer, also German Jews, arrived from

California to develop a wholesale dry goods business in Victoria. After flourishing for years, they were to move to the newly founded town of Vancouver, where they became two of its wealthiest citizens and David a celebrated mayor.[12]

And in the days of the rising Victoria business community there were, besides Sutros and Oppenheimers, men like Selim and Lumley Franklin, English-born Jews, who again came in the early wave from San Francisco. They were two of Victoria's first auctioneers, prospered in real estate and as commission agents, promoted shipping and cattle sales. Selim, moreover, sat for Victoria in the Vancouver Island legislature from 1860 to 1866, while Lumley was mayor of the city in 1865.[13] Still further, there were names like Ghiradelli and Antonovich, commission merchants, Jacob Sehl, furniture dealer from Coblentz, and P. Manciet, who kept the Hotel de France (a leading establishment in the sixties), all to demonstrate the variety of this new little urban business world.[14]

As for Americans, almost the most significant for the future was William Parsons Sayward, of New England origin. In 1858 he came up from a lumber business in San Francisco to found a similar one in Victoria. His wharf and yards grew over the years; but, more important, he went into sawmilling at Mill Bay in 1861, and ultimately became one of the chief figures in lumbering on the North Pacific coast.[15] Then, there was C.C. Pendergast, who opened an office for Wells Fargo in Victoria in 1858. From the start, Wells Fargo played a major part in banking, in exporting gold to San Francisco, and for some time in handling mail for the business community: all of which made "Colonel" Pendergast a man of wide regard.[16] Equally well regarded was T.N. Hibben, a South Carolinian whose stationery and bookselling firm, begun in 1858, would have a long existence in Victoria. Still others prominent in the American segment of the community were Edgar Marvin, hardware and farm machinery importer (an 1862 arrival who became United States consul), and J.A. McCrea and P.M. Backus, both auctioneers.[17] Theirs was an important occupation at the time, when so many cargoes as well as properties inland were disposed of through auction sales.

559

There were also agents of San Francisco shipping lines, wholesalers, and forwarding houses in the Victoria trade; for example, Samuel Price and Company, Dickson, De Wolf and Company, or Green Brothers. Sometimes their local representatives were Americans, but often instead they were Victorians of British background, serving as local partners in their firm — which itself might reach back far beyond San Francisco in a chain of interlocking partnerships to New York, Liverpool, and London. Dickson De Wolf, for example (locally Dickson and Campbell), was based on H.N. Dickson's of London, and also had houses or correspondents in Liverpool, Boston, and Halifax.[18] Yet from the time of the Fraser gold rush, a good deal of Victoria's expanding wholesale trade was handled by local commission agents and general merchants, who of course had San Francisco correspondents. And in this field it seems evident that the British segment of the business community became particularly important.

The relative prominence of British wholesale merchants in the basic import trades no doubt related to the fact of operating in British territory, and the likelihood of their securing better contacts with colonial authorities or the still influential Hudson's Bay Company — not to mention the possibility of their having useful business ties back to Great Britain herself, where some of them returned to visit. A good illustration is that of J.J. Southgate, an Englishman who had been a commission merchant and ship-handler in San Francisco, but moved to Victoria in 1858 with a letter of introduction to Governor Douglas. Southgate soon prospered there, gaining, for example, a contract to provision His Majesty's warships lying in nearby Esquimalt harbour.[19] He built a fine brick store (still standing), with financial backing from Commander H.D. Lascelles, R.N., dealt in real estate, took the lead in organizing a Masonic Lodge, and was elected to the legislature in 1860.[20] Another example is that of the Lowe brothers, Thomas and James, two Scots commission merchants in San Francisco, who similarly transferred their business to Victoria in 1861–62. Thomas was an old Hudson's Bay man who had close links with the Company trading network along the coast, and in the fifties had pioneered in selling coal from the Company's Vancouver Island mines in the San Francisco market.[21] It was notable, incidentally, that the Lowe firm wrote the letter of introduction that Southgate carried to Douglas.[22] Subsequently the brothers took over the latter's wholesale business when he was absent in England; and James Lowe became President of the Chamber of Commerce in 1866, though he failed to win election to parliament in 1869.

Among many other leading early British businessmen one may mention R.C. Janion, with Liverpool and Honolulu connections, J. Robertson Stewart, Robert Burnaby, and G.M. Sproat — President of the local St. Andrew's Society in 1863. Born in Kirkcudbrightshire, Gilbert Sproat had come to Vancouver Island in 1860 in the service of Anderson and Company, a big London firm of shipowners and shipbrokers who were developing a large steam sawmill at Alberni on the west coast of the Island. He became manager of the mill himself when its initiator, Captain Edward Stamp, resigned; but he also built up his own importing and insurance business in Victoria.[23] Another Anderson employee was to become Sproat's partner, Andrew Welch, an Englishman with a distinguished business career ahead of him. And Thomas Harris, also from England, Victoria's first butcher, grew to be a well-to-do provisioner and the city's mayor in 1862.

The British element was also found in banking, for the wealthy London-based and chartered Bank of British North America had opened a Victoria branch in 1859. A few months previous, however, the town's first private bank had already been established by Alexander Macdonald, an enterprising Scotsman who had come up from California with the gold rush in hopes of living by it. He did well at first, making advances in gold dust for sale in San Francisco. But in 1864 his bank was burgled (through the roof) of well over $25,000, which ruined him, and sent him fleeing back to California.[24] The Bank of British Columbia, again London-based with a royal charter of 1862, proved more substantial and reliable, helping to finance wholesale operations, and soon, indeed, the government itself.

"British" at this period quite properly could cover subjects of the Queen who came to Victoria from the eastern colonies of British North America. It is of interest to note that there was some (prospective) Canadian content in contemporary Victoria business and professional circles, as evidenced by Thomas Earle, wholesale grocer and later member of parliament, an Upper Canadian who arrived in 1862.[25] Gradually more eastern British Americans did appear, usually still by way of California; but one of the earliest significant indications of their coming was in journalism. The first newspaper, the *Victoria Gazette*, established in June, 1858, may have been an extension of American press enterprise, but it is worth observing that its publisher, James W. Towne of California, was born in Nova Scotia.[26] And the far more important David Higgins, who arrived in 1860 and subsequently would edit Victoria's enduring *Colonist* for many years, was similarly of Nova Scotian birth, if American upbringing.[27] Above all, there was the founder and first editor of the *British Colonist* (begun late in 1858), Amor de Cosmos, also a native Nova Scotian, who also came via California. His vehement and erratic career in press and politics may not suggest too close an analogy with Joseph Howe; but at least there was some Nova Scotian ingredient added to early Victoria, through this transplanting of Bluenoses from one coast to another.

561

The character of this business community, strongly associated with the American Pacific metropolis but also with the older British metropolis of the Atlantic, did not greatly change for years the stamp it had received in the gold boom era of the early 1860's. New men were to come forward, additional interests to develop; but the men largely emerged out of older firms and partnerships, and the broader economic developments did not alter Victoria's basic role as a maritime commercial entrepot serving a simple extractive hinterland. Of course, declining gold production from the mid-sixties onward, the coming of Confederation with Canada in 1871, and the mounting influence of Canadian metropolitan power thereafter — signalized by the National Policy of 1878 and the building of the Canadian Pacific in the next decade — all brought significant changes that inevitably affected Victoria business more and more. Yet well into the 1880's, and perhaps even to the nineties, the patterns of Victorian commercial society set between 1858 and 1864 continued as a basis; even while American or continental European elements within it decreased or were assimilated, and British and Canadian elements were enlarged. This, then, is the general framework for the next two decades. It remains to discuss the newer activities and the newer men that did emerge inside it.

The falling output of the gold mines after 1864, and the failure to find rich, easily workable new fields, did not seriously harm Victoria at first, still living on the momentum, so to speak, of the expectations of more finds, and with some stimulus to trade derived from the American Civil War. Falling gold revenues and heavy colonial debt burdens, however, did lead in 1866 to the union of Vancouver Island and British Columbia as an urgent move of retrenchment. And this union sharply affected Victoria by removing its privileges as a free port. It was almost the hand-writing on the wall; continental costs of development and need for customs duties had defeated the interests of maritime free trade. At the public proclamation in Victoria of the new united province of British Columbia, so the Colonist noted, members of the crowd variously informed the sheriff that he was reading his death-warrant, warned a red-nosed bystander that port was no longer duty-free, and urged "a seedy-looking individual" to hurry up Government Street and buy a suit while he could still save 15 per cent.[28] At least there was the consolation that Victoria remained provincial capital — to New Westminster's chagrin.

Activity in lumbering had offset in some degree the lessening role of gold. At Alberni, Gilbert Sproat's steam saw mill had reached a splendid peak in 1863, producing over eleven million feet of lumber, until the rapid exhaustion of timber close to water, accessible to the hand or ox-logging of those days, forced its closing by 1865.[29] However, the saw mill that W.P. Sayward had opened in 1863 up the Island's east coast near Cowichan thrived on a more accessible timber supply. In 1864 his mill alone brought two million feet to Victoria, and by the close of the decade put him into the export trade.[30] At the time of the union of 1866, moreover, there were six Vancouver Island saw mills in operation, much of their produce being marketed by way of Victoria. Furthermore, during the depression of the later sixties, they and the Burrard Inlet mills, that had now appeared on the mainland at Moodyville and Hastings, ended the former dominance of American Puget Sound mills over the import market.[31] While for some years following, Island lumbering failed to grow markedly, an important productive basis had been laid for future development, in which the Sayward milling and lumbering interests would play full part.

Then there was coal. In 1858 the Hudson's Bay Company had returned control of Vancouver Island to the Crown, and the next year its trading rights on the mainland had ended. Thereafter the Company had sought to concentrate on its original concern, the fur trade, divesting itself of other complicating ventures, such as its coal mines in the Nanaimo area. Thus in 1862 it sold these holdings to the Vancouver Island Coal Mining and Land Company, which was based in England and backed by British capital. (It also seems to have had an oddly literary connection, since T.C. Haliburton was its first chairman and among its investors were Agnes Strickland and the father of John Galsworthy.)[32] In Victoria, the thriving firm of Dickson, Campbell and Company served as its agents, George Campbell being made a director. Much of the Vancouver Coal Company's output went directly from Nanaimo to market, to San Francisco or the Royal Navy based at Esquimalt. But some as well went via Victoria, where Charles Wallace, also of Dickson and Campbell, managed the two ships that the Company bought for its trade in 1864.[33] The next year coal production rose to 32,000 tons; and to 44,000 in 1868.[34] But by 1870 it seemed to have reached a plateau, and in the following decade the Company ran into trouble, owing to lack of further capital to develop new mines, and competition not only in the American market but within Vancouver Island itself.

563

The latter competition came from Robert Dunsmuir, the son of a Scottish coal master, who had first been employed at Nanaimo in the Hudson's Bay Company mines, but had been engaged in his own independent workings there since 1855. In 1864 another English coal mining venture, the Harewood Company, was launched, backed by the Hon. H.D. Lascelles, commanding H.M.S. *Forward*, and Dunsmuir became its resident manager.[35] Though he drove his miners rigorously (which did not stop them entertaining him to a public tea that year),[36] he could not overcome the fact that the Harewood Mine, after starting well, began to peter out. Dunsmuir withdrew. In 1869, however, he discovered the truly rich Wellington Mine, and set up a company to work it, with financial aid from another naval officer, Lieutenant W.N. Diggle of the *Grappler*.[37] The Dunsmuir Company soon flourished, having one of the best coal seams on the coast and thus well able to stand the competition in the San Francisco market. Moreover, it undertook dock and railway developments at Nanaimo that ministered to that town's growth. And some of the benefit would redound to Victoria, since it kept much of the supply trade of the area. Hence, by the seventies, at least, growth in this coal hinterland could help balance decline in the older one of gold.

And then there was shipping. During the 1860's Victoria became the centre of shipping and shipbuilding interests of its own. It started, of course, with the rush of mining traffic to the Fraser. At the outset the Hudson's Bay Company had commanded the transport service; its pioneer steamers, the *Beaver* and *Otter*, would long be famous around the coasts and up the lower reaches of the river. But because of the demands for transport during the gold rush, Governor Douglas had recognized the need to allow American steamboat captains to enter the river navigation. A number of veterans of Puget Sound or Columbia River steamboating thus came in, and largely found it practicable to make Victoria their base of operations, as the main terminus of the Fraser trade. Captain William Irving became the most prominent and enduring of them — but here again the description of "American" is misleading, since he was a Scot, with much seagoing experience behind him before he pioneered with the first steamboat in Oregon.[38]

Irving joined with another Scottish steamboat pioneer from the Columbia, Alexander Murray, to build the stern-wheeler *Governor Douglas* at Victoria in 1858, her engine being brought from San Francisco.[39] This "first steamer built in the province for the inland trade" was soon joined by a sister ship, the *Colonel Moody*.[40] The previously mentioned merchants, Thomas and James Lowe, invested in the vessels; James for a time was an agent for the line, as were the also-mentioned Samuel Price and Company.[41] Irving built still more ships at Frahey's yard in Victoria, the *Reliance* in 1862 and the *Onward* in 1865.[42] The Hudson's Bay Company also acquired new craft to meet their competition and that from American steamboats. But the fall in gold-mining activity after 1864 led American captains to leave the Fraser, so that for the rest of the decade Irving's and the Bay Company's ships between them controlled the river.[43] Indeed, this situation virtually continued until Captain Irving's death in 1872, and afterwards his son, John Irving, built a still larger shipping domain.

Joseph Spratt was significant also, because the Albion Iron Works, the foundry and marine machinery works he established in Victoria in 1862, became central to the subsequent growth of the city's shipping activities. After having had some training as a marine engineer in England, Spratt had gone to San Francisco, where he had opened a foundry and reputedly built the first steam locomotive on the Pacific coast.[44] As well as running his iron works, he went into shipbuilding, later salmon-canning and whaling, and organized a shipping line up the island's east coast. In any case, by the end of the 1860's he had added the beginnings of industrial enterprise to Victoria. And by that time, too, nine of the seventeen steamers trading to British Columbia and eighteen of the twenty-eight schooners were Victoria-built.[45]

As the sixties drew to a close, however, the city was in a state of depression. The newer activities in lumber, coal, or shipbuilding had not yet hit full stride, and what was still far more apparent was the passing of the gold frontier, with its consequent effects on the wholesale trade, real estate, and financial interests of the Victoria entrepot. Business in the city in 1869 was so slow, in fact, that thistles grew in the gutters along Government Street, while the population was falling back again to little more than three thousand.[46] In this condition, it is not surprising that the business community was considerably despondent, or that, in the midst of continuing discussions on joining the new and far-off Canadian Confederation, some of its members might look to the simpler, sharper release of annexation to the United States. At any rate, the Annexation Petition of 1869 appeared in Victoria in November, signed with 104 names in all.

It is true that this was a limited number; that many of the signers were small men, not leading merchants; and that they included a large element of foreign born who had no strong political positions, either anti-British or pro-American, but voiced what was indeed "primarily an expression of economic discontent."[47] It is also true that the essential issue in Victoria was union with Canada or no union; that annexation was never a real alternative. Yet it is possible, besides, that doubts and fears expressed in anti-unionism among Victorians found a sharper focus in some of those businessmen who did subscribe to annexation: a matter of choosing the devil you knew at San Francisco to the distant unknown one at Ottawa, especially when the former so obviously commanded power and fortune. And certainly one might see concern for the wholesale trade or property values in such substantial signatories as Isaac Oppenheimer and David Shirpser, dry goods merchants, W.H. Oliver and W. Farron, heavy investors in Victoria real estate, or Emil Sutro, tobacco merchant, and T.N. Hibben, the prominent stationer.[48]

565

At all events, the flurry passed with little consequence; and within a few months Confederation was settled policy. By the time it took place in July, 1871, a brighter Victoria was ready to welcome it, hopeful indeed of the terms that had been agreed upon, including a railway to link East and West. For it well might be expected that a Pacific railway would have its terminus in or near Victoria, crossing to Vancouver Island over the narrows at its northern tip. Certainly the fact that a survey party for the projected Canadian Pacific were present in Victoria for the celebrations that accompanied the proclamation of British Columbia's entry into Confederation did not lessen the festivity.[49] And Victoria's businessmen could thus anticipate that change would also mean improvement for their community.

As the 1870's opened, it was a good thing that Victorians did have expectations from Confederation, for times continued slow in many respects: their city's population only passed 4,600 by 1874.[50] However, they could look to some federal relief from the provincial debt burden, some aid from a broader union in meeting the high costs of developing transport in the rugged hinterland. And there was the prospect of the railway, which raised new visions of Victoria as the San Francisco of the North, with its own transcontinental rail link like the newly opened Union Pacific, and its own Pacific oceanic empire of trade. Politically, at least, the city had been connected into a new continental system. Now it looked for the necessary communication network to be constructed also, to put it on the highroads of world development.

Gradually, moreover, its basic hinterland trades improved.

Gold production, after reaching a low point in 1870, went up in 1871, and up still further in 1874–75, although it never came near the scale of the early sixties.[51] Coal output also began a steady climb from 1873 to 1879, though bigger years of growth would come in the next decade.[52] And if lumbering on the Island experienced no great advance yet, a new hinterland enterprise of considerable export potential made its appearance: salmon-canning. The salmon-canning industry had reached the American Pacific coast in the 1860's, from earlier beginnings in Maine and New Brunswick; but it was first established on the lower Fraser in 1870, independent of any American connection.[53] Victoria commission merchants effectively financed the Fraser river canneries and acted as agents in exporting their product directly to Great Britain.[54] For the canning process offered a means of overcoming the barrier of distance between a rich North Pacific food resource and a hungry industrial market. Furthermore, it produced a valuable trade that did not face the impediment of ever-rising American tariff barriers.

566

British Columbian salmon-canning grew slowly at first in the seventies, faster in the eighties, by which time the industry had spread northward to the Skeena (in 1877) and to the Nass and beyond. Victoria businessmen continued to play a major role in the enterprise: J.H. Todd provides a good example. Born in Brampton, Upper Canada, he had gone to Barkerville in 1863, speculated in mines and operated a successful merchandising business before moving to Victoria in 1872 to undertake another. Through profits from mining properties, and through acting as agent for canners on the Fraser, the Todd wholesaling firm was able to acquire two canneries there and another at Esquimalt. Subsequently it added a much larger one on the Skeena obtained from another prominent Victoria house of the day, Turner, Beeton and Company. Todd and Sons, in fact, continued to operate from Victoria as late as 1954, its fishing interests ultimately going to B.C. Packers.[55]

Furthermore, the redoubtable Joseph Spratt of the Albion Iron Works early entered the business. He developed the oilery (for pressing out herring oil) that he had opened on Burrard Inlet in 1868, at the site of the present city of Vancouver, into a floating salmon cannery.[56] Popularly termed "Spratt's Ark," it was a pioneer in the area's canning industry. More important in the long run, however, was R.P. Rithet, a Victoria wholesale merchant of widespread interests and enterprises. After acting as an agent for local Fraser river canners, he organized a number of them into the Victoria Canning Company in 1891, to meet the competition of two British-backed companies, British Columbia Canning and Anglo-British Columbia Packing, who had acquired virtually all the other canneries on the river.[57] That story, however, runs beyond this study, and it is more important here to examine the advancing career of Robert Paterson Rithet as an exemplification of Victoria business in itself.

Born in Scotland in 1844, he was in the Cariboo in 1862; but after a few years came to Victoria, still in his early twenties, to find employment in the wholesale trade. In 1868 he was working for Sproat and Company; indeed, was running its Victoria office, since Gilbert Sproat, a man of many parts — merchant, insurance agent, sawmill manager, lobbyist, author, and ethnologist — was then mainly in London, directing the Committee on the Affairs of British Columbia that he had organized.[58] The next year Rithet moved to San Francisco, to deal with the firm's interests there; evidently a promotion, for Sproat had sent him "kind words of confidence" by letter.[59] And here he came in close contact with Sproat's San Francisco partner, Andrew Welch. Welch, who had begun as a bookkeeper from England and worked with Sproat in the Alberni sawmill before entering into partnership in his wholesale business, was already emerging as a wealthy and prominent member of the San Francisco commercial elite. Before his death in 1889 he was to become a millionaire several times over, do much to develop the shipping trade between Victoria and that city, gain control of the Burrard Inlet mills at Moodyville, and thus build up a large-scale lumber export business.[60] Rithet could hardly have made a better connection. It resulted, eventually, in his own partnership with Welch.

567

Before that transpired, he returned to Victoria, still in Sproat's service; and there in 1870 had a stiff little encounter with a Mrs. Sutton, who did not approve of his attentions to her daughter. In fact, he broke his engagement to Miss Sutton by formal note to her mama — a Victorian touch in the wider sense of the term.[61] That year, moreover, Rithet left Sproat's firm to join that of J. Robertson Stewart, one of the old original British merchants in Victoria, who carried on insurance business for British and American companies, and helped direct the British Columbian Investment and Loan Society, as well as operating a large wholesale warehouse.[62] In May of 1871, Rithet was "at present managing his business" because of Stewart's illness.[63] The latter soon decided to dispose of his interests and retire to Scotland. Andrew Welch bought him out, with Rithet's cordial approval.[64] In fact, that August a new firm was announced in the press, Welch, Rithet and Company, successors to J. Robertson Stewart. "We began," wrote Rithet, "under very favorable auspices, when the colony seems to be about to enter an era of improvement and progress. . . . with houses in San Francisco and Liverpool we should be able to make a business, and our outside connections are also tip-top."[65]

Thereafter through the seventies, and on into the eighties, Rithet's interests continued to grow: in wholesaling, shipping, insurance, lumbering, canning, grocery importing, and generally financial investment in a wide range of enterprises. With Welch, he became engaged in the sugar trade of the Hawaiian Islands; they acquired control of plantations there.[66] He invested in the mills at Moodyville, the Albion Iron Works, in sealing, whaling, and in farming. He became president of the Board of Trade and a justice of the peace in the 1870's, mayor of Victoria in 1885, then was elected to the legislature in the 1890's.[67] And on Welch's death he took over as head of both Welch and Company, San Francisco, and R.P. Rithet and Company, Victoria.[68] There is no space to deal with his later ventures in the mining and railway development of the British Columbia interior, nor in the building of deepwater dock facilities at Victoria through his Victoria Wharf and Warehouse Company. All that can be noted is his connection with the continued growth of the city's shipping interests through the founding of the Canadian Pacific Navigation Company in 1883. And this brings in another of the leading Victorian entrepreneurs of the era, John Irving.

Irving had assumed control of his father's steamship company in 1872, although only eighteen years of age. Gold discoveries in the Stikeen and Cassiar districts in the seventies revived the coastal shipping trade, and Irving moved vigorously into competition, adding new boats to his fleet. At the same time growing settlement on the mainland and its expanding needs produced more traffic to the Fraser, while soon plans for the Pacific railway's construction brought a further stimulus. In 1878 Irving obtained a contract to carry the first shipment of rails from Esquimalt to Yale, and from then on increasingly left all rivals behind.[69] His chief competitor was still the Hudson's Bay Company's fleet. In 1883 he successfully arranged to merge it with his own.

It might not be without significance that a year earlier John Irving had married the daughter of Alexander Munro, Chief Factor of the Company in Victoria — nor that two of the bride's brothers worked for R.P. Rithet, who himself had married one of the Munro girls in 1875.[70] At any rate, the Canadian Pacific Navigation Company that now emerged to combine the lines under his management had Rithet as one of its directors and chief shareholders, along with Munro and that other noted business figure, Robert Dunsmuir of colliery fame.[71] Understandably, one of the line's fast ships was the *R.P. Rithet*. Irving's shipping empire (a far cry from Captain Cooper's little schooner, *Alice*) took over minor companies at the end of the eighties, and increasingly went into inland navigation on the lakes of the interior. It was ultimately bought out by the Canadian Pacific Railway as its coastal service in 1900. That, in itself, marked the passing of Victoria's as well as Irving's steamboat hegemony; but it had been a very good run indeed.

Meanwhile Robert Dunsmuir's coal operations had grown steadily. In 1873 his one mine, the Wellington, had turned out 16,000 tons (just entering full production) to 45,000 for all those of the Vancouver Island Coal Company's.[72] In 1880, his holdings alone produced 189,000 tons, and three years later he bought out his partner for $600,000.[73] He was well on his way to being the province's outstanding industrial capitalist, with a fleet of cargo vessels, a mine railway, and a large part of the

Albion Iron Works besides.[74] As if to fit the classic picture of the nineteenth-century capitalist, he had a hard reputation with labour. He faced strikes at the mines in 1877 and 1883, brought in strikebreakers, and on the former violent occasion, a gunboat and the militia also. Apart from this, Dunsmuir, now settled in Victoria, was also moving into railway promotions and construction. In 1883, the Esquimalt Railway Company of which he was president (it included the powerful figures, Leland Stanford and Charles Crocker of San Francisco, and C.P. Huntington of New York) obtained a contract from the federal government to build the Esquimalt and Nanaimo line, on terms that included a lavish grant of land.[75] Begun in 1884 under Dunsmuir's direction, it was finished in 1886, for the first time giving Victoria overland access to the coal hinterland.

Yet the seventy-mile Esquimalt and Nanaimo was a rather small consolation prize for Victoria not securing the Canadian Pacific — which was essentially what it had turned out to be. Through much of the seventies the city had envisioned and urged the transcontinental line by way of Bute Inlet and Seymour Narrows to Vancouver Island, and hotly protested proposals for a Fraser valley route to tidewater instead. In 1874 the railway on the Island was at least promised anew by the Mackenzie federal government, but the bill for it was defeated in the Senate, leaving Victoria bitterly disappointed, and much angry talk of secession in political and business circles. But though the dispute rose and fell in the ensuing years, with recurrent swells of separatism again, the fact was that the capital or the Island did not necessarily speak for the province as a whole; and the British Columbian mainland communities saw far more benefit to be gained from a Fraser valley rail route. Here was, indeed, still further indication that the island community of Victoria had been brought into a continental system, and now had little weight to bear against the whole thrust of Canadian metropolitan designs. The best that could be done was look for consolation prizes.

The Esquimalt dry dock and the E. & N. itself were two of these. And by the time that Dunsmuir undertook to build the latter (seeking truly magnificent consolation for himself and friends in terms for subsidies, coal fields, and lands), Victoria interests were ready to make the best of the inevitable. Hence, in 1884, when the C.P.R. was already well advanced in its building, both up the Fraser and into the Rockies from the east, a final settlement of terms was harmoniously achieved. Victoria still had a sizeable and prosperous maritime trading domain; its population stood at twelve thousand that year,[76] and the city was thriving and hopeful. For at least it would have its own Island railway now.

Not only was the Island railway opened in 1886, but the C.P.R. that year also carried its first through trains to the Pacific — to Burrard Inlet. And this really marked the ending of an era for Victoria, for now Vancouver's meteoric rise was under way, as the true beneficiary of the

569

transcontinental railway, the National Policy, and the forces of Canadian metropolitanism in general. The little lumber settlement on the Inlet had been launched into its role as Canada's chief western outlet and Pacific port of entry. Not till 1898 did the import trade of the upstart city pass that of Victoria's; yet the trend was there before that was to make Vancouver the new British Columbian entrepot and distributing centre.[77] In the later eighties and nineties Victoria would further develop its coal, salmon, and lumber trades, along with new growth in deep-sea fishing, scaling, and also in grain exports. But a reorientation of commercial patterns from sea to land was in process, in which Victoria could not hope to dominate great new hinterlands of deep-rock mining in the interior ranges or of agriculture on the prairies. A phase was over for the maritime city; and the completion of the transcontinental railway signalized it better than anything else.

There had not been want of energy or initiative in the Victorian business community. Men like Rithet, Dunsmuir, and Irving demonstrated that fact, as did W.P. Sayward, who had built a large new lumber mill at Victoria in 1878 — which by 1890, was cutting nearly eleven million feet a year itself, while Sayward's logging camps were scattered up the Island, feeding his large-scale export trade.[78] Others, perhaps, in the community had showed less enterprise, being more content with things as they were, in a pleasantly civilized little world readily open to greater worlds in San Francisco or London, but remote from the harder, cruder surroundings of the continental interior. Yet it would be difficult to prove such a point; and in any case it was not so much lack of enterprise as lack of situation and economic leverage that had placed it beyond the power of Victoria's businessmen to deal with changing patterns of trade. They had responded successfully to various favourable factors in the climate of enterprise; there was not much that could be done when the unfavorable overtook them.

There are many other names that could be singled out in the period of the seventies and eighties that would show the general stability and substance of this business community. Many firms from gold rush days continued in being, carrying on names like Southgate, Hibben, Dickson and Campbell, Sehl, Pendergast, Heisterman, and others. Some early merchants indeed had died, retired or left, the Lowes going, one to Scotland, one to San Francisco, in the seventies; David Oppenheimer shrewdly moving to Vancouver in 1886, to become "the father of Vancouver's jobbing trade."[79] Yet there were still others who had known Victoria's earlier days actively on hand, like William Ward, manager of the Bank of British Columbia since 1867 and clerk before that, or A.H. Green of Garesche and Green, whose large private bank had taken over from Wells Fargo in 1873 but who had worked for that agency previously.[80] A notable feature of the Victoria commercial community, in short, was still its continuity; new leaders largely rose from within its own ranks. But no doubt this was a result of there having been no spectacular advances since the gold rush to bring new groups of entrepreneurs. Victoria was already an "old," settled, quietly growing town, after less than three decades of urban existence.

Its ties with San Francisco and Britain remained fully evident. In 1886, the bulk of its external trade was still directed to the former, though British goods continued to be of much significance as imports, and exports of salmon to Britain (and eastern Canada) were fast rising. Offsetting San Francisco influence, of course, was British influence through politics, capital investment, business personnel, and the very dealings with major firms in San Francisco that were themselves part of a London–Liverpool and Glasgow metropolitan network; like Welch and Company, Dickson, De Wolf, Falkner Bell, and several others.[81] Noticeable, too, was the growth of eastern Canadian agencies and imports in Victoria by this time, behind the national tariff wall; but nothing comparable to the change effected in a few years through the C.P.R. — to which one might ascribe the fact that advertisements for Canadian firms and products clearly began to displace those of San Francisco in Victoria directories by about 1890.

571

And thus, in a sense, passed the San Francisco of the North, gradually to be replaced with today's centre of tourism and retirement enterprises, and of that truly big modern growth-industry, provincial government. Yet the businessmen who had seen Victoria rise from a fort or a gold rush tent town to a flourishing port city in well under thirty years, had no cause to minimize the comfortable affluence they had acquired, and done much to give to their adopted home.

What had the business community done for Victoria? In the first place — without at all forgetting other factors, the role of politicians and bureaucrats, of the labour force, or simply, the citizenry of consumers — they had essentially shaped its economic functions, furnished the bulk of jobs and services that made it an operative centre of urban population. In the second place, they had considerably influenced its political, social, and cultural life, businessmen having widely entered into provincial and municipal politics, benevolent and religious societies, educational movements, literary and musical organizations, and the like. To deal with this would be to write another chapter. All that can be said here is that the record of early Victoria's business community in participating in primarily non-economic activities in their society seems as good as, or better than, the record of similar groups in comparable Canadian cities at similar stages of development. And this, again, is not to see this very human collectivity of fallible, self-interested individuals as peerless visionaries and altruists. It may have been more a result of Victoria's relative isolation, insularity, and small size, whereby the entrepreneurial element readily came to know, and feel committed to, a fairly compact local society that did not soon become heterogeneous and amorphous through continued rapid growth.

In the third place, the business community marked Victoria's character in the broadest sense: in its identity, to use a not-unheard-of term. The city's affiliations with California that still exist surely relate not just to sea and sunshine (unlike the humidity of Vancouver and the northwest American coast) but to the historic communications and exchange that its merchants sustained with San Francisco. Victoria's oft-noted "British" attributes, also, may well be derived less from an obsolete Bay Company officialdom or a small emigrant English gentry than from the strongly British element in the dominant wholesale trades, which easily maintained the outlook and behaviour of the old gentry elite as it rose in wealth and social position. And finally, even the faint continuing touch of cosmopolitanism in an otherwise provincial city — which seems to give it a more mature ambiance than many an older Canadian town — assuredly may come from the original non-British, non-American component of the business community that largely persisted through Victoria's first formative decades. There is, then, much more in the early development of Victoria than the affairs of provincial governments or the vicissitudes of public men.

572

NOTES

[1] On the general significance of this theme, see D.T. Gallagher, "Bureaucrats or Businessmen? Historians and the Problem of Leadership in Colonial British Columbia," *Syesis* 3 (1970): 173–86.

[2] W.K. Lamb, "Early Lumbering on Vancouver Island," pt. 1, *British Columbia Historical Quarterly* (January 1938), 43.

[3] Lamb, "Early Lumbering," 46.

[4] *Gazette* (Victoria), December 25, 1858.

[5] Alfred Waddington, *The Frazer Mines Vindicated* (Victoria, 1858), 19.

[6] *British Colonist* (Victoria), June 12, 1860.

[7] *The British Columbian and Victoria Guide and Directory for 1863* (Victoria, 1863), 49.

[8] W. Ireland, "British Columbia's American Heritage," Canadian Historical Association, *Annual Report for 1948*, 68.

[9] Ireland, "British Columbia's American Heritage," 69.

[10] M. Ormsby, *British Columbia: A History* (Toronto, 1958), 141.

[11] R.E. and M.F. Stewart, *Adolph Sutro* (Berkeley, 1962), *passim*.

[12] "The Oppenheimers of Vancouver," typescript, British Columbia Archives (hereafter BCA).

[13] British Columbia Archives, Vertical Files (hereafter BCAVF).

[14] Edgar Fawcett, *Some Reminiscences of Old Victoria* (Toronto, 1912), 60; British Columbia Miscellany, Bancroft Library, Berkeley.

[15] Lamb, "Early Lumbering," pt. 2, *British Columbia Historical Quarterly* (April 1938), 114.

[16] Fawcett, *Some Reminiscences*, 64.

[17] BCAVF.

[18] *Prices Current* (San Francisco). See advertisements from 1853 onward, also E. Mallandaine, *First Victoria Directory* (Victoria, 1860), 42. For Samuel Price, *Gazette*, January 25, 1858 — J.N. Thain was the local representative.

[19] *Colonist*, February 2, 1865.

[20] Fawcett, *Some Reminiscences*, 62; *British Columbian and Victoria Guide*, 137.

[21] On the Lowes, see J.M.S. Careless, "The Lowe Brothers, 1852–70: A Study in Business Relations on the North Pacific Coast," *B.C. Studies* 2 (1968–69): 1–18.

[22] Careless, "The Lowe Brothers," 10.

[23] I.M. Richard, "Gilbert Norman Sproat," *British Colonial History Quarterly* (January 1937), 22–23.

[24] BCAVF.

[25] British Columbia Miscellany, Bancroft.

[26] BCAVF.
[27] BCAVF.
[28] *Colonist*, November 20, 1866.
[29] Lamb, "Early Lumbering," pt. 2, 105.
[30] Lamb, "Early Lumbering," pt. 2, 114.
[31] Lamb, "Early Lumbering," pt. 2, 121.
[32] BCAVF.
[33] P.A. Phillips, "Confederation and the Economy of British Columbia," in W.G. Shelton, ed., *British Columbia and Confederation* (Victoria, 1967), 51, BCAVF.
[34] Phillips, "Confederation," 51.
[35] Ormsby, *British Columbia*, 215.
[36] J. Audain, *From Coal Mine to Castle* (New York, 1955), 36.
[37] Audain, *From Coal Mine to Castle*, 51.
[38] M.A. Cox, *Saga of a Seafarer* (New Westminster, 1966), 8.
[39] E.W. Wright, ed., *Marine History of the Pacific North West*, by Lewis and Dryden (New York, 1961), 81.
[40] Wright, ed., *Marine History*, 81.
[41] Careless, "The Lowe Brothers," 10. Lowe Papers, BCA, T. Lowe to A.C. Anderson, July 2, 1859.
[42] Wright, ed., *Marine History*, 140.
[43] Wright, ed., *Marine History*, 82.
[44] BCAVF.
[45] Phillips, "Confederation," 57.
[46] S. Higgins, "British Columbia and the Confederation Era," in Shelton, ed., *British Columbia and Confederation*, 28.
[47] Ireland, "British Columbia's American Heritage," 71.
[48] BCAVF.
[49] *British Colonist*, July 20, 1871.
[50] *City of Victoria Directory for 1890* (Victoria, 1890), 122.
[51] *Annual Report of the Minister of Mines* (Victoria, 1900), chart, n.p.
[52] *Annual Report of the Minister of Mines* (Victoria, 1900), chart, n.p.
[53] Phillips, "Confederation," 55.
[54] K. Ralston, "Patterns of Trade and Investment on the Pacific Coast, 1867–1892: The Case of the British Columbia Salmon Canning Industry," *B.C. Studies* 1 (1968–69): 42.
[55] BCAVF.
[56] J.M. Grant, "British Columbia in Early Times," *British Columbia Magazine* (June 1911), 494.
[57] Ralston, "Patterns of Trade and Investment," 42–43.
[58] Richard, "Gilbert Norman Sproat," 22–29.
[59] BCA, *R.P. Rithet Letterbook* 1, Rithet to G. Sproat, December 11, 1868. BCAVF.
[60] *Rithet Letterbook* 1, Rithet to Mrs. Sutton, April 16, 1870.
[61] *British Colonist*, November 11, 1869.
[62] *Rithet Letterbook* 1, Rithet to R.P.D. Duff, May 9, 1871.
[63] *Rithet Letterbook* 1, Rithet to A. Welch, August 24, 1871.
[64] *Rithet Letterbook* 1, August 25, 1871.
[65] *Colonist*, July 26, 1889.
[66] BCAVF. See also *Victoria Illustrated* (Victoria, 1891), 77–78.
[67] BCAVF.
[68] BCAVF.
[69] BCAVF.
[70] *Colonist*, April 17, 1889.
[71] Wright, ed., *Marine History*, 303.
[72] Audain, *From Coal Mine to Castle*, 52.
[73] Audain, *From Coal Mine to Castle*, 65, 73.
[74] *Colonist*, April 13, 1889.
[75] Audain, *From Coal Mine to Castle*, 79.
[76] *City of Victoria Directory for 1890*, 122.
[77] *Annual Reports of the British Columbia Board of Trade, 1887–1900* (Victoria, 1900), tables, n.p.
[78] *Victoria Illustrated*, 50.
[79] L. Makovski, "Rise of the Merchant Princes," *British Columbia Magazine* (June 1911), 57.
[80] BCAVF. Francis Garesche was drowned in 1874, but the firm continued in both names.
[81] See directory and newspaper advertisements of period for indications of operations of these firms. On all three, for example, see *San Francisco Directory for 1873*, M.G. Langley (San Francisco, 1873), and on Falkner Bell specifically, W.T. Jackson, *The Enterprising Scot* (Edinburgh, 1968), 222, 374, *passim*. Falkner Bell also appears in the Lowe and Rithet letters — and Jackson's work notes that the Scottish American Investment Company, for and with which they dealt, bought extensive California ranch property on the recommendation of John Clay (who had been George Brown's estate manager in Ontario), as well as involving Thomas Nelson, the leading Edinburgh publisher, in its investments. Nelson was Brown's brother-in-law, who with Clay succeeded in restoring Brown's Bow Park estate to financial health after the latter's death. One can see many ramifications here worth tracing out!

The Character of the British Columbia Frontier

BARRY M. GOUGH

Chief among the concerns of historians studying the founding of new societies has been the concept of the frontier, and in the writing of the history of Canada, the United States, South Africa, Australia, and New Zealand, among others, the frontier has been a substantial theme.[1] "Frontier" itself has been variously defined — from the outer fringe of metropolitan influence, to the actual geographical area of control, to a zone to be occupied, to a border between states.[2] Usually such definitions tend to be Eurocentric and agrarian, describing the process of the founding of the new society in question in terms of the expanding society's change in new conditions, its occupations of lands suitable for agriculture, and its evolving legal systems. Often such historical inquiry neglects two essential ingredients: the contact of cultures and races within the zone of influence and the geographical features of the zone itself. By doing so, such studies frequently do violence to the important result of how the aboriginal society already occupying the land and exploiting its resources responded and changed in the face of new circumstances. And such research neglects the role of environment in the historical process.

Our study of the formative years of British Columbia history must, however, concern itself with the frontier, though an enlarged, more encompassing perspective is required than hitherto offered by historians of British Columbia.[3] Such an inquiry cannot be hagiographical in nature but must analyse the institutions and forces whereby British Columbia changed from Indian territory to fur trade realm, then to colony, and finally to province all within a brief span of forty years. During the years 1846 to 1871 an imperial tide lapped the shores of the Northwest Coast and in doing so changed the character of human occupation, and it brought with it at the flood new political, legal, and social institutions whose legacies are still apparent. This process forms a "frontier" and for the purposes of this paper "frontier" will be taken to mean the zone of influence of imperial administration emanating from London and from the colonial capitals of Victoria and New Westminster. Also for the purposes of this essay "frontier process" will be taken to mean the methods by which Europeans extended their jurisdiction, occupied land, managed a resource base, developed an Indian policy, and established sites for

From *B.C. Studies* 32 (1976/77): 28–40. Reprinted with permission.

the exploitation of the sea coast and the interior land mass. The first section of this essay examines environmental determinants, the second explores British and American influences, and the third provides a summary of the character of the British Columbia frontier and its legacies.

I

From the earliest European contact with the Northwest Coast, explorers understood that the nature of the environment would determine the type of human occupation in that locale. The European reconnaissance of British Columbia in the late eighteenth century revealed that the environment was generally devoid of level land suitable for agriculture. Rather they found a mountainous terrain bordering the Pacific, a land whose scale was impressive, whose physical landscape was varied. Rugged off-shore islands, inshore channels and inlets, coastal mountains and lowlands, river deltas, interior plateaus and narrow river valleys testified to the lack of level land at low elevation. Yet the sea and land provided resources for exploitation — sea otter and beaver, salmon, timber, and spars — and from the very beginning of European contact with this portion of the Northwest Coast the exporting of primary resources formed the central feature of white–Indian trade relations. Moreover, the potential resource wealth of the region brought international rivalry among Russia, Spain, Britain, and the United States, and by 1846 the present boundaries of British Columbia had been largely determined in this first rush for spoils.[4]

575

The British Columbia frontier properly dates from 1846 for it was in that year that British sovereignty over the region was determined by Anglo-American treaty, presumptuously without any compliance on the part of the Indians who now found that they had new political institutions with which to deal. That treaty had, the British government hoped, secured a great fur-trading preserve north of the boundary for the Hudson's Bay Company. The Oregon Boundary Dispute had underscored the conflict between fur trade and settlement on the Pacific slope: its resolution had left the Americans with lands more suitable for agricultural settlement, and it gave the British the rich fur preserve of the north.[5] Moreover, the dispute resulted in the retreat of the Hudson's Bay Company and its agricultural subsidiary, the Puget's Sound Agricultural Company, north from its Oregon holdings; and in the process the Company developed new sites of occupation and its agricultural subsidiary farmed some of the best lands available in Vancouver Island, then virtually the sole lands known to be suitable for settlement. Other lands might be available, but in some areas such as Cowichan the Indians were known to be hostile[6] and in others the availability of scarce land suitable for tillage was not discovered until the Vancouver Island Exploration Expedition of 1864. Perhaps in the end it was the mountainous, non-agrarian character of the British Columbia frontier that saved the area from American squatter settlement. Now the Hudson's Bay Company's dominance of the Pacific slope had to be confined within new political boundaries.[7]

Within this area the Hudson's Bay Company had already established a commercial network of posts, trails, and shipping routes. In 1843 Fort Victoria had been built as the focal point of Company seaborne commerce, and subsequently Forts Rupert and Nanaimo had been established to mine and market steamer coal. Forts Hope and Yale had been built to provide new transportation links north of the forty-ninth parallel.[8] Fort Langley acquired new importance on the lower Fraser while Port Simpson at the entrance to Portland Inlet became the focal point for northern trade extending to the Queen Charlotte Islands, Alaska, and the continental interior.

The patterns of resource exploitation, of corporate dominance, and of cluster settlement in and around forts had begun to appear long before miners searched tributaries of the Fraser River in 1858 for gold. The gold seekers, too, had to face environmental realities; the weather and climate were different than in some areas of California they had mined previously. Though on the lower reaches of the Fraser miners could use the "rocker" or "cradle;" on the upper Fraser they were obliged to tunnel into the pay-channel lying below the creekbed. In the dry diggings they engaged in sluicing, using quicksilver brought from California. But again, the environment determined that gold extraction would necessitate expensive hydraulic equipment and substantial financial outlay. These features influenced the early demise of the individual miners' rush of 1858–59 and the rise of companies such as the Van Winkle Company that prospered into the 1870s.[9] And not least among the geographical influences was the isolation of the area from California, the eastern seaboard of North America, Europe, and Asia — an isolation that determined costs of transportation, slowness of communication, modes of travel, and, for the early settlers, political and social perspectives. Not least, it influenced the character of official response, whether from the imperial or colonial capitals, when a threat to sovereignty within or on the border of British territory seemed real or when "troubles" with Indians in British or adjacent territories threatened the peaceful repose of the settler communities.

Environmental determinants also meant that governments had to put a premium on encouraging means of transportation. Coastal and river navigation had to be made safer by surveys and markers. River channels had to be widened and cleared of debris. New wagon roads beyond the headwaters of sternwheeler navigation had to be built and these required large government outlays that in some cases had to be recovered by a tolls system. And new way stations and administrative systems for a growing colonial bureaucracy had to be built to serve a governmental network

576

that now, in the early 1860s, encompassed the Cariboo within its zone of influence.

By this time also the "heartland" of the region was the Georgia Strait area with its administrative and political leadership extending over a network of rivers and roads into the cordillera.[10] The Cariboo rush of the 1860s and the growth of lumbering on Vancouver Island extended commercial links inland and on the seaboard, and until the Canadian Pacific Railway reached Pacific tidewater and the Panama Canal shortened links with the Atlantic, Victoria remained the focus of the region. Vancouver City, important in the diversification of economic activities, was a latter-day corruption on this frontier. A functional unity based around the Fraser — Britain's Columbia, if you will — already existed by 1871.

II

Tempting as it might be to argue that the character of the British Columbia frontier was shaped by environmental realities, such a conclusion would exclude any study of the type of persons who came to British Columbia in its formative years and the form of government and authority emerging as a result of their migration. No sooner had the British government acquired sovereignty to Vancouver Island and continental territory north of the 49th parallel than it set about to establish means of countering the frontier tendencies of Americans.[11] Vancouver Island was established as a colony proper in 1849 to counter the threat of American squatter settlement, and the Hudson's Bay Company was assigned the task of developing a colony under strict regulations. Such a policy intended, at once, to encourage British immigration and to safeguard the interests of the Indians. The Colonial Office exhibited naivety on both counts, but it is important to note here that from the very beginning of settlement, the patterns of land occupation were government-directed.[12] Land by pre-emption was not available at first. Indian land title was alienated only in a few cases. The result was a different type of society than that emerging in adjacent American history.[13]

The second phase of government desires to protect British territory from American interest occurred only a few years later, in 1850 and 1851, when Victoria's political jurisdiction was extended to the Queen Charlotte Islands. London elevated the territory into a colonial territory administered by the Governor of Vancouver Island as a separate Lieutenant-Governorship, and the reason for this was that London intended to protect sovereignty there from "marauders without title."[14] In an age of American filibustering, Britain could take no chances. Gunboats were sent and signs erected in the islands, but the gold of the islands that had attracted five or six American ships out of San Francisco proved insufficient for economical exploitation and the environment proved unattractive to settlers. Nonetheless, an additional territory had been added to the formal British Empire's jurisdiction.

Two similar extensions of the imperial frontier subsequently occurred: first in New Caledonia with the establishment of the Colony of British Columbia in 1858, the second in the Stikine Territory in 1862 when a reorganization of British Columbia's boundaries allowed for the extension of imperial jurisdiction north to 60° North latitude (except to the Alaskan panhandle) and west to include the Queen Charlotte Islands.[15] The union of the colonies of Vancouver Island and British Columbia in 1866 was a natural successor to the administrative growth and consolidation that had gone on since 1849. In short, the means of formal control had been extended within a territory already British in sovereignty, and in every case the government's actions were motivated by a desire to pre-empt American squatter settlement and to protect the interests of the Crown.

578

Yet at the very same time, what Professor John S. Galbraith has rightly called "the imperial factor" — the Hudson's Bay Company — was fighting a rearguard action change.[16] The Company gave little encouragement to settlement on Vancouver Island. It sought to monopolize gold extraction from the Queen Charlotte Islands. It endeavoured to control means of transportation to the Fraser gold districts. It acted in a similar way during the Stikine rush of 1862. In each case it sought to exploit the resources of British Columbia in its own way as best it could, and it did so in an age when metropolitan and colonial critics of monopoly and of chartered companies — in others words, advocates of free trade — were making themselves heard in London. Indeed, from the very beginning of colonization on Vancouver Island, critics of the restrictive nature of Company control (particularly in land alienation and transportation control) objected to the domineering manner of the Company.[17] The Colonial Office's desire to end the Company's control on Vancouver Island was well advanced by the mid-1850s, and in 1856 the first legislative assembly met in Victoria — the first representative political institution in the Colony. In the following year a British parliamentary inquiry pointed to the end of Company monopoly in New Caledonia, and the Colonial Office was seeking ways of phasing out Company control on the mainland at the very time news reached London of the great rush to the Fraser in 1858. The result this time was a Crown Colony: a formal jurisdiction in which the colonial governor was answerable to London within rather confined limits. Now the governor was solely an imperial representative, and in a series of political moves initiated by London the Hudson's Bay Company's imperium came to an end. In its place London's authority held sway, more paternalistic than the Company regime and more anxious as time progressed to make the colonies on the Pacific seaboard not only united but self-sufficient and members of a British North American confederation.

By creating British Columbia as a colony proper, the imperial government could increase British executive control because, as the preamble to the 1851 act stated, "it is desirable to make some temporary provision for the Civil Government of such territories, until permanent settlements shall be thereupon established, and the number of Colonists increased . . . ."[18] Self-government was deliberately withheld because the Secretary of State for the Colonies, Sir Edward Bulwer Lytton, thought "the grand principle of free institutions" should not be risked "among settlers so wild, so miscellaneous, perhaps so transitory, and in a form of society so crude."[19] The Undersecretary of State for the Colonies, Herman Merivale, believed that only by providing security for settlers and affording the appropriate political climate could a responsible government free from the factiousness of American politics be fostered.[20] Moreover, central authority would provide trusteeship over the Indians, and prevent "cruelties and horrors that had been perpetrated in the early days of our colonies" and in the western United States.[21] In these respects, the British government devised a form of government that they thought suitable for the circumstances: it was arbitrary government, they admitted, but one in which there could be a relaxation of executive powers with the changing circumstances.[22]

This metropolitan form of control allowed the governor, James Douglas, and the first chief justice, Matthew Begbie, to establish a uniform judicial system throughout the colony. Californians, who formed the large majority of migrants into this frontier, by and large came to respect British law on this far western frontier. The reason for this, Begbie argued, was that the populace had willingly submitted to the powers of the executive — powers which, no matter how contrary to their wishes, were clearly and directly expressed.[23] At the same time Douglas devised a licence scheme (based on a system used in New South Wales in 1851 and the Colony of Victoria, Australia, in 1854) for miners that enabled the government to raise revenue for administration and public works, to keep a record of the number of adventurers entering the gold region, and to provide salaries for law enforcement officers and gold commissioners. Douglas attempted to establish a boat licence whereby the public were to observe the Company's exclusive rights of trade with the Indians, its rights of sole navigation to the mining region and elsewhere within its territories, and its requirement that all non-Company trading vessels possess licences issued by the Company. The Colonial Office declared this proclamation invalid because the Company's monopoly extended only to British trade with the Indians and instructed Douglas that it be removed. However, in the four-month interval that it was in force it alienated miners who rightly saw the governor acting for the private interests of the Company rather than the public interests of the Crown.[24] Another measure of the colonial government to regulate the activities of miners within their jurisdiction, the establishing of mining boards, provided the miners with regulation over the matters they were most concerned with — the size of claims and sluices and the rules for working and holding them. These boards provided a vent for miners' complaints and thus aided the British in their local administration.

In Indian relations as well, the executive exercised the initiative. Its principal aim was to prevent whites and Indians from taking the law into their own hands. Interracial conflict did occur during this critical phase of British Columbia's government, but a show of force was made by the governor, who took pains to explain to persons of both races that British law allowed for the protection of all men regardless of race. He appointed prominent members of Indian tribes as magistrates to keep order among the Indians and appointed justices of the peace at various places on the Fraser River to whom whites and Indians alike could apply for redress of grievance. The governor's diplomacy among Indian peoples was important but the forbearance of the Indians themselves[25] allowed for the peaceful resolution of difference so uncharacteristic of race relations in adjacent American territory.

Certainly Californians who entered British territory objected to the domineering influence of the Company and Crown in British Columbia, but they came to respect the strong role of the executive. They found the boat licence "outrageous." They objected to the tolls of roads. They disliked mining licences. But they came to respect in British Columbia, as in New South Wales, Western Australia, and Victoria, the type of frontier government emanating from an empire that had once ruled their own country. They found the colonial government well managed, void of the graft and corruption of California politics, and contributory to the common good of the populace and the growth of the economy.[26]

There were, however, exceptions to the willingness of Californians to submit to British regulations. Case studies show that some Americans with not a little bravado attempted to violate British regulations in the Fraser River. Others attempted to continue the feuding of California mining camps in British territory. Still others of a criminal nature continued their careers north of the border. Many of them were opposed to British regulations *per se*; they were spirited gold seekers willing to "twist the Lion's tail" if they got the chance.[27] They were individuals bent on fortune, and they did not form a group which might combine to subvert British authority as officials in Victoria and London feared. The United States Consular resident in Victoria, John Nugent, did attempt to marshal American complaints against the colonial government and courts with a view to fostering an annexation movement. But Douglas, in his own defence, prepared a lengthy memorandum for the British government in which he documented how American citizens in British Columbia were treated in a comparable manner to British citizens in California. Subsequently in Washington, D.C., General Lewis Cass, the United States Secretary of State, acknowledged that the regulations prevailing in British Columbia respecting the rights of foreign miners were in fact more liberal than those in force in California. As for Nugent, he was branded as a subversive by British colonial officials who believed that he intended to provoke a filibuster under the guise of protecting Americans from misrule. No such action occurred, Nugent returned to San Francisco, and the only organized American political protest against British rule in the region — a protest by and large the work of one man and without the support of the press — came to an end.[28]

The Nugent case and those of various Americans opposing British law and order tended to underscore the fears of British officials that Americans would indeed subvert the government unless checked by a strong executive authority. It has tended to glorify Douglas and Begbie as guardians of constitutional rights at the expense of ignoring how both had their critics within the ranks of British and Canadian colonists who did not believe that their rights as Englishmen were being protected by an arbitrary government. The birth of the *British Colonist*, a Victoria newspaper, came precisely from this political quarter, and for many years political factions took as their main point of contention the role of the executive in colonial government. The 1858 rush, therefore, had brought important American influences into British territory: influences that authorities feared, and influences which they used to establish strong, centralized administrations to prevent Americans from undermining legal authority.

581

The British Columbia frontier, then, was a British imperial frontier — a counterfrontier, so to speak, projected from London and Victoria in response to influences and pressures from neighbouring frontiers, particularly from Oregon in the case of Vancouver Island and California in the case of British Columbia. The frontier process occurred in a zone already occupied and exploited by the Hudson's Bay Company, and for a time (particularly on Vancouver Island and for a brief moment in British Columbia) a type of double-image executive authority existed whereby the interest of Company and Crown were often inseparable and often confused. The imperial government, however, forced the clarification of responsibilities between the two. Indeed, the 1858 rush afforded the Colonial Office the opportunity of pressing for full imperial jurisdiction in New Caledonia.[29]

This imperial extension of control allowed for the opening up of the colonies by new transportation routes and by settlement of lands hitherto controlled by the Company. These measures were undertaken by government in response to fears that large numbers of Americans and other foreign land or gold seekers might squat on British territory, establish a popular government and drumhead court, invoke their own crude legal remedies for existing lawlessness, and treat Indians in a violent and inhuman way. These interrelated forces — squatter settlement, the filibuster, and lawlessness — became in their own ways material determinants on the British Columbia frontier. They forced colonial and imperial governments to establish regulations, introduce judicial systems, and provide military aid in support of the civil power in order that similar developments could be avoided in British territory.[30] It was precisely the American frontiersman's propensity to manage his own political affairs (in Frederick Jackson Turner's words, "to preserve order, even in the absence of legal authority"[31]) which most disturbed governors of Vancouver Island and British Columbia and a succession of British Colonial Secretaries and Undersecretaries during the course of the timespan considered by this essay. Officials wanted a self-sufficient territory free from American lawlessness, and they responded in a fairly regular and predictable way in the founding of the Colony of Vancouver Island, in the extension of jurisdiction to the Queen Charlotte Islands, in the constituting of the gold colony of British Columbia, and in the extension of boundaries in the Stikine. Government's concerns for securing the boundaries of British Columbia adjacent to the Alaska Panhandle and the Yukon as well as in the San Juan archipelago were merely extensions of government's attempts to secure the outer fringes of the imperial frontier.

582

In this way the British Columbia frontier was markedly similar to that of the rest of Canada. It was structured, to employ the words of the Canadian economic historians Easterbook and Aitken, in "the interests of a unity threatened by United States' penetration." The American frontier, by contrast, with its security against outside intervention, constituted an expansive, emerging force which greatly accelerated the rate of economic advance."[32] The structured unity of the British Columbia frontier was provided by London, erected on foundations supplied by the Hudson's Bay Company, and made secure by the material means which the British government was able to provide in the form of ships of the Royal Navy and men of the Royal Marines and Royal Engineers. London provided the finance, the manpower, and, not least, the psychological support rendered by the world's pre-eminent nation and empire that made the British Columbia frontier an imperial frontier.

But such metropolitan dominance on this western North American frontier also meant that arbitrary government enjoyed a lingering death; responsible government did not appear until British Columbia joined the Canadian confederation in 1871. Myths of suspected American takeovers continued for some time.[33] The founding fathers of the new colonies, Douglas and Begbie, were lionized at the expense of others, such as Richard Blanshard and Amor de Cosmos, who fought for more democratic causes. Above all, metropolitan influence tended to reinforce colonial perspectives whereby things British were, as a colonist wrote enthusiastically, "burnished and made the most of!!!"[34] In these ways the metropolitan origins of the British Columbia frontier did much to define the uniqueness of that province in relation to adjacent American states, and, for that matter, to other provinces in Canada or to certain Commonwealth countries. The unique environment of the Pacific slope meant obviously that the founding of a new society in the area now known as British Columbia would be influenced by geographical features, particularly in land occupation, resource extraction, and spatial functions of hinterland and metropolis; but the British role in the extension of political jurisdiction and sovereignty, a role undertaken to counter American influences, also shaped the character of the political society emerging in this most distant west.

NOTES

[1] For reviews of the literature on Canadian frontiers, see J.M.S. Careless, "Frontierism, Metropolitanism and Canadian History," *Canadian Historical Review* 35, 1 (March 1954): 1–21, and Michael Cross, *The Frontier Thesis and the Canadas: The Debate on the Impact of the Canadian Environment* (Toronto, 1970), 1–7, 186–88.

[2] The typology provided by the frontier thesis of Frederick Jackson Turner as given in his "Significance of the Frontier in American History" (1893) and his *Significance of Sections in American History* (New York, 1932) has long been discredited by American historians. Nonetheless, American frontier experiences still invite comparative studies with adjacent Canadian territories and other former British Empire countries. See the guidelines offered by Paul Sharp, "Three Frontiers: Some Comparative Studies of Canadian, American, and Australian Settlement," *Pacific Historical Review*, 24 (November 1955): 369–77. The best interpretive work on comparative frontiers is Robin W. Winks, *The Myth of the American Frontier: Its Relevance to America, Canada and Australia* (Leicester: The Sir George Watson Lectures, 1971). These suggestive inquiries invite further empirical research.

[3] See, for instance, the narrow constitutional approach provided by W.N. Sage in "The Gold Colony of British Columbia," *Canadian Historical Review* 11 (1921): 340–59.

[4] R.W. Van Alstyne, "International Rivalries in the Pacific Northwest," *Oregon Historical Quarterly*, 46 (1945): 185–218.

[5] The outcome of the dispute also gave both nations access to ports in the lower straits area separating Vancouver Island and the mainland and freedom of navigation there. Norman Graebner, *Empire on the Pacific* (New York, 1955).

[6] Eden Colvile to Sir John Pelly, 15 October 1849, in E.E. Rich, ed., *London Correspondence inward from Eden Colvile, 1849–1852* (London: Hudson's Bay Record Society, 1956), 19: 5.

[7] Not that the Company could not trade in American territory, but the United States government undertook to indemnify the Company for loss of their property in Oregon, and American politicians were anxious that the removal of the Company be effected as soon as possible. John S. Galbraith, *The Hudson's Bay Company as an Imperial Factor, 1821–1868* (Berkeley and Los Angeles, 1957), ch. 13.

[8] The new routes through the Similkameen Country were developed, in part to provide security for Company brigades so that they would not have to travel through the Cayuse Territory where an Indian War was in progress in the late 1840s. Gloria Griffin Cline, *Peter Skene Ogden and the Hudson's Bay Company* (Norman, Oklahoma, 1974)

[9] H.A. Innis and A.R.M. Lower, eds., *Select Documents in Canadian Economic History, 1783–1885* (Toronto, 1933), 771–77, 780–90, and W.J. Trimble, *The Mining Advance into the Inland Empire* (Madison, Wisconsin, 1914).

[10] J. Lewis Robinson and Walter G. Hardwick, *British Columbia: One Hundred Years of Geographical Change* (Vancouver, 1973), 12.

[11] W.P. Morrell, *Colonial Policy in the Age of Peel and Russell* (Oxford, 1930), 444–46.

[12] Land alienation was partially based on the theories of Edward Gibson Wakefield, whereby land was fixed at the "sufficient price" of £1 per acre. Land prices later were reduced in efforts to encourage colonization.

[13] The bailiff system attempted to introduce established society and deferential relationships into the Vancouver Island colony. Partially successful (though in a very small way), it tended to encourage the idea of a landed gentry in the Victoria area.

[14] James Doublas to Earl Grey, 29 January 1852, C.O. 305/3, Public Record Office, London; Lord Malmesbury to Admiralty, 23 June 1852, Admiralty Correspondence, vol. 1, Provincial Archives of British Columbia, Victoria.

[15] W.E. Ireland, "Evolution of the Boundaries of British Columbia," *British Columbia Historical Quarterly* 3 (October 1939): 263–82.

583

[16] Galbraith, *Hudson's Bay Company*, *passim*.

[17] Governor Douglas' identification with the Company was so strong that independent colonists tried to short-circuit imperial communications by sending delegations and petitions to London. During the Parliamentary Inquiry into the Company's affairs in 1857 the same critics were able to make their complaints known to the government.

[18] Great Britain, Statutes at Large, 21 and 22 *Vic.*, c. 99.

[19] Great Britain, *Hansard's Parliamentary Debates*, 3rd ser., 151 (1858), 1102.

[20] These views are set forth in E. Bulwer Lytton to Colonel Moody, 29 October 1858, C.O. 60/3. See also Merivale's article in *The Edinburgh Review* 107 (April 1858): 295–321.

[21] Hansard, 3rd ser., 151 (1858), 2102.

[22] Hansard, 3rd ser., 1769.

[23] M.B. Begbie, "Journey into the Interior of British Columbia," *Journal of the Royal Geographical Society* 3 (1861): 248.

[24] F.W. Howay in F.W. Howay, W.N. Sage, and H.F. Angus, *British Columbia and the United States* (Toronto and New Haven, 1942), 147.

[25] Indians have argued that the peace on the frontier was owing to their forbearance and willingness to allow whites "to use that country on equal terms with ourselves." One tribe, the Couteau, "saved the country from war when the Indians were about to combine and drive out the Whites." Evidence of Chief John Tedlenitsa of the Couteau tribe, in deputation to Sir Wilfred Laurier, 27 April 1916, in Borden Papers, MG 26 H 1(a), vol. 38, pp. 16394–5, Public Archives of Canada.

[26] W.E. Ireland, ed., "Gold Rush Days in Victoria, 1858–1859," *British Columbia Historical Quarterly* 12 (July 1948): 241. Also, Rodman W. Paul, " 'Old Californians' in British Gold Fields," *Huntington Library Quarterly* 17 (1954).

[27] Barry M. Gough, "Keeping British Columbia British: The Law-and-Order Question on a Gold Mining Frontier," *Huntington Library Quarterly* 38 (1975): 269–80.

[28] R.L. Reid, "John Nugent: The Impertinent Envoy," *British Columbia Historical Quarterly* 8 (1944): 53–76.

[29] John S. Galbraith, "Bulwer-Lytton's Ultimatum," *The Beaver*, Outfit 268 (Spring 1958), 20–24.

[30] On the question of military support for the civil power, see Barry M. Gough, " 'Turbulent Frontiers' and British Expansion: Governor James Douglas, The Royal Navy and the British Columbia Gold Rushes," *Pacific Historical Review* 41 (1972): 15–32.

[31] Turner's statement is quoted in H.C. Allen, *Bush and Backwoods: A Comparison of the Frontier in Australian and the United States* (East Lansing, Mich., 1959), 101.

[32] W.T. Easterbrook and H.G.J. Aitken, *Canadian Economic History* (Toronto, 1958), 356.

[33] W.N. Sage, "The Annexationist Movement in British Columbia," *Proceedings and Transactions of the Royal Society of Canada*, ser. 3, vol. 21 (1927), sec. 2, 97–110.

[34] Quoted in M.A. Ormsby, *British Columbia: A History* (Toronto, 1958), 107.

National Archives of Canada/C733.

Convention at Charlottetown, Prince Edward Island, of delegates from the Legislatures of Canada, New Brunswick, Nova Scotia, and Prince Edward Island, to take into consideration the Union of the British North American Colonies. Photograph by George P. Roberts, September 1864.

What is remarkable is not that there was opposition to Confederation in the Maritimes but how ineffectual it was. . . . Unlike other areas of the world forced into federation on terms considered unjust, the Maritime opposition to Confederation was remarkably weak and evaporated remarkably quickly.

Phillip Buckner, "CHR Dialogue: The Maritimes and Confederation: A Reassessment"

Topic Fifteen

Why Was Confederation Accepted?

The union of British North America had been considered as far back as 1790. A renewed interest arose in the 1850s, when increased tension between British North America and the United States, and the emerging political deadlock in the Canadas, made the option of a larger colonial union attractive.

In the mid-1860s, the right conditions prevailed for the politicians of the Canadas, New Brunswick, and Nova Scotia to bring about Confederation. The details of union were worked out at two important conferences in 1864. At the Charlottetown conference, in September, the delegates agreed in principle on a number of the important features of the eventual federation, including the regional representation of the upper house (Senate) and "representation by population" in the lower house (House of Commons). They also arrived at the nature of the division of powers between provincial and federal governments. A second conference at Quebec, in October, finalized these understandings in the Seventy-Two Resolutions, the basis for the British North America Act. Between 1864 and 1867, the politicians worked to convince their respective colonial assemblies to adopt Confederation.

In Canada West, there was widespread support for Confederation, which was seen as a solution to the perennial problem of political deadlock in the Canadas. Moreover, union would work to the economic advantage of Canada West, as the largest and most commercially advanced of the provinces. Union would also provide increased military protection for the inland province in the event of an American attack. Canada West would also benefit from any eventual expansion of the new nation across the continent, particularly into the Northwest.

The idea of Confederation was strongly opposed in Canada East. In "Confederation and Quebec," a chapter from his book *The French-Canadian Idea of Confederation, 1864–1900*, Arthur Silver points out that French Canadians in the St. Lawrence Valley judged the proposal mainly in terms of its potential impact on French-Canadian nationalism. While the *bleus* (under George-Étienne Cartier) were convinced that the proposed union guaranteed the autonomy of Quebec, in Silver's words, "in the promotion and embodiment of the French-Canadian nationality," the *rouges* (under Antoine Dorion) remained unconvinced, and opposed the scheme.

In the Atlantic region of British North America, Confederation met with a mixed response. In New Brunswick, a pro-Confederation government was initially defeated, and subsequently re-elected, on the Confederation scheme. In Nova Scotia, Charles Tupper, leader of the Confederation forces, refused even to bring the issue to a vote in the Legislature. Yet, as Phillip Buckner points out in a paper reproduced here from a "CHR [*Canadian Historical Review*] Dialogue" entitled "The Maritimes and Confederation: A Reassessment," perhaps the Maritime support for Confederation has been underestimated. Both P.W. Waite and William M. Baker, in their replies to Buckner's paper, comment on his objection to the stereotype that has developed in Canadian history about the Maritimes — namely, in Baker's words, that they were "lethargic, conservative, parochial communities which had to be pummelled into accepting Confederation."

588 Many excellent books exist on the subject of British North American federation. A good starting point is Donald Creighton's *The Road to Confederation* (Toronto: Macmillan, 1964). W.L. Morton's *The Critical Years, 1857–1873* (Toronto: McClelland and Stewart, 1968) is also helpful. A lively account of the Confederation movement in the Canadas and the Atlantic region is P.B. Waite's *The Life and Times of Confederation, 1864–1867* (Toronto: University of Toronto Press, 1962). P.B. Waite has edited the original debates in the United Canadas in *The Confederation Debates in the Province of Canada, 1865* (Toronto: University of Toronto Press, 1967). *Confederation*, edited by Ramsay Cook (Toronto: University of Toronto Press, 1967), contains important articles on the subject, including the essay on New Brunswick by Alfred G. Bailey, "The Basis and Persistence of Opposition to Confederation in New Brunswick," and George F.G. Stanley's "Act or Pact: Another Look at Confederation." Ged Martin has edited a more recent collection, *The Causes of Canadian Confederation* (Fredericton: Acadiensis Press, 1990). For Canada East's response, see Marcel Bellavance, *Le Québec et la Confédération: Un choix libre? Le clergé et la constitution de 1867* (Sillery, Que.: Septentrion, 1992). An older treatment of the same subject is Jean-Charles Bonenfant, *The French Canadians and the Birth of Confederation*, Canadian Historical Association, Historical Booklet no. 21 (Ottawa: CHA, 1966). J.M.S. Careless's *Brown of the Globe*, vol. 2 (Toronto: Macmillan, 1963), and Donald Creighton's *John A. Macdonald*, vol. 1, *The Young Politician* (Toronto: Macmillan, 1952), review the ideas and the important role of these leading figures in the Confederation movement. A useful article on the background to Confederation is Ged Martin's "Launching Canadian Confederation: Means to Ends, 1836–1864," *The Historical Journal*, 27, 3 (1984): 575–602. W.L. Morton's "British North America and a Continent in Dissolution, 1861–71," *History* (new series) 47 (1962): 139–56, also continues to be of value.

Confederation and Quebec

A.I. SILVER

When French Lower Canadians were called on to judge the proposed confederation of British North American provinces, the first thing they wanted to know was what effect it would have on their own nationality. Before deciding whether or not they approved, they wanted to hear "what guarantees will be offered for the future of the French-Canadian nationality, to which we are attached above all else."[1] From Richelieu's Rouge MPP to Quebec's Catholic-Conservative *Courrier du Canada*, everyone promised to judge the work of the Great Coalition according to the same criterion.[2] Even Montreal's *La Minerve*, known to be George-Étienne Cartier's own organ, promised to make its judgement from a national point of view:

589

> If the plan seems to us to safeguard Lower Canada's special interests, its religion and its nationality, we'll give it our support; if not, we'll fight it with all our strength.[3]

But this quotation reminds us that concern for the French-Canadian nationality had geographical implications, that Canadians in the 1860s generally considered French Canada and Lower Canada to be equivalent. When French Canadians spoke of their *patrie*, their homeland, they were invariably referring to Quebec. Even the word *Canada*, as they used it, usually referred to the lower province, or, even more specifically, to the valley of the St. Lawrence, that ancient home of French civilization in America, whose special status went back to the seventeenth century. Thus, when Cartier sang "O Canada! mon pays! mes amours!" he was referring to the "majestic course of the Saint-Laurent";[4] and Cartier's protégé, Benjamin Sulte, versifying like his patron, also found French Canada's "Patrie . . . on the banks of the Saint-Laurent."[5]

Throughout the discussion of Confederation, between 1864 and 1867, there ran the assumption that French Canada was a geographical as well as an ethnic entity, forming, as the *Revue Canadienne* pointed out optimistically, "the most considerable, the most homogeneous, and the most regularly constituted population group" in the whole Confederation.[6] *La Minerve*, which, as has been seen, characterized Lower Canada by a religion and a nationality, referred also to a "Franco-Canadian nationality, which really exists today on the banks of the St. Lawrence, and which has affirmed itself more than once."[7] Nor was the equation of Lower

From *The French-Canadian Idea of Confederation, 1864-1900*, by A.I. Silver (Toronto: University of Toronto Press, 1982), 33–50. Reprinted with the permission of University of Toronto Press Incorporated.

Canada with French Canada only a pro-Confederationist notion. The editors of the *Union Nationale* also maintained that the way to defend the French-Canadian nationality was to defend the rights of Lower Canada.[8]

It followed from this equation that provincial autonomy was to be sought in the proposed constitution as a key safeguard of the interests of French Canada. "We must never forget," asserted the *Gazette de Sorel*, "that French Canadians need more reassurance than the other provinces for their civil and religious immunities. . . . " But since French Canada was a province, its immunities were to be protected by provincial autonomy; hence, "this point is important above all for Lower Canada. . . . "[9]

On this key issue, French Canadians felt themselves to have different interests from those of other British North Americans. Thus, Cartier's organ:

590

> The English . . . have nothing to fear from the central government, and their first concern is to ensure its proper functioning. This is what they base their hopes upon, and the need for strong local governments only takes second place in their minds.
>
> The French press, on the contrary, feels that guarantees for the particular autonomy of our nationality must come before all else in the federal constitution. It sees the whole system as based on these very guarantees.[10]

Le Courrier de St-Hyacinthe agreed that "we do not have the same ideas as our compatriots of British origin concerning the powers which are to be given to the central government. . . . We cannot consent to the loss of our national autonomy. . . . "[11] The Rouges also saw opposition between French- and English-Canadian interests. It was because of this opposition, they commented pessimistically, that George Brown had been able to reveal details of the Quebec Resolutions in Toronto, to the evident satisfaction of Upper Canadians, while in Lower Canada the ministers refused to make any information public.[12]

New Brunswick's governor, A.H. Gordon, in whose house Cartier had been a guest after the Charlottetown Conference, also saw an opposition between English- and French-Canadian aspirations. He reported to the Colonial Secretary that while the former seemed to expect a very centralized union, " 'federal union' in the mouth of a Lower Canadian means the independence of his Province from all English or Protestant influences. . . . "[13]

This was, indeed, what it seemed to mean to the French-Canadian press. Thus:

> We want a confederation in which the federal principle will be applied in its fullest sense — one which will give the central power control only over general questions in no way affecting the interests of each separate section, while leaving to the local legislatures everything which concerns our particular interests.[14]

A confederation would be a fine thing, but only "if it limited as much as possible the rights of the federal government, to general matters, and left complete independence to the local governments."[15] As early as 1858, French-Canadian advocates of a British North American confederation had argued that "it would certainly be necessary to give the separate [provincial] legislatures the greatest possible share of power," and even that the federal government should have its powers only "by virtue of a perpetual but limited concession from the different provinces."[16]

While most papers did not go so far as to support the provincial sovereignty which that last implied,[17] they did opt for co-ordinate sovereignty:

> The federal power will be sovereign, no doubt, but it will have power only over certain general questions clearly defined by the constitution.
>
> This is the only plan of confederation which Lower Canada can accept. . . . The two levels of government must both be sovereign, each within its jurisdiction as clearly defined by the constitution.[18]

What, after all, could be simpler than that each power, federal or provincial, should have complete control of its own field?

591

> Isn't that perfectly possible without having the local legislatures derive their powers from the central legislature or vice versa? Isn't it possible for each of these bodies to have perfect independence within the scope of its own jurisdiction, neither one being able to invade the jurisdiction of the other?[19]

To be sure, the fathers of Confederation were aware that French Canadians would reject complete centralization. John A. Macdonald told the Assembly that though he would have preferred a legislative union, he realized it would be unacceptable to French Canadians. Nevertheless, he felt the Quebec Resolutions did not provide for a real federalism, but would "give to the General Government the strength of a legislative and administrative union." They represented "the happy medium" between a legislative and a federal union, which, while providing guarantees for those who feared the former, would also give "us the strength of a Legislative union."[20] In short, he appeared to understand the Quebec scheme to provide for the closest thing possible to a legislative union, saving certain guarantees for the French Canadians' "language, nationality, and religion."

This interpretation was hotly rejected by French Canadians of both parties, including those who spoke for Macdonald's partner, Cartier:

> Whatever guarantees may be offered here, Lower Canada will never consent to allowing its particular interests to be regulated by the inhabitants of the other provinces. . . . We want a solid constitution . . . but we demand above all perfect freedom and authority for the provinces to run their own internal affairs.[21]

Let there be no mistake about it: anything close to a legislative union "cannot and will not be accepted by the French-Canadian population." A centralized union would be fatal to the French-Canadian nationality.[22] The *Courrier de St-Hyacinthe*, in fact, summed up the whole French-Canadian position when it said:

> But whatever guarantees they decide to offer us, we cannot accept any union other than a federal union based on the well-understood principles of confederations.[23]

In taking this view, French Canadians were led to reject another position adopted by John A. Macdonald: that the United States example proved the necessity of a strong central government. He argued that the Civil War had occurred there because the individual states had too much power under the American constitution — power which had given the federation too much centrifugal thrust. To avoid this, British North America must have a dominant central authority.[24]

In French Canada, even *La Minerve* considered Macdonald's reasoning to be nonsensical. "We believe that this is a specious argument. The United States have a strongly centralized government, which is even capable of acting despotically, as we can see every day." If you gave a central government too much power over too many localities, it would inevitably antagonize some of them.

> This is precisely what happened in the United States, where the war was caused not by the excessive power of the local governments, but by the central government, whose tyrannical actions came into direct opposition to the particular interests of a considerable part of the confederation.[25]

Le Journal de Québec agreed wholeheartedly. The causes of the American Civil War were to be sought, not in the powers of the states, but in "the awful tyranny which the central government of the United States imposes on the state authorities, by taking them over and stealing their most inalienable powers. . . . "[26]

There was agreement between Bleus and Rouges that the autonomy of a French-Canadian Lower Canada was the chief thing to be sought in any new constitution. Accordingly, the Confederation discussion revolved around whether or not the Quebec plan achieved that aim. As far as the opposition was concerned, it did not. The Rouges maintained that this was an "anglicizing bill,"[27] the latest in a line of attempts to bring about the "annihilation of the French race in Canada," and thus realize Lord Durham's wicked plans.[28] And it would achieve this goal because it was not really a confederation at all, but a legislative union in disguise, a mere extension of the Union of 1840.[29] "It is in vain," cried C.-S. Cherrier at a Rouge-sponsored rally, "that they try to disguise it under the name of confederation. . . . This *quasi* legislative union is just a step toward a complete and absolute legislative union."[30]

The evidence of Confederation's wickedness could be seen by its opponents on every hand. Did it not involve representation by population — the dreaded "Rep by Pop" which French Canadians had resisted so vigorously till now?[31] And were not English Canadians proclaiming that centralization was to be the chief characteristic of the new régime? The Canadian legislature had even ordered the translation and publication of Alpheus Todd's essay on the provincial governments — an essay which included the remark that these would be "subject to the legal power of the federal parliament."[32] Indeed, argued the Rouges, it was hardly worth while for Quebec to have such an elaborate, two-chamber parliament as was proposed, since, as Todd made clear, the federal legislature "will be able to quash and annul all its decisions."[33]

The Quebec Resolutions themselves indicated that Todd was right, that the provincial powers would be scarcely more than a mirage:

> Mind you, according to everything we hear from Quebec, the prevailing idea in the conference is to give the central government the widest powers and to leave the local governments only a sort of municipal jurisdiction. . . . [34]

Le Pays had been afraid of this from the time the Great Coalition had announced its programme. "Without finances, without power to undertake major public works, the local legislature will hardly be anything other than a big municipal council where only petty matters will be discussed."[35] When the Quebec Conference had ended, opposition papers still had the same impression: "In short, the general parliament will have supreme control over the local legislatures."[36] Even provincial control of education was an illusion, since the governor-general at Ottawa could veto any provincial legislation in the field.[37]

Finally, English-Canadian talk of creating a new nationality only strengthened Rouge fears that Confederation meant centralization and assimilation. When the legislature refused to pass A.-A. Dorion's resolution of January, 1865, that Canadians neither desired nor sought to create a new nationality, his brother's newspaper became convinced that it was all over for Lower Canada and its French-Canadian nationality.[38]

In answering all these opposition arguments, the Bleus certainly did not attempt to defend the notion of a strong or dominant central government. But, they maintained, that was not at all what British North America was going to get. Lower Canada, liberated from the forced Union of 1840, would become a distinct and autonomous province in a loose and decentralized Confederation — that was the real truth of the matter.

The defenders of Confederation refuted the opposition's arguments one after another. Did the Rouges speak of Rep by Pop? Why, any schoolboy ought to see the difference between Rep by Pop, which the Bleus had opposed as long as the legislative union remained, and a "confederation which would give us, first of all, local legislatures for the protection of our sectional interests, and then a federal legislature in which the most populous province would have a majority *only in the lower house*."[39] As long as there was only a single legislature for the two Canadas, Rep by Pop would have put "our civil law and religious institutions at the mercy of the fanatics." But Confederation would eliminate that danger by creating a separate province of Quebec with its own distinct government:

593

> We have a system of government which puts under the exclusive control of Lower
> Canada those questions which we did not want the fanatical partisans of Mr.
> Brown to deal with. . . .
>
> Since we have this guarantee, what difference does it make to us whether
> or not Upper Canada has more representatives than we in the Commons? Since
> the Commons will be concerned only with general questions of interest to all
> provinces and not at all with the particular affairs of Lower Canada, it's all
> the same to us, as a nationality, whether or not Upper Canada has more
> representation.[40]

This was central to the Bleu picture of Confederation: all questions affecting the French-Canadian nationality as such would be dealt with
at Quebec City, and Ottawa would be "powerless, if it should want to
invade the territory reserved for the administration of the local governments."[41] As for the questions to be dealt with at Ottawa, they might
divide men as Liberals and Conservatives, but not as French and English
Canadians. "In the [federal] Parliament," said Hector Langevin, "there
594   will be no questions of race, nationality, religion or locality, as this Legislature will only be charged with the settlement of the great general
questions which will interest alike the whole Confederacy and not one
locality only."[42] Cartier made the same point when he said that "in the
questions which will be submitted to the Federal parliament, there will
be no more danger to the rights and privileges of the French Canadians
than to those of the Scotch, English, or Irish."[43] Or, as his organ, *La
Minerve*, put it, Ottawa would have jurisdiction only over those matters
"in which the interests of everyone, French Canadians, English, or
Scotch, are identical."[44] For the rest — for everything which concerned
the French Canadians *as* French Canadians — for the protection and
promotion of their national interests and institutions, they would have
their own province with their own parliament and their own government.

And what a parliament! and what a government! Why, the very fact
that Quebec was to have a bicameral legislature was proof of the importance they were to have. "In giving ourselves a complete government,"
argued the Bleus, "we affirm the fact of our existence as a separate nationality, as a complete society, endowed with a perfect system of organization."[45] Indeed, the very fact that Ontario's legislature was to have
only one house while Quebec's had two served to underline the distinctiveness, the separateness, and the autonomy of the French-Canadian
province:

> It is very much in our interest for our local legislature to have enough importance
> and dignity to gain respect for its decisions. . . . For us, French Canadians,
> who are only entering Confederation on the condition of having our own leg-
> islature as a guarantee of our autonomy, it is vital for that legislature not to
> be just a simple council whose deliberations won't carry any weight. . . .
>
> The deeper we can make the demarcation line between ourselves and the other
> provinces, the more guarantee we'll have for the conservation of our special
> character as a people.[46]

Here was the very heart and essence of the pro-Confederation argument in French Lower Canada: the Union of the Canadas was to be broken up, and the French Canadians were to take possession of a province of their own — a province with an enormous degree of autonomy. In fact, *separation* (from Upper Canada) and *independence* (of Quebec within its jurisdictions) were the main themes of Bleu propaganda. "As a distinct and separate nationality," said *La Minerve*, "we form a state within the state. We enjoy the full exercise of our rights and the formal recognition of our national independence."[47]

The provinces, in this view, were to be the political manifestations of distinct nationalities. This was the line taken in 1858 by J.-C. Taché, when he wrote that in the provincial institutions, "the national and religious elements will be able to develop their societies freely, and the separate populations realize . . . their aspirations and their dispositions." And it was widely understood that Taché had played a vital role in influencing the course of the Quebec Conference.[48] Cartier himself had told that conference that a federal rather than a unitary system was necessary, "because these provinces are peopled by different nations and by peoples of different religions."[49] It was in this light that *La Minerve* saw the Quebec programme as establishing "distinctly that all questions having to do with our religion or our nationality will be under the jurisdiction of our local legislature."[50] All the pro-Confederation propagandists were agreed that "the future of our race, the preservation of everything which makes up our national character, will depend directly on the local legislature."[51] It was the Lower Canadian ministers who had insisted, at the Quebec Conference, that education, civil, and religious institutions should be under provincial jurisdiction, in order that Quebec should have the power to take charge of the French-Canadian national future.[52] Indeed, that power extended well beyond civil and religious institutions. It included the "ownership and control of all their lands, mines, and minerals; the control of all their municipal affairs"[53] — everything "which is dearest and most precious to us"[54] — all power, in fact, necessary to promote the national life of French Canada.

All these powers were to be entrusted to the government of a province in which French Canadians would form "almost the whole" of the population, and in which everyone would have to speak French to take part in public life.[55] Yes, Confederation, by breaking up the union of the two Canadas, would make the French Canadians a majority in their own land,[56] so that "our beautiful French language will be the only one spoken in the Parliament of the Province of Quebec. . . . "[57]

What was more, the control which French Canadians would exercise over their wide fields of jurisdiction would be an absolute control, and "all right of interference in these matters is formally denied to the federal government."[58] The Bleus, in fact, claimed to have succeeded in obtaining a system of co-ordinate sovereignty. "Each of these governments," they

595

explained, "will be given absolute powers for the questions within its jurisdiction, and each will be equally sovereign in its own sphere of action."[59] Some over-enthusiastic advocates of the new régime even claimed that the provinces alone would be sovereign, "the powers of the federal government being considered only as a concession of specifically designated rights."[60] But even the moderate majority was firm in maintaining that the provinces would be in no way inferior or subordinate to the federal government, that they would be at least its equal, and that each government would be sovereign and untouchable in its own sphere of action:

> In the plan of the Quebec conference there is no delegation of power either from above or from below, because the provinces, not being independent states, receive their powers, as does the federal authority, from the imperial parliament.[61]

596

Politicians and journalists expressed this same view, in the legislature as well as in print. Thus, Joseph Blanchet told the Assembly: "I consider that under the present plan of confederation the local legislatures are sovereign with regard to the powers accorded to them, that is to say in local affairs."[62]

It may be that French-Canadian Confederationists went further than they ought to have done in interpreting the Quebec Resolutions the way they did. Part of the reason for this may have been ignorance. A Bleu back-bencher like C.B. de Niverville of Trois-Rivières could admit in the legislative debates that he had not read the resolutions, and what's more, that his ignorance of the English language had prevented him from following much of the debate. In this very situation he saw — or thought he saw — an argument for Confederation. For as he understood it, the new arrangement would remove French-Canadian affairs from an arena where men such as he were at a disadvantage, and place them before a group of French-speaking legislators:

> Indeed, what sort of liberty do we have, we who do not understand the English language? We have the liberty to keep quiet, to listen, and to try to understand! [Hear! hear! and prolonged laughter.] Under Confederation, the Upper Canadians will speak their language and the Lower Canadians will speak theirs, just as today; only, when a man finds that his compatriots form the great majority in the assembly in which he sits, he'll have more hope of hearing his language spoken, and as they do today, members will speak the language of the majority.[63]

Such an argument seems virtually to have ignored the very existence of the federal parliament, or at least of the authority it would have over French Canadians.

The case of de Niverville may have been extreme, but it was certainly not the only case of Bleus interpreting the Confederation plan in such a way as to maximize the powers of the provinces and minimize those of Ottawa far beyond anything we have been accustomed to. The federal power to raise taxes "by any mode or system of taxation" was interpreted so as to exclude the right of direct taxation.[64] The federal veto power was represented not as a right to interfere with provincial legislation, but only as an obligation upon Ottawa to act as "guardian of the constitution" by keeping clear the distinction between federal and provincial jurisdictions.[65]

But more important than any of these *specific* arguments was the wide-ranging exuberance of pro-Confederation propaganda. Here was a source of rhetoric that seemed to be promising that Confederation would give French Canadians virtual independence. Quebec was "completely separated from Upper Canada and has a complete governmental organization to administer *all its local affairs* on its own."[66] In the legislative council, E.-P. Taché interrupted his English-language speech on Confederation to tell his French-Canadian followers in French: "If a Federal Union were obtained, it would be tantamount to a separation of the provinces, and Lower Canada would thereby preserve its autonomy together with all the institutions it held so dear."[67] This could not be too often repeated: "The first, and one of the principal clauses of the constitution is the one that brings about the repeal of the Union, so long requested by the Rouges, and separates Lower Canada from Upper Canada."[68] What patriotic French Canadian could fail to be moved by what the fathers of Confederation had achieved?

> We've been separated from Upper Canada, we're called the Province of Quebec, we have a French-Canadian governor . . . we're going to have our own government and our own legislature, where everything will be done by and for French Canadians, and in French. You'd have to be a renegade . . . not to be moved to tears, not to feel your heart pound with an indescribable joy and a deserved pride at the thought of these glorious results of the patriotism and unquenchable energy of our statesmen, of our political leaders, who . . . have turned us over into our own hands, who have restored to us our complete autonomy and entrusted the sacred heritage of our national traditions to a government chosen from among us and composed of our own people.[69]

This sort of exaggerated rhetoric invited an obvious response from the opposition. If you really are serious about separation from Upper Canada, they asked, if you really do want to obtain autonomy for French Lower Canada, then why not go the whole way? Why not break up the old union altogether, instead of joining this confederation? "Everyone is agreed that only the repeal of the union would give us the independence of action needed for the future of Lower Canadians."[70] If necessary, some sort of commercial association would be sufficient to satisfy Upper Canada in return for political separation.[71]

The Confederationists answered this, not by saying that Quebec's independence was an undesirable goal, not by saying that French Canadians wanted to join together with English Canadians to form a Canadian nation, but by claiming that complete independence was simply not practicable:

> The idea of making Lower Canada an independent State . . . has appealed to all of us as schoolboys; but we don't believe that any serious adult has taken it up so far. . . . We simply cannot do everything on our own. . . . [72]

This was, perhaps, a temporary condition, and it was to be hoped that one day Quebec *would* be in a position to make good her independence. Yes, French Canada "can and must one day aspire to be come a nation";[73] for the moment, however, "we are too young for absolute independence."[74] Of course, whoever says "we are too young" implies that one day we shall be old enough — and Confederation, in the mean while, would preserve and prepare French Quebec for that day of destiny.[75]

One obvious reason why complete independence was not a realistic goal for the present was that Lower Canada was still part of the British Empire, and imperial approval, without which no constitutional change was possible, could not be obtained in the face of intense English-Canadian opposition.[76] But beyond that, it should be clear that an independent Quebec would inevitably be gobbled up by the United States. "We would be on our own, and our obvious weakness would put us at the mercy of a stronger neighbour."[77] French Canadians must understand, therefore, that, "unless we hurry up and head with all sails set toward Confederation, the current will carry us rapidly toward annexation."[78]

The weakness of an independent Quebec would be both military and economic. The first of these weaknesses could hardly be more apparent to Quebeckers than it was in the mid-1860s, for just as the Anglo-American frictions created by the Civil War were impressing upon them the dangers arising from American hostility, the desire of British politicians to disengage themselves from colonial defence responsibilities was causing Canadians to think as never before of their own defences. Intercolonial co-operation seemed a natural response to the situation:

> No-one could deny that the annexation of the British colonies, either by their consent or by force, is intended and desired by the northern states; it is a no less evident truth that, as things stand today, we could resist their armies with help from Europe; but that on their own, without a political union, without a strong common organization, the colonies could, in the foreseeable future, sustain such a combat — that is something which no-one would dare to maintain. . . . [79]

It was in these circumstances that the Confederation project presented itself. Only weeks after the end of the Quebec Conference, the St. Alban's raid brought the fear of imminent war with the United States. Yet at the same time, recent British military reports on colonial defence made Quebeckers wonder how much help they could expect if war broke out. "We must not place unlimited hopes on the support of the mother-country in case of war with our neighbours. Circumstances more powerful than the will of men could render such confidence illusory."[80] Yet the prospect for the separate British North American colonies without British

598

support was bleak: "separate from each other, we'd be sure to be invaded and crushed one after the other."[81] Not only would Confederation give Quebec the advantage of a joint defence organization with the other colonies, but also, by this very fact, it would make Britain willing to give more help in case of war than she would have been willing to give to the isolated and inefficient defence effort of a separate Quebec.[82]

Quebec's economic weakness could be seen already in the flood of emigration directed toward the United States. Clearly, French Lower Canada's economy was not able, on its own, to support all its population. To keep her people at home, the province must co-operate with others to create opportunities. As French Canadians went to seek manufacturing jobs in New England, manufacturing must be established in Lower Canada;[83] by 1867, Quebec papers were appealing to outside capital to set up mills in the province.[84] Long before, Hector Langevin, in a prize-winning essay, had looked to the development of the St. Lawrence transportation system to check emigration by providing jobs in commercial enterprises.[85] But the St. Lawrence was an interprovincial organization — even more in the era of railroads than in that of the canal.[86]

599

Thus, the need for economic viability dictated some form of central authority and prevented Quebec's independence from being complete:

> The more provinces there are gathered together, the greater will be the revenues, the more major works and improvements will be undertaken and consequently, the more prosperity there will be. What Lower Canada was unable to do on its own, we have done together with Upper Canada; and what the two Canadas have been unable to do together will be done by the confederation, because it will have markets and sea ports which we have not had.[87]

The British North American provinces had been endowed with resources enough. If they worked together to develop them, they could enjoy abundance, material progress, and even economic power.[88] But if they failed to co-operate, if they remained separate and isolated, then their economies would be weak, and inevitably they would become dependent on the United States, the prosperous neighbour to the south. "But we know that where there is economic dependence there will also be political dependence. . . . "[89]

There were strong reasons, then, why Quebec's independence could not be complete, why the nationalist longing for separateness had to compromise with the practical need for viability. But if some form of association with the rest of British North America was necessary, the degree of unification must be the minimum required to make Quebec viable. In the spring of 1867, on his way home from London, where he had helped write the BNA Act, Cartier told a welcoming crowd at a station-stop in the Eastern Townships that his main preoccupation had always been to protect the French-Canadian nationality, language, and institutions. "That is why I was careful to make sure that the federal government would receive only that amount of power which was strictly necessary to serve the general interests of the Confederation."[90] This meant, as E.-P. Taché had explained in 1864, that Ottawa would have enough power "to do away with some of the internal hindrances to trade, and to unite the Provinces for mutual defence," but that the provinces would remain the agencies to which the "majority of the people" would look for the protection of their "rights and privileges" and "liberties."[91]

Perhaps this arrangement was not *ideal*; perhaps, even, Confederation was only "the least bad thing in a very bad world."[92] The French-Canadian leaders, after all, had not been alone at the constitutional conferences, and French Canada's own needs and aspirations had had to be reconciled with "our condition of colonial dependence and the heterogenous elements which make up our population."[93]

Nevertheless, it had to be admitted that, despite Rouge protestations to the contrary, the old union could not have continued longer,[94] that the only alternative to Confederation would have been Rep by Pop,[95] and that, whatever degree of central authority there might be in the confederation, the patriotism of French-Canadian leaders could be relied on to promote the interests of their nationality, just as their patriotism had already won so much for French Canada in the making of the confederation.[96]

And what, then, in the final analysis, had they won? According to Bleu propaganda, Confederation was to be seen as an "alliance" or "association" of nations, each in its own autonomous province, and co-operating for the common welfare.[97] And this "alliance with your neighbours,"[98] this *"federal alliance* among several peoples,"[99] was to be regulated by the terms of a treaty or pact drawn up freely among them. Even the imperial authorities, according to Cartier, in preparing and passing the British North America Act, had accepted that they were only giving the official stamp of approval to an interprovincial compact. "They understood . . . that the Quebec plan was an agreement among the colonies, which had to be respected, and they respected it."[100] Confederation had, thus, been achieved because four separate colonies had formed "a pact" among themselves.[101]

And in the federal alliance thus formed, Quebec was to be the French-Canadian country, working together with the others on common projects, but always autonomous in the promotion and embodiment of the French-Canadian nationality. "Our ambitions," wrote a Bleu editor, "will not centre on the federal government, but will have their natural focus in our local legislature; this we regard as fundamental for ourselves."[102] This was, no doubt, an exaggerated position, like the statement of de Niverville in the Canadian legislature, but what it exaggerated was the general tendency of the Confederationist propaganda. It underlined the Quebec-centredness of French Canada's approach to Confederation, and the degree to which French Quebec's separateness and autonomy were central to French-Canadian acceptance of the new régime.

NOTES

[1] *La Gazette de Sorel*, 23 June 1864.

[2] Perrault quoted in the *Gazette de Sorel*, 3 Sept. 1864; *Le Courrier du Canada*, 24 June 1864.

[3] *La Minerve*, 9 Sept. 1864. After the Quebec Resolutions were known, journalists, politicians, and clergy still claimed to judge them by the same criterion. See, e.g., *Le Journal de Québec*, 24 Dec. 1864; Joseph Cauchon, *L'Union des provinces de l'Amérique britannique du Nord* (Quebec: Côté, 1865), 19, 41; *Nouvelle constitution du Canada* (Ottawa: Le Canada, 1867), 59.

[4] Most relevantly quoted in Auguste Achintre and J.B. Labelle, *Cantate: La Confédération* (n.p., n.d.), 4. Cartier, indeed, saw French Canada as geographically defined. J.-C. Bonenfant claims that while he fought for the French Canadians, "seuls à ses yeux comptent ceux qui habitent le Bas-Canada." See Bonenfant's article "Le Canada et les hommes politiques de 1867," in the *RHAF* 21, 32 (1967); 579–80. At the 1855 funeral of Ludger Duvernay, the founder of the Saint-Jean-Baptiste Society, Cartier had warned that every nationality, including French Canada, must possess an "élément territorial" in order to survive. See Joseph Tassé, ed., *Discours de Sir Georges Cartier* (Montreal: Senécal et Fils, 1893), 95. Cartier also used the very expression "French Canada" in a geographical sense, meaning Lower Canada. See, e.g., Tassé, *Discours*, 83.

[5] *La Revue Canadienne* 1 (1864): 696.

[6] Ibid., 4 (1867): 477.

[7] *La Minerve*, 25 Sept. 1865.

[8] *L'Union Nationale*, 3 Sept. 1864. All of these quotations, of course, are merely variations of Louis-François Laflèche's statement (in *Quelques considérations sur les rapports de la société civile avec la religion et la famille* (Trois-Rivières, 1866), 43, "Les Canadiens-français sont réellement une nation; la vallée du St-Laurent est leur patrie."

[9] *La Gazette de Sorel*, 14 Jan. 1865; also, *La Minerve*, 10 and 14 Sept. 1864.

[10] *La Minerve*, 14 Sept. 1864.

[11] *Le Courrier de St-Hyacinthe*, 23 Sept. 1864; also *Le Journal de Québec*, 4 July 1867.

[12] *Le Pays*, 8 Nov. 1864.

[13] In G.P. Browne, ed., *Documents on the Confederation of British North America* (Toronto: McClelland and Stewart, 1969), 42–43; also, 47, 49, 168 for Gordon's other assertions on the matter.

[14] *Le Courrier de St-Hyacinthe*, 2 Sept. 1864.

[15] *La Gazette de Sorel*, 30 July 1864.

[16] J.-C. Taché, *Des Provinces de l'Amérique du Nord et d'une union fédérale* (Quebec: Brousseau, 1858), 147, 148.

[17] Some did support provincial sovereignty, however — at least at times. See, e.g., *La Gazette de Sorel*, 27 Aug. 1864.

[18] *Le Courrier de St-Hyacinthe*, 2 Sept. 1864; also, 28 Oct. 1864.

[19] *Le Journal de Québec*, 1 Sept. 1864; also, 6 Sept. 1864; *Le Courrier du Canada*, 30 Sept. 1864, and 10 Oct. 1864.

[20] In P.B. Waite, ed., *The Confederation Debates in the Province of Canada, 1865* (Toronto: McClelland and Stewart, 1963), 40, 41, 43. Macdonald's belief that he had obtained something more centralized than a federation is dramatically expressed in his well-known letter of 19 Dec. 1864 to M.C. Cameron (PAC, Macdonald papers), in which he predicts that within a lifetime, "both local Parliaments and Governments [will be] absorbed in the General power."

[21] *La Minerve*, 15 Oct. 1864. See also *Le Courrier de St-Hyacinthe*, 2 Sept. 1864.

[22] *Le Courrier du Canada*, 16 Sept. 1864.

[23] *Le Courrier de St-Hyacinthe*, 18 Oct. 1864. See also *Le Pays*, 13 Oct. 1864; *L'Ordre*, 14 Oct. 1864; *Contre-poison: La Confédération c'est le salut du Bas-Canada* (Montreal: Senécal, 1867), 9.

[24] The argument is stated clearly and briefly in the letter to M.C. Cameron mentioned above, 36n. See also Donald Creighton, *John A. Macdonald*, 2 vols. (Toronto: Macmillan, 1966), 1: 369, 375–76, 378–80; P.B. Waite, "The Quebec Resolutions and the *Courrier du Canada, 1864–1865*," in the *CHR* 40, 4 (Dec. 1959): 294; etc., etc.

[25] *La Minerve*, 15 Oct. 1864.

[26] *Le Journal de Québec*, 27 Aug. 1864. See also Cauchon, *L'Union des provinces*, 39. *Le Courrier du Canada*, far from seeing the U.S. constitution as embodying the error of excessive decentralization, found it an apt model for the Quebec Conference to follow. See J.-C. Bonenfant, "L'Idée que les Canadiens-français de 1864 pouvaient avoir du fédéralisme," in *Culture* 25 (1964): 316. Some Rouges, notably Médéric Lanctôt in *L'Union Nationale*, went so far as to maintain that it would be more desirable for Lower Canada to join the U.S. than the British North American Union, precisely because it would have more autonomy as an American state.

[27] *Le Pays*, 27 Mar. 1867.

[28] Ibid., 2 Apr. 1867; also, 23 July 1864; and *La Confédération couronnement de dix années de mauvaise administration* (Montreal: Le Pays, 1867), 5.

[29] *La Confédération couronnement*, 5, 8; *Le Pays*, 12 Nov. 1864, 9 Feb. 1865, 2 Apr. 1867.

[30] C.-S. Cherrier, et al., *Discours sur la Confédération* (Montreal: Lanctot, Bouthillier et Thompson, 1865), 13.

[31] *Le Pays*, 23 and 28 June, 14 July, 8 Nov. 1864; *L'Ordre*, 27 June 1864; *L'Union Nationale*, 8 Nov. 1864; *Confédération couronnement*, 13.

[32] Alpheus Todd, *Quelques considérations sur la formation des Gouvernements locaux du Haut et du Bas-Canada . . .* (Ottawa: Hunter, Rose et Lemieux, 1866), 5.

[33] *Le Pays,* 28 July 1866; also, 27 Sept. 1864, and 19 July 1866.

[34] *Le Pays,* 25 Oct. 1864.

[35] Ibid., 23 July 1864; also, *L'Ordre,* 22 July 1864.

[36] *L'Union Nationale,* 11 Nov. 1864; also, 3 Sept. 1864; *Le Pays,* 14 and 23 July 1864.

[37] *L'Ordre,* 14 Nov. 1864.

[38] *Le Déficheur,* 25 Jan. 1865. All these fears which inspired the opposition also provoked doubts in the minds of some people who were otherwise supporters of the government. "Nous avons toujours dit," remarked *Le Canadien,* on 3 Aug. 1866, "que dans le plan de confédération actuel, on n'avait pas laissé assez de pouvoir aux gouvernements locaux et trop au gouvernement général." See also, e.g., 3 Feb. 1865.

[39] *Le Journal de Québec,* 5 July 1864.

[40] *Réponses aux censeurs de la Confédération* (St-Hyacinthe: Le Courrier, 1867), 47–49.

[41] *La Minerve,* 20 Sept. 1864; also, *Le Courrier du Canada,* 11 July 1864.

[42] *Parliamentary Debates on the Subject of the Confederation of the British North American Provinces* (Ottawa, 1865), 368.

[43] Ibid., 54–55.

[44] *La Minerve,* 15 Oct. 1864.

[45] Ibid., 17 July 1866.

[46] *Le Journal des Trois-Rivières,* 24 July 1866. Also, *Le Courrier de St-Hyacinthe,* 10 July 1866.

[47] *La Minerve,* 1 July 1867; also, 2 July 1867: "[Comme] nation dans la nation, nous devons veiller à notre autonomie propre. . . . "

[48] Taché, *Des Provinces,* 151: "Les éléments nationaux et religieux pourront à l'aise opérer leurs mouvements de civilisation, et les populations séparées donner cours . . . à leurs aspirations et à leurs tendances." During the Confederation Debates, Joseph Blanchet claimed that the Quebec Resolutions were, essentially, the very sceheme which Taché had presented in his 1858 pamphlet (p. 457 of the Ottawa edition of the debates). Joseph Tassé asserted in 1885 that Taché had acted as special adviser to the Canadian ministers at the Quebec Conference. (See J.-C. Bonenfant, "L'Idée que les Canadiens," 314.) And Taché's son told an interviewer in 1935 that his father (whose uncle, Sir E.-P. Taché, had repeatedly recommended the nephew's scheme to the conference) had several times been called into the sessions, "vraisemblablement pour donner des explications sur son projet." See Louis Taché, "Sir Etienne-Pascal Taché et la Confédération canadienne," in the *Revue de l'Université d'Ottawa* 5 (1935): 24.

[49] In Browne, *Documents,* 128.

[50] *La Minerve,* 30 Dec. 1864. See also *Le Journal de Québec,* 24 Dec. 1864.

[51] *Le Courrier de St-Hyacinthe,* 28 Oct. 1864; also, 23 Sept. and 22 Nov. 1864.

[52] *Le Courrier du Canada,* 7 Nov. 1864. See also 11 Nov. 1864.

[53] *Le Courrier du Canada,* 13 Mar. 1867; also, 28 June 1867.

[54] *La Minerve,* 1 July 1867; also, 2 July 1867; and the speech of Sir Narcisse Belleau in the *Confederation Debates* (Waite edition), 29.

[55] *Le Courrier de St-Hyacinthe,* 10 July 1866.

[56] Cauchon, *L'Union,* 45.

[57] *Contre-poison,* 20. See also *Réponses aux censeurs,* 48.

[58] *Contre-poison,* 20; also, *Le Journal de Québec,* 15 Nov. 1864, and 24 Dec. 1864; Cauchon, *L'Union,* 45–46; *L'Union des Cantons de l'Est* (Arthabaskaville), 4 July 1867; Governor Gordon in Browne, *Documents,* 75; Bishop Larocque in *Nouvelle constitution,* 75.

[59] *Le Courrier de St-Hyacinthe,* 28 Oct. 1864.

[60] E.-P. Taché, quoted in Bonenfant, "L'Idée que les Canadiens," 315.

[61] Joseph Cauchon, *Discours . . . sur la question de la Confédération* (n.p., n.d.), 8: "les provinces, n'étant pas des états indépendants, reçoivent, avec l'autorité supérieure, leurs organisations politiques du Parlement de l'Empire. Il n'y a que des attributs distincts pour l'une et pour les autres." See also Cauchon, *L'Union,* 40, 52; *Le Courrier du Canada,* 7 Nov. 1864, and Waite, "Quebec Resolutions," 299–300.

[62] Joseph Blanchet in *Débats parlementaires sur la question de la Confédération des provinces de l'Amérique Britannique du Nord* (Ottawa: Hunter, Rose et Lemieux, 1865), 551.

[63] Ibid., 949.

[64] *L'Union des Cantons de l'Est,* 12 Sept. 1867. This argument about direct taxation will not be as unfamiliar to historians as to other payers of federal income tax.

[65] *La Minerve,* 3 Dec. 1864; also, 11 Nov. 1864; *Le Courrier de St-Hyacinthe,* 22 Nov. 1864; *Le Courrier du Canada,* 7 Nov. 1864.

[66] *Contre-poison,* 13.

[67] *Confederation Debates* (Waite edition), 22.

[68] *Contre-poison,* 11. Episcopal statements recommended Confederation on the same basis. Bishop Baillargeon of Tloa, who administered the diocese of Quebec, noted in his pastoral letter that, although there would be a central government, Confederation would, nevertheless, comprise four distinct provinces. "C'est ainsi que le Bas-Canada, désormais séparé du Haut, formera sous le nouveau régime

une province séparée qui sera nommé 'la Province de Québec'" (in *Nouvelle constitution*, 53).

[69] *Contre-poison*, 3.

[70] *L'Union Nationale*, 3 Sept. 1864; also, *Confédération couronnement*, 5.

[71] *L'Union Nationale*, 7 Nov. 1864. Even the pro-Conservative *Gazette de Sorel* admitted, on 23 June 1864, that it had always preferred a straightforward breakup of the union as the best solution for French Canada. Also, 30 July 1864.

[72] *La Minerve*, 5 Jan. 1865.

[73] *Le Journal de Québec*, 17 Dec. 1864.

[74] *Le Pionnier de Sherbrooke*, 9 Mar. 1867.

[75] See Cauchon, *L'Union*, 29.

[76] *La Minerve*, 28 Sept. 1864.

[77] *Le Courrier de St-Hyacinthe*, 25 Nov. 1864; also, *Le Courrier du Canada*, 10 Oct. 1864.

[78] Cauchon, *L'Union*, 25. Cartier put the same alternative to the legislative assembly, when he said: "The matter resolved itself into this, either we must obtain British American Confederation or be absorbed in an American Confederation." (*Confederation Debates*, Waite edition, 50.) See also *La Minerve*, 13 Jan. 1865; and *Nouvelle constitution*, 60, 66–67, 78ff.; *La Revue Canadienne* 2 (1865): 116, on Confederation as an alternative to "le gouffre et le néant de la république voisine."

[79] *La Revue Canadienne* 2 (1865): 159.

[80] *La Minerve*, 7 Dec. 1864. The danger of war with the U.S. was announced not only by *La Minerve* in December 1864, but also by *Le Courrier du Canada*, 26 Nov. 1866, and *La Gazette de Sorel*, 19 Nov. 1864, while the need to prepare for British disengagement was urged by the *Journal de Québec*, 17 Dec. 1864, and *Le Courrier du Canada*, 5 Oct. 1864.

[81] Cauchon, *L'Union*, 32. See also Jules Fournier, *Le Canada: Son présent et son avenir* (Montreal: La Minerve*, 1865), 4.

[82] *Contre-poison*, 8.

[83] *L'Union Nationale*, 19 July 1866.

[84] *L'Union des Cantons de l'Est*, 3 Jan. 1867.

[85] Hector Langevin, *Le Canada, ses institutions, ressources, produits, manufactures, etc., etc., etc.* (Quebec: Lovell et Lamoureux, 1855), 96.

[86] *L'Union des Cantons de l'Est*, 8 Aug. 1867.

[87] *Contre-poison*, 48–49.

[88] Taché, *Des provinces*, 10–11; *Le Courrier de St-Hyacinthe*, 23 July 1867; *Réponses aux censeurs*, 3–4; Achintre and Labelle, *Cantate*, 2–3, 8; Cauchon, *L'Union*, 3; Henry Lacroix, *Opuscule sur le présent et l'avenir du Canada* (Montreal: Senécal, 1867).

[89] *La Revue Canadienne* 2 (1865): 103. See also Fournier, *Le Canada*, 2–3, who argued that as long as Canada was economically dependent on overseas trade, she would be politically at the mercy of the U.S., unless she had her own all-British rail link with an ice-free port in New Brunswick or Nova Scotia. See also Cauchon, *L'Union*, 34–35.

[90] *L'Union des Cantons de l'Est*, 23 May 1867.

[91] Taché was speaking at the Québec Conference. In Browne, *Documents*, 127–28.

[92] Quoted in Waite, "Quebec Resolutions," 297. See *Le Courrier du Canada*, 11 Nov. 1864.

[93] *Le Courrier de St-Hyacinthe*, 22 Nov. 1864. The opposition tried to stress the weakness and isolation of the French-Canadian delegates to the constitutional conferences as a reproach to them. E.g., *Le Pays*, 13 Oct. 1864. But Confederationists thought it only reasonable to take realities into account. E.g., *La Minerve*, 25 Feb. 1865; *La Gazette de Sorel*, 1 Sept. 1866.

[94] *La Gazette de Sorel*, 23 June and 23 July 1864, 14 Jan. 1865; *Le Courrier du Canada*, 24 June 1864; *Le Courrier de St-Hyacinthe*, 8 Nov. 1864; *L'Union des Cantons de l'Est*, 4 Apr. 1864; *La Minerve*, 9 Sept. and 30 Dec. 1864; *Le Journal de Québec*, 15 Dec. 1864; Cauchon, *L'Union*, 19; *Contre-poison*, 7; the pastoral letters of Bishops Cooke and Larocque, in *Nouvelle constitution*, 58–59, 68.

[95] *La Minerve*, 28 Dec. 1864; *La Gazette de Sorel*, 30 July 1864; Louis-François Laflèche and Bishop Baillargeon, quoted in Walter Ullmann, "The Quebec Bishops and Confederation," in the *CHR* 44, 3 (Sept. 1963), reprinted in G.R. Cook, ed., *Confederation* (Toronto: University of Toronto Press, 1967), 53, 56, 66.

[96] *Le Courrier du Canada*, 22 June 1864; Bishops Baillargeon and Cooke in *Nouvelle constitution*, 54–55, 60; E.C. Parent to J.I. Tarte, Ottawa, 4 Sept. 1866, in PAC, Tarte papers (MG 27, 11, D16). Just as they had promoted French-Canadian interests at the constitutional conferences, Quebec's sixty-five MPs would watch over French Quebec's interests at Ottawa. For they would be sent to Ottawa as representatives of Quebec, the French-Canadian province, and their responsibility would be toward that province and its autonomy. See Bonenfant, "L'Idée que les Canadiens," 317; *Le Courrier de St-Hyacinthe*, 22 July 1864.

[97] *La Gazette de Sorel*, 25 Feb. 1865; *La Minerve*, 1 July 1867. It was perfectly clear, of course, what Quebec's nationality was considered to be. It was French-Canadian. But what nationalities were to be attributed to the other provinces was never certain. French Canadians were aware of distinctions among the English, Scottish, and Irish nationalities, and they may have seen the other provinces as having unique national characters determined by their respective blends of these various elements. But they were always vague on this point. Cartier, however, did suggest a similar distribution of religious characteristics when he said (in the legislative debate on the Quebec resolutions) that Ontario

603

would be Protestant, Quebec Catholic, and the Maritimes pretty evenly divided between the two denominations (e.g., in Tassé, *Discours*, 422).

98 *L'Union des Cantons de l'Est*, 4 July 1867.

99 *Contre-poison*, 8; also, 10.

100 *L'Union des Cantons de l'Est*, 23 May 1867.

101 *Le Journal de Québec*, 4 July 1867. See also the Bishop of St-Hyacinthe, in *Nouvelle constitution*, 65. J.-C. Taché had assumed, in 1858, that a confederation would necessarily be brought about by an intercolonial pact. See his *Des provinces*, 139.

102 *Le Courrier de St-Hyacinthe*, 10 July 1866. We shall find this point of view adopted not infrequently by French-Quebec journalists in the first decades after Confederation.

CHR Dialogue: The Maritimes and Confederation: A Reassessment

PHILLIP BUCKNER, with P.B. WAITE and WILLIAM M. BAKER

604

A number of years ago Ernie Forbes, in an important article, challenged the stereotype of Maritime conservatism and attempted to show how it had distorted the way in which the history of the Maritimes has been portrayed in the post-Confederation period.[1] Yet it can be argued that this stereotype has also influenced our interpretation of the pre-Confederation era in a variety of ways. Nowhere is this more true than in studies of the role of the region in the making of Confederation. The failure of the Maritime colonies to respond enthusiastically to the Canadian initiative for Confederation in the 1860s has come to be seen as yet another example of their inherent conservatism. The impression that emerges from the literature is of a series of parochial communities, content with the status quo and trapped in intellectual lethargy, who were dragged kicking and screaming into Confederation. This stereotype leads to several misleading conclusions. First, it encourages historians to underestimate the degree of support which existed within the Maritimes for the ideal of a larger British North American union and to exaggerate the gulf that divided the anti-confederates from the pro-confederates. Second, it oversimplifies and trivializes the very real and substantive objections which many Maritimers had to the kind of union that they were eventually forced to accept. Recent American historiography has led to a substantial rethinking of the debate that took place in the United States over the ratification of the American constitution in the 1780s, and a similar reassessment of the debate over the Quebec Resolutions in the Maritimes in the 1860s is long overdue.

The first studies of Confederation, in fact, devoted little time to this issue. Reginald George Trotter, in *Canadian Federation: Its Origins and Achievement* (Toronto, 1924), barely mentions the debate over Confederation in the Maritimes, and M.O. Hammond, in *Confederation and*

From *Canadian Historical Review* 71, 1 (March 1990): 1–45. Reprinted with the permission of University of Toronto Press Incorporated.

Its Leaders (Toronto, 1917), simply ascribed the views of anti-confederates such as Albert J. Smith to their "opposition to change of any kind" (237). In the first scholarly article on "New Brunswick's Entrance into Confederation," George Wilson assumed as a given New Brunswick's hesitancy and focused on the factors — the loyalty cry, Canadian campaign funds, and the "educational work of Tilley" (24) — which he saw as critical in persuading New Brunswickers to vote for union.[2] D.C. Harvey also concentrated on the idealism of the expansionists in his paper on "The Maritimes Provinces and Confederation" in 1927.[3] Writing at a time when there was a feeling in the Maritimes that Confederation had not delivered what had been promised,[4] Harvey stressed that union could have been accomplished relatively easily if the "factious" opponents of federation had not been "able to whip up an opposition that caused no end of trouble to the unionist statesmen and left behind a legacy of suspicion and ill-will which has been like an ulcer in the side of the Dominion" (44). Harvey called for Maritimers to "recapture" the initial enthusiasm of the pro-confederates and to abandon the tendency to blame Confederation for their problems. By implication, then, the critics of Confederation both in the 1860s and the 1920s lacked vision and statesmanship.

605

This perspective was also implicit in William Menzies Whitelaw's *The Maritimes and Canada before Confederation.*[5] In his preface, Whitelaw declared that he had focused the book around "the struggle between an incipient nationalism and a rugged particularism" (xix). The book was published in 1934, after the collapse of the Maritime Rights Movement and the onset of the Great Depression, at a time when most Canadian historians were beginning to see the advantages of a strong central government and Maritimers were again discussing the chimera of Maritime Union. Not surprisingly, Whitelaw approached the topic with a strong bias in favour of Confederation and preferably a highly centralized federal system. From the beginning the emphasis of the book was on the relative backwardness of the Maritimes and the persistence there of "early particularism," the title of one of the first chapters. Whitelaw ended his study in 1864, with an insightful chapter on "Maritime Interests at Quebec," which showed how the Canadians manipulated the Quebec Conference and outmanoeuvred the divided Maritimers.[6] Interestingly, he did not discuss the actual debate over the Quebec Resolutions but concluded with a brief lament over the decision to abandon Maritime Union. In his review of the book in the *Canadian Historical Review*, Chester Martin with some justification declared that Whitelaw "leaves an impression not only of 'particularism' but of parochialism: of particularism run to seed, too inert to defend or even to discern their own interests in the presence of the expansive forces then abroad in Canada and the United States."[7]

In the 1940s, A.G. Bailey contributed two important articles to the small corpus of serious scholarly literature on the Maritimes and Confederation.[8] In "Railways and the Confederation Issue in New Brunswick, 1863–1865," he focused rather narrowly on the debate over the western extension, which he argued was the "most potent" factor behind the opposition to Confederation in the colony (91).[9] The problem with explaining the debate in New Brunswick in these terms is that many pro-confederates wanted the western extension, not a few anti-confederates wanted the Intercolonial, and a large number of New Brunswickers wanted both, although they could afford neither.[10] In his next article, "The Basis and Persistence of Opposition to Confederation in New Brunswick," Bailey adopted a broader approach. Although starting from the assumption that "in the early stages of the union movement there was a misapprehension of its significance, together with some degree of apathy, rather than a reasoned opposition" (93), he went on to explore with some subtlety the roots of anti-Confederation sentiment. The rapid collapse of the anti-confederate government he again ascribed primarily to its failure to complete the western extension, but he also emphasized mounting pressure from the imperial government as well as "the exaggerated menace of Fenian invasion" (117) and Canadian campaign funds. He also recognized that many of those who opposed union "directed their attacks not so much against the principle of Confederation as against the specific terms of union which had been embodied in the Quebec Resolutions" (115). Indeed, the failure of the pro-confederates to make substantial alterations in those resolutions in London accounted, he suggested, for "the remarkable persistence of opposition" to Confederation after 1866 (116). But he did not emphasize this point, which is made as a kind of aside in the conclusion of the article.

The next major study of Confederation came from Chester Martin. In *Foundations of Canadian Nationhood* (Toronto, 1955), he dismissed the opposition to Confederation in the Maritimes as "too general to be the result of personalities or sheer parochialism" (347). This insight might have provided the basis for a fundamental reassessment of the debate in the Maritimes, but Martin quickly reverted to the stereotype of Maritime conservatism. Indeed, one of the major subthemes in the book is that the original decision to partition Nova Scotia into a series of smaller units had inevitably promoted parochialism: "Where local division had been deliberately planted and thriven for three-quarters of a century, provincialism was only too apt to degenerate into sheer parochialism" (290). Because he saw Confederation as forced upon the British North American colonies by (in what was the *leitmotif* of this section of the book) "events stronger than advocacy, events stronger than men" (291) and the opposition to it as a natural instinct (see 297), Martin also accepted that "there were solid reasons for resistance based upon conflicting interests and a long train of policy" (355). Nonetheless, the clear implication of his approach was that the fundamental motivation behind the widespread Maritime opposition to the Quebec Resolutions was the deep-seated conservatism of the region.

During the early 1960s, writing on Confederation became a growth industry as Canada approached its centennial. Since most Canadian historians were still influenced by the consensus approach, which minimized the significance of internal conflicts by focusing on the things which united Canadians and distinguished them from other people, they tended to downplay regional concerns and to interpret the making of Confederation as a success story of which all Canadians should be proud.[11] The best of these studies was P.B. Waite's *The Life and Times of Confederation, 1864–67*, and it is a tragedy that it has been allowed to go out of print.[12] Although Waite does not indicate that he was directly influenced by Chester Martin, there are a number of parallels in their interpretations. Like Martin, Waite saw Confederation as forced upon the British North Americans by external pressures. Although he was less deterministic and did not see Confederation as an inevitable response to these pressures, he concluded that Confederation was "imposed on British North America by ingenuity, luck, courage, and sheer force" (323). Like Martin, he argued that the opposition to Confederation was rooted in the "innate conservatism" of the smaller communities across British North America (14) and that this conservatism was particularly strong in the Maritimes. But reflecting the spirit of the 1960s, Waite also saw the tentative stirrings of a sense of Canadian nationalism in the 1860s. By 1864, he concluded, "Whether for good or ill, there was a national spirit stirring in the Maritime provinces" (72); in fact, the Maritime pro-confederates were even more eager than the Canadians to escape from "the littleness of provincial pastures" (89).

607

Since Waite clearly accepted that Confederation was necessary and desirable and that the Quebec Resolutions were an imaginative and ingenious recipe for union, he had limited patience with the anti-confederates, who are seen as "men of little faith."[13] His impatience with their unwillingness to accept the Quebec terms is revealed in his treatment of the "Poor, tired, rather embittered" Joseph Howe, who might "have supported Confederation had he had an opportunity similar to Tupper's" (210). And it is even more clearly revealed in his assessment of L.A. Wilmot: "It may have been that Wilmot was perfectly genuine in his conversion to Confederation. But if so, it was not his main motive. With Wilmot perquisites usually triumphed over policies" (256). Waite accepted that Nova Scotians had some reason for resentment, since the Quebec Resolutions were imposed upon them against their will, but he did not extend the same sympathy to New Brunswick and Prince Edward Island, which he described as totally mired in an all-pervasive parochialism: "Of both Fredericton and Charlottetown Goldwin Smith's unrepentant aphorism is not altogether inappropriate: 'The smaller the pit, the fiercer the rats'" (233).[14] It was the "ferocity of politics" which accounted for the "primeval character" of the discussion of Confederation in New Brunswick (233–34). As for Prince Edward Island, their opposition is more simply explained. Most Islanders had never been away from the Island in their lives (at least according to George Brown) and they had "had little opportunity to cultivate larger loyalties." "Like the Acadians a century before, they simply wanted to be left alone" (180–81).

Waite's emphasis on the parochialism and conservatism of New Brunswick and Prince Edward Island was reinforced by two more specialized studies which appeared in the early 1960s. There was always a curiously ambivalent attitude in the work of W.S. MacNutt towards his adopted province. Because he was disappointed with the province's performance in the post–World War II era, he took up the cause of Maritime unity in the 1950s and railed against those local politicians who were obsessed with the distribution of local patronage and lacked a vision of grandeur.[15] In *New Brunswick: A History: 1784–1867* (Toronto, 1963), he projected this anger backwards and his impatience with the provincial politicians shines through. Although MacNutt felt it was "difficult to allow very much praise for the politicians" of the province (460), at least "a few leaders of imagination and daring had made themselves the instruments of the grand idea that was British North America's response to the problems of the time, the urge for mergers and the manufacturing of great states" (454). Francis W.P. Bolger adopted a not dissimilar approach in *Prince Edward Island and Confederation, 1863–1873* (Charlottetown, 1964). During the years that Confederation was discussed, Island politics, he noted, "remained personal, parochial, and violent" (14), and it was inevitable that the Island would resist with all its might the pressures for union.[16]

It is difficult not to come away from these works with the impression that there was virtually no support for Confederation in the Maritimes, except for a handful of prescient individuals who had the imagination to accept the leadership of the more far-sighted and progressive Canadians. Yet all three studies revealed very clearly that anti-Confederation sentiment in the region was generated as much by the unpalatability of the Quebec Resolutions as by opposition to the idea of Confederation itself. All three historians also accepted that the terms adopted at Quebec City reflected Canadian needs and Canadian priorities and, like Whitelaw, they clearly assumed that the Maritime delegates to Quebec had failed to secure better terms because of the superior acumen and organization of the Canadian delegation. It is, of course, true that the exigencies of Canadian politics forced the members of the Great Coalition to adopt a relatively united front on the constitutional issues under discussion at a time when the Maritime delegations were divided both internally and among themselves at Quebec. But one could as easily attribute the failure of the Maritime delegates to their realism and to the extent of their desire for some kind of union. Their basic problem was that the two regions were of such unequal size. At Philadelphia in 1787 the Americans were forced to resort to equal representation in the Senate, not solely to appease the small states but also for reasons of "*regional* security," in order "to safeguard the most conspicuous interests of North and South."[17] In the end it was the comparative equality of the two regions which compelled the delegates at Philadelphia to agree to the "Great Compromise." No such pressure existed at Quebec in 1864. Because of the uneven size and power of the two regions, the Maritime delegates were compelled to agree to union on Canadian terms, if they wanted union at all.

The leading Maritime politicians at Quebec had no illusions about the limited room they had for manoeuvre. Even at Charlottetown, Samuel Leonard Tilley and W.H. Pope opposed the suggestion that Maritime Union should precede Confederation on the grounds that the Maritime provinces would be able to arrive at better terms with Canada by negotiating separately rather than united.[18] Indeed, Charles Tupper believed that the gradual withdrawal of Britain had made the subordination of the Maritimes to Canada inevitable and that the goal of the Maritime delegates at Quebec must be to gain the best terms of union that they could.[19] The Maritimers did try to offset their weakness in the House of Commons by insisting on sectional equality in the Senate, and the majority of them also sought to ensure that the provinces would be left with control over those local matters of most immediate concern to their constituents. Although Jonathan McCully failed in his attempt to have agriculture removed from the list of federal responsibilities, Tilley persuaded the delegates to transfer control over roads and bridges to the provinces.[20] Indeed, upon returning to New Brunswick, Tilley worked out that only five of the fifty-nine acts passed by the New Brunswick legislature in the previous session would be found *ultra vires* of the provincial government under the proposed division of powers.[21] And both Tilley and Tupper pointed out forcefully at the London Conference that their intention had not been to create a "Legislative Union."[22] Yet, even after it became clear to them how unpopular the Quebec Resolutions were, the pro-confederate leadership recognized that there were limits to the concessions the Canadians could make without destroying the fragile unity of the great coalition. Reluctantly, therefore, they accepted that, if Confederation was to take place in the 1860s, "it is the Quebec scheme & little else we can hope to have secured."[23]

Although the pro-confederate leadership was probably right in this assumption, the Quebec Resolutions weakened the potential support for union in the region. Many of those sympathetic to the ideal of Confederation felt that a second conference should be called to renegotiate the terms of union.[24] Both Bailey and MacNutt attributed much of the lingering resentment to Confederation in New Brunswick after 1866 to the failure of the efforts of the New Brunswick delegates at the London Conference to make substantial alterations in the unpopular Quebec plan.[25] Bolger also accepted that the Island rejected the initial proposals because they were not "sufficiently attractive."[26] Much of the debate

609

in the Maritimes revolved not around the issue of whether union was desirable but around that of whether the Quebec Resolutions adequately met Maritime needs and concerns. The strength of the anti-confederate movement throughout the region was that it could appeal both to those whom Waite describes in Canada West as the "ultras," who opposed Confederation on any terms, and the "critics," who had specific objections to the Quebec scheme although they were not opposed to Confederation on principle.[27] In Canada West, most of the critics were easily convinced to put aside their objections; in the Maritimes, the proponents of the Quebec Resolutions had an uphill battle to bring the critics on side. Unfortunately, Waite does not present the struggle in the Maritimes in quite these terms but lumps the critics together with the ultras, thus creating the impression that die-hard opposition to union was stronger than it was. He therefore concludes that "New Brunswick was pushed into Union, Nova Scotia was dragooned into it, and Newfoundland and Prince Edward Island were subjected to all the pressure that could be brought to bear — short of force — and still refused."[28] In a literal sense these comments are true, but they gloss over the fact that what the Maritimes were pushed, dragooned, and in the case of PEI "railroaded" into was a union on Canadian terms.[29] MacNutt and Bolger also admitted that there were severe imperfections in the Quebec Resolutions from the perspective of the Maritimes, but they too ignored the implications of this argument and bunched together all anti-confederates as conservatives who lacked foresight.

This was also the conclusion of Donald Creighton in *The Road to Confederation: The Emergence of Canada, 1863–1867* (Toronto, 1964). As in all his works, Creighton's writing was infused with a strong moral tone and a rigid teleological framework which emphasized that Confederation was the logical destination at the end of the road. Those who stood in the way of his vision of what was both right and inevitable were dismissed as narrow-minded obstructionists, and he began his book by approvingly paraphrasing Arthur Hamilton Gordon's description of the Maritimes as "half a dozen miserable fragments of provinces" where the "inevitable pettiness and the lack of talented and devoted men in public life could not but make for parochialism, maladministration, and low political morality in every department of provincial life" (8). Throughout the book, Creighton contrasted "the lofty nationalist aims of the Canadians" (154) with the parochialism of the Maritimers. "If the Charlottetown Conference was likely to end up as an open competition between confederation and Maritime union," he wrote scornfully, "the Maritimers seemed placidly unaware of the prospect, or disinclined to get excited about it. They appeared to be simply waiting without much concern, and even without a great deal of interest, to see what would turn up" (91). To Creighton, the opposition of the Maritimers to Confederation was almost incomprehensible. Since "Maritimers showed, again and again, that they could not but feel their ultimate destiny lay in North American union" (75), their opposition could only be based upon a natural lethargy. A much more sophisticated study of the Confederation era was W.L. Morton's *The Critical Years: The Union of British North America, 1857–1873* (Toronto, 1964). But Morton too had limited sympathy with the Maritimers' failure to see what he described as the "moral purpose of Confederation" (277). New Brunswick's opposition he ascribed to the lack of moral integrity of its politicians and the lack of principle of its electorate, which "was largely composed of individuals who were politically indifferent, or took no interest in politics except to sell their votes" (172).

The later 1960s and the 1970s also saw a considerable number of more specialized studies, mainly by academics coming from or living in the Maritimes, and they usually took one of two forms. On the one hand, some of these historians attempted to show that Maritime pro-confederates had played a more significant role in the Confederation movement than had previously been assumed, although they did not question the view that the pro-confederates possessed a larger vision than the vast majority of the inhabitants of the region.[30] Del Muise in his study of the debate over Confederation in Nova Scotia took a different and much more significant tack. Moving beyond the narrow political boundaries in which the whole debate had come to be cast, he argued that the battle over Confederation was between the proponents of the old maritime economy of "wood, wind and sail" and the younger, more progressive members of the regional elites, who were prepared to make the transition to a continental economy based on railways and coal and committed to industrialization.[31] Muise's interpretative framework was particularly convincing in explaining — really for the first time — why pro-confederates such as Tupper, who were from areas with the potential for industrialization, were prepared to support union even on the basis of the somewhat unpalatable Quebec Resolutions, and he successfully established that "certain regions and interests in the Province wanted and carried Confederation."[32] Muise's thesis also helped to explain why those most committed to an international economy based on shipping and shipbuilding were so vehemently opposed to Confederation on almost any terms. By rescuing the debate from a narrowly political framework and focusing on the economic interests of the participants, Muise challenged the stereotype that most Maritimers were motivated by a rather simple-minded conservatism. Yet he also fell into the classic trap by identifying the pro-confederates as younger men, while their opponents come across as conservatives resisting the forces of change. The work of the Maritime History Group has undermined this fallacious dichotomy, for they have shown that those who remained committed to the traditional economy — or at least to the shipping and shipbuilding industries — were among the most dynamic economic entrepreneurs in the region and that they were motivated not by a misplaced conservatism but by a sensible analysis of the economic benefits still to be derived from investing in the traditional sectors of the economy.[33] Although it was not his intention, by portraying the division of economic interests in the province in terms of the old versus the young (and by implication those representing the future against those wedded to the past), Muise's thesis thus inadvertently reinforced the stereotype that the anti-confederate forces were motivated by parochialism and unprogressive attitudes.

Moreover, the attempt to divide the whole province into pro-confederates and anti-confederates on the basis of their commitment to the economy of wood, wind, and sail was too deterministic. By the 1860s there was a growing desire to participate in the evolving industrial economy, but, as Ben Forster has pointed out in his recent study of the rise of protectionist sentiment in British North America, the Saint John manufacturing interests "had divided opinions as to the value of Confederation." Pryke makes the same point about Nova Scotian manufacturers.[34] Public opinion in those communities tied to wood, wind, and sail was also more deeply split than Muise's thesis allowed. After all, as he admitted, when Stewart Campbell introduced his resolution against Confederation in March 1867, only nine of the sixteen members of the Nova Scotia legislature who supported it were from areas committed to the traditional economy, and while twenty-five of the thirty-two members who supported it represented areas "with at least some commitment to the emerging economy of coal and railroads," the degree of that commitment varied considerably.[35]

Although Muise's approach was extremely valuable in helping to explain the extremes of opinion — the views of the ultras on both sides — it could not adequately explain the motives of the large body of men who were prepared to consider union with Canada but who disliked the Quebec Resolutions. We do not know precisely how many Maritimers fell into this category and we may never know, since the issue of accepting or rejecting the Quebec Resolutions temporarily forced most Maritimers to identify themselves as pro- or anti-confederates on that basis. What is certain is that a variety of interests and ideological and cultural perspectives were represented in both camps. Years ago, Bailey pointed out that in New Brunswick, "the cleavage of opinion seems not to have followed either occupational or class lines," and suggested that there were strong ethnic and religious overtones to the struggle.[36] Subsequent studies of New Brunswick have reaffirmed Bailey's insight and have emphasized cultural over economic factors, and similar patterns can be found in the other Maritime provinces. Traditionally, Canadian historians have emphasized the growing independence of the British North American colonies after the grant of responsible government. Yet these were also decades when, in a variety of ways, the colonies were becoming increasingly Anglicized.[37] The Quebec Resolutions, which so clearly sought to follow

612

imperial and British institutional models, appear to have been most strongly supported by those who welcomed movement in this direction and particularly by the British-born; they were less enthusiastically endorsed by the native-born, of whom there was a much larger number in the Maritimes than in Canada West, and were viewed with greatest suspicion by cultural minorities such as Irish Catholics and Acadians. Nonetheless, as William Baker has shown, "the whole idea of a monolithic response by Irish Catholics to Confederation is highly questionable."[38] Desirable as it may be to come up with matching sets of dichotomous interests or ethno-religious categories, one can do so only at the risk of obscuring the diversity that existed on both sides in the struggle.

The second major emphasis of the more recent scholarship has been on analysing the position of those Maritimers who opposed union. J. Murray Beck spent most of a life-time trying to correct the negative image of Howe embodied in the literature, although he did not deny that Howe "set store by the wrong vision."[39] Similarly, Carl Wallace dissected the motives of Albert J. Smith, who, he claimed, "exemplified the true mentality of New Brunswick 'in this era' and who, like New Brunswick, turned to the past, unable to adjust to the changing present."[40] Other historians, strongly influenced by the debate over the continuing underdevelopment of the region and a feeling that Maritimers may have made a bad deal when they entered Confederation, produced a series of studies that were more sympathetic to the anti-confederate position. Baker wrote a finely crafted book on Timothy Warren Anglin, pointing out that "in his original criticism of Confederation Anglin had been correct on many counts."[41] Robert Aitken supplied a sympathetic portrait of Yarmouth, that hotbed of anti-Confederation sentiment.[42] David Weale resurrected Cornelius Howat as the symbol of the desire of Prince Edward Island to retain control of its own destiny and, in *The Island and Confederation: The End of an Era*, produced with Harry Baglole a lament for the decision of the Island to enter Confederation.[43] Ken Pryke contributed an extremely balanced and very sophisticated study of Nova Scotia in *Nova Scotia and Confederation* (Toronto, 1979). Although he argued that Nova Scotians "had little alternative but to acquiesce" in a plan of union designed to meet Canadian needs, he explained the willingness of Nova Scotians to accept their "unwelcome subordination" to Canada by factionalism among the anti-confederates and imperial pressure. His conclusion was that "by default, then, Nova Scotia entered into and remained in Confederation" (xi). Whereas earlier historians had consigned the Maritime anti-confederates to the dustbasket of history, the revisionists rescued them from obscurity and emphasized that they were the true standard-bearers of the wishes of the majority of the population. Unfortunately, revisionism carries its own risks, for this approach often portrays the most vehement of the die-

613

hard anti-confederates as the legitimate voice of the Maritimes. More-over, once again inadvertently, the revisionists also tended to reinforce the image that Maritimers were motivated by an all-pervasive paroch-ialism and stubborn conservatism, which explained the depth of anti-confederation sentiment in the region.

It is time to challenge this stereotype. If one turns the traditional question on its head and asks not why were so many Maritimers opposed to Confederation but why so many of them agreed so easily to a scheme of union that was clearly designed by Canadians to meet Canadian needs and to ensure Canadian dominance — which virtually everybody who has written on the subject agrees was implicit in the Quebec scheme — then the Maritime response to the Canadian initiative looks rather different. It may be true that there had been little discussion of the idea of an immediate union before the formation of the Great Coalition made Confederation an issue of practical politics, but the idea of British North American union, as Leslie Upton pointed out years ago, had been in the air since the arrival of the Loyalists.[44] In an unfortunately much neglected article written in 1950, John Heisler concluded from a survey of "The Halifax Press and British North American Union, 1856-1864" that "it seems unlikely that a sense of British North American Unity had ever been wholly obscured."[45] Many Maritimers appear to have thought like the anonymous correspondent to the *Provincial Wesleyan* who, in 1861, referred to "our home" as "Eastern British America," thus implying some sense of a common destiny with Canada.[46] As Peter Waite pointed out, the initial response of the Maritimers at Charlottetown and in the regional press was certainly not unfavourable to the idea of union. Even Anglin, perhaps the most committed anti-confederate elected to the New Brunswick legislature, admitted that he did "not know of any one opposed to union in the abstract."[47] Indeed, Anglin himself be-lieved union was desirable as a future goal, though on terms so favourable to New Brunswick that they were undoubtedly impracticable.[48]

It was the terms agreed upon at Quebec which hardened Maritime attitudes as the ranks of the ultras swelled with support from the critics of the Quebec scheme, to use Peter Waite's terminology. Even then, what is surprising is how much support the pro-confederates had. In New Brunswick, the only province in which the issue was put to the electorate, the supporters of the Quebec plan were initially defeated at the polls but, for their opponents, it proved to be a pyrrhic victory.[49] From the beginning the new government included a large number of men who were sympathetic to the idea of Confederation, if not to the Quebec Res-olutions, and who were converted fairly easily into pro-confederates, once it became clear that union was not possible except on the basis of those resolutions. The attitude of the premier, A.J. Smith, towards Confed-eration was somewhat ambiguous, and he was surrounded by others like R.D. Wilmot who were even more clearly critics of the Quebec scheme

614

rather than die-hard opponents of union.[50] Ultra sentiment may have been more widespread in Nova Scotia than in New Brunswick, but the victory of the anti-confederate forces at the polls in 1867 was roughly of the same dimensions as in New Brunswick two years earlier. This result may have been distorted by the legitimate feeling of outrage that many Nova Scotians felt against the undemocratic way they had been forced into the union and by the fact that the Nova Scotia election took place after it had become certain that there would be no substantial alterations in the Quebec plan.[51] In any event, any anti-confederate government in Nova Scotia would have suffered from the same internal divisions as did the Smith government in New Brunswick and would probably have met much the same fate in much the same way. At least that is a viable reading of Pryke's study of what happened to the deeply divided anti-Confederation movement after Confederation. Indeed, Pryke suggests that those who advocated "an extreme stand towards union during the election represented a small minority of the anti-confederates."[52]

615

Even Prince Edward Island's opposition is easily exaggerated. There is in Island historiography a powerful tradition of Island "exceptionalism" and there is undeniably some justification for this approach. Prince Edward Island was small, its future on the edge of a large continental nation was bound to be precarious, and opposition to the idea of union was stronger than on the mainland. Yet it is doubtful whether the Islanders' commitment to the protection of local interests differed more than marginally from a similar commitment by other British North Americans.[53] After the Charlottetown Conference, the majority of the Island's newspapers came out in favour of a federal union "upon terms that the Island may reasonably stipulate for," and at Quebec the PEI delegates never opposed the principle of union.[54] Of course, the support of the Island elite for union was not unconditional and the forces favouring Confederation would have faced a difficult battle in persuading the majority of Islanders that Confederation was necessary in 1867. But what appears to have decisively swayed Island opinion was the failure of the Quebec Conference to respond sympathetically to any of the Island's needs.[55] Thanks to the resistance of the French Canadians and the Maritimers, the preference of some of the delegates for a legislative union was abandoned. But to the Islanders' requests for changes in the composition of the Senate and an additional member of the House of Commons (or even for a larger House in which the Island would have six representatives), for a recognition of the peculiar financial position of the Island with its very low debt and limited sources of potential revenue, and for financial assistance to resolve permanently the land question, the delegates from the other colonies turned a deaf ear. It is easy to dismiss the Island's demands, particularly the desire for adequate representation in the new federal parliament, as unrealistic. But during the discussions at Quebec, Alexander Tilloch Galt offered an alternative system of representation in the House of Commons that would have given the Island the six federal representatives they wanted, and an additional senator for the Island was surely not a radical demand.[56] Indeed, after Confederation, the principle of "rep by pop" was abandoned to meet the needs of the west.[57] It was the obduracy of the Canadians and the refusal of the other Maritime delegations to support PEI's demands, not the latter's unwillingness to compromise, that isolated the Islanders and delayed the Island's decision to enter Confederation.

Not surprisingly, the Islanders refused to consider the degrading terms which were offered to them and defiantly declared in the famous "no terms" resolution that they would never enter Confederation. Although in 1869 they again rejected a set of marginally better terms offered by the Macdonald administration, they found themselves inevitably drawn within the orbit of Canada. They adopted the Canadian decimal system of coinage and were forced to follow Canadian policy in regulating the Atlantic fisheries.[58] Unable to negotiate reciprocity on their own and eager for an infusion of money to resolve the land question, the Island leadership did not abandon negotiations with Canada. Undoubtedly the financial crisis generated by the building of an Island railway explains the timing of Confederation, but, as the debate in 1870 when the legislature rejected Canada's 1869 offer shows, the number of MLAs prepared to accept Confederation if the terms were fair was growing steadily even before the Island approached insolvency. When the Canadian government offered "advantageous and just" terms in 1873, giving the Island much of what it had demanded at Quebec in 1864, the opposition to Confederation evaporated.[59] If Cornelius Howat was the authentic voice of the ultras on the Island, his was very much a voice in the wilderness by 1873.

From a longer perspective, what is remarkable is not that there was opposition to Confederation in the Maritimes but how ineffectual it was. In Ireland, the union with Britain was never accepted and ultimately resulted in separation and partition. Even today there are secessionist movements in Scotland and in Wales. The imperial government was so impressed with the success of the Canadian experiment that it would try to reproduce it elsewhere, but except for Australia and South Africa — and in the latter it was imposed by force — few of the federations it created survived for long. In fact, unlike in other areas of the world forced into federation on terms considered unjust, the Maritime opposition to Confederation was remarkably weak and evaporated remarkably quickly. Although there remained pockets of secessionist sentiment, Maritime separatism has never been a potent force.[60] Of course, the simple explanation of this phenomenon is to explain it by the willingness of the Maritime leadership to sell their birthright for a mess of Canadian pottage. But the assumption that Maritime politicians and the Maritime electorate were more venal and more corrupt than politicians elsewhere is an assumption which cannot be sustained. Historians have for too long quoted enthusiastically the comments of Arthur Hamilton Gordon and other imperial visitors to the colonies. Inevitably, they were critical of what they saw, since they came from a more patrician political culture controlled by an elite who feared any movement in the direction of democracy. But much of what they disapproved of — the scrambling of different interest groups, the narrow self-promoting nature of much of the legislation, the continual catering to popular demands — is what popular politics is all about. The ideal of the disinterested gentleman-politician made little sense in colonies where there were virtually no great landed estates, limited inherited wealth, and no hereditary ruling caste. Much of the opposition to the Quebec scheme seems to have come from those who feared, legitimately, that it was designed to create just such a caste and to place power in the hands of an elite which professed the ideal of disinterestedness while lining their own rather larger pockets.[61]

The belief that politics in the Maritimes were individualistic and anarchic is also mythical. During the transition to responsible government, the Maritime provinces had begun to evolve parties in the legislatures at pretty close to the same pace as they evolved in Canada. In the decades before Confederation, all these provinces were in the process of developing party systems with roots deep in the constituencies, even New Brunswick.[62] If Confederation disrupted this development and brought about a major political realignment and considerable political confusion, it was because of the far-reaching implications of the measure, not because of the inherent pliability or lack of principle of Maritime politicians. It had the same effect in Ontario and Quebec, which also had their share of loose fish. Similarly, the belief that Maritimers were either by nature or because of the scale of their political structures more susceptible to patronage and corruption should be challenged. Gordon Stewart has advanced the claim that the Canadian political system before Confederation was more corrupt and more patronage-ridden than in the Maritimes, since Canadians had adopted the spoils system with greater enthusiasm and consistency during the transition to responsible government.[63] In fact, there may be a reverse correlation between size and patronage in pre-industrial societies. In a larger political unit, politicians are more remote from the people they serve and less likely to be drawn from a clearly defined local elite. They cannot command the same degree of deference and therefore require access to a larger fund of patronage to cement the more impersonal bonds of party loyalty. Certainly those Maritime politicians who held posts in the new federal administration — Tilley and Tupper, for example — claimed to be appalled by the ruthlessness of the Canadians in distributing patronage along party lines, although they soon began to pursue similar policies to ensure a fair distribution for their own constituents and their own re-election.[64] By proving that the system was not totally biased in favour of the Canadians,

617

the Maritime political leadership did something to dissipate the lingering fears that the new political system would be dominated by Canadians and Canadian needs. But this evidence cannot be used to explain the success of the pro-confederates in the first place, nor does it adequately explain the rapidity with which integration took place.

The degree of support for Confederation in the region can be explained only by abandoning the notion that all but a handful of Maritimers were inherently parochial and conservative. Maritimers did not live in a dream world. Although they had experienced a period of rapid economic and demographic growth, they were aware of the changes taking place around them. They were acutely aware that external events had made some form of larger union desirable in the 1860s. British pressure, the American civil war and the cancellation of reciprocity, and the Fenian raids helped to drive home this message, as they did in the Canadas. But no external pressures could have compelled the Maritimes to join Confederation if, ultimately, they had not been convinced that it was in their own interests to do so. That is the lesson which can be drawn from the failure of the earlier initiatives on Confederation in the 1830s and 1840s.[65] In all these cases, despite the strong advocacy of the Colonial Office and enthusiastic support from British officials in the colonies, the union movement collapsed because of lack of colonial support. Similarly, the Maritime Union movement, despite strong imperial pressure, collapsed because of lack of colonial enthusiasm. Undoubtedly imperial support helped to sway the more conservative groups in the colonies, such as the hierarchy of the Catholic church.[66] But imperial interference could also unleash a colonial reaction. As allies, men like Gordon were a mixed blessing, and it is quite possible that the pro-confederates won their victory in New Brunswick in 1865 despite, not because of, Gordon's interference in the politics of the province.[67] The combined pressures generated by the American civil war and the British response to it were critical factors in the timing of Confederation. Without those immediate pressures, union might not have come about in the 1860s and it would certainly not have come about on the basis of the Quebec Resolutions, since it was those pressures which persuaded so many Maritimers to accept union on those terms. But since the idea of Confederation does seem to have had widespread and growing support, at least from the elites in the region, it does not follow that in the 1870s negotiations between the Canadians (now presumably united in their own federal union) and the Maritimers could not have been successful, albeit on a somewhat different basis.

By the 1860s, a variety of indigenous forces were, in fact, leading an increasing number of Maritimers to the conclusion that some form of wider association was desirable. The restlessness of provincial elites may have been, as Waite suggested, part of the reason for the enthusiasm for a larger union, but this restlessness cannot be related solely to their political ambitions and their immediate economic self-interest. Support for the idea of union was, indeed, too widespread for it to be simply the result of individual ambition. Clearly there must have been some correlation between an individual's socio-economic position and his response to the Confederation issue, but it would be foolish to revert to the kind of Beardian analysis which American historians have come to find less and less useful.[68] In any event, without the support of a wide cross-section of the articulate public, any effort at union wold have been pointless.

It can hardly be denied that much of the support for a larger union came from those who equated consolidation with material progress and modernization, as most historians have recognized. What they have been less willing to accept is that these intellectual pressures were growing stronger in the Maritimes, as in the Canadas, and affected many of the opponents of the Quebec scheme as well as its advocates. Even prior to Confederation, governments in the Maritimes took on new responsibilities as the nineteenth-century revolution in government filtered across the Atlantic.[69] Maritimers shared with other British North Americans an enthusiasm for railways, for expanded and more highly centralized school systems,[70] for improved social services, and for governments with enhanced access to credit. In a recent book entitled *Inventing Canada: Early Victorian Science and the Idea of a Transcontinental Nation* (Toronto, 1987), Suzanne Zeller has argued that the diffusion of early science was another of the pressures encouraging the establishment of larger units of government, and that the inventory methods of Victorian science "laid a conceptual and practical foundation for the reorganization of British North America" (9). Unfortunately, Zeller focuses almost exclusively on developments in the United Province of Canada. But the Maritimes had its share of scientists influenced by similar notions and a wider political community similarly affected by the diffusion of scientific knowledge, and it seems likely that the same developments were occurring there.[71] Nonetheless, Zeller's book points to the direction which studies of the movement for Confederation must now take. What is required are detailed analyses of the intellectual milieu in which literary figures and the growing number of professionals functioned, of clerical thought, and indeed of changing views of the role and function of the state held by entrepreneurs and by other groups in society. One suspects that such studies will reveal support, in the Maritimes as elsewhere in Canada, for the emergence of larger and more powerful institutional units of government.

Yet it does not follow that all of the supporters of Confederation were on the side of an expanded role for government and material progress, while all of those who opposed the Quebec scheme were not. The most vehement opposition to Confederation in the Maritimes came, as Muise correctly pointed out, from those whose economic interests seemed

619

most directly threatened by union with Canada. It is, however, far from self-evident that they were opposed to the other changes that were taking place in their colonial societies. Some of the opposition to Confederation in the Maritimes, as in the Canadas, probably did come from those whose social ideal was reactionary and anti-modern in several respects, but not all anti-confederates, perhaps not even a majority, opposed commercial development or technological change. There does appear to have been an overlap between those who resisted government intervention, feared increased taxation, and resented outside interference with community institutions and those who opposed Confederation. Yet many pro-confederates shared these concerns. In summarizing the vast literature dealing with the politics of the early American republic, Lance Banning points out the futility of trying to describe the Republicans and Federalists as liberal and conservative and their opponents as conservative and reactionary: "if revisionary work has taught us anything, it has surely taught us that both parties were a bit of each."[72]

620

It has long been known that the Fathers of Confederation were not democrats and that they were determined to secure the protection of property and to create barriers against the democratic excesses which, in their minds, had led to the collapse of the American constitution and to the American Civil War.[73] For this reason they limited the size of the House of Commons so that it would remain manageable, chose to have an appointed rather than an elected second chamber, and sought to ensure that both houses of the proposed federal legislature were composed of men who possessed a substantial stake in society. Most of the Maritime delegates at the Quebec Conference shared these anti-democratic and anti-majoritarian objectives. So, of course, did many of the most prominent anti-confederate leaders — even that tribune of the people, Joseph Howe. Ironically, a considerable part of the initial opposition to the Quebec Resolutions came from those — for instance, Howe and Wilmot — who, like the leading pro-confederates, were wedded to British constitutional models but who rejected the Quebec plan for not establishing a legislative union or because they feared it might lead to the disruption of the empire. But once convinced that legislative union was impracticable, primarily because of the determined opposition of the French Canadians, and that Britain was solidly behind the Quebec scheme, many of these critics were converted fairly easily into supporters of union, although they continued to ask for marginally better terms for their provinces.

The more serious and determined opposition came from those who believed that the Quebec plan would create a monster, an extraordinarily powerful and distant national government, a highly centralized federal union in which Maritimers would have limited influence. It is easy to dismiss these arguments as based on paranoia, irrational fears, or perhaps some kind of psychological disorder, particularly since the worst fears of the anti-confederates were not realized. But the opposition to centralizing power in a distant and remote government was deeply rooted in Anglo-American political thought. Elwood Jones has described this attitude as "localism," as a world view that was held by many articulate conservatives and reformers on both sides of the Atlantic and was "an integral part of the British North American experience."[74] This approach has the merit of indicating the considerable overlap between those who supported and those who opposed the Quebec Resolutions. Those resolutions were capable of more than one interpretation, and many of the Canadian pro-confederates supported Confederation because it promised more, not less, autonomy for their provinces.[75] Nonetheless, the term "localism," with its implication of parochialism, to some extent distorts the nature of the opposition to the Quebec Resolutions. It reinforces the notion that the pro-confederates were drawn from the men of larger vision, usually described in American historiography as the cosmopolitans, while their opponents were men of more limited experience and a more local, and thus more limited, frame of reference.[76] In American historiography, however, the "men of little faith" are now taken more seriously than they used to be and it is time to reassess the criticisms made by those who fought hardest against the Quebec scheme.[77]

621

Only a minority of the Maritime anti-confederates appear to have denied the need for some kind of union, but since the Maritimers were not, like the Canadians, trying simultaneously to get out of one union and to create another, they were less easily convinced of the merits of the Quebec Resolutions. Following the Charlottetown Conference, the *Acadian Recorder* expressed the belief that when "the delegates . . . have to let the cat out of the bag," it would be found that the cat was "a real sleek, constitutional, monarchical, unrepublican, aristocratic cat" and that "we shall ask our friends the people to drown it at once — yes to drown it."[78] It will not do to create yet another oversimplified dichotomy, pitting democratic anti-confederates against aristocratic pro-confederates. Yet clearly the anti-confederates did attract to their cause those who were suspicious of the aristocratic pretensions of the designers of the new constitution. Whether such critics were true democrats or simply adherents of an older classical republican tradition, whether they drew upon English opposition thought, classical liberalism, or Scottish common-sense philosophy, or whether they simply drew eclectically upon the host of Anglo-American intellectual currents available to them cannot be established until more detailed studies have been completed of their rhetoric.[79] But it does seem likely that it is on the anti-confederate side that one will find most of those who were most sympathetic to wider popular participation in government and to the movement towards democracy already under way in the Maritimes.[80] And such men surely had good reason to be suspicious of the ideological goals of those who had drafted the Quebec Resolutions.

The critics of the Quebec Resolutions were also surely correct to believe that the proposed constitution went further in the direction of centralization than was necessary or desirable in the 1860s. The real weakness in the analysis of most of what was written in the 1960s, and it is particularly apparent in the work of Morton and Creighton, is that it focuses too much on the twentieth-century *consequences* of what was done rather than on the more immediate *context* of the late nineteenth century.[81] The Quebec plan, after all, never worked out as the far-sighted Macdonald and his associates hoped. Despite Macdonald's expectations, the provincial governments did not dwindle into insignificance after Confederation. Because of pressure from the provinces and the decisions of the Judicial Committee of the Privy Council, as well as Macdonald's own retreat from an extreme position on such issues as the use of the power of disallowance, the power of the federal government to interfere with the activities of the provinces was constrained in the late nineteenth century and the constitution was effectively decentralized. This decentralization made considerable sense at a time when, by our standards, the people and politicians had a remarkably limited concept of the role of government in society, particularly of the role of a remote federal government.[82] Twentieth-century historians such as Creighton and Morton may, for very different and to some extent contradictory reasons, lament the fact that those who lived in the late nineteenth century were not prepared to accept a twentieth-century role for the federal government, but it does not alter the reality. In fact, Macdonald shared with his contemporaries this limited conception of the role of the federal government. He did not wish a highly centralized federal system, either to introduce the degree of control over the economy that Creighton longed for in the 1930s or because of any commitment to the nation-wide bilingualism and biculturalism policy that Morton espoused in the 1960s when he was converted to a Creightonian conception of Confederation. It is time to abandon the Creightonian myth that Macdonald and the other advocates of a federal union that was a legislative union in disguise were simply practical politicians engaged in the necessary work of building the Canadian nation.[83] Confederation certainly did not require that the federal government should attempt to "treat the provinces more 'colonially' than the imperial authorities had latterly treated the provinces" through its control over the lieutenant-governors and the resurrection of the anachronistic power of reservation.[84] The Fathers of Confederation were not philosopher-kings, but neither did they live in the intellectual vacuum that much of the traditional literature seems to assume existed throughout British North America, particularly in the Maritimes. In fact, the roots of the thought of the exponents of centralization emerged not out of a vacuum but out of a body of conservative thought that was deeply suspicious of democracy, and their opponents were surely correct to place little faith in the motives of such men and the scheme they proposed. Many of the anti-confederates were clearly marching to a different drummer.[85]

Ideological and sectional considerations did not take place in isolation from each other and what initially united the Maritime anti-confederates, regardless of their ideological differences, was their feeling that the Quebec Resolutions did not adequately protect their sectional interests. As the anti-confederate newspaper the *Woodstock Times* noted, "union is one thing and the Quebec scheme is quite another."[86] The scheme that emerged out of the Quebec Conference was designed to mollify its potential critics in two ways: by ensuring that sectional interests would be protected through federal institutions such as the cabinet and the Senate and through the creation of a series of provincial legislatures with control over local matters. Yet those critics who argued that the Senate would be too weak and ineffectual to defend regional interests would be very quickly proved correct after Confederation. Indeed, by making the Senate an appointed body, the Fathers of Confederation had intentionally ensured that the decision-making body in the new federal system would be the House of Commons. This was no accident, for, as Robert MacKay pointed out, Macdonald's intention was to grant "the forms demanded by sectional sentiments and fears," while ensuring "that these forms did not endanger the political structure."[87] Traditionally, Canadian historians and political scientists have laid great stress on the principle of sectional representation in the cabinet as one of the primary lines of defence for the protection of regional interests. Yet this argument ignores the fact that, however important individual ministers may be, the policies that emerge from the collective decisions of the cabinet must inevitably reflect the balance of power in the House of Commons. The fears of the Maritime critics of the proposed constitution were undoubtedly exaggerated, but they were surely correct to believe that in the long run there was no effective guarantee that their vital interests were adequately protected at the federal level.[88]

623

Similarly, they were surely correct to be suspicious of federalism as it was presented to them in the 1860s. The question of whether the anti-confederates leaned towards a different and less centralized model of federalism than the supporters of the Quebec scheme is a controversial and ultimately unanswerable one, since it depends upon which group of anti-confederates one takes as most representative. In Halifax, as Peter Waite showed, there was considerable support for a legislative union, at least as reflected in the city's newspapers.[89] But outside of Halifax and in New Brunswick and Prince Edward Island there seems to have been considerably more sympathy for the federal principle.[90] Federalism was viewed suspiciously by conservatives, who believed that it would leave the government without the power to govern, and such fears were expressed by both sides in the Confederation debate. They were, however, most forcefully expressed, in Halifax and elsewhere, by the pro-confederates, and the Quebec Resolutions went a long way to pacifying most of those who wanted a purely legislative union. But the Quebec Resolutions did little to mollify those who feared that the proposed provincial legislatures would be nothing more than glorified municipal institutions and that all real power would be concentrated in the federal parliament. As Richard Ellis points out, during the debate over the American constitution, the supporters of ratification "preempted the term 'Federalist' for themselves, even though, in many ways, it more accurately described their opponents."[91] Until detailed studies of the Confederation debate in the three Maritime provinces have been completed, it would be premature to assume that the Maritime anti-confederates anticipated the provincial rights movement of the 1880s and argued for a form of co-ordinate sovereignty. But many of the critics of the Quebec Resolutions in the region clearly believed that their provincial governments would be left with inadequate powers and resources. In this regard they were also more prescient than the pro-confederates. The Maritime governments required special grants to cover their deficits in the later 1860s and 1870s and were forced to turn time and again to the federal government for financial assistance. We know little about how Maritimers responded to the provincial rights movement of the 1880s, since the literature assumes that Ontario and Quebec were the key players while the Maritimers were motivated solely by the desire for larger subsidies, but it is plausible to assume that the movement was supported in the region by many of those who had resisted the Quebec scheme of union.

If the enthusiasm of Maritimers for Confederation upon the basis of the Quebec Resolutions was less pronounced than in Canada (or at least in Canada West), it was, then, not because they lagged behind intellectually but because they obviously had more to lose in a federation which was not designed to meet their needs. It was not an obtuse conservatism which led many Maritimers to oppose the terms that were initially offered to them in 1864 but a feeling that those terms were patently unfair. They were motivated not by an intense parochialism which manifested itself in separatist tendencies but by a desire to find a place for themselves in a union which protected their interests. Under the pressure of events, the majority, at least in New Brunswick and Prince Edward Island, did agree to union on terms which they did not like.[92] But what most Maritimers sought in the Confederation era was not a failure for themselves outside of Confederation but a more equitable union than seemed to be promised by the Quebec Resolutions.[93]

P.B. Waite

Phillip Buckner's spacious survey of the historiography and argument of Confederation is refreshing. However, if some old books are not wholly anachronistic, the authors are apt to be. There is some irony in being asked to review an article that reveals Professor Buckner's grasp of the field and this author's failure to keep steadily up with it.

The most telling argument in Buckner's article is his turning the usual thesis inside out. Instead of asking why so many Maritimers opposed Confederation, he asks why so many agreed to accept it and, especially, a union that so clearly reflected the exigencies of the Province of Canada. Professor Buckner has cast his mind over the Maritime region and pulled diversities together. In other words, he says, if anti-confederates won 58.1 per cent of the popular vote in Nova Scotia and 50.8 per cent in New Brunswick, it is also true that confederates won 40.9 per cent in the former and 46.7 per cent in the latter.[94] It is a position not to be underestimated.

Nevertheless, there is no use in blinding oneself to the bitterness of the time, whatever the outcome in the long run. Perhaps it might all have been less traumatic had there been, after 1 July 1867, healing and hope from the new dominion government in Ottawa over the heart-burning in Nova Scotia and in New Brunswick. There wasn't. The Maritimes had but 33 seats in the Canadian House of Commons of 181 (in 1872 it was 37 in 200), and that elemental datum helped determine Macdonald's still limited perspective. The Maritimes also discovered that Canadian administrators were both tougher and more efficient at administering what were now Canadian laws. This was not only true of administration of the Customs; the criminal law was tightened; offences that Maritimers had been inclined to treat in a milder fashion were dealt with more rigorously by Ottawa. New and more onerous tariffs also bedevilled the Maritimers' first years in Confederation.[95]

625

It seemed to prove that the Canadians had learnt little from the tumultuous process of Confederation, other than the clear recognition of their own needs and a determination to realize them. For the "Pacification of Nova Scotia" — Creighton's expression in his *Macdonald*, volume 2 — began with Tilley, not Macdonald. It was Tilley who wrote, from Windsor, N.S., in July 1868, these stern lines: "I am not an alarmist, but the position can only be understood by visiting Nova Scotia. There is no use crying peace when there is no peace. We require wise and prudent action at this moment; the most serious results may be produced by the opposite course."[96] The plain good sense of that letter Macdonald did, indeed, pay attention to.

This judicious review by Buckner, while it redresses a balance long in need of it, does not quite translate the anger and frustration in Nova Scotia and New Brunswick before and after 1867. That was not going to simmer down for some time. Anti-Confederation in Nova Scotia, and to some degree in New Brunswick too, was like malaria: whenever the patient became run-down, or weak, the disease would surface; the patient would develop a temperature and have fevered visions of Maritime union,

Greater Nova Scotia, or fighting Ottawa. It was endemic. W.S. Fielding eventually became Canadian, after 1896; but in 1892 he felt constrained to refuse, politely enough, an invitation to a July 1st celebration at Canada House, London, because there would be toasts that he would be obliged, publicly, to disagree with. There was the old man in Halifax, whom George Wilson remembered in the federal election of 1925, who got up and exclaimed, "I voted against Confederation and the Tories in 1867 and, by God, I'll do it again!"

Something of this, and Wilson's delight in pulling away illusions, was in his article on New Brunswick and Confederation in 1928. There was ruthlessness, and some *Schadenfreude*, in exposing the machinations in New Brunswick to a Canada recently filled with the rhetoric of the 60th, Diamond, Jubilee of Confederation in 1927. What won New Brunswick, Wilson was saying in 1928, was power and manipulation. Arthur Gordon used both, with the British government and the Canadians backing him to the hilt. Wilson's article was a blockbuster and it was intended to be. Of course Buckner is right in saying that there was no use in Great Britain's commanding a British North American union if there did not exist the local will, and acceptance, to realize it. That difficulty was well known at the Colonial Office and was illustrated in Prince Edward Island and Newfoundland. The Fenians, and Canadian cash, had not reached either.

626

One need not accept Buckner's ingenious explanation of the allegedly superior skill of Canadians (West and East) at patronage. In the Atlantic provinces we had a 100-year running start at it even before Confederation, and there are delicious examples. A.H. Gillmor of Charlotte County, N.B. ("I goes for Charlotte," as he delicately put it); or the great five-cent stamp escapade (also in New Brunswick), where the postmaster general thought patronage of himself was superior and put his visage eloquently on the new New Brunswick stamp; and, of course, both before and after Confederation we have those native geniuses out of Cumberland County, N.S., the Charles Tuppers, senior and junior. Even Sir John A. Macdonald, hardened as he was, blanched at the full range of Charles Hibbert Tupper's exigencies in Pictou County.

As to Professor Chester Martin, it is proper to say that those graduate students who took his seminar on Canada, 1760–1867, were impressed with his scholarship; the trouble was it seemed twenty-five years, or more, old. Martin had done tremendous work in his time; but when a graduate student's paper came on that broached a new view of one of Martin's favourite themes, out would come those dog-eared notes from his inside pocket, and he would prove to his own certain satisfaction that you were wrong and he was right. You had not got the balance right, or had not put the right weight on the right documents. The granite of his face revealed the rock-like character of his mind. Both had been set many years before.

Donald Creighton was not like that, at least not in the 1950s when he was at the height of his powers. Few historians were more conscientious with their sources. There may be historians now who take their page proofs to the archives to check the accuracy of quotations, but I personally don't know of any. In seminar, unlike Martin, Creighton would accept anything if you could properly document it. The only occasion I saw him bulldoze a student was in the face of simple incompetence of research. His supervision of more than one Ph.D. thesis was constant, conscientious, patient, impeccable, even when he was away from Canada. And there is something else. It was well known by the early 1950s that as soon as he had finished *Macdonald* he was going to do a major new history of Confederation. My thesis was squarely across his project; yet he was the first to urge me to get it published. Not all professors would be high-minded enough to encourage that or avoid stealing some of it. There was never repining from him when *The Life and Times of Confederation* came out only two years before the appearance of his book on virtually the same field. Still, his *Road to Confederation* of 1964 deserves Buckner's strictures.[97]

627

There is one weakness in the historiography of the period that Phillip Buckner does not comment on: the absence of any detailed studies of the first real round of Confederation talk, 1857–60. One still has to assume that the difference between the Confederation movement of 1858 and that of 1864 was due to the shift of a whole set of variables in those six years, some domestic, others external: the grid-lock of the political system of the Province of Canada; the American Civil War; and not least Cardwell and the British government, whose relentless policy was sustained across three successive ministries. It is a pity more has not been done to develop or criticize that argument, those assumptions.

Professor Buckner is generous to the *Life and Times of Confederation*, but he gives me credit for more sophistication than I had. He suggests that I may have been influenced by Cecilia Kenyon's 1955 article "Men of Little Faith" in the *William and Mary Quarterly*. I had heard of the quarterly, but that much only is true. Indeed, aside from reading a great deal of American history for my Dalhousie classes, I deliberately avoided reading American learned articles. They carried the taint of American thought. My peculiar frame of mind derived from the fact that Confederation in its political ideology was in many ways a revolt against American ideas and American influences. I wanted my history pure; right or wrong, I was imbued with a strong determination to let the argument of the thesis (and the book) grow out of the vast and multifarious native sources that were available, the newspapers of the time. I did not want to be influenced by secondary literature. Frankly, I was afraid of it, of being turned by it, of having the raucous voices in the newspapers that came so vociferously muted by reflections engendered by modern minds, especially American ones. I wanted to be soaked in the British North

America of the 1860s and to make myself, if that ever could be possible, the means by which that world might be transmuted into the 1960s.

That was, of course, romantic and naïve. But then so were the 1860s as they came through the newspapers. What was overwhelming was the exhilaration of it. One was driven to the newspapers, to the Parliamentary Library, to the St. John's library, to the hot little sheds on Pinnacle Street, Belleville, Ont., not by the exigencies of a Ph.D., but by adrenalin.

For there was the nationalism of it, as well. That, I suppose now, is where one's historian's control slipped a little. One slackened the reins and the powerful steed took over. One was caught, as the newspapermen of the time were, by the sheer magnitude of Confederation, of colonials meeting and greeting each other for the first time, a bit star-struck some of them, the way the writer was, who'd caught it too. It made for peculiar history, nationalism reined in with difficulty by the historian's discipline, a discipline furnished, it is right to say, by the unrelenting intellectuality of D.J. McDougall and others, who ministered to that Ph.D. at the University of Toronto.

And there may be, *horrible dictu*, a philosophical question in all of this. Who, what, made the running in 1864? Was it men? Or was it events, according to Chester Martin, "stronger than advocacy, stronger than men"? Abraham Lincoln would have agreed with Martin. "I claim," Lincoln said in 1864, "not to have controlled events but confess plainly that events have controlled me." That view of life, history, and the Civil War, reminiscent of Tolstoy in *War and Peace*, may be reasonable enough, from the White House, with telegraphs, interviews, letters, streaming in upon one's consciousness. Still, it underestimates Lincoln's use, adaptation, of events, which in some critical cases was far from being passive. That small, low, island in the roadstead of Charleston, South Carolina, is a case in point. Lincoln's move to notify Governor Pickens of South Carolina at the end of March 1861 that the federal government would supply Fort Sumter with provisions only, not with arms, was brilliant. It was carefully weighed and pondered. It forced the South to make war first.

Does the Confederation movement suggest that men shape their own destinies? Does it argue, for example, that without George Brown Confederation might not have happened when and how it did? Or that without Anne Nelson Brown, George would not have offered coalition in June 1864? Is Frank Underhill's suggestion of the "Mother of Confederation" merely ironic?

These are questions that certainly I did not ask, and which one thinks of now. Confederation is susceptible to interpretation as dialectic between men and events, to prove (disprove) that action is possible. Different positions on that question might well have been taken by Tupper (who probably believed he could do anything), by Macdonald, or by Tilley. Perhaps it could be said that all men in political life prefer to live and work with the fundamental assumption not only that is action possible, but that it matters. Probably the basic apposition of men *vs.* events is too crude. Wilhelm Dilthey fairly meets something of this difficulty: "The historian must therefore understand the whole life of an individual as it asserts itself at a certain time and at a certain place. It is also the whole clutch of connections that goes from individuals . . . to the cultural systems and communities and eventually to the whole of mankind, which makes up the character of society and history. Individuals are as much the logical subjects of history as communities and contexts."[98]

William M. Baker

Dear Phil:

How delighted I was when Colin Howell phoned to ask if I'd participate in a CHR Dialogue focused on your paper. I felt sure that your essay would be both challenging and enlightening. I was not disappointed. The thrust is bang on. I agree that a negative stereotype has existed about the response of Maritimers to Confederation, that this stereotype should be "put down" as a stray dog, and that new and broader approaches need to be taken in examining the topic. Yet, as you note regarding the response of Maritimers to Confederation, it's one thing to agree in principle to a general proposal but quite another to accept a set of specific resolutions. In that spirit let me share with you some of the thoughts, questions, and concerns that came to my mind in response to your paper.

You begin by claiming that there is a stereotype about the Maritimes and Confederation — that the Maritimes were lethargic, conservative, parochial communities which had to be pummelled into accepting Confederation — and that this stereotype leads historians (1) to underestimate the support for Confederation in the Maritimes, and (2) to oversimplify and trivialize what actually were valid objections to the particular proposal for union. It struck me that this is an elaboration upon your feisty 1988 paper in the *Journal of Canadian Studies* objecting to an interpretation of the Atlantic provinces as conservative, parochial, and backward. The chief villains in your *JCS* article are the historical mandarins residing at the core of the empire (187). You don't say much in that article about BNA union per se but you do distance yourself from the anti-confederate movement, more or less equating it with separatism (194). Is that not rather like the very oversimplification and trivialization of objections to Confederation that you complain about in this *CHR* paper? Given the obvious distaste you expressed in the *JCS* article towards any dismissal of Maritimes as backwards or venal, however, I think that your denigration of the "antis" must have been a momentary

629

though not an inconsequential slip, which demonstrates both that the pervasive negative bias against the "antis" could be present in a passionate defender of the region and that in protesting your loyalty to the nation you were ready to shun a movement which was assuredly regional. The conclusion to your *JCS* paper was that nationalism and regionalism are not incompatible. That assumption, it seems to me, underlies your views on the Maritimes and Confederation in the present article.

After the initial statement of your thesis, you probe the existence of the stereotype and its corollaries by examining the historical literature. Since I assumed that these views existed, it was really out of a sense of duty that I turned to a sample of your sources. What I found surprised me.

To my mind Wilson's 1928 *CHR* article neither conformed to the stereotype you postulated nor underestimated support for Confederation. Although Wilson's statement that "the original apathy of the people to the question of federation had been replaced by a more unfriendly feeling" (8–9) may have given the impression that Maritimers were a naturally sleepy bunch, it also undermines your claim that Wilson "assumed as given New Brunswick's hesitancy." So too does Wilson's considerable discussion of the apparent willingness of the "anti" government to take up the union cause.

Harvey's brief 1927 Historical Association paper both confirms and denies the stereotype. On the one hand, in a simplistic and unconvincing explanation of the Maritime reaction to the union plan, he dismissed opposition to Confederation as factious; on the other, he provided evidence that, far from being conservative and parochial, Maritimers were visionary expansionists of a sort. Nor does his analysis underestimate support for Confederation. He argued virtually the opposite when he stated that "the Maritimes were honest dupes of their own enthusiasm as much as of the promises of Canadian Delegates" (43). Finally, I think your comment about Harvey urging Maritimers not to blame Confederation for their difficulties and suggesting that they replicate the enthusiasm of the pro-confederates is quite misleading. The thrust of Harvey's argument is that while Confederation shouldn't be blamed for all the woes of the Maritimes, Ottawa damn well better do something to improve conditions in the Maritimes. Only then would Maritimers "be able to recapture some of the enthusiasm" for Canada (45).

In Whitelaw's 1934 book I did not see much about the backwardness of the Maritimes. On page 20, for example, he describes the expansive vision of Nova Scotia in the 1850s. "Particularism" is used as a concept — based on geography, history, and economics — to explain the lack of unity within the Maritimes (and thus the failure of Maritime Union) rather than as an intentionally demeaning term. In fact, it's rather like the concept of "limited identities." Actually, Whitelaw's thesis is quite amorphous (the preface describes the enormous convolutions the project had taken from its original focus on the Quebec Conference). Nevertheless, on the key matter of "rugged particularism" *vs.* "incipient nationalism," he seems to be saying that both were evident in the Maritimes. That is, the contest was not between Canadian nationalism and Maritime particularism but between the two impulses within the Maritimes. He did assert that "up to the very turn of the mid-century provincial particularism was still at the flood" (7), implying that by the 1860s particularism was in decline while nationalism was in ascent. Although this might be taken to demonstrate Whitelaw's bias against particularism, to my mind that would be pushing the point too far. Furthermore, I think that your use of Martin's 1935 *CHR* review to describe Whitelaw's perspective is unfair. What you quote was not Whitelaw's view but Martin's. Martin was not happy with Whitelaw's failure to designate particularism as backwardness, and he explicitly stated that the evidence suggested "another interpretation" than that presented by Whitelaw (72). The view that Whitelaw was a pro-confederate with a centralist bias, in fact, is a much more plausible interpretation of his 1938 *CHR* article on the Quebec Conference than of the 1934 book itself. I'd venture that the 1938 article was significantly influenced by the concerns of the Rowell-Sirois Commission.

631

Well, Phil, I shouldn't belabour this line of examination, for I'm beginning to feel like Eugene Forsey. Scrutinizing your use of sources under a microscope seems a bit picayune. Every historian knows how devilishly difficult it is to summarize a mass of material in a few sentences and how one historian will interpret evidence in a different way from another. The fact that I read the sources somewhat differently from you may not, in the final analysis, be consequential. I do believe that the stereotype exists. I run into it each year in my classes at the University of Lethbridge. In spite of my students' easy acceptance of the validity of western grievances against Ottawa, they are surprised that any legitimate argument against Confederation from a Maritime point of view could have been made. The stereotype exists, all right, just as other stereotypes exist about other regions of the country (lotus eaters, red necks, fat cats, pea soupers).

The problem, I think, is in your attempt to locate the stereotype in highly specialized academic literature. It's probably more prevalent in the public mind and in sources more general than the ones you've examined. The specialized sources (even Martin) are less stereotypical than you suggest. At the same time, the pre-1967 history textbooks that I pulled from my shelves come closer to confirming your point. Where had these ideas come from? The stereotype may have been absorbed by historians from widely held popular views. Indeed, an examination of public attitudes towards the Maritimes since the 1860s likely would uncover the roots of the stereotype.

The second point I want to raise relates to your rather static view of the literature from the 1920s to the late 1960s. If historical writing reflects the contemporary concerns of both historians and the society in which they reside, then one might expect to find fluctuations in interpretation. Donald Creighton, the historian who probably contributed most to furthering the stereotype, was clearly upset with the drift of the nation at the time he wrote *The Road to Confederation*. He wished to revive the dream of the Fathers as he interpreted that vision. Those who did not share his dream were next to traitors. The Maritime "antis" of the 1860s, of course, were not the only ones he rebuked (remember his 1966 *Saturday Night* article, "The Myth of Biculturalism or the Great French-Canadian Sales Campaign"?). W.L. Morton shared Creighton's deep concern about the future of the country. In the same year as *The Critical Years* was published he wrote that "the country is so irradiated by the American presence that it sickens and threatens to dissolve in cancerous slime." Historians concerned with the survival of Canada were not likely to give much credence to the Maritime "antis" who had questioned the deal at the very beginning. This concern influenced social democrats as well as conservatives. I remember being quickly shut up by Frank Underhill when, as a Master's student, I had the audacity to suggest that there was legitimacy to the "anti" position and that it might be useful for historians to be more questioning of the virtue of Confederation itself. He dismissed the comments as obviously absurd. For Creighton and Underhill, the problems of the 1930s greatly influenced their view of the nation and the constitutional division of powers. They came out of the Depression decade as centralists. It is my sense that the stereotype of the Maritimes and Confederation emerged among academic historians in connection with the concerns of that decade, particularly in the Rowell-Sirois Commission and its studies, including Creighton's *BNA at Confederation* (which is an unfortunately neglected monograph) and Saunders's *Economic History of the Maritime Provinces*. Even in these volumes, however, the stereotype is more a conclusion that might be drawn by unreflective readers than one articulated directly in the works themselves.

The connection between the historian and the times might also be applied to the "revisionists" of the 1960s and beyond. Most of these people had grown up in the post–World War II era, were less wedded to the centralist view of the country, and were critical, perhaps even cynical, about government and the Canadian state. How else to explain my own work? I had been raised as a typical middle-class WASP in Toronto and attended only Ontario universities. Yet the questioning of established authority inherent in the movement for civil and minority rights obviously had an influence on me. My research on Timothy Anglin, Irish Catholic "anti" in New Brunswick, provided an opportunity to comprehend someone who represented a minority and challenged "the establishment" and its designs. The weakness of that work was not that it depicted the "antis" as parochial and unprogressive but that it was too dismissive of the pro-confederates and their cause. The view that

632

emerges from *Anglin* is that Confederation was a "snow job" imposed upon Maritimers by villainous Upper Canadians through a "dirty tricks" campaign. Perhaps that is forgivable in a biography of an "anti," but you've convinced me that such a portrait of the Maritimes and Confederation significantly underrates the force of the pro-confederate movement within the Maritimes.

Indeed, I'm not the only historian at fault in this regard. Much of the writing on the Maritimes and Confederation has underestimated or trivialized one side or the other. What I'm suggesting is that individual works usually present not both of the corollaries to your stereotype but only one of them. It's only when the literature as a whole is combined that both fallacies are present. To identify the stereotype as you have done, therefore, involves excluding the counter evidence that exists in the same body of material. Clearly what is required is another type of combination, a different sort of approach from that of choosing sides, of trying to determine who was right and who was wrong.

633

Figuring out who were the winners and who were the losers is not as simple as it first appears, even if it were appropriate to do so. Yesterday's loser may be today's winner; today's winner might lose tomorrow. Indeed, what is considered parochial, backward, and conservative at one time may be viewed as "natural," forward-looking, and progressive in another era. In fact, it can be argued that those who represented Maritime interests, whether for or against Confederation 1864–73, were not losers. If it is correct, as you argue, that a more decentralized union than that based on the Quebec Resolutions would have better suited the Maritimes and would likely have emerged had union taken place in the 1870s, then that is what happened before the turn of the century. The provincial rights movement of the 1880s had a lengthy and mixed ancestry, but certainly found some of its roots in the Maritimes and not just among the "antis." Tilley and Tupper, as you point out, had declared at the London Conference that they did not intend to create a legislative union, whatever Tupper's personal views on the matter might have been. The financial terms of the 1864 deal, which drew considerable fire in the Maritimes, were also amended in the years after 1867. In short, many of the Maritime objections to the Quebec Resolutions were redressed over time.

In fact, even the view that the Quebec Resolutions obviously favoured the needs of the Canadas to the detriment of the Maritimes (an article of faith in discussions of the Maritimes and Confederation) needs to be questioned. You hint at this but do not press the point. Were the Maritime politicians at Charlottetown, Quebec, and London so naïve or unskilful that they could neither identify nor protect Maritime interests? Many of the "concessions" given to the Maritimes were granted from the very beginning. After all, the Canadians came to Charlottetown and Quebec needing to sell the scheme. Not only did they promote a grand vision which appealed to expansionist views but they proposed a federal system which preserved local legislatures, offered an economic alternative to insecure British and American markets, provided financial support for both levels of government, and established a guarantee for the building of the Intercolonial Railway. While these arrangements may not have been ideal for the Maritimes, they were also not ideal for the Canadas. They met basic Maritime requirements. As you note, Tilley succeeded in winning for the provinces control over roads and bridges, and he calculated that virtually all of the powers exercised by the New Brunswick legislature would remain intact. How would a Union scheme developed in the 1870s or later have differed substantially from the Quebec Resolutions and given the Maritimes a better shake? What would have been significantly different about a plan prepared by Maritimers rather than Canadians? Surely most of the key items would have been the same, though Quebec City might have been favoured as the capital. Even the residual power and a "peace, order, and good government" clause likely would have been granted to the federal government, although the debate would have been more searching than it was at a time when the U.S. Civil War seemed to present a clear warning against states' rights. Perhaps the view that Maritimers got a raw deal under the Quebec Resolutions, then, is based less upon reality than upon its continuing political unity. Were Creighton alive he might pen an article entitled "The Myth of Maritime Rape or the Great Maritime Sales Campaign" (on the use of the term *rape* in this connection, see Underhill's *The Image of Confederation*, 4).

634

If the Quebec Resolutions were not as hostile to Maritime interests as has been assumed, this fact would lend support to your argument that there was more Maritime support for Confederation than many accounts have recognized. It would also help to explain why Maritimers so easily accepted the Confederation scheme. Yet, one has to be careful with the latter point. Opposition to the Quebec Resolutions was very intense. Nevertheless, once the deal had been accepted, strenuous agitation ceased. Your comparison of the Maritimes' acquiescence in Confederation and the continuing and violent Irish opposition to the 1801 union is very instructive. It demonstrates not only vastly divergent attitudes towards these respective unions but also the very different circumstances under which the two unions had taken place.

Your Irish example reminds us that external pressures alone could not have compelled Maritimers to join Confederation, or at least to acquiesce so readily. Yet those pressures were enormous and provided a tremendous impetus for Maritimers to see where their interests lay. A contemporary analogy is perhaps in order. Let us suppose that in the recent free-trade election the system had not returned a Conservative majority but had reflected the approximately 60 per cent of voters who favoured the Liberals and the NDP (the same percentage of New Brunswickers and Nova Scotians who apparently opposed the Confederation plan). A Liberal/NDP government was formed but was unable to get a better free-trade package from the United States, which began to impose a variety of protective barriers. International financiers refused to lend money; the United States and NATO indicated that Canada couldn't expect to be protected by the alliance and had better look after her own defences; the United Nations and other international authorities such as the Group of Industrialized Nations declared that the free-trade deal was in the best interests of Canadians and the world economy; the governor general vowed to find the first opportunity to overturn the government and kept Mulroney on as a privy councillor; public works were stalled because of financial difficulties; and armed raiders resident in the United States wishing to "free" Cuba were carrying out military attacks on Canada while the U.S. turned a blind eye to the skirmishers. Then, in a subsequent election campaign brought about by the intervention of the governor general, ethno-religious antagonism was raised, those opposing the deal were labelled as traitors, and the Mulroney government detached itself from the earlier free-trade deal and stated that a new one would be negotiated. Would one not expect the Canadian electorate to have "seen the light"? The parallel is speculative and inexact but not far off the mark. External pressures on the Maritimes were formidable, indeed absolutely crucial in securing Confederation in all three Maritime provinces. As Chester Martin pointed out, Maritime Union might have become a reality had it been pushed as vigorously as Confederation (*CHR* 1935, 73–74).

635

Saying that, however, by no means invalidates your claim that politics in the Maritimes were no more parochial or venal than elsewhere in British North America. Quite the contrary, for in accepting Confederation the politicians and people of the Maritimes made a rational choice. After all, what were the alternatives? Imperial union was impossible; annexation to the United States was repugnant; and the status quo was obviously a less and less viable option. Adjustments had to be made by the Maritimes. Seen in this light, BNA union might be viewed as the least worse choice for the Maritimes. It involved the least amount of change and offered some potential advantage. Accepting Confederation on these grounds was not the same as choosing it with exuberant enthusiasm; nor was it being "bought off" or even "knuckling under." Maritimers, like British North Americans elsewhere, were simply adopting a measure of *realpolitik*.

Your assertion that the Maritime response to Confederation was not a result of anachronistic attitudes and venal politics is so well made that I merely want to add some support to your contention that a democratic and anti-elitist thrust was an important component of the "anti" argument. Anglin, for example, objected to the plan of the confederates not to submit the plan to the electorate: "This is clearly a conspiracy to defraud and cheat the people out of the right to determine for themselves whether this Union shall now take place." He also complained that the scheme would "retard our progress by assuming the burdens of Court extravagance and standing armies." But, as you say, neither is it simply a case of aristocratic pro-confederates *vs.* democratic anti-confederates. Anglin himself was a cautious political democrat and never a social leveller. In fact, during his declining years he listed his occupation as "Gentleman." You are also correct in noting that there was no necessary correlation between opposition to Confederation and opposition to economic and political "modernization." Anglin had long projected a boosterist outlook on material development and in 1865–66 called for state ownership of the projected western extension railway. It wasn't that he consistently championed government intervention, but what nineteenth-century British North American did? All argued for laissez faire when it suited their interests and took the interventionist stance when it seemed advantageous to do so.

636

Your point that the views of Maritime "antis" and "pros" were not always dissimilar is a good one. I want, however, to examine this point in regard to the constitutional arrangement, for I find your stand on this issue somewhat confusing. You seem to say that the Quebec Resolutions were excessively centralist, that the Fathers favoured centralization, and that the constitutional balance which emerged after 1867 was more appropriate. But it is important to remember the atmosphere of crisis, to use C.P. Stacey's words, in which the Quebec Resolutions were drafted. It is commonplace wisdom that in times of external threat, power flows to the central government. Why not take the same view of the 1860s themselves? Perhaps what is more surprising is that national power wasn't augmented further. One must remember that not only did the plan call for a federal rather than a unitary system but also that the Fathers allowed a direct contradiction to be placed in the heart of the BNA Act. Ottawa was given the power to override provincial legislation but the provinces were given exclusive jurisdiction over their enumerated powers, which, as Tilley's statistical exercise pointed out, were substantial. Just as few "antis" were opposed to union on any terms, few of the Fathers were uncompromising centralists. Both centralism and localism were imbedded in the constitution and in the minds of its creators. It seems to me that although the Fathers established guidelines by which the game would be played, they understood that circumstances would determine the outcome. George Brown put it this way: "You will say our constitution is dreadfully Tory — and so it is — *but we have the power in our hands* (if it passes), *to change it as we like*. Hurrah!" To think that the Fathers had a clear, unambiguous view of federal-provincial authority is to ignore, among other pieces of evidence, the extraordinary debate that took place on the second-last day of the Quebec Conference. Chandler from New Brunswick objected to residual powers being granted to the federal government, saying that it created a legislative union rather than a federal union. Tupper favoured a legislative union. Brown stated that he could agree with Chandler, except that the local legislatures had been granted "sufficient powers." Macdonald favoured concentrating power at the centre but also cited the case of New Zealand, where the central government apparently could sweep away powers granted to the local legislatures: "That is just what we do not want. Lower Canada and the Lower Provinces would have no such thing." Without even hearing from Cartier and the rest, we can see that collectively the Fathers had some sensitivity to regional concerns. And, of course, don't forget Brown's comment in a letter to his wife at the end of the Quebec Conference which expressed his delight at the prospective separation of the Canadas: "French Canadianism entirely extinguished!" In short, while I agree that the constitutional balance which emerged by the turn of the century was an appropriate reflection of a regionally diverse country, that's not the same as saying that the BNA Act and the Fathers were necessarily or even overwhelmingly centralist in 1864. Indeed, as you indicate, Macdonald and the other Fathers were full participants in the post–1867 evolution of the constitution. It was Macdonald who refused to interfere with provincial educational powers in the New Brunswick Schools' Question even when he had highly plausible grounds for doing so, and it was Macdonald who enshrined regional representation in the federal cabinet from the very beginning. If one judges by his actions, Macdonald realized that Canada could be threatened not only by sectionalism run rampant, but also by governments failing to take into account regional concerns.

637

Maritimers and Canadians, anti-confederates and pro-confederates alike, shared many common convictions. There were elitists and democrats to be found among both the supporters and the opponents of the scheme. "Rugged particularism" and "incipient nationalism," to use the words and insight of Whitelaw, were found in every region. Many Maritimers viewed the scheme as unfair and there was considerable legitimacy to their concerns. Yet Maritimers after 1867 evidently did not find living with the Canadians so very difficult. If one combines the results for the Maritimes over the eight elections from 1872 to 1900, one finds that, both in popular vote and in party members elected, the Maritimes very closely paralleled national patterns. Indeed, the percentage of members returned as supporters of the government elected (61 per cent) was identical to that of the nation as a whole.

Still, Confederation has generally been studied as a contest between competing teams, and within both a sectional framework and a restricted period of time. What is now needed is an examination of what the Confederation story tells us about the nature of Canadian society as a whole and over a broader time frame. Currently there are many groups that are practically invisible in Confederation studies: urban workers, native people, women, and children — indeed, the vast majority of the population. The other day the PEI Advisory Council on the Status of Women, in objecting to a re-enactment of the Fathers of Confederation landing in Charlottetown, stated that the event "blatantly ignored the contribution that many courageous women made to help build this country" (*Maclean's* 10 July 1989, 8). Though ridiculous in one way — does our annual celebration connected to the birthday of Queen Victoria ignore the contribution of males? — the comment is also insightful. What the re-enactment demonstrates is the exclusion of women from formal involvement in political life, but not their irrelevance to the society in which Confederation took place. In the United States and Europe, historians have used the revolutionary era to illuminate the role and function of women and thereby enhanced our comprehension of the meaning of the eighteenth-century revolutions. Canadian historians should do the same, addressing how Confederation was shaped in ethnic, gender, and class ways.

638

So, Phil, that is my eclectic response to your paper. I think you can see that I found it highly stimulating. It forced me to re-think the whole business of Confederation, not merely the response of Maritimers. I am confident it will have the same effect on other readers. For that, we are grateful, for it is high time that the topic was re-examined. That re-examination should be enriched by the insights provided by Canadian and international scholarship over the last two decades, so it can illuminate the nature of British North American society in the second half of the nineteenth century.

Best regards,

Bill

NOTES

An earlier version of this paper was delivered at the seminar on "The Causes of Canadian Confederation: Cantilever or Coincidence?" at the University of Edinburgh, 9 May 1988, and I am grateful to Ged Martin for asking me to give a few "general comments" on this subject. I am also grateful to a number of colleagues and friends for agreeing to comment on that earlier draft, including Ernest Forbes, William Acheson, David Frank, Ken Pryke, Jack Bumsted, and Brook Taylor. I hasten to add that none of them agreed with everything I have said, although no two of them disagreed with the same thing.

[1] E.R. Forbes, "In Search of a Post-Confederation Maritime Historiography, 1900-1967," *Acadiensis* 8, 2 (Autumn 1978): 3-21.

[2] *Canadian Historical Review* (*CHR*) 9 (March 1928): 4-24.

[3] Canadian Historical Association, *Annual Report*, 1927: 39-45.

[4] The roots of this sentiment are discussed in E.R. Forbes, *Maritime Rights: The Maritime Rights Movement, 1919-1927* (Montreal, 1979).

[5] I have used the reprint edition, which contains a valuable introduction by Peter Waite (Toronto, 1966).

[6] Whitelaw pointed out that there was only one recorded vote at Quebec on which Canada was outvoted by the four Atlantic provinces voting together. See *The Maritimes and Canada before Confederation*, 240.

7 *CHR* 16 (March 1935): 72, cited in Waite's introduction to *The Maritimes and Canada before Confederation*, xv. Waite includes this excerpt as "an illustration of the best and the worst of Chester Martin — that is, of the comprehensiveness of Martin's thinking and his inability to change it." Yet it seems to me a fair interpretation of Whitelaw's perspective.

8 One might include James A. Roy, *Joseph Howe — A Study in Achievement and Frustration* (Toronto, 1935) as a serious study, but it is a perverse work that simply reiterates the myths about Howe perpetuated in earlier studies. For a critique of the book, see J. Murray Beck, "Joseph Howe and Confederation: Myth and Fact," *Transactions of the Royal Society of Canada*, 1964, 143–44. Perhaps because the issue of Confederation was not put to the electorate in Nova Scotia as it was in New Brunswick, the early writing on Nova Scotia focused almost exclusively on the perversity of Howe in opposing Confederation.

9 "Railways and the Confederation Issue in New Brunswick, 1863–1865" and "The Basis and Persistence of Opposition to Confederation in New Brunswick" first appeared in the *CHR* 21 (1940): 367–83, and 23 (1942): 374–97, and both are reprinted in Bailey's *Culture and Nationality* (Toronto, 1972), from where the quotations in the text are drawn.

10 For example, Timothy Warren Anglin was not opposed to the Intercolonial, although he thought the western extension should be the priority. See William M. Baker, *Timothy Warren Anglin, 1822–96: Irish Catholic Canadian* (Toronto, 1977), 54. Baker also notes that many pro-confederates supported the western extension, although frequently as a second choice (55).

11 The concept of a consensus approach is, of course, taken from American historiography but, as I have tried to argue elsewhere, it seems to be applicable to Canadian historiography. See my " 'Limited Identities' and Canadian Historical Scholarship: An Atlantic Provinces Perspective," *Journal of Canadian Studies* 23, 1 & 2 (Spring–Summer 1988): esp. 177–78.

12 I have used the second printing (Toronto, 1962), which contains "a few minor corrections" (preface, vi). As will become apparent, I have drawn heavily upon Waite's sources in the discussion which follows.

13 I do not know if Waite had read Cecelia M. Kenyon, "Men of Little Faith: The Antifederalists on the Nature of Representative Government," *William and Mary Quarterly*, 3d ser., 12 (1955): 3–43, but his approach was certainly in line with the American historiography of the period.

14 I attempted to trace the context of Goldwin Smith's remark, but Waite's source was G.M. Wrong, "Creation of the Federal System in Canada," in Wrong et al., *The Federation of Canada, 1867–1917* (Toronto, 1917), 17, and Wrong does not indicate his source. It seems likely, however, that the quote referred to Canadian politics in the post-Confederation era and reflected Smith's somewhat biased view of his adopted home.

15 Forbes makes the same point about J. Murray Beck in his "In Search of a Post-Confederation Maritime Historiography," 55.

16 Bolger also contributed the chapters on Confederation to *Canada's Smallest Province: A History of Prince Edward Island* (Charlottetown, 1973), where his larger work is synthesized.

17 See Jack N. Rakove, "The Great Compromise: Ideas, Interests, and the Politics of Constitution Making," *William and Mary Quarterly*, 3d ser., 14 (July 1987): esp. 451.

18 See G.P. Browne, ed., *Documents on the Confederation of British North America* (Toronto, 1969), 38–39.

19 See Ken Pryke, *Nova Scotia and Confederation* (Toronto, 1979), 190.

20 See Browne, *Documents*, 77–78.

21 Ibid., 171.

22 Ibid., 211. Tupper personally supported the idea of a legislative union, but he was undoubtedly influenced by the knowledge that this position was not shared by most Nova Scotians.

23 McCully to Tilley, 8 June 1866, quoted in Pryke, *Nova Scotia and Confederation*, 28.

24 See Pryke, *Nova Scotia and Confederation*, 22–23, 26.

25 Bailey, "The Basis and Persistence," 116; MacNutt, *New Brunswick*, 456–57.

26 Bolger, *Prince Edward Island and Confederation*, v, 293.

27 See *Life and Times of Confederation*, 122.

28 Ibid., 5.

29 "Railroaded" is the clever aphorism used by Peter Waite in his chapter in Craig Brown, ed., *The Illustrated History of Canada* (Toronto, 1987), 289.

30 See Alan W. MacIntosh, "The Career of Sir Charles Tupper in Canada, 1864–1900" (Ph.D. thesis, University of Toronto, 1960), and Carl Wallace, "Sir Leonard Tilley: A Political Biography" (Ph.D. thesis, University of Alberta, 1972). MacIntosh presents a very traditional portrait of Tupper, who is seen as accepting and following the overweening vision of Macdonald. Wallace makes a more successful effort to place Tilley in a regional context, but he too believes that "a good argument can be put forward to prove that Confederation was little more than a smokescreen for a diversity of local issues" (209).

31 This argument is presented in "The Federal Election of 1867 in Nova Scotia: An Economic Interpretation," *Collections of the Nova Scotia Historical Society* (1968): 327–51, and developed at greater length in "Elections and Constituencies: Federal Politics in Nova Scotia, 1867–1878" (Ph.D. thesis, University of Western Ontario, 1971).

32 Muise, "Elections and Constituencies," iv. For an application of the Muise thesis, see Brian Tennyson, "Economic Nationalism and Confederation: A Case Study in Cape Breton," *Acadiensis* 2, 1 (Autumn 1972): 38–53.

639

33 This argument is developed in a variety of works published by members of the group but most recently and fully in Eric W. Sager and Gerry Panting, "Staple Economies and the Rise and Decline of the Shipping Industry in Atlantic Canada," in Lewis R. Fischer and Gerald E. Panting, eds., *Change and Adaptation in Maritime History: The North Atlantic Fleets in the Nineteenth Century* (St. John's, 1985). For an interpretation which incorporates this approach, but one that builds upon Muise's insights, see John G. Reid's *Six Crucial Decades: Times of Change in the History of the Maritimes* (Halifax, 1987), esp. 113-16.

34 Ben Forster, *A Conjunction of Interests: Business, Politics, and Tariffs, 1825-1879* (Toronto, 1986), 62. On Nova Scotia, see Pryke, *Nova Scotia and Confederation*, 107, 190-92.

35 Muise, "The Federal Election of 1867 in Nova Scotia," 337-38.

36 Bailey, "The Basis and Persistence," 99. Peter Toner emphasizes "the Irish threat, real and imagined" in his discussion of the politics of Confederation in New Brunswick in "New Brunswick Schools and the Rise of Provincial Rights" in Bruce W. Hodgins, Don Wright, and W.H. Heick, *Federalism in Canada and Australia: The Early Years* (Waterloo, 1978), esp. 126-27.

37 The increased Anglicization of the Thirteen Colonies in the decades prior to the American Revolution is a major theme in Jack P. Greene, "Political Mimesis: A Consideration of the Political Roots of Legislative Behaviour in the British Colonies in the Eighteenth Century," *American Historical Review* 75 (1969-70): 337-67. It is a theme which has yet to be adequately explored in the evolution of *British* North America in the mid-decades of the nineteenth century.

38 Baker, *Anglin*, 79.

39 "Joseph Howe and Confederation: Myth and Fact," 146, and *Joseph Howe*, vol. 2, *The Briton Becomes Canadian, 1848-1873* (Kingston and Montreal, 1983), 211.

40 Carl Wallace, "Albert Smith, Confederation and Reaction in New Brunswick: 1852-1882," *CHR* 44 (1963): 311-12. An extended version of this argument is contained in "The Life and Times of Sir Albert James Smith" (M.A. thesis, University of New Brunswick, 1960), which concludes with the statement that "he lacked the depth and vision to be a great statesman" (210).

41 Baker, *Anglin*, 116.

42 Robert M. Aitken, "Localism and National Identity in Yarmouth, N.S., 1830-1870" (M.A. thesis, Trent University, n.d.).

43 David Weale, *Cornelius Howat: Farmer and Island Patriot* (Summerside, 1973), and David Weale and Harry Baglole, *The Island and Confederation: The End of an Era* (n.p., 1973).

44 L.F.S. Upton, "The Idea of Confederation, 1754-1858," in W.L. Morton, ed., *The Shield of Achilles: Aspects of Canada in the Victorian Age* (Toronto, 1968), 184-204.

45 *Dalhousie Review* 30 (1950): 188.

46 *Provincial Wesleyan*, 16 Jan. 1861. I am grateful to John Reid for supplying me with this reference.

47 Baker, *Anglin*, 103. I am grateful to a student in one of my seminars, Mary McIntosh, for supplying me with this reference.

48 See ibid., 58, 64-65.

49 Historians remain divided over the scale of the victory. Waite suggests in *The Life and Times of Confederation*, 246, that the election results were comparatively close, but Baker, in *Anglin*, 75, argues that the anti-confederates won at least 60 per cent of the popular vote.

50 Once again historians are not agreed on whether Smith did convert to Confederation prior to the defeat of his government. Baker, in *Anglin*, 102, argues that he did not, but Wallace feels that Smith was willing to lead the province into union. See "Albert Smith, Confederation and Reaction in New Brunswick," 291-92. In his "Life and Times of Smith," Wallace points out that as early as 1858 Wilmot had indicated his belief in the inevitability of British North American union (see 23).

51 Del Muise points out that about 60 per cent of the Nova Scotia electorate voted for anti-confederates in 1865, which is roughly comparable to Baker's figure for New Brunswick.

52 See *Nova Scotia and Confederation*, 49.

53 For a different point of view see Weale and Baglole, *The Island and Confederation*. I have two major disagreements with the authors. First, they create an image of harmony and unity on the Island that ignores the very real ethnic, religious, and class divisions which existed and thus postulate a unified response to Confederation. Second, they imply that Islanders had developed a strong desire to be separate that almost amounted to a sense of Island nationalism. But the Island had never been an independent and autonomous state and there is no evidence that any sizeable number of Islanders ever wanted it to become one. Indeed, the tendency to equate resistance to Confederation in the Maritimes to a kind of "provincial nationalism" is, I believe, utterly wrongheaded. What most Maritimers wanted, and Prince Edward Islanders were no exception, was to protect the corporate identities of their long-established assemblies. For a development of this theme in American historiography, see Jack P. Greene, *Peripheries and Center: Constitutional Development in the Extended Politics of the British Empire and the United States, 1607-1788* (Athens, GA, 1987).

54 Bolger, *Prince Edward Island and Confederation*, 59, 61, 86.

55 Unfortunately, most of the literature on Confederation, including Bolger, simply dismisses the Island's needs as irrelevant. See ibid., 68ff.

56 For Galt's plan and the discussion of the extra senator, see Browne, ed., *Documents*, 106. Today we accept much wider departure from the principle of rep by pop than PEI requested in 1864.

57 David E. Smith, "Party Government, Representation and National Integration in Canada," in Peter Aucoin, ed., *Party Government and Regional Representation in Canada* (Toronto, 1985), 14.

[58] See Frank MacKinnon, *The Government of Prince Edward Island* (Toronto, 1951), 132.

[59] Bolger, *The Island and Confederation*, 210, 262.

[60] The only serious expression of separatist sentiment was the repeal movement of the 1880s. It was in part, indeed perhaps in large part, simply a strategy for better terms. See Colin Howell, "W.S. Fielding and the Repeal Elections of 1886 and 1887 in Nova Scotia," *Acadiensis* 8, 2 (Spring 1979): 28-46.

[61] I have drawn for inspiration in these comments on Gordon S. Wood, "Interest and Disinterestedness in the Making of the Constitution," in Richard Beeman, Stephen Botein, and Edward C. Carter II, eds., *Beyond Confederation: Origins of the Constitution and American National Identity* (Chapel Hill and London, 1987), 69-109.

[62] See Gail Campbell, " 'Smashers' and 'Rummies': Voters and the Rise of Parties in Charlotte County, New Brunswick, 1846-1857," *Historical Papers* (1986): 86-116.

[63] Gordon Stewart, *The Origins of Canadian Politics: A Comparative Approach* (Vancouver, 1986), 88-89.

[64] The latter statement is based upon an examination of the patronage files in the Tilley and Tupper papers held in the National Archives of Canada, during the 1870s. I discuss the question of patronage at more length in "The 1870s: The Integration of the Maritimes," in E.R. Forbes and D.A. Muise, eds., *The Atlantic Provinces in Confederation* (in press).

[65] On the earlier attempts to achieve Confederation, see Ged Martin, "Confederation Rejected: The British Debate on Canada, 1837-1840," *Journal of Imperial and Commonwealth History* 11 (1982-83): 33-57, and B.A. Knox, "The Rise of Colonial Federation as an Object of British Policy, 1850-1870," *Journal of British Studies* 11 (1971): 91-112. My interpretation of Ged Martin's "An Imperial Idea and Its Friends: Canadian Confederation and the British," in Gordon Martel, ed., *Studies in British Imperial History: Essays in Honour of A.P. Thornton* (New York, 1985), 49-94, is that while British support was essential for Confederation, it was the circumstances within British North America which gave the British something to support.

[66] For example, Bishop MacKinnon wrote to Tupper that "Although no admirer of Confederation on the basis of the Quebec Scheme; yet owing to the present great emergency and the necessities of the times, the union of the Colonies upon a new basis, we receive with pleasure" (Pryke, *Nova Scotia and Confederation*, 27). MacKinnon's reservations are not spelled out, but they were likely similar to those of Archbishop Connolly, who wrote that "the more power that Central Legislature has the better for the Confederacy itself and for the Mother Country and for all concerned." Connolly to Carnarvon, 30 Jan. 1867, in Browne, ed., *Documents*, 262. See also K. Fay Trombley, *Thomas Louis Connolly (1815-1876)* (Leuven, 1983), esp. 302-44.

[67] Wallace, "Life and Times of Smith," 47.

[68] The reference here is, of course, to Charles Beard's economic interpretation of the making of the American constitution. As Richard Beeman notes in his introduction to *Beyond Confederation*, 14, the prolonged historiographical debate over Beard's interpretation has come to be seen as important by "ever-decreasing numbers" of American historians.

[69] See Rosemary Langhout, "Developing Nova Scotia: Railways and Public Accounts, 1849-1867," *Acadiensis* 14, 2 (Spring 1985): 3-28.

[70] As Ian Robertson points out, Prince Edward Island claimed to be the first place in the British Empire to introduce "a complete system of free education" with the adoption of the Free Education Act of 1852, and Nova Scotia was the next British North American colony to follow suit, in 1864. See "Historical Origins of Public Education in Prince Edward Island, 1852-1877," unpublished paper given at the Atlantic Canada Studies Conference, University of Edinburgh, May 1988, 3, 5.

[71] A.G. Bailey points out that the Maritime universities, like the central Canadian universities, "tempered their concern for the classics with a lively concern for the sciences" during the Confederation period. See "Literature and Nationalism in the Aftermath of Confederation," in Bailey, *Culture and Nationality*, 66.

[72] Lance Banning, "Jeffersonian Ideology Revisited: Liberal and Classical Ideas in the New American Republic," *William and Mary Quarterly* 43, 1 (Jan. 1986): 14.

[73] See Bruce Hodgins, "Democracy and the Ontario Fathers of Confederation," in *Profiles of a Province: Studies in the History of Ontario* (Toronto, 1967), and "The Canadian Political Elite's Attitude toward the Nature of the Plan of Union," in Hodgins et al., eds., *Federalism in Canada and Australia*, 43-59.

[74] Elwood H. Jones, "Localism and Federalism in Upper Canada to 1865," in Hodgins et al., *Federalism in Canada and Australia*, 20.

[75] See Arthur Silver, *The French-Canadian Idea of Confederation, 1864-1900* (Toronto, 1982), 33-50, and Robert Charles Vipond, "Federalism and the Problem of Sovereignty: Constitutional Politics and the Rise of the Provincial Rights Movement in Canada" (Ph.D. thesis, Harvard University, 1973), 82-87.

[76] In American historiography, the notion of the federalists as cosmopolitans and the anti-federalists as provincials, found, for example, in Jackson Turner Main's *The Antifederalists: Critics of the Constitution, 1781-1788* (Chapel Hill, NC, 1961) and *Political Parties before the Constitution* (Chapel Hill, NC, 1973), has been challenged by Wood in "Interest and Disinterestedness in the Making of the Constitution."

[77] See, for example, James H. Hutson, "County, Court and Constitution: Antifederalism and the Historians," *William and Mary Quarterly*, 3d ser., 38, 3 (July 1981): 337-68; Isaac Kramnick, "The 'Great National Discussion': The Discourse of Politics in 1787," ibid. 45, 1 (Jan. 1988): 3-32, and

641

Richard E. Ellis, "The Persistence of Antifederalism after 1789," in Beeman et al., eds., *Beyond Confederation*, 295–314.

[78] *Acadian Recorder*, 12 Sept. 1864, quoted in R.H. Campbell, "Confederation in Nova Scotia to 1870" (M.A. thesis, Dalhousie University, 1939), 80.

[79] I am, of course, calling for the kind of intellectual history associated with American scholars such as Bernard Bailyn and Gordon S. Wood and British scholars such as J.G.A. Pocock. The only serious attempts to apply this approach to the Confederation era have been by Jones, "Localism and Federalism," and by Peter J. Smith, "The Ideological Origins of Canadian Confederation," *Canadian Journal of Political Science* 20, 1 (March 1987): 3–29. Unfortunately, both efforts seem to me flawed by the effort to deal with too wide a time frame and to apply to the mid-nineteenth century categories developed for the eighteenth century.

[80] It is worth noting that the Maritimes were at least as far, if not further, advanced in this direction than the Canadas. According to John Garner, *The Franchise and Politics in British North America, 1755–1867* (Toronto, 1969), Nova Scotia had been "the first colony in North America to introduce manhood suffrage" (33). Although Nova Scotia subsequently drew back from the experiment, all of the Maritimes had wide franchises and Prince Edward Island had virtually universal male suffrage by the 1860s. After Confederation, when the federal government decided against vote by ballot, there was an outcry from New Brunswick, which had adopted the ballot in 1855. Indeed, it was this increasingly democratic climate that annoyed men like Gordon and that perhaps accounts, at least in part, for the desire of some members of the colonial elites for a wider, and preferably a legislative, union.

[81] I have been influenced here by Beeman, Introduction, *Beyond Confederation*, 5–8.

[82] There has been a heated debate over the role of the Judicial Committee of the Privy Council, but much of the controversy centres around the consequences in the 1930s of the decisions taken under very different circumstances in the 1880s and 1890s. For a summary of the recent literature see Frederick Vaughan, "Critics of the Judicial Committee of the Privy Council: The New Orthodoxy and an Alternative Explanation," *Canadian Journal of Political Science* 19, 3 (Sept. 1986): 495–519. Unfortunately, Vaughan is also primarily concerned with the implications of the decisions, this time in the 1980s, and expresses the fear that the JCPC "left us with a federal system that is seriously lacking an institutional body by which to bind the several provinces at the centre so as to ensure the continued existence of Canada as one nation" (505).

[83] This point is also made in Smith, "The Ideological Origins of Canadian Confederation," 3–4.

[84] Vipond, "Federalism and the Problem of Sovereignty," 128–29.

[85] James H. Hutson in "Country, Court and Constitution" has suggested that the division over the constitution in the United States in the 1780s was between those committed to a Country ideology and those committed to a Court ideology. The Court party supported commercial expansion and was profoundly statist in orientation, while their Country opponents defended agrarian interests and feared any substantial increase in state power. These categories have some value, but British North America in the 1860s was not the United States in the 1780s. There were very few self-sufficient agricultural communities, even in the Maritimes in the 1860s, and it is doubtful whether the majority of the anti-confederates were any less market-oriented than their opponents. Ideological determinism is as distorting as any other kind and there is the danger of turning all the pro-confederates into Hamiltonians and all the critics of the Quebec Resolutions into Jeffersonians.

[86] Quoted in Waite, *The Life and Times of Confederation*, 252.

[87] See Robert A. MacKay, *The Unreformed Senate of Canada*, rev. ed. (Toronto, 1963), 43.

[88] This is one of the major themes in Forbes, *Maritime Rights*, and is implicit in T.W. Acheson, "The Maritimes and Empire Canada," in David Bercuson, ed., *Canada and the Burden of Unity* (Toronto, 1977).

[89] See "Halifax Newspapers and the Federal Principle, 1864–1865," *Dalhousie Review* 37 (1957): 72–84.

[90] See Waite, *Life and Times of Confederation*, 238–39, on New Brunswick. Vaughan in "Critics of the Judicial Committee of the Privy Council" argues that the main anti-confederate alternative to Confederation in the Maritimes was an imperial union (510), but then admits a few pages later that an examination of the Confederation debates in the Maritimes shows that much of the resistance there was based on a clear perception of the centralist philosophy which lay behind the Quebec Resolutions (512).

[91] Ellis, "Persistence of Antifederalism," 302.

[92] In his study of the persistence of sectionalism in Britain, *Internal Colonialism: The Celtic Fringe in British National Development, 1536–1966* (Berkeley and Los Angeles, 1975), Michael Hechter concludes that "the persistence of objective cultural distinctiveness in the periphery must itself be the function of the maintenance of an unequal distribution of resources between core and peripheral groups" (37). That periodic outbursts of regional discontent in the Maritimes are rooted in such an unequal distribution seems unquestionable, but the very ease with which the Maritimes was integrated into Canada and the weakness of secessionist movements seems to me to imply that most Maritimers have always seen and continue to see themselves as part of the core rather than the peripheral group in Canada.

[93] I have not dealt with Newfoundland in this paper because it seems to me that it was the one place where, for a variety of historic reasons, these generalizations may not apply.

P.B. Waite

[94] The figures are from J.M. Beck, *Pendulum of Power* (Toronto, 1968), 12; for a more extended analysis, see Del Muise, "The Federal Election of 1867 in Nova Scotia: An Economic Interpretation," Nova Scotia Historical Society, *Collections* (1968): 327–51.

[95] P.B. Waite, "Becoming Canadians: Ottawa's Relations with Maritimers in the First and Twenty-first Years of Confederation," in R. Kenneth Carty and W. Peter Ward, *National Politics and Community in Canada* (Vancouver, 1986), 153–68.

[96] Tilley to Macdonald, 17 July 1868, cited in Joseph Pope, *The Memoirs of Sir John A. Macdonald*, vol. 2 (Ottawa, 1895), 27–28.

[97] The powerful drama of *Road to Confederation* helps disguise its teleology. Opponents of Confederation were nearly always wrong-headed. Joseph Howe, for example, is described as "tired, disappointed, unfulfilled, troubled by a haunting sense of lost causes and unused abilities, he had to look on enviously" (225).

[98] Wilhelm Dilthey, *Gesammelte Schriften*, vol. 7 (Stuttgart, 1961), 135. The German is as follows: "Der Historiker muss daher das ganze Leben der Individuen, wie es zu einer bestimmten Zeit und an einem bestimmten Ort sich äussert, verstehen. Es ist eben der ganze Zusammenhang, der von den Individuen . . . zu Kultursystemen und Gemeinschaften, schliesslich zu der Menschheit geht, der die Natur der Gesellschaft und der Geschichte ausmacht. Die logischen Subjekte, über die in der Geschichte ausgesagt wird, sind ebenso Einzelindividuen wie Gemeinschaften und Zusammenhänge."

643

Contributors

T.W. Acheson is a member of the History Department at the University of New Brunswick, Saint John.

William M. Baker is a professor of history at the University of Lethbridge.

Phillip Buckner is a professor of history at the University of New Brunswick, Saint John.

J.M.S. Careless is Professor Emeritus at the University of Toronto, where he taught Canadian history.

Ann Gorman Condon teaches Canadian Loyalist history at the University of New Brunswick, Saint John.

William Cronon teaches in the Department of History at the University of Wisconsin.

W.J. Eccles is Professor Emeritus at the University of Toronto, where he taught Canadian history.

Jane Errington is an associate professor at the Royal Military College of Canada, in Kingston, Ontario.

Daniel Francis is a Vancouver writer and the former editorial director of *Horizon Canada*.

R. Louis Gentilcore taught in the Geography Department at McMaster University. He is now retired.

Barry M. Gough teaches Canadian history at Wilfrid Laurier University, Waterloo.

Allan Greer teaches Canada history at the University of Toronto.

Naomi Griffiths teaches Canadian history at Carleton University, Ottawa.

Cole Harris is an associate professor in the Geography Department at the University of Toronto.

José Igartua teaches history at l'Université du Québec à Montréal.

A.J.B. Johnston is a researcher, writer, and editor at the Fortress of Louisbourg National Historic Park.

John McCallum is Chairman of Economics at McGill University.

Keith Matthews taught history at Memorial University, Newfoundland.

Jan Noel teaches women's studies at Trent University, Peterborough.

Fernand Ouellet teaches Canadian history at York University, Toronto.

Frits Pannekoek is the Director of Historic Sites and Archives Services for the Department of Alberta Community Development.

645

George A. Rawlyk teaches Canadian history at Queen's University, Kingston.

Arthur J. Ray teaches Canadian history at the University of British Columbia.

Elinor Kyte Senior (1926–1989) taught history at St. Francis Xavier University, Antigonish, Nova Scotia.

A.I. Silver teaches Canadian history at the University of Toronto.

Irene M. Spry is Economics Professor Emeritus at the University of Ottawa.

C.P. Stacey (1906–1989) was Professor Emeritus at the University of Toronto, where he taught Canadian history.

S. Dale Standen teaches Canadian history at Trent University, Peterborough.

C. James Taylor is a historian with the Historic Parks and Sites Branch of Parks Canada, Western Region, Calgary.

Bruce G. Trigger teaches in the Department of Anthropology at McGill University.

Gerald Tulchinsky teaches history at Queen's University, Kingston.

L.F.S. Upton taught history at the University of British Columbia.

Sylvia Van Kirk teaches Canadian history at the University of Toronto.

P.B. Waite is Professor Emeritus at Dalhousie University, Halifax, where he taught Canadian history.

Richard White teaches in the Department of History, University of Washington.

David Wood teaches in the Geography Department at York University.

Graeme Wynn teaches in the Geography Department at the University of British Columbia.

Reader Reply Card

We are interested in your reaction to *Readings in Canadian History: Pre-Confederation*, 4th ed., by R. Douglas Francis and Donald B. Smith. You can help us to improve this book in future editions by completing this questionnaire.

1. What was your reason for using this book?

   ☐ university course   ☐ college course
   ☐ continuing education course   ☐ professional development
   ☐ personal interest   ☐ other _____

2. If you are a student, please identify your school and the course in which you used this book.

3. Which chapters or parts of this book did you use? Which did you omit?

4. What did you like best about this book?

5. What did you like least about this book?

6. Please identify any topics you think should be added to future editions.

7. Please add any comments or suggestions.

8. May we contact you for further information?

   Name: _____

   Address: _____

   _____

   Phone: _____

(fold here and tape shut)

MAIL **POSTE**

Canada Post Corporation / Société canadienne des postes

Postage paid
If mailed in Canada

Port payé
si posté au Canada

Business
Reply

Réponse
d'affaires

0116870399   01

0116870399-M8Z4X6-BR01

Heather McWhinney
Publisher, College Division
HARCOURT BRACE & COMPANY, CANADA
55 HORNER AVENUE
TORONTO, ONTARIO
M8Z 9Z9

Instructor Reply Card

We are interested in your reaction to *Readings in Canadian History: Pre-Confederation*, 4th ed., by R. Douglas Francis and Donald B. Smith. You can help us to improve this book in future editions by completing this questionnaire:

1. For what type of course did you use this book?

   ☐ university course   ☐ college course
   ☐ continuing education course

2. How long was the course?

   ☐ one semester   ☐ two semesters   ☐ other _____

3. How many students were enrolled in your class?

4. What was the total *annual* enrollment for *all* sections of this course?

5. Which articles did you like best? Which ones did you assign?

6. Which articles did you like least? Which ones did you omit?

7. Please identify any readings or topics you think should be added to future editions.

8. Please add any comments or suggestions.

9. May we contact you for further information?
   Name: _____

   Address: _____

   _____

   Phone: _____

(fold here and tape shut)

Heather McWhinney
Publisher, College Division
HARCOURT BRACE & COMPANY, CANADA
55 HORNER AVENUE
TORONTO, ONTARIO
M8Z 9Z9